I0606370

CATHOLIC THEOLOGICAL FORMATION SERIES

General Editor: Kevin Zilverberg

The Catholic Theological Formation Series is sponsored by The Saint Paul Seminary School of Divinity, the graduate school of theological formation for Roman Catholic seminarians and laity enrolled at the University of Saint Thomas in Saint Paul, Minnesota. As a premier institution of theological formation for the region and beyond, The Saint Paul Seminary School of Divinity seeks to form men and women for the task of fulfilling the specific call God has for them, a call grounded in their common baptismal vocation to serve one another in Christ.

The school is intentional in its commitment to priestly and diaconal formation; as an institution of graduate theological education, it also prepares the laity to make Christ known and loved in the world. Although the students prepare for diverse ministries, all enroll in a curriculum of theological formation within the context of holistic and integrated Catholic formation.

It is this challenge of theological formation—the challenge to faithfully inform one's understanding—that serves as the focus of this series, with special attention given to the task of preparing priests, deacons, teachers, and leaders within the Roman Catholic tradition. Although the series is academic in tenor, it aims beyond mere academics in its integrative intellectual approach. We seek to promote a form of discourse that is professional in its conduct and spiritual in its outcomes, for theological formation is more than an exercise in academic technique. It is rather about the perfecting of a spiritual capacity: the capacity on the part of the human person to discern what is true and good.

This series, then, aims to develop the habits of mind required of a sound intellect—a spiritual aptitude for the truth of God's living Word and his Church. Most often, it will draw from the more traditional specializations of historical, systematic, moral, and biblical scholarship. Homiletics and pastoral ministry are anticipated venues as well. There will be occasions, however, when a theme is examined across disciplines and periods, for the purposes of bringing to our common consideration a thesis yet undeveloped.

Despite the variety of methodologies and topics explored, the series' aim remains constant: to provide a sustained reflection upon the mission and ministry of Catholic theological formation of both clergy and laity alike.

The general editor of the Catholic Theological Formation Series, Fr. Kevin Zilverberg, serves as associate professor of Sacred Scripture and the founding director of Saint Paul Seminary Press at The Saint Paul Seminary School of Divinity.

Worthy Lamb

An Exegetical-Spiritual Commentary on John's Apocalypse

Andreas Hoeck

SAINT PAUL, MINNESOTA • 2024

Cover image: Lamb of God window, St. Peter Catholic Church, St. Charles, Missouri
Cover design by Willem Mineur

Published 2024 by
Saint Paul Seminary Press
2260 Summit Ave., Saint Paul, Minnesota 55105

Library of Congress Control Number: 2024934805
LC record available at https://lccn.loc.gov/2024934805

Catholic Theological Formation Series
ISSN 2765-9283
ISBN 978-1-953936-12-7 (paperback)
ISBN 978-1-953936-62-2 (ebook)

Nihil Obstat:
Reverend Evan Koop, STD
Censor Librorum
Imprimatur:
Most Reverend Bernard A. Hebda, JCL, JD
Archbishop of Saint Paul and Minneapolis
April 9, 2024

spspress.com

Contents

Preface

Jesus is the first and the last name mentioned in the Book of the Apocalypse, solemnly pronounced no fewer than four times in its two opening (1:1–2) and closing verses (22:20–21). And just as he is, therefore, the beginning and the end of his Revelation to John, so he is also the all-embracing Alpha and Omega of God's historical dealings with the human family (22:13), making both ipso facto Christocentric. Unquestionably the most challenging book of the New Testament, its narration is of irresistible fascination to reader and interpreter alike. As the saying goes, truth is stranger than fiction; so also the Apocalypse as a veritable kaleidoscope of preternatural visions, brimming with intriguing and often breathtaking images more thrilling than any fable or fantasy, unveiled to John to faithfully report to us. We can intuit how much is at stake, and rather than being ill at ease with it, we are invited to approach it with thoughtfulness, creativity, and imagination. Such pondering is far removed from any literalist or unspiritual reading of the tea leaves or crystal-gazing, but rather seeks to grasp its divine message involving time and eternity.

When considered in this way, the Book of Revelation can never be passé; on the contrary, its attractiveness will continue to grow. Given the radical paucity of eschatological thought in the ancient world, it marks the defining highpoint of the biblical theology of history. Indeed, it superbly unfurls what was presaged about the panhistorical struggle on earth between happiness and rebellion especially in Psalms 1–2, or between the Church and the infernal gates as foretold at Matthew 16:18. And by keeping an unwavering focus on the apocalyptic Lamb, we will witness the victory of righteousness in the end.

This book is born out of three decades of personal studies of John's Apocalypse, including my doctoral dissertation on the topic of the New Jerusalem at the Pontifical Biblical Institute in Rome back in 2001, preceded and followed by many uninterrupted years of research and seminary teaching. But what triggered the thought of writing this commentary were those reiterated inquiries of my students over the years: "What do all these apocalyptic symbols mean for our lives today?" So, the intention was to point to the vast horizon of connections between a close reading of the text of Revelation and Christian spirituality, with no claim whatsoever to exhaustiveness.

Some initial vistas and patterns of interpretation are offered here, in hopes that they may incentivize the reader to carry on and go deeper in his own right, ideally with a Bible at hand to look up at least some of the numerous scriptural cross-references. *In puero homo*, "in the infant is hidden the adult," goes the adage attributed to Leonardo da Vinci, putting in a nutshell the truism that seminal realities mature and reach a fuller potential as our lives go on. May this exegetical-spiritual exposition of the Apocalypse in some small ways illumine the reader's thinking, to recognize ever more readily the paradigm of that epic conflict between the forces of light and darkness, between the dragon and the Lamb, playing out not only in the vicissitudes of the world today, but also in one's personal life.

But you, dear reader, may be wondering why there is yet another commentary on top of hundreds written over the centuries already, starting from the earliest surviving complete Latin commentary by the late third-century ecclesiastical writer Victorinus of Pettau, and the oldest Greek patristic one by the seventh-century Andrew of Caesarea, up to the almost uncountable, interdenominational, and highly respected ones of our own time. To answer this very justified question, allow me to point to three methodical traits whose combination, I believe, lends to the one you are holding in your hands a touch of uniqueness.

Casting about for perhaps novel ways to benefit from Revelation as an inexhaustible repository of insights for our Christian spirituality, I *firstly* decided to write from a Catholic vantage point. And what is meant by that is that the conclusions drawn from the interpretation of its symbolism invariably flow into reflections of a spiritual nature that will boil down to tenets of Catholic faith and morals. As a *second* methodological determination, this present commentary aims at enriching the interior life of the baptized soul. Hence, it will not be a matter of entertaining contemporary or futuristic geopolitical speculations, but rather of receiving a salvific message for the Christian heart through a close present-centered reading, attempting to actualize its timeless truths.[1] Tied into this is the *third* hermeneutical criterion underlying this book, and that is its preference for an idealist point of view that does not attempt to identify apocalyptic imagery with concrete historical events. Rather, symbols, figures, and metaphors are viewed as paradigmatic of the epic battle between good and evil that await their careful application to the interior life of the disciples of Christ of all times and places. Yet that mindset does not exclude an occasional reference to a more historicist reading of John's text.

And by choosing this allegorical-spiritual line of thought, we insert ourselves into a tradition that has the influential fourth-century Latin theologian Tyconius as one of its earliest proponents. But what is perhaps most singular about this present commentary[2] is that I have preferentially drawn, among others, on two far less known representatives of the idealist school, making them Archimedean points of comparison, namely, Rupert of Deutz and Adrienne von Speyr. The former, classically known as Rupertus Tuitiensis (d. 1129), was the Abbot of St. Heribert's Monastery in Cologne, present-day Germany. He became widely known as an influential Benedictine theologian during a period dominated by the Cluniac Reforms in Europe, a diligent and passionate figure of pre-scholastic medieval exegesis.[3] His hitherto untranslated Latin commentary on the Book of Revelation that I consulted (*In Apocalypsim Joannis Apostoli commentaria*) is heavily indebted to the interpretation of three foregoing Benedictines, namely, St. Bede the Venerable, Ambrose Autpert, and Haimo of Auxerre.[4] In this book he will be referred to simply as Rupert and quoted under the acronym RD. The Servant of God Adrienne von Speyr (d. 1967) in turn was a Swiss Catholic physician, prolific writer, and theologian. She creatively collaborated with the work of Hans Urs von Balthasar and is considered to have been a mystic and stigmatist, whose profound convictions of faith were brought to maturity amid the calamities of the Second World War. I draw on her spiritual reflections on the Book of Revelation from the original German commentary (*Apokalypse: Betrachtungen über die Geheime Offenbarung*), referring to her simply as Adrienne, henceforth cited under her initials AvS.

1. Cf. Craig R. Koester, *Revelation and the End of All Things* (Grand Rapids, MI: Eerdmans, 2001), 2–8.

2. Distinguishing it from similar ones, e.g., Stephen C. Doyle, *Apocalypse: A Catholic Perspective on the Book of Revelation* (Cincinnati, OH: St. Anthony Messenger, 2005).

3. Cf. Benedict XVI's General Audience on Rupert of Deutz (December 9, 2009).

4. Cf. Ian Boxall and Richard M. Tresley, *The Book of Revelation and Its Interpreters: Short Studies and an Annotated Bibliography* (New York: Rowman & Littlefield, 2015), 227.

All that said, an explanatory word concerning the book's purpose, intended readership, and recommended usage is in order. Beginning with its purpose, the subtitle speaks of an exegetical-spiritual commentary, which means that the entire Apocalypse, chapter and verse, will be interpreted by paying close attention to the text's linguistic and literary traits. This scrutiny of its grammatical, syntactical, and vocabular features will then inform inferences and speculations of a theological nature, highlighting its biblical meaning proper. But the goal is to take those scriptural expositions or findings and apply them to the realm of Christian spirituality. Thus, we are aiming not only at deciphering apocalyptic imagery, but at understanding its significance and relevance for one's personal life as a baptized member of God's people. And this no doubt must be considered to have been the intention of the sacred author, to not only communicate sterile symbolisms but to inspire his readers to reform their lives and pursue virtue and holiness.

And that brings me to the intended readership: As alluded to in the second paragraph above, the book was conceived as a written response, as it were, to conversations with seminary students over the years. I had them in mind primarily when I decided to illustrate the connection between apocalyptic metaphor and their future priestly life. Consequently, it presupposes at least some prior familiarity with biblical matters, and with the Book of Revelation and its interpreters in particular. But such an ideal background should not stop any other reader from delving in. As a matter of fact, I do believe that it holds an appeal for a wider audience of college students, Catholic Christians, and all Christians alike, and that it could even serve as a textbook for a course or seminar on John's Apocalypse. But ultimately, anybody of goodwill and interest in the Sacred Scriptures, regardless of background, should feel invited to engage in reading this exegetical-spiritual commentary. Allow me to channel that childlike sing-song voice that impelled St. Augustine to open the Bible and be enriched by its wisdom: *Tolle lege, tolle lege!* (Latin for "Take up and read, take up and read!").[5]

At this point, may I also add a few practical recommendations on how to make good use of the pages of this book: In order that the forest not be missed for the trees, it will be of great benefit to keep a close eye on the detailed outline of the Book of Revelation found in the Appendix, which will serve as an exoskeleton, as it were, ensuring structural logic and a clearer train of thought. Its headings and subheadings offer guidance through the multiplicity of Revelation's image-fields. They caption major thematic threads such as the septets of

5. Augustine, *Confessions*, 8.12.

letters, seals, trumpets, plague-bowls, and makarisms, but also the quartets of dirges, Hallelujahs, and wisdom calls, as well as the various stages of the Church as *expectans* ("awaiting"), *militans* ("militant"), *pressa* ("persecuted"), *triumphans* ("triumphant"), *sponsalis* ("espoused"), and *consummata* ("fulfilled"). Also, at the beginning of several chapters, a narrative summary is included to make sure the larger apocalyptic plot is not overlooked. I have opted against headlining the spiritual reflections, since they are interwoven into each passage of exegetical and theological exposition. Hence, they form a textual unity requiring the reader to proceed patiently and meditatively, also mindful of the many included biblical cross-references to verify intertextual meaning.

In terms of the book's methodology, we choose to forego a more comprehensive isagogics to the literary and exegetical science behind the Book of Revelation, including its place within the broader category of Judeo-Christian apocalyptic thought and its function during first-century Christianity, which, I believe, would be redundant considering that these have already been expansively dealt with in numerous other modern commentaries. Suffice it to reference the superb introductions, inclusive of extensive bibliographies, contained in Beale (*Book of Revelation*), Harrington (*Revelation*), Williamson (*Revelation*), as well as Muller (*History of the Book of Revelation*).[6]

Nevertheless, here is a preliminary review of a few general principles that undergird the organization and method of exegesis of this present book. Beginning with its format, instead of selecting and isolating certain passages for interpretation,[7] an attempt has been made to comment on every single verse of Revelation. All theological or spiritual inferences will be based on a meticulous analysis of the vocabular-literal meaning of words and sentences, in consultation with dictionaries such as Liddell and Scott's *Greek-English Lexicon*, or digitized resources such as Accordance Bible Software and BibleHub.

Although rooted in the soil of intertestamental Judeo-Christian apocalypses, John's Apocalypse stands out by its uncompromising Christocentrism as well as its markedly solecistic style. Teeming as it does with non-Greek phraseology and downright grammatical irregularities, its language betrays a

6. G. K. Beale, *The Book of Revelation*, NIGTC (Grand Rapids, MI: Eerdmans, 2013 [reprint]); Wilfrid J. Harrington, *Revelation*, SaPaSe (Collegeville, MN: Liturgical Press, 1993); Peter S. Williamson, *Revelation*, CCSS (Grand Rapids, MI: Baker Academic, 2015); David G. Muller, *Testing the Apocalypse: The History of the Book of Revelation* (Bloomington, IN: WestBow [Nelson & Zondervan], 2016).

7. E.g., A. Robert Nusca, *The Christ of the Apocalypse: Contemplating the Faces of Jesus in the Book of Revelation* (Steubenville, OH: Emmaus Road, 2018).

strong Semitic influence.[8] One can only imagine how its linguistic harshness must have provoked strong reactions from an early Hellenic-Christian audience, and by the same token it makes the book even more thought-provoking, analogous to its theological and spiritual provocativeness. As he struggles to put his otherworldly visions into human words, the apostle's speech becomes meta-conceptual and trans-historical, so to speak, inserting himself into the stream of mystics as the "calligraphers of the ineffable."[9]

Since in the Catholic Church the 1986 New Vulgate[10] (*editio typica altera* or revised version) is the official Latin text, it will be our exegetical fulcrum, while we translate and analyze the Koine Greek version and an English rendition, that is, the New Revised Standard Version Catholic Edition, accordingly. Much more than any other New Testament book, John's Revelation is a masterpiece of intertextuality, a veritable tapestry of approximately one thousand innuendos to the Old Testament.[11] His thought-world is shaped by the book of Exodus, by the prophecies of Daniel, Ezekiel, and Isaiah, as well as by the Wisdom books. Also, the epistolary format and the Asian provenance of Revelation suggest a profound Pauline affinity.[12] With amazing originality, he frequently gives these influences a paradoxical twist, always delighting in vivid and dramatic imagery. And it is not an exaggeration to say that the Old Testament is sufficient to unlock every single apocalyptic simile. It is for this reason that plentiful biblical cross-references were added in this book, to stimulate the reader's imagination, to facilitate further reflection, and to aid in tying the scriptural-spiritual threads together.

Moreover, what has been upheld for nearly two thousand years of Catholic tradition is that the visionary who authored the Apocalypse and who restates his personal name "John" four times in it, is identical with John the Evangelist, the son of Zebedee, the brother of James, the beloved disciple and apostle of Christ Jesus.[13] And that is also the premise endorsed in this commentary,

8. Cf. Edwin A. Abbott, *Johannine Grammar* (London: Adam and Charles Black, 1906); Steven Thompson, *The Apocalypse and Semitic Syntax* (New York: Cambridge University Press, 1985).

9. Cf. William Harmless, *Mystics* (Oxford: Oxford University Press, 2007), xiv.

10. In this book also called Nova Vulgata and Neo-Vulgate.

11. Cf. Colin J. Hemer, *The Letters to the Seven Churches of Asia in Their Local Setting* (Grand Rapids, MI: Eerdmans, 2001), 210; G. K. Beale and D. A. Carson, *Commentary on the New Testament Use of the Old Testament* (Grand Rapids, MI: Baker Academic, 2007), 1082.

12. Cf. Garrick V. Allen, *The Book of Revelation and Early Jewish Textual Culture*, SNTSMS 168 (Cambridge, UK: Cambridge University Press, 2017).

13. For instance, the Divine Office's Latin hymn of the Morning Prayer on the feast day of St. John (December 27) appears to confirm that Johannine authorship: "Tu, raptus in sublimia,

enabling us to study his Revelation in theological closeness to his Gospel and Letters.[14] Not only does he lend his apostolic authority to the Lord's dictate, but his love for him and his Boanerges zeal for his Kingdom, too, and his acute discernment of spirits (Mark 9:38), make him an inspiring exemplar of how to receive his writing.

Another methodic postulation is the centrality of the heavenly liturgy, meaning that the cosmic worship that unfolds unceasingly before the Lamb's throne is all-encompassing and all-important both for the ecclesial community as well as for the individual Christian. It is the native setting for the proclamation, the hearing, and the understanding of God's Revelation, also granting us a glimpse into the Ephesian church shepherded by John.[15] Hence, it is not at all unexpected that the overarching spiritual conflict hinges on the true adoration of the Most High and his Anointed One, in opposition to the blasphemous worship of the dragon and his beastly minions.

Furthermore, in its well-structured outline, the apocalyptic plot advances not so much in chronological linearity of ever-new scenes, but mainly in a logic of circularity or spiraling recapitulation, presenting the same epic conflict between the dragon and the Lamb from ever-varying angles.[16] And so, we will follow its canonical sequence of chapters and visions, highlighting the various tercets, quartets, and septets, seeking to unpack each one as a vignette representing a different stage in the Christian's interior life. What is more, the Apocalypse cannot be deciphered except by a hermeneutics of "signification" (*sēmaínō*, σημαίνω, *significare*, Rev 1:1) or symbolism.[17] John's metaphorical world incorporates anthropological (humanity-related), arithmetic[18]

/ arcana caeli conspicis; / Agni sed et mysteria / Ecclesiaeque percipis" (author's translation: "Raptured into sublimity, you saw the secrets of heaven, but also received the mysteries of the Lamb and of the Church").

14. Cf. Stephen S. Smalley, *The Revelation to John: A Commentary on the Greek Text of the Apocalypse* (Downers Grove, IL: InterVarsity Press, 2005), ix.

15. Cf. Patrick Henry Reardon, *Revelation: A Liturgical Prophecy* (Yonkers, NY: St Vladimir's Seminary Press, 2018), 9–33.

16. Cf. Augustine, *De civitate Dei* 20.17; Williamson, *Revelation*, 24.

17. A symbol being "something chosen to stand for or represent something else, usually because of a resemblance in qualities or characteristics." A. H. Marckwardt et al., *Funk & Wagnalls Standard Dictionary of the English Language*, International Edition, vol. 2 (New York: Funk & Wagnalls, 1967), 1270.

18. Where, for instance, "one" can stand for divine excellence or unity, "three" for the Trinity, "three and a half" for a limited time, "four" for creation or universality, "six" for imperfection, "seven" for fullness or salvation, "eight" for regeneration, "nine" for mystery, "ten" for restricted world-power, "twelve" and "twenty-four" for God's people, "forty" for the Church's

(number-related), chromatic (color-related), cosmic (cataclysm-related), and theriomorphic (animal-related) symbols. Oftentimes, he employs them in a cumulative fashion, blending elements that would be incompatible on earth, to underscore divine transcendence.

Moreover, Revelation represents a worldview of relative ethical dualism where evil makes war against the principles of good while God remains in control at all times and into eternity. It seems to place an exclamation mark behind Malachi's prediction, "Then once more you shall see the difference between the righteous and the wicked, between one who serves God and one who does not serve him" (Mal 3:18). However, unlike an absolute dualism of manichaeistic fashion, where this conflict would perpetuate itself *ad infinitum*, the apocalyptic dualism witnesses how history repeats itself in that struggle, but that after the eschatological turning point of Christ's Resurrection, everything becomes an anticipation of his eventual victory at the end of history.

Before we absorb ourselves in the sacred text, however, I must express my gratitude to those who helped make this book possible. First and foremost, I am filled with thankfulness toward my late father and my mother who were the ones who first placed a Bible into my hands as a child; this book is dedicated to them, *parentibus pietate*. I am also indebted to the late Fr. Ugo Vanni, SJ, my esteemed former professor of John's Apocalypse and doctoral director at my beloved alma mater, the Pontifical Biblical Institute in Rome, back in the 1990s. His love for Revelation and his wisdom in teaching it kindled a fire in me to take up this magnificent book of Scripture and scrutinize it myself, and that flame has only increased over the years; may the good Lord richly reward him for his mentorship. Another debt of gratitude is owed to Fr. Daniel Leonard, the current rector of Saint John Vianney Theological Seminary of the Archdiocese of Denver, who granted me a sabbatical leave for the fall of the academic year 2022: that gift turned out to be just perfect timing to advance the writing of this book, begun in early 2020. A heartfelt thanks goes also to our academic dean, Dr. Alphonso Pinto, for his support, to the Theology faculty who graciously covered my coursework during my absence from the classroom, and to the kind staff of our seminary library, especially Stephen Sweeney and Tamara Conley. I am very appreciative, too, of the magnanimity, expertise, and outstanding knowledgeableness of the reviewers as the manuscript underwent a double-blind peer review. A sincere thank you also to Erika Zabinski, the copyeditor, who made it so easy and pleasant to work through the final corrections

trials, and "one thousand" for an extended but not endless period; cf. Jean-Pierre Prévost, *How to Read the Apocalypse*, trans. John Bowden (New York: Crossroads, 1993), 33.

and ready the manuscript for printing. I thank Kathryn Wehr, who carefully proofread the manuscript, even checking the Greek diacritics. I am also much obliged to Deacon Larry Boldt, pastoral associate of St. Peter Catholic Church in St. Charles, Missouri, for going out of his way to provide me with the lovely photography of the Apocalyptic Lamb stained glass window featured on the book's front cover. Likewise, I am grateful for the professional and patient work of the *censor librorum*, Fr. Evan Koop, instrumental in granting the *Imprimatur* from the Archdiocese of Saint Paul and Minneapolis. Last but not least, my deep gratitude goes to Fr. Kevin Zilverberg for having so generously accepted this book for publication in his Catholic Theological Formation Series; and the fact that he is an alum of our seminary and my former student adds much joy to my thankfulness, but words fail to describe his Godsent kindness and helpfulness in carrying this project across the finish line.

And I cannot close these opening remarks without mentioning St. Joseph. As a minuscule token of filial devotion, I would like to entrust this book and its readers to him as the patron saint of the universal Church, who like John was instructed by God about Jesus through an angel in dreams (Matt 1:20). In due season, that Son of the carpenter, while speaking to all only in parables, would explain everything in private to his disciples (Mark 4:34); and so, may he now be at our side and in our mind to help unseal the mysteries of his Apocalypse to us.

Fr. Andreas Hoeck
November 1, 2023
Solemnity of All Saints

Abbreviations

ACCS	Ancient Christian Commentary on Scripture
ACT	Ancient Christian Texts
ANF	Alexander Roberts, James Donaldson, A. Cleveland Coxe, and Allan Menzies, eds., *Ante-Nicene Fathers* (Buffalo, NY: Christian Literature Publishing Company, 1885–1897)
AUSDS	Andrews University Seminary Doctoral Dissertation Series
AvS	Adrienne von Speyr, *Apokalypse: Betrachtungen über die Geheime Offenbarung*, 4th ed. (Freiburg: Johannes Verlag Einsiedeln, 2019)
BECNT	Baker Academic Commentary on the New Testament
CCC	*Catechism of the Catholic Church*, 2nd ed. (New York: Doubleday, 1997)
CBQMS	Catholic Biblical Quarterly Monograph Series
CCSS	Catholic Commentary on Sacred Scripture
CTh	Cahiers Théologiques
ECF	Early Christian Fathers Series
GNS	Good News Studies
IVPNTC	New Testament Commentary Series
JSOTS	Journal for the Study of the Old Testament Supplement Series
McANTC	MacArthur New Testament Commentary
NIGTC	New International Greek Testament Commentary
NPNF 2	Philip Schaff and Henry Wace, eds., *A Select Library of Nicene and Post-Nicene Fathers. Second Series* (Buffalo, NY: Christian Literature Publishing Company, 1890–1900)
NRSVCE	New Revised Standard Version, Catholic Edition
NTT	New Testament Theology
NVg	Neo-Vulgate
PG	*Patrologia Graeca*, ed. Jacques-Paul Migne (Paris, 1857–66)
PL	*Patrologia Latina*, ed. Jacques-Paul Migne (Paris, 1841–55)

RD	Rupert of Deutz, *In Apocalypsim Joannis Apostoli commentaria* (AD 1129), PL 169
SaPaSe	Sacra Pagina series
SBLit	Studies in Biblical Literature
SNTSMS	Society for New Testament Studies Monograph Series
SC	Sources chrétiennes
SST	Studies in Sacred Theology
TCS	Teams Commentary Series
ZS	Zacchaeus Studies

PART I

1:1–8, Unveiling of the unknown

Apocalyptic chain of communication (1:1–2)

[1]The revelation of Jesus Christ, which God gave him to show his servants what must soon take place; he made it known by sending his angel to his servant John, [2]who testified to the word of God and to the testimony of Jesus Christ, even to all that he saw.[1]

As is the case with most biblical books, whose opening verses are of programmatic importance,[2] so, too, it is with the Apocalypse of St. John, also known as the Book of Revelation. Its prologue (vv. 1–3) presents the reader with four features that set the inspirational stage for the lifelong adventure of a Christian's inner life according to these revelations, and on which the epilogue (22:6–21) will expand. The sacred author begins by indicating the overall title: "Revelation of Jesus Christ" (v. 1a). By choosing the name "Apocalypse" (*Apokálypsis*, Αποκάλυψις),[3] he pledges that otherwise hidden things can and will be revealed. As such there is the guarantee right from the start that we are not dealing with a concealing[4] or obstructing of the person of Christ Jesus to the point of disappearing like a passing mirage. With that in mind, we can confidently delve into the chapters of this last biblical book, reassured that things yet unseen and unknown will be uncovered and become visible and understandable.

1. The passages from the Book of Revelation cited at the beginning of each section are from the NRSVCE; the more literal translations provided during the discussion sections are by the author.

2. E.g., Gen 1:1–2; Job 1:1; Ps 1:1–2; Ezek 1:1; Luke 1:1–4; John 1:1–18; Heb 1:1–4.

3. The Greek noun for "revelation, disclosure, uncovering, appearance," deriving from the preposition *apó* (ἀπό), "away from," and the verb *kalýptō* (καλύπτω), "to cover," hence, "to reveal, remove the veil, uncover"; it recurs four times in the Septuagint, and eighteen times outside this book in the New Testament.

4. I.e., *apókrypsis* (ἀπόκρυψις), as the lexical antonym to the above *apokálypsis* (ἀποκάλυψις), cf. Henry George Liddell and Robert Scott, *A Greek-English Lexicon*, 9th ed. (Oxford: Clarendon, 1940), 204.

Evidently, too, the act of lifting the veil of secrecy means that its content would not have been accessible or comprehensible to the human mind, and that we depend totally on God's initiative in this regard. At the same time, these are words of prophecy (v. 3), underlining that the prediction of future events is their essence. A second aspect made prominent in this foreword is the chain of command, or rather the chain of communication (v. 1) that begins with God the Father as its ultimate origin. He is the one to "grant" (*édōken*, ἔδωκεν, *dedit*) this revelation to his Son. And what exactly did he give to him? Well, technically, the epexegetical genitive in the Greek text can mean either an objective revelation made by Christ, or also a subjective revelation of or about Christ. Now, since God the Father has already been identified as the source of this unveiling, it is more plausible that this *apokalypsis* uncovers the very mystery of Jesus Christ.

Yet if this book has as its content the revelation about Christ (1 Cor 1:7), then he truly receives absolutely everything from his Father, including the knowledge regarding the essence of his very self.[5] Given the Apocalypse's placement at the end of the New Testament canon, this revelation must, therefore, be the crowning gift of the Father to his Son. One might say that in the Gospels, the Son reveals the Father, while in this book, the Father reveals the Son. As a logical consequence, our Christian life, especially the hidden life of our soul, cannot be understood outside of the Father's revelation to us, which will also remain the guiding principle throughout these following reflections.

Mirroring the movement of the Incarnation, the destination or audience of this revelation are the heavenly Father's servants (v. 1). And two additional links in the middle complete the chain of communication, namely, the Father's angel, who is also Jesus' angel (22:16), sent to one of his servants, namely, the apostle John.[6] Rupert is of the opinion that this angelic messenger appeared to the apostle in the form of Christ himself.[7] Only genuine servants acknowledge God as their Creator and Lord, and consequently, the truths of these revelations can be fully received only by servant-minded souls. Such spiritual servanthood also implies that John had no say in the unfolding of the visionary plot. Saintly indifference in complete oneness with the will of the Lord was required

5. Rupert of Deutz, *In Apocalypsim Joannis Apostoli commentaria*, PL 169:828 (hereafter RD; all translations are by the author).

6. The 1916 apparitions of the angel of peace to the children of Fatima in Portugal as a prelude to Our Lady's apparitions in 1917, could serve as a more recent example of that logic of revealing and communicating of hidden mysteries.

7. "In figura Christi," cf. RD, 829.

on his part in receiving and faithfully transmitting the visions, a veritable mysticism of service and love.[8]

If Mary's *Fiat* in response to the annunciation of the angel Gabriel set in motion the Incarnation and eventually the holy Gospels, so also now, John's obedience gives the angel the opportunity to communicate the Apocalypse. And to stay with the Marian theme, similar to Mary's contemplation of the divine fruit of her womb, the apostolic visionary is now completely focused on this revelation of Mary's Son in the darkness of service, until he will cry out in proclaiming it to the Church, giving spiritual birth to Christ again in many souls.[9] If service, however, is an expression of authentic love, then John becomes an exemplar of humanity's love for the Lord, love that in the end turns into faithful witness. His testimony is not selective, but he narrates "all that he saw" (v. 2) in the objectivity of love and mission. This is the spiritual logic in the chain of communication of Christ's revelation, which will find its closing counterpart in the book's afterword (22:6–21).

First makarism: Liturgical reception (1:3)

[3]Blessed is the one who reads aloud the words of the prophecy, and blessed are those who hear and who keep what is written in it; for the time is near.

As a third postulate within Revelation's preamble, John envisions an ecclesial assembly as the primary place of proclamation of his visions, implied by the grammatical singular of "the one who reads" (*qui legit*) and the plural of the "those who hear" (*qui audiunt*) in v. 3.[10] This is a hint at the liturgy of the Word during the Holy Eucharist as it was celebrated by the early Church and until today.[11] St. Paul had already affirmed that the proclaimed word of God effects and creates faith as it arises from hearing as a gift from God (Rom 10:17). By

8. Cf. Adrienne von Speyr, *Apokalypse: Betrachtungen über die Geheime Offenbarung*, 4th ed. (Freiburg: Johannes Verlag Einsiedeln, 2019), 15–19 [hereafter AvS; all translations are by the author].

9. Cf. AvS, 37–43.

10. Cf. *Catechism of the Catholic Church*, 2nd ed. (New York: Doubleday, 1997), §§103, 1100.

11. "Revelation was specifically designed to be read aloud in the liturgy (1:3), and it is spangled with heavenly liturgies. It has been plausibly suggested that 1:4–8 might be read as a liturgical dialogue." Wilfrid J. Harrington, *Revelation: Proclaiming a Vision of Hope* (San Jose, CA: Resource Publications, 1994), 100; see also Ugo Vanni, "Un esempio di dialogo liturgico in Ap 1,4–8," *Biblica* 57, no. 4 (1976): 453–67.

emphasizing this ecclesial hearing, the upcoming letters (chs. 2–3) become an exordium to the salvific story to be heard in the main part of the Apocalypse (chs. 4–22).[12]

Detached from such a liturgical communion with other Christians, the soul will not be able to decipher what God the Father "indicates through signs" (v. 1). It is critical to fully grasp the meaning of the Greek verb *sēmaínō* (σημαίνω) in this verse, cognate to the nouns *sêma* (σῆμα) and *sēmeîon* (σημεῖον), i.e., "sign, signal, symbol, visual guidance"; it speaks to the notion of producing an image or impression to communicate an idea. That "signification" (*significare*, v. 1) includes the prophetic foretelling of things in the traditional biblical sense.[13] Hence, what is made known about the God-Man[14] will be given by way of symbols that require spiritual decoding and exegeting. This is crucial for the correct interpretation of this biblical genre, and most of all, it is pivotal for the benefit of our interior life.

Indeed, it is chiefly during our liturgies as a hermeneutic framework that the symbolic "words of the prophecy" (v. 3) are unveiled to us.[15] Adrienne rightly posits that they are addressed primarily to the human spirit rather than to the person's mere intellectual comprehension.[16] To make the reception of this apocalyptic message complete, the soul is to "protect" it (*tēréō*, τηρέω, *servare*, v. 3), as if to respect and keep inviolate the sovereignty of the divine word. In so doing, one will experience the otherworldly happiness, a foretaste of heavenly bliss (*makários*, μακάριος, *beatus*) of its interior presence, constituting the first of seven beatitudes in Revelation.[17]

One more spiritual aspect can be highlighted within this prologue, namely, that John seems to convey an urgency about the imminence of fulfilment when he says "what must soon take place" in the opening verse (v. 1b), and reiterates the concept here: "For the time is near" (v. 3; cf. 22:10).[18] Faith, therefore, is not just testimony to what happened in the past, but also embraces the things

12. Cf. Jerome H. Neyrey, *Hearing Revelation 1–3: Listening with Greek Rhetoric and Culture*, CQBMS 56 (Washington, DC: Catholic Biblical Association of America, 2019), 12–13.

13. John employs this word three times in his Gospel, incidentally, in places where it is a matter of predicting the manner of Jesus' or Peter's death (John 12:33; 18:32; 21:19).

14. A title for Christ (*Theánthrōpos*, Θεάνθρωπος) first used by Origen (cf. *De principiis*, 2.4).

15. Cf. Pierre Prigent, *Apocalypse et Liturgie*, CTh 52 (Neuchâtel: Delachaux et Niestlé, 1964).

16. Cf. AvS, 41.

17. Cf. 14:13; 16:15; 19:9; 20:6; 22:7, 14.

18. In contradistinction to the prophecy in Dan 2:28, which envisions a distant future.

that are yet to happen in the future. There is a sense of inevitability, too, regarding those events that are not subject to change or adaptation but are presented as accomplished and finished. That puts the reader in a position to reflect on human history from the vantage point of its finish line, as it were. It is described as still evolving and simultaneously already perfected.

Time and space assume a mystical relativity, as it were, with events taking place as if in a fourth dimension, appertaining neither to past, present, or future, nor to heaven, earth, or underworld, before they resolve at the end of time.[19] This pressing "soon" is not tied to a chronological before and after; it will remain an eschatological "soon" throughout the pilgrimage of the Church through centuries and millennia, making the apocalyptic images both contemporary to concrete events and timeless. For the interior person, it is the "soon" of proximity, or rather the presence, of Jesus Christ, "the same yesterday and today and forever" (Heb 13:8). The soul becomes increasingly aware of being surrounded by eternity, bound to render an account of its life on earth, as the prophet Zephaniah asserts (Zeph 1:14). Ergo, "soon" is interchangeable with "near" in the sense of accountability regarding the word received: out of love for us, Jesus exhorts us to be watchful.

Life with the Triune God (1:4–8)

[4]John to the seven churches that are in Asia. Grace to you and peace from him who is and who was and who is to come, and from the seven spirits who are before his throne, [5]and from Jesus Christ, the faithful witness, the firstborn of the dead, and the ruler of the kings of the earth. To him who loves us and freed us from our sins by his blood, [6]and made us to be a kingdom, priests serving his God and Father, to him be glory and dominion forever and ever. Amen. [7]Look! He is coming with the clouds; every eye will see him, even those who pierced him; and on his account all the tribes of the earth will wail. So it is to be. Amen. [8]"I am the Alpha and the Omega," says the Lord God, who is and who was and who is to come, the Almighty.

These verses can be described as an epistolary preface to the letters that the apostle John is about to address to the seven churches in Asia Minor, in accordance with the orders to be received (vv. 11, 19). With words of great solemnity, he now addresses himself to "the seven churches that are in Asia" (v. 4; cf. 1 Cor

19. Cf. RD, 897; AvS, 16.

16:19), and according to the underlying numerical symbolism, so characteristic of this apocalyptic genre, the number seven represents fullness and perfection. Rupert sees this foreshadowed in the seven nations conquered by Israel.[20] Writing as he does to the entire Church of all generations, and through her to the whole world,[21] John's succinct epistles as well as the ensuing visions are intended to draw a picture of how she will reach the point of her own universal and saintly consummation. As she walks with humanity through history, she attains to her own perfection. Consequently, we as members of this Mystical Body of Christ will find in this book a sure path to perfection, an inspired message of how we ourselves are meant to reach the goal of spiritual completeness.[22] We should not hesitate, therefore, to turn to the Apocalypse with confidence in search for that integrity and perfection of our Christian interior life, for we are those "seven churches."

What follows in vv. 4–8 amounts to a fascinating portrait of the very essence of the Blessed Trinity. Given its multiple facets, we will reflect separately on the three divine Persons in the order in which they appear in this biblical passage.[23] What will be the pivot of this scrutiny is the personal relationship we are called to discover and nourish with each of the three persons in that Triune God. Beginning with God the Father: the fact that the phrase "from him who is and who was and who is to come" (v. 4)[24] is solecistic in its Greek original, intimates that God is transcendent, and that his substance cannot be captured in the syntactic correctness of human language; he remains supernatural, and therefore also meta-conceptual, so to speak.[25]

Thus, God is the infinite present (*qui est*), existing from eternity (*qui erat*),[26]

20. Cf. RD, 832; see also Deut 7:1; Acts 13:19.

21. "For John also in the Revelation writes indeed to seven churches, yet speaks to all." Muratorian Canon, in Lee Martin McDonald, *The Formation of the Christian Biblical Canon* (Nashville, TN: Abingdon, 1988), 4 (p. 36); see also AvS, 80.

22. Cf. the words that the bishop addresses to the candidates after they make their promises of prayer, celibacy, and obedience, at the Mass of priestly ordination: "May God who has begun the good work in you bring it to fulfillment."

23. Adrienne speaks of a "tenfold Trinity," since it manifests itself in this paragraph as God the Father, the Holy Spirit as a septet of spirits, and the Son as God and man; she contends that whereas the Gospels depict neat differences among the three divine Persons, Revelation remains more fluid in its trinitarian delineation, cf. AvS, 45–46.

24. Cf. 1:8; 4:8; 16:5; 17:8, 11.

25. Cf. *CCC*, §206.

26. In the Greek, the expression *ho ēn* (ὁ ἦν) incorrectly couples a definite article with the imperfect tense of the auxiliary verb "to be" (*eînai*, εἶναι), a grammatical roughness that is smoothed over in the New Vulgate rendition.

and he will come to us in an unspecified future on the border between history and eternity (*qui venturus est*). There is only one other passage in the New Testament that speaks about God the Father coming into this world, i.e., John 14:23 (cf. Mic 1:3), and this wording sounds like a deliberate counterclaim to a title ascribed to the pagan god Zeus, "the one who was and who is and who will be." For the Christian reader this is of great relevance, since it confirms in the most straightforward terms that God the Father is our origin, our present life, and one day our destiny for ages unending. To spiritually relate to him means to embrace the divine purpose for one's existence on earth.

Indeed, he is the "Alpha and Omega" for each one personally (v. 8), and one's life is supposed to melt into the divine "I am" (*Egó eími*, 'Εγώ εἰμι, *Ego sum*). This is the only time, except for 21:5–6, when God the Father speaks in the first person. Just as the ancient rabbis used to arrange many of their Hebrew proverbs in acrostics (e.g., Ps 119), so also here, the first and last letters of the Hellenic alphabet become symbols of "the beginning and the end." Borrowing from the numerical interpretation of Scripture or gematria,[27] Rupert suggests that "Alpha" with its alphanumeric value of "one" represents the Father's only-begotten Son, and that "Omega," which is also "eight hundred," signifies all the redeemed who lived by the eight Gospel beatitudes, thus completing the Mystical Body of Christ. Be that as it may, for us to believe in God as "Alpha and Omega" means to profess our Creator and Restorer, our past, present, and future, resulting in a truly three-dimensional spirituality.[28]

In intimate union with the Father emerges the Holy Spirit, who dwells as "seven spirits" before his throne (v. 4).[29] Verse 4:5 will expand on this image, stating that "in front of the throne burn seven flaming torches, which are the seven spirits of God." Featured again is the plenary number "seven" that echoes the gifts of the Messianic Spirit (Isa 11:2–3). Repercussions of this pneumatic digit can be found in the Lamb's seven horns and seven eyes, which are the seven spirits of God sent out into all the earth (5:6). In addition to that, sevenfold will be the lampstands, stars, angels, churches, seals, trumpets, and bowls. Eastern traditions of biblical exegesis have recognized in those spirits an allusion to the angels, who are the closest associates of the divine Spirit.[30] In a similar vein, Adrienne maintains that these are seven ministers of Christ,

27. Cf. Keith D. Stanglin, *The Letter and Spirit of Biblical Interpretation: From the Early Church to Modern Practice* (Grand Rapids, MI: Baker Academic, 2018), 24.

28. Cf. RD, 831–33.

29. Cf. RD, 835–36.

30. Underscored by the liturgical presence of these vv. 4–6 in the Evening Prayer of the Liturgy of the Hours on the Feast of the Archangels (September 29).

representing the Holy Spirit and his sevenfold grace.[31] Hence, by anchoring our faith in this third divine Person, we grow in the spirit of adoration and spiritual worship before the throne of the Most High, illumined and strengthened by the manifold gifts of the Holy Spirit.[32]

Next, beginning in v. 5a, we find a vivid portrait of the second divine Person, the Son, the eternal Word, Jesus Christ. John reveals him with a climactic trifecta as "the faithful witness," "the firstborn of the dead,"[33] and "the ruler of the kings of the earth." One could argue that the "firstborn of the dead" implies that Christ grants resurrection to those born before his Incarnation, too.[34] Note that the consecration of the "firstborn" is rooted in the very Passover night and the ensuing exodus of the Hebrews from Egypt (Num 3:13). Also, the title "ruler of the kings of the earth" anticipates the majestic Rider on the white horse of the end-time battle, the "King of kings and Lord of lords" (19:16). As baptized Christians, therefore, we are consecrated into his eschatological witness, his resurrection of the flesh, and his universal dominion.

Accentuating the exceptional pulchritude of the subsequent vv. 5b–6 is the circumstance that they constitute the only New Testament doxology addressed exclusively to Jesus. Moreover, contained in this praise is another trilogy, this time aimed at Christ's relationship with individual souls: he loves us, he sets us interiorly free by dying a sacrificial death for each one of us, and he even makes us to be a kingdom of priests for the sole purpose of offering our lives in service to his beloved Abba. Hence, as a mother nourishes her child with her own blood and milk, so Christ shed his blood for us, giving him a certain maternal touch, too.[35] And Rupert points out the strident contrast between the Lord's infinite love for us and the tyranny of so many worldly kingdoms of all ages.[36]

Continuing the above thought, we can live in the certitude that Christ's filial love can transform us into worthy children of his Father, that we share in his victory over sin and death, and that our every word and action can be sacerdotal in nature to build up his reign on earth. Relatedly, Adrienne expresses the winsome thought that if Christ decides to save us by his blood, we can only receive it, surrender to him, and not fight against his gift of redemption.[37] And by doing so, our reciprocating love will contribute to his "glory and

31. Cf. AvS, 47.

32. Cf. *CCC*, §1830.

33. See the antithetical precedent at Job 18:13, where it implies a deadly disease.

34. Cf. AvS, 48–49.

35. Cf. Chrysostom, *Catecheses* 3.16.

36. Cf. RD, 839.

37. Cf. AvS, 49–51.

dominion,"[38] which knows no end (v. 6). Our inner life must be defined by looking forward to his coming at the end of time: "Amen!" (v. 6), "yes, indeed, so I believe!" (v. 7). These closing Amens bundle John's faith, hope, and love as if into a sheaf for the harvest.

Before moving into the opening vision at vv. 9–20, let us briefly ponder two of the finest gifts showered on us by each of the three divine Persons, namely, "grace and peace" (v. 4). The former, "grace," has a wide lexical spectrum in the Greek original *cháris* (χάρις, *gratia*):[39] on the one hand it signifies God's graciousness and goodwill toward his creatures, suggested also by the forceful dative pronoun "to you" (*vobis*), but also his immense attractiveness, generosity, and helpfulness. On the other hand, it instills delight in the soul, while at the same time producing exceptional effects of light and life in it. In response, the human heart is impelled to acknowledge not only the sheer gratuitousness and beneficence, but also the power of the divine Giver by acts of gratitude.

Along with grace, we are endowed with supernatural peace (v. 4), too, whose original vocable, *eirēnē* (εἰρήνη), carries a similarly rich spectrum of signification. As a state of mind, it is the opposite of inner conflict, indicating cessation of perceived hostility. It can figuratively refer to an agreement between persons,[40] in contrast to division and dissension. As a disposition of the soul, it is characterized by inner rest and harmony, wellbeing, and freedom from anxiety. This interior health is the outcome of reconciliation with God, but also of peaceful personal relationships which accept one another in justice, in turn bringing about tranquility and common welfare.[41] Not to be omitted is its connotation of messianic salvation of the end-time or eschaton (Luke 2:14). John seems to refer also to the grace of our Christian calling, and to the peace of reconciliation.[42] Adrienne comments that grace is given by Christ to his Church, and that peace is given back to him from all his cooperative and grateful churches.[43]

38. Literally, "empire" (*imperium*), from the Greek *krátos* (κράτος), denoting total power and supremacy.

39. In Greek mythology, Cháris is one of a group of goddesses personifying grace, fertility, and beauty, her name referring to the charming appearance of a fertile field or garden; cf. "Grace," Encyclopædia Britannica online.

40. The Proto-Indo-European term **pehₐḱ-* ("agreement, peace") is at the root of the Latin noun *pax* and the English "peace"; its verbal inflection *pactum*, therefore, has to do with "making a pact."

41. Evocative of the Latin adage *opus iustitiae pax*, "the work of justice shall be peace."

42. Cf. RD, 834.

43. Cf. AvS, 53.

1:9–20, The Church of the Son of Man

Brethren and partakers (1:9–12)

[9]I, John, your brother, who share with you in Jesus the persecution and the kingdom and the patient endurance, was on the island called Patmos because of the word of God and the testimony of Jesus. [10]I was in the spirit on the Lord's day, and I heard behind me a loud voice like a trumpet [11]saying, "Write in a book what you see and send it to the seven churches, to Ephesus, to Smyrna, to Pergamum, to Thyatira, to Sardis, to Philadelphia, and to Laodicea." [12]Then I turned to see whose voice it was that spoke to me, and on turning I saw seven golden lampstands.

The strong identity marker "I am" spoken by God the Father himself in the previous v. 8, redolent of Yahweh's revelation to Moses at the burning bush (Exod 3:14), is now imitated in the way the apostolic visionary introduces himself: "I, John" (v. 9). As the last surviving member of the college of the Twelve toward the end of the first century AD, he has already attained to such trans-regional renown that all he needs to mention is his first name for all the churches to know that it is the beloved disciple of the Lord speaking. Although declining any ecclesiastical rank or title, John does cite his name four times in Revelation.[1] Perhaps the three citations in this opening chapter alone are meant to underscore the veracity of his witness, not in self-aggrandizement but to protect the significance and authenticity of these precious visions, and ultimately to preserve them within the New Testament canon.[2]

Yet, despite his apostolic eminence he humbly calls himself "your brother" (v. 9). If the reader knew already from v. 1 that John is first and foremost God's servant (cf. Rom 1:1), then here he unassumingly asserts his status as a member of God's family, the Church, one with the many brethren. Complementing this,

1. Cf. vv. 1, 4, 9; 22:8.
2. Cf. RD, 848–49.

he is also our "partner" (*sygkoinōnós*, συγκοινωνός, *particeps*).[3] Likewise, as baptized children of God, we are led to boldly appreciate our own identity: we bear an individual Christian name that reminds us of the holy life of an angel or saint, we act in obedience to the dictate of a well-formed conscience like servants of the Lord, we recognize one another as brethren in God's ecclesial household, and we willingly become participants of her mission in this world.

Partaking of the "Kingdom" (v. 9) involves the experience of "tribulation," that is, suffering brought on by outward circumstances, as well as the inward anguish due to persecution. These inescapable afflictions must be met with Christlike patience and endurance. We should also point out the lexical range of the Greek *hypomonē* (ὑπομονή, *patientia*): this noun has to do with the capacity to "remain or persist" (*ménō*, μένω) "under" (*hýpo*, ὑπο) the weight of difficult conditions, or the adherence to a course of action despite challenges, and thus, the frame of mind of showing resilience and perseverance in the face of adversity. In this sense it is a component of the virtue of fortitude, combined with confidence and long-suffering. And it is sustained by the expectation that God will bring about realization in due time. He appears to strike a wise balance in making us always share in both the tough ("tribulation"), but also the joyful things ("Kingdom") of our Lord's life.[4]

Humanly speaking, John is in a terrible predicament, having been deported to the island called Patmos because of the word of God and the testimony of Jesus (v. 9). Patmos, even though geographically close to Asia, must have been all but unknown to the inhabitants of those lands. It is one of the Dodecanese, belonging to the wider southern Sporades island group in the Aegean Sea, and had been designated by the Romans as a penal colony: a convict would have been sentenced to forced labor in the local marble quarries.[5] While the exact circumstances of his banishment during the severe Christian persecution under the Roman emperor Domitian (reigning until AD 96) are not known, John must have been considered an enemy of the state and a criminal due to his loyalty to the Gospel.[6]

Yet, it is precisely in this most distressed situation that John "finds himself

3. A designation recurring at Rom 11:17; 1 Cor 9:23; Phil 1:7.

4. Cf. AvS, 72–73.

5. Also known as "damnation to the metals" (*damnatio ad metalla*), among the two most dreaded forms of punishment in ancient Rome, virtually tantamount to a death penalty; the other one was the "damnation to the beasts" (*damnatio ad bestias*), i.e., being thrown to the wild animals for public spectacle; according to tradition, the aged apostle miraculously survived his captivity, being able to return to Ephesus.

6. Cf. Pliny the Elder, *Natural History*, 4.23.

in the Spirit on a Sunday" (v. 10). The Greek verb *gínomai* (γίνομαι, "to become, to be") indicates that he entered a new state, that of spiritual ecstasy, but it also implies that when he wrote he was no longer held by it. This phrase "in the Spirit" will be repeated like a narrative bookmark at 4:2, 17:3, and 21:10. In this his visionary lot, the apostolic seer is preceded by the patriarch Jacob who saw Yahweh while in exile at Bethel (Gen 35:9); also in exile, Moses encountered the angel of the Lord at the burning bush (Exod 3:2); likewise, the prophet Elijah experiences God's nearness in exile at Mount Horeb (1 Kgs 19:12); Ezekiel, on his part, saw visions of God while in Babylonian captivity (Ezek 1:4); and Daniel watches the Son of Man approach the Ancient One (Dan 7:13).

There seems to be a divine pattern, namely, that for those to whom a home is denied on earth, the heavens open up for them. In other words, the more we are oppressed in this world and hemmed in from all sides, the more abundantly heavenly secrets will be revealed to us. Unquestionably, the time indicated is of relevance, too: just as Abraham sees the angels at noon, i.e., in the heat of the day (Gen 18:1), indicative of the fervor of his faith, so also John is drawn into his ecstasy on a Sunday, as if to underline his hope in the Risen Lord. One could distinguish three types of visions, namely, corporal, spiritual, and intellectual ones: the latter means that the mind is directly illuminated by the Holy Spirit to comprehend visionary images, as in the case of the patriarch Joseph and the prophet Daniel in the Old Testament.[7] It is also possible that the Holy Spirit took possession of the seer's mind, mystically removing him from himself, and thereby empowering him to experience things that go beyond the capacity of his mere human spirit. Or else, John may have been physically overpowered by an irresistible divine force, becoming completely controlled by the third divine Person.

Caught up in that Spirit, therefore, John "hears behind him a loud voice like a trumpet" (v. 10), a sound that is adapted to the imagination of the brethren (Heb 12:19). It is instantaneous and commands the entire message to be written down in a scroll (v. 11). This must have been a non-sensory articulation because John paradoxically "turns to see the voice that spoke to him" (v. 12), reminiscent of Moses "turning aside" to the burning bush (Exod 3:3), of Ezekiel's visionary experience as he is carried by the Spirit into exile (Ezek 3:12), but perhaps also of Mary Magdalene trying to catch a glimpse of the Risen Lord (John 20:14, 16). Emphasis is given to this movement of the apostle "turning around" (*convertere*) since it is reiterated in the same verse, as if to insist on a certain spiritual conversion before being able to receive the apocalyptic

7. Cf. RD, 852.

messages.[8] And what first meets his eye are seven golden lampstands,[9] which will be further commented on in vv. 13, 20.

Thus, this text inspires us to convert by prayer and fasting to a more purified faith in the Church, symbolized by those golden lamps (1 Pet 1:7). And why not think of a spiritual hearing and seeing at the same time by obediently investing ourselves into the reception of the word of God in faith and love? We must go out of our way, allow ourselves to be shaken out of daily routines and complacency, away from the ordinariness of everyday life. Only in this way can we become fully available in mind, will, and senses, to be open to the unexpected, the transcendent "Thou." In this way, John's physical turning around becomes emblematic of the Gospels' demand for personal *metanoía*, since Jesus' actions and teachings consistently exceed human expectations. By doing so, we signal our readiness to be transformed into ever more selfless instruments of God's grace.[10]

Three Christian offices (1:13–16)

[13]And in the midst of the lampstands I saw one like the Son of Man,
clothed with a long robe and with a golden sash across his chest. [14]His
head and his hair were white as white wool, white as snow; his eyes
were like a flame of fire, [15]his feet were like burnished bronze, refined as
in a furnace, and his voice was like the sound of many waters. [16]In his
right hand he held seven stars, and from his mouth came a sharp, two-
edged sword, and his face was like the sun shining with full force.

John is promptly rewarded with a magnificent vision, a symbolic depiction of Christ in glory, also known as the inaugural vision of the Son of Man (vv. 13–16). Amidst the many facets of it, there are the signs that reveal the three offices or *munera* of Jesus as our Priest, King,[11] and Prophet. First, his ankle-length robe denotes his dignity as the High Priest (Exod 28:4). As the apostle's gaze steadily moves upwards, he sees his chest girdled with a golden sash declaring his regal authority as King, chiefly to eviscerate the reign of sin and death. That royal

8. Cf. RD, 854–55.

9. Resonant of the menorah (Exod 25:31), the six-branched ancient Hebrew candelabra holding seven lamps, made of pure gold, and used in the tabernacle in the desert and later in the Temple in Jerusalem; it has remained a symbol of Judaism to this day.

10. Cf. AvS, 81–83.

11. In the Liturgy of the Hours, this pericope was chosen for the Office of Readings on the Solemnity of Christ the King.

band is actually placed across his chest (*ad mamillas*), which is the place of the beating heart, as if to showcase the seat of his person, full of everlasting life and divine love. Both the garment covering his whole body, as well as the girdle surrounding his thorax, manifest the Holy Spirit possessed by the Lord, containing and embracing his heart. And this pneumatic presence is the consubstantial sustainer of holiness and purity in the Body of Christ.[12] Among Jesus' insignia is also "a sharp, two-edged sword" coming from his mouth (v. 16), showing him to be the Prophet of God's word, judging the living and the dead,[13] and justly combating falsehood and impenitence. This divine word is prophetically completed in dogma and the teachings of the saints, and is echoed by the chorus of all nations who repeat and reflect on it until the end of time.

In addition to these images of the three *munera* of our Redeemer, and to round out the picture, there are signs indicating that he is at the same time divine and human (vv. 14–16). His divinity shines through the brilliance of his face, while the snow-white hair expresses eternity (Dan 7:9). His eyes like a flame of fire portray his omniscience, and his face like the blazing sun is indicative of his work of salvation, providing healing, warmth, and growth to the heart. Moreover, his feet of refined bronze display his immutability, and finally the seven stars secured by his right hand, i.e., the hand of power and authority, signal universal dominion.

By tentatively comparing Christ's nature to that of a Son of Man (*quasi*, "like," v. 13), the seer underlines his humanity, inviting our personal act of faith. His metallic feet are figurative of his Incarnation, with his body made redemptive in the furnace of his Passion and Resurrection. These glowing feet also seem to evince the missional zeal and loving obedience of the Church's outreach to all peoples. The Lord presents himself with the attributes of a spiritual director of the churches, too, clad in the regalia of his priestly, royal, and prophetic ministry, now ascended into heaven and united to the Father and the Spirit, but hypostatically retaining the self-effacing robe of his flesh once assumed through Mary his Mother.[14]

Returning to our spirituality as baptized children of the Church, this text inspires us to be mindful and proud of our affiliation with the threefold office (*munus triplex*) that makes all of us priests, kings, and prophets in the Kingdom already here on earth. That also means that we are called to officiate in daily spiritual sacrifice (Rom 12:1), to rule through kind and loving service, and to

12. Cf. AvS, 86.
13. Cf. RD, 859.
14. Cf. AvS, 89.

boldly proclaim the Good News in this world.[15] Faced with such burning luminosity, purifying integrity, and all-consuming eye contact with him, there is no room for indifference; each one is impelled to remove any obstacles, to surrender, and to be set ablaze by the God-Man Jesus Christ.

Mystery of the Church (1:17–20)

17 When I saw him, I fell at his feet as though dead. But he placed his right hand on me, saying, "Do not be afraid; I am the first and the last, 18 and the living one. I was dead, and see, I am alive forever and ever; and I have the keys of Death and of Hades. 19 Now write what you have seen, what is, and what is to take place after this. 20 As for the mystery of the seven stars that you saw in my right hand, and the seven golden lampstands: the seven stars are the angels of the seven churches, and the seven lampstands are the seven churches.

As a critical closing insight of this first chapter, the mystery (v. 20)[16] of the seven stars and the seven golden lampstands is revealed (vv. 12–13, 20): it is the hidden dimension of the Body of Christ, disclosed in the Church's teaching, known and practiced by persons who have been initiated through sacramental rites involving purification (baptism), corroboration (confirmation), and sacrifice (Eucharist). This mystery also alludes to what the influential fourth-century North African Donatist Tyconius called a bipartite Church (*ecclesia permixta*),[17] hinting at the mingling of the pious and the impious within the people of God, as also illustrated by the parable of the wheat and the tares growing together until the end (Matt 10:24–30). Thus, the Apocalypse describes the Church's

15. "The anointing with sacred chrism, perfumed oil consecrated by the bishop, signifies the gift of the Holy Spirit to the newly baptized, who has become a Christian, that is, one 'anointed' by the Holy Spirit, incorporated into Christ who is anointed priest, prophet, and king." *CCC*, §1241.

16. The Greek noun *mystḗrion* (μυστήριον) stems from the verb *mýō* (μύω), meaning "shut eyes, closed mouth," alluding to the lips closed in the protecting silence of the arcanum, or to the eyes shut until they are opened by sacred rites, or also to a person recollected in awe and inner meditation; moreover, the related verb *myéō* (μυέω) signifies "to initiate into the *mystéria*"; cf. Liddell and Scott, *Greek-English Lexicon*, 1150, 1156–57. The New Vulgate renders it in the Old Testament as *sacramentum* (Wis 2:22).

17. See the "Second rule" in his *Liber Regularum*, as mentioned by St. Augustine (*De doctrina Christiana*, 3.30–37) and quoted by Bede the Venerable (*Explanatio Apocalpsis*, PL 93:130–32); unfortunately, Tyconius' groundbreaking nonliteral or typological commentary on the Apocalypse is no longer extant.

historical and spiritual trajectory from her beginnings toward perfection. She is at the same time objectively holy in her divine Founder, yet subjectively sinful in her members. In his ecclesial hermeneutics, Tyconius also contrasts this mysterious body of the Church with the body of the devil waging war against faithful Christians on earth.[18] That reality will also be given expression in the opposing mystery of the great harlot seated on the beast (17:7), endorsing and promoting the agenda of the antichrist.

As baptized sons and daughters of the Church, we experience this mystery in a threefold way: *first*, we are spiritually shepherded by the hierarchical order of the bishops who are like stars in the night (v. 16), symbolized by the angels of the seven churches (v. 20);[19] they lead us with steadfastness like mystagogues, since they themselves are firmly held in the hand of Christ. Naturally, the lampstands are also a fitting image for each one of us as we strive to give glory to God by a life of obedient virtue and witness.[20] As is implied by the number "seven," this spiritual life within the communion of all the saints takes place under the constant overshadowing of the Holy Spirit. The *second* way to live the ecclesial mystery is the assurance that we belong to the Risen Lord: "I am the living one. I was dead, and see, I am alive forever and ever!" (v. 18). He may have been dead, hated and rejected by the many, yet Jesus is irrevocably alive, especially in the Eucharistic mystery of his real presence among us; and in him our earthly life is transformed into life eternal. And the *third* experience of a "mysterious" Church is that we do not have to live in fear any longer: "Do not be afraid!" (v. 17) since the God-Man has the keys of Death and of Hades (v. 18). Although, under the various burdens of daily living, we may be tempted, like John, to fall at the Lord's feet as though dead (v. 17; cf. 22:8), we believe that in him we are able to overcome death (*mors*) and avoid hell or Hades[21] (*inférnum*; cf. 6:8; 20:13–14). To thoroughly turn to God means to die to the world, which then carries the promise of interior rebirth. Jesus is always present to place his right hand on us (v. 17) and sustain us on our earthly pilgrimage. His right hand is all-powerful, because it not only holds the seven stars, but also secures the key to the underworld which he visited during his

18. Cf. "Seventh rule" in his *Liber Regularum*.

19. Origen, on the other hand, holds that they are the guardian angels of the churches (cf. *Homiliae in Lucam* 13; *Homiliae in Numeros* 20), which, however, makes it difficult to explain how, among numerous other interpretive shortcomings, they could have fallen from their first charity (2:4).

20. Intimated also by the symbolism of the Easter candle and baptismal candles.

21. "Hades" is the god of the dead and sovereign of the netherworld in Greek mythology, and as such, it is related to the Hebrew notion of Sheol, i.e., the house of the dead.

descent on Holy Saturday. From then on, he has the power to unlock it and restore life: he *is* the key![22]

Thus, this opening chapter of John's Apocalypse, that is, "what you have seen" (*quae vidisti*, v. 19a), encapsulates what is essential to Christian spirituality. Only to John on Patmos was it given to see the various labors of the eschatological Church, and that in her "evil persons will be commixed with the good unto the end of the world."[23] But he has written down what he saw, and as we now pass into the second and third chapters of his Revelation, we will hear the words of Christ to his churches, words that reveal "what is" (*quae sunt*, v. 19b), namely, the status quo of ecclesial communities in the late first century AD, but also of the eschatological "today" of our lives with Christ. This will then lay the foundation for understanding the prophetic part of the book in chs. 4–22, that is, "what is to take place after this" (*quae oportet fieri post haec*, v. 19c). And we will discover how these three dimensions, past, present, and future, are deeply interrelated in the Apocalypse.[24] But let us now listen to what the Lord and his Holy Spirit wish to communicate to the Church then and now.

22. Cf. AvS, 106.

23. As stated by Bede the Venerable in his *Exposition of the Apocalypse*, 110–96 in *Latin Commentaries on Revelation*, ed. and trans. William C. Weinrich, ACT (Downers Grove, IL: IVP Academic, 2011), 117.

24. Cf. RD, 863; AvS, 109.

2:1–3:22, Hear what the Spirit says!

Ephesus: Recoup the first love (2:1–7)

[1]*"To the angel of the church in Ephesus write: These are the words of him who holds the seven stars in his right hand, who walks among the seven golden lampstands:* [2]*"I know your works, your toil and your patient endurance. I know that you cannot tolerate evildoers; you have tested those who claim to be apostles but are not, and have found them to be false.* [3]*I also know that you are enduring patiently and bearing up for the sake of my name, and that you have not grown weary.* [4]*But I have this against you, that you have abandoned the love you had at first.* [5]*Remember then from what you have fallen; repent, and do the works you did at first. If not, I will come to you and remove your lampstand from its place, unless you repent.* [6]*Yet this is to your credit: you hate the works of the Nicolaitans, which I also hate.* [7]*Let anyone who has an ear listen to what the Spirit is saying to the churches. To everyone who conquers, I will give permission to eat from the tree of life that is in the paradise of God.*

When John is instructed to communicate the Holy Spirit's message to the angels of the seven churches (v. 1), one must remember that this is a figurative and even poetic way of describing how the Triune God transmits salvific directives and admonitions to the universal Church. In that sense, the "angel" represents the bishop as the spiritual leader of his local diocesan community, but also the latter's guardian angel. These seven angels symbolize, too, the corporate spirituality and mindset of each church, as well as its collective area of struggle against damaging or even destructive spirits, seeking to hinder its Christians from becoming holy and perfect.[1]

1. Cf. T. Scott Daniels, *Seven Deadly Spirits: The Message of Revelation's Letters for Today's Church* (Grand Rapids, MI: Baker Academic, 2009), 7.

John's first addressee is the church in Ephesus, and it seems only fitting to start by reminding us of the fascinating background of this city, situated on a great trade highway between East and West. Ephesus was one of the most important cities of ancient times, also known as "the light of Asia." In it was found the temple of the Greek goddess Artemis, the home of the magic arts (Acts 19:19, 35) and of the mystery cults. In the New Testament era, Paul chose it as a temporary center for his apostolic activities, founding its church together with Aquila, Priscilla, and Apollos, and ordaining Timothy as its first bishop. It is the place where John preached in his old age, residing there together with Mary, the Mother of Christ, and writing his Gospel and Epistles here around AD 90–100.[2] Among those who heard him before and after his exile on Patmos were Polycarp of Smyrna, Ignatius of Antioch, and Papias of Hierapolis. In due course, the city hosted the Ecumenical Council in AD 431 that proclaimed Mary as the "Birth-Giver of God" (*Theotokos*). After having become part of the Patriarchate of Constantinople, Ephesus eventually surrendered to the Ottomans in AD 1304, and henceforth its Christian community gradually dwindled. Sadly, Jesus' caveat concerning the removal of this church (2:5) has come true. Thus, we should all have an affectionate spiritual bond with the Ephesian church cherishing its memory, but also be aware that ecclesial communities can disappear if they cease to practice their faith or else are overcome by persecution.

And permit one last observation here before we delve into the message itself. There is a near-symmetrical format to the following seven letters, each comprised of seven sections: (a.) greetings for each of the seven churches, (b.) a descriptive title for Jesus who dictates the letters, (c.) insights into the life of the churches, (d.) necessary critique, except for Smyrna and Philadelphia, (e.) admonitions or instructions, (f.) final exhortations, and (g.) promises and assurances. This literary homogeneity in and of itself helps the reader comprehend that one's inner life should likewise aim at good order and harmony. Commentators agree that these seven missives to the churches are mere cover letters affixed to a copy of the entire book addressed to them. And again, just think of how John must have felt a profound loneliness and perhaps fear, caught between earth and heaven, in communicating with the sinless angels: what a special grace and true privilege among the apostles, redolent of the young Joseph receiving "one portion more than his brothers" (Gen 48:22).[3]

2. In fact, at least eleven of the twenty-seven New Testament books can be associated with this city and its surrounding region: Gospel of John, Luke-Acts, 1 Cor, Eph, Col, 1–2 Tim, 1–3 John, Rev.

3. Cf. RD, 862; AvS, 114–16.

Jesus now reintroduces himself as the one "who walks among the seven golden lampstands" (v. 1), that is, he is continually present in the center of his local churches, moving from one to the next. And if Christ is "always present in his Church, especially in her liturgical celebrations,"[4] then he makes himself present in the hearts of all his faithful, too. Consequently, everything and everyone is drawn into the middle, which is Christ's heart.[5] This heart of his is an all-knowing heart, as underlined by his avowal "I know" (v. 2):[6] he possesses absolute clarity regarding all the facts of life as they happen in the hearts of the individual members of that community. Given Christ's knowledge of hearts, something he has graciously shared with a number of saints in the form of cardiognosis, we can learn from him the gift of spiritual discernment.[7] Moreover, what will become evident throughout these seven letters is an extraordinary emphasis on "works," in perfect continuity with the teachings of John's and Paul's writings, only to be brought to completion and fruition at the very end of the book (22:12). Works here are understood as our faith-imbued conduct in the service of the Gospel. And among other possible areas of discernment, the Lord invites us to cultivate a spirit of wise boundary-keeping, to not tolerate the sins of evildoers, and to test those who are given to mendacity (vv. 2, 6). Jesus himself hates[8] the teachings of those Nicolaitans that had crept also into the church at Pergamum (vv. 6, 15).[9]

Verses 4–5 are a veritable testament to Christ's patience in awaiting the fruits of a soul's spiritual conversion. And so, after having praised the church, he now submits a reproach: "I have this against you" (v. 4). Praise and rebuke will continue to alternate throughout the seven letters, showing him to be a wise pedagogue; and as a matter of fact, throughout the entire Apocalypse, scenes of light and darkness will take turns, just as consolations and desolations succeed one another in our spiritual lives. A principal danger in the life of the baptized is to "abandon the first love" (v. 4): Jesus is acutely aware of what is praiseworthy and what is blameworthy, and here he testifies that he

4. Second Vatican Council, *Sacrosanctum Concilium* (December 4, 1963), pp. 13–58 in *The Sixteen Documents of Vatican II* (Boston: Daughters of St. Paul, 1965), §7.

5. Cf. AvS, 103.

6. Reiterated at the beginning of all seven letters (2:9, 13, 19; 3:1, 8, 15).

7. Cf. AvS, 121.

8. This is the only mention of Christ's personal hatred in Scripture; he detests, of course, only their heresies, not their persons, as a last resort for inviting them back into his love.

9. On Nicolaus as a heresiarch, cf. Irenaeus (*Adversus haereses*, 1.26.3), Hippolytus of Rome (*Refutatio*, 7.24), and Clement of Alexandria (*Stromata*, 3.2).

is personally affected by their cooling love.[10] Even though our external works can be good and acceptable, the interior disposition at the same time may not be in order. The soul cannot only receive divine love; it must exercise itself in it, too, just as the mutual relationship of love between God the Father and his Son is eternally active.[11] This first love is the strongest proof of the new life in Christ, but it can wane despite doctrinal orthodoxy. Abandoning it is equal to relinquishing a good friend, or like falling off a steep cliff into a deep valley (v. 5), and part of a new start is remembering that event with urgency, "Remember then!" Sound spiritual discernment must begin with a process of remembering and scrutinizing one's past actions. Once this is accomplished, the next step is to convert.

In order to better understand what that means, it is helpful to recall the extra-biblical background of the Greek word here chosen, namely, *metanoéō* (μετανοέω), meaning "to change one's mind about something": in classical literature it was often personified as an ethereal goddess dwelling in twilight, shrouded and mournful, who escorted Kaíros, the god of opportunity, spreading compunction and instilling penitence for the missed moment. Hence, changing one's heart has to do with thoughtful regret and contrition, leading to various degrees of transformation toward a more conscientious use of our precious time on earth to serve God and neighbor. That is what is implied in the Lord's exhortation, "Do at once the works you did at first!" (2:5b). Christ's call for the Ephesian Christians to practice *metanoía* can also be related to the penitential rite at the beginning of the Roman Catholic Mass.[12]

From a state of fallenness (v. 5), down in the valley of tears, the Lord wants us to look up to the cliff where pure love is; we need again and again to climb back up to gain height.[13] Nothing can replace this process of discernment and conversion of the heart in our life as Christians, and sincere *metanoía* remains the normative path of salvation. Its alternative is simply unacceptable and truly dismal, to wit, the soul's "removal" (v. 5). On the contrary, to heed the Lord's advice by "listening to what the Spirit is saying to the churches" (v. 7),[14] means "to conquer" (1 John 5:4), and eventually "to eat from the tree of life that is

10. The loss of love was probably also due to persecutions under Emperor Nero, as well as the influence of the early Gnostics (Nicolaitans?).

11. Cf. Matthew Lewis Sutton, *Heaven Opens: The Trinitarian Mysticism of Adrienne von Speyr* (Minneapolis, MN: Fortress, 2014), 103–25.

12. Cf. AvS, 116.

13. Cf. AvS, 127–29.

14. A sapiential appeal reminiscent of the Synoptics (e.g., Matt 11:15), yet not found in the Fourth Gospel.

in the paradise of God" (Rev 2:7) which is symbolic of partaking in the Holy Eucharist on earth, and enjoying the beatific vision of God one day in heaven.[15] The admittance into Eden, that is, into the spiritual paradise[16] which is the Church, is more marvelous than Adam's original innocence and justice, it is victory in love.

Smyrna: Fearless in affliction (2:8–11)

[8]"And to the angel of the church in Smyrna write: These are the words of the first and the last, who was dead and came to life: [9]"I know your affliction and your poverty, even though you are rich. I know the slander on the part of those who say that they are Jews and are not, but are a synagogue of Satan. [10]Do not fear what you are about to suffer. Beware, the devil is about to throw some of you into prison so that you may be tested, and for ten days you will have affliction. Be faithful until death, and I will give you the crown of life. [11]Let anyone who has an ear listen to what the Spirit is saying to the churches. Whoever conquers will not be harmed by the second death.

Proceeding about thirty-five miles north from Ephesus along the ancient semicircular mail route a courier would have taken to deliver the letters to the seven churches of the Roman province of Asia, we arrive at the city of Smyrna. Originally established around 1000 BC by Aeolian Greek settlers, it developed into a wealthy seaport at the mouth of a great Anatolian trade artery. The reference to Jesus as the one "who was dead and has come to life" (v. 8) may allude to its history of recurrent decline followed by resurgence. At the time the local church was founded during Paul's third missionary journey (Acts 19:10), Smyrna was a polytheistic city of many magnificent temples, of a fusion of cultures, and a bustling commercial center. That proliferation of pagan worship may have prompted the expression "synagogue of Satan" (v. 9). One can only imagine how St. Polycarp as a young man was sitting among the Christian faithful when the Book of Revelation was read there for the very first time; he had known

15. Cf. RD, 870–71.

16. The biblical term "paradise" is inherited from the ancient Persian word *paridayda*, signaling a "walled enclosure"; by the fifth century BC, emperors constructed magnificent gardens held in such high esteem that they wished to be remembered as "gardeners," and it is from this usage that the garden of Eden and of the Kingdom of Heaven derives (Gen 2:8; Luke 23:43; 2 Cor 12:4).

and been taught by the elder John, who also ordained him as his first apostolic successor, bishop of Smyrna.

In reflecting on the spiritual message presented in this the shortest of the seven letters, let us receive again Jesus' gentle commendation, "I know your affliction and your poverty, even though you are rich" (v. 9). Perhaps the local Christian community refused to take part in the religious ceremonies of the trade guilds of the day, and consequently suffered economically. What comes to mind when looking at the contrast between poor and rich is the first Gospel beatitude about the poor in spirit inheriting the Kingdom (Matt 5:3). If God knew their works, then he surely knows our works; indeed, he also knows our thoughts. He therefore is divinely knowledgeable regarding the happiness and inner peace that is brought about by the inner mindset of evangelical poverty. How does the Lord know? Because he himself chose to abase himself in his Incarnation, becoming poor for our sakes to enrich us by his poverty (2 Cor 8:9). Hence, despite appearances to the contrary, we do own the treasures of God's salvation, making us rich in grace.[17] This realization will also be instrumental in resisting the contemporary spirit of mindless greed and consumerism.

Written during a time of ruthless persecution of Roman Christians, the church at Smyrna faced even more opposition than most, due to the strong influence of emperor worship there, which at the time was required by law and enforced by threat of imprisonment or even death. Yet, strengthened by that interior richness, Christians could look to the future with confidence: "Do not fear what you are about to suffer" (v. 10). That suffering would have included slander, hostility, persecution, imprisonment, and worse. However, these various forms of oppression take on an ulterior meaning for the faithful, namely, they put our loyalty to Christ to the test. An intentional denial would be tantamount to membership in that ruinous assembly of Satan (v. 9; cf. 3:9). No matter how vicious the affliction may be, its duration in our lives will be limited to "ten days" (v. 10; cf. Dan 1:12). It is surely telling that this is the first of seven references to the number ten (*déka*, δέκα, *decem*) in Revelation, the remaining six all depicting the horns of the dragon and its beasts in chapters 12–13 and 17, suggesting that the tribulation is whipped up by the forces of evil. According to apocalyptic numerology, "ten" amounts to a limited period of time on earth, permitted by the Lord, who knows exactly how much suffering is necessary to bring the soul into a more perfect union with him.

Most heartening is Jesus' closing promise that "whoever conquers will not be harmed by the second death" (v. 11). Full credence must be given to it, as the

17. Cf. AvS, 137–38.

one speaking is "the First and the Last, who was dead and came to life" (v. 8), and we are here to keep the memorial of his Death and Resurrection eternally alive. If this "second death" refers to eternal damnation,[18] anticipating 20:6, 14; 21:8, 19, then the first death refers to both the spiritual death of the soul in the state of mortal sin, and to the physical death of the human body. Hence, the text implicitly encourages us to make every effort to eschew occasions that can result in falling into that serious sin which spells the spiritual death of our soul (1 John 5:16–17), obviously a key to all Christian spirituality. Christ's word to the angel of the church in Smyrna contains no criticism and no censure; it is a vademecum for those who wish to be prepared for the hour of spiritual battle, intrepidly aware that God uses trials to purify and sanctify us: "Thy will be done," even when it hurts. But let us continue the journey and visit the third church addressed by the exiled apostle.

Pergamum: False toleration (2:12–17)

[12] *"And to the angel of the church in Pergamum write: These are the*
words of him who has the sharp two-edged sword: [13] *"I know where you*
are living, where Satan's throne is. Yet you are holding fast to my name,
and you did not deny your faith in me even in the days of Antipas my
witness, my faithful one, who was killed among you, where Satan lives.
[14] *But I have a few things against you: you have some there who hold*
to the teaching of Balaam, who taught Balak to put a stumbling block
before the people of Israel, so that they would eat food sacrificed to idols
and practice fornication. [15] *So you also have some who hold to the teach-*
ing of the Nicolaitans. [16] *Repent then. If not, I will come to you soon and*
make war against them with the sword of my mouth. [17] *Let anyone who*
has an ear listen to what the Spirit is saying to the churches. To everyone
who conquers I will give some of the hidden manna, and I will give a
white stone, and on the white stone is written a new name that no one
knows except the one who receives it.

Situated around forty miles past Smyrna along an ancient Roman postal road, we now arrive at Pergamum (v. 12), at John's time a wealthy Greek city, the northernmost of the seven churches of Asia. It was one of the most dazzling and influential cities in Hellenistic antiquity and in the Roman Empire. Since the first temple of the imperial cult was built here in honor of the deities Roma and

18. Cf. RD, 875.

Augustus around 29 BC, in due course it became the capital of Caesar worship, a touchstone of civic loyalty under Domitian. This may have prompted the ominous identification as the "throne of Satan" and the place "where Satan settled down" (v. 13) of a cluster of pagan temples that was devoted to idolatrous cults of the likes of Zeus, Athena, Dionysus, and Asclepius. Of Pergamum an ancient writer said it was "given to idolatry more than all Asia."[19] Paul passed through the region of Mysia, where the city was located, and probably founded the Pergamene church during his ministry at Ephesus (Acts 19:10) when the Gospel was preached throughout Asia. As a regional hub of trade and culture, the innovative people of Pergamum, among other things, perfected a parchment made out of calfskin[20] and prided themselves on a ten-thousand seat amphitheater.

To this ecclesial community the Lord reveals himself right away as the one "who has the sharp two-edged sword" (v. 12). Originally a long Thracian javelin, such a *romphæa* later came to describe a large combat sword, and by metonymy, "war." We remember that this sword issues from his very mouth like his breath or word (1:16), and anticipating v. 16, it becomes the specter of actual warfare. With its twofold efficacy of being "two-edged" and "sharp," it is a powerful symbol of spiritual discernment and judgment. Simeon's prophecy to Mary confirms that association: "A sword will pierce your own soul, too, so that the inner thoughts of many will be revealed" (Luke 2:35). No matter how it is wielded, it will inflict painful wounds on the good and the bad. Jesus clearly indicates the desired outcome of any Christian discernment, namely, to hold fast to his name, and not deny our faith in him, even in the days of martyrdom.[21] Since the Church and the devil ironically reside in close quarters, Christ the divine warrior teaches acute discernment between faith and unbelief.[22]

As sons and daughters of the Church, we constantly need to monitor what we allow to influence us. Two erroneous teachings are pointed out by Christ under the onomastic symbolism of "Balaam" and the "Nicolaitans" (vv. 14–15): while Balaam symbolizes those who cause the scandal of idolatry and incitement to fornication,[23] the Nicolaitans embody those who abuse the notion of

19. John MacArthur, *Revelation 1–11*, McANTC 32 (Chicago: Moody, 1999), 84.

20. Due to the shortage of papyrus in the region this new material was developed, and was called *pergamena* after the city, a name that has become the anglicized "parchment."

21. Antipas as Jesus' faithful martyr (v. 13), not to be confused with Herod Antipas the tetrarch (Matt 14:1), was the first bishop of Pergamum; he is remembered by the Church in her Roman Martyrology on April 11.

22. Cf. AvS, 147.

23. It is possible that the Balaamites were a variety of the Nicolaitan sect (v. 6); regarding these names, some speculate about internal leadership crises of the church, e.g., Paul B. Duff,

Christian freedom. Against any false spiritual toleration, Jesus urges again to repent (v. 16), that is, to discern in light of his sword, which is the word of God, to firmly reject heretical and sectarian ideas on the one hand, and to choose orthodox faith and morals on the other.[24] Are we always on our guard against manipulative leaders within our ranks? Are we sure to worship God the Most High and him alone? What worldly and satanic philosophies have we allowed to creep in? Such infidelities amount to enmity against God. Our fight is not so much against people but against scandal and heresy as such. "Listen to the Spirit!" (v. 17), that is, pay attention even to the limit of one's capacity, hold on to sound doctrine, exercise prudence, avoid immorality[25] in purity of heart.

To incentivize the best within us, his beloved "conquerors" (v. 17), Jesus promises the reward for all our goodwill and effort in discerning the spirits. He desires to share with us already now in this life the "hidden manna" of chastity in mind and body, made possible by the participation in the sacrament of his hidden yet real presence in the Eucharist.[26] Just as the desert gift of manna signaled the first manifestation of God's love for his covenanted people (Ps 78:24–25), so also today, it is the supernatural bread of pilgrims, members of his Mystical Body.[27] This is complemented by the reception of a "white stone," evocative of the bright amulet often used in antiquity as a password or entrance ticket for public games, suggestive of innocence, victory, and joy.[28] Paired with the connotation of a glistening gem, the metaphor is that of rising to new life and being admitted into the deeper mysteries of God's loving plan for us. It may also allude to the Urim and Thummim worn by Israel's high priests (Exod 28:30) and would again speak of the priestly mission of the baptized, as well as their access to the presence of God.

This exquisite stone, however, would be incomplete without the "new name" engraved in it (cf. Exod 28:21). That name is known only to the one who receives it, since it epitomizes the profound mystery of his or her rebirth in Christ, becoming a child of God. From now on this soul has its individual story of experiencing the love of Christ, just as lovers on earth exchange nicknames

Who Rides the Beast? Prophetic Rivalry and the Rhetoric of Crisis in the Churches of the Apocalypse (Oxford: Oxford University Press, 2001). Balaam is considered a biblical prototype of the religious compromiser, warlock, and deceiver (Num 25:1–3; 31:16; Josh 13:22; 2 Pet 2:15; Jude 11).

24. Cf. RD, 875–76.

25. The lexical meaning of *porneúō* (πορνεύω, v. 14) is the practice of sexual immorality, fornication, and prostitution; metaphorically, it alludes to the sin of idolatry (e.g., 17:2).

26. Cf. RD, 880.

27. Cf. AvS, 156.

28. Cf. *CCC*, §2159.

that express their mutual affection. What is happening is a perpetually renewed love-secret between the Lord and the human heart; in other words, the Divine becomes total gift and dedication to the person's humanity. As a lifelong adventure, one is to learn to enter into that name, receive it, explore it, and remain docile to its calling. We began with the wounding sword of spiritual discernment, and the letter to the Pergamene Christians ends with the reassurance that the Trinity handpicks a name for us that summarizes the soul's loving relationship with the Father, Son, and Holy Spirit. It is now time to move on to the next church in Asia Minor.

Thyatira: Hold fast till I come (2:18–29)

18“And to the angel of the church in Thyatira write: These are the words
of the Son of God, who has eyes like a flame of fire, and whose feet are
like burnished bronze: 19“I know your works, your love, faith, service,
and patient endurance. I know that your last works are greater than
the first. 20But I have this against you: you tolerate that woman Jezebel,
who calls herself a prophet and is teaching and beguiling my servants
to practice fornication and to eat food sacrificed to idols. 21I gave her
time to repent, but she refuses to repent of her fornication. 22Beware, I
am throwing her on a bed, and those who commit adultery with her I
am throwing into great distress, unless they repent of her doings; 23and
I will strike her children dead. And all the churches will know that I am
the one who searches minds and hearts, and I will give to each of you as
your works deserve. 24But to the rest of you in Thyatira, who do not hold
this teaching, who have not learned what some call ‘the deep things of
Satan,’ to you I say, I do not lay on you any other burden; 25only hold
fast to what you have until I come. 26To everyone who conquers and con-
tinues to do my works to the end, I will give authority over the nations;
27to rule them with an iron rod, as when clay pots are shattered 28even as
I also received authority from my Father. To the one who conquers I will
also give the morning star. 29Let anyone who has an ear listen to what
the Spirit is saying to the churches.

By far the longest letter is addressed to a church in the most insignificant of the seven cities, judged from a historical standpoint, namely, Thyatira (v. 18), situated in the confines of Mysia and Ionia. As the courier's circuit now turns southwards, this city is close to the Roman road between Pergamum and Sardis. Founded probably by the Lydians, it became a Macedonian colony about 290 BC. Worship of the national deity of the Greeks, the sun-god Apollo, was prominent, possibly prompting Jesus to introduce himself to that church as the "Son of God, who has eyes like a flame of fire." The city was famed for trading the purple cloth it produced; indeed, more guilds are known there than in any other city of the Roman province of Asia of the time, including wool-workers, robe-makers, tanners, potters, bakers, and bronze-smiths.[29] It was from there that Lydia the purple-seller of Philippi hailed, Paul's first European convert (Acts 16:14). In all likelihood, she was linked to the industrial syndicate of scarlet dyers, and her presence in Philippi is an illustration of the ancient trade relations between Greece and Asia Minor. To her, the Christian community at Thyatira may have owed its beginning.

At this midpoint within the septenary of letters, given its unusual length, let us focus on just four vistas of its spirituality. To begin with, "works" are mentioned no fewer than five times, namely, right at the outset (v. 19) and toward the end of the epistolary body (v. 26), as well as twice in between (vv. 22–23). That conspicuous placement and repetition makes it the most emphasized concept, meaning, that to work for the Kingdom is paramount, embracing all the other virtues; these works are the fruit that allows one to tell the quality of the tree (Matt 7:20). Works like "love, faith, service, and patient endurance" (v. 19) will be the main criteria for Jesus' final reward to us (v. 23). Moreover, these faithful "works to the end" are in reality the works of the Lord himself (v. 26). Of them he is speaking when he enjoins on those Christians to "hold fast to what you have until I come" (v. 25). While Jesus himself will deal with the sinners in the community, the faithful ones are admonished to simply persevere until his parousia, meaning his coming in a moment of grace or in the hour of death.[30] Taking an even closer look, an increase is noted from our "first" to our "last" works (v. 19), in apparent contrast to the loss of first love and works in Ephesus (vv. 4–5). Perhaps the spiritual trajectory from faith-filled fear toward loving service is implied.[31] By the same token, the Thyatiran church is earnestly cautioned not to engage in the Jezebelian "works" of immorality and idolatry (v. 22). If they remain faithful to the end, the Lord will bestow supernatural authority in this world (v. 26), drawing the soul into his own obedience toward the Father (v. 28). And what a reversal of fortune it will be, from witnessing his

29. Cf. William Mitchell Ramsay, *The Letters to the Seven Churches of Asia and Their Place in the Plan of the Apocalypse* (London: Hodder & Stoughton, 1906), 324–35.

30. Cf. AvS, 177.

31. Cf. RD, 882.

crucifixion to partaking in his rule over the world.[32] And the "morning star" (v. 28)[33] is given to the one who labors in the night and vigil of faith, until the morning of everlasting life dawns.[34] It promises to be a day of victory, consolation, and rest, since to work for God every day of our lives is demanding and difficult: "Let anyone who has an ear listen!" (v. 29).

A second spiritual lesson is contained in Jesus' stern reprimand of the church's toleration of "that woman Jezebel" (v. 20). Similar to the Balaamists and the Nicolaitans in Pergamum (vv. 14–15), she is a false prophet, trying to deceive the good Christians, having them indulge in immorality and idolatry.[35] While the Thyatiran Jezebel may have been a historical figure, she also recalls the evil character of King Ahab's wife, instrumental in instituting the worship of Baal and Ashtaroth on a national scale, promoting fornication in Israel, as well as attempting to violently purge the prophets of Yahweh.[36] Elijah fought mightily against her machinations (1 Kgs 18), just as Phineas did against Moab's King Balak with zeal (Num 25). It is noteworthy that God punished Jezebel's misdeeds by annihilating her husband's dynasty, as well as permitting her own ignominious death by defenestration. Christ scolds the bishop of Thyatira for being too permissive (v. 20) toward that personification of erroneous doctrine and sin, that new Jezebel, that human conduit of "the depths of Satan" (v. 24),[37] that sinister adumbration of Babylon the great harlot (ch. 17). As hierarchical shepherd, he has failed to provide protection and guidance in faith for his flock, to do spiritually what Elijah did with the sword (1 Kgs 19:1). He has the sacred duty to conscientiously screen out deceptive teachers from his local church. Relatedly, Christians should not always compromise with and assimilate the dominant dictates of the culture that surrounds us.[38] Also, we are to strike a balance between laxity and rigor in applying moral principles, always loving the sinner, yet detesting sin. Genuine discernment of spirits will be attentive

32. Cf. AvS, 178.

33. Cf. Balaam's messianic oracle in Num 24:17, "I behold him, but not near, a star shall come out of Jacob."

34. Cf. RD, 889.

35. Reversing the word order of idolatry and immorality from 2:14, and thereby giving more emphasis to the first notion, that is, the practice of fornication.

36. Cf. 1 Kgs 16:31; 18:19; 21:25.

37. To become acquainted with the depths of divinity was a crucial ambition of the Gnostics of that era (cf. Irenaeus, *Adversus haereses*, 2.22.1); curiously, the Neo-Vulgate translates the adjective *bathýs* (βαθύς, "deep") as "heights" (*altitudo*), indicating the peak of satanic pride, trying to equal the Most High.

38. Cf. James L. Resseguie, *The Revelation of John: A Narrative Commentary* (Grand Rapids, MI: Baker Academic, 2009), 93.

to the link between orthopraxy and orthodoxy, meaning that only by embracing the true faith one is able to live a morally upright life. Otherwise, one will inevitably fall into heteropraxy due to heterodoxy. One thing is certain, that Christian witness often runs counter to contemporary culture, and that tolerant conformism or some sort of privatized faith can never be the answer.

Thirdly, although the cursed Jezebel is an emblem of malice, heresy, and impenitence in the Bible, the Lord gives her "time to repent" (v. 21). This is simply astounding since he usually demands immediate *metanoía*. His forbearance may have to do with his gratitude for whatever good she has done in the past, but it certainly also highlights the fact that true conversion is typically a slow process. What follows is like a tug-of-war between a forgiving God and a recalcitrant soul: in response to its refusal to repent and to adapt to God's will, God intensifies the trials without necessarily taking the sinner out of his or her habitual environment. Hence, the bed of adultery now becomes a place of suffering, and those who are implicated in a person's sin may experience great trouble (v. 22). Willful repudiation of conversion can engender an even heavier cross of testing, and the soul now needs to muster more strength to resist sin, "unless they convert." Jesus here acts like a wise novice master, who arranges for suitable tests and humbling trials, looking for signs of spiritual growth in the novice.[39] Shockingly, his pedagogy of grace can involve even the death of one's children (v. 23), which must have been dreadful for the beloved disciple to hear. It may be an allegory, too, for the ultimate necessity to die to oneself by being vetted by Christ. Divine punishment should occasion prayer and self-scrutiny; it is the time to repent. In all this, God will always be "slow to anger," or literally, "have a long nose" (Exod 34:6). For persons entrusted with spiritual direction, it will be critical to understand that it is the Lord himself who scrutinizes and tests the soul; one does not have to come up with various clever trials to impose on the directee, provided he or she is willing to trustingly submit to the Lord.

Related to the above, we can glean a fourth and final spiritual insight from this remarkable letter to the Thyatiran church, and it has to do with Christ being "the one who searches minds and hearts" (v. 23). The apostle has already spoken about his omniscient and all-consuming eyes like a flame of fire, and the cauterizing effect of his feet like burnished bronze (v. 18), leaving a glowing trace wherever he goes, his humanity hypostatically engulfed in his divine personhood. It comes as no surprise that "the Son of God"[40] is the perfect

39. Cf. AvS, 170–71.

40. Unlike the most common title "Son of Man," the phrase "Son of God," while frequent in the Gospel and Epistles of St. John, occurs only here in the Apocalypse.

knower of hearts. While it is true that he rules with earth-shattering strictness as with an iron rod (2:27), he primarily discerns between insincere repentance, symbolized by "kidneys" (*renes*), and sincere conversion, signaled by "hearts" (*corda*, v. 23).[41] Augustine's memorable words come to mind: "You [God] were more inward to me than my most inward part, and higher than my highest."[42] What adds to the weight of this divine discernment is that Jesus and the Holy Spirit speak with one voice (vv. 18, 29). But let us now travel on to the Christian community in the neighboring city to the south.

Sardis: Walk with me (3:1–6)

1 "And to the angel of the church in Sardis write: These are the words of
him who has the seven spirits of God and the seven stars: "I know your
works; you have a name of being alive, but you are dead. 2 Wake up,
and strengthen what remains and is on the point of death, for I have not
found your works perfect in the sight of my God. 3 Remember then what
you received and heard; obey it, and repent. If you do not wake up, I
will come like a thief, and you will not know at what hour I will come to
you. 4 Yet you have still a few persons in Sardis who have not soiled their
clothes; they will walk with me, dressed in white, for they are worthy. 5 If
you conquer, you will be clothed like them in white robes, and I will not
blot your name out of the book of life; I will confess your name before my
Father and before his angels. 6 Let anyone who has an ear listen to what
the Spirit is saying to the churches.

Sardis, capital of the ancient Lydian monarchy in western Asia Minor, was nestled in a plain watered by the auriferous river Pactolus, and is known to history as the place where modern currency was invented due to its technical ability to mint gold and silver coins. An earthquake in AD 17 destroyed the urban perimeter, followed by a devastating pestilence. Yet, before the date of this apocalyptic letter the city seems to have recovered its prosperity, appearing alive. In the second century AD, the Apostolic Father Melito was bishop of Sardis, holding a prominent place among Christians in Asia, both in personal influence and in literary work. He may have been the immediate successor of

41. Cf. RD, 886.

42. Augustine, *Confessions*, trans. Hal M. Helms, *The Confessions of St. Augustine: A Modern English Version* (Orleans, MA: Paraclete, 1996), 3.6.11 (Latin original: "interior intimo meo et superior summo meo").

the "angel" bishop to whom this fifth missive is addressed. This church garners almost unalloyed disapproval from "him who has the seven spirits of God and the seven stars" (v. 1), were it not for those few persons there that are found "worthy" (v. 4). Those spirits and stars amalgamate 1:4, 16, 20, symbolizing the Holy Spirit and the angels of the churches; Jesus at this point carries and externalizes this combined spiritual force, showing it forth as an encouraging and guiding light in the night of human history, a beacon that eventually leads back to him.

Not long in coming is the first reproof: "You have a name of being alive, but you are dead" (v. 1). Regrettably, Sardis's interior state of affairs does not match its reputation. Even "what remains, is on the point of death," because its works are "incomplete before God" (v. 2). Christians there apparently did not finish what they started; they were about image and not substance. Although nothing can be concealed from Christ's gaze, he counsels gently and respectfully without revealing the exact nature of their sin.[43] We are put on guard by his word, to not turn into mere facades or whitewashed tombs. The soul knows when it is spiritually moribund or already deceased, and it can choose to persist in this sad situation, mistakenly thinking that it is less painful than being alive. Self-reference and indifference can cause spiritual death. Oftentimes, too, it is the absorption in exterior activity that suffocates the interior recollection of the soul, triggering lethargy and numbness. Or perhaps the inner torpor is the result of avoiding the challenges and demands of one's authentic Christian vocation.[44] Either way, we are called to pay close attention to the state of vitality of our souls, sustained by divine grace and virtue; everything else in the end becomes irrelevant.

Priestly work is not complete if it does not counsel the remedy, or if it does not result in the forgiveness of sins and amendment of life. And so, the Lord proceeds to advise the soul to "wake up" from its spiritual apathy, to "strengthen" what may still have an ounce of life in it (v. 2), to "remember" what was received, and to "preserve it" (v. 3). Timeless counsel, indeed: the inner life cannot survive, let alone advance, without vigilance ("wake up"), self-mastery ("strengthen"), frequently poring over the Sacred Scriptures and dogmatic or catechetical truths ("remember"), and putting them into practice ("keep"). At this juncture we should also call to mind that "remembering" is among the great covenant virtues of the Old Testament: "I will call to mind the

43. Cf. RD, 891.
44. Cf. AvS, 182–83.

deeds of the Lord; I will remember your wonders of old. I will meditate on all your work, and muse on your mighty deeds" (Ps 77:11–12). In the adverse event of not heeding Jesus' counsel, he will unpleasantly surprise those who slumber, barging in like a thief (v. 3), instead of arriving like a bridegroom who visits those who keep watch.

Before moving on to the church in Philadelphia, let us briefly address the repeated mention of "soiled" and "white robes" in vv. 4–5; commentators have taken this to be an image for the Christian virtue of chastity.[45] It may not be a coincidence that Christ broaches this topic at this location: for one, Sardis was the great commercial hub of dyed woolen textiles, the many Phrygian sheep supplying the raw material; in fact, the art of dyeing is said to have been invented here, forming the cornerstone to a thriving manufacturing community producing multicolored carpets or mats. Additionally, the pagan worship of the Anatolian mother goddess Cybele was the prevailing one; its cultic rites, like those of Dionysius and Aphrodite, involved and encouraged physical impurity. It is precisely here that Christ promises that "you will be clothed in white robes" (v. 5): just as Elohim "made garments of skins for the man and for his wife, and clothed them" (Gen 3:21), so also in our lives the chaste integrity of body and soul will always be a gift of God's grace to us. In that sense, it is sobering to read that there are only "a few people" (v. 4) who live that marvelous virtue of purity within the Sardisian church. Then and now, chaste conduct is among the traits that distinguishes Christians the most from their secularized environment. Spiritual progress will always be inextricably associated with it: "Blessed are the pure in heart, for they will see God" (Matt 5:8), enabling us to walk with the Lord the walk of faith (v. 4). And of course, "white" is also symbolic of joyous victory and new life, announcing the immaculate bodies that are destined to rise on the last day (v. 5), to share in that purest intimacy between the Trinity and the holy angels.[46] But let us now listen to what the Spirit has to say to the penultimate of the seven churches.

45. Cf. RD, 890; AvS, 188.
46. Cf. AvS, 189.

Philadelphia: Unclosable door (3:7–13)

7 "And to the angel of the church in Philadelphia write: These are the words of the holy one, the true one, who has the key of David, who opens and no one will shut, who shuts and no one opens:

8 "I know your works. Look, I have set before you an open door, which no one is able to shut. I know that you have but little power, and yet you have kept my word and have not denied my name. 9 I will make those of the synagogue of Satan who say that they are Jews and are not, but are lying, I will make them come and bow down before your feet, and they will learn that I have loved you. 10 Because you have kept my word of patient endurance, I will keep you from the hour of trial that is coming on the whole world to test the inhabitants of the earth. 11 I am coming soon; hold fast to what you have, so that no one may seize your crown. 12 If you conquer, I will make you a pillar in the temple of my God; you will never go out of it. I will write on you the name of my God, and the name of the city of my God, the new Jerusalem that comes down from my God out of heaven, and my own new name. 13 Let anyone who has an ear listen to what the Spirit is saying to the churches.

Lydian Philadelphia,[47] literally meaning "brotherly love," was a city in west-central Asia Minor, about twenty-five miles southeast of Sardis, on the road to Laodicea. It derived its name from Attalus Philadelphus, the king of Pergamos, who died 138 BC. Given the volcanic nature of the region, the town had a long history of earthquakes, which may lie behind the reference to making her church a permanent "pillar in the temple of my God" (v. 12). Among the many local pagan temples were those that housed an imperial cult, the survival of which until the sixth century AD intimates that the city never entirely converted to Christianity. Since numerous fugitive Jews had settled here after the destruction of Jerusalem, whether the mention of the "key of David" (v. 7) and "Jerusalem" (v. 12) had any connection with that Jewish colony remains unclear; it is conceivable, however, that the church was mostly Jewish Christians.[48] Philadelphia gains Christ's unalloyed praise,

47. Not to be confused, among others, with the Cilician Philadelphia, also recorded as Philadelphia Minor.

48. The *Epistola ad Philadelphenses*, attributed to St. Ignatius of Antioch, besides encouraging unity and ecclesial respect, also warns the Philadelphians not to listen to Jewish Christians who were advocating that Christians ought to observe the Torah.

and of all the seven churches, it enjoyed the longest period of prosperity as a Christian city.

John receives this letter from "the Holy One, the True One" (v. 7). Holiness and truth form a perfect union in Christ, and indeed, he is their quintessence. In the upper room he had already reassured Thomas, and through him all of us, that he is "the Way, the Truth, and the Life" (John 14:6). Only in him we find consummate holiness as truth, and the complete truth as holiness, and they are forever subsumed in a person, in the God-Man Jesus.[49] By addressing the bishop of Philadelphia and the corporate spirit of its local church, he continues to instill this true holiness into the One, Holy, Catholic, and Apostolic Church. From then onwards, the individual soul can no longer find holiness outside the truth, and only full doctrinal and moral truth will propel it into the realm of personal holiness. Yet above all, one cannot attain to it without being intimately drawn into the very person of Christ: that is the innermost secret of Christian holiness.

Still referring to himself in the grammatical third person, the Lord declares that he carries "the key of David, who opens and no one will shut, who shuts and no one opens" (v. 7), validating the messianic passage from Isaiah 22:22.[50] One might say that King David had figuratively received authority from God the Father like a treasurer or custodian of the future Messiah; now in turn, the Son receives it from David, his ancestor according to the flesh (Matt 1:1), to bring the Father's designs to fulfilment in the Church, and confirming the continuity of the Old and New Testaments.[51] In light of Christ's promise to Peter (Matt 16:19), this salvific key can symbolize, besides the eventual passage through the gates of heaven, three components of our Christian spirituality. For one, it is the supernatural grace that opens the mysteries of Holy Scripture to us, making them truly food for the journey.[52] On the other hand, it implies the Church's power of absolution of personal sins, encouraging us to take regular advantage of the sacrament of penance and reconciliation. No genuine progress can be made without that grace of Confession, since it prevents us from falling into greater sin, as the proverbial stitch in time that saves nine. Thirdly, it intimates

49. Unmasking the sophistry of Pontius Pilate's inquiry "*what* is truth?" (John 18:38); he failed to realize that truth is not some philosophical construct, but a divine Person, responding to "*Who* is the truth?"

50. On this typological use of the Old Testament, cf. G. K. Beale, *Handbook on the New Testament Use of the Old Testament: Exegesis and Interpretation* (Grand Rapids, MI: Baker Academic, 2012), 140–48.

51. Cf. AvS, 190.

52. Cf. RD, 894.

that Jesus is the one who opens the doors of human hearts to listen to him (v. 8), as we engage in the work of evangelization.

Moreover, the Son of God pledges inner solidity and stability to those who undertake the spiritual conquest: "I will make you a pillar in the temple of my God; you will never go out of it" (v. 12). Like those structural buttresses of a physical edifice, the human heart will be made unshakable and nearly impregnable, without stifling, however, its spiritual growth and development. That interior firmness enables us not to be afraid of or confused by the various adversaries that we may have to face. On the contrary, they will one day be forced to bow down at the believer's feet and "learn that I have loved you" (v. 9), which appears to be an allusion to the final judgment due to the hyperbolic use of the Latin verb *adorare* ("to adore"). Even major trials that can befall the human body and spirit will not succeed in distracting us from that calm focus on our Lord, not least because he himself will "protect us" (v. 10). Our house will not be built on sand, but rather be founded on rock (Matt 7:24), so we do not have to fear in the end. The paternal name of God the Father, the maternal name of the New Jerusalem, and the fraternal name of Jesus is written on it (v. 12).

While so many more spiritual aspects could be discussed in all these letters, we don't want to be too long-drawn-out; instead, let us now visit the last of "the seven churches that are in Asia" (1:4).

Laodicea: Standing at the door (3:14–22)

14 "And to the angel of the church in Laodicea write: The words of the
Amen, the faithful and true witness, the origin of God's creation: 15 "I
know your works; you are neither cold nor hot. I wish that you were
either cold or hot. 16 So, because you are lukewarm, and neither cold nor
hot, I am about to spit you out of my mouth. 17 For you say, 'I am rich,
I have prospered, and I need nothing.' You do not realize that you are
wretched, pitiable, poor, blind, and naked. 18 Therefore I counsel you
to buy from me gold refined by fire so that you may be rich; and white
robes to clothe you and to keep the shame of your nakedness from being
seen; and salve to anoint your eyes so that you may see. 19 I reprove and
discipline those whom I love. Be earnest, therefore, and repent. 20 Behold!
I am standing at the door, knocking; if you hear my voice and open the
door, I will come in to you and eat with you, and you with me. 21 To the
one who conquers I will give a place with me on my throne, just as I
myself conquered and sat down with my Father on his throne. 22 Let any-
one who has an ear listen to what the Spirit is saying to the churches."

Laodicea, meaning "justice of the people," on the river Lycus in Phrygia, lay south of Philadelphia on the way to Ephesus where the apocalyptic journey began (2:1). Its original name was Dióspolis, the "city of Jupiter-Zeus," in honor of its tutelary deity. Advantageously positioned on a trade route, it became a flourishing center of commerce, sharing with Thyatira and Sardis in the wool and dye trade. Destroyed by an earthquake in 62 AD, it was rebuilt by its wealthy citizens without the assistance of the state.[53] Their affluence contributed to the advancement of art, belles-lettres, and science, including an influential medical school. In addition to a sizeable Jewish community, early Christianity was burgeoning there, following the evangelizing efforts of Paul[54] and Epaphras.[55] Tradition has it that Archippus (Col 4:17) became the first bishop of the Laodicean church, and thus may have been the original recipient of this apocalyptic message.[56] Even though the last and worst of the seven churches of Asia, Christians later throve there, even celebrating a fourth-century regional synod. By the thirteenth century, when the city was razed during the Mongol invasions of Anatolia, Christianity had waned, suffering the same fate as Ephesus. It remains, however, a titular see in the Catholic Church, like the other six churches.

Not having anything virtuous to commend, Jesus the "Amen" or infallible truth,[57] the "Witness" and "Origin" (v. 14), commences by censuring Christians in Laodicea for being tepid (vv. 15–16), uncovering a morbid spirit of self-sufficiency. What follows is among the most graphic images ascribed to Christ in the New Testament, namely, the metaphorical act of vomiting, spitting out those who show no sincere dedication to him. Not to fully surrender to him can ultimately mean to be violently separated from him, and indeed, be expectorated through his divine mouth with utter disgust.[58] The image is that of a pot of water that was supposed to be either hot or cold to be useful, but instead turned lukewarm and insipid, having naturally adapted itself to the surrounding temperature. Symbolically, it denounces all those who are half-hearted or refuse to become more loyally involved, in the affairs of a local parish, for instance. These souls are in the sorry state of fluctuating between listlessness and an occasional

53. Cf. Tacitus, *Annals*, 14.27.

54. Cf. Acts 16:5–6; 18:23; Col 2:1; 4:15–16.

55. Cf. Col 1:5–8; 4:12–13.

56. Cf. the fourth-century AD *Apostolic Constitutions*, 7.46.

57. Cf. RD, 899–900; AvS, 203.

58. Lev 18:28 carries this warning in the context of sexual immorality among the covenant people: "Otherwise the land will vomit you out for defiling it, as it vomited out the nation that was before you." (see also Lev 20:22).

burst of fervor, living a spiritual paralysis that may have sprung from worldly prosperity and intellectual pride (v. 17).[59] Jesus' disdain for material wealth appears to be so pronounced that he can unequivocally say that the poor are rich, and that those in mundane affluence and economic success are internally impoverished and associated with the vain ostentations of Babylon the great harlot (chs. 17–18).[60] His advice to the Laodiceans is timeless, namely, to take note of their wretchedness and impoverishment, as well as their radical need to purchase from him gold refined in the crucible to yield spiritual dividends. And we leave the Lord with no choice, so to speak, but to reject any indifference and self-righteousness in us: he does not want us to be unwilling or spineless or noncommittal, but on the contrary, he needs to see in us an ardent dedication to his work of salvation, that is, to "be zealous" (v. 19).

Shaken at the thought of Christ's possible revulsion at us, we are reminded of the recommendation of today's Church to take advantage of spiritual direction. Just as he assisted the Laodicean church with his divine counsel (v. 18), we can rest assured that our pilgrimage on earth will be more manageable and joyful if accompanied by a wise person who is able to periodically give good spiritual advice. As the popular saying goes, our life is "not a sprint but a marathon." Many are the examples in the lives of the saints, where the Holy Spirit spoke through a personal spiritual director,[61] developing a course of action for the soul to follow in humble docility. Invariably, inner peace and serenity are the outcome.

But returning to v. 18, Jesus counsels us to draw on his own riches and healing, which he is willing to share with those who obey: a veritable treasure-trove prepared in the crucible of his Cross, symbolized by the refined gold, white robe, and soothing collyrium. Those will help to overcome the frustrating obstacles of material satiety and other self-imposed limitations. In the process, we will also come to the happy realization that the heavenly Father's gift always outdoes our own actions and sacrifice. To converse with a spiritual mentor involves obedience that enables us to adjust our eyes to the vision of the Church, and indeed, it is the grace of seeing the Father through the eyes of the Son.[62] And *en passant*, in searching for the right director, why not turn to

59. Cf. AvS, 206.

60. Cf. Mark D. Mathews, *Riches, Poverty, and the Faithful: Perspectives on Wealth in the Second Temple Period and the Apocalypse of John* (New York: Cambridge University Press, 2013), 3–5.

61. John of the Cross directed Teresa of Ávila, and Francis de Sales and Vincent de Paul advised Jane Frances de Chantal, to mention but two such instances.

62. Cf. AvS, 212.

the tried and true devotion of Eastern Christians to Our Lady of the Way (Virgin Hodegétria) or the Western one to Our Lady of Good Counsel.

Coupled with the above is this secret that the Lord reveals to us: "I reprove and discipline those whom I love" (v. 19). For better understanding of this divine insight, let us briefly delineate the meaning of two Greek verbs in this verse: first, *elénchō* (ἐλέγχω), which conveys the idea of evaluating our soul in response to incorrect or sinful behavior. Thus, Jesus is telling us that in his love, he will bring to light any wrongdoing by offering convincing evidence. His disapproval, as intimated by the voice of our conscience, will spur us on to address and remove whatever might obstruct the path of his grace into our hearts. And second, *paideúō* (παιδεύω), stemming from the noun *paîs* (παῖς), "child," primarily signifies the instructing of an infant and adolescent, steering him or her toward adulthood by educating the person in all human virtue, even to the point of heroism. Thus, comprehensive ethical maturity is the goal, which at times can imply parental discipline. This latter sense is highlighted by the Neo-Vulgate's translation as *castigare*, that is, "to punish." The God-Man, therefore, reveals his love for us by teaching us how to be his perfect disciples. He is like a skilled physician who cures the body by excising a malignant tumor. In this way, our spiritual path retraces that of his own experience as the Suffering Servant taught by Yahweh: "He made my mouth like a sharp sword, in the shadow of his hand he hid me; he made me a polished arrow, in his quiver he hid me away" (Isa 49:2). Such tough love, so to speak, is also what unites us to the fruitfulness of his Cross.[63] Conversely, to be left untroubled in our sins should cause alarm, that perchance God no longer pursues us with love. Becoming aware of that sternness of divine pedagogy, Teresa of Ávila, as the hagiographic accounts relate, wittily exclaimed heavenwards: "If this is how you treat your friends, no wonder you have so few!"

But among the most endearing images in this entire septenary of letters is no doubt this exhortation: "Behold! I am standing at the door, knocking; if you hear my voice and open the door, I will come in to you and eat with you, and you with me" (v. 20). Illustrated so charmingly by W. H. Hunt in his 1853 painting "The Light of the World," depicting Jesus, crowned with gold and thorns, like a beggar in the night, gently and pensively knocking on a door. That door, however, appears to have been shut for a long time, since it is overgrown with vegetation; but even more beguilingly, it has no exterior handle: it can only be opened from the inside. What an artistic master-stroke to symbolize our freedom to choose. And so, one could say that the nuptial (Cant 5:2) and

63. Cf. AvS, 215.

Eucharistic Jesus always takes the initiative, he is ever near the door of our soul, waiting patiently. All one needs to do is open up and allow him to enter as a humble guest, enjoying the reciprocity of love and peace. Subsequently, he will draw us into his own place, the realm of his and his Father's throne, making us equal to him in his Kingdom (v. 21). At that point, Christ will have shared with us everything he himself owns, so that no deeper intimacy need be awaited.[64] This will be the completion of our spiritual journey,[65] and in some way it foreshadows the sabbatical rest of heaven. And this concludes the septet of letters to the churches in Asia, and through them to the universal Church; here also begins the visionary part proper of John's Apocalypse.

64. Thomas à Kempis' *Imitation of Christ* comments on this interiority: "If you prepare within your heart a fitting dwelling place, Christ will come to you and console you. His glory and beauty are within you, and he delights in dwelling there. The Lord frequently visits the heart of man, and there he shares with man pleasant conversations, welcome consolation, abundant peace, and a wonderful intimacy" (Lib. 2.2; trans. Leo Sherley-Price [New York: Dorset, 1986]).

65. Cf. AvS, 218; RD, 902–3.

PART 2

4:1–11, Otherworldly throne hall

Heaven in the human heart (4:1)

[1]After this I looked, and there in heaven a door stood open! And the first voice, which I had heard speaking to me like a trumpet, said, "Come up here, and I will show you what must take place after this."

If already the palaces and throne rooms of earthly royalty can dazzle us, then how much more must this vision of an open heaven in 4:1–11 strike us with awe. God's supernal dwelling and the place of his *basileía,* that is, his Kingdom and its worship, are described in time-honored language for otherworldly majesty. If during the inaugural vision (1:12–16) John was on earth, he is now invited up into heaven, overtaken by the heavenward force of the Spirit.[1] His exclamation "after this I looked," inspired by Daniel 7:6, and reiterated at 7:1, 9; 15:5; 18:1; 19:1, seems to mark a decisive turn to the future. Indicating a heavenly door standing open is common within the apocalyptic genre (e.g., Ezek 1:1), not least because the ancients viewed heaven as a solid vault, entered by way of actual doors. Its openness inverts the idea of a heaven closed due to the world's sin.[2] In the context of 3:20, this door can be interpreted as symbolizing Christ himself who opened it in his Passion, Death, and Resurrection.[3] His ascended and glorified Body is now the open door to heaven; from then onward his reign is in us (Luke 17:21), and "heaven" signals our supernatural life in the Risen Lord. By extension, we are reassured that in God's grace many scriptural arcana will be disclosed to our understanding, resulting in a universal proclamation of the mystery of Christ. To "ascend" here means to exceed all bodily senses and to contemplate spiritual realities. John's ecstatic state allows him to reveal to us what happens after this, as indicated already in 1:19.

1. Cf. AvS, 222.

2. Cf. Luke 4:25; Jas 5:17–18; see also Grant R. Osborne, *Revelation*, BECNT (Grand Rapids, MI: Baker Academic, 2002), 224.

3. Cf. RD, 903–4.

Faith, matured and joyous (4:2–4)

[2]At once I was in the Spirit, and there in heaven stood a throne, with one seated on the throne! [3]And the one seated there looks like jasper and carnelian, and around the throne is a rainbow that looks like an emerald. [4]Around the throne are twenty-four thrones, and seated on the thrones are twenty-four elders, dressed in white robes, with golden crowns on their heads.

After he enters the heavenly door, John's visionary gaze passes from the throne to the One seated on it, surrounded by a rainbow. Also encircling the Divine are twenty-four elders symbolizing the twelve patriarchs[4] and the twelve apostles[5] in representation of God's saving action in the Old and New Testaments. At the same time, these elders are wise kings seated on thrones and wearing crowns. Exercising a cultic role, they form the celestial counterpart of the pilgrim Church on earth, for after their "Amen-Alleluia" in 19:4, they are heard of no more, being absent from the New Jerusalem. Their white-golden appearance could be taken as an allegory of our faith, matured, joyous, and leading to eternal life.[6] That same gift of faith helps us to be victorious over mundane attachments, transcend earthly allegiances, and attain to the fruition of our share in the triple *munus* of Christ in his Kingdom without end.[7]

What takes center stage in the heaven of the human heart is the "throne" of the Church, and it is through the Church that already on earth we enjoy paradise, fixing our eyes on the very face of God. Under the image of a throne, the Church militant and the Church triumphant are united in the absolute power of the Almighty.[8] Still, part of our earthly condition is that we cannot see the face of the Lord directly; hence, the visionary on Patmos helps us perceive the presence of the Divine by way of the pulchritude of precious stones and a rainbow. Since similar gems were mounted on the priestly breastplate representing the twelve tribes of Israel,[9] they convey the Lord's holiness, power, and zeal for his chosen people. Jewels were also employed to describe Eden, and they now

4. Additional interpretations include their identification with the twelve Judges of Israel, with the twenty-four classes of priests in 1 Chron 14:1–19, or as signaling all sainthood in the people of God.

5. Which would imply that St. John at that moment has a vision of himself enthroned among the other apostles.

6. Cf. RD, 908–9.

7. Cf. AvS, 225–26.

8. Cf. RD, 906.

9. Cf. Exod 28:17–21.

capture the splendor of transcendence itself. Joined to this image is that of the rainbow, reminding us of God's covenant with Noah, the eternal Judge mindful of his promise of mercy.[10] That forgiving compassion now surrounds the globe and transforms our souls toward eternal life.[11] Metaphorically, the seven colors of the rainbow indicate the sanctification at work in our lives through the seven gifts of the Holy Spirit.[12] We are called to be signs of reconciliation with God.

Grace, robust yet fragile (4:5–6a)

[5] Coming from the throne are flashes of lightning, and rumblings and peals of thunder, and in front of the throne burn seven flaming torches, which are the seven spirits of God; [6a] and in front of the throne there is something like a sea of glass, like crystal.

Three images, when taken together, appear to symbolize the Church's sacrament of baptism with its sanctifying grace. First, there are the "flashes of lightning, and rumblings and peals of thunder" coming from the throne; they are not only reminiscent of God's encounter with his people at Mount Sinai, but also signal the preaching and miracles of the apostles by which they spread the Gospel and instituted the sacraments. Second, John explains how right in front of the throne burn seven flaming torches, embodying the seven spirits of God.[13] Here we have an allusion to the fiery effusion of the Holy Spirit on the day of Pentecost and his seven gifts, making the heavenly Father the most hidden person of the Blessed Trinity.[14] Capping this three-faceted baptismal canvas is the fact that in front of the throne, too, there is "something like a sea of glass, like crystal." While the sea recalls both the primordial waters above and beneath the firmament (Gen 1:6–7), and the passage of the Israelites through the Red Sea (Exod 14:22), its vitreous appearance speaks to the pure light of grace, to the transparency of our interior life, and, rather paradoxically, to its simultaneous

10. All judgment on earth is framed by the protological one in the diluvial water, and the eschatological one by fire; and between these two, the Lord grants times of repentance.

11. Cf. RD, 907.

12. Cf. Isa 11:2–3; see also AvS, 224. From a scientific perspective, the rainbow colors are sevenfold due to water droplets that break the white sunlight into the seven colors of the spectrum, i.e., red, orange, yellow, green, blue, indigo, and violet; and, figuratively speaking, the whiteness of divine holiness is mirrored in the sevenfold color scheme of the angels and saints.

13. See also the seven archangels of Judeo-Christian tradition.

14. Cf. RD, 910; AvS, 228–29.

solidity and fragility.[15] Tied into the baptismal symbolism is also the vanquishing of the sea serpent (cf. Gen 1:21): "And the sea was no more!" (21:1c). Baptism destroys the power of the devil and blots out original sin. In that same sense, the sea of glass reappears in 15:2, this time mixed with fire, and all those who have conquered the beast and its image standing beside it singing the song of victory (cf. 15:3).

Worshipful vigilance (4:6b–8a)

6b Around the throne, and on each side of the throne, are four living creatures, full of eyes in front and behind: 7 the first living creature like a lion, the second living creature like an ox, the third living creature with a face like a human face, and the fourth living creature like a flying eagle. 8a And the four living creatures, each of them with six wings, are full of eyes all around and inside.

The four living creatures, translated as *animalia* by the Nova Vulgata, are yet another reality impressed on the eyes of the apostolic seer as he continues to sketch this supernatural tableau in broad brushstrokes. Even though they are in the middle and around God's throne, that is, attending to its four sides, suggesting their centrality, their true nature remains largely elusive. As is typical for him, John appears to combine several descriptive elements found in Ezekiel 1:5–21,[16] Isaiah 6:2,[17] and Daniel 7:3–8,[18] simplifying and reworking them into the innovative portrayal of the four living beings in his own vision. In their originality, they may be distinct and even superior to the ranks of ordinary angels.

The relative scarcity of information about them has spawned a variety of interpretations over the centuries: commentators have thought of the six wings

15. Rupert recognizes this double entendre of the symbol of "glass," explaining that the saints are always lucid in mind and speech, yet fragile in the body; however, once they arrive in heaven, they will be radiant and incorruptible. On earth, eternity is clothed in the robes of mortality, but the Divine shines through their humanity, cf. RD, 911.

16. God's throne bearers, sometimes equated with the angelic choir of the Thrones, also known as *ophanim*, "spheres," *galgalim*, "wheels," or *merkabah*, "heavenly chariot," identified as cherubim in Ezek 10:14–17, 20; 41:19; in the Qumran manuscript of the Songs of the Sabbath Sacrifice they are construed as simple angels (cf. 4Q405).

17. Seraphim or angels of fire supporting God's throne, guardians of his temple, ranked first in the Jewish angelic hierarchy.

18. Four great beasts.

(vs. four wings in Ezek 10:21) as three pairs indicating the Blessed Trinity and the fulfillment of all Christian potential, active and contemplative. Those same wings have also been taken as symbols of the living Christ and his universal authority, the many eyes signifying his eternal wisdom. Rupert opines that they represent his four principal actions, i.e., Incarnation (human), Passion (bullock), Resurrection (lion), and Ascension (eagle).[19] Most modern authors view the living creatures as chief agents within the created order in complete harmony with its Creator,[20] calling on every existing thing to worship him, and merging heavenly (wings, eyes) with earthly traits (three animals and human). Others again see in them super-angelic powers who direct the physical world in its nobility (lion), strength (ox), intelligence (human being), and agility (eagle).

On a more metaphorical level, they highlight qualities of the Church on earth, such as her royal dignity (lion), humble weakness (human), sacrifice (ox), and her destiny in the heights of heaven (eagle). It seems possible, too, to envision their fourfoldness as symbolic of good hierarchical administrators (man), contemplative souls (eagle), teachers (lion), and compassionate religious superiors (calf).[21] In due course, Victorinus and Irenaeus popularized the allegorical tetramorph of the four evangelists, Matthew, Mark, Luke, and John. According to Rupert again, they symbolize the four Gospels that allow us to walk safely, and to know where we come from and where we are going.[22] One might also find a metaphorical allusion to the four cardinal virtues as an expression of all Christian life. In a way, Psalm 103:22 sums up the essence of these mysterious creatures: "Bless the Lord, all his works, in all places of his dominion."

Among their most prominent features is their ocular totality, as they are replete with eyes all around, inside and out, fully immersed, as it were, in the vision of God, and at the same time participating in his omniscience and cardiognosis. Their superabundant wings could be taken as a reflection of divine mobility and omnipresence. Moreover, the living beings are obediently moving in every direction that God will send them, while at the same time reverently and modestly serving in his presence.[23] They carry the supreme gift of life, like a pure embodiment of faith, love, and service.[24] Alert and knowledgeable, they

19. Cf. RD, 912.

20. Cf. *CCC*, §1138.

21. Cf. RD, 916.

22. Cf. RD, 917; for Adrienne, the eagle signals the swift and farsighted reception of the Gospel, cf. AvS, 232.

23. Evocative perhaps also of a winged Sphinx of the ancient Egyptian culture.

24. Cf. AvS, 230–31.

are designed by the Most High to witness everything, and to be attentive to the state of the world and the Church in general.[25]

At the same time, they possess perfect self-knowledge, teaching us to monitor the state of our own heart with its various passions and appetites, affections, and thoughts.[26] In their untiring vigilance and circumspection, those living beings are not only focused on God, but also no wile of the spiritual enemy will escape their notice. Coupled with their unparalleled visionary capability is their incessant worship, offering praise to the Lord God, remaining altogether restless in their divine adoration and service. Likewise, we should pray always, and strive to proclaim Christ's Gospel unceasingly.[27]

Cosmic hymnody (4:8b–11)

8b Day and night without ceasing they sing, "Holy, holy, holy, the Lord God the Almighty, who was and is and is to come." 9 And whenever the living creatures give glory and honor and thanks to the one who is seated on the throne, who lives forever and ever, 10 the twenty-four elders fall before the one who is seated on the throne and worship the one who lives forever and ever; they cast their crowns before the throne, singing, 11 "You are worthy, our Lord and God, to receive glory and honor and power, for you created all things, and by your will they existed and were created."

It is anything but silent in the proximity of the heavenly throne, because in addition to the voices and thunders of v. 5a, something is happening that can best be described as a cosmic liturgy expressed in hymns.[28] Leaning in a little closer, one notices two choruses that chant in unceasing alternation, namely, the hymn of the living creatures (vv. 8b–9), and the responsorial praise by the elders (vv. 10–11). Unsurprisingly, the former give "glory, honor, and thanks" (v. 9) to the Triune God enthroned in unending life, by acclaiming "Holy, holy, holy, the Lord God the Almighty, who was and is and is to come" (v. 8c). When it comes to glorifying his throne, these *animalia* consistently take the lead in

25. Recalling the wakeful *egrēgoroi* or "watchers," who never close their eyes (Dan 4:13, 17, 23).

26. Cf. AvS, 234.

27. Cf. RD, 919.

28. Cf. Robert E. Coleman, *Singing with the Angels* (Old Tappan, NJ: Fleming H. Revell, 1998).

celestial worship (4:6–9; 5:8–9; 19:4). Although the Trisagion (cf. Isa 6:3) is three-dimensional, the coda of this doxology "who was and is and is to come"[29] refers chiefly to the Father as the Godhead. While "glory and honor" regards the divine perfections, "thanksgiving" refers to the divine gifts in creation and redemption.

Seamlessly picking up on this quasi-Eucharistic praise of the Creator are the elders who offer their hymnic response: "You are worthy, our Lord and God, to receive glory and honor and power, for you created all things, and by your will they existed and were created."[30] In a complementary fashion, they exchange "thanksgiving" (v. 9) for the acknowledgment of the Lord's "power" (v. 11). In keeping with their cultic function throughout Revelation, these twenty-four representatives of God's covenant with humanity, join in the universal worship of the All-Ruler. Just as ancient vassal kings removed their crowns when coming into the presence of the emperor, these noble men and women lay their diadems of victory before their Lord. Their prostration in profound adoration reveals perfect love and complete abandonment to the Divine, as they surrender their crown of holiness to the one who bestowed it on them.[31]

"Our Lord and God" (*Domine et Deus noster*, v. 11a) may be in retort to the idolatrous title of the Roman Caesar Domitian of John's time. As baptized Christians, we are drawn into this eschatological liturgy, praising the Almighty who creates and re-creates everything.[32] Unlike us humans who are unworthy (cf. 5:2, 4, 9), he is truly worthy of our worship (cf. 5:9, 12). That has become even more cogent ever since Christ's incarnate and glorified humanity through his Paschal Mystery was subsumed into that supernal timelessness. Creation forever reminds heaven of God's all-powerful will, but also of humanity's calling into his Kingdom, a Kingdom desirous of incorporating everything created.[33] Our destiny is divine doxology, yet already now we are invited to learn this language of heaven and join in this cosmic hymnody by giving witness through blameless lives.[34]

29. Changing the word order from the a-chronological "who is and who was and who is to come" at 1:4, to the chronologically ordered "who was and is and is to come" in this present verse; notice that at 11:17 and 16:5 "will be" is omitted.

30. The unexpected sequence "they existed and were created" denotes God's universal providence and timeless power; see a similarly illogical word order, "birth-conception," in Ps 7:15.

31. Cf. AvS, 236.

32. Cf. RD, 924.

33. Cf. AvS, 237.

34. Cf. RD, 921.

5:1–14, Worthy Lamb

Scriptural seals (5:1)

[1]Then I saw in the right hand of the one seated on the throne a scroll written on the inside and on the back, sealed with seven seals.

Aided by that magnificent chanting before the divine throne, our eyes are still riveted on "our Lord and God" (4:11a), but now John invites us to zoom in on a particular detail of God's presence, that is, his open right hand, as visualized by the Greek preposition *epí* (ἐπί, "upon"). In common experience, the right hand is the one of a trusted greeting or agreement, of honest work, of revered authority, and of captivating power (cf. 1:16; 2:1). Here it also conveys the certainty of God's openness to and intimacy with us his children.[1] Resting in this benevolent hand is a "scroll," which in the original is called by the diminutive or endearing term for *bíblos* (βίβλος), namely, *biblíon* (βιβλίον). Immediately the Bible itself comes to mind, either as the Book of Life (cf. 3:5; 13:18), or as the Old Testament unsealed in the New, making up the Sacred Scripture as we know it today.[2] It is God's preordained plan for this world to be revealed and carried out by the Lamb, to return humanity to the Lord as his sole possession. Curiously, this book is so replete with words that the content spills onto the outside, it is "written on the inside and on the back" (v. 1b). This copiousness of messaging could allude to the literal and spiritual sense of the divine word.[3] It is the superabundance of what the Holy Spirit has to say to us about the Father and the Son. Also implied is that God in his omniscience knows the human heart inside and out (cf. John 2:25).

1. Cf. AvS, 238.

2. Cf. RD, 924.

3. Cf. RD, 925; Origen in a like manner comments that "the whole Scripture is what is revealed by the book which has writing on the front because its interpretation is easy, and on the back because it is hidden and spiritual." *Commentary on John* 5.6, quoted from Ronald E. Heine, *Origen: An Introduction to His Life and Thought* (Eugene, OR: Cascade, 2019), 62.

Access to it, however, is far from easy, since it is hermetically closed and hidden by seven seals.[4] Not only is the Scripture like a vessel that contains the sevenfold wisdom of the Holy Spirit,[5] but it also holds the plenitude of Christ's mysteries from his Incarnation to the eschatological establishment of his Kingdom.[6] Thus, nothing can supersede the importance and confidentiality of this book. Figuratively speaking, since the heavenly Father is occupied with holding it, and the Holy Spirit with concealing its contents, only the Son is available to open it.[7] On a spiritual plane, we should have the daily desire to read this sacred word, to be illumined and nourished by its wonder.

Tearful surrender (5:2–4)

[2]*And I saw a mighty angel proclaiming with a loud voice, "Who is worthy to open the scroll and break its seals?"* [3]*And no one in heaven or on earth or under the earth was able to open the scroll or to look into it.*
[4]*And I began to weep bitterly because no one was found worthy to open the scroll or to look into it.*

Yet, before the contents of this book can be viewed, a truly kerygmatic question must be answered (*praedicare,* v. 2a), a question concerning worthiness.[8] This inquiry is of such cosmic proportions that it takes a mighty angel to execute it. His inquiry "Who is worthy?" could be said to represent the entire Old Testament. Tragically, out of all the angels in heaven, the righteous on earth, and the patriarchs and matriarchs in limbo, none was capable of opening nor even looking at the scroll.[9] All of creation with its threefold biblical division of heaven, earth, and underworld, are not weighty enough to break open those

4. Also, according to ancient Roman inheritance law, a last will and testament was officially registered and filed with seven seals, involving up to seven witnesses; it is also known that the scrolls of Roman emperors, such as Augustus and Vespasian, were sealed seven times.

5. Just as the throne in 4:3–6 was surrounded by seven celestial insignia (jasper, carnelian, rainbow, emerald, thunderstorm, torches, glass-sea), so also here, the scroll and the praises (v. 12) are of a septenary format; cf. RD, 923.

6. Identified as Incarnation, Passion, Resurrection, Ascension, sending of the Paraclete, calling of the Gentiles, parousia; cf. Apringius of Beja, in William C. Weinrich, ed., *Revelation,* ACCS (Downers Grove, IL: InterVarsity Press, 2005), 69.

7. Cf. AvS, 239.

8. This Greek adjective *áxios* (ἄξιος) stems from the verb *ágō* (ἄγω), describing something that draws down the scale; hence, it signifies an entity that has "weight, worth, value."

9. Cf. RD, 927.

seven seals. And John's reaction is heartbreaking: his mind anointed by the Holy Spirit is overwhelmed, his emotions are overcome with sadness, and he weeps profusely. His tears are not flowing due to frustration, but because human history remains indecipherable and therefore incomprehensible. These are bitter tears of human longing, including the Old Testament yearning for Christ. These are the tears of the Church, too, who experiences epochs of powerlessness and persecution; she also weeps at her own sins, and beseeches the Lord for her redemption.[10] As her sons and daughters, we join in the seer's anticipation and surrender, waiting for God's Testament to be unsealed in the presence of his prime witness, his only-begotten Son.

Lion and Root (5:5)

[5]Then one of the elders said to me, "Do not weep. See, the Lion of the tribe of Judah, the Root of David, has conquered, so that he can open the scroll and its seven seals."

Instead of having our eyes blurred with tears, however, we should fix them on Jesus who alone has won the battle against cosmic doom and vanquished the darkness of sin and death. By this unique victory, a deeper meaning of human history can now be disclosed to us. His all-decisive conquest, brought about in his Resurrection, was prepared by God from the earliest times of the Old Testament. As a descendant of one of Israel's ancestral tribes, he would be the Lion of Judah.[11] Patriarch Jacob envisioned his son Judah as a lion's whelp (Gen 49:9), and in due course it would become the symbol of that tribe, emblazoned on its standard within Israel's encampment.[12] In the fullness of time Christ was to be born of this leonine tribe, and was to be a great Conqueror. His might, courage, and sovereignty will enable us to share in his victory, provided we maintain undistracted eye contact with this divine Lion.

Since this tribe was also representative of the royal house of David, son of Jesse, the messianic title Root of David is intimately connected with it. Several prophets of old had described him as a righteous Branch springing from the ancient stock, as a shoot sprouts from a fallen tree (Jer 33:15). It turns out that he who is the Branch is also the Root; he who is King David's Son in his humanity,

10. Cf. AvS, 242.

11. Mentioned fourth in lists of the twelve tribes, following his older brothers Reuben, Simeon, and Levi (cf. Deut 27:12–13), yet placed first in Rev 7:5.

12. See *Palestinian Targum* on Num 2:2.

is also his Lord by virtue of his divinity. It could be argued, too, that related to the image of the branch is that of the ruler's scepter (2:27): the Son of David is the true source of spiritual power, not only for his ancestral tribe and dynasty, but even more so for all who look to him for strength. And as that Davidic scion he has the right to occupy the throne and rule over the new people of God. It is only just that he receive the task of opening the seven seals of the mysterious scroll. From now on, he will reign over the earth, and indeed, over the entire universe. With that in mind, may we never cease to behold (*ecce*, v. 5b), that is, to contemplate Christ as our Victor and Ruler.

Slain yet standing (5:6–7)

[6] Then I saw between the throne and the four living creatures and among the elders a Lamb standing as if it had been slaughtered, having seven horns and seven eyes, which are the seven spirits of God sent out into all the earth. [7] He went and took the scroll from the right hand of the one who was seated on the throne.

As the exiled visionary on Patmos looks up to see the Lion of Judah and the Root of David, he instead is shown a little innocent Lamb,[13] in the very center of the throne, surrounded by the living creatures and the elders. What a mind-wrenching rebirth of imagery: biblical precedent and Christian tradition teach us that the Lamb is an image for Jesus as Savior, and it becomes his main title in Revelation, too, reiterated no fewer than twenty-eight times. A wealth of Old Testament passages is blended into one, namely, the paschal lamb without blemish whose blood made Israel triumphant over captors and oppressors (Exod 12:1–27), the lamb of expiation and daily sacrifice (Lev 14:10–20), the suffering Servant of God (Isa 53:7), but also the Lamb of God who takes away the sin of the world (John 1:29), who one day will victoriously shepherd his people in paradise (7:17).

Unique, however, is the way St. John presents the Lamb as if in an artist's collage, merging images of power and awe with those of redemptive immolation. Each part of this symphony of symbols should be analyzed individually to extract its *sensus plenior*: the Lamb's position in the middle of the throne, living beings, and elders, conveys his absolute centrality, evocative, too, of the

13. The Greek noun *arníon* (ἀρνίον) is the diminutive form of the regular *arḗn* (ἀρήν, cf. Luke 10:3; John 21:15), signifying "a little lamb"; notice the cognate term *amnós* (ἀμνός) at John 1:29; it figuratively conveys a person with gentle and virgin-like intentions.

personified Wisdom assisting at God's throne (Wis 9:4). He could be called the fulcrum of the Kingdom of Heaven in a cosmic (living beings) and soteriological sense (elders). Mind-boggling and genuinely meta-conceptual is the idea of a little lamb that is slaughtered (*occisum*), yet at the same time standing up on its feet (*stantem*).[14] It metaphorically points to Christ's Death and Resurrection; he is paradoxically forever dead and alive at the same time, Victim and Victor. Furthermore, John's newborn Lamb, mystically alluding to Jesus' infancy, bears a strong resemblance to an adult male sheep, a ram, since it has horns. What cannot be found in nature, however, is the number of horns, namely, seven, imaging the fullness of divine power. Likewise, his seven eyes indicate his wisdom and omniscience.[15] At this juncture, the seer offers his own interpretation, just as he frequently does in his Gospel (e.g., John 2:21–22, 24–25). He reassures his readers that the horns and eyes coalesced are a figure of the seven spirits of God sent out into the world, an allusion certainly to the eschatological mission of the Church impelled by the Holy Spirit.

After having meditated on some of the biblical implications, let us now try to make more explicit the spiritual message of the Lamb to each one of us. Although God's features are not discernible except for his being seated on a throne, the Lamb by contrast is in sharp view, revealing his Father's nature to us.[16] As he approaches him to receive the sealed scroll from his right hand, he does so as divine Heir, prime Witness and Executor of his Will and Testament. The Father's plan was conceived before creation, and the Son will inherit everything, since he is the origin, too (3:14). He is completely resigned to his Father's will, and just as the Lamb suffered slaughter, so also his Father bears with the removal of the scroll from his almighty hand. Evidently, there is perfect harmony of will and action in the Trinity, bringing all things to completion.[17] Enlarging this perspective, St. Paul exclaims: "That very Spirit bearing witness with our spirit that we are children of God, and if children, then heirs, heirs of God and joint heirs with Christ, if, in fact, we suffer with him so that we may also be glorified with him" (Rom 8:16–17).

Additionally, how can one ignore the tremendous tension implied in

14. Both verbs in Greek are inclined in the perfect tense (*hestēkós, esphagménon*), implying that Christ's Paschal Mystery has been accomplished in the past, but has an inerasable effect in the present, as well as for all eternity.

15. Cf. 1:14; Zech 4:10; Isa 11:2–3; see also RD, 929.

16. Cf. AvS, 245.

17. Cf. AvS, 246–47.

Christ's contrastive characterization as Lion-Lamb?[18] Deemed worthy due to his lamb-like meekness in his Passion, Jesus also resembles a lion that captures the prey, sending out the roar of evangelization and final judgment across the globe. He dies innocently like a lamb yet conquers death with a lion's fierceness. He is a lamb toward the world, but a lion toward the devil.[19] The purpose and the reward of his victory is to open the scroll; thus, by his death he conquered, as it were, the Father and the Holy Spirit so that they release the secret of this book.[20] Henceforth he will be central to the communion of angels and saints, in his glorified wounds still bearing the trophies of his crucifixion, grace for the redeemed, but a cruel reminder for his enemies. Each one of us, baptized into the Church, is called to live in that tension, the boldness of the Lion and the humility of the Lamb, slain yet standing erect: his grace empowers us and weakens us all at the same time (2 Cor 12:9). Jesus promised to send us out like lion-lambs into the midst of ravenous wolves in sheep's clothing (Matt 7:15).

Moreover, like the Lamb under the unction of the Spirit, we strive to incorporate the active and the contemplative life, represented by the seven horns and seven eyes. And like the Holy Spirit, who is sent out into all the earth, yet always remains in heaven, we should retain a good measure of recollection of the presence of God, even amid the countless distractions of daily life. Why not also ask him to destroy in us by his power all worldly attachment, and to rule over our inner passions? Lastly, commentators have noted that the Aramaic word for "lamb," *tályā* (טַלְיָא),[21] can also mean "youthful servant" (*puer*[22]), which adds another layer of meaning to the image, namely, that the followers of the Lamb are also imitating his servanthood (Matt 20:26b–28). This humble service is illustrated by the magnificent tapestry of all the saints, confessors, virgins, and martyrs.[23]

18. Notice also the complementary theological angles on Jesus; while the Letter to the Hebrews highlights him as the High Priest, the Book of Revelation sheds light on him as the Victim-Lamb.

19. Cf. RD, 928.

20. Cf. AvS, 243.

21. The related diminutive noun *talítha*, literally "little lamb," is a term of affection toward a child, cf. Mark 5:41.

22. Which in turn connotes divine Wisdom: "Give me the wisdom that sits by your throne, and do not reject me from among your servants [NVg: *pueris*]," Wis 9:4.

23. See also a summary on the Lamb in John D'Souza, *The Lamb of God in the Johannine Writings* (Allahabad: St. Paul Publications, 1968), 168–72; see also Eric Edward May, *Ecce Agnus Dei: A Philological and Exegetical Approach to John 1:29,36*, SST 5 (Washington, DC: Catholic University of America Press, 2013).

Triple regal chorale (5:8–14)

[8]When he had taken the scroll, the four living creatures and the twenty-
four elders fell before the Lamb, each holding a harp and golden bowls
full of incense, which are the prayers of the saints. [9]They sing a new song:
"You are worthy to take the scroll and to open its seals, for you were
slaughtered and by your blood you ransomed for God, saints from every
tribe and language and people and nation; [10]you have made them to be
a kingdom and priests serving our God, and they will reign on earth."
[11]Then I looked, and I heard the voice of many angels surrounding the
throne and the living creatures and the elders; they numbered myri-
ads of myriads and thousands of thousands, [12]singing with full voice,
"Worthy is the Lamb that was slaughtered to receive power and wealth
and wisdom and might and honor and glory and blessing!" [13]Then I
heard every creature in heaven and on earth and under the earth and in
the sea, and all that is in them, singing, "To the one seated on the throne
and to the Lamb be blessing and honor and glory and might forever and
ever!" [14]And the four living creatures said, "Amen!" And the elders fell
down and worshiped.

Revelation grants periodic glimpses into that cosmic liturgy happening in front of the divine throne, including frequent songs of worship that underscore the luminous face of history. Especially when the plot turns dark, disturbing, or even depressing, these moments of pure exultation lift us up, helping us to keep a transcendent perspective on our world with its eschatological vicissitudes. These moments of universal praise not only teach us a deeper understanding of God's sovereign designs, but they invite us also to join in and partake of the adoration. Now, the second half of this fifth chapter, i.e., vv. 8–14, is taken up entirely by such acts of worship, and there are three of them to be precise, a grandiose treble glorifying the Blessed Trinity.

First, there is the song that exalts the perennial newness of our redemption (vv. 9–10), proffered by two groups that wholly belong to the realm of eternity, that is, the four living creatures and the twenty-four elders. They symbolize not only creation itself, but also all the saints on earth, and their liturgy involves physical attributes such as prostrations, harps, and golden thuribles from which arise aromatic incense. By offering these prayers, the elders exercise their priestly office of mediation. Rupert explains that these harps indicate humanity praising God, while the incense symbolizes their wide-open hearts, filled with intercession and charity.[24] Adrienne adds that they summon the earthly Church onto a heavenly level in purity of conscience.[25] In Judaism, incidentally, this mediatorial role is attributed to Michael and the archangels.[26] This awe-inspiring scene seems to anticipate the liturgical action described at 8:3–5. And indeed, the Church appears to have adopted all these signs, such as bodily postures, sacred music, and incense, to be performed during the sacramental ceremonies in our cathedrals, churches, and chapels. Along with the new name (2:17), the new heaven and new earth (21:1), and the New Jerusalem (21:10), this new song (v. 9) forms part of the unfading newness of conciliation between the Blessed Trinity and redeemed humanity; it is ever new because renewed from generation to generation.[27]

Quite illustrative is the Greek word here used for "redemption," namely, the verb *agorázō* (ἀγοράζω), which stems from *agorá* (ἀγορά), meaning the central square in ancient cities where assemblies were held. Implied is the idea of making a purchase in that place, transferring ownership from sellers to buyers. Hence, in addition to the reality of ransom (Latin *red-émere*, "to buy back, release from captivity"), it points out how the Christian believer now belongs to the Lord as his supernatural acquisition. By his Paschal Mystery, Jesus has satisfied all the responsibilities and acquired all the rights that make us his beloved brethren. Pivotal to the abiding newness of this redeeming act is the painful price that was paid, namely, the blood of the God-Man, buying us back for his Father from every tribe and language and people and nation. We must profess that only God can redeem so magnificently and universally. Now a Kingdom of priests, they shall reign over the earth: although they live in this world, their faith makes them conquer and transcend it already. Kingdom and priesthood also epitomize the very essence of the One, Holy, Catholic, and Apostolic Church in her objective sanctity. On the night before the Lord was to suffer, the apostle John was an eyewitness of her humble beginnings in the upper room, resting his head on Jesus' heart; and now he recognizes her eschatological grandeur, modeled on heavenly realities. Music, incense, and blood could be said to express the nature of the people of God until the end of time.[28] Enthused by this new song of the *animalia* ("living beings") and *seniores*

24. Cf. RD, 932.

25. Cf. AvS, 248.

26. Cf. Tob 12:12, 15; Testaments of the Twelve Patriarchs, *Testament of Levi*, 3:5–6; 3 Bar 11.

27. Cf. AvS, 249.

28. Cf. AvS, 250.

("elders"), let us appreciate with ever greater fervor and gratitude the undying novelty of the gift of our redemption.

Second, with the praise of the countless host of angelic beings (vv. 11–12), distinguished from the living beings, a new feature is introduced. Looking and listening at the same time, the apostolic seer recounts the colossal volume of voices, a refrain of worship, coming from those choirs concentrically surrounding the throne of God. It completes the thread of reflection regarding the worthiness of knowing, revealing, and executing God's eternal plan. The mighty angel had challenged John by inquiring: "Who is worthy?" (v. 2), to which John despondently submitted, "No one is worthy!" (v. 4). But a happy denouement was indicated when the living beings and elders addressed the Lamb directly, "*You* are worthy!" (v. 9), only to receive a jubilant subjoinder now from the innumerable multitude of angels, "Worthy *is* the Lamb!" (v. 12). That sequence makes their doxology sound like a responsorial acclamation, so fitting for this cosmic liturgy.

Before moving on, however, to reflect on the tenor of their chanting, it is important to take stock of the vast number of those angelic beings.[29] According to scholastic theology, each one of them is a person created by God with an individual character. In their totality, they amount to ten thousands of ten thousands[30] multiplied by thousands of thousands,[31] resulting in a truly astronomical host of good spirits, so appropriately compared to the stars (1:16, 20; 2:1). And still, it remains finite, and not limitless, subject to the dominion of the Lord God. With much ardor (*voce magna*) they now exalt seven attributes of the slain Lamb, namely, his power (*virtus*) and wealth (*divitia*), his wisdom (*sapientia*) and might (*fortitudo*), his honor (*honor*) and glory (*gloria*), as well as his blessing (*benedictio*). While the first four appear to highlight his qualities as Savior, the last three praise his divine attributes. Also noteworthy, both here and in the third song (cf. v. 13b), is the absence of any signs of devotion toward the gift of redemption, since only the elders in the first hymn (vv. 9–10) are the beneficiaries of Christ's work of salvation, while the fallen angels and lower creation are not directly affected by its justifying grace. The most fulsome of all the doxologies in the Apocalypse,[32] through its seven elements it carries the

29. Cf. Dan 7:10; Jude 14; 1 Enoch 40:1.

30. Keeping in mind that *myriás* (μυριάς), i.e., 10,000, was the highest Greek numeral at the time.

31. The numeral *chiliás* (χιλιάς) stands for 1,000.

32. See 7:12, which also has seven elements, but in a different order and with a distinct terminology, and on that occasion the praise will be addressed to God (see also 1 Chron 29:11 with its fivefold adoration).

absolute plenitude of worship. By extension, these attributes equally glorify the Father and the Holy Spirit, worthy of every glorification. As Christians, we can learn from this comprehensive act of angelic praise, imitating it in our personal and communal prayer.

Third and last, like a second echo reverberating from the song of the living creatures and the elders (vv. 9–10), as well as from the responsorial hymn of the angels (v. 12), John hears the one pronounced by all creation (vv. 13–14). Left earlier in a state of confusion and frustration when no one in heaven or on earth or under the earth was able to open the scroll or to look into it, the seer is now entranced to hear for the first time every creature in heaven and on earth and under the earth and in the sea, singing. This time, even the creatures contained by the world's oceans join in the joyful strains, surpassing the threefold division of heaven-earth-underworld (v. 3) by a fourfold one, adding the sea. Not without a poetic touch, creation is personified in singing common praise, albeit not in a rational or vocal way, but by the natural state of each creature's existence.[33] As they climax into this cosmic summons to worship, they accomplish all manners of praise. Divine liturgy is now fully revealed as the all-encompassing and defining reality of absolutely everything there is in the *ordo naturae*. In fact, doxology proves to be the most profound purpose of the entire cosmos. Unsurprisingly then, this is the only song within this treble of chorales that is addressed primarily to the one seated on the throne, that is, the Father of all creation, complementing the first two songs addressed exclusively to the Lamb. Nevertheless, the indirect speech ("to the One seated on the throne") carries in it the unfathomable chasm established between the Divine and the Created (Luke 16:26). At the same time, by paralleling the Father and the Lamb, the sacred author subtly conveys that creation and redemption are centerpieces of the entire *opus Dei*. God alone, and he as trinitarian Creator, Redeemer, and Sanctifier, is all-deserving of worship; and if that is true, then creation is already absorbed, *hic et nunc*, into the sphere of infinity.[34]

Seamlessly resuming the chant of the angels (v. 11), therefore, every creature now offers a fourfold act of worship, beginning with benediction or blessing, which was the last sentiment of the song above. Then, honor and glory, reflective of the second- and third-last attributes of the preceding hymn, while might echoes the fourth item in both songs. Not only are these last two chants intimately coupled, but the three together (vv. 8–10; vv. 11–12; v. 13) make up a single unity of praise, as can be seen from the way the four living creatures

33. Cf. RD, 938.
34. Cf. AvS, 254.

say "Amen!" in confirmation, and how the elders fall down in worship (v. 14). Indeed, that prostration attributes the three songs to the one God in three persons, coming full circle. During his earthly life, very few prostrated themselves before the Son of Man, but now, lo and behold, every knee bends in adoration, in heaven, on earth, and under the earth, and every tongue confesses that Jesus Christ is Lord, to the glory of God the Father (Phil 2:10–11).[35] For all eternity, the ontological difference between Creator and creature can only be expressed in humble adoration. Every created being will take part in the whole-hearted "Amen" of the Son toward his heavenly Father, vicariously voiced by the living beings.[36] And so, through Christ, our own personal "Amen" is spoken to the glory of God (2 Cor 1:20). May this stir in us the desire to make of our lives an ongoing doxology to the Blessed Trinity.

35. Cf. RD, 931.
36. Cf. AvS, 255.

6:1–17, Trials on earth

First seal: White horse of conquest in faith (6:1–2)

[1]Then I saw the Lamb open one of the seven seals, and I heard one of the four living creatures call out, as with a voice of thunder, "Come!" [2]I looked, and behold, a white horse! Its rider had a bow; a crown was given to him, and he came out conquering and to conquer.

We are now arriving at the prophetic, and, therefore, most difficult part of this mysterious book. Chapters 6–16 contain a series of three sets of seven elements or septenaries: seven seals (6:1–8:1), seven trumpets (8:2–11:19), and seven bowls (15:1–16:21). As an aside, it could be argued that their imagery bears resemblance to end-time events prophesied in Jesus' Olivet Discourse (Matt 24–25; Mark 13; Luke 21), namely, the rise of false religions, increase of wars, diseases, famines, natural disasters, loss of faith, intensified persecution, and martyrdom. In any event, the above septets, even though mostly ominous in nature, are unfailingly punctuated by scenes suggesting the triumph of the Lamb in heaven and his witnesses on earth.[1] Since Revelation's narrative plot progresses in a circular, rather than a rectilinear movement, each of these sets of seven signal the entire end-time or eschaton, that is, the time of the Church until Christ's return. Simultaneously, when contemplated in their succession, they seem to illustrate how the trials on earth intensify as history moves closer to its resolution, especially in chs. 17–22: the fall of the worldly city, a final battle, universal judgment, and separation between heaven and hell imaged by a fiery lake (20:15) and the New Jerusalem (21:2). With its imagery adapted from the prophet Zechariah (1:8–17; 6:1–8), vv. 1–8 of this sixth chapter depict four horsemen, commonly viewed as harbingers of the Last Judgment.[2]

1. E.g., chs. 7, 10.

2. It is conceivable that one single horseman, be it Christ himself, or the Gospel, or the Holy Spirit, or the antichrist, or even worldly empires, is riding these four horses successively,

Immediately after receiving the cosmic homage while taking possession of the scroll, the Lamb now starts to break open its first seal, thunderously summoning both the seer and the first horseman through one of the living creatures, likely the lion (4:7), into complete obedience and availability: "Come!" At last, the sinners' alienation from God begins to be reversed, and through the necessary trials of war and pestilence, they are readied for the coming of the Lord Jesus.[3] Resonating in this voice is also God's longing for the return of his children. Making its appearance now is a white horse, a symbol of pure faith in Christ: what a sight to behold (NVg: *ecce*). Could it not also be a sign of the carnal impulses deep within the human heart, to be dominated by supernatural virtue? According to its chromatic symbolism, white always points to realities pertaining to the heavenly realm.[4] The rider is brandishing a bow,[5] meaning the word of the Gospel, and the arrows of its doctrines (cf. Hab 3:9). Swift is their motion, sudden their striking, laying open the secret thoughts of a person's interior (cf. Heb 4:12), and causing him or her to submit to the rule of Christ's Kingdom (cf. Ps 45:4–6).

While this apocalyptic rider comes into view already armed with the bow, this crown, either that of a king or of an honored soldier (4:4), is bestowed on him afterwards, expressive of assured conquest and dominion (cf. Dan 7:4, 6, 14).[6] Given to him by God the Father, it symbolizes Christ's regal authority, his dignity, and his victories. His coming out "conquering and to conquer" has an air of inevitability, that is, our faith becomes inherently victorious if practiced well (cf. 1 John 5:4). And among his greatest victories are indubitably the conversion of nations, as well as the martyrdom of countless Christians. One could identify this first horseman also with the person of Jesus himself, who received the Kingdom from the Father, and is now the warrior-like Ruler of all nations, the *Rex Universorum*. Although the gradual consolidation of his reign throughout the centuries is certainly not uncontested, his ultimate triumph remains an absolute certainty.

representing different aspects of one and the same tribulation. Rupert interprets them as four phases in the Redeemer's life, namely, his Incarnation, Passion, Resurrection, and Ascension, cf. RD, 939.

3. Cf. AvS, 256.

4. Cf. 1:14; 2:17; 3:4–5, 18; 4:4; 6:11; 7:9, 13; 14:14; 19:11, 14; 20:11.

5. Perhaps in allusion to the ancient Parthians, the only mounted archers of the first century AD, native to the eastern frontier of the empire, and constituting the single greatest threat to Roman sovereignty; see also 9:14; 16:12.

6. At ancient Roman triumphs, the victorious general would wear a crown of laurels, riding in a four-horse chariot in procession with his army, captives, and his spoils of war.

Second seal: Red horse of unbridled passion (6:3–4)

[3]When he opened the second seal, I heard the second living creature call out, "Come!" [4]And out came another horse, bright red; its rider was permitted to take peace from the earth, so that people would slaughter one another; and he was given a great sword.

Following the first apocalyptic rider is the dramatic opening of the second seal, accompanied by another living creature's command, "Come!" This second one is probably the bullock of 4:7. Heeding this word is another horseman, coming forth and ready to run his course. Most disturbingly, however, his horse is of the same red color as the upcoming "other sign in heaven," namely, "the great dragon" (12:3), the only other recurrence of the adjective "red" in the New Testament. If the white horse represented prosperity and happiness, then this one, especially since the rider is given a great sword, announces discord and bloodshed.[7] Allegorically ridden by the devil, worldly powers have a tendency to take away peace and security by the sword of persecution of Christians. While the first seal may be a vision of the Church's triumph over Satan in apostolic times, in the second one, the martyrdom of Christians in the age immediately following is portrayed.[8]

Viewed on a spiritual plane, the fiery red horse reveals all the unchecked passions battling in the depths of our soul, causing inner disquiet as well as outer quarrels (Jas 4:1). As an emblem of justice, the sword also spurs us on to fight indifference, and to be intolerant toward lukewarmness. It aims at demolishing all forms of idolatry and immorality in our hearts, and through spiritual battles it will overcome corruption and temptation.[9] Christ himself made it clear that he intends to cause division and trigger discernment in our interior life (Matt 10:34). Quite telling in this context is the pairing of the noun *máchaira* (μάχαιρα), that is, a sacrificial or pruning knife, with the rare verb *spházō* (σφάζω), exclusively employed by John to speak of sacrifice. There may even be a relationship with the aforementioned ox as the second of the *animalia*. Just as Abraham was willing to offer up his own son Isaac, raising the knife of immolation over him (Gen 22:10), so we also ought to be resolved to surrender ever more perfectly to the will of the Father. On the other hand, there is Cain, who schemed to slay his innocent brother Abel (1 John 3:12), and

7. In consonance with the first two woes of the Synoptic apocalypse, i.e., wars and international strife (Luke 21:9–10).

8. Cf. RD, 943.

9. Cf. AvS, 258–59.

who should be a reminder for us to wield the sword not against our neighbor, but much rather against our own inner imperfections and sinful inclinations, imitating the oblation of the divine Lamb himself. Last but not least, the sword functions as a sign of God-given authority on earth (Rom 13:40), reassuring us that progress in the spiritual life is facilitated by just laws laid down by church and state.

Third seal: Black horse of principled justice (6:5–6)

[5] *When he opened the third seal, I heard the third living creature call out, "Come!" I looked, and there was a black horse! Its rider held a pair of scales in his hand,* [6] *and I heard what seemed to be a voice in the midst of the four living creatures saying, "A quart of wheat for a day's pay, and three quarts of barley for a day's pay, but do not damage the olive oil and the wine!"*

Without missing a beat, John witnesses the third living being, probably the one with the human face (4:7), calling forth the third apocalyptic horseman, riding on a black horse, and holding a pair of scales in his hand. His appearance is noteworthy in that it is accompanied by an unidentified yet audible intervention, originating from among the four living creatures, and thus, close to God's throne. He is ordered to drive up the prices of wheat and barley, to the point of becoming exorbitant, and thus placing them out of reach of the ordinary working citizen. At the same time, he is to leave oil and wine supplies unaffected, perhaps also related to the more resilient roots of olive trees and vines. On that occasion, food will be rationed and sold at prohibitive or even extortionate prices, causing workers to struggle to feed their families. This third horseman could be taken as a personification of God's resolve to punish the world with famine as a usual accompaniment of war in antiquity (Ezek 14:21), precipitating want and calamity for humanity (Matt 24:7).

Furthermore, a pair of scales is a common symbol of justice, and therefore, in complementarity to the sword of discernment, this apocalyptic rider reminds the world of the principle of Christian justice and equity, of work and just wages, of grace and merit. He could also be understood as the embodiment of Christ as the divine Lawgiver who secures the scales of eternal justice. As such, he oversees the progression of Christian values in this world and in each individual soul, the virtues of religion, faith, self-mastery, as well as social justice. That we are encouraged to avoid all forms of injustice in our lives is implied by the verb *adikéō* (ἀδικέω), meaning "to act contrary to or ignore justice."[10] Also, the Greek noun for balance, i.e., *zygós* (ζυγός), primarily denotes a yoke. Hence, just as the farmer places heavy yokes on the oxen's necks to till the soil, so also a life lived in accordance with God's justice in this world means to carry a heavy responsibility: only by abiding by the teachings and laws of the Church, symbolized by the one quart, and by remaining firmly anchored in the Blessed Trinity, signified in the three quarts, can one hope to share in the one prize of redemption, foreshadowed in the one denarius, that is, the gift of immortality.[11]

Taking up yet a different vantage point for a moment, one could argue that the fire-red horse of discernment is followed by the black horse of spiritual darkness and starvation. Christians must expect to see times of scarcity of Gospel proclamation, of spiritual distress in the world and even in the Church. And is not the self-indulgent opulence of the few, so starkly contrasting with the poverty of the masses, precisely the result of the prevalence of irreligious principles? Do they not give proof that the *regula aurea*, the golden rule of Christ (Matt 7:12), is not yet understood and lived? There can be no doubt that recurring global manifestations of selective shortage stem from injustice and corruption, already denounced by the prophet Hosea (12:7). Alternatively, the figurative preservation of oil and wine in this apocalyptic vision may hint at the protection of the Church herself. More specifically, the Catholic faithful will always enjoy a certain measure of immunity during periods of spiritual dearth, since they partake of the bread and wine of the Holy Eucharist, transubstantiated into the Body and Blood of Christ by the anointed hands of bishops and priests. And finally, individual souls, even when the light of the Gospel seems eclipsed in the dark night of faith, will be lifted up by the spiritual wine of consolation and the oil of compassion.[12]

10. While the New Vulgate's translation, *laedere*, signifies "to strike, hurt, harm, offend, thwart, betray."

11. Cf. AvS, 260.

12. Cf. RD, 944–45.

Fourth seal: Green horse as death's pathway (6:7–8)

[7]When he opened the fourth seal, I heard the voice of the fourth living creature call out, "Come!" [8]I looked and there was a pale green horse! Its rider's name was Death, and Hades followed with him; they were given authority over a fourth of the earth, to kill with sword, famine, and pestilence, and by the wild animals of the earth.

Compared to the previous three, the content of this fourth seal could be called the most ghoulish. At its opening and at the invitation of the fourth living being, likely the eagle (4:7), another horse bursts into the visionary foreground, this one sickly pale, intimating the greenish pallor of a corpse in decomposition. To describe the posture of its rider, the seer employs the odd phrase "the one seated on top of it," or even "above it" (*desuper*[13]), suggesting the specter of a skeleton, or perhaps a demon, not mounting astride and dexterously reining his horse, but eerily crouched and hovering over the mount's back, like a ghastly phantom. Among all these apocalyptic horsemen, only this one is given a name, and a most unflattering one at that, namely, Death, symbolizing utter destruction. He is the unrivalled king of tyranny and terror. Unlike the previous three, this last rider does not brandish a weapon, or some other object given him, an absence that has tempted many an artist to depict him as a grim reaper carrying a scythe.[14]

Instead, he is followed by Hades, who, in ancient Greek mythology, is the god of the dead and the king of the underworld.[15] The synonymous place functions as the abode of disembodied spirits, the Greco-Roman equivalent to the biblical *sheol* (שְׁאוֹל), signaling the earthly grave as an intermediate condition of the dead between death and final judgment.[16] Even though a locale of punishment, it signals not yet the absolute and eternal condemnation, but rather a foretaste of the final sentence. This personified Hades is imagined on foot as the entourage of Death, singlehandedly gathering up the lifeless bodies ravaged by plague, sword, and famine, as one collects the spoils of war. As Death strikes down victim after victim, the dead become so abundant at the going forth of

13. For the first three horsemen, John had employed the simple preposition *super*, cf. vv. 2, 4–5.

14. See, for instance, the 1865 engraving titled "The Fourth Horseman, Death on the Pale Horse" by French illustrator Gustave Doré.

15. In its older version, the noun *Haidēs* (Ἀΐδης) derives from the privative prefix *a-* and the verb *ídein*, "to see," literally meaning "unseen world."

16. Related to it are other New Testament concepts such as Gehenna (hell), Abyss (unfathomable depth), and Tartarus (a bottomless dungeon).

this horseman, that hell can no longer contain them, and this vast retinue of cadaverous nations accompanies him on earth in monstrous celebration. Still, these two are mere instruments in God's hand, as evinced by the passive voice in the phrase "they were given authority,"[17] meaning, they have become tools of his wrath, channeling his rulings on earth. We can rest assured, however, that the Father of mercies and God of all comfort will not sit in judgment until and unless humanity is thoroughly deserving of it (2 Cor 1:3).

Ezekiel 14:21 makes for a clear backdrop regarding the afflictions brought about at the opening of the fourth seal, corresponding to God's four judgments, namely, sword, famine, pestilence, and wild beasts. They mark the pinnacle of the evils visited on humanity by the three earlier horsemen. But even if only a fourth of the earth will be affected by them, then we must envision a period of great slaughter and devastation that does not spare the consciences or spiritual lives of men and women. While it is true that the precise seasons of these four seals cannot be ascertained, one could argue that the annihilation of thousands of Christians during the early persecutions by the Roman empire has already fulfilled this apocalyptic vision. Nonetheless, those were a mere prelude to countless acts of oppression perpetrated against the followers of Christ over the centuries and to this present day. This last seal also represents every guise of heresy, which brings about a falling away from Christ in spiritual death.

On a metaphorical level, the quadripartition of the earth suggests that a quarter of a person's worldly mind suffers damage and even extermination.[18] But more generally, these four seals taken together could be read as cyclical representations of the entire mission of the Church, intimately influencing her faithful children. In that vein, the fourth seal would highlight death as the unavoidable pathway from this perishable life on earth to an imperishable one in heaven. This certitude of dying is compounded by one's innate abhorrence of mortality, also implied by the horse's ashen color. However, when viewed through the lens of faith, we realize that death is the ultimate transitioning to a new and definitive existence, in the all-sustaining embrace of our Lord.[19] Indeed, what awaits us is the simultaneous and total possession of an illimitable life.[20] This conviction also undergirds the Christian spirituality of a saintly death:

17. Cf. 6:4; 9:1, 3, 5; 13:5, 7, 14–15.

18. Cf. RD, 947.

19. Cf. AvS, 261–62.

20. According to the well-known definition of "eternity" by the Roman philosopher Boethius (†524): "Aeternitas igitur est interminabilis vitae tota simul et perfecta possessio" (*De consolatione philosophiae*, 5.6).

> In [Christ] the hope of blessed resurrection has dawned, that those saddened by the certainty of dying might be consoled by the promise of immortality to come. Indeed, for your faithful, Lord, life is changed not ended, and, when this earthly dwelling turns to dust, an eternal dwelling is made ready for them in heaven.[21]

As an overarching insight concerning these first four seals, we are reminded that God maintains sovereignty over both human history and individual destinies, and that he ultimately checks the activities of the evil one in this world.

Fifth seal: *Ecclesia expectans* (6:9–11)

*9 When he opened the fifth seal, I saw under the altar the souls of those
who had been slaughtered for the word of God and for the testimony
they had given; 10 they cried out with a loud voice, "Sovereign Lord, holy
and true, how long will it be before you judge and avenge our blood on
the inhabitants of the earth?" 11 They were each given a white robe and
told to rest a little longer, until the number would be complete both of
their fellow servants and of their brothers and sisters, who were soon to
be killed as they themselves had been killed.*

At the undoing of the fifth seal, one realizes that it is wholly different from the preceding four, making those apocalyptic horsemen a clearly distinguished group within this septet of seals. Something similar, albeit less pronounced, will take place within the septenary of trumpets, since there, too, will be a caesura after the first four (8:7–12), while 8:13 will solemnly introduce the remaining three. This narrative logic of decrease, or "four plus three" pattern, will have disappeared by the time the angels pour out on the earth the seven bowls of God's wrath (16:1–21). Thus, the first septet of the seven letters (chs. 2–3), as well as the last one, the plague-bowls (ch. 16), show perfect uniformity, while the middle two are broken up in that "four plus three" arrangement. Accordingly, the reader is invited to consider both, the group of four and the one of three, as units of spiritual message within the larger span of the septet. With that in mind, let us delve back into the visionary scene.

John's eyes become immediately riveted by an object not seen until now, namely, the heavenly altar, the consecrated place of encounter between God and humanity. It appears to be a supernatural copy of the altar of incense that

21. Roman Missal, *Preface I for the Dead.*

stood in the sanctuary of Israel's Temple (Exod 30:1; Luke 1:11). Christ promised that when he was lifted up on the altar of the Cross, he would draw all to himself (John 12:32), and that prophecy comes true in this vision of souls at the foot of the heavenly altar, that is, at the feet of Christ. They find themselves underneath the altar, as if sheltered by God's providence.[22] How amazing, though, that these souls and their inner lives suddenly become visible to John's inspired eyes. It is possible that they include all the righteous men and women, heroes of faith, of the Old Testament (Heb 11). Their bodily lives had been taken away in imitation of the Lamb himself, evoking the primeval fratricide suffered by Abel at the hand of his brother Cain. Yet, what was their crime in the eyes of the world? Why were they hated to the point of being slain? It is their love for the word of God, and their courageous witness to it, which is precisely the cause of the apostle's own exile on Patmos. Although they perished during the various tribulations along the centuries of human history, sharing in Christ's testimony and sacrifice, they now find themselves intimately associated with his victory.[23]

Far from being in some comatose state until the resurrection of the flesh, these souls of the deceased prove that they are fully awake, able to articulate their longing for the truth with earsplitting voices. To be sure, this cry began under Roman repression, especially during the Diocletian persecution in the early fourth century, which was the most severe of all. Yet now, these souls are not afraid to turn with their worry to Jesus himself, addressing him as Sovereign Lord. In doing so, they call out as slaves to the Master of the household, but also as the beloved to their divine Bridegroom.[24] "How long?" is an exclamation filled with yearning and ache, echoing throughout the Old Testament.[25] Christ seems to respond to it in his Sermon on the Mount, "Blessed are those who hunger and thirst for righteousness, for they will be filled" (Matt 5:6), but also by instructing us to fervently pray, "Your Kingdom come!" (Matt 6:10). These Christian victims of earthly violence are eager to witness the execution of God's justice, vindicating their blood (Luke 11:50–51). They plead, too, for the consummation of the saints in this world, for the redress of harm incurred, and for the eradication of demonic influence in the world. Just as the blood of Abel cried out to Yahweh-Elohim from the ground of the field (Gen 4:10), and

22. Cf. RD, 949.

23. Cf. AvS, 263.

24. Since the Greek noun *despótēs* (δεσπότης) in v. 10 derives from *pōsis*, meaning "husband."

25. E.g., Pss 6:3; 13:1–2; 22:1; 94:3; 119:84.

as the blood of the sacrificial animals was poured out at the foot of the altar to atone for sin (Lev 4:7), so also the blood of the martyrs offers expiation for the inhabitants of the earth.[26]

God responds to their plea with a gesture and with a word, both carrying a profound spiritual lesson for us today. First, he gives each of them a glistening white robe (cf. 3:4–5; 7:13–14), as if to grant justice and patience. Just as he clothed our protoparents with garments of skin (Gen 3:21), so now he confers the attire of immortality on his faithful as a reward for their oblation.[27] These are robes of righteousness and of honor, because the ones who wear them have become like God, seeing him as he is, reflecting his image. The whiteness of their stoles speaks to their distinction as innocent conquerors, but also to their blessedness in glory. Accompanying this divine gesture is the imperative "rest a little longer!," that is, until the number of their fellow servants is complete. While it is true that they loved their enemies and entreated for them on earth, now, placed so near the eternal Judge himself, they are impatient to see justice realized, in exaltation of the holiness and truth of their Lord.[28] For now, these souls are to learn from God's own patience in his exercise of justice, recompense, and retribution. In his mysterious designs, times of repentance and mercy must run their course, before forgiveness or condemnation can be considered. We, too, are to live in patient hope, always looking out for the well-being of our brethren, members of the Church as God's family. And even if the completion of the number of the elect (v. 11) cannot refer to a predetermined multitude, the intercession of the martyrs and saints does hasten the end of the eschaton.

Sixth seal: Removing mountains of pride (6:12–17)

12 *When he opened the sixth seal, I looked, and there came a great earth-*
quake; the sun became black as sackcloth, the full moon became like
blood, 13 *and the stars of the sky fell to the earth as the fig tree drops its*
winter fruit when shaken by a gale. 14 *The sky vanished like a scroll roll-*
ing itself up, and every mountain and island was removed from its place.

26. Note that the relics of canonized saints are enshrined within the altars of Catholic churches of the Roman rite, kept in a cavity known as the *sepulcrum*; likewise, priests of Eastern rite churches celebrate the Divine Liturgy upon a silk cloth called the *antiménsion*, depicting the burial of Christ, and into which relics of martyrs and saints are sewn.

27. Cf. RD, 952–53.

28. Cf. AvS, 265.

[15] Then the kings of the earth and the magnates and the generals and the rich and the powerful, and everyone, slave and free, hid in the caves and among the rocks of the mountains, [16] calling to the mountains and rocks, "Fall on us and hide us from the face of the one seated on the throne and from the wrath of the Lamb; [17] for the great day of their wrath has come, and who is able to stand?"

In literary proximity to the first half of the Matthean Olivet Discourse with its portrayal of end-time trials (Matt 24), the opening of the sixth seal seems to describe an approaching day of reckoning for the whole world. The enumeration of seven creational items in vv. 12–14 (earthquake, sun, moon, stars, sky, mountains, islands), mirrored in the seven social classes of humanity at v. 15 (kings, nobles, generals, rich, powerful, slaves, free), symbolizes the all-embracing nature of God's judgment. What is more, cosmic upheavals attending the Day of the Lord are very much part of ancient prophetic language,[29] signifying the irruption of divine action into human history. In that sense, the apostle Peter on Pentecost declared that the cataclysm described in Joel 2:28–32 was in fact fulfilled during that day's effusion of the Holy Spirit over the nascent Jerusalem Church (Acts 2:16–21). In a way, it also hints at a reversal of creation, disrupting its primordial order (Gen 1), only to usher in a new creation. Rupert finds in them the persecutions of Christians, coming to a head in the time of the antichrist.[30] Earthquakes, according to the apocalyptic genre, also denote great spiritual agitations and convulsions on the earth. These ongoing paroxysms, companions of history, always involve the fallen stars of overthrown rulers, often unfaithful Christians, instigated by diabolical forces.

Astral bodies abruptly losing their usual luster suggest the darkness[31] of mourning, penance, chastisement, and insecurity, all permitted by God. Initially made to mark times and seasons (Gen 1:14), sun and moon are now obscured not by the sackcloth and blood of faithful witness, but by the violence and rebellion of evil forces at work in history. That distortion of their primordial purpose also alludes to the extent of disruption of the God-willed natural and supernatural order.[32] And this painful turmoil in the Church and in individual souls involves the concealing of truths and the obscuring of sound doctrine.

Even good Christians are not immune from falling like unripened fruit

29. E.g., Ps 18:7–19; Isa 2:19; 13:10; 34:4; 50:3; Ezek 38:19; Amos 8:8–9; Joel 2:10; 3:3–4.
30. Cf. RD, 954.
31. The color of traditional sackcloth was dominated by the hair of black goats.
32. Cf. AvS, 268.

(v. 13). However, these winter figs epitomize mainly those whose religiosity is unequal to the stress of trial, and who fail in the corporal or spiritual crises with which they are faced. Symbolized by the removal of the very skies (v. 14) is the overt separation between God and humanity, a ruptured relationship that spells devastation. It is as if even the heavenly powers were grieving the falling away from the faith, angels seemingly unable to bear the abuse suffered by Christ and by his Church. All presumptive security is not only shaken but outright discarded. Mountains and islands of sinful pride are displaced.[33] Similar cosmic upset will recur at 16:20 and 20:11, seeking to gradually eradicate human vainglory and insubordination against its Creator and Redeemer.

Listing the various ranks representative of whole societies underlines the universality of terror at the impending doom (v. 15). At the same time, those social distinctions will be forgotten in the frantic attempt to escape it. Communication with God is replaced with the futile attempt to talk to mountains and rocks. People express their longing to die, rather than focus on the countenance of the Father and the wrath of the Lamb (v. 16). Of course, a wrathful Lamb is a deliberate paradox, a contradiction in terms, since little lambs are never associated with extreme anger. Yet precisely that incongruity of language shows forth the Lamb's otherworldly nature: our merciful Savior is also the eternal Judge of the living and the dead. Hence, the Trinity is united not only in love but also in righteous indignation.[34]

Enhancing the picture of John 5:22, where the Son is the exclusive Judge, here the Father as well as the Lamb are revealed in judgment. Faced with that reality, humans are filled with fear and a desire to hide, reenacting our protoparents' vain attempt to escape accountability and personal ruin (Gen 3:8). In fact, they are partaking of the devil's own terror in God's presence (Mark 5:12). The moment a person refuses God's love, he or she will know his wrath, disrupting their false spirituality of self-centeredness. As a result, the inner life is thrown off kilter, no comfort zone remains, and the human heart becomes fatally estranged from its Maker.[35] "Who is able to stand?": this conscience-stricken alarm can lead either to repentance or to despair.

At this juncture, let us draw three spiritual lessons from this sixth seal. As his death was imminent, Jesus pleaded: "My Father, if it is possible, let this cup pass from me; yet not as I will, but as you will" (Matt 26:39). Notwithstanding the Son's begging, his Father did not spare him from death, but rather

33. Cf. RD, 957.
34. Cf. AvS, 270–71.
35. Cf. AvS, 272–73.

strengthened him, knowing that his dying was necessary for our salvation. He did not grant deliverance *from* death, but rather deliverance *through* death. Likewise, Christians are called to profess their faith in Christ and his truth with boldness and candor before the world, regardless of the consequences. Whatever we may have to endure, the temporary contempt of this world, or even imprisonment and death, must be borne courageously to avoid the shame that is everlasting.

This vision also teaches us that God has ways to demolish all forms of vainglory and pride, turning them into utter dismay and consternation. Therefore, knowing full well that all forms of self-glorification are doomed to failure, we should constantly remind ourselves of St. John's directive in his first epistle:

> Do not love the world or the things in the world. The love of the Father is not in those who love the world; for all that is in the world, the desire of the flesh, the desire of the eyes, the pride in riches, comes not from the Father but from the world. And the world and its desire are passing away, but those who do the will of God live forever (1 John 2:15–17).

For our own advantage, as creatures graced with free will and intellect, let us be resolved to make ourselves completely dependent on the will of God, and always content ourselves with promoting his glory alone.[36]

Perhaps a third spiritual insight can be gained from this penultimate seal, namely, that the Church can undergo periods of hiding (v. 16). By adopting an attitude of discretion and caution, or hiddenness, she may be able to avoid untimely or unnecessary situations of trouble and persecution, mindful of Jesus' own instruction: "If anyone will not welcome you or listen to your words, shake off the dust from your feet as you leave that house or town" (Matt 10:14). In fact, the early Christians humbly, yet astutely, concealed themselves in the Roman catacombs, and the Mexican martyr Blessed Miguel Pro exercised his priestly ministry disguised as a car mechanic and similar camouflages, to be less exposed to the maltreatment of the reigning power of the day. Likewise, over the centuries, millions of Christian men and women have sought protection from worldly tyranny in underground and exile.

36. A thought expressed in St. Teresa of Avila's (†1582) poem *Nada te turbe*: "Let nothing disturb you, let nothing frighten you, all things pass away: God never changes; patience obtains all things; he who has God finds he lacks nothing; God alone suffices."

7:1–17, Interlude: Assurance from heaven

Expectant silence on earth (7:1)

[1]After this I saw four angels standing at the four corners of the earth, holding back the four winds of the earth so that no wind could blow on earth or sea or against any tree.

In continuation of the sixth seal, and before the seventh seal will be opened at 8:1, ch. 7 answers the second and last question of the previous chapter, at the same time solemn and distressed: "Who is able to stand?" (6:17). So far, John's mystical experience, like an electromagnetic wave, appears to oscillate between heaven and earth: beginning with his vision of the heavenly Son of Man in ch. 1, then descending to the earth in writing to the seven churches in chs. 2–3, he again ascends back into the heavenly throne hall in chs. 4–5, reverting to mostly earthbound trials and vicissitudes in ch. 6 (excepting the fifth seal, vv. 9–11), only to be transferred again from earth to heaven at 7:4. Unsurprisingly, the visions concerning heaven are moments of reassurance and spiritual anointing, to harden us, as it were, for our ongoing Christian warfare. Whenever desolation reaches new degrees of intensity, the seer, and we ourselves through him, are granted moments of consolation, lifting us up from darkness into the light. Ch. 7 is such a heartening foretaste of God's care. As a narrative interlude, it contains visions, an audition, and even a dialogue with one of the elders. To be precise, it consists of two parts, the first being 7:1–17, followed by the second at 8:1–5, coinciding with the opening of the seventh seal, and ushering in the series of seven trumpets (8:6). A similar twofold entr'acte will separate the sixth and seventh trumpets in 10:1–11 and 11:1–14, as if to give more emphasis to that impending seventh element.

Hence, in addition to the "four plus three" pattern in ch. 6, we also have a "six plus one" arrangement that keeps the reader in suspense, eager to learn the story's punch line. God's wrath, manifested in the sixth seal, shook humanity to its core and out of its smugness and delusional sense of security; but his punishing action is now interrupted by an intermezzo that highlights celestial peace, salvation, and glory. At least momentarily we can turn away from the menacing roar of our earthly journey toward the beatific worship awaiting us before the throne of the Lamb. There is no better way to brace for more trials and ever-renewed cycles of temptations, than a glimpse of otherworldly bliss.

Although still part of the sixth seal, the phrase "after this I saw," just as in 4:1, conveys both continuity and a subtle caesura in the vision sequence. It introduces not only a new scene, but also a sense of the passage of time, without defining the length of a given interval. Even though it may not necessarily indicate the historical succession of events, it nevertheless marks the order in which John received these blessed dreams. What he sees are four angels standing at the four corners of the earth, evoking the four living creatures and the four horsemen.[1] More quadruple groups will be added as the plot progresses, such as for instance the four angels bound at the Euphrates (9:14–15), and the four horns of the altar (9:13).

Contrasting with the angel of the rising sun in v. 2, these angelic spirits are focused on the earth, as is made clear by the triple reiteration of the noun *terra* in this verse. They exert all their power in containing the four winds of the earth.[2] Positioned as they are at its four corners, they remind us of a biblical idea that regarded the earth as a table of rectangular surface, similar to an altar (cf. Gen 13:14; Isa 11:12). Conceivably, this language also allegorizes an edifice with its four corners, since one also spoke of the bases or cornerstones of the earth.[3] Moreover, the notion that angels of the lower orders guarded elemental forces was current (cf. 14:18; 16:5), and in Hebrew tradition, the cardinal winds blowing from the four directions were considered harmful, unlike the beneficial winds arriving from the sides. Besides, the eschatological discourse predicts that once the Son of Man comes on the clouds of heaven, he will send out his angels to gather the elect from the four winds (Matt 24:31).

Before we draw another spiritual lesson, this time from the image of the four angels governing the winds, let us reflect on two biblical presuppositions. First, the earth can symbolize our human life, body and soul (Ps 143:6), based also on the fact that God formed Adam from the dust of the ground (Gen 2:7).

1. Some expositors, and quite arbitrarily so, equate the four horsemen with these angels of the four winds (v. 1).

2. Cf. Ps 104:4; rabbinic wisdom often associated the four cardinal directions with the archangels Michael (South), Gabriel (West), Raphael (East), and Uriel (North). And on an extra-biblical note, the ancient Greeks and Romans arranged the winds in four classes, under the stewardship of King Aeolus, namely, Zephyrus, Boreas, Notus, and Eurus.

3. E.g., Ps 104:5; Prov 8:29; Job 38:4; Jer 31:37; Zech 12:1.

Christ himself, in his Parable of the Sower (Matt 13:1–23), compares our soul to the soil of the land, supposed to bring much fruit through the word of God. As a second assumption, the winds are emblems of days of trouble and judgment. Just as they clear the air and drive away the chaff, so do judgments try the godly and the ungodly alike.[4] To hold them back would mean a delay of commotion and destruction; or, put differently, these winds signal a state of peace and tranquility, but also of profound silence across the earth of our souls, which is about to be complemented by the heavenly silence (8:1).[5]

A sense of anticipation is in the air, too, as the soul eagerly awaits God's action. Equally foreshadowed in that quaternity of directions is the aspect of cruciformity, which means that the human spirit is sheltered in and secured by the Cross of Christ. Just as Yahweh shielded the tree of life and the tree of knowledge of good and evil (Gen 2:9, 17; 3:22, 24), so also the fruits of his grace are given the opportunity to ripen in us, before any adverse winds can shake them off, causing them to rot away prematurely. To remain silent in the Cross also entails a suspension or even erasure of punishment for our personal sins, as if the scorching wind of the Holy Spirit had been paused.[6]

Thus, this apocalyptic vignette contains a veritable spirituality of patient silence: these are times of eager anticipation, protection, and deep inner peace, born from one's union with the crucified One. Interior quiet, unlike mere physical muteness or petulant taciturnity, enables us to stay attuned to the divine Spirit and his holy angels. Scripture hereby teaches us to regularly seek out moments of stillness: "I wait for the Lord; my soul does wait, and in his word I put my hope" (Ps 130:5). And yet another psalm comes to mind: "Be still and know that I am God; I will be exalted among the nations, I will be exalted over the earth" (Ps 46:10).

Servanthood confirmed (7:2–3)

[2]I saw another angel ascending from the rising of the sun, having the seal of the living God, and he called with a loud voice to the four angels who had been given power to damage earth and sea, [3]saying, "Do not damage the earth or the sea or the trees, until we have marked the servants of our God with a seal on their foreheads."

---

4. Cf. Jer 49:36–37; Dan 7:2; Zech 6:5.

5. Rupert likens the winds and accompanying rainy clouds to the fecundity of apostolic preaching down the centuries, and how many kingdoms refuse to listen to them, cf. RD, 959.

6. Cf. AvS, 275.

Another angel enters John's field of vision, not statically positioned in the cardinal directions like the previous four, but rather dynamically arising from the east. His ascending movement seems embedded within the sunrise itself, which must have been a spectacular sight to behold, even dazzling to an unbearable extreme. After that sackcloth-like blackening in 6:12, now this principal light source is shining again, giving proof of the recapitulatory or spiral logic of the image pattern in Revelation. Scripture's first mention of the east is when God planted a garden in Eden and there put the first man (Gen 2:8). In doing so, he undoubtedly made it prominent among the directions, foreshadowing messianic developments in eras to come. Tragically, however, following the expulsion of the postlapsarian Adam, he had to place the cherubim and a flaming, turning sword at the east of the garden to guard the way to the tree of life (Gen 3:24). A long time afterwards, in conceptualizing the glory of a future temple, Ezekiel calls attention to God dwelling in its eastern quarter (Ezek 43:1–4). In due course, Zechariah, filled with the Holy Spirit, presages that the Savior himself would appear from the East (Luke 1:78–79).[7] Thus, it would not be far-fetched to recognize in this good spirit a representative of the God-Man himself. His ascending movement, related to the descending one of the Christomorphic angel in 10:1, is allusive to the splendor of the Lord's Resurrection. Furthermore, his authority over those angelic devastators (cf. vv. 2–3) seems to manifest the very will of God, binding them in obedience by the seal of his superior mission.[8]

Complementary to the earlier silence on earth is the image of the *sigillum* held by the heliacal angel (v. 2). It is rather paradoxical, however, that while the breaking of the sixth seal is still in progress, this seal implies the opposite, namely, the simultaneous sealing up or concealing of something. In biblical times, a seal often meant a signet ring[9] or stamp, engraved with a royal crest, impressed on soft wax or clay and affixed to a document or other valued object. By doing so, the king attested to his ownership, authenticated a letter's content, and kept it confidential and unchangeable. Serving as a legal signature in the ancient world, this token guaranteed the contents' credibility as well as the sender's trustworthiness. Hence, when this angel carries the seal of the living God, he is really representing Christ, the guarantor of the Father's unending life. That this seal is primarily trinitarian, embodying the Father, Son, and Holy

7. Ironically, danger, too, will arise from the east, cf. 16:12.

8. Cf. AvS, 276.

9. E.g., Pharaoh's signet ring put on Joseph's hand (Gen 41:42–43), or King Ahasuerus's given to Haman (Esther 3:10); see also Dan 6:17; Matt 27:66.

Spirit, can also be gathered from the teachings of St. Paul (e.g., 2 Cor 1:21–22; Eph 1:13–14; 4:30; 2 Tim 2:19).

This mark will be placed on the foreheads of the servants of God, which is prefigured by the shielding mark put on Cain (Gen 4:15), as well as the *thau* on the forehead of Jerusalem's faithful (Ezek 9:4). This sacred sign has been interpreted as an emblem of the Cross, imaging life and property of God. It must be on the person's forehead so that it can be plainly seen by friends and foes alike, but not by the protégé himself—except when mirroring himself contemplatively in God's word, at which moment one realizes that it signifies the name of the Lamb and his Father (14:1). Before the imminent crises, the goodness of God's servants as well as the world's evil must be clearly discerned. Before the tempests of manifold trials will blow, the elect will be revealed: once the ultimatum expires, however, and amidst violent winds, they shall enjoy the indemnity of their God. Calamitous cyclones shall be restrained so as not to shake too soon the immature fruit. Christian servanthood means sustenance and survival in tribulation rather than complete preservation from hardship, as already portended by the paschal blood on the Hebrews' doorposts prior to their exodus from the house of oppression.

Also suggested is the spiritual immunity of the righteous remnant, awaiting their reward from the living God (Luke 21:18–19). Of course, this seal denotes our Christian vocation and mission under the sign of the Cross, too, hand in glove with its inner justification and merit.[10] But the ultimate source is the inner sacramental mark of belonging to God, indelibly conferred on the soul at the reception of baptism, confirmation, and the priesthood. In his Bread of Life discourse, Jesus hints at a connection between the seal and the Eucharist, too: "Do not work for the food that perishes, but for the food that endures for eternal life, which the Son of Man will give you. For it is on him that God the Father has set his seal" (John 6:27). Thus, imprinted with God's effigy and assured of filial adoption as his beloved children, we are confirmed in servanthood, and bear witness to his promise of life.

Israel's lasting election (7:4–8)

*[4]And I heard the number of those who were sealed, one hundred for-
ty-four thousand, sealed out of every tribe of the people of Israel: [5]From
the tribe of Judah twelve thousand sealed, from the tribe of Reuben
twelve thousand, from the tribe of Gad twelve thousand, [6]from the tribe*

10. Cf. 1 Cor 9:2; see also RD, 960.

of Asher twelve thousand, from the tribe of Naphtali twelve thousand, from the tribe of Manasseh twelve thousand, [7]from the tribe of Simeon twelve thousand, from the tribe of Levi twelve thousand, from the tribe of Issachar twelve thousand, [8]from the tribe of Zebulun twelve thousand, from the tribe of Joseph twelve thousand, from the tribe of Benjamin twelve thousand sealed.

One hundred forty-four thousand are the ones that are sealed, a number referring to two distinct yet related groups in the Apocalypse, the first being the twelve tribes of Israel (vv. 4–8), and the second being the assembly close to the Lamb (14:1). This number is symbolic, composed of "three," hinting at the Divine, times "four," suggestive of creation; the square of the resulting twelve is one hundred and forty-four, which in turn relates to the New Jerusalem (21:17). The latter is then multiplied by a thousand, signaling a very large yet finite crowd. By the inherent limitation of this numerical statement, the idea of election is combined with that of its antithesis, i.e., reprobation (cf. Rom 9:27). Compared to the billions of human beings that have ever lived so far, the quantity is infinitesimal, evoking Jesus' word about his little flock (Luke 12:32).

To understand this privileged sealing of the people of Israel, one must recall the mystery proclaimed by Paul concerning their eschatological return in Romans 11:25–26. They are sealed into the everlasting love of God, who through their end-time conversion confirms their beloved election (Rom 11:28) and their unregretted[11] gifts and calling (Rom 11:29). Premised on Malachi 4:5–6, a tradition speaks of Elijah returning at the end of time prior to the antichrist, to call Jews to the Christian faith.[12] John only hears the number of these elect, but does not see them, which may be hinting at their elusiveness, since many appertain to the distant past of the Old Testament, and many others are yet to convert in the imminence of Christ's parousia (Matt 24:3). Hence, Israel here should be understood in both its literal and spiritual sense. By choosing a perfectly equal number of persons from each tribe, that is, twelve thousand, evenly framed by the verb "sealed" (vv. 5, 8),[13] the vision appears to underscore God's

11. The Neo-Vulgate renders the verbal adjective *ametamélēta* (ἀμεταμέλητα) with *sine paenitentia*, literally, "without repentance," and hence, "irrevocable."

12. According to Sir 48:10, Elijah's mission as a future herald of the eschaton will include calming God's fury, as well as restoring the twelve tribes of Jacob.

13. Differing from the depiction of their military enrollment by Moses in the wilderness, where their draft numbers starkly vary from tribe to tribe, from 32,200 to 95,300 (Num 1:20–45).

supernatural fairness and infinite justice. While spiritual matters often remain obscure and imprecise on earth, especially when it comes to the inner secrets and movements of the human heart, there is nothing vague about the exact number recorded in heaven, that is, of Jews that have converted and will convert to Jesus as their Savior.[14]

It should not astound us either to find Judah listed first, ahead of the first-born Reuben (Num 1:5–15), since in due course it became the quintessential messianic tribe. Not included in the selection of the twelve tribes, however, are the names of Ephraim and Dan, although their names feature among the tribes that settled in the Promised Land. This could be due to their pagan practices later in history, which led St. Irenaeus to speculate about the antichrist tragically arising from the tribe of Dan.[15] One might also recall the acts of idolatry of the Danites as a disqualifying criterion.[16] Their omission would explain Jesus' own prophecy, anticipating that in the Kingdom of God his disciples will sit on twelve thrones judging the twelve tribes of Israel (Matt 19:28), meaning that the unfaithful part of these religious ancestors shall one day be asked to render an account. Then, in the vision of the heavenly Jerusalem, their names summarily reappear, inscribed on the city gates (21:12–13). Inspired by this apocalyptic image, our Christian spirituality is constantly enriched by remembering our Hebrew-Jewish heritage with sincere appreciation and reverential love. Even if we cannot regularly be in contact with these our "elder brothers,"[17] we should make an effort to read and reflect upon their wisdom, contained primarily in the historical, prophetic, and sapiential books of the Old Testament. Together with the contemporary Jewish people all over the world, we Christians treasure their beloved election and unregretted vocation.

New Israel's *Sukkot* (7:9–10)

[9]After this I looked, and there was a great multitude that no one could count, from every nation, from all tribes and peoples and languages, standing before the throne and before the Lamb, robed in white, with

14. Cf. AvS, 278.

15. Cf. Irenaeus, *Adversus haereses*, 5.30.2.

16. Cf. Mark W. Bartusch, *Understanding Dan: An Exegetical Study of a Biblical City, Tribe and Ancestor*, JSOTS 379 (Sheffield: Sheffield Academic, 2003); see also the ominous allusion to "snake and viper" in Jacob's patriarchal blessing (Gen 49:17), as well as the setting up of an idolatrous golden calf in Dan (1 Kgs 12:28–30).

17. Expression used by St. John Paul II, spoken during his historic visit to the Grand Synagogue in Rome on April 13, 1986.

palm branches in their hands. [10]*They cried out in a loud voice, saying, "Salvation belongs to our God who is seated on the throne, and to the Lamb!"*

While only hearing the number of those who are sealed, the apostle now sees a great multitude: this visionary crescendo extends not only to the size of the crowd, since the previous one hundred and forty-four thousand are surpassed by a throng of people impossible to count,[18] but it also involves their global provenance. John offers the fourfold portrayal of persons hailing from every nation, from all tribes and peoples and languages. What he is really seeing is the matured fruit of Israel, its spiritual offspring having now grown into the all-embracing New Israel of the apostolic Church.[19] St. Paul calls her the Israel of God (Gal 6:16).[20] To the elect from the covenanted people of old are now added those who are chosen from the whole human family in all its ethnic and cultural richness.[21] Yet this vast crowd of the universal Church is envisioned no longer as militant or suffering on earth, but rather it is gathered triumphant in the glory of heaven, right in front of the throne of God the Father, and of his Son, the Lamb.

Three characteristics regarding these people are made explicit: they are robed in white, with palm branches in their hands, and they cry out in a loud voice, all of which are features of the ancient Hebrew Feast of Tabernacles, or Sukkot, the most popular among the three pilgrimage feasts.[22] Originally an occasion of thanksgiving for abundant harvest, the great autumn festival recalled God's providence during Israel's sojourn in the wilderness. Eventually, it was celebrated in terms of the end-time and its accompanying messianic expectations. People, young and old, would leave their houses and dwell in booths to commemorate their time in the desert; the streets were bursting with celebratory multitudes carrying branches of palm, olive, and myrtle; everywhere the sounds of rejoicing and singing were heard (Neh 8:14–17). At the same time, four rituals were performed at the Jerusalem Temple: first, the

18. Reminiscent also of God's covenant promise to Abraham (Gen 13:16; 15:5; 17:2, 4; 22:17; 32:12).

19. Cf. Second Vatican Council, Decree on the Mission Activity of the Church *Ad gentes* (December 7, 1965), §5; see also *CCC*, §877.

20. On the Catholic Church being the organic continuation of Israel, see also Eph 2:12–22; 1 Pet 2:9; Jas 1:1.

21. Cf. AvS, 277.

22. Cf. Lev 23:39; Judg 21:19; 1 Kgs 8:2; 2 Chron 7:8; Neh 8:14; Isa 30:29; Ezek 45:23; Flavius Josephus, *Antiquities*, 8.101.

water libation, where a priest, accompanied by Levites, daily drew water from the well of Siloam, and poured it out in the temple court by the altar of burnt offering. They would send up prayers for rain and commemorate the Mosaic water miracle (Exod 17:1–17), while the people sang the words of Isaiah 12:3 (cf. John 7:37–39). Second, there was the ceremony of light (cf. John 8:12; 9:5), followed thirdly by the rite of turning their backs toward the rising sun and facing the Temple in atonement for idolatry committed in the past (Ezek 8:16). And fourth, the people would carry palm branches and chant joyously, something that occurred also during Jesus' triumphant entry into the Davidic City, Jerusalem (John 12:13).[23]

Jewish tradition viewed Sukkot as foreshadowing the end of history and the coming of God's Kingdom, which might prompt us to apply this imagery to the spiritually prosperous state of the Church at the end of so many grievous sufferings and historical persecutions: the troubles of the wilderness are finally ended, the sowing days are over, and that great multitude of peoples reaps what it sowed, delighting in the glorious consummation of their harvest-home, the Church. God himself tabernacles among his beloved servants (v. 15),[24] and they are shepherded and protected by the Lamb (v. 17), just as the sealing of Israel's tribes reminded us of the protecting sign on the lintels of their houses on Passover. Additionally, the white robes signal the princely and priestly character of redeemed humanity, and the waving of palm branches becomes an emblem of victory. Thus, ancient Jewish institutions and customs find their eschatological fulfilment in this vision on Patmos.[25] This heavenly festival of Tabernacles is a celebration of unending life, joy, and salvation.

Whereas the twelve tribes of Israel are sealed in silence, this innumerable crowd cries out: "Salvation belongs to our God who is seated on the throne, and to the Lamb!" (v. 10). An analogous hymn of praise will resound at the fall of the dragon (12:10) and of the godless city of Babylon (19:1). With intense devotion they ascribe all delivering grace to God and to the Lamb.[26] It is worthwhile remembering that the noun *sōtēría* (σωτηρία, *salus*) here transmits the

23. Cf. Francis J. Moloney, *The Gospel of John*, SaPaSe 4 (Collegeville, MN: Liturgical Press, 1998), 233–36.

24. Not least because of this apocalyptic figure, in the center of all Catholic churches around the world, one finds the Eucharistic tabernacle, housing the Real Presence of our Lord and God among us, his pilgrim children.

25. Cf. Gale A. Yee, *Jewish Feasts and the Gospel of John*, ZS (Wilmington, DE: M. Glazier, 1989), 82.

26. The present tense of the Greek verb *krázousin* (κράζουσιν) and of its Latin rendition *clamant*, vividly conveys the unceasing nature of their worship.

idea of safety and welfare, which, coming of age as a Christian concept, signifies victorious deliverance from sin, death, and eternal punishment, and the gracious admission to eternal life. Although the Holy Spirit is the one that teaches and sustains this cosmic prayer, he remains self-effaced in divine humility; his seemingly subordinate nature was already revealed by the seven spirits before the throne (1:4; 4:5). Nevertheless, no explicit praise is ever offered to him, either here or throughout the entire Apocalypse. In any event, may the reflection on this sublime vision spur us on to look forward in Christian hope to the day when we can join in the everlasting celebration of the Feast of Tabernacles before the throne of God, jubilantly surrounded by all the sons and daughters of the New Israel.

Antiphonal Amen (7:11–12)

[11]And all the angels stood around the throne and around the elders and the four living creatures, and they fell on their faces before the throne and worshiped God, [12]singing, "Amen! Blessing and glory and wisdom and thanksgiving and honor and power and might be to our God forever and ever! Amen."

Many angels had been glorifying the Lamb before (5:11–12), but now all of them do so together, as they encompass the throne, the elders, and the living creatures, reaching the summit of divine worship, and falling on their faces, extolling God the Father himself. Their validating initial "Amen!" is in direct response to the acclamation of the great multitude in vv. 9–10, while their ovation of blessing and glory seamlessly resumes the ending of the sevenfold chant in 5:12. Wisdom and honor appear in the same position, i.e., third and fifth, of both septuple heavenly paeans. Unique to the latter is the central placement of "thanksgiving," replacing the previous "wealth" (5:12). Two distinctive marks, namely, the insertion of the Greek definite article before the sevenfold attributes, and the concluding "Amen!," lend to this doxology a sense of definitiveness and universality.

Angels throughout Scripture are messengers of God's plans for humanity, and by their own ways of doing obeisance to the Lord, they can enhance our spiritual life in this world. By not remaining on their feet but choosing to fall on their faces in adoration,[27] they tutor us to focus on what is essential in total

27. John employs the Greek verb *proskynéō* (προσκυνέω) to portray this angelic act of veneration; it is composed of the preposition *prós*, "toward," and *kynéo*, "to kiss"; hence its literal

self-effacement and self-forgetfulness. Their gesture should also become ever more incentivizing for the contemplative Church here on earth.[28] Outstanding, too, is the angels' gratitude in reflection of the sacramental Eucharist. In other words, in their astounding unselfishness they express their gratitude for a sacrament that was not instituted to their advantage, but solely for the good of God's people on earth.

Their magnanimity also impels them to confirm human salvation by adjoining their own repeated "Amen," fully aware that it was never meant to alter their faithful status as spiritual beings in the Lord's presence. In the same vein, they offer praise to "our God," just as humanity did earlier (v. 10), underscoring their intimate union with us, and bringing the covenant to fulfillment (21:3). Thus, the world of angels accomplishes its eternal service to God, but at the same manifesting its marvelous oneness with the human family. In fact, this text seems to strongly favor Thomas Aquinas's opinion that they, too, are part of the Mystical Body of Christ.[29] In sum, this hymnodic praise is bound to snowball into an unending avalanche of cosmic worship before the throne of the Most High.[30]

Bathed in blood (7:13–14)

13 *Then one of the elders addressed me, saying, "Who are these, robed in white, and where have they come from?"*
14 *I said to him, "Sir, you are the one that knows." Then he said to me, "These are they who have come out of the great ordeal; they have washed their robes and made them white in the blood of the Lamb.*

As on a previous occasion (5:5), one of the twenty-four elders draws near to offer his assistance in interpreting the vision. If indeed the elders represent the

meaning "to kiss the ground when prostrating before a superior"; this is reflected in the Latin *adorare*, which stems from the preposition *ad*, "toward," and the noun *os*, "mouth," literally, "turning one's mouth toward [God]."

28. Cf. AvS, 282.

29. *Summa Theologiae* III, q. 8, a. 4: "But it is manifest that both men and angels are ordained to one end, which is the glory of the Divine fruition. Hence the Mystical Body of the Church consists not only of men but of angels. Now of all this multitude Christ is the Head, since he is nearer God, and shares his gifts more fully, not only than man, but even than angels; and of his influence not only men but even angels partake." Trans. Fathers of the English Dominican Province, 2nd rev. ed. (London: Burns, Oates, & Washbourne, 1924) (all subsequent quotations are from this edition).

30. Cf. AvS, 284–85.

twelve patriarchs and the twelve apostles, then it is at least a possibility that Peter himself or John's brother James approached him, which adds to the fervor of their dialogue. When the New Vulgate says *respondit* (v. 13) to describe the moment the elder approaches the seer, it implies that he is here to "respond" to John's innermost thoughts, as well as his desire to know more, as he continues to marvel at the enormous multitude of humans, angels, elders, and living beings. Anticipating the apostle's inquiry into those uncountable people gathered before the Lamb, robed in white, the elder challenges him to reflect not only on their identity, "Who are these?," but also on their origin, "Where have they come from?" By striking up a conversation (Zech 4:4–7; 6:4–6; Ezek 37:3), he establishes a bridge between the realm of heaven and the world to which John belongs. This wondrous connection between the supernatural and the natural order adds vividness to the point under consideration.[31] To interact with a heavenly citizen, and to be asked this question, is tantamount to inculturation or naturalization into heaven, that is, the apostle now possesses full rights to speak and socialize there. God's throne and its environs become a locale of familiarity and trust with all their interpersonal dimensions, and nothing is covered up.[32] And the seer engages in the dialogue with great deference: "My lord, you are the one that knows," giving proof of his deep intuition that the elder's answer will confirm his own knowledge, and pave the way for him to proclaim it to his churches on earth with full assurance.

Resolutely the elder replies: "These are they who have come out of the great tribulation" (cf. Dan 12:1; Matt 24:21). Christians, therefore, are promised to emerge triumphantly from all sorts of ordeals and persecution, sparked by their faithfulness to the Lamb. Upon further scrutiny, the Greek participle in the present tense, *hoí erchómenoi* (οἱ ἐρχόμενοι), suggests that the visionary watches in the moment as Christians and martyrs of all ages emerge from their struggle and enter into their heavenly inheritance. A complementary explanation is given by Rupert when he states that this great tribulation signifies humanity afflicted by original sin.[33]

Carrying on with his description, the elder declares that they have washed their robes and made them white in the blood of the Lamb. A crucial insight

31. Cf. Elisabeth Schüssler-Fiorenza, "Composition and Structure in the Book of Revelation," *CBQ* 39 (1977): 344–66; Amos N. Wilder, *Early Christian Rhetoric: The Language of the Gospel* (Cambridge, MA: Harvard University Press, 1971), 46; Terence Craig Voortman and Jan A. du Rand, "The Language of the Theatre in the Apocalypse of John: A Brief Look at the Apocalypse as Drama," *Ekklesiastikos Pharos* 79, no. 1 (1997): 78–93.

32. Cf. AvS, 286.

33. Cf. RD, 967.

can again be gleaned from the original language, in that twice the verbal active voice is employed when illustrating the washing and whitening of their garments (*laverunt, dealbaverunt*), which associates them with the splendor of Christ himself, transfigured on Tabor (Mark 9:2–3). In other words, Christians are expected to actively cooperate in overcoming the effects of original and personal sin, and of all forms of oppression and persecution. What is rather baffling is the color or chromatic symbolism expressing the paradox of achieving a linen's whiteness by dipping it into the redness of the Lamb's Blood, foreshadowed in Jacob's patriarchal blessing over his son Judah (Gen 49:11). Yes, we are to be proactive by using the sacramental means of purifying our souls, but ultimately it is the indispensable act of Christ's redemption that makes them radiant and pleasing to God.[34]

In fact, any maltreatment here below only increases the desire for spiritual purity, to pass toward heavenly integrity by maintaining the sheen of the baptismal robes of sanctifying grace.[35] Also, the soul is bathed in the divine Blood whenever we communicate from the sacred chalice of the Blessed Sacrament of the Altar. One additional benefit deriving from that human-divine synergy in keeping the vestment of our souls unblemished is the forthcoming promise of being invited into the future New Jerusalem: "Blessed are those who wash their robes, so that they will have the right to the tree of life and may enter the city by the gates" (22:14). All temporal trial will then have finally turned into everlasting bliss.[36]

The Lamb redeems the sheep (7:15–17)

[15]For this reason they are before the throne of God, and worship him day and night within his temple, and the one who is seated on the throne will shelter them. [16]They will hunger no more, and thirst no more; the sun will not strike them, nor any scorching heat; [17]for the Lamb at the center of the throne will be their shepherd, and he will guide them to springs of the water of life, and God will wipe away every tear from their eyes."

That thought of being admitted into the heavenly city is expanded on by the elder, still talking to the exiled visionary; and in these remaining verses of the

34. On the feast day of the Holy Innocent Martyrs (December 28), the Roman Missal presents this Alleluia antiphon: "The white-robed army of martyrs praises you."

35. Cf. AvS, 287–88.

36. Notice, incidentally, the many close parallels between the heavenly scene of 7:13–17, and the depiction of the New Jerusalem at 21:2–22:5.

chapter, we see a renewed concentration on the divine throne. Although primarily envisioning the *Ecclesia triumphans,* that is, all the redeemed who have been found worthy of eternal life, prior to the final judgment at the end of time, what is said of them here is equally motivating for us today. They are engaged in one unceasing act of worship in God's sanctuary, expressed by the present tense of the verb *latreúō* (λατρεύω, *servire*), the singular explicit reference to divine worship in the Apocalypse aside from 22:3. The idea is that of a vast congregation occupied with the priestly ministry[37] of rendering homage to the Most High with sincere hearts and willing minds.

Eloquent is the etymological background of the noun *látris* (λάτρις), signifying a qualified servant, hired to accomplish a technical task. As Christians we should think of our lives as one extended opportunity to eradicate all forms of idolatry, and to love and serve God with all our strength. Sacramental liturgies in our cathedrals, parish churches, and oratories simply anticipate the soul's *opus Dei* that we are called to render day and night within his temple. While we assemble spiritually "before" (*ante*) his throne "within" (*in*) his temple, God, besides dwelling in us, also tabernacles "over" (*super*) us (v. 15). By pitching the tent of his unmediated presence and protection above us, he lives in intimate communion with us, his beloved children, further augmenting the imagery of the heavenly Feast of Tabernacles (vv. 9–10; John 1:14). Humanity's destiny, therefore, is to dwell forever in God's *shekhinah* (שכינה), worshipfully reflecting his light and enjoying his loving closeness.[38]

Once we have reached the boundaries of history, however, and all things have been subjected to Christ (1 Cor 15:28), there will be no temple in the city, for its temple is the Lord God the Almighty and the Lamb (21:22). Those four emphatic negations in v. 16 (cf. 21:4) underscore how none of the privations which the faithful have endured for Christ's sake shall trouble them any longer, none of the dissatisfactions of life shall afflict them. For the weariness of hunger, thirst, and fatigue will be no more; indeed, the former things will have passed away (Isa 25:8; 49:10). No desire remains unfulfilled, body and soul will no longer experience discomfort; on the contrary, scorching heat will have turned into eternal *refrigerium.*[39]

The visionary lens pans, as it were, between the Lamb and God the Father in vv. 14–15, and it now swivels back toward the Lamb at the beginning of v. 17,

37. Even though the more specific term *leitourgéō* (λειτουργέω, *ministrare*), which is at the root of the word "liturgy," does not occur in Revelation.

38. Cf. AvS, 289.

39. See the Commemoration of the Dead in the Roman Canon (Roman Missal).

only to focus all the attention on God again at the verse's end. In a flashback to 5:6, the elder from v. 13 concludes his elucidations by reminding John that the Lamb is stationed in intimate proximity to the Father, i.e., in the center of his throne.[40] That centrality appears to fulfill Jesus' promise to make himself present in the midst of his disciples (Matt 18:20), and to walk in the middle of the seven golden lampstands of his Church (1:13; 2:1). Putting the accent on his leadership (*poimaíno*) rather than the act of feeding (*bósko*), like a Shepherd he pastors his sheep, guarding their movements during the day, and directing his flock back to its fold for the night, lest they go astray (John 10:11; Pss 23:1–4; 49:14). Thus, paradoxically, the Lamb has redeemed the sheep (*Agnus redemit oves*).[41]

Even more communicative of Jesus' leadership is the second of the three verbs in this v. 17, namely, *hodēgéō* (ὁδηγέω, *deducere*), which implies the guidance and instruction given by a skilled teacher. It is a rare biblical word that conveys the idea of being led by the Holy Spirit in the path to eternal life. With surety and knowledge, the divine Lamb leads the sheep of his Christian flock on their way to a vast terrain around the throne that has become their feeding grounds, drinking the water of life from the inexhaustible springs of God the Father. One might say that henceforth, the very essence of the Blessed Trinity will serve as their nourishment.

Our journey from earth to heaven is such a pilgrimage, and we will not flounder or stumble, so long as we follow the One who can lead us home (John 14:6). He who produced water from the rock in the wilderness (Exod 17:1–7), who made his people drink from the stream by the wayside (Ps 110:7), and who gives to those who come to him the water which alone will quench their thirst (John 4:13–14), he now makes them drink also from the river of his delights (Ps 36:8). Eloquently enough, these springs of life-water have their origin in the throne itself (22:1), prefigured by the brook that Ezekiel saw issuing from below the threshold of the temple toward the east (Ezek 47:1). Nevertheless, since in the New Jerusalem there will be no temple (21:22a), we are carried straight up to the throne of God to savor the wellsprings of every gladness.

This noble emblem of water again alludes to the ancient festival of Tabernacles, marking the definitive end of our earthly desert sojourn. Complementing the element of water, and still referencing Sukkot, God himself, with the tenderness of a parent, will wipe away every tear from their eyes (cf. Isa 25:8).

40. Literally, "above the center" of the throne, *aná meson toû thrónou* (ἀνὰ μέσον τοῦ θρόνου), which he shares with the four living creatures (4:6).

41. From the Easter sequence *Victimae paschali laudes*.

At that point, the beatific vision will have completely supplanted any grief and discomfort (Matt 5:4).[42] Indeed, no one will be able to weep, because sin as the source of all sadness will be cut off, and the Paraclete's holiness and consolation will be consummated in his children (John 14:26). Thus, the divine Lamb-Shepherd, Jesus, offers redemption as guidance toward life, leaving nothing to be desired, neither unslaked thirst nor unrequited love. In that sense, this chapter is a veritable foretelling of the New Jerusalem as depicted at 21:1–22:5.[43] And herewith the elder's remarks to the apostle are rounded off; their extraordinary beauty is a testament to the former's prodigious insight into God's purpose and principle of salvation.

42. Cf. AvS, 291.

43. Proven by no fewer than seventeen concepts that are found in both scenes: "God" (7:2–3, 10–12, 15, 17 || 21:2–3, 7, 10–11, 22–23; 22:1, 3, 5); "Lamb" (7:9–10, 14, 17 || 21:9, 14, 22–23, 27; 22:3); "washed white or clean" (7:9, 13–14 || 21:27); "nations" (7:9 || 21:26; 22:2); "throne" (7:9–11, 15, 17 || 21:3, 5; 22:1, 3); "water or book or tree of life" (7:17 || 21:6, 27; 22:1–2); "tears" (7:17 || 21:4); "thirst" (7:16 || 21:6); "day and night or sun/moon" (7:2, 15, 16 || 21:23; 21:24–25; 22:5); "temple" (7:15 || 21:22); "their God, his peoples" (7:9–10, 12 || 21:3, 7, 26); "seven" (7:12 || 21:9); "angel" (7:1, 2, 11 || 21:9; 22:1); "glory" (7:12 || 21:11, 23, 24, 26); "honor" (7:12 || 21:26); "worship" (7:11, 15 || 22:3); and "face" (7:11 || 22:4).

8:1–13, Stillness begets cataclysm

Seventh seal: Heavenly silence (8:1–2)

[1]When the Lamb opened the seventh seal, there was silence in heaven for about half an hour. [2]And I saw the seven angels who stand before God, and seven trumpets were given to them.

As the spotlight shifts from God (7:17) back to the Lamb, we see him opening the seventh seal, providing closure to that series begun at 6:1, and at the same time prompting a period of silence in heaven. This quietude briefly arrests the plot before it ventures into the next septenary, that of the trumpets (v. 2). Why not use this narrative hiatus to insert some remarks concerning the emerging structure of these chapters? A triple cycle of septuple visions, consisting of the seals (chs. 6–7), the trumpets (chs. 8–11), and the bowls (ch. 16), signals past, present, and future events in the eschaton. Not repetitive but synchronous with one another, each septet seems to trace the course of divine action up to the consummation of all things under a different aspect. In other words, they relate to the history of humankind from the beginning to the end of time, which in turn marks the ushering in of eternity. While the seals, with their general cues concerning God's judgments, delineate the way through earthly trouble to eternal rest, the upcoming trumpets unveil our path through hardship to triumph. In principle, although specific events in history may be partial realizations of apocalyptic prophecy, the actual fulfilment is spread out across all generations.

Again, the seals depict the tribulation befalling the Church because of the world, while the trumpets display the plights affecting the secular world due to the Church's progressive conquest of it, redolent of Israel's advance toward full possession of the land of promise and all the battles that had to be fought along the way. Speaking of Old Testament antetype, the employment of trumpets for seven days at the destruction of Jericho (Josh 6:1–21), a symbol of worldliness, may have inspired the format of this present vision, announcing a final judgment and destruction of the world. Furthermore, there is a correlation between the arrangement of seals and trumpets, since in both cases two subordinate visions are introduced after the penultimate element of the series: just as the sixth seal was followed by the vision of ch. 7, the sixth trumpet will dovetail with the ones in 10:1–11:1–14. These interpolations serve a similar purpose, namely, to give the reader an encouraging insight into the growth of Christ's Church.

It could be argued, too, that the first six items of each septet describe more external aspects such as afflictions as somber companions of world history, whereas the interposed visions exhibit a more spiritual dimension such as the work and victory of the children of God. In any event, these sevenfold series illustrate how the Lord in his providence summons the earth's population to surrender to him. Yet another resemblance between the seals and the trumpets can be found in the separation between the first four and the last three: just as the first four seals were presented by the cry "Come!," so also the last three trumpets will be introduced by the threefold cry of "Woe!" (cf. 8:13). What we will be able to gather from these trumpets is that they herald the transformation of all the kingdoms of this world into the one supernal reign of Christ, the King of the universe.

But back to the actual text of this new chapter: As the Lamb opens the final seal, a concurring surge and lag of silent prayers, reflection, and expectancy is triggered. A greater contrast than between this half-hour silence on the one hand, and the previous electrifying chant by men and angels (7:10, 12) on the other, is hard to imagine. Logically, the breaking open of this last seal completes all the others, and that mysterious scroll in the Father's hand (5:1) becomes fully decipherable at last. This seal, however, also introduces the septet of trumpets subsumed under it, as in turn the seventh trumpet will launch the bowls of wrath. Hence, the absolute duration of this seal is much lengthier and encapsulates many more events than any of the six earlier ones, taking us all the way to the close of ch. 11.

Is this silence in v. 1 the calm preceding the storm? Before answering this question, let us recall that a Jewish tradition speaks of a primeval silence heralding the first day of creation.[1] Also worth recalling is Wisdom 18:14–16, often applied to the moment of the Incarnation of Christ, the virtual beginning of

1. "And the world shall be turned back to primeval silence for seven days, as it was at the first beginnings; so that no one shall be left" (4 Ezra 7:30).

God's work of re-creation.[2] Moreover, Zephaniah relates suspenseful silence to God's judgment (Zeph 1:7). Silence could, therefore, be seen as the ritual prelude to eschatological woes that are about to unfold.[3] As is often the case, the most obvious interpretation is likely the accurate one, and that is, these metaphorical thirty minutes are expressive of a solemn foreboding regarding the great events about to be unveiled, although the Trisagion of the angels and saints probably echoes without intermission. Indeed, the Church triumphant reverently anticipates that something decisive is taking shape on the horizon.[4] This heavenly silence could also be viewed as a grace period or a time of wordless acclimatization to a new reality (7:1).

Before addressing one more aspect of this mystifying silence, we should ask ourselves how this apocalyptic image can spur us on to accompany any spiritual and physical trials with moments of recollection, taking good advantage, too, of liturgical silence in our churches. Such godly tranquility of soul will result in renewed serenity and fortitude (cf. Isa 30:15; Ps 62:1). And so, in addition to the above interpretations, this silence is also reflective of the sepulchral stillness of Holy Saturday before Easter. It becomes a temporary silencing of the enemies of Christ and his Church before the eternal Sabbath rest of the people of God; then, when all sorrows are no more, the righteous will rest on the breast of God as the beloved disciple did during the Last Supper. Hence, we are inspired to cultivate a habitual homesickness, allowing our hearts to quietly yearn for our true and lasting home.

With his attentiveness heightened due to the surrounding quiet, John now sees seven angels standing before God (v. 2). They are positioned nearest to God to receive their trumpets, the sounding of which is to bring down woe upon woe on an impenitent earth. That they have been standing there for a long time is underscored by the perfect tense of the verb *hestēkasin* (ἑστήκασιν). They are possibly the seven "angels of the presence" (Tob 12:15; Luke 1:19), who according to Jewish tradition are archangels by the name of Michael, Gabriel, Raphael, Uriel, Raguel, Sariel, and Remiel.[5] However, just as we took the seven spirits at 1:4 (cf. 4:5; 5:6) to be symbolic of the Holy Spirit, so also here can

2. In a similar vein, an ancient homily on Holy Saturday highlights the silence before Christ's Resurrection: "Something strange is happening, there is a great silence on earth today, a great silence and stillness. The whole earth keeps silence because the King is asleep" (PG 43:439).

3. Cf. RD, 970.

4. See also the silence of the Judeo-Christians assembled in Jerusalem after hearing from Peter about God's design to henceforth include all Gentiles into the Church (Acts 11:2, 18).

5. Cf. Bruce Manning Metzger and Michael David Coogan, eds, *The Oxford Companion to the Bible* (London: Oxford University Press, 1993), 54.

we interpret the seven angels as representatives of the complete power of God over the world, including his authority to judge at the end. Adrienne recognizes in them the angels of the seven churches (chs. 2–3), guarantors of that pneumatic connection between divinity and humanity in the Church.[6]

What is more, their septuplicity might be a clue that God prefers to unleash his wrath on a stubborn world not all at once, but in slower and more measured degrees, as it were. In his immeasurable mercy he appears disinclined to inflict sudden judgments on his beloved creatures, giving them opportunities to repent until the very end. As the angels are being furnished with those trumpets, we can expect a boisterous end to the silence, as well as the closeness of deafening cataclysms. These instruments in the Old Testament were also used as summons for worship and warfare, as well as to mark the steady advancement of Israel's desert encampment toward freedom and lasting peace. In this present context, the trumpets seem to announce the approaching Day of the Lord with its judgment on this world.[7] They are the harbingers of the postlude to world history, an inflection point when Christ will quell all idolatry, apostasy, and hostility. Standing ready for his parousia and our universal homecoming to the heavenly city, we are determined to maintain our quiet vigilance.

Ascending prayer, descending fire (8:3–5)

[3]*Another angel with a golden censer came and stood at the altar; he was given a great quantity of incense to offer with the prayers of all the saints on the golden altar that is before the throne.* [4]*And the smoke of the incense, with the prayers of the saints, rose before God from the hand of the angel.* [5]*Then the angel took the censer and filled it with fire from the altar and threw it on the earth; and there were peals of thunder, rumblings, flashes of lightning, and an earthquake.*

These verses are the direct preface to the upcoming trumpets, an inkling of the horrors looming on the earth; for now, there are mere dashes of fire (v. 5), announcing the real barrage of God's wrath (vv. 7–10), long pent up, but poured out at last. When we learn of this scene at the heavenly altar, the incense offering[8] at the *shekhinah*, the tabernacle where God dwelt with his people in the

6. Cf. AvS, 293.

7. Cf. Isa 27:13; Joel 2:1; Zeph 1:16; Matt 24:31; 1 Cor 15:52; 1 Thess 4:16.

8. To be distinguished from the biblical burnt offering or holocaust (Hebrew עלה, *`olah*, from the verb "to cause to ascend," thus, "to burn"). Especially as an animal sacrifice, it was

desert, comes to mind. Inside it, next to the curtain dividing it off from the Most Holy, the gilded incense altar was located (Exod 30:1–3, 20). A similar altar stood in Solomon's temple in Jerusalem where this perfumed offering was accomplished before the morning and after the evening sacrifice (1 Chron 28:18). While the sacrifices were made, voices could be heard and the trumpets sounded, and the people outside prayed in silence (Luke 1:8–11). Once a year, on the Day of Atonement, coals from the altar were taken in a censer together with two handfuls of incense into the Holy of Holies to be burnt before the mercy seat of the ark of the testimony (Lev 16:12–13).

Now, however, the altar of incense is located right before the throne of God, the veil having disappeared. Another angel approaches this altar (v. 3), holding a golden censer at the golden altar (Exod 30:3), symbols of what is divine and heavenly. He is reminiscent of Gabriel the archangel in Luke's Infancy Narrative. He presents himself at the altar like a priest, and rises above it,[9] to plead with God, to intercede on behalf of his own or for his enemies. Does he symbolize Christ the High Priest himself (cf. 10:1), sanctifying all his faithful by his self-sacrifice? Well, if the Lamb was emblematic of Jesus as our sacrificial victim, then this angel betokens him in his priestly *munus*, offering up to God the prayers of all the saints. Clasping a golden censer would signify his mediatorial office exercised at the altar of the Church, offering his Body like aromatic incense.[10]

That censer is the link between the throne of God and his judgments upon the earth, prepared by the prayers of the angelic priest (v. 4). The notion of such angelic mediatorship[11] surfaces in postexilic Judaism with the belief that the prayers of the righteous win special efficacy when presented to God by angels such as Gabriel, Raphael, or Michael. Illumined by this passage of the Apocalypse, we in our own day should never cease to entrust our spiritual life to the guidance and intercession of these good spirits, especially to our personal guardian angel, asking him to always lift up and multiply our prayers before the throne of the Most High.[12]

"Many incenses" are supplied by God (v. 3), giving off garlands of fragrant smoke. This abundance denotes the mediator's great merits and intercessory

consumed totally by fire, and considered the greatest form of sacrifice offered at the temple (cf. Lev 1).

9. As suggested by the Greek preposition *epí* (ἐπί), meaning "upon, over, on, above," translated in the New Vulgate as *ante*, "before, in front of."

10. Cf. RD, 971–77.

11. Cf. AvS, 297.

12. Cf. *CCC*, §§336, 350; Thomas Aquinas, *Summa Theologiae* I, q. 114, a. 3, ad 3.

power before God. He in turn gives it to the prayers of all the saints (cf. 5:8), commingling them with his own. And if our prayers are weak and flawed, the fragrant cloud of divine grace will absorb whatever is earthly, carnal, or unbelieving in them, making any imperfections disappear. Nothing is left behind but the sweetness of Bethany's precious spikenard filling the heavens (cf. John 12:3).[13] At last, the anguished *usquequo, Domine?* of 6:10 is answered, together with all the anonymous prayers of the Bride of Christ. Our pleas, mingled with those of others, are now rendered acceptable, as they rise into the Lord's presence.

Due to the priestly character of the Church, as Christ continues to offer his very Body to the Father, filling the Church with the Holy Spirit, we can be assured that none of our prayers is ever lost. Even though some of them may seem to have been long unanswered, they are never forgotten, they never fail to move God's fatherly heart. No prayer recommended by the angels has ever been denied a hearing and acceptance. On the contrary, history itself is influenced by the prayers of the saints; like weapons in the hands of Christ's soldiers, they become mightier than any earthly armaments. In this way, John consoles the followers of Jesus, assuring them that their prayers for the coming of the Kingdom are never sighed in vain. All our supplications are safely deposited on the golden altar before his throne, waiting to be answered often in wondrous and unexpected ways.

Having emptied the golden thurible of its incense, the angel now fills it with fire from the altar and hurls it toward the earth, or rather "into" it, as implied by the Greek preposition *eís* (εἰς, NVg: *in*; v. 5). It becomes obvious that it is impossible to lock up the power of that incense, this devouring fire of love and judgment, within its liturgical receptacle. Many are the Old Testament antetypes of this fiery scene,[14] but in particular, John enhances the scattering of burning coals over Jerusalem in Ezekiel 10:2 with the casting of fire onto the whole earth. And that results in peals of thunder, rumbling voices, flashes of lightning, and an earthquake, like a clamorous prelude to something even more dreadful, namely, the seven trumpets with all their woes (cf. Wis 19:13). That cacophony of voices conveys utter chaos on earth, in contrast to the peaceful silence in heaven. The world below is no longer a reliable haven of life and happiness; everything is unhinged now, everything has to be reevaluated.[15]

13. Cf. AvS, 294–95.

14. E.g., Gen 15:17–18; Exod 9:8–10, 23; 19:16; Lev 9:24; 16:12; Num 16:37; 1 Kgs 18:38; Judg 13:20–21; Isa 6:6–7.

15. Cf. AvS, 299.

Hosts of holy prayers had lain dormant on the heavenly altar, but now they bestir themselves, and without delay the mighty works of God, his mercy and judgment, are manifested on earth. Here we have proof of the effectiveness of prayer, capable of producing tremendous changes on earth. One could contend that the Christian religion, celestial in its origin and destiny, keeps colliding with the passions of sinful humanity, resulting in riotous phenomena, just as the Lord prophesied in Luke 12:49–51. Hence, this blazing action means that God's judgments are about to descend on the earth (2 Thess 1:7–8), a token of his acknowledgment of the prayers of the saints, and a powerful incentive for us to pray. However, this fire from the altar also communicates the Almighty's loving mercy and merciful love. Indeed, it is one and the same tool that warms the hearts of the faithful and executes vengeance on God's enemies. Christ's glowing love translates into humanity's faith, and conversely, God is in need, as it were, of our prayer to advance the work of his Son on earth. These supplications are then purified to become light for the soul and a searing tool of his judgment.[16] Thus, this apocalyptic image of fire could be said to illustrate the correlation between God's mercy and justice.

First Trumpet: *Zikkarōn*, aridity, compunction (8:6–7)

[6]Now the seven angels who had the seven trumpets made ready to blow them. [7]The first angel blew his trumpet, and there came hail and fire, mixed with blood, and they were hurled to the earth; and a third of the earth was burned up, and a third of the trees were burned up, and all green grass was burned up.

Nothing escapes the visionary's eye, and so now he watches the seven angels grasping their instruments in such a way that they can bring them up to their mouths, ready to blow. Perhaps this angelic phalanx (cf. 2 Chron 13:12) is also arranging itself in the order in which they are to sound, bringing the half-hour silence in heaven to a thrilling end. Since the biblical trumpet fanfare is often synonymous with the proclamation of God's mysteries,[17] humanity is about to be reminded that there is a Kingdom that cannot be shaken. Although the first four trumpets seem to reverse the phases of the first creation account or *hexameron* (Gen 1), what is about to unfold is the great advancing of Christ's reign (vv. 7–12). Another commonality is that their judgments affect natural

16. Cf. Pseudo-Chrysostom, *Homilia* 6, *De precatione*: PG 64:462–66.
17. Cf. Beale, *Book of Revelation*, 468–72.

objects necessary for life, i.e., the earth, trees, grass, the sea, rivers, fountains, the light of the sun, moon, and stars. Contrasting with these are the last three, the so-called woe-trumpets (9:1, 13; 11:15), that will afflict humanity's spiritual life with pain, death, and hell, in judicial retribution.

With language borrowed from the ten plagues of Egypt, the first trumpet resembles the seventh plague (Exod 9:23–26). Unlike on that occasion, however, where the havoc was mainly wrought by the hail, here it is brought about by fire, reiterated three times in this verse (*combusta est*). Peculiar to Revelation is the miraculous mixture of blood with the hail and fire (Wis 16:15–24), possibly triggered by the destructive power of the large hailstones (cf. 16:17–21; Josh 10:11). And it is precisely this resemblance to the history of the Hebrews in the land of oppression that offers us a hint, in that it carries us back to the past, and asks us to remember the mighty works of God. This memorialization is known among the Jews as *zikkarōn*,[18] whose purpose is to glorify God, proclaim the defeat of the enemy, and to celebrate the victory of the Lord and his people. Moreover, this act of recalling past *magnalia Dei* ("wondrous works of God," Sir 18:5), and asking him to be mindful of his covenant, is believed to make one partake in those same graces in the present, as well as preparing the people to receive them in the future. Thus, as a first spiritual lesson drawn from this trumpet septenary, Christians prayerfully cultivate this interior remembrance of all the good that Jesus has done in their lives and reflect on his continuing love and mercy. This habit of personal *zikkarōn* will always be crowned by the Eucharistic memorial, recollecting the Lord's Death and Resurrection, liturgically reenacting its grace, and venerating his Real Presence until he comes again.

No longer merely a fourth part (6:8), but now a third of the earth is hit (Zech 13:8–9). Perhaps the agency of three elements, namely, hail, fire, and blood, affecting three other worldly features, i.e., earth, trees, and green grass, functions as an intimation of this trumpet's source in the designs of the Blessed Trinity.[19] That the totality (*omne*) of verdant grass is incinerated tips the reader off as to the universal scope of this cataclysmic visitation, affecting material fruitfulness, human productivity, and necessary food supplies. Already during the opening of the third seal (6:6), the issue of famine was broached, and

18. This Hebrew noun (זִכָּרוֹן) stems from the verb *zakār* (זָכַר), meaning, "to remember."

19. Rupert refers it to all humanity, comprised of three parts, that is, the righteous, the penitent, and the impenitent; to his mind, the third part that is burnt up are the impenitent descendants of Noah's cursed son Ham, leaving the remaining two, Shem and Japheth, unscathed, cf. RD, 978–79.

again, the upcoming plague of famine will be seen as a direct result of burning fire (18:8). Bearing in mind the maximal importance of wood and livestock-supporting grass, the only possible conclusion is that their partial destruction implies starvation, destitution, and the undermining of any hope for a prosperous future.

How much more punishing can it get than a concoction of cold, heat, and bloody liquid dropping down from the skies with mighty impact? Hail spells inevitability, fire signals human passion and divine retribution, while blood evokes the vengeance of Abel's murder.[20] Eventually, fire wins out over hail and blood, charring a third of the earth. Could the supervening dearth and hunger indicate those inescapable periods of spiritual aridity? As the soul progresses in holiness, it experiences times of dryness, darkness, or disturbance, in which it seems unable to derive any consolation or satisfaction even from prayer. This lack of interior gratification may make it harder to carry on with one's customary religious practices.[21] Instead of giving in and taking the bait of lessening one's effort to pray, we do well to insist more on meditation, examen, and suitable ways of doing penance. Among the surest ways to face desolations courageously, is to abstain ever more from mundane things, to heed the loud trumpet sound of God's presence and wisdom, to take advantage of the sacrament of Confession, and to frequently move toward the unscorched pastures of the Holy Eucharist. Hence, this first trumpet nudges us to accept and embrace the recurring periods of interior barrenness, taking advantage of them by fixing our inner eyes more keenly on Christ Jesus.

There is a third implication that may be more obvious than the ones pondered above, and that is the message of divine judgment, the frightful Day of the Lord. As a matter of Old Testament precedent, one notices the combination of fire and blood in the context of judgment already in Joel 2:30–31, quoted by Peter on the day of Pentecost (Acts 2:19). And of course, the destruction of Sodom and Gomorrah by a rain of sulfur and fire became proverbial (Gen 19:24). As early as the time of Job, hail was understood to be an indicator of divine displeasure, and an instrument of punishment (Job 38:22–23). Hail as a symbol of divine vengeance is present also in Isaiah 28:2, Ezekiel 13:11–13, and Haggai 2:17. In any case, this first apocalyptic trumpet with its amalgamation of these diverse scriptural antecedents, signals a judgment precipitated on earth through the ordinary powers of nature. John is warning humanity, instilling a

20. Cf. AvS, 301–2.

21. Ignatius of Loyola describes in the Fourth Rule of his *Spiritual Exercises* how the trial of desolations aids us in growing closer to God.

healthy dose of alarm in each one of us, not to harden our hearts like the Egyptian Pharaoh, but to repent.

Fire then turns into a figure of continual cleansing, not unlike gold that is purified in the crucible, aiming at compunction and submission to God's will. In this way, we make ready for the climactic Last Judgment, not being caught off guard, red-handed, or otherwise unawares.[22] As mentioned above, the Lord's ire will always be intertwined with his infinite mercy, and the graduality of inflictions carries the overtone of God restraining his indignation to grant time for repentance.[23] The menace of chastisement is really intended to turn into the gift of conversion and the experience of divine forgiveness. As a concluding thought on this first trumpet, if the trees emblematize the great ones in human society, and if the grass signifies the common people, then no one shall be exempted from the personal and universal judgment prepared by our Father in heaven, and the eschaton in which we live is a chance to work out our salvation with fear and trembling (Phil 2:12).

Second Trumpet: Humility, fortitude, generosity (8:8–9)

[8]The second angel blew his trumpet, and something like a great mountain, burning with fire, was thrown into the sea. [9]A third of the sea became blood, a third of the living creatures in the sea died, and a third of the ships were destroyed.

In continuity with and complementarity to the imagery of the first trumpet, at this juncture another third of the planet is harmed: instead of the earth, now the world's oceans with their marine life and seafarers suffer mighty spoilage. John must have thought of the first plague of Egypt as a backdrop (Exod 7:14–25), which, in apocalyptic dramatization, he transforms into two vexations, and their sheer vehemence and magnitude betray their purpose as eschatological judgment. Unlike in 6:14–16, however, where actual mountains and rocks are portrayed, the seer is careful to add that this otherworldly body was "like" (*tamquam*) a great mountain burning with fire. Which is to say, it was not a real mountain, but had the characteristics of an active volcano, appearing as an immense rock or a blazing asteroid (cf. 18:21).[24] The Bible frequently

22. Cf. AvS, 300–303.

23. Cf. RD, 971.

24. Cf. 1 Enoch 18:13; 21:3, depicting the fallen angels under judgment as "great mountains burning with fire."

presents mountains as metaphors for kingdoms and cities (e.g., Jer 51:25). In other places the image of a quaking rugged mountain indicates something remarkable or mysterious, the sign of divine power, often overwhelming the enemies of Israel and erasing the high places of pagan worship (e.g., Nah 1:5). In Isaiah 2:2, the "mountain of the Lord" signifies the Church and her Lord himself. One may therefore conclude that a judgment of great magnitude is foretold in this vision.

Moreover, since the Greek verb *bállō* (βάλλω), "to cast," calls for a forceful hurling or swinging, only God and his angels would be capable of tossing a mountain like a toy, a fact that is expressed in the passive voice of this phrase (*missum est*). All the notable events in the Old Testament that occurred on or near mountains, including the Garden of Eden (Ezek 28:13–15), Abraham's sacrifice of Isaac, and Moses at the burning bush, connote a transcendent encounter with the Divine; yet now they have been perverted into a chasmic distance from the Most High. Sacred mountaintops like Horeb, Sinai, and Zion, that celebrated redemption and communion with God, are now implicitly desecrated as a place of desolation, judgment, and even condemnation. Most spectacular is the distortion of a luminous Tabor into a fiery mountain banned from God's presence, indicative of the debasement of the worldly. Jesus' solitary nightly communing with his heavenly Father (Matt 14:23) has now changed into an image of passionate eviction and obliteration of whoever or whatever is hostile to God. Ergo, the immense wealth of mountain symbolism has been turned upside down and into its opposite.

Now, in light of Christ's temptation, during which the devil took him up to a very high mountain to show him all the kingdoms of the world and their glory (Luke 4:5), here the mountain must be interpreted as a symbol of Satan's pride. If we then take the fire to be a figure of jealousy, then there is a joint metaphor for the sinful arrogance of the individual soul, worsened by diabolical envy. Additionally, its precipitous falling mirrors the banishment of the great red dragon from the celestial sphere (12:3–4, 9, 13), made complete by the fall of its diabolical kingdom on earth, also known as the spiritual Babylon: "Fallen, fallen is Babylon the great!" (14:8). Thus, one might say that the crashing mountain represents the evil one's intent to inflict spiritual death through pride and jealousy. Consequently, all such tendencies, especially self-importance and conceit, will have to be annihilated from the inner landscape of one's soul. Relying on the grace of God, we will attempt to always practice Lamb-like humility as a sure protection against the enemy, as shown by a word attributed to St. Anthony the Great: "I saw all the snares that the enemy spreads out over the world and I said groaning, 'What can get through from such snares?' Then I heard a voice saying to me, 'Humility.'"[25]

Upon the impact of this smoldering mountain in the apostle's vision, something distressing happens: a third of the sea becomes blood (cf. 11:6; 16:3; Exod 7:17). This largest of all earthly bodies of waters, emphatically restated three times in vv. 8–9, symbolizes humanity, as will be revealed in 17:15. And if the living creatures[26] are viewed as representative of all the untold members of the earth's population (cf. Ezek 29:4),[27] then a third of humanity (cf. 9:18; 12:4) is brutishly affected by the satanic onslaught. A third, too, of the natural waters turns into blood. A subtle textual development can be observed in that the blood was eventually consumed by the fire in v. 7, whereas now it prevails over the fire and even acquires oceanic proportions.[28] Taking into consideration that in Babylon the blood of the slain prophets and saints will be found (18:24), we can apply the imagery again to our spiritual lives. If indeed the oceanic blood stands for the violent dying of Christians in this world, then we ought to regularly pray for those persecuted for their faith, but we should also be aware that the prospect of persecution and even martyrdom can never be completely dismissed from the horizon of our daily lives. Hence, we should ask for the grace of fortitude and perseverance to face whatever hardship may be in store for us with courage and trust. We are interiorly consoled by the thought that the blood of the martyrs will always be the seed of new Christians.[29]

Bearing as it does the imprint of trinitarian justice, the second trumpet not only devastates the sea and its marine life, but also a third of ships, another indication of the overpowering force and extent of the punishment. Before analyzing the image of the ships, however, let us first resolve the vocabular meaning of the Greek verb at the closing of v. 9, which is a compound of the intensifying prefix *diá* (διά), "thorough, total," and *phtheírō* (φθείρω), "to destroy": what it denotes is a process of completely corrupting something. Especially against the

25. *The Sayings of the Desert Fathers: The Alphabetical Collection*, trans. Benedicta Ward (London: Mowbray, 1984), 2.

26. Not to be confused with those otherworldly living beings (*animalia*) that are introduced at 4:6, and are modeled on the *ḥayyōṯ* in Ezek 1:5. Of note is also the solecism in the Greek phrase *tá échonta* (τὰ ἔχοντα), "those having [life]," which should be a genitive rather than a nominative, to agree with its antecedent *tôn ktismátōn* (τῶν κτισμάτων), "of the creatures"; this lack of syntactic agreement may be due to Semitic influence, since Hebrew has fewer declined forms than Greek; cf. Beale, *Book of Revelation*, 477–78.

27. Cf. RD, 980.

28. Cf. AvS, 304.

29. Tertullian: "Semen est sanguis Christianorum," *Apologeticus*, 13.

intertextual backdrop of its only other recurrence in the Apocalypse at 11:18, pointing to those who destroy the earth, John seems to allude to an ethical wasting away due to the influence of moral depravity. This connotation is not as strongly reflected in the Neo-Vulgate's rendition of *interiit,* which simply focuses on the ships' demolition.

But what do those ships represent in this scene? In the Bible, an arch can be spanned from the ark of Noah to the bark of Peter, signifying places of safety amid flood or storm. Jesus called his first disciples when they were busy mending their nets close to their boats, and he himself taught from one on the lake of Galilee with the crowds in attendance on the shore.[30] With this in mind, the ships embody the universal Church, and their annihilation would mean that a substantial fraction of dioceses and their parishes have gone or will go under. And so, places that are supposed to offer refuge from the storms of life, are failing, leaking, and capsizing right into the abyss.[31] Additionally, the commercial function of ships invites the metaphorical association with the sin of greed. Also, considering their immemorial involvement in warfare, they emblematize worldly power and riches. Which reminds us that we are not supposed to trade the sacred things of God: "Freely you have received; freely give!" (Matt 10:8). Chapter 18 will demonstrate how global economics, symbolized by Babylon, will eventually meet their demise, and the present obliteration of a third of all ships foreshadows that collapse, as well as its ensuing famine. Sadly, many Christian churches are infected with that greed of the great harlot, focusing on fiscal profit, fame, or false prosperity gospels, and thereby commercializing God's Kingdom (1 Tim 6:5–10). Instead of bowing to the pressures of mammon, this apocalyptic imagery reminds us to practice the opposite virtue, that is, generosity coupled with personal frugality, especially when it comes to sharing with the brothers and sisters the manifold gifts of our faith.

Third Trumpet: Poisonous hedonism (8:10–11)

[10] The third angel blew his trumpet, and a great star fell from heaven,
blazing like a torch, and it fell on a third of the rivers and on the springs
of water. [11] The name of the star is Wormwood. A third of the waters

30. The Greek word for these ships in the Apocalypse is not the most common one, but the one used in the Gospels of the apostolic vessel in which Christ sat and spoke, namely, *ploíon* (πλοῖον), rendered as *navis* by the Neo-Vulgate.

31. See the titular sees in Catholic tradition that memorialize defunct local churches.

became wormwood, and many died from the water, because it was made bitter.

Not only the second, but also the third trumpet can claim the first Egyptian plague, part of the larger Exodus motif, as their biblical matrix, having in common the undrinkable water of the river (Exod 7:21; Ps 78:44). But the torch-like star, called Wormwood, evokes not only the seven stars in Christ's right hand, said to be the angels of the seven churches (1:20), but also the crown of twelve stars glorifying the head of the celestial woman at 12:1. It also resembles the fall of a third of the angels, swept down to the earth by the tail of the great red dragon (12:4). Moreover, it relates to the morning star as the reward for victory in faith, that is Christ himself (2:28; 22:16), as well as to the one who holds the key to the shaft of the bottomless pit (9:1). And since the present star's luminescence is compared to a blazing torch, it has an undeniable affinity with the Holy Spirit who dwells in front of the throne under the guise of seven flaming torches (4:5). How can one not recall the star as a figure for the Messiah, exemplified in Balaam's prophecy (Num 24:17), but also of his second advent (Matt 24:29)?

Several textual clues, however, make this star a sign of diabolical influence and a manifestation of God's wrath.[32] For one, the focus is on its free fall from heaven,[33] like a blazing meteorite shooting through the sky, associating it with the above-mentioned fall of Satan and his demons (12:4, 7–9). This is now the third trumpet that inflicts fire as a partial judgment, this time on rivers and springs of water. Since it is delineated as a "great" star, its evil nature is magnified and its symbolic closeness to the great red dragon (12:3). Isaiah's taunt against the king of Babylon comes to mind (Isa 14:12–15), and, given the imminent appearance of an eagle in v. 13, Obadiah's oracle against the enemies of God's people is of significance, too (Obad 1:4). A star is also a natural symbol of a person distinguished by rank or by talent, and hence, this tumbling star may point to the downfall of many human potentates and other celebrities in this world, albeit often admired as luminaries. Burning with lust for power and fame, and consumed by arrogance and the fanaticism of evil ideologies, they will be removed from their seats among the stars.

32. Cf. RD, 981.

33. Accentuating the active voice of the verb *píptō* (πίπτω), "to fall," by placing it at the beginning and repeating it shortly after in that same verse, unlike the deemphasized placement of the passive voice of *bállō* (βάλλω), "to throw," in the middle of v. 8: God appears to allow the devil to plummet toward the earth without any further divine or angelic influence.

Most revelatory, however, is its name, the "Wormwood" (*Absinthius*), the epitome of bitterness and corruption.[34] This shrubby plant has an extremely spicy-bitter taste, and it even holds toxic components that can be damaging to the human body.[35] The Old Testament employs it allegorically, similar to gall, to castigate four transgressions and their bitter consequences, namely, idolatry (Deut 29:17–18),[36] heresy (Jer 23:15), the perversion of justice (Amos 5:7), and calamity due to wrongdoing (Jer 9:12–15). As this star crashes into a third of the rivers and springs of water on earth, it transforms them into absinthe, causing many people to perish from their toxic bitterness. This plague could be interpreted as the reverse miracle of Moses' healing of the waters at Marah (Exod 15:22–25), and of Elisha restoring the spring of Jericho (2 Kgs 2:19–22). Moreover, the spoiled taste of this water evokes Moses' grinding of the golden calf to powder, casting it into the brook, and making the children of Israel drink of it (Exod 32:20). Its deadly nature certainly stands in stark opposition to the life-giving waters mentioned elsewhere in Revelation, representative of the reward of eternal life (7:17; 21:6; 22:1). In the last analysis, *Absinthius* conveys the radicality of God's wrath that will not spare even the most ordinary sources of life.

On an anagogical level, several applications of this vision seem plausible: wormwood is the conflagrant star of Babylon, the world-city, and by its idolatry, heresy, and injustice it poisons the source of its own life, cajoling the nations into the misery of spiritually undrinkable water.[37] These corrupted waterways also denote any self-referential intelligence that departs from God, falsifying eternal truths, and thus falling from heaven. One might also see here an image of Christian churches in the end-times that become acerbic in their adherence to heterodoxy, plunging into spiritual unfruitfulness, hopelessness, and death (Heb 12:15).[38] Then there is the realization that the moral implosion of formerly pious Christians has the potential to harm many others, just as the innumerable pseudoprophets over the centuries have defiled the waters of sound doctrine

34. The fact that this name carries a definite article and is capitalized in the original Greek shows that bitterness is its very nature, comparable to "I am the Resurrection and the Life" (John 11:25), or "I am the Immaculate Conception!" (Mary's greeting to St. Bernadette Soubirous in Lourdes on March 25, 1858).

35. Its species name according to the binomial nomenclature is *Artemisia absinthium*, the latter term being translated as "without sweetness."

36. Most Exodus plagues were designed as judgments on false Egyptian gods and their idolaters, cf. John James Davis, *Moses and the Gods of Egypt* (Grand Rapids, MI: Baker, 1971).

37. Cf. RD, 981.

38. Cf. AvS, 306.

(Jude 13). In this regard, St. Bede the Venerable writes, "Heretics falling from the summit of the Church, attempt with the flame of their wickedness to taint the fountains of divine Scriptures."[39] Surely, those poisoned rivers also refer to all demonic temptation, which, if given in to, turns into a venom paralyzing the soul, shutting down the inner faculties, and ultimately leading to spiritual asphyxiation. In addition, it would not be too far-fetched to think of how sinners allow themselves to become embittered at the glory of the saints. But perhaps the most straightforward perspective on this third trumpet is the truism that an over-indulgence in worldly pleasures generates bitter disappointment. In fact, ancient and modern iterations of hedonism at first feel like a fountain of sweet satisfaction, but soon turn into acrid self-destruction. On the other hand, a person who wishes to pursue the interior life in Christ must steer clear of even the semblance of profligacy and self-centered high living, because clearly, they are forms of idolatry. God's judgment can be as rapid as a shooting star, and as absinthial as wormwood.[40] Enlightened by this apocalyptic imagery, we pray for the awareness that sin can be punished at any time, and that living in a state of sin offers no real inner or outer security.

Fourth Trumpet: Ecological conversion (8:12)

[12] *The fourth angel blew his trumpet, and a third of the sun was struck, and a third of the moon, and a third of the stars, so that a third of their light was darkened; a third of the day was kept from shining, and likewise the night.*

To situate this fourth trumpet within the overarching storyline of Holy Scripture, let us begin with the Old Testament, where there is again a similarity with one of the plagues of Egypt. This time, the dimness vanquishing the lights of the firmament carries us back to the ninth plague, that of regional darkness (Exod 10:21–23), which now under John's pen assumes a universal and eschatological reach. Furthermore, two of the Minor Prophets, namely, Joel and Amos, comment on the imminent day of the Lord as being a day of darkness and gloom that spreads like blackness across the mountains (Joel 2:1–2, 10, 31; Amos 8:9). One should also point out that already in Wisdom literature these phenomena are taken as a metaphor for divine punishment of idolatry and

39. Cf. Heinrich Meyer, *Critical and Exegetical Commentary on the New Testament* (Springfield, OH: Funk & Wagnalls, 1893), on Rev 8:10.

40. Cf. RD, 982.

oppression of the ancient Hebrews (Wis 14–17). As we turn to the New Testament, we observe a parallel pattern between Jesus' Olivet Discourse on the one hand (Luke 21), and Revelation's septets of seals (ch. 6), trumpets (ch. 8) and bowls (ch. 16) on the other. Sequentially akin is the movement from wars, pestilence, and famine to cosmic cataclysms that see the powers of heaven shaken (Luke 21:25–26).

That these Johannine visions must be read in a mostly trans-temporal and meta-conceptual key becomes abundantly clear when we consider that the skies were already cleared of their stars at 6:13. In a recapitulating fashion, this fourth trumpet is contemplating God's partial judgments from yet another vantage point. What is unique about it is that a previous total obscuration as during the opening of the sixth seal (6:12–13) is now replaced by a simple dimming of those cosmic luminaries, striking down a mere third of sun, moon, and stars, redolent of the three-day limitation of the ninth plague in Egypt (Exod 10:23). That incompleteness of judgment is made emphatic by the fivefold restating of *tertia* in this verse. Sun, moon, and stars could be understood as allegories for Christ, his Church, and divine grace, obscured in history and not embraced by many.[41] Likewise, the blocking out of some of the natural light could be referred to the Church, darkened by false brethren and hardened unbelievers, spiritually separated from Christ. This eclipse could also be explained as punishment of the ungodly for oppressing the Church and the saints.

Moreover, darkness usually signals some satanic scheme of deception, intended to confuse and destabilize us earth-dwellers. Could it also allude to the seasons in our Christian lives when it is harder to find the way to God, or worse, when he is perceived as absent? There is perhaps the anxiety of running out of time, of missing out on the Divine, or times when worries and labor prevail.[42] It resembles the three-hour eclipse on Calvary (Mark 15:33), and it also reminds us of the dark night of the senses and of the soul, so thoughtfully analyzed by the Doctor of the Church, St. John of the Cross. Why did he call the soul's journey toward a mystical union with God the "dark night," if not because the destination and its path is humanly unknowable; indeed, we walk by faith and not by sight (2 Cor 5:7). Additionally, the person must experience necessary purgations or "nights," both active and passive. Those nights involve the cleansing of the senses or sensory part of the soul, and of the spirit. They

41. Cf. RD, 984.
42. Cf. AvS, 307.

characterize one's earthly pilgrimage toward more perfect illumination and divine union.

However, these phases should not be conceived of as running consecutively, but rather as simultaneous experiences of the soul in the state of grace and desirous of perfection. One might say that during those periods the only light is that which burns inside the heart, tying back into the tertiary shadowiness of this fourth trumpet. Besides, the nights of the bodily senses and of the soul are not so much a spiritual crisis as the daily dying to oneself and to the comforts and pleasures of the flesh, and the gradual detachment from all reliance on this perishable world.[43] Also, some may be vexed by thoughts of doubt concerning the existence of God, struggling to assent to them intellectually or volitionally. One should reckon extraordinarily challenging or painful times in one's life as such a night of the soul, like, for instance, after the death of a loved one, a difficult marriage, or the diagnosis of a life-threatening illness. It should also be mentioned that while these "nights" are usually temporary, they may occasionally last for a long time.

In any event, such occasions of lightlessness and sorrow must take place, since it is through seasons such as these, when the lights of human wisdom and of spiritual guidance seem shrouded, that the human spirit matures, and the Catholic faith is deepened. Just as primeval chaos and obscurity preceded God's work of embellishing his creation (Gen 1:2), in a like manner, we must pass through interior and exterior diffuseness into the illumination of holiness and happiness, ultimately toward our own death and resurrection. Attached to this is the recognition that Yahweh protected the ancient Hebrews, long before they became his beloved people at Mount Sinai, from the Egyptian plagues by the blood of the Passover lambs, exterminating the firstborns only of those households that were unmarked. Likewise, if we persevere in prayer, in receiving the sacraments, and in works of charity, our faith will be preserved from deception and destabilization, and we will be strengthened even through the dark nights of soul and senses.

These first four trumpet visions all display disruptions of the order of creation. When read side by the side with the early pages of the Book of Genesis, also known as the creation accounts (Gen 1–2[44]), they seem, although arranged differently, to depict the undoing of what God accomplished *ex nihilo* ("out of nothing") on those six days of creation: the vegetation is smitten, the earth

43. In consonance with St. Teresa of Avila's well-known motto, *Aut pati aut mori*, literally, "Suffer or die."

44. With Gen 2, the second account, arguably being just a more in-depth look at Day 6.

and sea are intermingled, the living things in seas and streams are subverted, and the lights of the heavens are darkened; ergo, a veritable de-creation. These God-permitted disturbances of the cosmos could be viewed as a retribution in kind, that is, the elements that were abused are now inflicting pain and punishment on their abusers. Such disruptions, especially the ones caused by a diminished brightness of the heavenly bodies, are bound to strike extreme perplexity in the human heart. It can also be proven from Scripture that the distortion of astral light-sources equals judgment on the chosen people for violating covenant obligations (e.g., Jer 31:35–36). In other words, God alters fixed patterns of the created world regulating human wellbeing to cause discomfort in those whose moral order is disturbed by infringing on his laws.

Taking one step further, the biblical texts also affirm an intimate link between human moral conduct and the natural order (Rom 8:20–22), allowing us to draw another critical lesson, this time regarding the Church's teachings on ecology, understood as the preservation of harmonious relationships between living organisms, including humans, and their physical environment. Christians are bound to respect ecosystems and biospheres, appreciating their marvelous biodiversity but also their inherent fragility, and to protect them is a grave responsibility for the common good.[45] The cataclysms and environmental disasters of our own times are stark reminders for us to act as good stewards of creation, that is, of our mother, the earth. As a matter of fact, all are called to an ecological conversion,[46] developing a personal spirituality that makes us choose a lifestyle of sustainability and frugality vis-à-vis the use of material things. We ought to prayerfully discern the accountability that God places on our shoulders, avoiding any semblance of wasteful or exploitative consumerism. Instead of squandering and demolishing earthly resources, genuine disciples of Christ exemplify by their lives how to preserve and protect them for humanity's posterity.

On that note, it is crucial to realize that the fourth trumpet also announces the selfsame features that will beautify the cosmic woman in heaven, that is, sun, moon, and stars (12:1).[47] Originally created on the fourth day and placed in the expanse of the sky to distinguish between the day and the night and to mark the seasons (Gen 1:14), these lights are disrupted by the fourth trumpet,

45. Cf. Pontifical Council for Justice and Peace, *Compendium of the Social Doctrine of the Church*, 2nd ed. (Rome: Libreria Editrice Vaticana, 2005), §§166, 299, 340, 359, 461–86.

46. Cf. Pope Francis' 2015 encyclical letter *Laudato si'*, as well as his 2023 apostolic exhortation *Laudate Deum*.

47. Cf. Jon Paulien, *Decoding Revelation's Trumpets*, AUSDS 21 (Berrien Springs, MI: Andrews University Press, 1987).

yet they are ultimately meant to glorify Mary, the Mother of the Church and representative of all humanity in heaven. Only in the New Jerusalem will their splendor be surpassed by God's own glory (22:5). And in wrapping up our reflections on these first four trumpets, one might say that they are timely reminders not only of our personal death and final judgment, but also of the radical insufficiency of the material creation, which longs to be transformed at the end of days. In response to this biblical message, we continue to humbly place all our faith and trust in God.

Eagle of justice (8:13)

[13]Then I looked, and I heard an eagle crying with a loud voice as it flew in mid-heaven, 'Woe, woe, woe to the inhabitants of the earth, at the blasts of the other trumpets that the three angels are about to blow!'

Naturally, John has been observing and listening all along, and with rapt attention, but after his spiritual eyes had adapted, so to speak, to the cosmic penumbra in the preceding verse, he now seems to be startled by the zenithal incandescence that suddenly compels him to turn to this new sight, at the same time in continuity with the foregoing, and yet offbeat: the shatteringly bright image of an eagle. Of note here is the absence of the comparative adverb *hōs* (ὡς, *tamquam*, "similar to"), connoting a crystal-clear perception on the visionary's part. Eagles[48] are not only majestic apex predators in the avian world, but they are also featured as omens of doom and vengeance in several Old Testament prophecies (e.g., Hos 8:1). And despite its visual clarity, opinions diverge as to its nature: Could it be the fourth living creature (4:7)?[49] Or is it the great eagle that will transport the woman into the wilderness (12:14), or is it an angel,[50] or else, is it purely symbolic of an eternal Gospel (14:6)? This bird and its symbolism are deeply ingrained already in the Exodus tradition (Exod 19:4, Deut 32:11–12). It also evokes certain covenant curses that include corpses being eaten by raptorial birds (cf. Ezek 39:17–20). In direct antithesis to the meekness of a dove, it remains a prominent biblical image of divine judgment, soaring

48. The Greek noun *aetós* (ἀετός) can be translated both as "eagle" and as "vulture" (cf. Luke 17:37); the Nova Vulgata opts for the former term (*aquila*).

49. As a matter of fact, the fourth trumpet and this flying eagle are comparable to the fourth seal introduced by the fourth living creature, 6:7–8.

50. "Eagle" is read in the oldest and most authoritative manuscripts such as ℵ, A, B, Vulgate, Syriac, Coptic, etc., while "angel" is found in P, 1, 16, 34, 47, etc.; one manuscript (13) carries *aggélou hōs aetoū* (ἀγγέλου ὡς ἀετοῦ), "an angel like an eagle."

high with all-seeing eyes, hovering over the prey, and then inescapably swooping down from on high to pounce on it.

Flying most conspicuously across the meridian altitude of heaven, that is, closest to the sun at noonday, it can be seen and heard by all to whom its message pertains, and that is, by the entire human family (14:6; 19:17). This its flight in mid-heaven at the brightest hour of the day seems to hint at a climactic judgment, recalling the first coming of the Son of God in the fullness of time (Gal 4:4). Crying with a loud because anguished voice, "Woe!" three times, either to show the greatness of the calamities looming on the horizon, or in correlation to the number of the angels yet to sound their trumpets. "Woe! woe! woe!" likely represents three separate catastrophes: the first woe will be finished at 9:12, the second, following the interlude of 10:1–11:13, will conclude at 11:14, whereas the third and final woe, 11:19, released by the seventh trumpet blast at 11:15, will have no distinct ending, but will flow into the new visionary segment at 12:1. In the meantime, this eagle expresses not only the sorrow of the angels, but also warns of impending fiascos.

Passing through the center of heaven, this aquiline herald not only lends intensity and urgency to its ill-boding proclamation, but by reiterating the woes three times, it also reminds us of the trinitarian design of what is coming next. As if the first four trumpets had not been terrible enough, the anticipation of the remaining three is truly horrifying, knowing that it has to do with the imposition of divine justice on the inhabitants of the earth.[51] Does not the very appearance of the eagle in full flight, especially by its magnificent black-yellow contrasted eyes and regal wingspan, communicate something of the transcendence of the all-knowing and all-powerful God? It also implies that his judgments arrive with swiftness and certainty. This conviction should be on the mind of every Christian, as we make good use of our time on earth, watching and praying (Matt 26:41).

51. Cf. AvS, 308–10.

9:1–12, Fifth trumpet: First woe

Antipole of heaven (9:1)

[1]And the fifth angel blew his trumpet, and I saw a star that had fallen from heaven to earth, and he was given the key to the shaft of the bottomless pit.

In marking off this remaining triplet of trumpets by the specter of 8:13, Revelation seems to prepare the reader for an even greater harshness of judgment than in the first four. As discussed already at the fifth seal (6:9–11) and at the beginning of ch. 7, here we have the second and last instance of the "four plus three" pattern, with its heightened sense of anticipation. Another pointer is the lengthier descriptions of the approaching triptych of woes, just as the upcoming depiction of the bowls in ch. 16 will swell from one verse in the first two, to five verses at the closing two bowls. Such a literary intensification has its precedent in the steady deterioration of the ten plagues of Egypt (Exod 7–11). Moreover, if the previous four trumpets involved natural elements of the visible creation, then the last three suggest direct demonic activity aimed at readying for an eternal judgment. Thus, in the fifth and sixth trumpets (9:1–21), satanic beings will concentrate their tormenting and slaying power on humanity. But before moving on, let us acknowledge that we are facing an increasingly complex symbolism in these remaining trumpets. And in response to that, we will break down larger scenes into smaller components, try to decipher each figure, and then step back and look at the larger picture again.

Even with minimal knowledge of modern astrophysics, it is obvious that it is wholly implausible for a fixed star to crash-land on earth, given its disproportionate size and heat that on approach would utterly carbonize and pulverize our planet way before impact. And yet, that is precisely what John is seeing in this vision. Given that astronomical unreasonableness, one can only turn to its symbolism. As an initial consideration, the Greek perfect tense of the verb *peptōkóta* (πεπτωκότα, *cecidísse*), "had fallen," conveys the idea of that star having fallen already in the past, and being now in a state of fallenness, rather than depicting its actual flight path from heaven to earth as in 8:10. By choosing this word, we are also made to understand that this was not a smooth descent ending in a soft touchdown, but a harsh and punishing plunge, all of which would clearly apply to the fall of Satan at the dawn of time. In fact, the wording suggests that he was thrown down, possibly at God's command for a definite purpose. Second Temple Judaism, too, represented fallen angels as stars.[1]

Jesus himself alludes to this event: "I watched Satan fall from heaven like a flash of lightning" (Luke 10:18). This irruption onto the earth can only be imagined as widespread destruction and contrary to the gentle arrival of God's good angels (1:1; 10:1; 20:1–3; 21:9; 22:6, 16). And if this fallen star is indeed the devil, then this verse anticipates and complements what will be said of him and his minions at 12:4, 7–10, 12–13.[2] The question that remains unanswered for now is, why God would permit the precipitation of this star? What is clear at this point is that whatever visitations will be unleashed against earthly degeneracy, they will be judgments coming from the divine throne. But then again, precisely this closeness to God has led many expositors to take this star to be Christ himself (22:16), his fall referring to his incarnation, and the key given him as a sign of his power over life and death (1:18; 3:7; 20:1). However, there is a far-reaching difference between the use of the key by the star here, opening the pit and letting out smoke and locusts, and the angel at 20:1–3, who apprehends the dragon and shuts him up: the latter suits Christ well, while the former does not. At any rate, the figure of a star underlines the deceptiveness of the demon, capable of transforming himself into an angel of light (2 Cor 11:14), who knows that his promises of power, prestige, and pleasure are nothing but empty masquerade.

Next up is the metaphorical gesture of granting him a key, the verb being parsed in the passive voice, *edóthē* (ἐδόθη, *data est*), like the one at the opening of the fourth seal (6:8). It is another divine passive, meaning that the key is given to the devil by God, which is of great theological significance: the Almighty appoints an infernal entity to play a major role in the execution of his designs, allowing him to lock up those who are already there, that is, the demons and the souls of the damned, or else to set them free. Put differently, he will have God-given authority during these end-times to turn loose the evil

1. Cf. Isa 14:12–15; applied to false teachers in the early Church, cf. Jude 13; see also some Jewish traditions that explain those mysterious "nephilim" of Gen 6:1–4 (נְפִילִים, γίγαντες [LXX], *gígantes*) as fallen angels and later inhabitants of Canaan (cf. 1 Enoch 6–13).

2. Cf. RD, 986; AvS, 312.

spirits for them to mete out pain and punishment. Yet by the same token, these forces of darkness are being taught that they can only act so far as they have permission, and can always be restrained and shut up again, at the good pleasure of the Lord. Also implied by this figurative key is the reassurance that in a Christian's life nothing will happen outside of divine approval, as expressed already at 1:18. And if indeed the divine passive presupposes Christ's victory on the Cross,[3] then we are made to understand that evil will always remain under control also in one's personal life (1 Cor 10:13), especially if we persevere under the auspices of the keys of the Kingdom entrusted to Peter (Matt 16:19).

Armed with this key, the devil can lock or unlock that region under the earth containing a lake seething with brimstone and fire, called the abyss. Harking back to Gen 1:2, the Hebrew *tĕhôm* (תְּהוֹם) in the Old Testament is ordinarily rendered by *abýssos* (ἀβύσσος) in the Septuagint, a word that originally means "without any bottom."[4] Hence, the primary lexical connotation is that of an unsearchable pit or void, located in the underworld. Here it refers to Sheol or Hades, as the abode of the devil and his angels (11:7; 17:8; Luke 8:31; 2 Pet 2:4), the darkest depth of the natural earth, the bottomless zone of the dead. The apostle conceives of it as a subterranean cavern filled with fire whose only connection with the earth's surface is a kind of mine shaft or *phréar* (φρέαρ, *puteus*, lit. "dungeon, well, cistern") that can be kept under lock and key. That narrow channel with a mouth at its top is the murky orifice of hell allowing ingress and egress.[5] It will be Satan's provisional prison for the thousand years of the Church's eschaton along with his fallen angels (20:1, 3, 7–10; 2 Pet 3:8).

If heaven is an invisible yet real world, which one day will become visible as a new heaven and new earth, so also the abyss is an unseen, yet real world of the ungodly, which will also become a visible reality as shown in these apocalyptic visions (14:10). And this verse presents us with the most extreme contrast imaginable, as the luciferian star plunges from the heights of heaven down into this world, ready to open the netherworld. This trajectory, however, has been traversed already by the divine Word, born of the Father in heaven, incarnate on earth, and descending into hell. Unfathomable is the pit that represents the most perverted antipode of a boundless heaven.[6] As Christians, we must grow in our awareness that the human heart can be such an abyss, too (NVg: Ps 64:7;

3. Numerous are the passages that highlight his conquest of death and hell, e.g., Luke 23:43; Rom 6:23; 1 Cor 15:55; 2 Tim 1:10; Heb 2:14; 1 Pet 3:18.

4. From the alpha-privative *a* (α), "not," and *býthos* (βύθος), "depth, bottom."

5. Poetically reflected in Dante Alighieri's concentrically narrowing circles of hell (cf. *Divine Comedy*, *Inferno*).

6. Cf. AvS, 312.

Jer 17:9). Therefore, the heart as the inner *sanctum* of our very being, not only "conceals the fathomless mysteries of human desires, motivations, and yearnings,"[7] but it also carries within it the potentiality of darkness and evil. In dealing with God, with oneself, and with one's neighbor, one must always be conscious of this persistent drive toward wrongdoing, especially when the shaft to the pit becomes unsealed.[8] This innate tendency to sin[9] can only be curbed and healed by a robust faith in our Redeemer, Jesus Christ (Rom 10:6–9).

Smoke and mirrors (9:2)

²He opened the shaft of the bottomless pit, and from the shaft rose smoke like the smoke of a great furnace, and the sun and the air were darkened with the smoke from the shaft.

Smoke in the Bible is often an indicator of God's mighty presence, shrouding a quivering Sinai (Exod 19:18), accompanying the outpouring of the Holy Spirit on Pentecost (Acts 2:19), rising from angelic hands in the form of incense with the prayers of the saints before the throne of God (8:4), and filling the heavenly temple with divine glory (15:8). However, the moment that satanic meteorite opens the nether-shaft, John witnesses the diffusion of so much smoke that it cloaks the sun and pollutes the atmosphere. While in the vision of the fourth trumpet, the obscuration of light is caused by the smiting of the celestial bodies (8:12; 6:12–14), in this one, occultation arises from these external fumes. In addition to representing divine displeasure (Ps 18:7–8), this apocalyptic smog is symptomatic of ever-widening divine judgment (9:3, 17–18; 14:11; 18:9, 18; 19:3). The devil likes to ape what is godly, and here we are looking at diabolical anti-smoke, counterfeiting sacred incense, and evoking the haze that once wiped out Sodom and Gomorrah (Gen 19:28). Lamentably, the pristine air made gladsome by the rays of the sun is now obfuscated, making all beauteous things on earth appear hideous and bleak. All pulchritude created by God appears vitiated into ugliness.

This filthy vapor, produced by fire, beclouding and penetrating everything,

7. St. John Paul II's address to the participants of the Roman Symposium on Cardiology (May 30, 1989), no. 2; English trans. "Address to Participants in a Cardiology Symposium Urging Them to Continue to Defend Life in All Its Phases," *L'Osservatore Romano*, English Edition 1096 (July 3, 1989): 5.

8. Cf. AvS, 312.

9. Augustinian and Thomistic theology propose the term *concupiscéntia* to describe this mysterious inclination.

evinces all evil. Although troublesome to the eyes and nose, it is of a perishing nature and will soon vanish. Likewise, metaphorically speaking, evil is doomed to be crushed and banished before long. Then, on an ecclesial level, this image is illustrative of that never-ending war which the Church is waging with the world, the struggle between good and evil, destined to culminate in the victory of all truth. Christ's faith has come to be the light of the world (Matt 5:14–16), yet in its advancement through time in this world, many mundane lights fall, and the deceptive glare of pseudo-prophecy (Matt 24:11), rising like a smoke-screen from the furnace of heresy, will eventually evaporate. Hell does not unlock itself, but there will always be some false teacher to do so. Undeniably, the enemy of the Body of Christ is at work, seeking to obscure its light by the dissemination of opaque theories, and diffusing a nebulous spirit of falsehood and hostility against God and man. Just as dense smoke hinders the sight, so do errors shade the understanding (2 Cor 4:4; 2 Thess 2:9–11). Doctrinal error will forever originate in the unlatched pits of the hearts of demons and sinners, seeking to eclipse the perennial faith of the Church.

Lastly, regarding the individual soul, smoke remains a token of the hellfire of passions and desires in the depth of our being, constantly generating fumes of foolishness and darkness.[10] Coupled with the devil's drive to rebel, our sinfulness tends to be diffusive of evil. Hence, this smokescreen is thrown up by the hordes of the abyss, to limit our vision, to hide the radiance of the Lord's face, to cover up the origins of sinful rebellion, to lure us into fallacy, to promote ignorance and confusion, and to complicate any spiritual discernment.[11] To escape from such infernal exercises of smoke and mirrors, the soul does well to turn its inner eyes toward the Sun of Justice and Star of David, Jesus the Lord. By daily engaging in prayer and charity, and by being faithful to the reception of the holy sacraments, we can thwart, or at least counteract, Satan's attempts at blinding us spiritually.

Facets of rebellion (9:3, 7–11, 17–19)

[3]Then from the smoke came locusts on the earth, and they were given authority like the authority of scorpions of the earth.

[7]In appearance the locusts were like horses equipped for battle. On their heads were what looked like crowns of gold; their faces were like human

10. Cf. RD, 987.
11. Cf. AvS, 314.

faces, [8]their hair like women's hair, and their teeth like lions' teeth; [9]they had scales like iron breastplates, and the noise of their wings was like the noise of many chariots with horses rushing into battle. [10]They have tails like scorpions, with stingers, and in their tails is their power to harm people for five months. [11]They have as king over them the angel of the bottomless pit; his name in Hebrew is Abaddon, and in Greek he is called Apollyon.

[17]And this was how I saw the horses in my vision: the riders wore breastplates the color of fire and of sapphire and of sulfur; the heads of the horses were like lions' heads, and fire and smoke and sulfur came out of their mouths. [18]By these three plagues a third of humankind was killed, by the fire and smoke and sulfur coming out of their mouths. [19]For the power of the horses is in their mouths and in their tails; their tails are like serpents, having heads; and with them they inflict harm.

Locusts coming upon all the land of Egypt during the eighth plague (Exod 10:12–20)[12] were Yahweh's punishing response to Pharaoh's hardened heart, and they form the backdrop to John's vision in vv. 3, 7–11. It is not necessary to look for major historical events to give exhaustive meaning to this vision. Instead, true to the image of the human heart as an abyss (see above), we recognize in the imagery of this chapter the horrible nature and result of personal sin. What the upcoming metaphors express, therefore, is the soul in a state of rebellion against God, in contrast to the four living creatures, symbolic of creation in harmony with its Maker. With that in mind, we watch those baleful insects emerge from the smoke and spread across the earth (v. 3). Given the implausibility of these denoting deceased human beings,[13] most interpreters have opted for a demonic explanation of these locusts.[14] Given their proverbial destructiveness due to a catastrophic voracity, they were considered a principal scourge to land and population (Deut 28:38, 42; 1 Kgs 8:37; Joel 2:25). But

12. Mentioned, too, as part of prophetic announcements of the Day of the Lord (Joel 1:4, 15; Amos 7:1), and Midrashic reformulations of the event can be found in Wis 11:15–19; 12:8–9; 16:9.

13. Biblical episodes like the one involving the Endorian sorceress (1 Sam 28:3–25), or the bodies of many saints rising from their tombs in Jerusalem following the Crucifixion (Matt 27:52), must be considered rarest exceptions.

14. It is not altogether inconceivable that John the Baptist symbolically proved his exorcistic power by consuming them (Mark 1:6).

before proceeding with the discussion of their attributes, the case can be made that the fifth and sixth trumpets depict the same reality from different angles, just as several features of the four horsemen overlapped. Hence, we will reflect on the imagery of locusts (vv. 3, 5, 7–11) and cavalries (vv. 16–19) as one larger unit of meaning due to the obvious similarity of their traits.

Unlike genuine locusts,[15] these are given the power of scorpions (v. 3), which again stresses the fact that they are mere instruments of God's purpose. This reiterated divine authorization clause ("it was given," *data est*) intimates some sort of permission to execute their task while God retains absolute sovereignty. It turns out that their power consists in tails armed with harmful stingers (vv. 10, 19). Here it is worth recalling that the sting of a scorpion occasions intense suffering, similar to that of a bee, bringing about throbbing numbness, swelling for days, and a feeling of wretchedness throughout the body. Applied to the soul, this venom epitomizes the malicious energy of sin, multiplied by the endless number of locusts, making it revolt against God for as long as one lives on earth (Ezek 2:6; Luke 11:12). What is indicated by their crossbred appearance is sin's propensity to pull the wool over the eyes of the soul, and eventually subjugate it in unholy servitude.

Another conceivable implication of the scorpion tail is any deceitful backstabbing present in heart and mind when in the state of sin. Not only does the sinner often experience unbearable pain in his own presence, but now it is made worse by the poison's potency at work in the recesses of the soul. And it is precisely this shrouded activity on the inside that makes it so difficult for another person to diagnose its nefarious effects.[16] Just as the scorpion's sting causes local pain that quickly spreads to the whole organism, so sin also gnaws away at body and soul.[17] Indeed, nothing is harder to bury than the tail of a sinful habit, like a whale that is not free for its life while the barbed harpoon is hooked in its skin and a tenacious line tethers it to the whaler's boat. Grotesquely affixed to this image is that their tails are headed serpents (v. 19), obviously compounding their lethal impact.[18] To sin means to tacitly join forces with the countless minions of Satan, the leviathan of cosmic evil (Gen 3:1; Job 41:1).[19] It will expose the soul in varying degrees to the devil's guile concern-

15. See their status as "clean" in Lev 11:22.

16. Cf. AvS, 329–30.

17. Cf. AvS, 321.

18. Possibly allusive to warfare tactics of Parthian dynasties, or to the Amphisbaena of Greek mythology; see also Num 21:6; Deut 32:24; Jer 8:17.

19. On the metaphorical associations of snakes and scorpions with doctrinal deception and judgment in the Bible and Judaism, see Beale, *Book of Revelation*, 515–17.

ing God-like immortality and omniscience (Gen 3:4–5).[20] In the process, the human heart suffers real spiritual harm: "The one who sins against me [God], injures himself; all who hate me love death" (Prov 8:36).[21]

In addition, the locusts are like horses equipped for battle (v. 7). Now, horses occupy a place of prominence in Revelation, recurring no fewer than sixteen times. They are arranged in a narrative crescendo, from the four apocalyptic riders (6:1–8), through the devilish armies in this present chapter (vv. 7, 9, 16–19), toward the cathartic action of the heavenly cavalry (19:11, 14, 19, 21). The seer's portrayal of a demoniacal militia owes much to the insect swarms of Joel 2:1–11, whose message is centered on the imminence of the fearsome Day of the Lord. Beyond being the frightful agents of divine judgment,[22] these equine monsters symbolize the sinful mind, which, the more it is overwhelmed by God's punitive justice, the more it seeks to rationalize and to resist it. A soul in the state of sin adopts attitudes of infernal aggression, like war stallions ready to charge.[23] Hence, in continuity with the four horsemen, the image of warhorses signals habitual sin and, in its wake, vile passions and idolatries, as if ridden by evil spirits.[24]

Our hearts are like battlefields assailed by the constant threat of imminent attacks and stinging defeats.[25] And contrary to the hideousness of their serpentine tails, the heads of these gargoylian beasts are wearing crowns of gold (v. 7; cf. 6:2), signifying all the various sins committed out of intellectual pride and carnality. Since such diadems are insignia of royalty or victory, this image also suggests that the soul enjoys a false sense of dignity, security, and even invincibility, basking in the trivial attention garnered from others. John continues in his description: "Their faces were like human faces" (v. 7), employing a word of comparison (*similitudo, similis, tamquam, sicut*) for the fifth time in this verse, and it will be reiterated in vv. 8–10. His struggle to put into words exactly what he observes must be due in part to the smoke-blurred scene, but mostly because of the preternatural images shown him. For us, these humanoid facades communicate the anthropological dimension of evil in history, the

20. Cf. RD, 1003.

21. Also expressed by the verb *adikéō* (ἀδικέω, *nocēre*) in vv. 4, 10, 19, literally meaning to "to act unjustly and to inflict hurt by ignoring God's justice."

22. Incursions of barbaric cavalries were a standing feature of Jewish imagination ever since the Parthians loomed on the political horizon; cf. the first-century Jewish apocryphal work *Assumption of Moses*, 3.1.

23. Cf. AvS, 339–40.

24. Cf. RD, 1000.

25. Cf. AvS, 323–24.

result of human uprising against God. In his pretense of reason, man ultimately falls for Satan's primal slogan *Non serviam!* ("I shall not serve").[26]

Acting as mirrors, these anthropoid visages reflect that dark aggressiveness against God in each one of us, obliging us to face the abyss of our finite and puny Ego. Any type of refusal to contemplate the Divine means being condemned to look at oneself, and never finding authentic peace or joy.[27] On the contrary, this egocentric mindset is twisted into a hellish vision of one's sinful "I," away from the redeeming "Thou."[28] Enhancing this symbolism is that the hair of these creatures resembles the hair of women (v. 8), which by the way is an exclusive Johannine feature without biblical parallel.[29] At the same time beautiful and terrible to look at, this hair could be a symbol of all diabolical allurement and seduction that tempt the soul to turn its back on Christ. To counter such temptation, we ought to remember that we bear the indelible mark of warriorship through sacramental confirmation, and we soldier on as members of a Body whose head is disfigured by a crown of thorns.

Not to be confused with the first living being (4:7), and as a parody of Jesus or his angel (5:5; 10:3), those locusts' teeth resemble the teeth of lions (v. 8), and the heads of the horses are like lions' heads, too (v. 17), anticipating the beast rising out of the sea with a lion's mouth (13:2). Lions, best known for their untamable ferocity, appear in Greek mythology as the chimera, a fire-breathing female monster with a lion's head, a goat's body, and a snake's tail. And in foretelling the eschatological *Dies Domini*, the prophet Joel says: "A nation has invaded my land, powerful and innumerable; its teeth are lions' teeth, and it has the fangs of a lioness" (Joel 1:6). The leonine features of these hybridized bands symbolize cruel mindsets and ideologies born from sinful hearts; they are like lions ever ready to tear to pieces and to devour whatever is human, even to the point of self-destruction. Left to our own devices, we would not be able to escape from this metaphorical pride of rapacious lions or a team of swift war-stallions, but that is precisely the situation the soul is in when falling into sin and vice.[30] These forces of hell bear a semblance of inescapability, and their relentless charges will be shut down only by the heavenly army in 19:18.

Moving on to the next facet, namely, their body-armor like iron breastplates (v. 9; cf. v. 17): in these we can discern the ungodly soul ensconced as

26. Cf. RD, 991.

27. The cardiognostic St. John Vianney, for instance, often included thoughts about the dreadful state of a lukewarm soul in his parish catecheses.

28. Cf. AvS, 325–26.

29. Evocative again of the long-haired Parthians.

30. Cf. AvS, 337.

it were in an impenetrable shell, pretending to be invincible, becoming hardened and defensive about its depraved state, and belligerent at the same time against God and his saving grace. Adding to the monstrosity is the noise of their wings like the racket of many chariots with horses rushing into battle (v. 9; cf. Joel 2:5),[31] denoting the rapidity with which sin conquers ever new spaces in the human heart if left unchecked. This numbing rumble could also symbolize any interior arrogance and pride, not to mention the soul's constant distraction springing from the lack of spiritual stillness. Aside from that, the ongoing interior cacophony fosters an inner state of terror, making one's cries for help increasingly inaudible, as well as compounding fear and anxiety in the face of the approaching battle; all of which will in the long run result in an intensified sense of loneliness, inertia, and even paralysis.[32] In terms of coloration of the unidentified riders' armor (cf. 4:2, 9–10; 20:11), their triple hue is fiery red, sapphirine blue,[33] and sulfurous yellow. Fire and sulfur are common biblical figures for divine judgment (20:10–15; Gen 19:24), and applied again to the spiritual life, fire may be a simile for concupiscence, the smoky hyacinth for human pride, and the bright yellow brimstone for immorality.[34] This splash of colors could be taken, too, as symbolic of the gaudy lifestyle often chosen by persons who have habituated themselves to the state of sin.[35]

Matching these three colors is the tripartite stream of destructive breath going forth from their mouths, an exhalation of fire and smoke and sulfur (vv. 17–18).[36] Once inhaled, sin punishes the soul with a foretaste of hell; to sin is like stepping into billowing smoke that becomes thicker and ever more dangerous: likewise, unrepented sin takes vengeance on the sinner in the end, and becomes more and more self-destructive. Also, deadly fumes like these may allegorize types of false speech and ideological errors, leading to the extermination of entire populations.[37] By repeating this phrase, John seems to stress their lethal impact, namely, the sensation of despair and suffocation due to lack

31. The winged divine horse Pegasus of Greek mythology proves that this figure was already part of human imagination.

32. Cf. AvS, 329.

33. Literally, *hyakínthinos* (ὑακίνθινος, *hyacinthina*), referring to the plant of blue or dark purple, bordering on black; Exod 28:33 uses it to describe Aaron's priestly vestment.

34. Cf. RD, 1000.

35. Cf. AvS, 337.

36. *The Shepherd of Hermas,* Vision 4.1:6, "Then Lo! A huge beast arose like a Leviathan, with fiery locusts flying from its mouth." In *Shepherd of Hermas: The Gentle Apocalypse,* adapted and introduced by William Jardine (Redwood City, CA: Proteus, 1992).

37. Cf. RD, 1002.

of spiritual oxygen to breathe, so far removed from the enlivening breath of the Holy Spirit.[38]

"Locusts have no king" (Prov 30:27), moving about in swarms without being under the direction of any one ruler. So it must have struck the seer as a peculiarity that these hordes of demonic grasshoppers very much do have one: "They have as king over them the angel of the abyss" (v. 11). Tellingly, the title *basileýs* (βασιλεύς, "king") was used of the Roman emperor of the time, influencing the way early Christians interpreted this image as pointing to Satan himself, who has control over his kingdom of corruption, and to whom can be traced all the destruction that ensues from his rising out of the abyss. As per the apostle's usual practice to give two names (e.g., John 1:42), he promptly adds that his name in Hebrew is Abaddon (v. 11). Conveying the idea of destruction, the Semitic noun אֲבַדּוֹן can be found almost exclusively in Wisdom literature as a designation for the region of the dead, synonymous with Sheol or Hades.[39] Perdition, therefore, is the overarching rule of this prince of darkness.

Adjoined is the Greek translation of his name, i.e., Apollyon, meaning, the destroying one, not to be confused with the name of the Greek god Apollo. There may, however, be a pun, since the first-century AD emperor Domitian adopted the divine name Apollo, claiming to be his incarnation.[40] Both haunting names are reminders of the angel of death of the Passover night (Exod 12:23; Heb 11:28).[41] Incidentally, the Book of Jubilees identifies this angel as Mastema,[42] another name for Satan. Apollyon is the devil himself, out to destroy his own followers, confirming the words of our Lord that he is a murderer from the beginning (John 8:44), although remaining forever under God's vigilant authority.[43] In his ambition to cause widespread devastation, he appears to be the exact antithesis of Isaiah's Angel of Great Counsel (cf. Isa 9:6 LXX).[44]

What can be gleaned from this apocalyptic imagery is that postlapsarian humanity is embroiled in a spiral of sin that is not undesigned but rather the brainchild of a hidden yet well-organized force. The battle happens not only on the surface, such as revolutions, tyrannies, and networks of international crime,

38. Cf. AvS, 338.

39. E.g., Prov 15:11; Qumran's Thanksgiving Scroll presents Abaddon as the hellish home of Belial, the satanic asp (1QH 3:16, 19, 32).

40. Apollo had the locust as his symbol, too; cf. Osborne, *Revelation*, 374.

41. Cf. RD, 993.

42. He was known as the angel of disaster, the father of all evil, a flatterer of God, chief of the *nephilim*, executor of divine punishment, and tempter of humanity.

43. Cf. AvS, 330–31.

44. Cf. RD, 992.

but it involves spiritual principles, tokens of the epic psychomachia between the Spirit of salvation and the spirit of destruction, between Christ and Belial, God and Mammon, the Angel of Great Counsel and Abaddon-Apollyon. Satan is the inspiring genius from below, the prince of the underworld, a ruthless despot who continues to marshal his troops. Personal sin is the acknowledgment of Abaddon's kingdom in one's heart and mind, an act of allegiance to Apollyon, in the end becoming like him, detestable, hopeless, and miserable.[45] In the final analysis, we must choose to rally with the camp of the saints (20:9), and against God and Magog (20:8).

Thus, all these diabolical armies are not so much metaphors of past or modern warfare, but rather depict attacks on the Christian soul, reflected on the disfigured face of Christ: *Ecce Homo!* These hordes of monsters are among the most outlandish images in the Apocalypse, and they are recorded as an urgent invitation to conversion. In their wide spectrum of details there is a parable, as it were, of the phases of sin: from the initial temptation to deliberate consent, from shameful commission to sudden horror, complete with remorse and shame in its aftermath.[46] Furthermore, the devil is unambiguously pictured in this text to be a person endowed with will and intellect, as consistently taught by the Church.[47] And hence, our minds and hearts should always be drawn away from the misguided curiosity that seeks to match these eschatological images with some external historical event, and instead be sensitive to their symbolism, encouraging spiritual vigilance and the pursuit of self-mastery. John's intention is not to warn against invading armies of geopolitical enemies, but to signal various forms of evil and the terrible influence and consequences of all sin. And may the interior battlefield of our conscience, purified and fortified by baptismal grace, witness an ever-stronger resolve to resist evil, and conquer the abaddonic-apollyonic spirit.

Sealed by God or marked by the beast (9:4)

[4] They were told not to damage the grass of the earth or any green growth or any tree, but only those people who do not have the seal of God on their foreheads.

---

45. Cf. AvS, 330.

46. Cf. AvS, 327.

47. "Evil is not an abstraction, but refers to a person, Satan, the Evil One, the angel who opposes God. The devil (*dia-bolos*) is the one who 'throws himself across' God's plan and his work of salvation accomplished in Christ." *CCC*, §2851.

The fact that a third of the earth, the trees, and all grass was burned up already at 8:7 only adds further proof to Revelation's spiral or recapitulatory storyline. In contrast to the eighth plague that left no green on tree or plant in the fields anywhere in Egypt (Exod 10:15), the hellish cavalries of this first woe-trumpet, in perversion of their natural instincts, avoid all vegetation and turn against humanity itself. A noticeable shift of focus is taking place, moving away from other parts of creation, and zeroing in on humans, in subtle continuity with the mission of the pale green horse (6:8), inflicting harm that can be deemed both punitive and remedial. Furthermore, we find here a most astounding division of humanity into two classes, in tune with typical Johannine dualism: there are simply those who are sealed and those who are not. A careful distinction is made, however, between the seal of God (*signum Dei*) and the mark of the beast (*character bestiae*), recurring at 13:16–17; 14:9, 11; 16:2; 19:20; 20:4. While the former is imprinted only on the person's forehead, the latter can appear either on someone's forehead or on the right hand (13:16). Later we will learn that it is identical with the beast's name and its number (13:17–18). But if that is the case, then the seal of God is likely indistinguishable from the name of God, too.[48] This drastic antithesis and fundamental separation running through the human family is also expressed by the binary expressions "I will not erase his name from the book of life" (3:5) on the one hand, and "Everyone whose name has not been written in the book of life" (13:8; 17:8) on the other.

Furthermore, it is no coincidence that all are sealed on their foreheads, since that is the most visible part of the face,[49] denoting one's intellectual and volitive capabilities, expressive of personality and character. Given this high visibility, it is conceivable that the identifying and safeguarding seal might become visible to humans at the time of the infliction of judgment upon the ungodly. As a reminder, those who receive the seal of the living God (7:2), are the one hundred forty-four thousand righteous men and women of the Old (7:4) and New Covenants (14:1), contemplated as one united multitude of the redeemed at 22:4. Just as in Luke 10:17–20, there is a link between Satan's fall (9:1) and the providential protection of those who are faithful to Christ. Hence, no matter what the damage might be, it cannot injure God's children. Or put differently, those who soil their baptismal vows, do not enjoy immunity from the locusts' maleficence. Without a doubt, it is stupefying that the unfaithful, those who

48. Cf. *CCC*, §1296. 22:4: "And they shall see his face; and his name shall be in their foreheads"; 2:17: new name.

49. The Greek noun *métōpon* (μέτωπον, *frons*, "forehead") is composed of the preposition *metá* (μετά), "after," and the noun *óps* (ὤψ), "eye," signifying the space between a person's eyes.

remain intractable in their unbelief, are singled out and struck directly. At that moment those who are protected and observe the wounding of the unsealed, will realize how sin liquidates not only their relationship with God, but also with the surrounding creational order. It will strengthen their resolve to avoid near occasions of sin, while the unshielded will progressively sink into deeper demoralization and agony, which they are at a loss to explain.[50] Ergo, we are taught that God preserves his own, although it may at times appear to them as though the innocent suffer with the guilty. But then again, the quintessence of the seal is not to bestow complete invulnerability from physical distress or death, since that would contradict the tenor of 6:11. Rather, it emblematizes our defense against Satan's ruse that always aims at making us lose our covenant-love for the Lord Jesus. So let us prayerfully welcome tests and trials to prove our loyalty to him and his Church.

One hundred and fifty, déjà vu (9:5)

[5]They were allowed to torture them for five months, but not to kill them, and their torture was like the torture of a scorpion when it stings someone.

Five months (cf. v. 10) is the prefixed length of time during which the apocalyptic hoppers are permitted to torture the part of humanity that accepts the mark of the beast. Five months, of course, amount to one hundred and fifty days, and the earliest biblical archetype for that period is the deluge that saw the waters swell and prevail on earth (Gen 7:24). Only Noah, his family, and specimens selected from the entire animal kingdom, were preserved by taking refuge in the ark. Also, on a biological plane, five months is the approximate life cycle of insects like cicadas, or the timeframe of their ravages of vegetation, typically between May and September. But viewed through the lens of numerical symbolism as a trait of this apocalyptic genre, five represents half of the worldly number ten, indicating the quality more than the quantity of an incomplete or relatively short time,[51] unlike seven, suggestive of divine

50. Cf. AvS, 317–18.

51. As such, it frequently appears in the New Testament, namely, for the five foolish and five prudent virgins (Matt 25:2), the five talents gaining another five (Matt 25:15–16), the five sparrows (Luke 12:6), the five divided against one another in one household (Luke 12:52), the five yokes (Luke 14:19), the five brothers of the rich man (Luke 16:28), the five minas and five cities (Luke 19:18–19), the five husbands (John 4:18), the five porticoes (John 5:2), and the five fallen kings (Rev 17:10).

completion. In that sense, five is related also to one thousand two hundred and sixty days as half of seven years (11:3; 12:6), connoting the entire eschaton of the Church. In addition to this chronological limitation to a mere five months, God's control is also highlighted by his command to torment but not to kill, just as he had imposed constraints on the scope of devastation caused by the plagues in Egypt (e.g., Exod 7:17), as well as on Satan's power over Job's life (Job 1:12; 2:6).

When meditating on the spiritual message of this verse, there is the realization that the Lord in his boundless mercy[52] spares the natural life even of the greatest sinners, granting more time for grace than destruction. Personal sin can be likened to torture that God can turn into a force for our conversion.[53] Five months become his offer to a wayward person to accept a given trial as a test, embracing physical, emotional, or spiritual pain[54] as an opportunity to avoid the second death on judgment day, whose eventual infliction God reserves to himself. Such temporary affliction serves the purpose of awakening the inveterate sinner, giving him or her another chance to redirect their steps away from wicked ways and resume a lifestyle of religiosity. John seems to repeat the Greek noun *basanismós* (βασανισμός) and its derivative verb *basanízō* (βασανίζω) three times in this verse deliberately. It formerly described the process of testing out precious metals, especially alloys of gold and silver, by moving them up and down on a touchstone as on a file. When a piece of fine-grained dark schist was used for that purpose, the metal would leave a mark on it, whose color could be observed and assessed in terms of market value. Implied here is the idea of verifying moral worth by applying pressure. Complementing this interpretation is the fact that the New Vulgate translates this word with the noun *cruciatus* and the related verb *cruciare,* which stem from the Latin *crux,* that is, "cross." In other words, the periodic or chronic "crosses" that we experience, saints and sinners alike, in the last analysis are divinely permitted standard tests by which one's Christian life can be evaluated.

52. Although the most prominent biblical word for mercy: *éleos* (ἔλεος; Hebrew *ḥesed,* חֶסֶד) is tellingly absent from Revelation.

53. Cf. AvS, 319.

54. Involving the five senses, possibly intimated by the five months.

Thwarted death-wish (9:6, 12)

6And in those days people will seek death but will not find it; they will long to die, but death will flee from them.

12The first woe has passed. There are still two woes to come.

To lend more expressiveness to his words, the sacred author here employs the literary device of a synonymous parallel.[55] There is a studied intensification going from "seeking" to "desiring,"[56] and from "not finding" to "fleeing from them." Additionally, the key notion of "death" is restated three times, in undeniable resemblance to the apparition of "Death" riding a pale green horse with "Hades" in tow (6:8), and to the desire of the ungodly for annihilation, not from the torment of their suffering, but from fear of God before whom they must appear (6:15–17). Instead of seeking death, every human being is endowed with the natural desire to live and will do everything to avoid death, while psychology talks about the extremely strong instinct of self-preservation that makes us behave so as to avert injury and maximize chances of survival. Besides, Scripture is replete with references to the sanctity and beauty of human life. This is why the desire to die is an aberration of the creational order, it is *contra naturam.*

However, we should point out a few biblical precedents, like King Saul begging his armor-bearer and later the Amalekite to slay him (1 Sam 31:4). Job, too, alludes to this nagging wish to no longer be alive (Job 3:20–22). The death-wish and suicide impulse, the contemplation of mortality due to a self-pitying state of mind, is notoriously found also in the prophets Elijah (1 Kgs 19:4), Jeremiah (Jer 20:14–15), and Jonah (Jonah 4:3, 8–9). But who is thwarting the anguished quest to die in the present verse? Could it be God himself ensuring that the suffering continues indefinitely, making Death's pale horse gallop in the opposite direction away from its potential victims? The text does not answer this question, and so the withholding of death enhances and refines the torture to be endured. To be sure, if the motivation is to find sweet relief from this world and its inherent trials, then that is not a legitimate reason to seek death. Nevertheless, we find a related longing in St. Paul, one with a completely different motivation: he does not seek to escape, but to be definitively united

55. A ubiquitous feature in the Old Testament, also found in the Gospel of John (e.g., John 6:55).

56. In keeping with the classical etymology of the Latin *desiderāre*, it has the original sense of looking up to the stars and awaiting what they will bring; composed of *de*, "from," and *sidus*, "star," this metaphor is born from ancient nautical practices and obsession with astrology.

with the Lord, a yearning springing not from desperation but from Christian hope (Phil 1:21–24). And so, each one of us should also have a robust desire to be once and for all made one with Jesus.

Moreover, and very much contrary to those deprived of the seal of God and marked by the devil, good Christians are able to find meaning and even spiritual satisfaction in earthly pain, which they take as an occasion to show their love for their crucified Master (Col 1:24). Even though the wicked are tested for only five months, in their sinfulness they are unable to realize the brevity and transitoriness of it all; they are imprisoned in their mistaken perception and raging desire to die. Is it not strange, though, that suicide is never contemplated in this passage? In this regard, one must remember that the demons first enslave the human heart, then they induce anxiety and hopelessness wedded to cowardly weakness, which will result in the self-centered unwillingness to commit suicide. Conversely, the theological virtues of faith, hope, and love mean existential openness to and encounter with the "Other," Divine and human. For Catholic Christians, the faithful reception of the holy sacraments will have the same effect, decentralizing us from ourselves, expanding the soul toward God and neighbor, and thereby putting to flight the temptation to despair or compulsive suicidal thoughts.

Since we have reflected on the locust cavalries already (see above, vv. 3, 7–11, 17–19), we now turn to the sixth trumpet: v. 12 concludes vv. 1–11 when it declares "The first woe[57] has passed"; and v. 12 also introduces what is next, "there are still two woes to come."[58] These are remarks by John and are not to be taken as spoken by the eagle, or any other heavenly messenger. They were added not only to distinguish the woes among themselves to emphasize each period, but also to suggest that some time will intervene between them.

57. The Greek *he ouaí* (Ἡ οὐαί) is an unusual combination of an indeclinable and genderless interjection, preceded by a feminine article; it is followed by the feminine cardinal number, *he mía* (ἡ μία), "the one" (cf. v. 13; 6:1), as opposed to the grammatically correct ordinal number *prôtos* (πρῶτος), "first"; the literal translation would be, "the one woe, that happens to be the first."

58. The anacoluthic singular verb *érchetai* (ἔρχεται) contains a hypallage, that is, a figure of speech in which the syntactic relationship between two terms is interchanged; here it concerns its incongruity with the plural "two more woes": syntactically less offensive since the verb precedes, it amounts to a parenthetical remark of the author, simply announcing something that is still in the future, devoid of any reference to its plurality yet, like saying colloquially, "Here it comes, two more woes!" Its objective textual roughness, however, is reflected in the variant reading that has the more logical plural *érchontai* (ἔρχονται), endorsed by the Neo-Vulgate's *veniunt*, to describe "two more woes forthcoming."

9:13–21, Sixth trumpet: Second woe

Horned altar as beams of the Cross (9:13)

[13] *Then the sixth angel blew his trumpet, and I heard a voice from the four horns of the golden altar before God.*

Since the reader has learned from the apocalyptic eagle that the trivium of woes concurs with the blowing of the last three trumpets (8:13), it is easy to delimit the textual perimeter of the second woe or sixth trumpet, spanning from 9:13 to 11:14. Now, in the interest of contextualizing the ongoing infliction of plagues on humanity, aimed at eliciting a conversion of heart (vv. 20–21), one must recognize that they originate in the Cross of Christ, symbolized by the horned altar. But what would be the correlation between the two? In Exodus 27:2, Moses is instructed to build a holocaustic altar for the desert sanctuary: "At its four corners you will make horns." Although this fourfoldness is not reflected in the Greek text of this verse, the Old Testament reference may have influenced the ancient variant reading "four horns" that is still mirrored in many English renditions.[1] And so, based on that implied quadruplicity, this horned altar indicates the four beams of the Cross of our Lord.

In addition to the practical purpose of keeping the sacrificial animals in place during their ritual immolation, there is a more profound meaning to the horns protruding from this altar. In general, the altar signals the intersection between the divine and human spheres, symbolizing priestly worship, sacrifice, consecration, and communion. And when Moses added horn-like projections to its four corners, the people would have naturally associated them with the strength of a bull.[2] Hence, the comparison to power and fertility, reaching

1. The Neo-Vulgate returned to the original reading of Codex Sinaiticus (*א), which does not include *tessárōn* (τεσσάρων), "four."

2. Divinized, for instance, in the ancient Egyptian religion as the sacred bull Apis, believed to have been sacrificed and reborn, serving as an intermediary between humans and other gods.

its pinnacle in the divine gift of salvation. Metaphorically, the horned altar becomes the destination of humanity's pilgrimage, a universal place of refuge and deliverance. "Four" also intimates the order of creation, disturbed by sin, and in need of redemption; it recalls that our faith is founded on the patriarchs and prophets, righteous kings, and judges of the Old Testament.[3] All of these realities are manifested in the seven horns of the Lamb (5:6), diabolically aped by the dragon (12:3) and its beasts (13:1, 11). Thus, John's vision of the altar, now transmigrated into heaven, suggests that by eating the blessed fruit of Jesus' Cross we will be empowered to endure the trials of life. Consequently, let us take hold of this altar's horns (1 Kgs 1:50–51) and receive God's grace to repent of our sins: "Behold the wood of the Cross, on which hung the salvation of the world; come, let us worship!"[4]

Strikingly, the altar is personified, and it speaks with one voice, perhaps indicating the oneness of God in three persons, meeting at and communicating from the heart of the Cross, where they are most united, and where their eternal volition becomes bundled into one.[5] At the same time, since the utterance comes from the golden altar positioned before God,[6] it could have been pronounced by any of those present in God's holy place, such as a living creature, an angel, or even one of the elders (16:7). While this supernatural voice shows God's displeasure at the offenses done to his majesty, it also stands for the preaching of the Church as she strives to uncover the lies of the antichrist. Not least, it appears to be God's gracious response to the petitions of the saints and martyrs resting under the altar (6:9–11; 8:3–5). Those fervent prayers, rising from the four quarters of the world, incensed and elevated by the angel, are now being heard and answered. This is the voice of Christ's mediation, now no longer supplicating, but commanding. And as long as we are pilgrims in this world, let us frequently open our inner ears and be transfigured by the Father's voice: "This is my Son, whom I have chosen; listen to him!" (Luke 9:35)

3. Cf. RD, 994.

4. From the liturgy of Good Friday (Roman Missal).

5. Cf. AvS, 332–33.

6. The Vulgate reads "before the eyes of God" (*quod est ante oculos Dei*).

River of good boundaries (9:14)

[14] Saying to the sixth angel who had the trumpet, "Release the four angels who are bound at the great river Euphrates."

Among the seven trumpet-bearing angels, this penultimate one is exceptional, in that he is called to take part in the action itself by releasing the four angels who are bound above[7] the great river Euphrates. His involvement appears to mark a latter stage in history, since the seventh trumpet will proclaim the passing from this world to the Kingdom of God (11:15). Extraordinary is also the pinpointing of the precise geographic region from where the apocalyptic devastation will be unleashed: it is the impressive Euphrates, by far the largest river in western Asia. From its source in the Armenian mountains to the Persian Gulf, into which it empties itself, it has a course of approximately 1,730 miles, defining an area on earth that has been called the cradle of civilization. Roman authorities designated it as the eastern frontier of their empire, attempting to fend off the constant threat of a Parthian invasion from beyond the river. At Genesis 2:6 we learn of a stream[8] rising from the earth that may be the primeval source of that river flowing from Eden to water the garden, and from there it divides to make four streams (Gen 2:10), the fourth of which is the Euphrates (Gen 2:14). Together with the third one, Tigris, it is one of the two defining watercourses of Mesopotamia, literally the region "between the rivers." It would later demarcate the northeastern border of the land promised by God to Abraham and his descendants as part of his covenant (Gen 15:18). In due course, King David's conquests would fulfill this stipulation and circumscribe his realm (1 Kgs 4:24). Just as the Nile represented the power of Egypt, so in the following centuries the Euphrates would embody Assyrian power (Isa 8:7; Jer 2:18).

As with the other toponymy in John's Apocalypse, the basis of any spiritual interpretation should be sought in these historical-geographical facts. And so, the Euphrates came to symbolize the natural military barrier between Israel and its perennial adversary Babylon, one of the most important urban centers of the ancient Near East. To the Old Testament prophets the Euphrates was the symbol of all that was calamitous about the divine judgments (e.g., Isa 7:20; 8:7; Jer 46:6, 10). In the entire New Testament, only here and in 16:12 is the river named, and on both occasions, it speaks of some warlike invasion. As a matter

7. Being true to the Greek preposition *epí* (ἐπί), "above" (*super*).

8. The Hebrew reads "mist" (*ēd*, אֵד) rendered by the Septuagint as "fountain" (*pēgḗ*, πηγή), and by the New Vulgate as "well" (*fons*).

of fact, the scene in 9:13–19 anticipates the sixth plague-bowl (16:12) with the drying up of its waters, that is, the annihilation of the protecting boundary, in preparation for the battle of Harmagedon.

Setting free the four angels, hitherto bound at this important river, can only signal disturbances on the great frontier between the City of God and the world-city. Blurring or altogether removing boundaries between truth and falsehood, between light and darkness, or between morality and immorality, is precisely that great spiritual combat, that epic war between the spirit of this world and the spirit of Christ. In our own days we are witnessing how ethical controversies have become more distinct and divisive. In response to this, the Christian ought to fight off the temptation of worldliness that is trying to creep into our hearts. Remember the sixth trumpet blast, for it is a declaration of war against religious indifferentism, moral relativism, and spiritual tepidity within the heart of each individual follower of Jesus. Once we have mystically crossed the Euphrates with Abraham, there is no going back to the idolatries of this world, threatening clergy and laity alike. Once we are initiated into the sacramental life of the Church, we have crossed the Rubicon of our spiritual journey.

We must draw a line, and at times it can be a fine line, between secular demands and church loyalty. And we can be sure of this, that there will be times when we must obey God rather than humans (Acts 5:29), object to "Caesar" in conscience, and courageously choose orthodoxy and orthopraxy over secularism, syncretism, and neo-paganism. We will not allow worldliness to dilute our Christian fervor (John 15:19). We refuse to be conformed to this world but choose to be transformed by the renewal of our mind (Rom 12:2). And since Christ's Kingdom is not native to this world, there should always be a spiritual Euphrates between our soul and all those who do not accept the Lord (John 1:11), so necessary for authentic missionary outreach.

And a time to die (9:15)

15 So the four angels were released, who had been held ready for the hour, the day, the month, and the year, to kill a third of humankind.

"Four" is the numeral in John's Apocalypse descriptive of the living creatures (4:6), the horsemen (6:1–8), the wind-restricting angels stationed at the four corners of the earth (7:1–2; 20:8), the horned heavenly altar, and these Euphrates angels now about to be released. In all these instances, it embodies God's creation, highlighting his presence and operation as they affect human existence and the course of history. At first, the two quartets of angels, the one in 7:1–2 and the one here, seem to be identical, yet upon further deliberation, one could make a case that the former represents good angels, whereas the latter is diabolical in nature. Buttressing this distinction are five possible arguments: *first*, they are situated in different locations, that is, at the corners of the earth (7:1) and at the Euphrates; *second*, they have different missions, namely, to hold back premeditated damage (7:3; 8:7–9) and to kill (9:15); *third*, they have distinct degrees of autonomy, the latter being bound, held back, and in need of being set free (vv. 14–15);[9] *fourth*, the former are addressed by another angel having the seal of God (7:2), while the latter are not; and *fifth*, the former are called to partake in the sealing of the servants of our God (7:3). Considering, therefore, the slavish restraint and lethal mission of the present four angels, they appear to be associated with the abyss (9:1) rather than with the divine altar (v. 13). Hence, they are symbolic of divine wrath and subsequent punishment as sanctioned by his providence. All that pent-up suspension will be eased, since they have stood ready for quite some time, and upon their release their destructive power will be unleashed in the four directions over the great river of this world.

Incidentally, that counterintuitive countdown of hour, day, month, and year[10] is unique in Scripture, consolidating all the prophecies and sayings involving "years," "months," "days," and "the hour" into one end apocalyptic event or reality. Four angelic spirits are held by four units of time, and the Almighty's power has kept them in readiness, reserved for this occasion. There is a touch of predestination and of inescapable certitude, accentuating again that compelling belief in divine providence that runs through Revelation, namely, that all forces of history are dictated by his sovereign design. And it is not only the good things that are under God's control, but also the delivery of chastisement and destruction.[11] These judgments appear to steadily increase in severity, and it is undeniable that the scope of this scourge is shocking and truly unprecedented, namely, the annihilation of a third of humankind. Equally frightening is the precision with which these angels of death execute their divine mandate, killing precisely every third human being (vv. 17–19).[12] This sixth trumpet is by

9. Cf. the divine passive implied in *dedeménous* (δεδεμένους, *alligati sunt*, v. 14), *elýthēsan* (ἐλύθησαν, *soluti sunt*), and *hetoimasménoi* (ἡτοιμασμένοι, *parati erant*, v. 15).

10. One would expect the more dramatic sequence of "year-month-day-hour"; and what is more, by omitting "week," the sacred author again breaks the scheme of logic as is customary in this genre.

11. Cf. RD, 996.

12. Cf. AvS, 334.

far the most lethal of them all, at least up to this point, reaching a high diabolical fever pitch.[13]

Common sense will tell us that over the course of bygone millennia, a third part of all previous generations has indeed died already, deaths permitted by God as a consequence of, and punishment for, their sins.[14] Two insights may help us live our Christian lives even more conscientiously, beginning with the thought that Satan and his angels desire our destruction and death. They pursue their fiendish goal by disseminating illness, injury, and dying. And they do so, waiting patiently for just the right hour, day, month, or year, to pounce on their victims like a roaring lion (1 Pet 5:8). It is of great importance to be aware of this insatiable and irrepressible lust to kill us, but the Lord created us for incorruption and will protect us from the devil's envy (Wis 2:23–24). Jesus does allow the unleashing of some demonic destructiveness for the testing of our faith and that of his Church, while at the same time reassuring us of his divine desire to draw us to himself forever (John 10:10).

In the second place, this page of the Apocalypse reminds each one of us of the sobering certainty that we will have to pass through the narrow gate of earthly death (6:11). Indiscriminately a third of humanity is being killed, and not just those who lack the sacred seal of God (9:4). Given the unavoidability of dying, what will matter most is to work on the inner state of grace, but also to pray for the sanctification of the hour of our death, preordained by God. To die in and with Christ is gain (Phil 1:21), and to know that the hour of our death is God-willed gives peace to the mind, since there is a time to be born and a time to die (Eccl 3:2). In this way we will have thwarted the devil's desire to make us perish, and death will turn into one's *dies natalis* or birthday into everlasting life. And may Mary, Mother of God and Mother of the Church, pray for us, now and in the hour of our death, Amen.

Goliath of cavalries (9:16)

[16] The number of the troops of cavalry was two hundred million; I heard their number.

Echoing the dual narrative arrangement of the fifth trumpet, that is, a bird's eye view (vv. 1–6) that flows into a closeup shot of those stallion-like locusts

13. See also the prominent role of destructive angels in Jewish demonology and eschatology.

14. Cf. RD, 997.

(vv. 7–11), the sixth one also passes from a summary sketch (vv. 13–16) to a detailed description of Satan's equestrian campaign, ultimately identical with the above monster-insects (vv. 17–19). The chapter is rounded off by an ethical verdict (vv. 20–21), giving ch. 9 a somewhat symmetrical structure. John employs again the term "myriad" (5:11) which in ancient Greek had three meanings: it designated at the same time a group of ten thousand, countless thousands, and was simply the largest number linguistically expressible. Parsed in the grammatical plural, multiplied by itself, and then reduplicated,[15] one arrives at an amount of at least two hundred million, or, at an incalculable number of cuirassiers.[16]

Resonating in it is Psalm 68:17 with its very similar wording, "The chariots of God are thousand upon thousand." Such an utterly bewildering figure, similar to the portrayal of immense swarms of locusts (v. 3), pointing to an absurdly large cavalry, with each angel commanding fifty million horsemen, must have sufficed to make commentators look for nonliteral interpretations of this image. Hence, this enormous quantity seems to stand for a preternaturally immense host of combatants with prolific powers of retribution, capable of bringing in the harvest of sin and inflicting large-scale tribulation in the process. The seer must have heard the number from the mouth of an angel since it is far beyond his capacity of computation, even though he will estimate the magnitude of Satan's armies at 20:8 by comparing them to the sands of the sea. Likewise astonishing is the unthinkable disproportion between this number and the much smaller numeral of the elect at 7:4, potentially allusive of the little flock of Christ that cannot be intimidated and is never to be afraid (Luke 12:32).

Such puzzling disequilibrium can help us again engage in a spiritual contemplation of this image. On the one hand, it may be true that the demons can inflict myriads of wounds on creation and on humanity, that there is power and relative indestructibility in their numbers, and that it is clearly an unwise undertaking to confront this enemy, but on the other hand we also understand that Satan has a penchant to make evil look larger than it really is. And in fact, his ultimate powerlessness is ringingly affirmed by Christ on the eve of his death: "Now judgment is upon this world; now the prince of this world will be cast out" (John 12:31). God's infinitely greater designs are impossible to grasp;

15. This singular scriptural phrase *dismyriádes myriádōn* (δισμυριάδες μυριάδων) is accurately rendered by the Neo-Vulgate as *vicies milies dena milia*, literally "twenty-thousand times ten-thousand."

16. The etymology of the feminine noun *myriás* (μυριάς) remains undecided, having been linked either to the waves of the sea, or also to ant-swarms.

when we are left to our own devices, the devil and his hordes can overwhelm the soul, yet we choose to put all our trust in God and not in ourselves.[17] By doing so, we will realize that his numbers are even greater than those of our foe (5:11), and that intrepid and invincible defense is very much on our side (19:14; cf. Matt 22:7; John 18:36; Jude 14–15).

Thus, no matter how ominous the enemy might appear in our lives, we believe that God is always greater,[18] a conviction that should imbue us with confidence and give us strength. It is with that same assurance that the prophet Elisha trapped the blinded Arameans (2 Kgs 6:15–17), that an undaunted David routed the hitherto undefeated Philistine giant Goliath (1 Sam 17),[19] and that the holy priest John Vianney refused to be demoralized by Satan's visitations. In fact, he even made fun of him, quipping: "Oh! the 'clawed boogie-woogie' and myself? We are almost chums!" For our interior life in union with Jesus we can learn that there is no such thing as an insurmountable juggernaut or inevitable *karma* that is bound to subjugate and enslave us; on the contrary, we overcome the world by faith (1 John 5:4) and will one day reach the City of the living God with its innumerable angels in festal gathering (Heb 12:22). And the best tactical gear to stay unflinching in the battle is to simply do good things for the Kingdom: "Do not be overcome by evil but overcome evil with good" (Rom 12:21).

Still worshipping demons (9:20)

[20] The rest of humankind, who were not killed by these plagues, did not repent of the works of their hands or give up worshiping demons and idols of gold and silver and bronze and stone and wood, which cannot see or hear or walk.

As one of the most picturesque chapters of the Apocalypse, deluging the reader with a veritable tidal wave of images, ch. 9 culminates in a tragic punch line: "Not even[20] then did they repent!" At long last, God's primary purpose in his

17. Cf. AvS, 336.

18. Cf. the traditional Latin adage, often ascribed to St. Augustine, *Deus semper maior*, paraphrased as "God is ever greater than what can be imagined."

19. The name Goliath may mean "Exile," from the Semitic noun *gōla* (גולה), "captivity," reinforcing his figurative status as an emissary of the devil who keeps on trying to ensnare us and lead us as captives away from our heavenly homeland.

20. True to the expressivity of the Greek negative conjunction *oudé* (οὐδέ, identical with *outé* [οὔτε], repeated no fewer than six times in vv. 20–21), deriving from the negative particle

judgments is laid bare, namely, his desire to bring us to conversion. Ghastly metaphors of demons are but a specter intended to shock humans out of their spiritual complacency and lethargy, to realize the danger lurking behind their long-indulged vice and their idols. Calamities and hardships are designed to bring about repentance, and to make us turn away from sin (Rom 2:4–5). Not in vain did John the Baptist and Jesus himself begin their public mission with this urgent appeal: "Repent, for the Kingdom of heaven has come near" (Matt 3:2). Similarly, Paul ties trials to penitence in 2 Corinthians 7:9–10. Evenly spread across Revelation, the notion of conversion or *metanoia* recurs in the Spirit's plea with the seven churches (2:5, 16, 21, 22; 3:3, 19), in this chapter, and again in 16:9, 11. It involves a determined pivoting away from worldliness and a radical turn toward God,[21] considering this present life as an opportune time or *kairōs* of salvation by faith in Jesus. Such an intentional self-extrication from the inclination to sin is articulated by the Greek phrase "repent out of, away from"[22] in vv. 20–21.

Additionally, true conversion rescues the soul from a perilous situation that can result in eternal damnation, comparable to someone holding on to a floating plank after a shipwreck, and waiting to be rescued.[23] Sadly, however, the surviving portion of humanity is not touched by God's fatherly love for sinners. Although they are grievously stricken, all these trials fail to bring them to their senses, a theme that reechoes throughout the Apocalypse from the unrepentant Jezebel (2:21–22) to the plagues of the fourth and fifth wrath-bowls (16:9, 11). This also appears to confirm Jesus' own relative pessimism regarding the chances of repentance in the rich man's five brothers (Luke 16:28–31). Such unwillingness to repent is rooted in a contumacious heart, a stubborn will, and the craftiness of sin itself (Rom 1:18–25), despite the abundant opportunities granted by God for personal reform. The apostolic visionary does not tell us whether people felt terror, or momentary qualms, or misgivings, but simply that they did not forsake sin in the end. Arguably the worst omen of spiritual doom is a lost sense of sin itself, feeding into diminished willpower to abhor evil (Ps 36:4). This is known as the mystery of iniquity (*mysterium iniquitatis*) of which Paul speaks in 2 Thessalonians 2:7,

oú (οὐ), "not," and the connective particle *dé* (δέ), "even, moreover": it properly means "not even, nor even, moreover not, neither indeed," introducing an emphatic negation; it is rendered well by the Nova Vulgata's *neque*.

21. See the Thomistic maxim "aversion from the world, conversion to God" (*aversio a mundo, conversio ad Deum*).

22. Cf. *metenóēsan ék* (μετενόησαν ἐκ, *paenitentiam egerunt de/ab*).

23. Cf. Jerome, *Epistle* 117.3.

fortunately counterbalanced by the mystery of piety (*mysterium pietatis*), as taught by St. John Paul II.[24]

Aside from original sin itself, idol worship and its colorful ramifications must be considered the root cause of all moral wrongdoing. What is so perspicacious about John's list of transgressions is that he establishes a direct link between demon-worship and idolatry. Copious are the biblical texts cautioning against the demonic forces ensconced behind idols, God's jealousy against them, and the strict prohibition of their adoration as an unwarranted compromise with heathendom. Idolatry is an error in diametrical opposition to the worship of the living God, and people who practice it debase themselves by various forms of polytheism, superstition, or outright apostasy (Exod 32:35). Ethical evils are not the fundamental sin, but merely symptoms of idolatry. Old Testament prophets and Wisdom writers already denounced the absurdity and ludicrousness of prostrating oneself in front of things made of gold, silver, bronze, stone, and wood,[25] unable to see or hear or walk.[26] Particularly the idols' inability to move around stands in striking opposition to the Son of Man constantly walking among his seven churches (2:1).

To be underlined is their ultimate powerlessness, lexically expressed by the neuter diminutive variant of the Greek feminine noun *daímōn* (δαίμων, "demon"), that is, *daimónion* (δαιμόνιον), which literally means "little devil." They may be evil spirits, fallen angels, inferior to God yet superior to man, gods of the Gentiles, and pervasively present in this world, but at the end of the day, they remain feeble and toothless, unable to measure up to Christ Jesus and his sovereign designs of redemption. Searching into one's own heart, one must again be conscious of the realness and seriousness of demonic deception: to displace God from the soul and replace him with earthly things means to go down on one's knees and do obeisance to Satan.[27] As a liar and the father of lies (John 8:44b), he shamelessly hides behind idols to anesthetize the unsuspecting human spirit into the slumber of ignorance and delusion, trip wiring it away from the truth (2 Tim 3:13). It will suffice to recall the alarming rise in cases of demonic possession these days, given the many ways by which one can become embroiled with the devil, eventually turning the person into the reality that he or she worships (Ps 115:8).

24. Cf. his 1986 encyclical letter *Dominum et vivificantem*, §32.

25. A narrative prolepsis toward the list of merchandise commercialized in the mighty yet fallen city, Babylon the great (18:2, 10–12).

26. E.g., Cf. Deut 4:28; Isa 2:8; 44:9–20; Ezek 22:1–4; Dan 5:4, 23; Hos 13:2; Pss 115:4; 135:15–17; Wis 13:10–15:17.

27. Cf. AvS, 341.

Most consternating, however, is that the vast majority remains impenitent. If a third lost their lives already at v. 18, then the rest of humankind not killed by those plagues logically amounts to a prodigious two thirds of all men and women on earth. This wholesale failure to be remorseful is foreshadowed by Pharaoh's unchanged heart following the slaughter of the firstborn after the tenth Egyptian plague (Exod 14:8). It also prepares for a necessary final judgment of incorrigible sinners (Wis 12:10–12). Likewise, only a remnant of the covenanted people believed in Jesus, the arriving Messiah, and that less than a majority will find eternal salvation must be considered a possibility, given his unambivalent teaching about the narrow gate and the hard road found only by a few (Matt 7:13–14; cf. Luke 18:8). And so, just as there are dark spots on the surface of the sun, likewise there are always areas in one's soul that tend to resist thorough evangelization, penance, and positive change. Those unrepentant recesses of the human heart should be a spiritual focus of ours. God is not only the giver of unmerited graces of conversion (Wis 12:19), but he himself turns away from his wrath when noticing a penitent heart (Jonah 3:10). All of which should be encouragement enough for us to have heartfelt sorrow for our sins, to listen to God's transformative voice (Ps 95:8), and to embrace the present moment as an opportunity to cooperate with the gift of his grace: "See, now is the acceptable time; see, now is the day of salvation!" (2 Cor 6:2).

Repentance refused (9:21)

[21]*And they did not repent of their murders or their sorceries or their fornication or their thefts.*

Not left unanswered is the question regarding the actual transgressions from which we are supposed to turn away: vv. 20–21 enumerate certain offenses that by their language hark back to the Old Testament and are representative of all human sin. While v. 20 could be characterized as an allusion to the first commandment of the decalogue, located on the first tablet and declaring the three principal sins against God (Exod 20:2–5), v. 21 is a singular rendering of some sins written on the second tablet, displaying the violations of neighborly charity.[28] By repeating in both verses the fact that surviving humanity does not

28. Surprisingly, the sacred author inserts "sorceries" after "murders," and he is also the only one to use the noun *porneía* (πορνεία, "fornication") instead of the verb *moicheýō* (μοιχεύω, "to commit adultery"); apart from these peculiar traits, his sequence of sins is similar

repent, a synthetic parallelism is brought about, rounding out the structure of the Ten Commandments, and anticipating a definitive exclusion of those transgressions from the New Jerusalem.[29]

A list of four serious sins is welded together by the vigorous negation "not" and "also not" (*non, neque*). Thus, despite all the intervening terror, humans do not repent from the heartbreaking legacy of Cain, the first in a continuous line of people who have shed their brethren's blood like that of Abel, in the final analysis attributable to the devil himself as the murderer from the beginning (John 8:44). Likewise mentioned in the ominous plural are sorceries, featured here as an extension, so to speak, of the sins of the first tablet in v. 20. To the ancient Greeks, the word *phármakos*[30] would have evoked anything from drug, medicine, poison,[31] enchantment, or aphrodisiac potion, to witchcraft, magic, charm, spell, or divination. It stood for the diabolical allure of inducing illusions and hallucinations in the search for power, knowledge, and pleasure derived from invisible worlds. One connotation, however, is of topical interest, and that is its association with abortifacient drugs in pagan and early Christian writings (Gal 5:20), where it is denounced among the works of the flesh.[32] If taken in that sense, that is, an innuendo to the grave moral evil of abortion,[33] it is quite fittingly placed here between murders and fornication as sins against one's neighbor.

The second-last offense listed is sexual impurity (*porneía*, πορνεία, *fornicatio*) parsed in the grammatical singular, amidst three plurals, to indicate that those lacking purity of heart indulge in one ongoing immoral act. Closing out this sorry lineup of transgressions against God's commandments are thefts, which lay bare somebody's covetousness and greed as the very essence of worldliness and moral bankruptcy. Tellingly, Paul ties it to fornication and idolatry itself (Eph 5:5; Col 3:5). And yet, even the inner torment and shame of thievery fails to bring evildoers to repentance. These last two are also contained

to the Hebrew original (Exod 20:13–15; Deut 5:17–19; Matt 19:18; Mark 10:19), but distinct from the Septuagint version, followed by Luke 18:20; Rom 13:9.

29. At 21:8 and 22:15, John will reference the persons who commit these sins, presenting them in yet another order, namely, murderers, fornicators, sorcerers, and idolaters.

30. This noun *phármakos* (φάρμακος, 21:8; 22:15) was originally used of people using drugs and religious incantations, called poisoners, sorcerers, or magicians. The related noun *pharmakeía* (φαρμακεία) pointed to the practice of using drugs, spells, or medicine for magical enchantment (18:23; Gal 5:20).

31. See the Neo-Vulgate's *venefícium*, meaning "venom."

32. Cf. Michael J. Gorman, *Abortion and the Early Church* (Downers Grove, IL: InterVarsity Press, 1982), 48.

33. Cf. *CCC*, §§2270–75.

in the catechetical list of capital or deadly sins. Undoubtedly, the surrounding pre-Christian society of his time with its excesses and debaucheries must have been on John's mind when prophesied that those vices will be perpetuated through the ages despite advancing cultures and civilizations.

Spiritual evils will afflict the ungodly soul in this life and give it a foretaste of its doom in the life to come. Sin frequently brings immediate unrest and trouble in its train. And since all sins are interrelated,[34] there is no viable compromise and no substitution for repentance. The sins enumerated in this verse all spring from a mind that is self-centered in glaring contrast to the selfless life of our Lord Jesus.[35] Uncompromising loyalty to the Church will keep him in the center of our heart and preserve us from the spiritual adultery of idolatry.[36]

In closing the reflections on these first six trumpets, we realize that they serve as a wake-up call to each one of us, a call to repentance. Each trumpet blast builds up anticipation and relentlessly brings with it a plague of a more disastrous nature than the one before it. That the narrative plot of the Apocalypse is not sequential but complementary or recapitulatory is proven also by the repeated descriptions of the same final period before Jesus returns, in this case the devil's release before the end of time, depicted again at 13:1–8, 16:12–14, and 20:7–9. Like a good mother giving loving guidance to her child or pleading with it to avoid danger, Revelation repeatedly nudges the soul to stay alert, to be willing to return to our Savior with acts of penance. That return will give joy and compassion to the Father's heart (Luke 15:7, 32). And if he permits the star to fall (v. 1), then he will also grant many graces to endure and to overcome every test.

34. Just as there is a connection among all the mysteries of our faith (*nexus mysteriorum*), there also exists a link among all the sins and vices (*nexus vitiorum*).

35. Cf. AvS, 342.

36. Cf. *CCC*, §2380.

10:1–11, Another interlude: Renewed prophecy

Christomorphic life (10:1–3)

> [1]*And I saw another mighty angel coming down from heaven, wrapped in a cloud, with a rainbow over his head; his face was like the sun, and his legs like pillars of fire.* [2]*He held a little scroll open in his hand. Setting his right foot on the sea and his left foot on the land,* [3]*he gave a great shout, like a lion roaring. And when he shouted, the seven thunders sounded.*

Narratively still part and parcel of the second aquiline woe, 10:1–11:14 represents another interlude, which, much like the previous one (7:1–8:5), is composed of a dual scene. First, there is the interstitial vision of a Christlike angel in 10:1–11, followed by the scene of two unknown witnesses at 11:1–13, trending toward the days when the seventh angel will blow his trumpet (11:15), a moment foretold as the grand consummation of God's mystery (10:7). These two pairs of twofold visions, the former mainly in heaven, the latter taking place on earth, rather than being merely parenthetical to the storyline, are intended to heighten the reader's suspense, but also to mark a steady transition from the sixth to the culminating seventh element of each septet, seals and trumpets. Not so much narrative digressions, they seem to run parallel to the main plot, showing forth the simultaneous and mutually conflicted realities of wickedness (6:1–17; 8:6–9:21) and godliness (7:1–8:5; 10:1–11:13) in the world. By inserting this second interlude, John once more breaks the septenary rhythm, interlocking the first with the second half of his book. This narrative device is augmented, as it were, by the visionary being recommissioned to prophesy before the inhabitants of the earth (cf. 10:11).[1]

All attention is now arrested by this new vision, so magnificent as if a new covenant or revelation were about to occur in the world. Descending from above is the most majestic angel in the entire Apocalypse, bearing a close affinity with

1. Cf. Beale, *Book of Revelation*, 520.

the ones in 1:1, 5:2, and 22:6, 8–10, so far removed from a petite baroque cherub. While clearly drawing on the imagery of Daniel 10–12, and inspired by what he saw during the inaugural vision (1:12–16), John models this angel on the same glorious insignia with which the Old Testament depicts Yahweh, and the New Testament presents the Son of God and Son of Man. Commentators have recognized the divine and Christic attributes of this angelic spirit, perfectly fused into an entity that can only be defined as an angelo-morphic Christ or a Christo-morphic angel, meaning, Jesus described with angel attributes or an angel looking like the God-Man.[2] Such a mystifying identity carries on the biblical tradition of the Angel of the Lord,[3] and prepares for the multifaceted nature of the apparitions of the cosmic woman as Eve, Israel, Mary, and the Church in ch. 12, as well as of the renewed cosmos as a Holy City, New Jerusalem, Bride of the Lamb, and re-found Paradise all at the same time, at 21:1–22:5. And if Paul exhorts us to put aside the old man and clothe ourselves with Christ (Rom 13:14) to partake in his identity as a new creation (2 Cor 5:17), let us meditate on the upcoming symbolism as an invitation to embrace a Christomorphic life.

This descending angel establishes an immediate rapport not only to 5:2 (see also 7:2; 8:3; 18:1; 20:1), but to that entire chapter as well. While the Greek verb for this solemn descent, *katabaínō* (καταβαίνω), dissociates him from the cataclysmal fall of the star at 9:1, it also associates him with the incarnational Verbum in the Fourth Gospel (e.g., John 3:13). It implies, too, that in the meantime the seer's visionary field has moved from heaven (4:1–2) back to the earth, continuing the oscillation of scenes between heaven, earth, and netherworld, between above and below, and between consolation and desolation. This angel is one of only three in the Apocalypse characterized as "mighty" (5:2; 18:21), making it possible that he is either the archangel Gabriel, whose name means "Strength of God" in Hebrew, or Michael, "Who is like God?" This power of his suggests that the mission to be accomplished is arduous, beyond mere human strength, and requires the overcoming of tremendous obstacles. In his coming down from on high he reassures us not only of the accessibility of the Divine, but also that the close of the eschaton is ever imminent. Discerning Christ in this figure, we are inspired to find strength in him, and to take care to remain available to our brethren in the Church by good works.

2. Cf. RD, 1005.

3. This harbinger of the Most High (Hebrew *malakh Yahweh*, מַלְאַךְ יְהוָה; Septuagint *ággelos Kyríou*, ἄγγελος Κυρίου) is a heavenly being appearing in the Old Testament on behalf of, and essentially indistinguishable from, the God of Israel, often referring to himself as divine in the first person (e.g., Gen 16:7–12).

This imposing angel is surrounded by four features associated with the sky through which he traveled on his way to earth, namely, cloud, rainbow, sun, and fire (v. 1). And so, what catches John's eye right away is that he wraps himself in a cloud like a glorious garment.[4] It also indicates God's protecting and guiding presence with his covenanted people (Exod 13:21), as well as his future coming as Judge (Matt 24:30). We are reminded of God's immanence in human hearts as in a temple (1 Cor 6:19), honoring him by a life of virtue, always watchful and mindful of the final judgment.

Next, there is an awesome rainbow, resumed from 4:3 (Ezek 1:28), spanning over the angel's head and signalizing that Jesus has taken over the reins of the Father, fulfilling his covenant-promise of reconciliation and peace for all generations (Gen 9:11–17). This aesthetic detail should inspire us to share in the Holy Spirit's faithfulness and patient mercy toward the repentant soul. Furthermore, the angel's face shining as the sun evokes the transfigured Lord on Tabor (Matt 17:2; see also Rev 1:16). And as Moses' face glowed in the radiance of Yahweh's own light (Exod 34:29–30), we are called to mirror Christ, the Sun of Justice (Mal 4:2), in our mind and body. Reflecting his light and warmth into this world and toward our neighbor, we do our part in the spiritual growth of the Christian community until we reach together our destination in heaven (Matt 13:43).[5]

An additional trait are the angel's legs[6] like columns of fire. This theophanic blaze recalls the giving of God's Torah on Mount Sinai (Exod 19:18), but also his illuminating and shepherding presence among the Israelites in the wilderness (Exod 13:21–22). These flaming columns symbolize the preaching of Christ's Gospel in the power of the Spirit,[7] encouraging each one of his followers to be ever ready to evangelize in communion with the Church, spreading the truth in love (Eph 4:15).

In the hand of this Christoform messenger there is a little scroll completely opened (v. 2). It is probably his left hand since he will soon raise his right hand to heaven (v. 5). To describe the scroll, John employs a noun that is exclusive to Revelation, namely, the diminutive (*biblarídion*; vv. 9–10) of a diminutive (*biblárion*) of a diminutive (*biblíon*; v. 8) of the regular *bíblos* (βίβλος),[8] a triple

4. Interpreted by Rupert as Christ's incarnational flesh (cf. RD, 1005), and by Adrienne as an indicator of his Mystical Body, the Church (cf. AvS, 343).

5. Cf. RD, 1006; AvS, 343.

6. Literally, "feet" (*pódes*, πόδες; *pedes*).

7. Cf. RD, 1006; AvS, 343.

8. Or rather *býblos* (βύβλος, possibly so called from the name of the Phoenician sea port Byblos), originally referring to the inner bark of a papyrus plant out of which paper was man-

diminutive, therefore, to capture the extraordinary smallness of this book, literally, a little papyrus-roll, or a miniature Bible (*libellum*), so to speak. Imagine just for a moment the extreme contrast between this tiny booklet and the gargantuan stature of the angel holding it! It looks purposely bite-sized since he will swallow it in v. 10, distinguishing it from the scroll of 5:1 that was not ingested but rather unsealed by the Lamb.[9] Perhaps it functions as a spiritual link between that one and the book of life (3:5), which in turn relates to the tree of life (2:7), the crown of life (2:10), the water of life (7:17), and the breath of life (11:11). In its bold disclosure it embodies the Gospel, which the followers of Christ love to internalize and by which they live. And it is no exaggeration to say that in every age the devout study of the Word of God has lent freshness to forgotten truths, has saved countless souls from the bondage of spiritual blindness, and has given rise to courageous witness for the Lord Jesus in this world.

John then watches this angelic colossus set his right foot on the sea and his left foot on the land (v. 2). Sea and land, reiterated four times in this chapter (vv. 5–6, 8),[10] are meant as *pars pro toto* to show the global extent of his mission, the universality of the Church's message, but also her dominance over the beasts rising out of the sea (13:1) and out of the earth (13:11). Like an indomitable conqueror taking possession of the whole world, the angel's fiery feet are firmly planted on its soil, and a spiritual storm of conquest is bound to be set off through the power of Christ. And in imitation of the Lord and his angel, each of us are called to make him known to all.[11] This is precisely his great shout like a lion (v. 3),[12] the cry of the dying Savior on the Cross (Mark 15:34), making hell tremble and heaven burst open, through an ever new and universal evangelization.[13] In response to the angel's booming voice there is the deafening sound of seven thunders,[14] that is, the clarion call of the Holy Spirit and his seven gifts, suffused in the preaching of all the saints. In the end, this angelo-morphic

ufactured; later, it connoted a scroll or a book. It is the very first word of the New Testament (Matt 1:1).

9. Cf. RD, 1006.

10. Depicting the Creator, their order is reversed into earth and sea in v. 6.

11. Cf. AvS, 344.

12. The verb *mykáomai* (μυκάομαι, *rugire*), occurring only here in Scripture, expresses the bellowing of a bull; Peter instead uses *ōrýomai* (ὠρύομαι, "to growl as a beast") to describe the roar of the lion (1 Pet 5:8).

13. Cf. RD, 1008.

14. Adding to the long list of seventeen septenaries in Revelation, i.e., churches (1:4), spirits (1:4), lampstands (1:12), stars (1:16), torches (4:5), seals (5:1), horns (5:6), eyes (5:6), angels (8:2), trumpets (8:2), thousands (11:13), heads (12:3), diadems (12:3), plagues (15:1), bowls (15:7), mountains (17:9), and kings (17:10).

Christ stirs our conscience and confirms our heart with these signs of power, truth, and love.

Hidden from your eyes (10:4)

[4]*And when the seven thunders had sounded, I was about to write, but I heard a voice from heaven saying, "Seal up what the seven thunders have said, and do not write it down."*

At first, the command from heaven to seal up seems puzzling, since whatever this blend of lion's roar and seven thunders may have been, it was perfectly intelligible[15] to John, and he was on the verge of writing down their utterances, which, by their very nature must have been of fearsome import. This episode proves that he has grown into the habit of recording his visions right at the moment they came to him or as soon as practicable, in accordance with the instruction at 1:11, 19. Now, however, an interruption is imposed, and by simply not taking notes he seals the content of the vision, evoking the prophet Daniel (Dan 12:4), yet contrary to 22:10. In absolute exclusivity, the message remains buried in the visionary's mind and heart, at least for now. That concealment is conveyed by another tautology, so characteristic of John's literary style: "Seal up—do not write it down!"[16] Hence, we are left in the dark concerning this message and, for that matter, the reason for suppressing it, a circumstance, nevertheless, that can lend itself to a spiritual reflection. Indisputably, the Lord has the right to reserve certain mystical experiences to the apostle only,[17] insights that are meant for him alone. On a narrative plane, this message may as well have been synchronous to the previous septets in a way that nothing new had been revealed at this instance, after all. There may also be the aspect of God graciously revoking and canceling his judgments, or, in his tender sympathy with our feeble condition as earthlings, not wishing to disclose terrifying things of the future. It is also conceivable that it relates to Jesus' own caution not to share mysteries with the unworthy: "Do not give what is holy to dogs; and do not throw your pearls before swine, or they will trample them under foot and turn and maul you" (Matt 7:6).

15. That familiarity is also expressed by the triple repetition of the definite article before the "seven thunders" (*hai heptá brontaí*, αἱ ἑπτὰ βρονταί), unlike at 19:6.

16. Since these seemingly redundant reiterations also signal advancement of thought or plot, Resseguie terms them "two-step progressions," cf. *Revelation*, 23–25.

17. Cf. AvS, 346.

More importantly, and akin to the primarily Markan motif of the Messianic Secret (e.g., Mark 1:43–45), by concealing himself and not revealing all his purposes, God keeps us depending on him. In many respects he remains the *Deus absconditus*, veritably a hidden God (Isa 45:15; cf. Rev 2:17), although on a surface level this may seem contrary to the obvious logic of this Book of Revelation. For us his creatures, there will always be that spiritual and intellectual struggle to accept his hiddenness, fundamental unknowability, and ineffability, spurring us on to discover him through humble prayer and meditation, and scrutinizing the historical traces of his divine actions, but in the end always acknowledging the subjective limit of our human knowledge. This concept became particularly relevant for great thinkers such as Clement of Alexandria,[18] Nicholas of Cusa,[19] and Blaise Pascal.[20] It also keeps us vigilant and prudent in our ongoing discernment of his perfect will, as Jesus attested to amidst tears: "If you, even you, had only recognized on this day the things that make for peace! But now they are hidden from your eyes" (Luke 19:42). Not to mention that our union with the Lord makes us partake in a mystical way in his concealment: "You have died, and your life is hidden with Christ in God" (Col 3:3). What remains for now is the sobering realization that we are metaphysically incapable of wholly grasping the mystery of God, leading us to appreciate the collective effort of Christians across the ages to receive, ponder, and share sacred knowledge throughout the eschaton (John 16:12–13).

Angel of time (10:5–6)

[5] Then the angel whom I saw standing on the sea and the land raised his right hand to heaven [6] and swore by him who lives forever and ever, who created heaven and what is in it, the earth and what is in it, and the sea and what is in it: "There will be no more delay."

Fixing his interior and inspired eyes again on this mighty angel, John observes how he is touching the three parts of the universe, i.e., air, earth, and water, descriptive of the entire cosmos (Dan 12:7). By pronouncing an oath to God eternal and almighty, he appeals to him as the supreme witness, as the One who

18. Proposing an apophatic approach to theology, also known as *via negativa* (cf. his writing *Protrepticus*); in his work *Stromata* he expresses an epistemological and empirical skepticism.

19. Cf. his minor works *De docta ignorantia* (1440), *De Deo abscondito* (1444), and *De quaerendo Deum* (1445).

20. Cf. *Pensées* (first published in 1670), 4.242–43.

is acquainted with the truth of what is said, and who will punish whosoever dares to swear in falsehood. To give it greater solemnity, and to honor God's will, the angel points his hand upwards to the Lord's dwelling place, establishing a figurative bridge toward him who in his everlasting power can reward or sanction according to the fidelity to the oath.[21] His direct speech in proclaiming the oath begins with a warning: "There will be no more delay!" (cf. Heb 10:37). Whereas the angel with the seal of the living God demands a grace period before the opening of the seventh seal to spiritually immunize the servants of God (7:2–3), this angel, on the contrary, denies any further room for repentance or respite for the ungodly, before the sounding of the seventh trumpet. This renewed urgency aligns itself with similar reminders of the relative shortness of time and opportunity to save one's soul (1:3; 12:12; 22:10), declaring that the judgment is near, just as Jesus himself inculcates the imminence of the final judgment (Matt 24:22). It should, however, also be tempered by the martyrs' cry for vengeance and their being told to rest a little longer (6:10–11). There are other indications, too, regarding God's enduring patience with the sinner (2:21), with the pilgrim Church (12:14; cf. Dan 12:7), and with Satan's scheme to carry on testing humankind, allowing him to be released for a little while as late as in 20:3. Peter explains this parousiac delay in these terms: "The Lord is not slow about his promise, as some think of slowness, but is patient with you, not wanting any to perish, but all to come to repentance" (2 Pet 3:9).

As intriguing as the complicated question of an eschatological delay may sound, there is a different angle to the warning "There will be no more delay," and to get to the bottom of it, one must analyze the original Greek which literally states, "Time no more shall be."[22] When read in this key, the phrase becomes more of a formal announcement of the outright cessation of time on the boundaries of world history, and consequently the start of eternity. This is not only logical in light of the successive v. 7, highlighting the consummation of God's designs,[23] but also complements the directly preceding cosmic description of the Creator as "the Living one for all ages" (*Viventem in saecula*). Jesus' self-designation further underscores the sovereign demarcation of time by him alone: "I am the Alpha and the Omega, the First and the Last, the Beginning and the End" (22:13). What is also eloquent in this regard is the choice of the

21. Cf. RD, 1011–12; AvS, 347.

22. Rendering the future indicative in *chrónos oukéti éstai* (χρόνος οὐκέτι ἔσται, *tempus amplius non erit*) in all its syntactic expressivity, including the emphatic placement of "time" at the beginning of the clause.

23. Cf. AvS, 349.

noun *chrónos* (χρόνος[24]) over *kairós* (καιρός[25]) here, two very distinct concepts in the Greek language, further suggesting that John has in mind the mystery of the eventual termination of time as we know it, and its being replaced by otherworldly timelessness. Although a dictionary definition of "time" may sound straightforward,[26] luminaries like St. Augustine of Hippo found the concept of time exceedingly challenging, and struggled to explain its aspects of mutability, rapidity, transitoriness, uniqueness, irreversibility, as well as its absolute beginning and its travel toward a definitive goal.[27]

Hence, some call the mighty messenger of 10:1 the Angel of Time since he indicates the closing epoch of the ages. If the Judeo-Christian patrimony views time as rectilinear and directional,[28] beginning with the act of creation by God, then this oath portrays its purposeful or teleological ending on the eschatological frontier. And while there may be a symbolic correlation between the elevated right hand of oath (v. 5) and the angel's right foot set on the waters of the sea (v. 2), intimating the fluctuation and instability of our human comprehension of the realities of time and eternity, one thing is certain, the apparent deferral of the Lord's parousia should never lower our fervent expectations, lessen our watchfulness, or limit our prayerful perseverance. Colloquially speaking, it is not "wither and die," but "grow and live!" Applied to our personal existence here below, we remain conscious of the fact that our own days are numbered, and the opportunities to return to the Lord are not unlimited.[29] May this biblical word motivate us to treasure every minute of *chrónos* that God grants us in this world as *kairós*, and spend it well by doing good (Acts 10:38), knowing that the Angel of Time has already spoken.

24. Identified in Hellenic mythology as personified time, commonly depicted as an old, wise man with a long, gray beard, the quintessential Father Time; the word itself denotes the numeric clock time or chronology (cf. 2:21; 20:3).

25. Etymologically associated with both archery and weaving, implying the moment an arrow is dispatched toward a target, or again, the instant the shuttle passes the thread on the loom; this noun signals the opportune season to live rightly (cf. 1:3; 11:18; 12:12, 14; 22:10).

26. As the continued sequence of existence and events occurring in an irreversible succession from the past, through the present, into the future, often referred to as a fourth dimension, accompanying the three spatial dimensions.

27. He ends up calling time a distention of the mind by which we simultaneously grasp the past in memory, the present by attention, and the future by expectation (cf. *Confessions*, 11; *De civitate Dei*, 12).

28. Unlike many ancient cultures (e.g., Babylonian, Greek, Incan, Mayan, Hindu, Buddhist) that propose the concept of a wheel of time, envisioning cyclical ages of the universe and of human life.

29. Cf. RD, 1013.

Mystery to fulfill (10:7)

[7]"But in the days when the seventh angel is to blow his trumpet, the mystery of God will be fulfilled, as he announced to his servants the prophets."

By now it has become abundantly apparent that the apostolic exile on Patmos constantly interweaves the narrative by recalling or anticipating various scenes. One such example is this verse, foretelling the days when the seventh angel is to blow his trumpet, which functions as a prolepsis toward 11:15–19.[30] When reading both passages together one learns that the consummation of God's mystery has to do with the beginning of the everlasting Kingdom of Christ (11:15), coinciding with the final judgment of the dead and the rewarding of his servants with the joys of heaven. This happens to be the blueprint for the remainder of this book, referring to the end of the present age when the forces of evil will be put down (17:1–19:4, 11–21; 20:7–10), and the establishment of God's reign when all will be created anew (21:1–22:5). Thus, the joyful completion of his mystery precedes his wrath (15:1), and even in 17:17 is pointed out as still in the future, further underlining the meta-chronological storyline of Revelation. Paul's prophetic word at 1 Corinthians 15:51–52 is a remarkable parallel to and confirmation of it. Yet, whenever he and the Synoptics speak of the "mystery," they tie it to its logical counterpart of "knowledge," meaning that the hidden designs of God can only be known by a divine act of lifting the secret (Matt 13:11).

Here, however, "mystery" (*mysterium*, cf. 1:20; 17:5, 7) is lexically somewhat mismatched with the notion of fulfillment (*consummare*), rather counterintuitive to the more logical correlation between mystery and revelation. According to Colossians 2:2, that mystery of God is Christ himself, which evokes another parallel, this time with Golgotha: describing the hour of Jesus' death, the Evangelist who stood at the foot of the Cross remembers that, before bowing his head and giving up his spirit, Jesus said "It is finished" (John 19:30), using that selfsame phrase, *consummatum est*, as here. And there seems to be a spiritual lesson contained in this biblical context: human etiology and teleology can superficially grasp a revealed divine mystery but can never fully comprehend it, and thus, like at 10:4, it is ultimately not about understanding everything, but about fulfilling the mysterious will of God. As Christians, we

30. Such a representation of an event as existing before it actually comes to pass is typical also of John's Gospel.

do so by daily uniting our lives to that of the Crucified Lord, experiencing with him the *Consummatum est,* as illustrated in the epistle to the Hebrews: "It was fitting that God, for whom and through whom all things exist, in bringing many children to glory, should make the pioneer of their salvation perfect (*consummare*) through sufferings" (Heb 2:10).

Paradoxically, even though the seventh trumpet has yet to sound in the future (11:15), the angel's oath speaks of the mystery's completion in the prophetic past, or rather the Greek aorist tense to be exact, and in the divine passive voice, i.e., *etelésthē* (ἐτελέσθη, *consummatum est,* v. 7b[31]), communicating the idea that God will be the one who fulfills the mystery of his will in us. Like an antique navigation telescope, extending out one stage at a time to eventually function at full capacity, so also in our spirituality, by resigning ourselves to the Cross, enduring the adversities of life, and conforming our will to Christ's in keeping his commandments (John 14:15, 21), we will gradually fulfill God's mystery. One might add that the perfecting force in this process will always be love (1 John 4:12, 17–18), which is at the same time the path and the goal. This is what is meant by God announcing the good news[32] *to* his servants the prophets (cf. 1:1; 22:6), and not just *through* or *by* them to others. To sum up, the consummation of God's mystery declared in this verse comes true in our lives not so much by trying to comprehend one and all supernatural secrets, but rather by intertwining our will with that of our dying Savior, breathing our *consummatum est* with him and in him, and so obtaining the Kingdom.

Sweet ingestion for bitter digestion (10:8–10)

8 Then the voice that I had heard from heaven spoke to me again, saying, "Go, take the scroll that is open in the hand of the angel who is standing on the sea and on the land." 9 So I went to the angel and told him to give me the little scroll; and he said to me, "Take it, and eat; it will be bitter to your stomach, but sweet as honey in your mouth." 10 So I took the little scroll from the hand of the angel and ate it; it was sweet as honey in my mouth, but when I had eaten it, my stomach was made bitter.

---

31. Apparently to smooth over this textual solecism, the Vulgate had the future tense, *consummabitur,* to keep it synchronous with the future trumpet blast.

32. Literally, "God evangelized the prophets," a textual roughness that was harmonized in the Vulgate by adding the preposition *per*: "He announced *through* his servants the prophets."

Among the most eye-catching interactions between the apostle and the supernatural world during his visions is this scene narrated in vv. 8–11.[33] The fact that he is both witness to and a character actively involved within the story makes him a homodiegetic narrator, solidifying the credibility of his narration.[34] It is both intensive and extensive in that it involves, more than anywhere else, the physical senses of his body: he listens, walks, speaks to the angelic expositor, takes, eats, digests, and reacts to the saccharine and acerbic sensations in his mouth and stomach. It is at the same time an enlivening and delaying interstice, and the course of visions will not resume until he has accomplished what is asked of him, namely, to retrieve the little scroll from the angel's left hand and swallow it. But without further ado, let us point out some possible spiritual ramifications of this captivating episode, starting with our own attentiveness to the inner voice of God reverberating especially in our personal moral conscience. Then there is also the perfect way in which John is available to and bound by the will of God, like the pure souls in heaven, able to execute it with docility and ease.[35] In that profound serenity of mind, he does not hesitate to draw near an angelic spirit and to address him fearlessly, while other distinguished personages in the Old Testament fainted in the presence of angels (e.g., Dan 8:17–18). Such marvelous vivacity reminds us of the ritual aspects of our Christian religion, inspiring us to infuse with meaning, for instance, the liturgical moments when we genuflect, kneel, fold our hands, raise our voices to praise God, or rise to listen to the Gospel.

Symbolically pregnant, too, is the complete swallowing of the little booklet in v. 10,[36] an image derived from the prophets Ezekiel (Ezek 2:9–10; 3:1–3) and Jeremiah (Jer 15:16). If we presume it to be the word of God, then consuming it means to feed the soul, to eat the bread of angels (Ps 78:25), and to completely master its content. This internalization also links the two New Testaments, that is, the one of the Word and the one of the Body and Blood of

33. The other eight occasions are 1:12, 17 (turning around and falling down at Jesus' feet, touched by his hand), 4:1 (spiritual rapture into heaven), 7:13–14 (dialogue with one of elders), 11:1 (given a measuring rod with an angelic allocution), 17:1–3 (angelic allocution and carried away into the wilderness), 19:9–10 (angelic allocution, prostration), 21:9–10 (transported by an angel unto a high mountain), and 22:6–10 (allocution, prostration).

34. Cf. Lourdes García Ureña, *Narrative and Drama in the Book of Revelation: A Literary Approach*, trans. Donald Murphy (New York: Cambridge University Press, 2019), 188.

35. Cf. AvS, 351.

36. The Greek reiterates the compound verb *kataphágō* (καταφάγω) in vv. 9–10, meaning "to devour, eat up entirely, swallow in a hurry, consume with eagerness or passion" (cf. 11:5; 12:4; 20:9; Matt 13:4; John 2:17).

the Lord (1 Cor 11:25). As we develop a spiritual hunger and thirst concerning Holy Scripture, we do well to continually absorb it within the intimate space of our hearts. Digesting, accepting, and assimilating its message, without picking and choosing, strengthens us in our mission to spread it among our brothers and sisters (Ps 119:11–13).[37] It should be our goal to be not just familiar with God's word, but to be fully saturated with it to the point that it is no longer some fossilized code of laws, but a steady instinct, a second nature, something that becomes our marrow and blood. Before being able to bring it to the others in our communities, we must naturally first be impressed and penetrated with it ourselves.

Next, let us briefly meditate on the bittersweet[38] nature of this divine word. After taking the little scroll from the angel's hand and swallowing it, John feels a sweet taste like honey in his mouth (Pss 81:17; 119:103), yet it soon turns bitter in his stomach. This mixture of sensorial sweetness and bitterness in his body could be taken as an invitation to studiously attend to inner responses or reactions to the divine word in us, to discern interior joys and sorrows. Such discernment will be instrumental in overcoming a basic distaste for supernatural things due to the fallen state of the human soul, but also in neutralizing the satanic absinthe of personal sin that tends to embitter the waters of the heart (8:11).[39] Very relatable is this pleasant realization of God's wisdom unfortunately mixed with a deep-seated grief, albeit usually subliminal, as we anticipate personal suffering and death.[40] Being attentive to the inner movements of consolation and desolation, and opening oneself to the delights of putting the word of God into practice, necessarily implies embracing the hardships that go with a mature Christian vocation.

While the hope of a final victory is palatable, the lingering certainty of disappointments and sufferings will always be perceived as disagreeable and acrid. While Christ's word may give indigestion to carnal-minded people, to those who espouse it with sincerity of heart it will introduce them to the nuptial drama of lover and beloved: "With great delight I sat in his shadow, and his fruit was sweet to my taste" (Cant 2:3). What the taste buds feel when savoring delicious food is naturally short-lived, but the acidity affecting the gut is enduring; likewise, the Lord makes us relish his goodness in fleeting bursts of joy

37. Cf. RD, 1014.

38. Verses 9–10 present the threefold chiasm of "bitter-sweet/sweet-bitter," "stomach-mouth/mouth-stomach," and "sweet honey/honey-sweet."

39. Cf. AvS, 353.

40. Cf. RD, 1015.

from time to time, yet he also allows a lasting thorn in the flesh (2 Cor 12:7), compounded by the anguish of witnessing the rise of apostasy and immorality in our days. At first, it may be easy to accept God's will, but it can become quite difficult once the worldly pushback sets in,[41] bringing about the paradox of being comforted in mourning, of being blessed when hungering and thirsting for righteousness, and when being persecuted for righteousness (Matt 5:4, 6, 10). What should always prevail in mind and heart is the joyous anticipation of the eventual overthrow of the wicked and the subsequent deliverance of the saints, or, in other words, the fall of the old Babylon and the descent of the New Jerusalem.

Every person tasked with preaching the word of God is familiar with this taste, too, the simultaneous satisfaction and sickness of the stomach. Not without reason does the Old Testament characterize a prophetic utterance or oracle as a burden,[42] reflecting the encumbrance many prophets felt at their divine calling, investiture, and mission. There is no arguing that preaching the Gospel is a burdensome labor of love, and the exile on Patmos no doubt bore his personal share of suffering for it (1:9). Christian tradition has it that, after arriving in Rome from Ephesus during the reign of the notoriously cruel emperor Domitian, he was thrown into a cauldron of boiling oil. And after he was miraculously saved from sure death, the spectators witnessing it all at the Colosseum were converted to Christianity. By the same token, one should feel honored at having been chosen by the Lord to be an instrument of his peace: "O Master, let me not seek as much to be consoled as to console."[43] A person ready to endure bitterness in fidelity to God must not only be permeated by his teaching, but must also have attuned the palate of their heart to the sweetness of the Word in order to persuade the listeners. Also, the souls who are most enthusiastic in their Christian love for neighbor and who understand how delightful their vocation is, are the most likely to suffer this apocalyptic bitterness. Their very charity makes all failure bitter to bear; yet it is precisely through this unbloody martyrdom that the finest victories are won.

It is a winning trait that the visionary does not take anything without permission: "I went to the angel and told him to give me the little scroll" (v. 9). This humble and modest way of surrendering to higher authority must have inclined the Lord to impart on him the blessing, privilege, and faculty to become the inspired writer of the Fourth Gospel. And this is also why his *Evangelium* is

41. Cf. AvS, 355.

42. Hebrew *massā* (מַשָּׂא), e.g., Isa 13:1; Nah 1:1.

43. Cf. the anonymous text usually called the "Prayer of St. Francis of Assisi."

utterly trustworthy since it is born out of the bittersweet experience of having received it from on high. In a like manner, all the baptized, and especially the ordained ministers of the Word, bishops, priests, and deacons, should go to Christ, to have their eyes opened and their intellect enlightened, so that they may explain the salvific mystery to others. Since the mouth is not only the organ of eating but also of speaking, may all be empowered to proclaim Jesus with sweetness, as is so splendidly epitomized by the last of the Church Fathers, St. Bernard of Clairvaux, the *Doctor mellifluous*.[44] If spiritual bitterness accompanies the Word's reception, then one can be assured that even greater suavity resides in its proclamation to others (Ps 19:9–10).

Evangelize anew (10:11)

[11] *Then they said to me, "You must prophesy again about many peoples and nations and languages and kings."*

"Then they said to me": but who are "they"? "They" are probably a combination of the voice heard from heaven in vv. 4, 8, and that of the booklet-bearing angel, now coalescing into one message. Leaving the speaker unidentified is a common biblical feature, a reverential way of pointing to divine inspiration and impulse, amounting to an idiomatic "I was told (by God)." To "prophesy again" is the divine command that could be regarded as a renewed commissioning of the apostle, a new phase in his life, solemnly reenacting the directive given to him at 1:11, 19, mirroring Old Testament priestly and prophetic investitures (e.g., Jer 1:7–8). Certainly not without merit is the opinion that this prophecy alludes to his eventual release from exile in Patmos and his return to Ephesus, as well as to his subsequent writing of the Gospel during the last decade of the first century AD. In the absence of any further divine instruction to John, it is plausible that chs. 11–22 are the implementation of the command to prophesy again, not to mention the prophetic mission of the Church herself over the millennia ever since. In any event, the prompt emergence of God's witnesses in 11:3 give this verse the appearance of a narrative transition.

What follows is a one-of-a-kind list of audiences destined to hear his

44. Cf. the homonymous 1953 encyclical letter of Pius XII: "His teaching was drawn, almost exclusively, from the pages of Sacred Scripture and from the Fathers, which he had at hand day and night in his profound meditations." *Doctor mellifluous*, 91–118 in *The Last of the Fathers: Saint Bernard of Clairvaux and the Encyclical Letter* Doctor Mellifluus, trans. Thomas Merton (New York: Harcourt, Brace and Co., 1954), §3.

message, namely, many peoples and nations and languages and kings. Notwithstanding the other six analogous enumerations in Revelation,[45] this one is unique in that it includes "kings," conceivably a preparation for their prominent role in ch. 17. John becomes the herald of a universal Gospel that will affect all generations, quite dissimilar, for instance, from Ezekiel's mission exclusively to the exiled Israelites (Ezek 3:11), which is still reflected in Jesus' own declaration, "I was sent only to the lost sheep of the house of Israel" (Matt 15:24). Again, the inclusion of kings on this list also dramatizes the scope of the apostle's task, called to humbly speak truth to power. Which may explain the otherwise puzzling preposition "from above, over, upon" (*super*; cf. 13:7; 14:6) on which the list is predicated. Rather than preaching "to," "about," or even "against" humanity, the Church is proclaiming the Good News "from above," in the sense that her eternal truths are communicated from a divine vantage point, mediating between heaven and earth, between God and humankind (2 Cor 5:20; 1 Tim 2:5; Heb 9:15). There might also be the connotation of Christ, the Truth, having the upper hand eventually over all falsehood in this world. And in that sense, the preposition *super* becomes an image of supernatural triumph.

On a more personal plane, just as God recommissioned his servant John to prophesy again, so he is calling each one of us every day to follow him. It remains imperative to stay attuned to his voice, prepared to recognize and welcome even the slightest stimuli of his grace, aiding us in new beginnings, improvements, and course corrections. Once called in baptism or priestly ordination, the soul is required to respond daily to Christ's calling (John 10:27). That way the relationship with him will stay lively, growing ever more mystical and stronger as time goes on. St. John Paul II once spoke of the necessity of returning to the initial grace of our personal vocation by meditating on the boundless love of the Lord, who has looked at each of us and called us by name: "Follow me!" (Matt 9:9). Such an ongoing conversion naturally involves zeal, prayer, the regular confession of sins, and continuous engagement with our spirituality, which the Saint captions as "constant training" (*formatio permanens*).[46] Such faithful pondering of the magnitude of our Christian calling will not fail to increase the very efficacy of our mission, too. And what is my mission? Not just to see but also to proclaim the prophecy like John does, inviting people to study the Bible and to discover or rediscover its truly incomparable

45. Set either in the grammatical plural (7:9; 11:9; 17:15) or singular (5:9; 13:7; 14:6), they all contain four items: "people" (*populus*), "nation" (*gens* or *natio*), "language" (*lingua*), and "tribe" (*tribus* or *turba*).

46. Cf. *Letter to all the Priests on occasion of Holy Thursday* (1979), §10.

and global significance for the present time.[47] Every generation of Christians, laity and clergy alike, must "prophesy again" by doing their part in the new evangelization,[48] not least to quell the pernicious influence of heresy, syncretism, and agnosticism that unfortunately spring up in every culture and every era of human history.[49] In closing, one should recall St. Paul's own ardor: "I am not ashamed of the Gospel; it is the power of God for salvation to everyone who has faith, to the Jew first and also to the Greek" (Rom 1:16).

47. Cf. AvS, 356.
48. Cf. Paul VI's 1975 Apostolic Exhortation *Evangelii Nuntiandi*, §2.
49. Cf. RD, 1016.

11:1–14, *Ecclesia militans*

Full measure of his stature (11:1–2)

[1]Then I was given a measuring rod like a staff, and I was told, "Come and measure the temple of God and the altar and those who worship there, [2]but do not measure the court outside the temple; leave that out, for it is given over to the nations, and they will trample over the holy city for forty-two months.

Just as 8:1–5 formed the second portion of the twofold interludial vision begun in 7:1–17, so also here, 11:1–14 complements the first half of the visionary interval starting at 10:1, and preparing for the seventh angel to blow his woe-trumpet (11:15). Thus, for the second and last time, the sixth and seventh elements of a septenary are separated by a narrative intermission that results in heightened suspense. No such entr'acte will take place between the penultimate and final bowls (16:12, 17), as if to convey some of the eschatological urgency before the epilogue of human history in the fall of Babylon (ch. 17).

With that in mind, let us rejoin the apostolic seer and reflect on the mystical significance of his vision. He recalls being given a measuring rod like a staff (v. 1). Forthwith, this has the appearance of a dramatization, beginning with a seemingly impersonal transaction, although v. 3 will imply that the agent is Jesus himself. At first sight, what is handed to him is a single stalk of a reed plant,[1] allusive to a pen as an ordinary writing implement (3 John 13), or also to the very canon[2] of Scripture as a lasting rule of faith. Moreover, it reminds us of the Lord's meekness as the Servant of God who refuses to snap a bruised reed (Isa 42:3), and of his Passion, too, during which the soldiers forced a reed into his right hand similar to a scepter to mock his Kingship, and even struck

1. The Greek noun *kálamos* (κάλαμος, *calamus*), denotes a plant with a jointed hollow stalk, growing in wet grounds.

2. The noun being derived from the Hebrew *qanē* (קָנֶה), meaning "reed."

his head with it (Matt 27:29–30). Then, in his last hour on the Cross, they put a gall-soaked sponge on such a reed to hold it up to his mouth to drink, to enhance his agony to an extreme (Matt 27:48). Upon further observation, however, John compares this fragile reed to a sturdy rod, amplifying the original symbolism. This reed, therefore, has the convenience, straightness, and handiness of a walking staff, the efficacy of a scourging utensil, the semblance of a regal scepter, and the dignity of a prophet's or priest's staff. Thus, there may be an allusion to Christ's triple *munus* as King, Prophet, and Priest.

After receiving this rod, the apostle receives a fourfold command "Rise!," "measure!," "cast out!," and "do not measure" (vv. 1–2). After having walked up to the angel to receive the scroll (cf. 10:9), he had probably sat down to write, and the excitatory "rise!" makes him get up again to play an active part in his own vision. First, he is asked to measure the temple of God and the altar and those who worship there, putting his measuring device to good use as a surveyor's rule, his initial exercise of the recently renewed prophetic investiture (10:8–11). In general, measuring evokes an architect and workers involved in the construction of a building, or also a tailor who is crafting a garment from carefully measured pieces of cloth. Additionally, it implies admiration for God's wisdom expressed in his creation (Isa 40:12, 15). Also suggested is the act of protecting and preserving a property from impending harm. In Revelation, it seems to further develop the concept of sealing, too (7:2–3).

Temple,[3] altar, and worshipers symbolize the people of God, especially in its inward being, but also in its outward, earthly and empirical, existence, owned by him, and protected from danger and desecration.[4] Until it will be assessed again as the New Jerusalem, this time at the hands of one of the bowl-angels with a golden measuring device (21:9, 15–17), the Church will be continuously assembled by the Lord as her Builder (Heb 3:3), in fulfilment of the prophetic blueprint of Ezekiel's utopian temple (Ezek 40–48). As mentioned above, the authoritative gauge of evaluating the Church will forever be the person of our Lord Jesus himself, as well as his divine word. Only in him can the true spiritual dimensions of the faithful members and their priestly sacrifice

3. There are two nouns in the Greek New Testament that are rendered as "temple": the first, *hierón* (ἱερόν), indicates the whole sacred enclosure, including the outer courts, porticoes, and other edifices attached to the temple itself (Luke 2:27); the other, *naós* (ναός), used in vv. 1–2, 19, is the sanctuary proper, where God himself resides, the Holy of Holies (Luke 1:21). That distinction, however, is no longer reflected in the Neo-Vulgate which translates both terms as *templum*.

4. Foreshadowed by the *shekhinah* in the wilderness whose measurements are indicated at Exod 26–27; 30:1–10.

be calculated. Tellingly, John does not record the actual outcome of his measuring activity, since for now those measures are known only to God, whereas for us it remains the *Mystical* Body of Christ.[5]

What is made explicit, however, is the paramount worth of the liturgy suggested by the altar and the worshipers surrounding it. By persevering in liturgical prayer and celebrating the holy sacraments, the inner life of Christians will not only be preserved but also grow into their ideal proportions toward their completion as willed by God the Father, true temples of the Holy Spirit, under Christ's watchful eye (Eph 4:13). Another way of putting it is that the temple represents the norm of faith laid down by the Father; the altar intimates both the Son's work of salvation, and the human heart called to relive his oblation to the Father; and the worshippers signal the Holy Spirit who dwells in them and congregates them into the Church, who in turn eucharistically reenacts, as it were, the Incarnation.[6]

If before there was the sharp contrast between "sealed" (7:3) and "not sealed" (9:4), now it is the no less stark dialectic between "measured" and "not measured," viewed from a different angle and spiced up with a forewarning, that is, not to measure the court outside the temple: "Cast that out, for it is given over to the nations, and they will trample over the holy city for forty-two months" (v. 2). True to the symbolism of this extensive simile with its cluster of images (vv. 1–13), the unmeasured tenants of the court outside[7] and the nations[8] are one and the same, pointing to all unbelieving walks of life, subscribers to falsehood, people with dissembling hearts, the heretical enemies of the Church of Christ.[9] They may once have belonged to her, but have since apostatized and been cast out from her communion with the same force by which the Lord exorcised the demons during his earthly ministry.[10] They are now purposely neglected as if the divinely appointed time to repent had already run its course. All that remains to be done is to expel their mendacity and disbelief.[11] Several

5. Cf. RD, 1017.

6. Cf. AvS, 357.

7. The noun *aulḗ* (αὐλή, *atrium*) generally denotes the uncovered courtyard of an ancient Mediterranean house, and specifically the roofless part of the temple outside of the sanctuary enclosed by a wall.

8. The noun *éthnos* (ἔθνος, *gens*) in the New Testament usually means a people distinct from Israel, i.e., the Gentiles.

9. Cf. RD, 1018.

10. The verb *ekbállō* (ἐκβάλλω, *eícere foras*), meaning "to banish, throw out," is employed on both occasions (e.g., Matt 8:16).

11. Cf. AvS, 358.

passages in the Gospels can elucidate this image, namely, where Jesus raises the specter of the heirs of his Kingdom being thrown into the outer darkness, where there will be weeping and gnashing of teeth (Matt 8:12); where he drives out the merchants from the temple (Matt 21:12); as well as where he predicts that Jerusalem will be trodden underfoot by the Gentiles (Luke 21:24). For those idolaters and hypocrites who show extreme disdain by trampling on the Son of God (Heb 10:29), the tide will turn on that one day when he will tread the winepress of the Lord's wrath (19:15). In addition to "temple, altar, worshipers," the "holy city" signifies the members of the Church, too. Founded in the historical Jerusalem, she will eventually grow into a heavenly city, the New Jerusalem,[12] contradistinguished from the worldly and benighted "Babylon the great" (17:5).

Yet this desolating time of testing will be limited to a relatively short forty-two months (cf. 13:5),[13] a biblical metaphor for the entire arc of Church history between the first and second advents of the God-Man Jesus.[14] It matches with the one thousand two hundred sixty days of the upcoming two witnesses (v. 3) and the woman's refuge in the wilderness (12:6), which in turn is interchangeable with three and a half years (Luke 4:25), and three and a half days (vv. 9, 11). All of these temporal indications are modeled on the original expression coined by the prophet Daniel, namely, "a time, two times, and half a time" (Dan 7:25; cf. Rev 12:14).[15] This archetypal season of trial and oppression for God's people may see the opponent, Satan, at times get the upper hand, but the Lord of history reserves the last word of vindication to himself.[16]

What spiritual message can be drawn from all this? All justifiable preterist or futurist interpretations aside, let us come back to the measuring-rod, which is the Gospel and the Christian Creed as abiding benchmarks of faith: through John, the angel prompts each of us, "Rise and measure," namely, to appraise our own spiritual growth and progress. When all is said and done, there should be a deep-seated desire to attain to that measure of mind and heart that our Maker

12. Cf. *CCC*, §117.

13. See the three phases of fourteen Old Testament generations, totaling forty-two, and leading up to the birth of the Messiah (Matt 1:17); then there is also the arithmetic symbolism of dividing forty-two by seven, equaling six, which signifies that this eschatological era falls short of the completeness of seven, or forty-nine months.

14. Cf. AvS, 359.

15. Or half of the perfect numerical symbol seven, which also happens to be the duration of the persecution of the Jews by Antiochus IV Epiphanes (Dan 12:7).

16. Cf. Klemens Stock, *Das letzte Wort hat Gott: Apokalypse als Frohbotschaft* (Vienna: Tyrolia, 1985).

has thought for each one of us, his children, before the foundation of the world, not least by faithfully worshipping at the altar of the temple of God. It will be crucial to stay alert in this regard, although the spiritual result of this measuring, that is, the precise state of one's interior relationship with the Blessed Trinity, is mercifully and wisely withheld from our eyes for now. Only in heaven will the breadth and length and height and depth of the love of Christ in the saints be revealed (Eph 3:18–19), which is the proper stage to be measured again, this time by the angel with a golden reed (21:15–16).

Sent out two by two (11:3–4)

[3]*And I will grant my two witnesses authority to prophesy for one thousand two hundred sixty days, wearing sackcloth."* [4]*These are the two olive trees and the two lampstands that stand before the Lord of the earth.*

Continuing this dramatic allegory about the Church's mission in this world, Christ himself appears to share this prophecy[17] with John (v. 3). Further expanding the pool of ecclesial images, he now adjoins his two witnesses to the temple, altar, worshipers, and holy city (vv. 1–2), all together epitomizing the people of God. Hence, they should not be taken in the narrow literal sense of two individuals,[18] but rather be interpreted in the broadest logic of the Greek noun *mártys* (μάρτυς, *testis*), meaning an eye- or ear-witness, human or angelic (19:10), who truthfully testifies. Obviously, this take is inclusive of the ultimate expression of testimony in holy martyrdom. In short, they represent the life and work of Christians in all of history, testifying to their Lord during the eschaton of the pilgrim Church when often unspiritual world-powers seem dominant. Inevitably, their attestations will sharpen the antagonism between good and evil in the human conscience, anticipating the Lord's parousia.[19]

17. See the future tense *dṓsō* (δώσω, *dabo*) of divine determination, so to speak.

18. Past commentators have propounded an intriguing host of interpretations, including Abraham and Lot, Moses and Aaron, Moses and Elijah, Caleb and Joshua, Elijah and Elisha, Enoch and Elijah, Zerubbabel and Joshua, Ezra and Nehemiah, Haggai and Zechariah, Peter and Paul, Paul and Barnabas, Old and New Testaments, Torah and Prophets, Israel and Church, Jewish and Gentile Christians, Eastern and Western churches, interior and exterior Christian life, saints and martyrs (cf. RD, 1022), mercy and grace, body and soul, Francis and Dominic, as well as the Hearts of Jesus and Mary.

19. Cf. AvS, 360.

Surely not without purpose is the numeral "two," which, other than highlighting the perennial fewness of authentic Christians (Luke 12:32), conveys the biblical legality of two competent witnesses to establish the truth (Matt 18:16). In other words, the Church will be able to rely on a sufficient quorum of evidence in proclaiming the truth regarding faith and morals for one thousand two hundred sixty days (v. 3), which is the same image as the limited trials of forty-two months in v. 2. Furthermore, only one external trait of these witnesses is portrayed, namely, the wearing of sackcloth, not dissimilar from the Baptizer's garment of camel's hair (Matt 3:4), signaling that those who bear witness will do so in a spirit of penance. This archaic garb of prophets[20] symbolizes the multidimensionality of *metanoía*, that is, the followers of Jesus mortify themselves to atone for their own sins and for those of others. Thus, fasting and grieving will be emblematic of their mission, evoking again Jesus' beatitude of mourning and consolation (Matt 5:4).

Furthermore, these witnesses are also identified with the two olive trees and the two lampstands that stand before the Lord of the earth (v. 4). Two other figures can now be appended to the lengthening list of symbols referencing the Church, i.e., temple, altar, worshipers, holy city, olive trees, and lampstands. Borrowing from the prophet Zechariah, where the menorah-like lampstand represents Israel, and the two olive trees feeding the lamp refer to the priest Joshua and to the prince Zerubbabel, John alludes to the sacerdotal and regal nature of the Church, anointed to be the light of the world.[21] Oil reminds us of the gifts of the Holy Spirit, his mercy, healing, and peace,[22] whereas the tree brings to mind the momentous Pauline prophecy of Israel's salvation to complete the Body of Christ at the end of time (Rom 11:17, 24–26). Not to be overlooked are the hint at the agony in Gethsemane at the foot of the Mount of Olives in Jerusalem, as well as the undamaged fruitfulness (6:6) of those who remain in the presence of "the Lord of the earth" (v. 4), for, in due course, he will be given glory as the "God of heaven" (v. 13). Thus, God's grace makes us strong to achieve our work in the building of that more glorious spiritual temple, set upon the foundation of patriarchs and apostles (21:12, 14), having Jesus himself as its cornerstone (Ps 52:8).

20. The Greek noun *sákkos* (σάκκος, *saccus*) describes a coarse black cloth commonly made of animal hair, used for sacks, for straining, and for mourning garments (6:12; Elijah, 2 Kgs 1:8; Mark 1:6).

21. This image is applied to Sts. Peter and Paul in the hymn of the Office of Readings (Latin Liturgy of the Hours) on June 29.

22. Cf. RD, 1025–27.

Before moving on to the next segment of this prolonged ecclesial parable, let us briefly come back to those two witnesses. In biblical hindsight, there has constantly been a commissioning of God's chosen messengers two by two, culminating in Christ's sending his disciples ahead of him in pairs to every town and place where he himself intended to go (Luke 10:1). Unquestionably, even to this day he continues to send us forth two by two, knowing well that none of us can accomplish the task alone or apart from the wider Christian community. Instead, it will always be beneficial for us to pray for the willingness to partner with the brethren in the Church to embark on and execute the common mission. Among the many advantages, there is the mutual support offered, but also the need for the alliance of two different characters in the same effort: the energy and the sympathy, the person of thought and the one of action, the apologist and the evangelist, the Son of Thunder (Mark 3:17) as well as the Son of Consolation (Acts 4:36). And why not also highlight the synergy between husband and wife in a Christian marriage, that nuclear driving force behind the new evangelization?

In a splintered world of excessive and self-pleasing individualism, the Lord desires this holy duality to be brought into play. By consenting to missionize together in his vineyard we also have an opportunity to atone for the cruel envy of Cain who refused to be a keeper of his brother Abel. What is more, interiorly imbued with the sackcloth of self-denial and austerity, spiritual teamwork will be able to withstand the diabolical duet of Gog and Magog and their siege of the camp of the saints (20:7–9). Let us be assured that the Lord is following hard on the heels of his diligent disciples, like a divine charioteer reining his horses. Thus, by remaining under his regimen and cooperating with his special graces,[23] we will be successful collaborators as his two witnesses in our present days.

23. As St. Bernardine of Siena confirms: "There is a general rule concerning all special graces granted to any human being; whenever the divine favor chooses someone to receive a special grace, or to accept a lofty vocation, God adorns the person chosen with all the gifts of the Spirit needed to fulfill the task at hand." Sermo 2, *De S. Ioseph*; trans. Eric May, *St. Bernardine's Sermon on St. Joseph*, (Paterson, NJ: St. Anthony's Guild, 1947), p. 5.

Kicking against the goads (11:5–6)

[5]*And if anyone wants to harm them, fire pours from their mouth and consumes their foes; anyone who wants to harm them must be killed in this manner.* [6]*They have authority to shut the sky, so that no rain may fall during the days of their prophesying, and they have authority over the waters to turn them into blood, and to strike the earth with every kind of plague, as often as they desire.*

To understand the next facet of the witnesses' portraiture one must remember their Old Testament adumbration in Moses and Elijah.[24] Just as the latter were exposed to the rage of enemies, so will also the former. By restating "wants to harm them," Jesus adds intensity to his warning, reflected also in the equally reiterated effect of being "consumed" and "killed." Nevertheless, the choice of the present tense verb *thélei* (θέλει, *vult*), and the subjunctive mood of the verb "to want," *thelḗsêi* (θελήσῃ, *voluerit*) in v. 5 intimates an intention or potentiality rather than the actual infliction of damage, as if to say, "if anyone ever intended to harm them." What is conveyed, however, is the alarming decrease of the level of immunity that was promised to those who are sealed by God (9:4, 10, 18). In any event, the two witnesses resemble Moses and Elijah who called down fire upon their adversaries (e.g., Num 16:35; 1 Kgs 18:38). Their fire was real, whereas the one issuing from the witnesses' mouth is symbolic of the word of God denouncing all opponents of true religion (1:14, 16). It dramatically sketches the fierce antinomy between the Church militant and surrounding societies in all generations, pitting fire against fire, as it were (9:17–18). This fire of the Gospel offers light to guide the steps of saints, to illuminate sinners, to detect errors, but also to expose immorality and idolatry. It purifies the soul and readies it for sincere worship. And indeed, those who wish to hurt the Church will be devoured by the unquenchable fires of correction in this world, and potentially of damnation in the next, truly an ironic and paradoxical pattern of justice.

Furthermore, Elijah serves as the antetypical backdrop also for the witnesses' authority to shut the sky, so that no rain may fall during the days of their prophesying (v. 6; 1 Kgs 17:1; 18:1). To shut up the heavens and to restrain the blessings of rain from descending on the soil of the earth can only mean drought; hence, during the time of the Church's proclaiming of the Word,

24. In late Judaism, it was believed that they would usher in the eschatological age, a view assimilated by early Christianity (cf. Mark 9:2–13; Luke 1:15–17; 4:25–26; 7:11–17; John 1:21).

divine protection shall be withheld from those who neglect and despise it. And when John says that the witnesses have power over the waters to turn them into blood, and to strike the earth at will, he derives those images from the life of Moses on the cusp of the Exodus (Exod 7:17). This ominous blood (8:7–8; 16:3) is at the same time a contrastive reminder of the sacrificial blood of the Eucharistic Christ, and of divine vengeance.[25] Those who reject the Blood of grace will have to drink from the blood of chastisement on humanity (Ps 75:8). When the Lord indicated earlier that he will grant the authority to prophesy (v. 3), he implied that now they have power (*potestas*) abundantly, since it is restated in this verse. Amazingly, they are empowered to unleash every kind of plague and as often as they want (*voluerint*, v. 6), all but neutralizing their enemies' machinations to mistreat or injure them, and, even more stunningly, God will oblige. But that will be the subject matter of ch. 16, where we learn of the seven bowls of God's wrath being spilled out over the earth.

There seems to exist an ethical conundrum, however. Jesus not only rebuked James and John for desiring to emulate Elijah calling down destructive fire from heaven (Luke 9:54–56), but during his Sermon on the Mount he proclaimed that his followers were no longer to avenge an eye for an eye and a tooth for a tooth; instead, they were to turn the other cheek to those who struck them (Matt 5:38–39). Even more radical is his exigency to love our enemies and do good to those who hate us (Luke 6:27). Although these commands sound oxymoronic, they simply reveal the revolutionary nature of Christianity, fundamentally reversing the Old Testament code of retributive justice that invited commensurate retribution.[26] Christians discard the reciprocity of "tit for tat," and in its place promote the ethics of "going beyond" what is demanded, yes, even beyond the Golden Rule. In the end, this is grounded in the covenantal actions of God himself, and it requires a counterintuitive act of the will, strengthened by the sacraments. So how does the seemingly vengeful attitude of the two witnesses square with the beatitude "Blessed are the meek, for they will inherit the earth" (Matt 5:5); is it not hopelessly antithetical to it?[27] True, it may be a contradiction, but there is no moral dilemma if read in a symbolic key, to wit, that the Church through the fire of the word of God dispenses spiritual life and death.

Each one of us, faithful members of the Body of Christ, must always

25. Cf. AvS, 363–64.

26. Also known as *lex talionis*, i.e., the law of retaliation (*tālio*, from *tālis*, "of such kind"); e.g., Exod 21:23–27.

27. Cf. AvS, 362.

practice the virtues of meekness and forgiveness (Matt 5:9). Meanwhile, the bark of Peter does exercise the power of binding and loosing with all the eternal consequences of good or ill attached to it (Matt 16:19). Ergo, while never inflicting physical harm, she can manifest the saving truth, but also the cost of rejecting it. Seeking to lash out at Christian testimony in this world can result in spiritual death, whereas following God's commandments implies dying to oneself to gain eternal life (John 12:25). Thus, the soul that wishes to be happy, should submit cheerfully to Jesus and to the authority he invested in his Church. Because the more one rebels against it, and the more one resists and violates the urgings of one's conscience, the more it will ache interiorly, and the more one will injure oneself. And of that ethical pointlessness of inner resistance, the Risen Lord himself reminded Saul at his Damascene hour: "It hurts you to kick against the goads" (Acts 26:14).

Uncomfortable truth (11:7–10)

[7]*When they have finished their testimony, the beast that comes up from the bottomless pit will make war on them and conquer them and kill them,* [8]*and their dead bodies will lie in the street of the great city that is prophetically called Sodom and Egypt, where also their Lord was crucified.* [9]*For three and a half days members of the peoples and tribes and languages and nations will gaze at their dead bodies and refuse to let them be placed in a tomb;* [10]*and the inhabitants of the earth will gloat over them and celebrate and exchange presents, because these two prophets had been a torment to the inhabitants of the earth.*

After testifying to the Lord in marvelous invulnerability and finishing their preordained course, the witnesses are faced head-on with the enemy, that is, the beast coming up from the abyss to make war on them and conquer them and kill them (v. 7). Suddenly introduced here for the first time in Revelation, the wild beast is presented as a known entity, since the Greek noun *thēríon* (θηρίον, *bestia*) is preceded by a definite article. As a stylistic trait of this book, subsequent prophecies are at times anticipated; in this case, the beast is a literary anticipation or analepsis toward 13:1, where it ascends out of the sea, and also to 13:11, where a second one rises out of the earth. To further showcase the trans-temporal nature of these visions, its ascent is still depicted as a future event in 17:8. There and here it rises out of the abyss, as also the swarm of locusts did earlier (9:1–3), pointing to its origin in the underworld as the realm of darkness and death. Even before its more exhaustive description in ch. 13, this beast is without a doubt an anti-Christian personification of the forces of evil, savage and bloodthirsty, manifesting itself in the guise of never-ending persecutions in this world. John tells us overtly that it will have its hour of triumph, wielding lethal power over the two witnesses who have taught the principles of religion. It surfaces for a triple nefarious purpose, namely, to make war, to conquer, and to kill (v. 7). One would be forgiven for thinking that these witnesses were invincible (vv. 5–6), but their overthrow in utter violation of their innocence signifies the temporary conquest of the spirit of irreconcilable antagonism against Christ. It is all-out war between veracity and mendacity, an endeavor to exterminate the Christian testimony by force, a last-ditch effort to destroy the saints.[28]

Unfortunately, perpetuated in human history is the postponement of moral and social advancement for centuries through the outbreak of some brutal and irrational ideology, or the reversion to forms of practical paganism. Did the Lord not put us on notice already: "When the Son of Man comes, will he find faith on earth?" (Luke 18:8). Does not also the Joban problem come to mind, namely, why do the righteous have to suffer (Job 27:1–6)? Conversely, why does evil prosper on earth? These are profoundly uncomfortable truths. And as if the scene was not awful enough already, the visionary goes on to observe how the corpses of those witnesses lie in the street of the great city (v. 8). By employing the collective noun *ptôma* (πτῶμα, *corpus*), which originally means "fall" or "offal,"[29] he suggests that Satan momentarily succeeds in associating the lifeless bodies of Christians with his own fall and that of his idolatrous city Babylon. Strewn across its central boulevard like refuse, the deceased witnesses are exposed to public ignominy in the sight of its inhabitants, who in their arrogance are still convinced that their city is great.

John adds the illuminating remark that this city is prophetically[30] called Sodom and Egypt, emphasizing its symbolic nature, to be discerned with the aid of God's Spirit. Read in light of the books of Genesis and Exodus, Sodom represents immorality, and Egypt stands for plagued tyranny against God's chosen people. Even Jerusalem itself becomes an ambiguous reality that can mean both, the blessed city of David, theater of our salvation and future glory (21:2,

28. Evocative of the quote attributed to Henry II of England preceding the death of Thomas Becket, the Archbishop of Canterbury, in 1170: "Will no one rid me of this meddlesome priest?"

29. Based on the Greek verb *píptō* (πίπτω), "to fall."

30. The adverb *pneumatikôs* (πνευματικῶς, *spiritaliter*), literally means "of the spirit," i.e., related to the Holy Spirit (cf. 1 Cor 2:14).

10), but also the place of apostasy in whose center square, no longer outside, Jesus is continuously crucified. In the last analysis, therefore, Babylon, Sodom, Egypt, Jerusalem, and by extension, Rome, all emblematize the ungodly part of the earth and its diabolically influenced communities that reject God and his beloved witnesses. Spiritually speaking, until the end of time, Christ the Lord will continue to be killed in the midst of a sinful world to complete the universal drama of redemption.[31]

Humanity was supposed to welcome the apostle's prophetic teaching (10:11), yet sadly many will gaze at their dead bodies and refuse to let them be placed in a tomb (v. 9). They do so for the limited period of three and a half days, redolent of Jesus' own sepulchral rest before Easter Sunday morning.[32] It is imaginable that the abrupt switch to the grammatical plural of "bodies" in this verse is intended to further accentuate the way that Christians' dying is intertwined with the Lord's own Death and Resurrection. To leave them unburied means to treat them with utmost indignity and contempt, a veritable climax of anti-Christian malice. History has given proof to the fact that martyrdom can indeed involve the ultimate profanation of dead bodies, denying them even the common human privilege of a burial (Tob 1:17). Contemplated, however, through a more mystical lens, these exposed cadavers could also hint at the persistence of the Catholic dogma refusing to be entombed and forgotten; on the contrary, it will remain ever open even under tragic circumstances, to be observed by all throughout salvation history.[33]

Yet to pile even more insult onto injury, the inhabitants of the earth will gloat over them and celebrate and exchange presents, because those two prophets had been a torment to the inhabitants of the earth (v. 10). Hardening their hearts, they unfortunately misjudge their opportunity to repent and to search for God's will,[34] and instead erupt in a celebratory atmosphere (Esth 9:18). At once perverse and childish, these spectators are rejoicing because the life and teaching of these two witnesses, who are now called prophets, meant continual torment to them, and the very sight of them had become a burden (Wis 2:10–24). It convicts their misinformed or otherwise twisted consciences and brings to light their defiance against the divine rule, as they eventually exchange the macabre gift of a Herod-Pilate agreement among themselves

31. Cf. RD, 1030.

32. The noun *mnēma* (μνῆμα, *monumentum*), "tomb, monument, memorial," accords with the narrative of Christ's burial (Luke 23:53; 24:1).

33. Cf. AvS, 366.

34. Cf. AvS, 367.

(Luke 23:12). Curiously, the inner voice of an anticipated judgment appears to simultaneously vex and delight those who are not open to the Gospel. Yet their schadenfreude will suffer a bitter reversal of fortune on the day the elect will make merry, while the condemned will be tortured (14:10), in fulfillment of the beatitude, "Blessed are you who weep now, for you will laugh; woe to you who laugh now, for you will mourn and weep" (Luke 6:21, 25).

To close again on a spiritual note, may this passage, "when they have finished their testimony" (v. 7), make us more aware of the fact that God gives us sufficient time to do good and to complete our Christian witness in this life.[35] In that certitude we can serenely embrace the thought that when God has no further need for our service here on earth, then our death will give him glory and yield its fruit for eternity. Here we should remember St. Thérèse of Lisieux, who in her childlike fervor, loved to imagine herself as a little toy ball, the plaything of the divine Infant, gladly abandoning herself to his wishes. What is critical for this present day is to work and wait patiently for him (Ps 130:6). That interior abandonment and forbearance should brim over in the form of compassion for perceived enemies, knowing that the preaching of the Gospel pains them. To love our enemies and do good to those who hate us (Luke 6:27) would imply that we pray for them. And if there is any bête noire in our personal life, it is our Christian duty to intercede for their conversion of heart and for inner peace.

Kenotic turning point (11:11–12)

[11]But after the three and a half days, the breath of life from God entered them, and they stood on their feet, and those who saw them were terrified. [12]Then they heard a loud voice from heaven saying to them, "Come up here!" And they went up to heaven in a cloud while their enemies watched them.

Having now traversed the valley of their lowest abasement during a fleeting period of earthly time, the two witnesses, who are also prophets, are at a turning point of exaltation through their miraculous resurrection (v. 11). Allusion is made to Genesis 2:7–8, where God breathes the breath of life into Adam's nostrils, making him a living being and putting him in Eden, the garden he had planted (Job 33:4). John must have been reminded of Ezekiel's vision of the dry bones, too (Ezek 37:1–10). Like the Lamb himself, these prophets are able rise

35. Cf. RD, 1029.

again to their feet,[36] instilling terror in those who watch them (18:10, 15), and unexpectedly turning their malevolent relishing into consternation. By making the witnesses ascend to heaven in a cloud, God preserves them from the rage of their enemies. Both the booming voice and the cloud[37] are Exodus and apocalyptic imagery for divine presence and action that cannot be fully grasped.[38] Moreover, the witnesses' spectacular ascension evokes Noah's antediluvian ancestor Enoch (Gen 5:24), the prophet Elijah (2 Kgs 2:11),[39] but most of all Christ himself (Acts 1:9). This episode appears to anticipate the male child being snatched away and taken to God and to his throne before his mother flees into the wilderness (12:5–6). While Elijah ascended in a whirlwind into heaven, his disciple Elisha watched (2 Kgs 2:12), but here, the witnesses' enemies watch them, as another inverse parallel to Jesus' Ascension (cf. Acts 1:11).

This hostility to the end finds its source in the proto-evangelic enmity between the woman and the serpent (Gen 3:15). With the spotlight alternating between witnesses and opponents in vv. 11–12, the choice of the verb *theōréō* (θεωρέω, *videre*), "to observe, to watch," seems relevant here, since lexically it has to do with an intentional beholding or contemplating for the sake of discernment, concentrating on the essence of what is unfolding; hence, these witnesses can be considered as the conscience of the world, just as the Blessed Trinity renders testimony to the truth in our personal conscience. On a similar spiritual plane, the Lord's witnesses must not be weary of service and suffering, nor hastily grasp at the reward, but must stay till their Master calls them. And this work is a participation in his own *kénōsis* or abasement (Phil 2:7), his *tapeinōsis* or deepest humiliation (Phil 2:8), his *hyper-ypsōsis* or super-exaltation (Phil 2:9), and finally his *doxōsis* or glorification (Phil 2:11).[40] Just as the witnesses' life, passion, death, revivification, and ascension is conformed to the Lord's own life, himself emphatically styled as the faithful and true witness in 3:14, so is ours, at least in a figurative or mystical way. And it is precisely by

36. The feet of Christ, Mary, or the angel, are focused on in the Apocalypse as a sign of power (1:15, 17; 2:18; 3:9; 10:1–2; 12:1; 19:10; 22:8).

37. See also the cloud of glory filling Solomon's temple (1 Kgs 8:10–11), the pneumatic overshadowing of Mary (Luke 1:35), the cloud on Tabor (Matt 17:5), and the parousiac Son of Man (Matt 24:30; Rev 1:7; 14:14–16).

38. Cf. AvS, 370.

39. According to Jewish tradition, Moses too was removed from the sight of his followers by a cloud (cf. Flavius Josephus, *Antiquities*, 6.8.48).

40. May the kind reader bear with this author for taking the liberty of phrasing these words in accordance with the Greek original, for the purpose of bringing out the biblical connotations of each phase of Christ's earthly career.

that union with Christ that everything we experience on earth becomes fruitful (John 12:24). As baptized witnesses and prophets, each of us must now look for the things that are above, where the Lord is, for we have been crucified with him and our life is hidden with him in God for glory (Col 3:1–4).

Refound fear of God (11:13–14)

[13]At that hour there was a great earthquake, and a tenth of the city fell; seven thousand people were killed in the earthquake, and the rest were terrified and gave glory to the God of heaven. [14]The second woe has passed. The third woe is coming very soon.

As if inching toward the tip of an arrowhead, the narrative zeroes in on that "hour," counted down from forty-two months (v. 2) or one thousand two hundred sixty days (v. 3), and from three and a half days (vv. 9, 11). This hour, the smallest unit of chronological reckoning in Revelation, and a typical feature of John's literary style, is the moment of a retributive warning on the worldly city where the two witnesses were slain. Assuredly, divine intervention is a thing of precision. While the seer's eyes are fixed on the prophets' ascension, there is a great earthquake like a mirror image of the repercussion of Christ's rising from the dead (Matt 28:2). Terror and confusion ensue, shaking the nations out of their spirit of worldliness and complacence. It is almost a geophysical approval of the saints' triumph, and perhaps even a cue to the resurrection of the flesh on the last day.[41] And as a tenth of the city falls, seven thousand fatalities occur: reminiscent of Abraham's pleading with Yahweh to spare Sodom for the sake of ten righteous (Gen 18:32), God still gives the remainder of humanity time to repent.

Given that ten in the Apocalypse is the number of the horns of the dragon and beast symbolizing world-kingdoms (17:12), this tenth part may point to the partial overthrow of the ungodly city amid anti-Christian turmoil. Looking back to the Old Testament, the tenth part often signifies the religious tithe, i.e., the portion due from the community to God or to the ruler (Gen 14:20). Hence, the Almighty appears to be exacting his due now, such that persons who previously refused to recognize him are now forced to acknowledge his sovereignty by the punitive exaction of a tithe, proving again that all and everything are under his divine sway. Furthermore, it is perfectly conceivable that seven thousand as one tenth refers to Jerusalem's demographics of the time,

41. Cf. RD, 1033.

that is, seventy thousand citizens. Is it coincidental, though, that those who fall are of the same number as those who did not bow to Baal (1 Kgs 19:18)? Be that as it may, it is an emblematic sum representing all social classes in large numbers, as expressed by "seven" multiplied by "thousand." What is literally spoken of are "names of humans" (*nomina hominum*), stressing the inalienable worth of every single person. To God nobody is nameless, certainly not those who testified to his name (2:13), and are to receive a new name (2:17), which makes one wonder whether those killed in the city are precisely those whose names will be erased from book of life (3:5): No one who is predestined to live will perish, and none escapes who deserves to be included.

After the previous cold-hearted and stone-faced non-repentance (9:20–21; 16:9), one could be forgiven for expecting the same outcome here, yet what happens next is astounding, since the sixty-three thousand survivors of the earthquake give glory to the God of heaven (14:7). And although their ulterior fate is not disclosed, what is unveiled is that like on the morning of the Lord's Resurrection, people are frightened (Luke 24:5, 37), and, at last, many use their second chances to glorify God. Nevertheless, they may also have merely stood in awe at what God was doing and acknowledged his power without necessarily repenting and becoming truly his friends. Their terror at his might to defeat death by raising the two witnesses from the dead (v. 11), and fright at the partial demolition of the worldly city (v. 13) show how estranged humanity can become and how difficult it is to find the way back to faith.[42] Jesus' parable of the impassable gulf between the rich man and Lazarus also makes the rather pessimistic point of how challenging it is to achieve conversion of heart and embrace true religion (Luke 16:31). In the same vein, that they praise not the "Lord of the earth" (v. 4) but the "God of heaven" (v. 13) at first seems hopeful and convincing, only to read later that they curse him in impenitence (16:11), dampening again their chances of salvation.[43] It is nonetheless fair to say that the early Christians probably would never have imagined that Western civilization, after having converted from heathendom to Christianity for millennia, would so foolishly and rapidly revert to paganism in our present age. Spiritually enlightening is the circumstance that some good can come from fright, especially when it is coupled with a genuine fear of God (Luke 5:26). Let us not postpone the day of repentance; may we never procrastinate in giving heartfelt glory to the God of heaven.

42. Cf. AvS, 368.

43. While the expression "God of heaven" is found only in these two places of the New Testament, it is not uncommon in the Old Testament (e.g., Ezra 1:2; Neh 1:4; Dan 2:18).

That rounds off the second woe (v. 14) which was the content of the sixth trumpet (9:12–13), and it also closes the entire second interlude that began in 10:1. Intervening is a narrative that demonstrates how kairotic opportunities of knowing God's will are given to humanity, as well as warnings of judgment in response to inflexible disobedience. Without missing a beat now, the sacred author adds, "Behold, the third woe is coming very soon" (v. 14). But if the exclamatory woe[44] is normally an expression uttered in grief or as a warning of impending chastisement, human or divine, then the events of 11:15–19 will not fit that description, as will be seen soon. And since John does not attempt to identify the exact scope of this third woe, nor indicate its precise ending, the reader should take it in the broader sense as being developed in chs. 12–20. This woe is reflected especially in the execution of the seven bowls of the wrath of God in 16:1–21, which will result in the fall of Babylon in chs. 17–18. Thus, there is a continuous crescendo, from seals to trumpets to plague-bowls, until God's grand finale in chs. 21–22. But reading the Apocalypse at the beginning of the third millennium only corroborates the relativity of the eschatological "very soon."[45]

44. The Greek *ouaí* (οὐαί, *vae* or *heu*) is an indeclinable interjection meaning "alas! woe!" with which the Septuagint translates the Hebrew *hoi* (הוי or אוי); it recurs no fewer than fourteen times in Revelation.

45. Aside from this mention in the middle of Revelation, the adverb *tachý* (ταχύ, *cito*), meaning "swiftly, quickly," and its cognate noun *táchos* (τάχος), signaling "quickness, haste," appear only in its opening chapters (1:1; 2:16; 3:11) and again in the final one (22:6–7, 12, 20).

11:15–19, Seventh trumpet: Third woe

Anointed coregency (11:15)

[15] Then the seventh angel blew his trumpet, and there were loud voices in heaven, saying, "The kingdom of the world has become the kingdom of our Lord and of his Messiah, and he will reign forever and ever."

Hurried away back to heaven, the exiled visionary observes the initial unfolding of the third woe. This seventh trumpet triggers the events of vv. 15–19 that resemble the opening of the seventh seal in 8:1–5. While it seems to bring us up to the final climax of salvation history, it will halt just short of it to retrace the ground for fuller details starting in 12:1. As implied in 7:10 and 16:17, v. 15 declares the end, underlining yet again that these septets of seals, trumpets, and wrath-bowls, are likely parallel and not successive scenes of one and the same reality, that is two kingdoms, one heavenly and divine, and the other worldly and demonic. Hence, the narrative plot must be typified as recapitulatory or perhaps upward spiraling, rather than rectilinear, as if tending unswervingly toward the boundary of history with the Lord's second advent as its Judge.

By blowing his trumpet, the seventh angel announces the fulfillment of God's mystery as heralded back in 10:7. This may also be the last trumpet on which Paul elaborates at 1 Corinthians 15:52.[1] According to the hexameron, that is, Genesis 1:1–2:3, six is the number of the world, now surrendering to judgment and the ushering in of the Creator's Kingdom, corresponding to the eternal sabbath (Heb 4:4).[2] Other Old Testament precedents include the seven

1. Cf. RD, 1003.

2. An ancient Jewish chronicle makes the world last six thousand years in reflection of the six days of creation: 2,000 years of "chaos" (*tôhu*), 2,000 years of the "law" (*tôrah*), and 2,000 years of the "days of the Messiah" (*yemot haMashīach*), the "desire of all the nations"; the seventh millennium will inaugurate the Messianic Age proper, perfecting six thousand years after creation, also known as *Anno Mundi* (cf. Babylonian Talmud, *Aboda Zara* 9a; *Sanhedrin* 97a–98a).

days of atonement during Aaron's priestly consecration (Exod 29:35, 37), as well as the fall of Jericho after seven days (Josh 6:15–16). Moreover, a striking contrast exists between the contemplative silence of the heavenly liturgy in 8:1, and the loud voices in heaven on this occasion. To whom these utterances belong is a question that is neither inquired about nor answered, but they could be ascribed to the four living beings, or to all the angels and saints in the celestial sphere. At any rate, what they proclaim is truly sublime, namely, the arrival of the Messiah's everlasting Kingdom.

This is also an anticipatory or proleptic celebration of holy dominion over a world that does not become God's and of his Anointed One until the victory over diabolical powers and the judgment, as depicted in chs. 19–20. Thus, in the same breath, this magnificent transition is stated as an already accomplished fact (*factum est*) and simultaneously reserved for an unstipulated future (*regnabit*), only to revert to the prophetic past (*regnasti*) in v. 17. This high tension between "already and not yet," so characteristic of the apocalyptic genre, has the capacity to involve readers of all ages to become active players in this drama. Also, these constantly fluctuating verb tenses betray the struggle of the apostolic seer to communicate meta-conceptual and trans-temporal visions in human language. Unique, albeit remarkably in line with Psalm 2, is the phrase "our Lord and his Christ," calling the paternal Godhead "Lord" (*Kýrios*), and unveiling something of a divine coregency, in which Father and Son are joint rulers (12:10).[3] Their reign (*regnum*) overrules the current dominion of world powers. Furthermore, for the first time since 1:1–2, 5 does Jesus receive the appellation "Christ" (*Christós*, Χριστός), that is, the Anointed One, which becomes an epithet for King, although biblical prophets and priests were also consecrated with sacred ointment. Hidden behind this solemn title, however, is the entire Christian people sanctified by baptismal chrism. Once inaugurated, this supernatural reign will have no end, but we will have to wait until chs. 20–22 to learn more about its state of consummation, when God rules supreme, and no further enemy can arise. What crystallizes immediately, however, is that the millennial reign, bespoken in 20:1–6, has begun already, and with that, the time of the first resurrection.

A spiritual takeaway could be our Christ-centered pride and satisfaction at the incredible honor of being called Christians, carrying on a humbling tradition that sprang up in Antioch two thousand years ago (Acts 11:26). We have been chosen to become veritable partners and more than partners of Jesus'

3. In addition to the passages where the Lamb is pictured as seated on the Father's throne (3:21; 5:6, 13; 7:10, 17; 12:5).

Kingdom (Rom 8:16–17). Already here and now, just as the heavenly Father and his Son experience blissful unity in exercising dominion after the Ascension of Christ, so should we enjoy prayerful intimacy with the Father and with the Son.[4] In that strength we can go forth and defend the royal dignity of all of God's children on earth, from the natural beginning of their life to their natural death, working to reverse trends of a culture of death, and diligently promote a culture of life.[5]

Raging nations meet God's wrath (11:16–18)

[16] Then the twenty-four elders who sit on their thrones before God fell on their faces and worshiped God, [17] singing, "We give you thanks, Lord God Almighty, who are and who were, for you have taken your great power and begun to reign. [18] The nations raged, but your wrath has come, and the time for judging the dead, for rewarding your servants, the prophets and saints and all who fear your name, both small and great, and for destroying those who destroy the earth."

Imitating all the choirs of angels (7:11), the twenty-four elders worship the Most High (v. 16), a gesture they perform routinely as can be deduced from 4:10; 5:14; 19:4. Chosen from both Testaments, Old and New, these blessed souls now represent the Church of God in all ages, and their most unassuming adoration corresponds to the highest revelation of God's glory and his subduing of all enemies. It is also quite fitting of them since they are particularly indebted to the Lord who establishes his Kingdom through the final victory of his Church. Now they enthusiastically voice their gratitude[6] as they address God with the most impressive title *Pantokrátōr* (παντοκράτωρ[7]), interchangeably designating the Father or the Son (v. 17). This name signifies the supreme Ruler of the universe, the almighty Sustainer of the World, who holds unrestricted sway. From now on the victorious saints may sit with Christ on his throne (3:21), even if it is still proleptic toward 19:1, when all this will finally take place. In that

4. Cf. AvS, 376.

5. Cf. St. John Paul II's 1995 encyclical letter *Evangelium vitae*.

6. This is the singular occurrence of the verb *eucharistéō* (εὐχαριστέω, *gratias agere*) in Revelation, denoting the acknowledgement of a "good grace, gift, blessing, favor," with its Eucharistic connotation in the New Testament (John 6:11, 23; 1 Cor 11:24).

7. This Greek noun, recurring nine times in the Apocalypse, is translated with the adjective *omnipotens*, "almighty," by the Neo-Vulgate; it is the Septuagint rendition of the Hebrew *Yahweh Sabaoth* ("Lord of Hosts") and *El Shaddai* ("God Almighty").

sense, God is no longer the One who is to come (1:4, 8), but simply the One who is and who was (16:5); indeed, he has already come to take possession of what is his, and to reclaim his creation.[8]

Both the prayers of the groaning Church,[9] and the cries of a travailing creation (Rom 8:19–22) have been heard. World history is rehashed as a theater of raging nations whose rebellious stage-play is finally headed into its catharsis and denouement, as it were. All antagonism has now been resolved by the divine protagonist and hero in his moment of wrath (v. 18). Linguistically, an irony is conveyed in the first of two wordplays in this verse, namely, at its beginning the repetition of the Greek word for anger, showing how the futile violence of humans will be silenced by the effective and definitive judgments of God (Ps 99:1–5). Then, at the end of the verse, forming a literary *inclusio*, we find the second pun in the reiterated notion of "destroying the destroyers" (*exterminare-exterminant*, v. 18b). Their anger is the result of moving away from their God, opposing his laws, persecuting his people, slaying his witnesses, and attempting to eliminate all vestiges of his wise authority on earth. Yet, how frivolous and petty humanity's rage turns out to be in the face of the Lord's impassioned acts of vengeance. And in Matthew 25:31–46, Jesus himself has given us already the most extensive advance description of that time for judging the dead and for rewarding his servants, the prophets and saints (v. 18).

At this juncture of John's Apocalypse, we find yet another proleptic scene, this time of the final judgment in 20:11–15. Unique is the listing of those servants of God awaiting to be rewarded for their decisions and actions on earth, to wit, prophets, saints, and all who fear his name. Especially the saints appear to partake of the holiness of God himself (4:8; 6:10), of the angels (14:10), and of the New Jerusalem (21:2, 10). And to be God-fearing certainly sums up what is essential about biblical religiosity. Almost as an afterthought the elders announce the destruction of the earthly destroyers which references already the collapse of Babylon (v. 18). Moral corruption and destructiveness (*exterminare*) have no place whatsoever in heaven (21:27).

Coming to a conclusion here is the first series of septenary and interludial visions referred to in the scroll that was resting in the palm of the Father's right hand, sealed with the seven seals (5:1). This present celestial liturgy (11:15–18) parallels the one at 7:9–12, proleptically closing the eschatological drama of seals and trumpets. Contrast the jubilant tenor of this Eucharistic thanksgiving (v. 17) with the strained foreboding sounded in 12:12, before the actual conflict

8. Cf. AvS, 377–78.

9. Cf. 5:10; Luke 18:7–8.

explodes in 19:19. But let us reflect for a moment on that human rage checked by God's wrath (v. 18). More than a final divine outburst of anger, is it not first and foremost a time of his greatest closeness to sinners, an expression of his long-suffering love, a revelation of a God who wants everyone to be saved and to fully understand the truth (1 Tim 2:4)? His disciplinary actions in our lives spring from his desire to have all of us bear fruit in repentance and conversion (Luke 19:10).[10] And finally, there is divine attention to both the small and the great (v. 18), and if we are predestined to be among those little ones, then let us remember what the Spirit told the church in Philadelphia: "I know that you have but little strength, and yet you have kept my word and have not denied my name" (3:8).[11]

Ark holding a golden urn (11:19)

[19] *Then God's temple in heaven was opened, and the ark of his covenant was seen within his temple; and there were flashes of lightning, rumblings, peals of thunder, an earthquake, and heavy hail.*

As if confirming the grateful carol of the twenty-four elders (vv. 16–18), the Lord's heavenly sanctuary is opened, and the ark of his covenant appears amidst cosmic rumblings. Since the septets of seals and bowls flow toward a similar highpoint (8:1–5; 16:17–18), there is again evidence that the seals, trumpets, and bowls are not so much consecutive but rather coterminous vignettes of apocalyptic symbolism, crescendos that apex in one and the same consummation. They also present the unfolding of God's plan of salvation until its grand conclusion from three different yet complementary vantage points. Rather than a postlude to the final trumpet, however, this vision should be viewed as a preface to 12:1, as it appears to begin a new theme (4:1–2; cf. Isa 6:1–5).

To describe what John is seeing here, two metaphors come to mind. First, that of a Russian nesting doll where a set of wooden figurines of decreasing size are placed one inside another, all with the same face. Then there is also the image of layers being peeled off an onion to eventually lay bare its core. Such is the fascinating sequence of heaven enclosing the temple, the temple carrying encased in it the ark of God's covenant, which in turn encapsulates a golden urn holding the manna, Aaron's budding rod, and the covenant tablets (Heb 9:4). When contextualized, this heavenly scene is even more thrilling considering

10. Cf. AvS, 380.
11. Cf. AvS, 383.

that both "ark" and "covenant" are the only occurrences of these words in Revelation, and that the temple will have altogether vanished from the New Jerusalem (21:22). This is now the third glimpse into heaven (4:1; 8:1), followed by two more (15:5; 19:11) as the fulsome result of opening the seven seals (5:2), leading up to the renewal of heaven and earth in 21:1. Disclosing the innermost recesses of the temple sanctuary, the Holy of Holies of the triumphant Church, Jesus invites us to one day pass with him behind the curtain (Heb 6:19; 9:3) as his beloved brethren and as the covenanted children of God. For now, Christians will find similar shelter in his Church on earth.

After disappearing during the demolishment of King Solomon's temple by the Chaldeans under Nebuchadnezzar in 587 BC (2 Kgs 25:8–17), the ark of the covenant was recovered by the prophet Jeremiah who hid it in a cave on Mount Nebo against the day of Israel's restoration, declaring that the hiding place was to remain unknown until God would gather his people again (2 Macc 2:4–8).[12] While, therefore, it was conspicuously absent from the second temple (Jer 3:16), the exile on Patmos now witnesses its dramatic reappearance, which will also be the last mention of it in the Scriptures. With the Holy of Holies thrown open, this gold-covered wooden chest with its elaborate propitiatory lid becomes visible to all, an important figure of God's abiding presence and continual help, his footstool (1 Chron 28:2) and seat of mercy flanked by two cherubim. In ancient days a signpost toward the Promised Land (Josh 4:7) and a rallying point in battle (1 Sam 4:3–5), it now symbolizes the ingathering of God's people through the remission of their sins.[13] Each septet closes with analogous cosmic manifestations, such as flashes of lightning, rumblings, earthquakes, and heavy hail, as if reducing creation to its primeval chaos, mirrored eventually in the coming of the Holy Spirit on Pentecost (Acts 2:2).[14] Thus, the abode of God is an open sanctuary to those who practice their faith, but it becomes a menacingly clouded and lightning-stricken Sinai to the faithless. These somber salvos of the heavenly hosts now drown out the fanfare of the last trumpet, setting the stage for the second half of the apocalyptic narrative starting in 12:1.

12. Jewish tradition has cherished the belief that the restoration of the people in the last days would be accompanied by the disclosure of the sacred ark in a cloud, together with the tabernacle and the altar of incense. The idea was that the disappearance of the ark from the Holy of Holies was a temporary painful setback which had to be righted before the final bliss could arrive (cf. Flavius Josephus, *Antiquities*, 18.4.1).

13. See also the ark's connection with the rituals of Yom Kippur, the Day of Atonement (Lev 16:14–15; Heb 4:6).

14. Cf. RD, 1040.

But before turning the page, let reflect on the spiritual meaning of the ark as a symbol of the Blessed Virgin Mary, especially after her Assumption into heaven.[15] It is as if the righteous of the Old Testament were saluting the Incarnation of Christ signaled by the open temple. Mary has given birth to Jesus, the golden urn holding the manna, Aaron's rod, and the covenant tablets. In other words, she has an intimate relationship with the Blessed Sacrament of the Altar; in fact she is the "Woman of the Eucharist"[16] who will not tire of teaching us how to draw strength from this hidden manna (2:17). She will remind us of the holiness of the priesthood in the hierarchical order of the Church, symbolized by the rod of Aaron, knowing that without it there would be no Eucharist as source and summit of all Christian life.[17] Mary is also the Mother of him who has chiseled his divine wisdom onto the tablets of our hearts (2 Cor 3:2–3; Heb 10:16). And lastly, the multiple envelopment of manna, rod, and tablets within the urn, contained in the ark, inside God's temple appearing in heaven, could be viewed as a token of maternal protection and safety, which Mary offers to her spiritual children, just as she carried the Son of God in her blessed womb.[18] These considerations prepare us for the next chapter with its detailed delineation of the Mother of God and Mother of the Church.

15. Cf. Pontifical Council for the Pastoral Care of Migrants and Itinerant People, "The Shrine: Memory, Presence, and Prophecy of the Living God" (May 8, 1999), §18.

16. Cf. St. John Paul II's 2003 encyclical letter *Ecclesia de Eucharistia*, §53.

17. Cf. *CCC*, §§1324–27.

18. See also the related ecclesial images of the ark of Noah (Gen 6:14), as well as the small basket hidden among the reeds of the river Nile, safeguarding the infant Moses (Exod 2:3).

PART 3

12:1–18, *Ecclesia pressa*

A great sign (12:1–2)

[1]A great portent appeared in heaven: a woman clothed with the sun, with the moon under her feet, and on her head a crown of twelve stars. [2]She was pregnant and was crying out in birth pangs, in the agony of giving birth.

Few will dispute that ch. 12 is not only the structural hub of, but also a theological key to the Apocalypse's entire narrative, unveiling the deepest dimension of a spiritual conflict that is more latent in chs. 1–11. This central section of the book, unfolding the initial sketch at 11:7–10, finally unmasks the evil one, disguised as a dragon opposing God and his people. While John is still raptly fixed on the theophanic ark in heaven, it fades away, and a related portent fades in like an added foil on an overhead projector. Crystallizing before his visionary eyes at this point is something even more impressive than the ancient ark, namely, a great sign in heaven (v. 1), which, together with the two other celestial signs (v. 3; 15:1), will turn out to be the most amazing embodiment of God's entire economy of salvation. And that it is a symbol of monumental impact is apparent from the fact that this is the first recurrence of the noun *sēmeîon* (σημεῖον, *signum*), "sign, miracle, sign-post, mile-marker," since its programmatic precedent in the form of a verb in 1:1 (*sēmaínō*, σημαίνω, *significare*). When used in the sense of a miracle, as John frequently does in his Gospel (e.g., John 2:11), it is a token of divine power or purpose, and sometimes it foreshadows future events, which seems to be the intended connotation here, too.

"A woman" is the sign, and she could be compared to an octahedron of at least eight basic biblical aspects. *First*, she reminds us of the first "woman" (*virago*, Gen 2:23), built from the rib of Adam and called mother of all the living (Gen 3:20), sadly instrumental, too, in the primordial fall of humanity into sin. *Second*, she symbolizes God's chosen people of the Old Covenant, Israel, also known as Daughter Zion (Isa 1:8) and Jerusalem (Gal 4:26), which in due course would bring forth the Messiah. *Third*, she appears to fulfill the image of Lady Wisdom in Old Testament sapiential literature (Prov 8:1), so utterly antithetical to Dame Folly (Prov 9:13–15). *Fourth*, this cosmic woman is a figure of the New Eve, the Blessed Virgin Mary, who encouraged her divine Son to perform his first public miracle at Cana's wedding, and would not abandon him on Golgotha, now dwelling in the very presence of God from whence the Son of Man had descended to the earth. Would it be too far-fetched to assume that John must have immediately recognized her since Jesus from the Cross had entrusted her to him?[1] In her untarnished beauty, she stands in absolute contrast to Babylon the great, mother of harlots (17:5) and the evil woman Jezebel (2:20). *Fifth*, she also represents the New Israel, God's beloved people of the New Covenant, the never-aging Bride of Christ and Mother of his spiritual children, the Church militant on earth.[2] *Sixth*, the apocalyptic woman signals the Church triumphant, decked out with victorious splendor in heavenly places. *Seventh*, this mystical *mulier* is symbolic of every single woman to ever live, be it as daughter, sister, bride, wife, mother, grandmother, unmarried or widowed. Among the metaphysical traits of womanhood, in contradistinction to man, is her God-given capacity of personal surrender and receptivity, which incidentally characterizes all human relationship to God: we are called to become subject to and receive life from him as his servants. This constitutes our faith by which the individual becomes a child of God. Conversely, all ill-construed autonomy of the human spirit subverts this fundamental religious attitude toward God. And just as woman is the physically weaker gender compared to man, so also the Church has usually exercised her spiritual power in societies through her perceived powerlessness and vulnerability. Which ties into the *eighth* and last metaphorical facet, namely, that in her femininity and nuptiality, the cosmic woman also epitomizes every human soul, yours and mine, created to enter a lasting spousal relationship with its Creator and Redeemer.

Marvelously, this woman is clothed with the sun, her natural feminine fragility now transcended by the meridian glory of the firmament, reflecting the light of her Maker and his eternal wisdom (Wis 7:26, 29). Unlike the great harlot, who embellishes herself with seductive worldly finery (17:4), this woman is clothed like a bride in beautiful raiment bedecked with the luminosity of Christ himself (19:8, 13). As the psalmist sings, she is wrapped in light as with a garment (Ps 104:2). She is also revealed as the Mother of the Sun of Justice

1. Cf. AvS, 390.

2. In the Third Vision of the early second-century Christian work *The Shepherd of Hermas* she is pictured as an elderly lady with a youthful countenance.

(Mal 4:2), sending out his rays of majestic and loving warmth, perpetually risen and transfigured with him. As such she is a paradigm of the Church or *Typos Ecclesiae*[3] that shines all supernatural light into this world by proclaiming the brightness of Gospel-truth.[4] Light is also indicative of this woman's immaculate virtues of purity, zeal, and holiness. Wherever she goes there will be the light of the day, and absent the darkness of the night, already exhibiting her future state of glory.[5]

In fact, the moon is found beneath her feet (v. 1), a sign of her absolute dominion over the night of sin. Sun and moon are cosmic insignia of the uncreated and the created light, and the differentiation between the former's incandescence and the latter's paleness only heightens the beauty of this truly iconic picture. Aside from that, the moon as a footstool signals her superiority above everything that remains subject to change.[6] In her diurnal and nocturnal dominance she overcomes the vicissitudes of time, her immovability counterbalances the mutability, defectiveness, and uncertainty of creation.[7] This ever-changing lunar shimmer occupies a position of inferiority since it gleams with borrowed light, perhaps an image of the relationship between the Old and the New Testaments. Given its dependence on another fixed star, the moon cannot dispel darkness and change it into day, symbolizing the non-Christian world in relation to the one true Church of Christ.[8] By the same token, the moon represents the Holy Spirit who, as the vicar of the Lord on earth (John 14:16) governs his Church as her soul. Yet similar reflections on sun and moon would remain incomplete if they did not include Mary, central to all creation, the first citizen of heaven, representing the earth and its population which are not otherwise mentioned in this verse.[9]

With supernal elegance, she freely walks along the orbits of the skies to

3. "This is the Church clothed in the Word of the Father, shining more brightly than the sun. This brilliance of the sun signifies likewise that she possesses the true knowledge of God and his laws and contains his revelations." Averky Taushev and Seraphim Rose, *The Apocalypse in the Teachings of Ancient Christianity*, 2nd ed. (Platina, CA: St. Herman of Alaska Brotherhood, 1998), 177.

4. See St. John Paul's 1993 encyclical letter *Veritatis splendor*.

5. Cf. AvS, 386.

6. Cf. Taushev and Rose, *Apocalypse*, 177.

7. Cf. Nicholas of Lyra, *Apocalypse Commentary*, trans. Philip Krey, TCS (Kalamazoo, MI: Medieval Institute Publications, 1997), 139.

8. Cf. the 2000 Declaration *Dominus Iesus* by the Congregation for the Doctrine of the Faith, on the unicity and salvific universality of Jesus Christ and the Church.

9. Cf. Lawrence R. Michaels, *Revelation in Its Original Meaning* (San Diego, CA: Bovee Productions, 1999), 83.

encounter her divine Bridegroom: "Who is she that looks forth as the morning, fair as the moon, clear as the sun, and terrible as an army with banners?" (Cant 6:10). Unhappily, however, her feet are not received by the earth, denoting a world that does not wait for its Savior (John 1:11).[10] To round out this cosmic display, the woman wears on her head a crown of twelve stars,[11] much more fulgent than the rainbow surmounting the angel's head (10:1), indicating her exceptional dignity as the only daughter of humanity not blemished by original sin.[12] These glittering crown jewels signal her exalted standing as the uncontested Queen of heaven,[13] sharing in the universal reign of her Son consisting in the communion of angels and saints, kings, prophets, and priests. By extension, the stellar diadem points to the Gospel, prepared by the patriarchs, and preached by the apostles,[14] going into all the world and proclaiming the Good News to the whole creation (Mark 16:15). At the dawn of history God made the heavenly bodies for signs, for seasons, and for days and years (Gen 1:14); but since at this present stage, time has slipped into the realm of eternity, at long last their true purpose is revealed, and that is to serve as perpetual trophies and ornaments, celebrating in grandiose stillness the victory of the Lamb and his Bride, the Church.[15] Now no longer tokens of separation but of unity[16] beyond good and evil, they give expression to all jubilation in the day of Christ in glory. Sun, moon, and stars will play an eschatological role framing the parousia of the Son of Man, too (Matt 24:29–30), yet once his enemies are put under his feet (Matt 22:44) after the consummation of history, there will be no need for them any longer in heaven (21:23; 22:5).

In direct fulfillment of the messianic prophecy at Isaiah 7:10, 14, this apocalyptic woman is pregnant and crying out in birth pangs, in the agony of giving birth (v. 2; cf. Mic 5:3). What can be heard in the background, as it were, is Eve's weeping after being cursed by the Lord God (Gen 3:16). Due to our

10. Cf. AvS, 391.

11. Cf. 1:20; 4:4; Matt 26:53; see also Balaam's prophecy of the messianic star (Num 24:17), and the twelve gems in the priestly breastplate (Exod 28:21).

12. Cf. AvS, 388–89.

13. Opposite to the idolatrous "queen of heaven" (Jer 7:18; 44:17–25; 2 Kgs 23:5), potentially fostering humanity's fascination with heavenly bodies, not least as reflected in the twelve signs of the zodiac cycle in Western astrology.

14. Cf. RD, 1041.

15. Notice the striking resemblance with the image of Our Lady of Guadalupe, imprinted on St. Juan Diego's tilma during her apparitions at Tepeyac, Mexico, in 1531.

16. Visually evocative of the 1781 Cowpens flag, an early version of the United States flag, where twelve white stars are arranged in a circle on a blue field with the thirteenth star in the center, denoting the original states of the American Union.

protoparents' sin, the whole creation groans and travails in pain together until now (Rom 8:22). Also reverberating is Israel's cry of yearning for the promised Deliverer (Rom 9:4–5), turning her covenanted history into one plurimillennial gestation.[17] Contemplating this multivalent image with Christian eyes, one sees Mother Church bearing children unto Christ (Gal 4:19). She is in agonizing pain to bring forth a holy family for God her husband (Isa 54:5; 62:5), constantly suffering to rise above spiritual barrenness, and generating the grace of conversion for the salvation of souls. She joins in the scream of the Crucified Lord[18] as she gives life to her children through the death and burial of baptism, by the proclamation of the Gospel, and through periods of persecution. Christ laid upon her this law of birth pangs until the end of time,[19] without which she cannot work deliverance.

It will always be the pain of rebirth from natural to supernatural children, transforming them into the image and likeness of Christ (Gen 1:27), whereas schismatics, heretics and apostates must be considered miscarriages. Thus, the triumphant image is still reflective of temporality, i.e., of the militant and suffering Church. Her stage of celestial victory in John's vision is merged with the stage of earthly suffering, symbolized by the Lamb slain and at the same time standing upright (5:6). She who once was so discreetly quiet in the Gospels now wails and writhes in agony,[20] and as such becomes the principal model of the new people of God as *Mater Ecclesiae*.[21] From a strictly Catholic vantage point, there seems to be an incongruity, however, between the studied fivefold reiteration of the verb *tíktō* (τίκτω, *pario*; vv. 2, 4–5, 13), meaning "to give birth," implying a labored birthing process on the one hand, and the inherent painlessness implied in the dogma of Mary's perpetual virginity on the other.[22] But this contradiction is only apparent since the image refers more to the mystical birth

17. Cf. RD, 1042.

18. Note the same verb *krázō* (κράζω, *clamare*) on Calvary (Matt 27:50).

19. All Greek verbs of this verse are in the present tense, conveying the idea of ongoing pain involved in birthing these spiritual children for the Church.

20. Notice how the phrase *en gastrì échousa* (ἐν γαστρὶ ἔχουσα, *in utero habens*), literally, "carrying in the womb," is part of both the Matthean Infancy Narrative (Matt 1:18, 23) and of the Eschatological Discourse (Matt 24:19).

21. Cf. Second Vatican Council, Dogmatic Constitution *Lumen gentium* (November 21, 1964), 107–90 in *The Sixteen Documents of Vatican II* (Boston: Daughters of St. Paul, 1965), §63: "As St. Ambrose taught, the Mother of God is a type of the Church in the order of faith, charity, and the perfect union with Christ."

22. The dogma that Mary was a Virgin before, during, and after the birth of Christ (*ante partum, in partu, et post partum*) was defined by Pope Martin I at the Lateran Council of 649, and restated by Vatican II, *Lumen gentium*, §57.

pangs that Mary undergoes in cooperating in God's plan of salvation and in bringing forth the sons and daughters of the Church,[23] and not so much to the actual nativity of Christ in Bethlehem likely surrounded by expressions of joy (Isa 9:6; 66:7). From a spiritual viewpoint, by this virginal birth, she becomes at the same time the Mother and Bride of her Son, while the God-Man is both her Son and Bridegroom. Lastly, this birthing image carries the eschatological overtone of the sudden arrival of the Day of the Lord (1 Thess 5:3). Thus, the woman that the apostle is seeing in his vision is so clearly a superhuman figure that can hardly be identified with any single human being; and indeed, she concurrently represents humanity in so far as it belongs to God, but also ancient Israel, the Church militant and triumphant, and the Blessed Virgin Mary herself.[24]

We would be remiss if we did not subjoin a word of encouragement to be cordially devoted to her, our Sister, Mother, and our Queen.[25] Just as she precedes her Son in Cana (John 2:1–2), so she is introduced in the Apocalypse ahead of him, which shows that she is forever the gateway to Jesus, as well as Christ's entryway into this world. As true children of the Church, we should always allow her to lead us to her Son: *per Mariam ad Iesum*. This magnificent revelation of the most graced Daughter of the human family should also be the primary inspiration for all women. In times when many are embroiled in anti-Marian forms of feminism, not to mention the diabolical gender confusion of our day, the Mother of God reminds especially women of their Christian nobility and dignity,[26] and how they ought to imitate her in their journey toward holiness, nurturing and sharing the fruits of their God-given feminine genius.[27] An ever more menacing tide of a culture of death can be countered only if women discover and rediscover their high vocation, and choose to model their lives on that of the Virgin of Nazareth, in order to promote a culture of life as daughters, sisters, wives, mothers, and grandmothers: indeed, Christian civilization cannot thrive without their example of holiness.

23. To give but one example for the many internal anguishes that she suffered, one can only imagine the excruciating pain of seeing Joseph her husband discerning the signs of her pregnancy, and not being able to explain the divine origin to him at the time (Matt 1:18–19). Worth noting here, too, is the devotion to the seven sorrows of the *Mater Dolorosa*.

24. Cf. William Barclay, *The Revelation of John*, vol. 2, 2nd ed. (Philadelphia: Westminster, 1960), 92.

25. Cf. the 1974 apostolic exhortation *Marialis cultus* by St. Paul VI; and the 1987 encyclical letter *Redemptoris Mater* by St. John Paul II.

26. Cf. the 1988 apostolic letter *Mulieris dignitatem* by St. John Paul II.

27. Cf. St. John Paul's 1995 *Letter to Women*, §12.

Another sign (12:3–4a)

[3]*Then another portent appeared in heaven: a great red dragon, with seven heads and ten horns, and seven diadems on his heads.* [4a]*His tail swept down a third of the stars of heaven and threw them to the earth.*

While John's eyes are still riveted on the cosmic woman caught in the throes of childbirth, another sign in heaven is shown to him with great insistence or even urgency: behold (*ecce*), a great fiery-red dragon! (v. 3). Mentioned here for the first time in the New Testament, it is pictured as floating in the air of the upper regions of the skies rather than the third heaven of blissful glory (Job 1:6–7; 2:1–2). Scripturally based on Genesis 3:1, 14 (cf. Exod 7:9), it symbolizes the person of the devil, the foremost spirit of enmity against God, instigator of all forces of evil, perpetual antagonist of good, root of every anti-Christian action, and the persecutor of the Church in all ages. Previously intimated at 6:8, 9:11, and 11:7, he is now finally uncovered. As the god of this world, he is fittingly likened to a dragon[28] for its cunning in circumventing and ensnaring Christians, for its cruelty and inhumanity in persecuting them, for its injecting into them the poison of idolatry, and for its intriguing yet unholy power.

The seer begins to describe this sheer mosaic of biblical imagery by pointing to this monster's flame-red color, redolent of the second apocalyptic rider (6:4), but also foreboding the scarlet beast (17:3). It is the sinister mark of the murderer from the beginning (John 8:44), causing oppression and bloodshed among the saints and martyrs. Tellingly, a purple toga was worn by the earliest persecutors of Christians, namely, the ancient Roman emperors and generals, in imitation of Mars, the god of war. Furthermore, this sanguinary monster has seven heads and ten horns, modeled on the many-headed leviathan (Ps 74:13–15): they are a simile for the consummate wiliness of a satanic mastermind, out to besiege the Mother and eliminate her Child. These heads are like hideous storehouses of overwhelming hatred toward their offspring (12:17).[29]

Mirroring the fourth beast of Daniel's vision (Dan 7:7) and aping the seven horns of the Lamb (5:6), the ten dragon's horns are symbols of its temporary power on earth, consistently antithetical to the "horn of salvation" (Luke 1:69).

28. The Greek noun *drákōn* (δράκων, *draco*) recurs in the Septuagint chiefly for the Hebrew *tannín* (תַּנִּין), "snake" (e.g., Pss 91:13); it is a probable derivation from the verb *dérkomai* (δέρκομαι), "to see, to look," denoting a mythical serpent believed to have phenomenal eyesight, able to see its prey from far away, spotting it in any hiding place.

29. Rupert explains them as representatives of all the generations of evil people, cf. RD, 1078.

They will resurface in the two beasts (13:1, 11) and are also reminiscent of the ten days of tribulation inflicted on the Smyrnaean church (2:10). Later, the mind of wisdom will identify heads and horns with successive kingdoms (17:9, 12), that is, forms of dictatorial governments seeking to destroy faith in Christ and culminating in the anti-Christian rebellion in the final days. At the time of John's writing, the imperial power on his mind would have been Rome, a city sprawled across seven hills, mightily presiding over the whole world.

Topping off this draconian portrait are seven diadems on his heads (v. 3), clashing with its ten horns in diabolical disparity, asymmetric confusion, and ugly self-contradiction.[30] One could discern in them a caricature of the seven Spirits of God.[31] As sevenfold badges of infernal royalty they may be figurative of the pseudo-fullness of the dragon's tyranny over the kingdoms of this world, as he animates them by his foul spirit.[32] He is the prince of this world (John 14:30), already condemned and cast out (John 12:31; 16:11). Thus, if the woman is a metaphor for the Kingdom of God, then the dragon represents the kingdom of the world. Nevertheless, the latter will always be surpassed and controlled by the King of kings and Lord of lords, who in his infinite majesty wears many diadems on his head (19:12, 16).

Besides, and with high drama, John depicts the dragon slithering along the vault of the sky, his tail sweeping down a third of the stars of heaven, throwing them to the earth (v. 4). This furious lashing and thrashing refers to the primeval seduction and destitution of "stars," that is, angels (1:20) from their heavenly ranks to serve his will rather than God's (Jude 6).[33] Merely alluding to the eerie outcome of this rebellion in heaven, the seer does not interrupt his narrative here to further expound, but will return to it in vv. 7–9, elaborating on the devil's enmity toward the Most High. Two-thirds of the angelic beings remain unscathed in this gargantuan struggle, whereas Jesus, interestingly, seems to point to an absolute majority of damned souls (Matt 7:13–14; 22:14). As it turns out, the tails of the locust-horses at the fifth trumpet (9:10, 19), the devastation of third parts under the second through fourth (8:7–12), and also the sixth trumpet (9:15, 18), all were adumbrations of this triple decimation of spirits. While leaving the radiance of the twelve stars of the woman's diadem

30. Cf. RD, 1046.

31. The Belgian Jesuit and Scripture scholar Jacobus Tirinus (d. 1636) compares the crowns to the seven deadly sins (cf. *Commentarius in Sacram Scripturam*).

32. For instance, the serpentine image often represented ancient Egypt, the principal foe of Israel (e.g., Isa 27:1), and Pharaoh's crown was wreathed with the ceremonial asp.

33. Evocative, incidentally, of the enmity between the Scorpion and Orion in Greek mythology and astrology, reflected in the *cauda* ("tail") of the constellation Scorpius.

undimmed, this act of primordial insurgency must have darkened the expanse of space. By managing to tear away one out of three, the serpent makes a frantic attempt to disparage the trinitarian principle of one God in three persons, and to slyly strike at the Holy Spirit, too.[34] There may be the added meaning of saints being killed across the centuries (Dan 12:3). And also, the plummeting stars could represent human beings fallen from grace, as well as those who apostatize from heavenly doctrine and fall into worldly error and spiritual death.

Now is a good time to also reaffirm that Satan is an actual person to be reckoned with, and not just an impersonal force of evil. He is indefatigable when it comes to ensnaring the human mind and heart, in trying to fascinate them with mundane power, pleasure, and prestige. His ultimate objective is to overthrow us, sweeping us off into the nether regions of sin, vice, and despair. Instead, let us set our minds on that which is above, and not on worldly things (Col 3:2). When tried and tempted by the devil, we should recall the ageless advice given by Paul to the Corinthians: "If you think you are standing, watch out that you do not fall. No testing has overtaken you that is not common to everyone. God is faithful, and he will not let you be tested beyond your strength, but with the testing he will also provide the way out so that you may be able to endure it" (1 Cor 10:12–13).

A Son, a male child (12:4b–5)

[4b]Then the dragon stood before the woman who was about to bear a child, so that he might devour her child as soon as it was born. [5]And she gave birth to a son, a male child, who is to rule all the nations with a rod of iron. But her child was snatched away and taken to God and to his throne.

As the narrative focus swings back toward the pregnant woman from v. 2, that diabolical stance in front of her is beyond suspenseful, it is downright terrifying (v. 4). Just as the expectant Mother, so also the dragon is expectant, only in a perverse way, namely, awaiting his opportunity to destroy the child. He is the embodiment of self-centered arrogance and menace, while her humility is the exact inversion of that fire-red pride.[35] Restaging the sinister confrontation between Eve and the serpent (Gen 3:1–5), and at the same time presaging Christ's own face-off with the tempter in the desert (Matt 4:3), her screaming

34. Cf. AvS, 393.
35. Cf. AvS, 392.

in travail takes on the added meaning of an urgent cry for help. Similarly, her celestial attributes of sun, moon, and stars now seem more like an array of armor and weaponry against the one who is hell-bent on annihilating the blessed fruit of her womb. Symbolized here is Satan's mortal enmity toward the Church, ravenous to persecute and brutalize her, to erase Jesus' name from human memory, and to thwart any spiritual gain due to his Incarnation and salvation (1 Pet 5:8–9). Unprovoked, he is the provocateur of all trial and oppression, diabolically watchful to crush the Christian religion. His voracity,[36] however, will be met by provisions of divine protection. True, Christ will be bitten by the serpent's fangs and devoured by death and tomb, but his Father will raise him up and seat him at his right hand, forever frustrating the ferocious attacks of his opponent.[37]

Despite his open hostility, the woman gives birth to a son, a male child, who is to shepherd[38] all the nations with a rod of iron (v. 5). A deliberate syntactic incongruency, i.e., adjoining a neuter adjective to a masculine noun in the guise of an apposition (*hyiòn ársen*, υἱὸν ἄρσεν, *filium masculum*),[39] lends extraordinary prominence to the gender of this divine neonate, literally "a son, a male child" or "a child of manliness."[40] By making his masculinity so explicit, it recalls the Genesis account of God creating Adam and Eve, "male and female he created them" (Gen 1:27), hinting at a new creation.[41] This virility of the woman's child identifies him with the Messiah, Jesus Christ, Son of God and Son of Man, underscoring, too, the innate vigor and robustness of his work of redemption (Luke 2:23).[42] In that manliness he also pastors all of humanity, or, to follow the apocalyptic language, the Lamb feeds the sheep.

His global dominion is predicted in Psalm 2:7–9, where his birth concurs with his royal inauguration and enthronement, receiving all the nations

36. See the recurrence of the verb *katesthíō* (κατεσθίω, *devorare*), "to devour," at the defensive events of 11:5 and 20:9; cf. also the related *katapínō* (καταπίνω, *absorbere*), "to swallow up," at 12:16.

37. Cf. RD, 1049.

38. Literal translation of the Greek verb *poimaínō* (ποιμαίνω), "to shepherd, feed," with its pastoral connotation; the Neo-Vulgate, instead, renders it as *regere*, "to rule, govern," with a pronounced regal undertone.

39. That it is indeed a studied exception to grammatical rule is proven by the circumstance that John employs the correct masculine gender, namely, *tòn ársena* (τὸν ἄρσενα, *masculum*), in v. 13.

40. Considering that the Greek noun *hyiós* (υἱός) denotes both "son" and "child."

41. Cf. AvS, 394.

42. Corresponding to the gender-specific messianic prophecy at Jer 31:22, "For the Lord has created a new thing on the earth: a woman encompasses a man (*femina circumdabit virum*)."

for his inheritance. That his rule will be supreme and unimpeachable is suggested by the iron rod that he wields over the good and the wicked, magnifying his priestly role, symbolized already by Aaron's rod. Moreover, if his scepter were to be interpreted as the Cross, then Christ's birth and his crucifixion are blended in this vision. Expression is given here to the fundamental idea of the entire Apocalypse, namely, the historical battle between light and darkness, which is the reason why Satan lays snares chiefly for the child, but later also for the woman and the rest of her children (v. 17).

Something marvelous and unexpected happens next: the Mother's child is snatched away and taken to God and to his throne (v. 5). Foreshadowed by Moses' escape from Pharaoh's selectively male infanticide (Exod 1:16; 2:3), by the Holy Family's flight to Egypt from Herod's murderous pursuits, but also correlated to the two witnesses' rapture away from the spiritual "Sodom and Egypt" (11:8, 12), the woman's blessed offspring evidently enjoys God's special protection. Without making his Death and Resurrection explicit, in a telescoped snapshot of his entire incarnational mission, Christ is taken up into heaven, to where he was before, that sitting on his Father's throne he may reign over all (Phil 2:9–11). His sudden rescue[43] from the fangs of the dragon means his preservation in the safest and most exalted place of refuge, that is, heaven, undergirding his own divinity. This breathtaking escape could be understood as a pledge that assures the ultimate safety and prosperity of the Church, no matter how much hardship she must endure along her pilgrimage on earth.

When compared to Gospel data, however, there appears to be a twofold incongruity regarding this image of the Ascension of our Lord. For one, the historical Jesus, after suffering the deepest abasement in his Passion, ascends into heaven like a successful military general crowning his victory with a triumphant parade (Acts 1:9–10; Col 2:15). Here, on the contrary, he experiences an abrupt escape from potentially lethal peril. Also, in the former ascension, the Son of Man is in his prime enjoying the full maturity of his faculties, whereas the latter sees a vulnerable infant being wrested from imminent danger to his life. But then again, this seeming incompatibility aids the reader to remain within the boundaries of the intended symbolism of this scene, namely, that God will shield and deliver his Church in times of persecution.

43. The divine passive of the Greek verb *herpásthē* (ἡρπάσθη, *raptus*) not only intimates the initiative taken by the heavenly Father in exalting his Son, but also carries the overtone of a violent rapture (cf. Matt 11:12; 12:29; 13:19; John 6:15; 10:12, 28–29).

And as it happened, the dragon did try its very hardest to eradicate nascent Christianity during the early centuries of its existence, until the Edict of Milan in AD 313 brought about religious toleration within the Roman Empire. Hence, the people of God are comparable to a feeble and oppressed woman, but her faith raises her up before God, placing her beyond the reach of every hostile power. Notwithstanding the jealousy and animosity of adversaries, the Mystical Body of Christ will continue to expand among the nations. While the Jesus of Nazareth is now seated as Pantocrator at the Father's right hand in heaven, his Church will remain on earth to assist us in our spiritual warfare (Eph 6:12), ever animating us to persevere until he comes again.[44]

Among the spiritual lessons that can be taken away from this Bible passage, one should point out the remarkable textual emphasis on the moment of birthing (vv. 2, 4–5, 13). No doubt, the serpent has in its crosshairs above everything else the seed of the woman, the child about to be born, putting himself right in front of the laboring mother, in order that, when she has given birth, he may devour the newborn. He is ever lurking to obliterate the first signs of human life, every token of goodness, and every resemblance to Christ in each one of us and in the world. And he does so out of jealousy over humanity's God-given gift of immortality and similitude to the Creator (Wis 2:23–24). In other words, out of envy at seeing the deserted angelic thrones in heaven repopulated with humans, the evil one will always attempt to prevent the increase of the Church and eliminate human life as early as in the maternal womb. This specific act of swallowing up is also known as abortion, one of the most heinous crimes and worst forms of murder, and one of the grimmest stigmas of modern societies.[45] And he obviously does not stop at feticide but unleashes his hostility against all the children of the Church (John 15:20).

In all this we can rest assured that as Mary's spiritual children we will be safeguarded amid the struggle, and that godlessness cannot arrest Christ, spiritually born into the minds and hearts of his hearers. And at some point, his rule will put an end to the dragon's conquests. Furthermore, Satan appears to victimize and hound the woman just because she is about to become the Mother of that child in his maleness. He does so with ferocious intentionality, targeting the maternal-filial relationship of a woman to her male child in their differentiated gender identity. Sacred Scripture distinguishes unambiguously between male and female (Gen 1:27), intended by the Creator to reflect his transcendent

44. Cf. AvS, 395.
45. Cf. *CCC*, §§2270–75.

nuptial love for his covenanted people.[46] The biblical clarity of that distinction must be regarded as the decisive remedy to all misguided gender ideology of our day, confusing those very boundaries to deleterious effect for marriage, family, and the wider civilization. Thus, in response to these verses of Revelation, with confidence let us take refuge in the Hearts of Jesus and his Mother Mary.

New Exodus (12:6)

[6]*And the woman fled into the wilderness, where she has a place prepared by God, so that there she can be nourished for one thousand two hundred sixty days.*

As a rule, these apocalyptic visions possess multiple layers of meaning, and they are narrated in a nonlinear chronology. And so, when John reports that this cosmic woman and Mother flees into the wilderness where God has prepared a place for her (v. 6), he projects already into v. 14. There, he explains the reason for her being driven into the wilderness, to wit, the imminent threat of persecution by the dragon, not only against her Son (v. 4), but now also against her own person. That narrative prolepsis is at the same time anachronistic regarding the war in heaven portrayed in vv. 7–9, since that took place at the dawn of creation, prior to the woman's very existence. This meta-historical presentation had John begin the chapter with the glorified Church of the time of fulfilment in v. 1, reflected in the heavenly proclamation of vv. 10–12, then oscillating backward to the birth of the people of God in history at v. 2, then swinging back even further to the primeval fall of the angels in vv. 3–4, only to advance again into the eschatological period of the Church in vv. 5–6. Said eschaton, therefore, is sandwiched between a contemplation of the original separation between good and evil in vv. 3–4 and vv. 7–9. Eventually, the visionary lens will swivel back to that historical pilgrimage of a persecuted Church in vv. 13–18. The apostolic seer uses this trans-temporal method of alternating between scenes precisely to demonstrate the intimate connection that exists among these epic events in creation and salvation history. What emerges in due course is a kaleidoscopic masterpiece of God's design.

At any rate, to better appreciate the image of the woman's retreat into the

46. Cf. the Instruction "Male and Female He Created Them: Toward a Path of Dialogue on the Question of Gender Theory in Education," by the Congregation for Catholic Education (Vatican City, 2019).

desert, one must remember the versatile nature of this biblical concept with its positive and negative implications. Firstly, it is a metaphorical region of God's first and tender love toward his people (Jer 2:2; Hos 2:14), of nuptial encounter (Cant 8:5), of divine care (Exod 16), as well as protection, serenity, and peace (Hos 13:5). Yet secondly, it is also the locality where the Lord sends trials to test his children's perseverance and where he exercises judgment (Exod 20:35). It is the theater of the people's rebellion against their covenant God (Exod 17; Heb 3:8) even to the point of apostasy (Exod 32:4). Not least, too, its extreme natural environment spells constant danger, desolation, and death (1 Cor 10:5). As such it is identical to the unmeasured and outcast courtyard of the gentiles (11:2), as well as the uncured wasteland where the great harlot has taken up her abode (17:3). According to the typology of Israel's Exodus, this wilderness becomes the traditional place of refuge for the afflicted after fleeing the house of oppression (Exod 3:9), as well as of pilgrimage en route to the Promised Land. Overlaid on this paradigm is a new Exodus, propounded mainly by Isaiah, envisioning the joyous return of the redeemed to Zion, as they march through a flourishing wilderness along a holy way (Isa 35:8).[47] On the threshold of the New Covenant, John the Baptizer becomes the new prototypical desert dweller, initiating, so to speak, the reversal of Adam's expulsion from paradise (Gen 3:23–24).

When describing the woman fleeing into the desert, the apostle seems to refer to ancient Israel, Mary as New Eve, and the Church, as almost indistinguishable entities. Contrary to those who flee from divine wrath (Matt 3:7), from suffering (Matt 26:56), or from their Christian calling, the people of God must continuously break away to find contemplative solitude[48] to remain faithful to its mission and become the Mother of many children (Gal 4:27).[49] God himself prepares a place for her where she can be nourished (vv. 6, 14),[50] that is, a tabernacle of safety (Ps 90:1). Detached from worldly comfort and pomp,[51] she is mysteriously nourished with the true Bread from heaven[52] and

47. Cf. David W. Pao, *Acts and the Isaianic New Exodus* (Grand Rapids, MI: Baker Academic, 2000).

48. The Vulgate renders the Greek noun *érēmos* (ἔρημος) as *solitudo*, "solitude."

49. As a contemporaneous example, one could cite the flight of Christians to Pella in the desert of the Jordan Valley before the destruction of Jerusalem in AD 70.

50. On the Greek noun *tópos* (τόπος, *locus*, "place") as a spiritual sanctuary, see Beale, *Book of Revelation*, 648–49; notable is also the absence of a place for the devil in 12:8.

51. Cf. RD, 1050.

52. Tellingly, Jesus chose a deserted place for his miracle of the multiplication of bread, foreshadowing the gift of the Holy Eucharist (Luke 9:12).

with the living water from the Rock (1 Cor 10:3–4). Does the seer imply that she is fed by the hand of angels, since he speaks in the plural (*pascant*)? This verb also recalls the miraculous feeding of the prophet Elijah (2 Kgs 17:4) and the bucolic figure of the Good Shepherd (v. 5). If the Almighty can sustain the birds of the air (Matt 6:26), then there is no question that he will provide for the Bride of the Son of Man and rear her children. Indeed, he will do so for one thousand two hundred sixty days, or circa three and a half years, or forty-two months, as opposed to the plenary seven years' period (v. 6; cf. 11:2), meaning, for the entire length of her earthly pilgrimage. Thus, there will never be an age in which the Church becomes extinct; instead, she will be nurtured and preserved until her New Exodus is accomplished at the end of time, and she emerges victorious to enter her eternal paradise.

After she carried the Son in her virginal womb, enabling her to entertain a mystical dialogue with him, now he carries her into utter loneliness.[53] This circumstance can be enriching to our own Christian spirituality: While the apocalyptic woman does not literally refer to the historical Mother of God, for the latter did not flee into the wilderness and stay there for that length of time, she does symbolize the Church and her children, and as such she is an emblem of our baptized soul sheltered in God himself. Moreover, there are symbolic overtones bound up with desert landscapes that help us understand our own spiritual journey toward the Promised Land. Among countless other occasions, whenever we enter the innermost chamber of our heart, shut the door, and pray to our heavenly Father (Matt 6:6), we experience the desert with the open skies overhead: protection from satanic plots, quasi-eremitic contemplation, subdued distractions, increased interior clarity and purity, and perhaps even the realization of obstacles and challenges. All of which calls upon the deepest reserves of the traveler's discernment and determination.

Good and faithful Christians regularly celebrate personal spiritual exercises or similar retreats, following the example of Jesus who allowed himself to the driven out by the Spirit into the wilderness to face Satan (Mark 1:12). On those blessed occasions we become like the proverbial sheep fleeing from the stranger (John 10:5), from immorality (1 Cor 6:18), and from idolatry. We also understand from reading the Gospels that Christ frequently slipped away to pray during the night (Luke 6:12) or before dawn (Mark 1:35), and he also took his apostles into deserted places to rest with him (Mark 6:31). Also coming to mind is St. Anthony of the Desert, who during his sojourn in the Egyptian wilderness for many years engaged in highly demanding spiritual exercises and

53. Cf. AvS, 396.

was subjected to fierce temptations by the devil.[54] His ascetic resistance against all demonic ruses, and his prayerful perseverance in this intense spiritual combat, redounded to his extraordinary holiness (Jas 4:7–8).

Who is like God? (12:7–9)

[7]And war broke out in heaven; Michael and his angels fought against the dragon. The dragon and his angels fought back, [8]but they were defeated, and there was no longer any place for them in heaven. [9]The great dragon was thrown down, that ancient serpent, who is called the Devil and Satan, the deceiver of the whole world, he was thrown down to the earth, and his angels were thrown down with him.

Interrupting the train of thought regarding the woman's flight into the wilderness and her persecution by the serpent, vv. 7–13 also brusquely change the visionary setting from earth back to heaven, a narrative shift that is caused apparently by John's desire to account in some degree for the unremitting hostility of the devil toward God and his Church. A case could be made that this angelic battle in the celestial sphere depicts the deathblow that the Incarnate, Crucified, and Risen Lord dealt to Lucifer (Luke 10:18; John 12:31). Figuratively, Michael would represent humankind which in the person of Christ is victorious over evil. Perhaps favorable to this explanation is also the mention of salvation as a gift already obtained in the Messiah as well as in the blood of the Lamb, in the hymnic acclamation of vv. 10–11. Despite this interpretive option, it seems more congruent with the tenor of this central chapter of the Apocalypse, that the seer compresses the entire arc of history into a single vignette, into one all-encompassing scene, that is, from the angelic conflict at the dawn of time (1 John 3:8) with the ensuing fall of the demons, all the way to the final triumph of the Church in heaven.

Carrying the water for this interpretive angle is the fact that the combat here is fought directly between Michael and the dragon, and not between Christ and the devil, as at the Incarnation and Resurrection. Likewise, Calvary was certainly not the instant of Satan's rebellion and expulsion from the heavens to the earth. Thus, at an unspecified point in time, following the creation of

54. Anthony died in 356 reportedly at the age of 105; "The Temptation of St. Anthony" was first discussed by his contemporary, St. Athanasius of Alexandria (d. 373), in his biography entitled "Life of Anthony" (*Vita Antonii*), a book that played a pivotal role in the spreading of the eremitic ideals in Eastern and Western Christianity.

the visible and invisible world (Gen 1:1), and without any hint of a *causa belli*, war broke out in heaven; Michael and his angels fought against the dragon, and the dragon and his angels fought back (v. 7). Obviously, a considerable contingent of recently created angels allowed themselves to think in ways that would cause a crack in their personal loyalty toward the Creator (Job 15:15; 4:18), and that interior disloyalty now suddenly erupts into open conflict among the spiritual hierarchies, denoting the origin of the biblical notions of evil and of holy war.[55] It is the only explicit reference in Scripture to such a primordial war in heaven, a seeming contradiction in terms since one expects nothing but peace in the presence of God. This brazen rebellion, even though the actual battle may have taken place in the lower regions of heaven rather than the divine habitation,[56] must have caused such an insult to the Almighty that it would only be atoned for in due course by Christ's glorifying return to his Father.[57]

Utterly intolerant of satanic pride, the good angels appear to fight with such vehemence that God did not even have to step in to banish evil. Lucifer's insolent *Non serviam!* ("I will not serve") is trounced by Michael's intrepid *Quis ut Deus?!* ("Who is like God?").[58] Led by this archangelic warrior, spokesperson and champion for God,[59] they seem to go on the attack in the strength of God himself, remaining faithful to his cause. Only in a spirit of unconditional service to him were they able to accomplish the enormous task of defeating all devilish anarchy and insurrection, sustained also by the grace of the Holy Spirit. Receiving humiliation on top of injury, Lucifer is vanquished by an angelic being who, although now captain of all celestial hosts (Jude 9), was created inferior to his own rank. By reiterating the word "fight" three times in this verse, John portrays an epic prehistoric tug of war between Michael and his angels and the dragon and his angels (Matt 12:24), resulting in the fall of those stars from v. 4, and explaining the existence of a dual angelic hierarchy ever since, that is, of good and of demonic spirits (Ezek 28:12–19).

55. "A consistent thematic, that of God's Holy War, pervades John's entire composition. This thematic serves to confirm the structural unity and coherence of Revelation and to impart to it a distinctive and dominant theological emphasis." Charles Homer Giblin, *The Book of Revelation: The Open Book of Prophecy*, GNS 34 (Collegeville, MN: Liturgical Press, 1991), 224.

56. What was known in ancient cosmologies as the empyrean heaven, from the Greek *émpyros* (ἔμπυρος), meaning "in the fire" (2 Cor 12:2, 4).

57. Cf. AvS, 398–99.

58. In translation of the Hebrew name "Michael" (מִיכָאֵל); cf. Gregory the Great, *Homilia* 34.8 (PL 76:1250).

59. Reminiscent of the "commander of the army of the Lord," with "a drawn sword in his hand" (Josh 5:13–15).

Not a lone wolf, but surrounded by his devilish pack, Satan is condemned to live in darkness, all the while unable to jettison his faith in God (Jas 2:19). Despite his viciousness, his collective might falls short and is no match for the armies of the Most High (v. 8). And there is no rallying after the floundering either, since there was no longer any place for them in heaven.[60] Exacerbating the first negation "he did not prevail" (οὐκ, *non*) is a second stronger one, "not *even* a place was found for them" (οὐδέ, *neque*), reinforcing the opposition to the woman who does have a place prepared for her by God (v. 6). So shamefully thorough was the dragon's ejection that he was no longer permitted to remain in heaven in any capacity (Isa 14:12), evincing an inherent weakness in all evil. Conversely, it faintly announces the grace of redemption. Thus, the ancient serpent is deprived of its heavenly excellence, and will be chained in a pit for the eschatological duration of the Christian people (20:1–3), then released for the short apocalyptic period (20:7), only to be cast into the fiery pit as his deepest and most torturous relegation forever (20:10).

As the intensity of spiritual warfare was conveyed by a triple restatement of "to fight" in the active voice (v. 7), so also the magnitude of demonic ruination is expressed by reiterating "thrown down" three times in the passive voice (vv. 9–10, 13). This underlines Lucifer's total departure from heavenly realities and full-scale turning to earthly affairs, becoming imprisoned in them. Something unique in Scripture is the aggregation of no fewer than five appellatives to capture the infernal nature and activity of the foe as exhaustively as possible: "great dragon, ancient serpent, Devil, Satan, deceiver of the whole world." This compact identification of the person of the devil stands in contrast to the otherwise unidentified cosmic woman, perhaps to place more emphasis on the communal aspect of the people of God. Be that as it may, the great dragon of v. 3 is now unmasked as the ancient serpent (Ps 74:13–14), hinted at already in 9:19. This is the singular occasion in the Bible where we are told explicitly that Eve's tempter in Eden was the devil (Gen 3:1; Wis 2:24), making the snake a symbol of the evil principle itself and of everything godless in history. His third cognomen is *diábolus*, literally, the slanderer or defamer or backbiter, that is, the one who unabatingly calumniates the innocent. Fourthly, he is called Satan, which in Hebrew (שָׂטָן) signifies an accuser (*accusator*, v. 10) or adversary, one who incubates never-ending opposition to God's loving and saving work in the world

60. When Satan appears among the sons of God again, presenting himself in heaven to accuse a saintly Job, it must again be interpreted as not signifying the highest heaven, and only until Christ's Incarnation (Job 1:6).

(Matt 16:23).[61] His fifth moniker is seducer (Matt 27:63), because his hellish trademark is to sow confusion to the point of engendering death, which is why Jesus himself labels him as murderer from the beginning,[62] liar, and the father of lies (John 8:44).[63] His repertoire of deceit includes idols, oracles, sorcery, soothsaying, magic, and all other guises of fraudulence perpetrated on earth. His agency of maligning, inculpating, and beguiling enwreathes the entire inhabited globe, wherever his minions roam. Put another way, the damage is no longer partial as under the sixth trumpet (9:15, 18), but total; he craves for the whole world (*universum orbem*) to worship himself and not God.[64]

What is spiritually reassuring, however, is that even though Satan's operations may be staggeringly insidious, he remains an adversary who has been fully conquered already. In fact, he has suffered a twofold cosmic excommunication, as it were, one in the beginning of time and again at the Resurrection of Christ, i.e., at the first and at the new creation. And it was Jesus, "the stronger than the strong one," who has overpowered him and taken away his armor (Luke 11:21–22). Now the demons have no choice but to await their final undoing at the end of time. Being born into this world means being introduced to the effects of that battle in heaven and on Golgotha, that is, the spiritual warfare between the angels of darkness and the angels of light, between Christianity and those who choose to stay impermeable to the pull of our Savior's amazing grace. On our part, as his baptized brethren, we are under a solemn vow to inflict as many defeats as achievable on the ancient serpent by resisting his temptations, and thereby earn heaven. If the *diábolos* is our accuser, then we have the Holy Spirit as our Paraclete, i.e., the Defender and Comforter, and the Blessed Virgin Mary as our Advocate (*Advocata Nostra*). With their assistance we are determined to tolerate less and less evil in our life, detesting every form of sin. Humility will outmaneuver Satan's "I will not serve," and the watchword should always be "Who is like God?!" Each time the soul manages to prayerfully withstand the devil's wiles, it throws him out of heaven and crushes his head all over again. Besides, with the discomfiture of the demons the former heaven was forever

61. A crucial part of the so-called Divine Courtroom Motif, also known as the *Rîb*-pattern, found especially in the Gospel of John.

62. As a matter of fact, the first death of humanity was not a natural death, but a murder, that of Abel (Gen 4:8).

63. Attempting as he does to mislead human hearts and minds by applying his threefold matrix of deceit, namely, to sow doubt concerning God's veracity (Gen 3:1), to deny the deadly consequence of sin (Gen 3:4), and to falsely promise greater knowledge and God-likeness (Gen 3:5).

64. Cf. RD, 1055.

changed, now awaiting a new heaven (21:1). And so, we recommit ourselves today to Christ, making every effort to one day fill the thrones that were abandoned by those fallen angels in heaven, in order that we might contribute to and partake of that blissful reconfiguration of Paradise.

Accusation quashed by exoneration (12:10–12)

[10]Then I heard a loud voice in heaven, proclaiming, Now have come the salvation and the power and the kingdom of our God and the authority of his Messiah, for the accuser of our comrades has been thrown down, who accuses them day and night before our God. [11]But they have conquered him by the blood of the Lamb and by the word of their testimony, for they did not cling to life even in the face of death. [12]Rejoice then, you heavens and those who dwell in them! But woe to the earth and the sea, for the devil has come down to you with great wrath, because he knows that his time is short!"

Witnessing the expulsion of those disloyal angels, heaven erupts in resounding celebration (vv. 10–12), evocative of the mirthful songs of Moses and Miriam at the Red Sea (Exod 15:1–18), of Deborah and Barak (Judg 5), and of David (2 Samuel 22). A more apposite occasion for such a canticle can hardly be imagined than the full-scale defeat of Satan and his mutinous hordes. This renewed heavenly hymn is an exergasia of similar chants in Revelation (7:10; 11:15; 19:1) and serves as an interpretive gloss regarding the preceding scene, illustrating God's microcosmic and macrocosmic dominion: "Now have come the salvation and the power and the kingdom of our God and the authority of his Messiah" (v. 10). This visceral shout is the answer to the Our Father, "Hallowed be thy name, thy Kingdom come, thy will be done on earth as it is in Heaven" (Matt 6:9–10), further unfolding the formulaic "already and not yet," so unmistakable in Johannine literature, also known as realized or inaugurated eschatology. It is also a sigh of liberation from the Luciferian prosecutor who accuses us day and night before God,[65] a dark counterpart, as it were, to the Holy Spirit as our divine Advocate (John 14:16).

For who shall lay anything to the charge of God's elect, when it is God

65. In rabbinic literature, Michael is called "the advocate" (*synēgor*, συνήγορ), standing as a pleading angel or protector of Israel in opposition to Satan the "accuser" (*katēgōr*, κατήγωρ), cf. Midr. Teh. Ps 20; 1 Enoch, ch. 9; Jewish tradition also maintains that Satan accuses humans every single day of the year, except on Yom Kippur, the Day of Atonement.

himself that justifies, when it is Christ that died (Rom 8:31–34)? The saints in heaven have conquered him by the blood of the Lamb and by the word of their testimony, for they did not cling to life even in the face of death (v. 11). Three are, therefore, the catalysts of triumph: first, Christians are assimilated to the blood of Jesus the Lamb of God (John 1:29), by whose efficacy they were saved (Phil 4:13). Second, they have given faithful witness to the doctrines pertaining to the work of the Redeemer and truthfully proclaimed by his Church (20:4). And third, knowing that the Lord loved them (1:5; 3:9), the saints did not love their own souls but became fearless even in the face of death, just as Christ taught them to hate their earthly life to obtain an amaranthine one in heaven (John 12:25; Luke 14:26). Countering the devil's efforts to drive religion from the world by deception and oppression, they execute in history what is being celebrated in the presence of God Almighty.

After which the seer still hears them sing: "Rejoice then, you heavens and those who dwell in them!" (v. 12). Heaven's riddance of the rebellious dragon is amplest reason to exult, in anticipation of the final restoration of creation (18:20), and of saints and angels living together like brethren. By using the Greek verb "to dwell in a tent, to tabernacle" here (*skēnóō*, σκηνόω; 7:15; 13:6; 21:3; John 1:14), John reconnects this scene not only with Yahweh's *shekhinah* or desert sanctuary after the Exodus, but also with the glorious ark in heaven (11:19), spelling unruffled rest and safety for those who formerly were burdened with the sorrows of the wilderness. It is a further confirmation, too, of heaven as an unending festival of Sukkot. Yet antithetical to these is the warning issued next: "Woe to the earth and the sea, for the devil has come down to you with great wrath" (v. 12), a final denunciation of the third and most grievous woe before the fall of Babylon (18:10). Unfortunately, between now and then, the earth must still witness the establishment of the ill-omened kingdom of the beast (13:1–10), spewing great rage.[66] Contrasting with his fall in vv. 9, 13, the verb "descend" in this verse seems to emphasize the demonic deliberateness and determination to wreak as much antichristic havoc on earth as possible. It also reminds the reader that John is positioned up high during this vision, gazing downward at the earth. Compared to eternity, the devil's time to destroy souls is short, and he knows it (v. 12), and after inflicting great misery, he himself will soon be miserable. Available to him is a little while (*modicum tempus*; 6:11), the same limited season elsewhere dubbed as time, and times, and half a time, forty-two months, one thousand two hundred sixty days, a thousand years, or

66. This is the first mention of the noun *thymós* (θυμός, *ira*), "wrath," in Revelation, denotative of divine judgment in the second half of the book (e.g., 14:10).

ten days. This little while may coincide with Satan's short release before the final judgment in 20:3. In sum, these periods signal the relatively fleeting time span of the world's existence from the fall of Satan till Christ's parousia. And this concludes the digression begun in v. 7, illustrative of the primeval angelic warfare, and heaven's reaction to Satan's overthrow.

For better spiritual assimilation let us briefly meditate on that accusatorial role of Satan. He and his demons are likely able to detect even the smallest infidelities in our service to the Lord, incriminating us about them and making us feel undeserving of divine blessing. Naturally, to some degree everybody can be accused of personal sins, even though many of them are due to diabolical deception and temptation. To harm Job, the adversary brought charges even against God, accusing him of bribing that just man (Job 1:9–12). Now, those diabolical aggressions constitute the test of our faith and hope here on earth; by resisting them we become stronger and more resilient like a well-trained athlete, or iron smithed on the anvil. Most of all, however, as Christians we believe in the glad tidings of redemption: after having sinned, our heart can convert and regain righteousness; indeed, the human soul is *sanābilis*, that is, salvageable by God's restoring grace (Wis 1:14). And against the one who renounces his love of life, the calumniator has no power. Moreover, although omitted in v. 10, the Holy Spirit is always present as a divine Protector to redress whatever damage the hellish faultfinder may have caused. By the same token, this passage of the Apocalypse teaches us not to accuse our neighbor unnecessarily, but rather to charitably defend and prayerfully intercede for all. Ultimately, we must keep clear of being dejected or intimidated by the Luciferian plaintiff, confident that "in all these things we are more than conquerors through him who loved us" (Rom 8:37).

Eschewing the pseudo-paradise (12:13–18)

[13]*So when the dragon saw that he had been thrown down to the earth,*
he pursued the woman who had given birth to the male child. [14]*But the*
woman was given the two wings of the great eagle, so that she could fly
from the serpent into the wilderness, to her place where she is nourished
for a time, and times, and half a time. [15]*Then from his mouth the serpent*
poured water like a river after the woman, to sweep her away with the
flood. [16]*But the earth came to the help of the woman; it opened its mouth*
and swallowed the river that the dragon had poured from his mouth.
[17]*Then the dragon was angry with the woman, and went off to make war*

on the rest of her children, those who keep the commandments of God and hold the testimony of Jesus. [18] *Then the dragon took his stand on the sand of the seashore.*

Having heard the proclamation of the woe concerning the devil's descent (v. 12), John now sees it unfolding in vision. Deposed from his throne as Lucifer because of his pride against God in heaven, unsuccessful in his direct warfare against the good angels, and foiled also in his assault on the male child, Christ Jesus (vv. 4–9), Satan now carries on his belligerence against the woman, that is, the Church (v. 13). Hence, the epic conflict between light and darkness in the invisible realm is now transferred into the visible world. Since Mary had conceived the Son of the Father through the Holy Spirit, the dragon now attacks her and her spiritual fertility.[67] Boundlessly envious of her who would bear many children to inherit the places left empty by his fall and the fall of the spirits siding with him, he persecutes her with equal malice, albeit not with equal power. She remains the main target of his frenzied assaults against life and salvation, as he continues to interfere with God's creation, that is, the metaphysical purpose for man and woman to symbolize God's loving covenant with humanity, and Christ's nuptial relationship with his Church.

Resuming the narrative plot from v. 6, and after explaining the reason why the woman is forced to flee (v. 13), John now comments on how she was given the two wings of the great eagle, so that she could fly from the serpent into the wilderness to be nourished there for a time, and times, and half a time (v. 14). Far beyond the natural spite between the eagle and the snake, this large and fast raptor is related to the harbinger of woes in 8:13 and encapsulates the way God assists the woman to outstrip her pursuer and to reach a place of safety. Yahweh had spoken of the swift deliverance of Israel from Pharaoh's oppression under a similar emblem (Exod 19:4). There is, however, a minute difference: during the Exodus, if God is said to have borne his people on eagles' wings, then here those very wings are given to the woman, suggesting a more intimate bond between divinity and humanity. Those aquiline pinions recall the loftiness of the living beings (4:8), perverted in the noisy wings of the locusts (9:9) and the two horns of the upcoming beast (13:11).

Thus, the Lord harnesses the willfulness and wickedness of the enemy to bring about good for his children. Just as the Israelites fled from Egypt, so does the Church exit the world-city Babylon to preserve pure religion. Her pilgrimage through the wilderness of history is also symptomatic of her perpetual

67. Cf. AvS, 418.

virginity, barren to earthly desires and vice. Individual Christians likewise flee from profane thoughts and idolatry by taking refuge in the solitude of their unworldly and patient hearts, knowing full well that persecutions will continue for all generations. As formerly in the desert-tabernacle and the Torah, the heavenly Father will not cease to nurture them by Word and Sacrament in the brokenness of this eschatological season, waiting for the three and a half times to pass into the "seven" of eternity (v. 14).[68] Meanwhile, shielded from the repulsiveness of the serpent's visage (*a facie serpentis*), God's sons and daughters look forward to contemplating his divine countenance, and worshipfully fall on their faces before his throne forever and ever (22:4).

After failing to ravage the woman by his draconian fierceness, the foe now harasses her with the shapeshifting and venomous cunningness of a serpent: "Then from his mouth the serpent poured water like a river after the woman, to sweep her away with the flood" (v. 15). This water-spewing monster reminds the reader of the primal separation of waters and dry land (Gen 1:9–10), but also implies Israel's dry-shod passing through the Red Sea (Exod 14:21–22). Also critical in interpreting this animal-related or theriomorphic symbol is the Joban Behemoth, representing primeval cosmic creatures, whose subjugation validates God's wisdom and power (Job 40:15–24). This snake also calls to mind those mesmerizing venom-spitting cobras, suggestive of the poison of falsehood and heresy which attempt to carry the Church away from the true faith.[69] Throughout Revelation, the "mouth" serves as a dialectic image of both truth (e.g., 1:16) and lies (e.g., 13:2). When it comes to the figure of the river, among the most pertinent connotations are invading armies (Dan 11:10), persecution (Ps 18:4), irreligiosity or idolatry (Cant 8:7), and judgment (Ps 42:7). Those who allow themselves to be carried away by its toxic waters will suffer a similar fate, as Jesus avows: "Because you are lukewarm, and neither cold nor hot, I am about to spit you out of my mouth" (3:16).

Within the Apocalypse, waters mainly signify peoples and nations (17:15), imagining an inundation of various nations instigated by the dragon to oppose and oppress the Christian religion. Historically, the first-century AD Roman Empire was such a torrent launching itself against the Church. Thus, the metaphor is that Satan will send his vassals after us as we try to focus on God, and he does so in the guise of popular uprisings, hostile public opinion, systems

68. Adrienne explains that "time" indicates early Church history, "times" suggest the bulk of the eschatological age, and "half a time" hints at a brief yet decisive end-time period immediately preceding the Lord's glorious return or parousia, cf. AvS, 409.

69. Cf. RD, 1060.

stacked against us, and people's general ill-will against Christianity. Unlike that life-preserving water provided by God from the rock (Ps 105:41), this ominous tidal wave is unmistakably intended to exterminate the woman by washing her away, mimicking the deluge of Noah's time (Gen 7:11–12). Even though a flash flood is diametrically opposed to the concept of a desert, the devil attempts to make her river-borne, that is, to gain buoyancy and float away on the watery surface (*potamophórēton poiḗsē*, ποταμοφόρητον ποιήσῃ, *trahi a flumine*), just as he does to the great harlot (17:1). Thus, the serpent tries to create a dystopia, a demonic scheme to fatally delude the woman by creating the impression of a temporal pseudo-paradise. In contrast to the Lord's enticing his people into the desert as the place of his first love for them (Jer 20:7), the Church is to be duped into believing that life on earth is a perpetual garden of Eden, watered by four rivers (Gen 2:10–14), as if humanity had never fallen into sin. However, the earth after the fall is no longer a paradise, but an austere spiritual wilderness. Redolent of those flattering words spoken in Eden by the primeval serpent to beguile the first woman, and reenacting Christ's temptation in the desert, Satan relentlessly aims at capsizing the bark of Peter in an inundation of error and heresy. He watches it with smugness to see whether it will give into the mirage of being carried along on a bed of comfort, and in due course make the Church oblivious of, and antagonistic to, the tribulations that are necessary companions during her earthly pilgrimage.

It is not difficult to imagine John being awestricken by what he sees next, how the earth comes to the help of the woman, opening its mouth and swallowing the river that the dragon had poured from his mouth (v. 16). This enigmatic detail has no parallel in Jewish or early Christian literature, recalling not so much Abel's innocent blood (Gen 4:11), nor the divine judgment on Dathan and Abiram (Num 26:10), but rather continuing the Exodus motif of the Red Sea engulfing the Hebrews' pursuers (Exod 15:12). It might also symbolize Christ's human nature devouring death by his own Incarnation, Death, entombment, descent to the netherworld, and Resurrection. A baffled dragon witnesses the earth becoming the woman's ally against his machinations and violence,[70] as if to signify that God through the interposition of creation and its natural law provides ultimate vindication for the truth. No doubt, the people of God is also rescued by its inherent and universal sense of faith (*sensus fidei*), absorbing and neutralizing threats of heresy. And by faithfully opening her mouth and proclaiming the Gospel, the Church

70. This verse marks the eighth time the aggressive Greek verb *bállō* (βάλλω, *míttere*), "to throw, cast," is employed between vv. 4–16 of this chapter.

frustrates the devil's corrupting purposes, and she can rest assured that she will always experience Christ's saving provisions until the day when she transitions into eternal life.[71]

In unequivocal reference to the lasting and mortal enmity between the serpent's and the woman's offspring spoken of in the Proto-Evangelium (Gen 3:15), "the dragon was angry with the woman, and went off to make war on the rest of her children, those who keep the commandments of God and hold the testimony of Jesus" (v. 17). Although the "many children" appear to contradict the tenor of an only-begotten son in v. 5, as well as the perpetual virginity of Mary, the Mother of Christ, the original can be taken to signify the "many" (*reliquis*) who issue "from her seed" (*de semine eius*), that is, from the person of Christ. Ergo, like in 12:1–2, the image is multivalent, suggesting the Church and the sum of her past, current, and future children. And again, having failed at obviating the mission of the male child (v. 5), and having been foiled in his attempts against the life of the woman (vv. 6, 13–16), Satan proceeds to attack her spiritual offspring, that is, the individual members of the Church.[72] Inflamed only to greater rage, he now turns on Christians, the elect remnant, leaving the other members of the human family largely unmolested.

Nevertheless, there is a noticeable deterioration from the enmity in Eden, and from the persecution of v. 13, to his all-out war in this verse, replicating on earth his previous unsuccessful warfare in heaven (v. 7), and thereby forcibly transforming the people of God into a Church militant. That is the truly epic dimension of our spiritual combat whose backbone will forever be the keeping of God's commandments and the testifying to Jesus. And under his protection and guidance we will be able to persevere until we are gathered into the New Jerusalem of an eternally triumphant Church. By taking his stand on the sand of the seashore (v. 18),[73] the dragon indicates his plan to fight against the multiplication of Abraham's descendants (Gen 22:17), and thereby against God himself who established that covenant with our father in faith (Rom 4:1). He also makes ready for the final battle against the camp of the saints (20:8). Yet, while the hazardous quicksand on the shore is shifting constantly, the Church as the people of God is founded on the unshakable rock which is Christ.[74]

71. Cf. RD, 1061.

72. Reminiscent of King Herod's attempt to destroy the infant Jesus (Matt 2:13).

73. Instead of the third person singular "he [dragon] stood" (*estáthē*, ἐστάθη, *stetit*), some Greek manuscripts read the first person singular "I [John] stood" (*estáthēn*, ἐστάθην), as if the apostle were speaking of his own positioning on the seashore, preparing for the next vision: "And I saw a beast rising out of the sea" (13:1).

74. Cf. RD, 1064.

In wrapping up our exegetical ruminations on this central chapter of John's Apocalypse, let us touch on a few aspects of spiritual interest contained in it. Conscious of the existence of an abiding anti-Christic and anti-Marian part of humanity, whose single goal is to wreck the ecclesial community, chiefly through the idolization of political power that easily decays into sacrificing Christians in its wake,[75] as the brethren of Jesus, we will overcome the world by the vision of God through the eyes of a pure heart. Knowing that our adversary, the devil, is condemned by God the Most High to use elements like water as a medium in trying to harm us, we see that he has given proof of his misery and powerlessness. Which also implies that any earthly opposition to God's truth is doomed to fail in the end. Nevertheless, to win this ongoing spiritual battle, instead of wanting to revert to the proverbial fleshpots of Egypt (Exod 14:12; 16:3), we must intentionally venture into and choose to remain in the desert, refusing to succumb to a self-delusional pseudo-paradise. What matters most is the choosing of desert-unpleasantness over world-comfort, preferring temporary cacotopia over demonic utopia, asceticism over mundane promises of peace and fruition. As children of an apocalyptic Virgin-Mother, we ought never to subscribe to the misconceptions of Babylon's great harlot, who in her inebriation pretends to forever rule as queen, never be widowed, nor at any time see grief (18:7). Conversely, half walking, half flying, the woman exalted by a mystical eagle is the beloved people of God that endures this arduous tension between heaven and earth.[76]

Faithful to her divine calling, this community of the followers of Jesus remains *Ecclesia pressa*, that is, the Church forever hard-pressed, never capitulating to any dreamlike place of definitive consolation and relief in this world, devoid of tears and death. Rather, in the absence of such a prospect for peace and justice in this world ahead of God's final triumph, she can conquer only by embracing her lot as a desert pilgrim: "Many waters cannot quench love, neither can floods drown it" (Cant 8:7). Moreover, she will be transfigured and transcend this present wilderness: "As they go through the valley of thirst, they make it a place of springs; the early rain also covers it with pools. They go from strength to strength; the God of gods will be seen in Zion" (Ps 84:6–7). The ebb and flow of spiritual combat, even demonic rip-tides, will bring the soul spiritual favors and miraculous deliverance that it would not otherwise have received except under such pressure and in persecution. Christ will

75. The noun *martyría* (μαρτυρία, *testimonium*) in v. 17 literally means "martyrdom."
76. Cf. AvS, 407.

always watch over his Bride, the Church, and each one of her sons and daughters, guarding them against any draconian fury and hurt: "He reached down from on high, he took me; he drew me out of mighty waters" (Ps 18:16). And he does so through the saving grace obtained on the Cross, symbolized by the eagle's majestic wingspan.[77]

77. Cf. AvS, 408.

13:1–10, Sea-beast

Conniving surrogate (13:1–2)

[1]And I saw a beast rising out of the sea, having ten horns and seven heads; and on its horns were ten diadems, and on its heads were blasphemous names. [2]And the beast that I saw was like a leopard, its feet were like a bear's, and its mouth was like a lion's mouth. And the dragon gave it his power and his throne and great authority.

Consecutive to the apocalyptic scene of the cosmic woman and the red dragon evicted from heaven is the emergence of two monsters, one from the sea and the other from the land, who with the dragon forge an evil triarchy, a satanic trinity, as it were.[1] Stationed upon the seashore, the serpent now summons its co-conspirators to execute another war-plan. By employing the stereotypical "And I saw" (*Et vidi*), John divides his upcoming visions into the following segments: 13:1–10 illustrating the sea beast, 13:11–18 adding the rise of the land beast, 14:1–5 turning to Mount Zion, 14:6–13 depicting the Gospel judgment, 14:14–20 mapping out the harvest of the Son of Man, and 15:1–4 announcing his final victory as the Lord and King. Here, at the beginning of ch. 13, and at the dragon's bidding, two monsters rise, one distinguished by more brutish, the other by more subtle power. Their surfacing, rage, and diabolic sway, however, was already contemporaneous with the trials featured in chs. 8–11. Himself residing on an island at the time of writing (1:9), the visionary's eye is now captivated by a ghastly spectacle when out of that sea a monster arises (v. 1). Cursed is the sea (12:12), the symbol of the bottomless pit (11:7), the source of the noxious flood issuing from the serpent's mouth (12:15), and the figurative womb of the earth into which the devil enters to be born, satirizing the pregnant woman (12:2). His origin is not heavenly but abysmal, fittingly confined to that abode of cold darkness, formlessness, and death.[2]

1. Cf. Bruce Manning Metzger, *Breaking the Code: Understanding the Book of Revelation.* (Nashville, TN: Abingdon, 1993), 72.
2. Cf. 20:13; Gen 1:2.

Compared to the land, the ocean is also metaphorical for unsettled and ungovernable humanity, the world's state of volatility and disarray. Endless waters stirred into waves by uncontrollable tempests signal ever-present errors and heresies in history, causing all sorts of confusion in opposition to the Church of God. As if aping the angel's ascent from sunrise (7:2) and Jesus' own Resurrection and Ascension, this beast surfaces from beneath, in blatant self-exaltation and auto-glorification.[3] Basing it on the Joban Behemoth and Leviathan (Job 40:15; 41:1), and creatively reworking the four Danielic monsters (Dan 7:1–7) into a single composite, John calls it "a little beast" (*thēríon*, θηρίον[4], *bestia*) to highlight its bruteness,[5] but also the fact that it only plays second fiddle in the shadows of the dragon, so to speak. Whatever power is looming here is one that rules not by love or right, but by fear and defiance, one that seeks to subdue in malice and savagery. It seems to signal the trans-historical and anti-Christian force of a world that in every age has been on the warpath against justice and humaneness. Starting with the dictatorial Roman empire of apostolic times, this beast is a principal, albeit not exclusive, expression of the dragon's operation on earth (Dan 7:17, 23). It or he and his Luciferian adepts arise from the fluid obscurity of the sea as their hideout, full of deceit and evil scheming against God, to enslave individuals and nations in death-dealing madness, the sum total of atheistic obstruction until the end of time. He is the infernal emissary of conflict against the Mother's offspring sojourning in the wilderness (12:17), mirroring the enmity between the Son of Man and the beasts in Daniel 7.

Continuing to paint his visionary canvas, John adjoins several details that enhance the overall symbolism of the looming monster. He observes that it has ten horns and seven heads (v. 1), timeless emblems of power and intellect. Confoundingly, and unlike the dragon (12:3), the portrayal of this beast is distorted by mentioning the horns prior to its heads, even though in the natural order most animals carry horns on their heads, and not vice versa. Genuinely grotesque is also the numerical disproportion between too many horns for the available heads, intimating that Satan's brute force outpaces his cognitive and volitive abilities (Dan 7:7). In other words, the devil and his minions lack both

3. Cf. RD, 1066.

4. A diminutive of *thḗr* (θήρ), "dangerous beast, venomous animal," hence, "a little animal"; it is related to the noun *thḗra* (θήρα), meaning "hunting, prey, entrapping, game, a net used for capture"; also, as a point of interest, "beast" never refers to animals set aside for ritual sacrifice in the Old Testament.

5. In contradistinction to *zṓon* (ζῷον, *animal*), from *záō* (ζάω), "to be alive," used for the living beings in their creaturely aliveness and astuteness (4:6).

reason and reasonableness: in the exercise of their might and insight they are conflicted within themselves, being ingrainedly unbalanced and dysfunctional. That this polycephalous brute is a God-opposing character can also be deduced from the number ten as a biblical symbol not so much of universality or totality, but rather of earthly sufficiency for a given purpose and its finiteness.[6] It is accompanied by the number seven, which in turn caricatures the seven Spirits of God, standing for the relative fullness of totalitarian rule on earth. One could also interpret them as the seven capital sins, self-sufficiently subverting the seven gifts of the Holy Spirit.[7] Hence, this sea-beast in its aberrancy and ugliness signals every tyrannical and idolatrous empire, essentially identical with the dragon himself. At 12:3, Satan was described in his personal character, whereas here he is plainly shown under the aspect of the persecuting power of the world, founded on passion and selfishness. In Scripture, the Kingdom of God, on the other hand, is never represented by the image of a beast. This embodiment of evil is like the bizarre body of Satan warring against the Mystical Body of Christ.

Continuing his description, the apostle notices ten diadems crowning the ten horns (v. 1), adapted from the seven crowns on the dragon's heads (12:3), and falling hopelessly short of the many diadems on the head of the white horses' Rider (19:12). These are signs of the devil's false claim to sovereign authority in rebelliousness against Jesus' plenitude as the King of kings and Lord of lords (19:16). Those three surplus crowns, since there are only seven heads, seem to take aim at the Blessed Trinity, to insult its eternal dominion.[8] Satan is known to deceive those in civil authority first, and primarily through them he then proceeds to persecute Christians.[9] Moreover, on the beast's seven heads were blasphemous names (17:3), suggesting its diabolical aspiration to be like God (Gen 3:5) as an act of utmost irreverence and profane infatuation. Blasphemy is the idolatrous and scurrilous language that switches right for wrong or wrong for right (Rom 1:25), epitomized in attributing divinity to someone or something that is not divine.[10] Such a calculating usurpation of supernatural honors

6. See also the brittle ten toes of the great statue in Nebuchadnezzar's troubled dream (Dan 2:41).

7. Cf. AvS, 405.

8. Cf. AvS, 414.

9. Cf. RD, 1067.

10. The blasphemous titles of *divus*, *dominus et deus*, and *Augustus* (from the Greek *Sebastós*, "venerable one") were assumed by Roman emperors since Octavian (d. AD 14), implying superhuman claims of imperial worship that did not fail to scandalize the pious feelings of Jews and Christians alike.

is inexplicable except on the supposition that mundane power carries within itself the potentiality of becoming a tool of the devil himself.

John must have been startled at the forthcoming vision, for who would expect such a crossbred monster to crop up from the sea? “And the beast that I saw was like a leopard, its feet were like a bear’s, and its mouth was like a lion’s mouth. And the dragon gave it his power and his throne and great authority” (v. 2). Conflating Daniel’s four great beasts, namely the eagle-winged lioness, the three-tusked bear, the four-winged and four-headed leopard, and the iron-toothed and ten-horned beast (Dan 7:2–7), into one, it represents all forms of world-power, ruthless in oppression and swift in bloodshed.[11] What distinguishes the leopard[12] is its well-camouflaged fur, opportunistic hunting behavior, muscular prowess in leaping on and subduing its prey, and ability to adapt to a wide variety of habitats. And further enhancing its predatory prowess in this vision are the powerful claws of a bear with their formidable force of laceration. There is the idea of coalescing their bloodthirstiness and dominance. Even though this monster has seven heads, mention is made of only one mouth, and it resembles that of a lion (9:8, 17). Leonine fangs are made to seize and hold their dying prey, featuring among the most redoubtable in the animal kingdom, expressive of fearless aggression and voracity. As such it becomes a sign of the callous exercise of tyrannical state power in this apocalyptic context. In the end, however, this wild beast remains an impotent mimicry of God’s superior agency, of the Lamb-Lion (5:5), of the first living creature (4:7), and of the Christomorphic angel (10:3), just as Pharaoh’s magicians were limited to aping the signs of Moses and Aaron (Exod 7:11–12).

Having failed in his lust to destroy the woman, yet not resigning himself to being a mere spectator but pretending to be the prince of this world (John 12:31), the dragon now attempts to delegate his futile power to this beast in the hope of annihilating the woman’s blessed offspring. It is being authorized as his vice-regent, as it were, in the struggle he has undertaken against Christian believers. In due course, he will unleash another beast and false prophet (13:11), as well as his servant, Babylon the great harlot (17:5); these four, incidentally, shall meet their demise in reverse order. Ironically, Lucifer has completely lost his angelic throne already (12:8), and whatever power he possesses is given to him by the Most High, yet now he is lying to his conniving surrogate about

11. Cf. Dante Alighieri, *Divine Comedy*, trans. Henry Wadsworth Longfellow (Aeterna, 2021), *Inferno*, Canto 1:10–15.

12. The Greek *párdalis* (πάρδαλις) is the feminine form of *párdos* (πάρδος, *pardo*), literally “leopardess, pantheress.”

his dismal status, namely, the complete absence of real authority. He had brazenly bluffed about it already before the God-Man when he took him to a very high mountain and showed him all the kingdoms of the world and their splendor, tempting him to demonic worship (Luke 4:6–7). Throughout Revelation, "power," "throne," and "great authority" symbolize God's exclusive and universal rule (e.g., 4:2; 20:11), and Paul points to him as the origin of all governance on earth (Rom 13:1–7). Hence, the satanic figment of might and its delegation to the sea-beast is a parody of God, who grants everlasting dominion to the Son of Man (Dan 7:13–14).[13] As Daniel's fourth beast was without a name (Dan 7:7), so this spooky ghoul is nameless, too, anonymously partaking of the nature and mission of the dragon, with its focus on sowing weeds among the wheat while everyone is asleep and then slyly slipping away (Matt 13:25).[14]

Looking back over these two opening verses of ch. 13, a few words should be said again about how they affect our spiritual life as followers of Christ in this world. For one thing, the devil clearly likes to change his appearance constantly. If he does not accost us in the intimidating disguise of a dragon or stalk us under the seductive mantle of a serpent, he tries to instill horror as a beast. This chameleon-like pattern of insinuation and temptation also involves the many heads that allow him to uncannily inspect and attack the soul from varying angles, like a professional pugilist, until a weak spot in us is detected for ultimate defeat and ruin. Continually prowling to assault us with feline, ursine, and leonine nimbleness, the evil one will not tire of testing us with every conceivable trial (Luke 4:13).[15] Nevertheless, the soul can take comfort from the realization that demonic forces in our lives, even though presenting themselves as quite fearsome, are small and have no actual power. And if their siren songs lure us into seeking personal fame, privilege, and wealth in this world, then we do well to remember that those, too, are mere lies and deceit. Instead, we should always nurture a healthy level of trepidation in God's presence as an antidote to any unholy fright (Matt 10:28). Let us also take note that all glamour of pride and sin arises from the abyss of the sea; and bragging about vice and corruption is the exact opposite of repentance. It would be indicative of those horns already having pierced our body and soul like devilish harpoons that cannot be easily extricated. To stay clear of those goring hooks we must refuse to love this world, that is, the concupiscence of the flesh, the desire of the eyes, and the boastfulness of riches, all of which are

13. Cf. RD, 1070.
14. Cf. AvS, 416.
15. Cf. AvS, 405–6.

ephemeral (1 John 2:16–17). But those who strive to do the will of God with a sincere heart will live forever.

Who is like the beast? (13:3–8)

[3]*One of its heads seemed to have received a death-blow, but its mortal wound had been healed. In amazement the whole earth followed the beast.* [4]*They worshiped the dragon, for he had given his authority to the beast, and they worshiped the beast, saying, "Who is like the beast, and who can fight against it?"* [5]*The beast was given a mouth uttering haughty and blasphemous words, and it was allowed to exercise authority for forty-two months.* [6]*It opened its mouth to utter blasphemies against God, blaspheming his name and his dwelling, that is, those who dwell in heaven.* [7]*Also it was allowed to make war on the saints and to conquer them. It was given authority over every tribe and people and language and nation,* [8]*and all the inhabitants of the earth will worship it, everyone whose name has not been written from the foundation of the world in the book of life of the Lamb that was slaughtered.*

As soon as John realizes that one of the beast's heads seemed to have received a death-blow (v. 3; cf. v. 12), he must have been reminded of the head of the primeval serpent already fatally bruised by the seed of the woman (Gen 3:15). This present lethal wound is caused by a sword, as we will learn at v. 14, yet it does not stop the monster from living and exerting its deleterious power. Is it not also conceivable that Michael's blow ejecting the dragon from heavenly regions (12:8–9) is revealed only now and perpetuated in this deadly trauma upon one of the heads of this its agent on earth? Even more compellingly, however, it could refer to the knockout dealt to the power of Satan by the Death and Resurrection of Christ, at least partially overthrowing worldly might founded on inordinate passion, self-sufficiency, and inhumanity? By employing the same word for "slaying" as in 5:6 (*spházō*, σφάζω, *occídere*), the beast makes himself a parody of the Lamb of God. Hence, not only does the dragon generate this beast as a further travesty of God creating humanity, and perverting fertility and generation into an impugnment of God's creativity,[16] but now he also apes the Lamb's work of redemption by having its mortal wound healed (v. 3). He clearly envies that wondrous coexistence of those two antagonistic qualities in

16. Cf. AvS, 419.

Jesus: "I was dead, and see, I am alive forever and ever" (1:18).[17] Thus, he camouflages his defeat as victory, to present evil itself as good (2 Cor 11:14).

All Satan can do is mimic the things of God's Kingdom, since he is metaphysically unable to create anything out of nothing (*ex nihilo*), counterfeiting Christ's triumph to deceive others, and in the process becoming the archetype of all antichrists. That the paroxysm of wounding and healing is a mere mockery of the work of redemption is proven by the fact that no scar remains in the beast, while the marks of our Lord's wounds visibly perdure (John 20:27). Some see in this imagery also an innuendo to the demise of the pagan Roman empire, as well as the rise of Christian civilization in the global West in the fourth century AD. Others have endeavored to relate the wounded head to a variety of historical figures, most notably the Roman emperor Nero, whose suicide in 68 AD resulted in a year of civil war that threatened the very survival of the empire. In his imperial successors Vespasian and Domitian, the beast came to life again, embodying all the cruelty and impiety of Nero, and spawning a popular legend that he would return from exile or even death to rule again to the amazement of the world. Among early Christians, this legend of a *Nero redivivus* shifted to a belief that he was the antichrist.[18]

World history teaches us that after momentary crises, including world wars, secular power experiences eras of relative peace, restoration, and reinvigoration. Especially totalitarian regimes will pose as defenders of the law, all the while misleading societies and individual souls by the promise of false regenerations. Likewise, "the whole earth marveled after the beast" (v. 3; cf. 17:6–8), again parodying the Lamb worshipped by his followers. Usurping the honor due to Christ alone, it shamelessly exacts quasi-liturgical homage and submission from the whole world, displaying its globalized seductive appeal for the length of the eschaton. Disastrously, the earth's populations, apart from all godly believers, fail to comprehend that the creeping in of the wrathful dragon means only woe for them (12:12). At any rate, his devious stratagem (Eph 6:11) will transpire ever more palpably: unlike fallen Adam who was redeemed and repatriated by the God-Man Jesus, the ancient serpent cannot be reinstated in heaven; as if grasping at straws then, he "creates" the beast to pursue exactly the opposite, namely, preventing human generations from returning to their Creator.

With undeniable indignation, the prophet on Patmos documents that "they worshiped the dragon, for he had given his authority to the beast, and

17. Cf. RD, 1071.

18. Cf. Augustine, *De civitate Dei*, 20.19.3.

they worshiped the beast" (v. 4). By claiming and receiving semi-religious worship, Satan and his underlings exercise considerable anti-Christian leverage. Wherever infatuated worldliness prevails along with statolatry in all its forms,[19] the spirit of the dragon and of the wild beast is adored, so contrary to the law of God and so much in derogation of his divine claims here on earth. In extreme folly the devil markets himself as being more potent than he really is,[20] and aims at deceiving and subduing the world by his uncontrolled power. The delusion of satanic incomparability and invincibility, "Who is like the beast, and who can fight against it?" (v. 4), is an ironical perversion of hymnic phraseology found in the Old Testament (e.g., Ps 35:10) and of the name of Michael the archangel who defeats Lucifer with the battle cry "Who is like God?" (12:7). Pretending to be omnipotent, the demons tend to fuse two traits into one, that is, blasphemy toward the Most High, and almost irresistible seduction exercised over the human heart.

Instigated by the dragon and with divine permission,[21] the beast's leonine mouth (v. 2) not only behaves in a cruel and voracious way, but it now is also given blasphemous soundbites dripping with egotism (v. 5). Such supercilious speech stands in direct opposition to the apostolate of the Church and her humble proclamation of Christ. What do these arrogant claims consist of, if not of the endless historical conga line of emperor worship, and of the manipulation of human liberty, personal property, and people's consciences? Among the many guises assumed by infernal agents are infiltration, trying to weaken the inner life of the Church, as well as outright assaults on the followers of Jesus, buoyed by absolutized injustice. Yet again, they can act only within the unassailable confines of divine authority (John 19:11).[22] Both the Woman and the antichristic beast have the same length of time to act, namely, the eschaton, understood as the historical lifespan of the Church between the two comings of the Lord, symbolized by forty-two months (v. 5).[23]

While the dragon was cast down from heaven, the beast challenges God by arrogating to itself all power in heaven, earth, and hell. It opens its mouth

19. By way of illustration, the imperial cult was ruthlessly enforced especially under the emperor Domitian, who like Antiochus IV Epiphanes, demanded that he be called by divine titles such as "our lord and god" and "Jupiter."

20. Cf. RD, 1072.

21. Connoted by the stereotypical repetition of the phrase "it was allowed to" (*kaí edóthē autô*, καὶ ἐδόθη αὐτῷ, *et datum/data est illi/ei*) in vv. 5, 7.

22. Mysteriously applied even to Christ and his ability to appear to carefully chosen witnesses only, following his Resurrection (Acts 10:40).

23. Cf. AvS, 422.

"blaspheming his name and his tabernacle, that is, those who dwell in heaven" (v. 6). "Tabernacle" here denotes the place where God is worshipped in the communion of all the saints. By extension, it is an image of the Church, the Mystical Body of Christ, pitched like a tent by the Father, in which the Godhead dwells bodily, tabernacling among us.[24] His Eucharistic presence in the countless tabernacles on earth is recognized by those whose citizenship is in heaven (Phil 3:20) and whose life is hidden from the diabolical persecutor in the tent of God's heart.

And yet, it must be acknowledged that the Christian faith will always be exposed to the veritable warfare of public slander.[25] Despite a providence and a sovereignty higher than his, Lucifer is allowed not only to make war on the saints, but also to conquer them (v. 7; 19:19; Dan 7:21), not excluding their murder (v. 15). Thus, John's realism does not hold out any unfounded hope of rescue from death for those whose fidelity is put to a toilsome test. Contrastingly, the Lamb and his followers conquer not by slaying but by dying (5:5; 12:11). And although the reach of satanic influence is universal (v. 7), not unlike that of the two witnesses, it will be overcome by those who obtain redemption. Nevertheless, in total antithesis to divine grace, and in satisfaction of his hellish pride, the devil will be adored by "everyone whose name has not been written from the foundation of the world in the book of life of the Lamb that was slaughtered" (v. 8). It is exegetically admissible to connect the phrase "from the foundation of the world" with the word "written" in this verse, signifying that the names of the predestined ones have been enrolled in the book of life from the very dawn of creation (Phil 4:3). If, however, "from the foundation of the world" is linked with "slain," as in the Geek and Latin texts (*esphagménou apò katabolē̃s kósmou*, ἐσφαγμένου ἀπὸ καταβολῆς κόσμου; *occisus est, ab origine mundi*) then the divine Lamb is conceived of as having been mysteriously offered by his heavenly Father from the foundation of the world (John 17:24; Acts 2:23). Whatever the preferred viewpoint may be, the verse proclaims God's eternal love for his faithful children.

How can these additional features of the apocalyptic sea-beast, chronicled in vv. 3–8, enlighten us regarding our interior life as baptized Christians? First, the survival of one of the seven monstrous heads (v. 3) may be metaphorical for the human heart's inclination to sin, a propensity that continues unabated even when momentarily interrupted by acts of penance and sacramental absolution. And if the seven heads (v. 1) are taken as an indication of the seven capital sins,

24. Cf. RD, 1075.
25. Cf. AvS, 423–24.

then the reviving of one head would imply the inherent vitality of the other six, compensating the loss by osmosis, as it were, and reaffirming the sinister interconnectedness of all sin in us (*nexus peccatorum*).[26] Like the proverbial nine lives of a cat, sin causes spiritual death, yet at the same time has the predisposition to thrive again and to chain-react through every type of sinful rebellion. There is consolation, however, in the awareness that God's permissive will, allowing the evil tempter to come after us, is outdone by his deliberate will by which he desires our sanctification and delights in it. Sin's grip on the soul is neither boundless nor compulsive, but kept in check by the veiled power of God. No matter how much Satan puffs himself up, the healing force especially of the Church's seven sacraments overpowers him. These also prevent us from falling for false ways to regenerate ourselves and rise from death: in its extreme ideation, postmodern transhumanism, for instance, becomes a futile quest for immortality outside of God's design of salvation. And we are compelled to reiterate the expression *extra Ecclesiam nulla salus*,[27] conveying the belief that the Church is directly or indirectly the indispensable vehicle for humanity to attain to eternal life.

May this passage of Revelation also inspire us never to engage in boastful or presumptuous, let alone blasphemous, speech, but rather renounce mundane vainglory by attributing all spiritual good to Jesus: "Let the one who boasts, boast in the Lord" (1 Cor 1:31). What is more, the "book of life" (v. 8), New Jerusalem's citizen registry, so to speak, based on the dual concept of good and bad books in Daniel 12:1–2, reminds us of the inscrutable mysteries of God's predestination, election, and predilection: at baptism, the Christian's name is registered in it, but it will take a lifetime of virtuous living to not have it blotted out in the end (3:5). Above and beyond the thorny theological issues involving divine omniscience, predestination, and human freedom, this thought springs from the entirely biblical notion that individual salvation is from start to finish the unmerited act of God. Everlasting life will forever depend on our generous and determined cooperation with his supernatural gifts: "By the grace of God I am what I am, and his grace toward me has not been in vain" (1 Cor 15:10a).

26. Cf. AvS, 417–20.

27. First proposed by St. Cyprian of Carthage (d. 258) in his *Epistle* 72.

First call: Endurance and faith (13:9–10)

[9]Let anyone who has an ear listen: [10]If you are to be taken captive, into captivity you go; if you kill with the sword, with the sword you must be killed. Here is a call for the endurance and faith of the saints.

Echoing Jesus' own summarizing exclamations or *epiphonemata* in the Gospel (e.g., Matt 11:15) and the Spirit's exhortation to the seven churches (e.g., 2:7), St. John invites persons of every age, ethnicity, and culture, that is, the entire human family, to pay close attention to both the preceding and the following messages: "Let anyone who has an ear listen!" (v. 9). It is a direct appeal to all seekers of God's wisdom to lend attentive and intelligent ears, i.e., ears worth having, open to truths that require more than ordinary powers of thought to comprehend, and to seriously weigh their importance. Taking careful heed means to not just perceive the sound of words, but rather consciously inquire into their doctrinal and mystical significance so they can be better understood and practiced. Is the seer not also intimating that he foresees that what he says would not be believed by all (Rom 11:8), but only by those whose spiritual ears and hearts God has opened to receive his mysteries? Also expressed is the fact that we are all predisposed by nature to learn God's commands, to diligently attend to and obey them.

Furthermore, inspired by Jeremiah's oracle against Jerusalem (Jer 15:2), the visionary forewarns: "If you are to be taken captive, into captivity you go; if you must be killed with the sword, by the sword you must be killed" (v. 10). He has just told us of the war waged by the world against Christians, and now he cautions against the futile attempt to defend ourselves by the use of the sword, knowing that "all those who take the sword will perish with the sword" (Matt 26:52). His purpose is to enforce an attitude of loyal endurance, a sharing in the Passion of Christ, to be resigned to our fate of suffering,[28] even if that should involve captivity or death by the sword. Thus, there are woes foreordained for the friends of Christ that they must courageously undergo without relinquishing the faith, nor meeting force with force, but remaining nonviolent (Luke 6:29).[29] Not only our patience but our faith is to be tested, as we bear evils that we cannot avoid. By willingly submitting to such tribulations, we imitate the Lord who embraced his Cross as a necessity according to his heavenly Father's

28. Manifested, for instance, in the aspirational words ascribed to St. Mary Magdalene Pazzi: "To suffer, not to die!"

29. Excepting, obviously, cases of legitimate self-defense.

will. Added is this consolatory word: "Here is a call for the patience and faith of the saints" (v. 10b).

This is the first of four such sapiential exhortations in the Apocalypse (13:18; 14:12; 17:9). Holding fast to the Gospel and true worship of God in the hour of trial is a spiritual trademark of the elect whose names are written in the book of life. For the staying power and the fidelity of the saints will be tested to the utmost, especially during the end-time reign of the beast. Of all the persecutions of the Church this will be the most severe, exceeding those of the early times both in degree and in duration. Hence the demand for interior stamina and resilience in nonresistance, enduring everything without grasping at worldly methods of pseudo-salvation. Faith remains the only true victory, sustained by the certainty of God's eventual vengeance on the oppressors. It is of utmost importance to remember that Christians will be saved *through* tribulation, and not *from* it, as experienced by the Lord himself, despite his dolorous plea: "My Father, if it is possible, let this cup pass from me; yet not as I will, but as you will" (Matt 26:39).

13:11–18, Land-beast

Surrogate of the surrogate (13:11–13)

[11]Then I saw another beast that rose out of the earth; it had two horns like a lamb and it spoke like a dragon. [1] It exercises all the authority of the first beast on its behalf, and it makes the earth and its inhabitants worship the first beast, whose mortal wound had been healed. [13]It performs great signs, even making fire come down from heaven to earth in the sight of all.

If the sea (v. 1) epitomized the multidirectional waves of peoples with their tumultuous impulses and passions, then this other beast rising out of the earth (v. 11) could symbolize the consolidated, ordered world of nations with their long-established cultures and learning. Both wild beasts rise from below, not from above,[1] suggesting that their wisdom is not divine but earthly, sensual, and devilish (Jas 3:15, 17). While Daniel's four successive beasts are all very different from one another (Dan 7:3), John's two monsters effectively resemble each other. This second one "had two horns like a lamb and it spoke like a dragon" (c. 11), aping not only the Lamb of God (5:6), but also mimicking the dragon itself. In this way, it is a demonic synthesis or compromise between Lamb and dragon, attempting to mislead humanity with an irreconcilable "both, and." Nevertheless, it is slightly less hideous in appearance than the first one; in fact, it could be labeled as almost human-like. Yet its two horns, reflective of the Danielic ram and male goat (Dan 8:3, 5), appear to mock the two olive trees and the two lampstands that personify the two dominical witnesses (11:3–4). What is now crystallizing before our eyes is a satanic travesty of the Blessed Trinity, with the dragon satirizing God the Father, the

1. According to apocalyptic tradition, on the fifth day God created two mythological monsters (Gen 1:21), Leviathan and Behemoth, one to inhabit the sea and the other the land (4 Ezra 6:49–52; 1 Enoch 60:7–10; 2 Bar 29:4).

sea-beast caricaturing the Son of God, and the earth-beast deriding the Holy Spirit.[2]

Spookily, the earth-beast "exercises all the authority of the first beast on its behalf, and it makes the earth and its inhabitants worship the first beast, whose mortal wound had been healed" (v. 12). Just as God the Father gave all authority in heaven and on earth to his Son (Matt 28:18), so the antichristic sea-beast receives power from the serpent (v. 4); and again, as the Holy Spirit glorifies Christ (John 16:14), so also the land-beast functions as the demonic propagandist and marketeer of the first beast, not so much succeeding as supporting it. As collateral damage, as it were, this perverted logic also parodies the apostolic succession established in the Catholic Church that hands on the grace of Jesus' priesthood in the Holy Orders of bishops, priests, and deacons. Evidently a figure of some earthly power tyrannizing men and women, this second beast acts as the sinister accomplice, interpreter, and *alter ego* of the first beast, attempting to lead people astray in idolatrous worship. This armor-bearer of the antichrist disguises itself as a pious follower of Christ while doing the work of the devil. That is why it will be identified afterwards with the traditional false prophet (16:13), since in the manner of a magician it accompanies the sea-beast, the false messiah.

If the first beast, namely, Lucifer's surrogate, is a political symbol, pseudo-regal and belligerent, it is the business of this second beast, as the surrogate's hellish surrogate, to stand as the standard of false religion, exercised in magic. To seduce souls, it does not refrain from performing "great signs, even making fire come down from heaven to earth in the sight of all" (v. 13). By doing so, it ironically and uncreatively apes Moses' portents in Egypt, including his discrediting of Pharaoh's magicians Jannes and Jambres (2 Tim 3:8). By counterfeiting the benevolent power of God himself, as the descent of fire was frequently a sign of his approval (Gen 15:17), the land-beast tries to validate its pretended authority similar to true prophets, such as Elijah in his day (1 Kgs 18:37–38; 2 Kgs 1:1–12). Recalled, too, is the vindictive intent of the Boanerges brothers, James and John, to consume the Samaritans in fiery judgment (Luke 9:54), and more notably, the flaming tongues of the Holy Spirit on Pentecost that the devil envies. Lastly, it should not go unmentioned that the land-beast's magic performance is the counterpart of the work of the two witnesses in 11:5, too.

At this point, the question becomes again how one can discern the operations of this second beast in our own life. To begin with, there is the obvious

2. Cf. AvS, 432.

recognition that human nature turns into something more animalistic and brutish when severed from God, who remains humanity's archetype and in whose image we were first made, and whose ideal is exhaustively realized in the God-Man Jesus Christ. By derivation, any world-power seeking its own glory, and not God's, represents a wild beast, as King Nebuchadnezzar harrowingly experienced, when in self-deification he forgot that the Almighty reigns supreme above the kingdom of mortals, and was driven away from human society to live with wild animals (Dan 4:17, 25, 33). A certain change of mode, but not of spirit, can be determined in this land-beast, as it proceeds with more refinement, intelligence, and civility; yet it is still the mundane power that is worshipped, a self-seeking idolization of honors and pleasures, springing from earth's dust and ending up among its ashes. This worldly wisdom is propounded through ideas and scientific cultivation, a rationalistic philosophy pandering to the semi-gnostic pretense of superior knowledge. "Your eyes will be opened!" was the infernal bait of the primeval tempter (Gen 3:5, 7), and this surrogate monster continues to display its seductive machinations before the eyes of the sea-beast and in the sight of all humanity.[3] Aiming at self-divinization through unmitigated worldliness, it will always enthrone the "isms" of every age that without fail plummet into the tyranny of atheistic materialism.

Moreover, if the first beast was seen attacking the saints from without (v. 7), this second one attempts to corrupt them from within, disseminating an ideological message of deception and obscurantism. Hence, to guard against false teachers in every generation, vigilantly resisting their malicious persuasiveness, remains an imperative for us Christians. In persevering noncompliance, we will not allow anybody to antagonize us against our Creator and Savior. And also, in its worst manifestation, this latest monster embodies the entire spectrum of what is known as black magic or *ars magica*,[4] all type of occultism that sins against the First Commandment, including divination, sorcery, witchcraft, augury, and spiritism.[5] These do not foster true divine worship but are designed to confuse us, to divert our attention from the Lord, and to do lasting harm to the soul. By entertaining that holy fire that set the lips and hearts of the saints ablaze, the servants of Christ reject the unhallowed Luciferian lights that burn upside down in disorientation (v. 13). Putting the Gospel into practice and

3. The adverb *enṓpion* (ἐνώπιον), from *én* (ἐν), "in," and *optánomai* (ὀπτάνομαι), "to see, appear," literally means "before the face, in the eyes" (*in conspectu*), and is emphatically repeated three times in vv. 12–14.

4. Cf. RD, 1079.

5. Cf. *CCC*, §§2115–17.

assiduously receiving the Sacraments will prevent us from making room for the devil (Eph 4:27).[6]

Imaging the substitute (13:14–15)

[14]And by the signs that it is allowed to perform on behalf of the beast, it deceives the inhabitants of earth, telling them to make an image for the beast that had been wounded by the sword and yet lived; [15]and it was allowed to give breath to the image of the beast so that the image of the beast could even speak and cause those who would not worship the image of the beast to be killed.

Shackled by its subservience to the first beast, and still operating only within the boundaries of divine permission, the second beast continues to deceive the inhabitants of the earth, telling them to make an image for the beast that was wounded by the sword and yet lived (v. 14). A pawn of Satan, its sole power lies in using treachery and fraudulence to enlarge its global strength. Its duplicity consists in manipulating humanity into confecting an icon (*eikóna*, εἰκόνα, *imago*) of the sea-beast. Besides implying the likeness of such an image to the original, the Greek word involves the idea of representation and manifestation, as was the case with Caesar's portrait on the denarius (Matt 21:20). Such an idolatrous statue signals yet another level of travesty, beginning with the generation of the eternal Word himself, Jesus, as the reflection of God's glory, the exact imprint of God's very being (Heb 1:3), as well as the Firstborn of all Creation (Col 1:15). It ridicules the procession of the Holy Spirit from the Father and the Son, and satirizes the issuance of all creation from the hands of its Maker. Additionally, it parodies the holy resemblance between the good angels and the Spirit of God. A charade is made of the coming of that Spirit as another Paraclete (John 14:16), as well.

How does it not also make a mockery of the forming of Adam in Elohim's likeness (Gen 1:27), and of the "constructing" of Eve from one of his ribs (Gen 2:22, *aedificavit*, lit. "built")? Additionally, this idolatrous image of the beast taunts the many statues of the Blessed Virgin Mary and of the angels and saints in churches and private homes around the globe.[7] And yet, legion are the replicas of this demonic phantom in history: King Nebuchadnezzar's golden statue (Dan 3:1), the idol of Bel among the Babylonians (Dan

6. Cf. AvS, 436.
7. Cf. AvS, 437.

14:3), Emperor Caligula's statue blasphemously erected inside the Jerusalem temple,[8] Domitian's gigantic statue at his Ephesian temple, and the Colossus of Rhodes, to mention but a few.[9] Here is the dogged attempt of an unenlightened humanity to restore and perpetuate idolatry, as already denounced by the apostle Paul: "They exchanged the glory of the immortal God for images resembling a mortal human being or birds or four-footed animals or reptiles" (Rom 1:23).

To make matters worse, the land-beast "was allowed to give breath to the image of the beast so that the image of the beast could even speak and cause those who would not worship the image of the beast to be killed" (v. 15). Conferring the breath of life summons up Adam's creation (Gen 2:7), but also the Resurrection of Christ, the sole true Firstborn from the dead (Col 1:18). Furthermore, is Satan scheming to outdo the miracle of the dry bones rising from the valley in Ezekiel's vision (Ezek 37:1–10), or outshine the resurrection of the two witnesses in the great city (11:11)? Also, does John suggest that the image's ability to speak amounts to an ongoing instigation to violent action against those who refuse to comply with the imperial cult? Of course, to render divine honors to idols has been and always will be utterly unacceptable for those who are baptized into Christ. Mindful of the Maccabean nightmare of discrimination and torture (2 Macc 6–7), we ought to recall how precisely the refusal of forced worship to the emperor's image was made the test of Christianity in the early Roman persecutions. Back then and down the centuries since, those who would not worship were oftentimes put to death. Instead, the one true God and his Incarnate Son prefer freedom of worship, and, indeed, Christ sheds his own blood, while the antichrist sheds the blood of others.[10]

When viewing this diabolical effigy of the sea-beast from a spiritual standpoint, it becomes clear that the lethal blow to one of the latter's heads (vv. 3, 14) is caused by the sharp, two-edged sword[11] issuing from the mouth of the Son of Man (cf. 1:16), signifying that one of the most efficient weapons in our fight against the intellectual stratagems of the evil one remains an intimate

8. Cf. Flavius Josephus, *Antiquities*, 18.261–62.

9. One reads in the pseudepigraphal *Ascension of Isaiah*, that Beliar, i.e, the devil, "sets up his image before him in every city," and "there will be the power of his miracles in every city and region" (4.10–11).

10. Cf. RD, 1083.

11. Exclusive to the Greek text, however, is the distinction made between Christ's "long sword" (*rhomphaía*, ῥομφαία, 1:16) and the devil's "short sword" (*máchaira*, μάχαιρα, 13:14), as if to suggest that the deathblow to one of the sea-beast's heads is the consequence of internecine warring among infernal factions, hinted at in Mark 3:23–26.

understanding and practicing of Holy Scripture (Eph 6:17). Moreover, the Christian soul must be on its guard not to compromise with perceived lesser or diluted forms of idolatry, intimated by the smaller copy of the beast. its aim is not to convince us to pay greater tribute to the first beast, but to mislead us into a demonic alternative, so that those who vacillate in their allegiance to the dragon's proxy might repress their scruples and cheat their own conscience by giving in to idolatrous worship of its "mere image," ultimately becoming ensnared in the same trap and incurring the same condemnation (2 Cor 4:4). Thus, these verses of Revelation teach us that those who by specious reasoning throw in their lot with the worldly in perhaps more covert ways, are equally guilty with those who are overt adherents of the first beast and of its master, the devil. Here we see the foul spirit of religious compromise, of mediocrity, and of minimalism. Instead, an authentic follower of Christ will persevere in addressing the root causes even of one's venial sins and imperfections and go on staunchly striving for spiritual perfection.

Second call: Wisdom and understanding (13:16–18)

16 Also it causes all, both small and great, both rich and poor, both free and slave, to be marked on the right hand or the forehead, 17 so that no one can buy or sell who does not have the mark, that is, the name of the beast or the number of its name. 18 This calls for wisdom: let anyone with understanding calculate the number of the beast, for it is the number of a person. Its number is six hundred sixty-six.

Cunningly, and in brazen usurpation of power, the land-beast manages to impose its will on humanity, trying to dictate their choices and enslave them in vv. 16–17. What is remarkable about the expression "it makes them all do" (*poieî pántas*, ποιεῖ πάντας, *facit omnes*) combined with the phrase "that they give themselves" (*hína dôsin autoîs*, ἵνα δῶσιν αὐτοῖς, *accipere*) in v. 16, is that it thinly cloaks infernal duress under the semblance of free human choice. Also, the unexpected way in which three distinct pairs of human society are presented, i.e., placing the perceived inferior element ahead of the superior in the first one (small-great), but then randomly placing the supposed upper class ahead of the lower one in the remaining two (rich-poor, free-slave; cf. 19:18), conveys the idea that such man-made disparateness is arbitrary and ultimately irrelevant in the eyes of God, for whom the last will be first, and the first will be last (Matt 20:16).

What is virtually forced on all humanity is an ominous mark (*chāragma*, χάραγμα, *character*) that seems engraved on their living bodies as if on lifeless sculptures or coins. At the time of his writing, John would have been reminded of the Roman custom of tattooing slaves, soldiers, or convicted criminals; likewise, temple devotees or superstitious votaries would sear their idol's cipher into their skin.[12] For us contemporaries, the branding of cattle on a ranch to designate a farmer's property comes to mind. That the beastly stamp is impressed on the right hand (v. 16), the symbol of human toil and interaction, caricatures the sacred right hand of God the Father (5:1, 7), of his divine Son (1:16–17, 20; 2:1), and of his angel (10:5). Likewise, the marked foreheads, representing human intellect, freedom, and dignity, ape the proud identification of the saints (7:3), but they also foreshadow the sinister mystery of Babylon (17:5) and her doomed children (14:9; 20:4).

As a counterpart to Israel's fidelity to the Torah (Exod 13:9), and in direct contrast to the seal of the Lamb, this satanic imprint is spiritual in nature, a parody of the indelible and unrepeatable character bestowed on a person in the sacraments of baptism, confirmation, and Holy Orders.[13] Just as the latter signals one's configuration to the Lord and to his Church (2 Cor 1:22), brought about by the anointing of the Holy Spirit as a grace granting divine protection, so also the devil brands his spoils, a harvest of subjugated souls. They are pressured into compromise and cooperation with evil, not to mention that the visible mark on them balefully betokens to whom they belong: these wearers of the unholy mark are under his patronage, swearing their allegiance to him. It surely also means their acquiescence in thought and action to the principles of any tyrannical world-power.

As the chief abettor of world-dominance, therefore, the land-beast seeks to impress a mark on all, under penalty of comprehensive social exclusion: "No one can buy or sell who does not have the mark, that is, the name of the beast or the number of its name" (v. 17). Lacking all creativity, it can only mimic the Lord's own gesture of writing his name on his beloved brethren (3:12). Trying to dominate the earth through an economic albatross, the antichrist claims jurisdiction over the traffic of wealth, and ventures to make it tributary to its own warped purposes. And as a matter of historical fact, Christian artisans in antiquity who wished to earn a livelihood by practicing their trade, would have had to join pagan guilds under the aegises of the imperial cult, and those

12. Such "cuttings," incidentally, were forbidden by Mosaic Law (Lev 19:28).
13. Cf. *CCC*, §1121.

who refused were subjected to economic discrimination and strain.[14] Satan's attempt at absolute control, however, will be thwarted when God lays waste to the riches of this world (18:11).

As if seeking eye contact with his audience of all generations, John turns to each one of us and avers: "This calls for wisdom: let anyone with understanding calculate the number of the beast, for it is the number of a person" (v. 18). Here we have another sapiential exhortation, the second of four, asking for our creative interpretation by tapping into the infinite wisdom of God, also implying that the intellectual grasp of this "mark-name-number" is humanly attainable. To scrutinize scriptural mysteries in general, and to compute this apocalyptic number in particular, is not futile but rather is recommended to us on divine authority. "Mark," "name," and "number" stand for the beast's identity, for the enemy's *modus operandi*. Since it is equivalent to a human being,[15] it suggests that Lucifer will always be represented by or hiding behind some anthropological reality here on earth, such as a charismatic leader or ideology.[16] It expresses all that is possible for the human intellect when dominated by an evil spirit, which is to achieve a state of pseudo-paradisiac perfection in history. After taking hold of culture and corrupting civilization, such persons will declare that faith in God is an insolence and the hope of a future life a vilification of those who seek present-day happiness. At this point only a wisdom descended from above will be able to unmask the infinite difference between life with faith and life without faith.

To say that "its number is six hundred sixty-six" (v. 18) means to speak about the least relevant aspect of the sea-beast's nature. In the quest for meaning, many have attempted to apply various cryptographic codes that assign a numerical value to a name according to its letters. However, there are simply too many historical personages whose letters will amount to "six-six-six," either in Hebrew gematria or Greek isopsephy, to make this a viable hermeneutic. As explained in most commentaries, a consensus has settled on the alphanumeric value of the Greek title "Nero Caesar" when transliterated into Hebrew script. This Roman emperor, therefore, would be one typological embodiment of beastly evil, a sad metaphor for abuse of political power. Yet, this application remains unconvincing, since the original language of Revelation is Greek

14. Such handicaps seem to have been foisted on them, for instance, during the Diocletian persecution, by requiring business transactions to be preceded by pagan credal formulas.

15. See also the identification of the human measure with that of an angel in 21:17b.

16. Jesus' revelation of the "enemy-human" (*echthròs ánthrōpos*, ἐχθρὸς ἄνθρωπος, *inimicus homo*) identified as the devil in his Kingdom parable (Matt 13:28, 39) seems to suggest that synergy between human and demonic agencies.

and not Hebrew, and in all likelihood, John would have indicated any supposed switch to a different language, as indeed he does at 9:11 and 16:16. Also, this would be the sole exercise of digital encryption and decryption in the Apocalypse, further weakening this hypothetical approach.

Hence, it appears more plausible, and also more in accord with the hermeneutics applied to all the other numerals in Revelation, to reflect on the generic symbolism of this truly infamous number. In principle, the triple repetition of "six" conveys utmost imperfection, a systemic falling short of a sacred and perfect "seven." Consequently, the beast symbolizes emphatic negativity in this world and in our lives, a veritable embodiment of the mystery of iniquity. Additionally, an antichristic stance is expressed vis-à-vis the God-Man Jesus, whose Greek name amounts to "eight-eight-eight," also hinting at his Resurrection on the eighth day. Perhaps there is also a hint at the serpent's brazenness to aspire to higher glory than God himself, whose trinitarian nature is implied by "three-three-three." One might even speculate that "human" (*ánthrōpos*, ἄνθρωπος, *homo*, v. 18), created on the sixth day, despite being very good (Gen 1:31), remains incomplete until humanity reaches its creatural finality on the seventh day, that is, the Sabbath of God's eternal rest (Gen 2:2–3). In that sense, "six hundred sixty-six" would be a chronological indication of Satan's imperfect reign, the eschatological period during which he will strive to obstruct humanity from attaining its fullness. Yet at the end of the day, the most enduring message passed on by this chilling and mesmerizing 666 is that as baptized Christians we are called to conquer the beast and its image and the number of its name (15:2).

Wrapping up this chapter on the two apocalyptic monsters, let us heed the call to be wise and ponder their impact on our interior lives. We could point to three areas that are affected, starting with the godless "mark-name-number" on right hands or foreheads as blasphemous travesties of the sacramental character. To counter any diabolical influence, each one of us is invited to continuously rediscover the spiritual potency of our baptism as our birthday into supernatural life. It will be most beneficial to study and reflect on the life of the saint whose name we or our parents chose at baptism. By knowing more about this heavenly intercessor and protector we will be able to imitate his or her ways of holiness. While the brutish mark also apes the signs of the Passion (John 20:25),[17] perverting it into an emblem of diabolical independence and rebellion, the apostle Paul points to the stigmata that he carries in his own body as proof for his being a servant of the Lord Jesus (Gal 6:17). It may be profitable

17. Cf. AvS, 438–39.

to also explore the saintly lives of some of the notable stigmatists venerated by the Catholic Church.[18] Obviously, the apocalyptic branding of a person's right hand and forehead intimates the submission of bodily and intellectual powers to the beast's domination. That is why we must cultivate more and more our intellect through habitual contemplation, and ennoble our hands through Christian action overflowing in good works.

A second point of consideration has to do with the Evil One's presumptive power over the material goods of this earth, as intimated by the phrase "buy and sell" (v. 17), in open defiance toward God the Maker of all earthly goods. Now, in one way or another, Christians will always be ostracized by worldly societies, declared a social nuisance, and shunned by the ungodly who prefer to pay allegiance to the beast. Notwithstanding such ongoing discrimination, subtle or unsubtle, as the case may be, we can be assured that the Lord himself will provide for his faithful ones, as he does for the woman in the desert (12:6). Evidently, his followers in the early Church did bravely refuse to pay homage to trade guild deities or Caesar's image, which subsequently brought poverty upon many of them. Yet Christ restores confidence by showing them their true inner wealth: "I know your affliction and your poverty, but you are rich" (2:9). Thus, Revelation motivates us to turn even more intently to Jesus and buy refined gold, white robes, and soothing salve from him (3:18), who by his blood bought us for God (5:9). Even though there may be times when we suffer serious deprivation, we know that we find plenty in him from whom we have all received, grace upon grace (John 1:16).

A third and final item to be spiritually ruminated upon in our quest for authentic wisdom is to decipher Satan's stratagems, to defeat his cold-blooded intellectual brilliance, his camouflaged maneuvering, and his tactics of deception under the patina of righteousness. In the soul's close combat with an enemy who does not respect human freedom, we must find shelter in the bulwark of divine knowledge, in order that we do not fall prey to him. By satanic self-mirroring and self-referentiality, he seeks to perplex us, inflating the trinitarian reality into an inadequate hextuple (666), while failing to embrace the salvific septuple, represented, for instance, by the Church's seven sacraments.[19] In some mysterious ways, this arrogant distortion of his does infiltrate the human nature, "for it is the number of a human" (*numerus enim hominis est*, v. 18), which in its most tragic instantiation can spawn demonic possession.

18. E.g., Sts. Francis of Assisi, Catherine of Siena, Rita of Cascia, John of God, Gemma Galgani, Mariam Thresia Chiramel, and Padre Pio of Pietrelcina.

19. Cf. AvS, 440.

One sure symptom that the monstrosity of the beast's number is still lurking in the human heart is indulgence in mundane distractions, sharing in the devil's restlessness that will not attain to the seventh-day rest of God.[20] "Here is wisdom [and] understanding" (v. 18), namely, to make time every day for prayer and contemplation, experiencing again and again that "the fear of the Lord is the beginning of wisdom, and the knowledge of the Holy One is insight" (Prov 9:10–11).

20. Cf. RD, 1085–86.

14:1–5, *Ecclesia triumphans*

Great assembly on Zion (14:1)

[1]Then I looked, and there was the Lamb, standing on Mount Zion! And with him were one hundred forty-four thousand who had his name and his Father's name written on their foreheads.

True to his narrative pattern of alternating between intimidating and consoling scenes, the prophet on Patmos, having related in chs. 12–13 the trio of enemies with which God's people must contend, now passes on to communicate the blessedness in store for faithful Christians. A foil to the preceding section, vv. 1–5 anticipate chs. 21–22 as a sort of tribute or encomium to the Lamb, no longer slain but triumphant. In attendance are his companions, the first fruits of the redeemed, who chose to worship him, and not the emperor, during their lifetime. This is the remnant around which the Kingdom will be rebuilt after the victory. Just as the pledge of salvation to the faithful (ch. 7) resulted in the excoriation of the ungodly (8:1–11:14) and in another glory-filled vignette of the saved (11:15–19), so also here the depiction of bliss on Mount Zion (14:1–5) is followed by the announcement of judgments coming upon the irreligious (14:6–18:24), leading once more to a snapshot of the saints in celestial splendor (ch. 19:1–8). So now, after stomaching the portrayal of the dragon and the beasts (chs. 12–13), we are surely ready for something joyous and uplifting.

After some indeterminate length of time, John's eyes are ravished away from the earthy beast (13:11) toward a festive spectacle on high, seeing the Lamb standing on Mount Zion surrounded by his faithful servants (v. 1). The stark contrast and unexpected relief can be sensed in the introductory phrase "And I saw, and behold!" (*Et vidi: et ecce*), also indicating a new phase of the vision (4:1). How overjoyed he must have been to see, instead of a warrior King, the Lamb coming into visual focus again for the first time since 8:1. This is Christ the Savior, in whose atoning blood his valiant soldiers find their victory, and he is now proudly positioned, and has been for some time,[1] as their leader on the citadel of the heavenly city. All satanic monstrosity has given way to divine pulchritude. Having left his position in the midst of the throne (5:6a) to open the seven seals (6:1), the Lamb now takes his stand on Mount Zion,[2] mentioned only here in the Apocalypse.

This biblical locality with its sacred aura has undergone a progressive spiritualization heavenwards. Of uncertain Semitic etymology (Hebrew צִיּוֹן), Zion originally referred to a specific acropolis on which the higher and more ancient part of the city of Jerusalem was built, in the proximity of Mount Moriah, also known as the Temple Mount,[3] the Mount of Olives, as well as Mount Golgotha. Later it came to designate the central area of Davidic Jerusalem where a fortress stood. King David captured this hill, placed the Ark of the Covenant upon it as a symbol of rest and royal glory (Ps 132:13–14), and chose it as the site for his palace, with the other city dwellings clustered around it. In due course, it became synonymous with Jerusalem's population itself, as well as with the entire land of Israel, poetically personified as "Daughter of Zion" (John 12:15). Centuries later, it stood as a traditional beacon of refuge and security for the true remnant being saved, the Israel of faith, rallied around it while awaiting the messianic reign (2 Kgs 19:31).

Further idealized as the seat of divine worship on earth, the immovable abode and throne of God, Zion stood as the epitome of divine presence, protection, and salvation both in the past and in the future end-times.[4] And here, the Lord is at the same time transcendent and manifest to his people. As such, in the grand scheme of the history of the chosen people, Zion is at the same time the serene and peaceful ennoblement of gloomy Sinai and the quintessential antipode to corrupt Babylon. Later, in its penultimate historical-spiritual rereading, it symbolizes the Church on earth, living her millennial reign of the eschaton.[5] In its final stage, John, as an authentic prophet of the New Covenant, idealizes Zion once more into a simile of the heavenly regions, blending effortlessly into the world to come, the New Jerusalem (21:10), its communion of

1. The perfect participle "standing" (*hestós*, ἑστός, *stans*) mirrors the perfect participle in 5:6 (*hestēkós*, ἑστηκός, *stantem*), whose linguistic aspect connotes duration and completion of an action starting in an unspecified past.

2. Emphasized with a definite article in the Greek (*tò óros Siṓn*, τὸ ὄρος Σιών; cf. Ps 101:14).

3. According to Gen 22:2, also the locale where Isaac was offered (cf. Book of Jubilees 18:7–16).

4. Dante Alighieri, *Divine Comedy*, *Inferno*, Canto 1:128, "He governs everywhere and there he reigns; there is his city and his lofty throne; o happy he whom thereto he elects!"

5. Cf. RD, 1089.

saints, and God's eternal dwelling place among them.[6] It is contemplated here as already accessible to believers, with an already-and-not-yet end time view in mind. This is the Church triumphant,[7] the ultimate antithesis to the fiery lake where the demons and damned souls will find themselves forever imprisoned (20:14–15).

Joining the Lamb are one hundred forty-four thousand (v. 1), that is, those who have been redeemed from the earth (v. 3), no longer seen in their exposure to worldly trials like those in 7:4, but now victorious.[8] Unlike the demonic unfinishedness of six-six-six, they represent the totality of saved humanity, having entirely grown into God's plan. They are reminiscent of that remnant of the twelve tribes chosen by Yahweh, and whose fullness, according to Romans 11, will again become the Lord's possession as his true Israel.[9] Here we see all those genuine followers of the twelve apostles, proliferated into a thousandfold over time, and thus, the Holy Church. Such prodigious increase can serve as an encouragement to the present-day reader of Revelation, invigorating him or her to become yeast mixed in with the flour of society till it is leavened all through (Matt 13:33).[10]

In a throwback to 7:4, and in anticipation of 22:4, but also in contradistinction to those who accepted the mark of the beast at 13:16–17, we learn that on their foreheads are written the names of the Lamb and of his Father (v. 1).[11] And so, this chorus of heavenly citizens is described not only in their concord, but more importantly, they are sealed as the inalienable property, that

6. "In Sion intellege caelicam civitatem," Origen (quoted from the *Liturgia Horarum*, Week 2, Feria III, *Laudes*, caption introducing Ps 64); see also 4 Ezra 13:25–52; 2 Bar 40:1.

7. Cf. AvS, 443; although the terms descriptive of the three states of the Church, i.e., "Church militant" as it exists on earth (*Ecclesia militans*), "Church suffering" as the souls in purgatory (*Ecclesia poenitens* or *expectans*), and "Church triumphant" as the saints in heaven (*Ecclesia triumphans*), are not explicitly cited in the Catechism of the Catholic Church, their teaching is implied at §954.

8. Since the same crowd is referenced, in the Greek text they are no longer preceded by the definite article *haí* (αἱ), just as in 17:3, the beast without the article *tó* (τό) is the same as the one who appears in 13:1.

9. There is also a subtle hue of the Trinity in the triple multiplication of twelve times twelve times one thousand, resulting in the above number, cf. RD, 1090.

10. Cf. AvS, 443.

11. Two variant readings should be mentioned here: first, the Ethiopic version adds "and of his Holy Spirit," probably to complete the trinitarian reference; second, a copyist must have misread the Greek *kaì tò ónoma* (καὶ τὸ ὄνομα), "and the name," as the almost identical looking *kaiómenon* (καιόμενον), "burnt," hinting at the way those names were potentially cauterized into their skin.

is, children, servants, and soldiers of God.[12] Even though the Holy Spirit is not made explicit on this occasion, he is present not only in the embrace between the Father and the Lamb, but also in the unity between God and man.[13] Evocative of the inscription "Holy to the Lord" (*Sanctum Domino*) on the high priest's miter (Exod 28:36), as well as the Torah frontlets between the eyes of the ancient Hebrews (Deut 6:8), the names tell of their eternal election received in the grace of baptism, which in turn inscribes their names in the Book of Life. Fully adopted by the Lord, they are no longer fearful slaves but are emboldened in their adoptive sonship, crying "Abba! Father!" (Rom 8:15).

It should instill confidence in us to understand that we no longer face the harshness of Mount Sinai, but are oriented toward the loving-kindness, peace, and serenity of Mount Zion (Heb 12:18–24). Christianity is a religion of human dignity, meekness, and inner strength, as is so fittingly sung by the psalmist: "Those who trust in the Lord are like Mount Zion, which cannot be moved, but abides forever. As the mountains surround Jerusalem, so the Lord surrounds his people, from this time on and forevermore" (Ps 125:1–2). And just as the prophets of old hinted at that cumulative idealization of Mount Zion, that is, from a topographic reality in the Holy Land to a symbol of the glorified people of God, so also is our interior life in union with Christ caught up in an ongoing process of spiritualization or transformation away from the affairs of this world, until it finally blossoms into the mystical Zion of imperishable bliss. To attain to the sanctity of those one hundred forty-four thousand, even beyond the holiness intimated by the letters to the seven churches (chs. 2–3), every servant of Christ Jesus is encouraged to give heartfelt and unabashed witness to their Catholic faith (Rom 1:16). Every day we choose to cooperate in the cause of God and of the truth, as if wearing his name or the sign of the Cross[14] visibly on our foreheads: "It is by believing with the heart that you are justified, and by making the declaration with your lips that you are saved" (Rom 10:10).

12. This scene finds a magnificent artistic expression in John and Hubert van Eyck's altarpiece "Adoration of the Mystic Lamb" (1432), preserved at St. Bavo's Cathedral in Ghent, Belgium.

13. Cf. AvS, 443.

14. Cf. RD, 1089.

Learning the new song (14:2–5)

[2]And I heard a voice from heaven like the sound of many waters and like the sound of loud thunder; the voice I heard was like the sound of harpists playing on their harps, [3]and they sing a new song before the throne and before the four living creatures and before the elders. No one could learn that song except the one hundred forty-four thousand who have been redeemed from the earth. [4]It is these who have not defiled themselves with women, for they are virgins; these follow the Lamb wherever he goes. They have been redeemed from humankind as first fruits for God and the Lamb, [5]and in their mouth no lie was found; they are blameless.

While John finds himself still on earth in his vision, his attention is now more fully drawn to the celestial sphere, hearing a voice from heaven like the sound of many waters, of loud thunder, and of harpists playing on their harps (v. 2). This sound (*vox*), whose vocable is reiterated four times in this verse, resembles the roar of the ocean or a mighty cataract of falling water (1:15). Tellingly, it is one of the Sons of Thunder (Mark 3:17) who compares this roar to yet another apocalyptic tempest that instills fright and trembling (e.g., 4:5). First perceived at a distance, the voices become ever crisper, and are at last identifiable as simultaneously vocal and instrumental: the mystique of thunderous waters blends with the sweet melodiousness of "harpers harping on their harps" (*citharoedorum citharizantium in citharis*).[15] So loud is the sound that it can be heard from heaven to earth (Ps 29:3–9), representing the irresistible and winning spread of the Gospel throughout the reign of the antichrist, being heard far and near. Rapid waters and reechoing thunder also allegorize Christ's judgment over humanity, whereas the harps convey the tuneful testimony of grace, truth, and reward for the righteous; they are a parable of the beauty of God's saints.[16] One also envisions the historical advancement of the Church's teaching voice from an indistinct rustling in the wilderness (12:6) to a strikingly efficacious doctrine down the centuries, tending toward the Jerusalem above (Gal 4:26). And indeed, Jesus' servants can at times be like the Boanerges brothers, able to shake up men's and women's consciences and make them cast

15. The biblical harp (*kithára*, κιθάρα, *cithára*, "lyre, zither"), a forerunner of the modern guitar, was a stringed instrument invented by Jubal (Gen 4:21) and commonly employed in sacred music (e.g., Ps 32:2); its ten strings were typically played by the hand (1 Sam 16:23); see also Flavius Josephus, *Antiquities* B. 10.12.3.

16. Cf. AvS, 444.

off sin, but at the same time through them resonates the sound of redemptive joy and consolation.

Assuming that the apostolic mystic is still looking at the one hundred forty-four thousand (v. 1), that is, the transfigured saints reigning with Christ, he now stirringly depicts how they sing a new song before the throne and before the four living creatures and before the elders (v. 3).[17] While this sweet strain evokes the scenes at 5:9–12, 7:9–12, and 11:15, it also paves the way toward 15:2–4 and 19:1–4. Voices and instruments make up one euphonious praise in the presence of God (Ps 150:3), the Lamb, the angels, all of creation, and the Church, whereas, by maximal contrast, the followers of the dragon and its satanic trinity are never said to sing in the Apocalypse. In comparison to the songs of Zion of old (Ps 137:3), this heavenly song is in some sense new (*quasi canticum novum*), and its unfading novelty lies in its overcoming of the order that existed prior to Jesus' work of redemption. Thus, this chanting is an unending celebration of the New Testament and its final triumph over the Church's foes. Never before were the saints able to laud the excellence of the Father's design and declare the worthiness of Christ to receive power, riches, and wisdom. Nor could the angels exalt him in these terms so exclusive to the salvific love bestowed on humanity alone. New is this worship, like the new name (2:17), because now it accompanies the putting on of the "new man" (Eph 4:22–24), i.e., our personal Christian vocation, including the virginal priesthood in the Church inaugurated by the apostle John.[18]

"No one could learn that song except the one hundred forty-four thousand who have been redeemed from the earth" (v. 3): That only the chosen ones can learn that song is due to the fact that faith is a gift of grace given more abundantly to those who conform their lives to the harpists of the Holy Spirit, that is, the evangelists. Flesh and blood, earthly desires, and world-noises dull the spirit in man (Ps 137:4), yet the Lord can open the ear to hear and the heart to rejoice in the ways of God (Isa 51:11). His purchasing blood enables the Christian soul to learn[19] the meaning of what is celebrated in the new song. Not even the angels can learn that song, for no experiential knowledge is given to them

17. Dramatically passing from the past tense *eídon* (εἶδον, *vidi*), "I saw," at v. 1, and *ḗkousa* (ἤκουσα, *audivi*), "I heard," in v. 2, to the historic present *ádousin* (ᾄδουσιν, *cantant*), "they sing," in this verse.

18. Cf. RD, 1092; AS, 448.

19. This is the only occurrence in Revelation of the verb *manthánō* (μανθάνω, *díscere*), "to learn," and its lexicality has to do with making certain of key facts, gaining fact-knowledge by experience, also involving personal reflection (Matt 11:29; 24:32; John 6:45).

about what it really means to be saved and to have washed one's robes in the blood of the Lamb (7:14).

Threefold is the quality of those who accept the grace of salvation, pinpointed by the triple demonstrative pronoun "these" (*hoũtoi*, οὗτοί, *hi*), beginning with the hallmark that "they have not defiled themselves with women, for they are virgins" (v. 4). Undoubtedly to be taken in a spiritual sense and not limited to the unmarried, childlike purity is intended here (Matt 5:8; 18:3–4; 25:1). It appears that one kind of sinful defilement[20] and the most alluring temptation, i.e., sexual immorality, metonymically stands for every other. Trying to overcome unchastity, and by God's grace abstaining from all lewdness in thought, word, and deed, sets Christians apart from the non-baptized world perhaps more than other moral aspects. Spiritual virginity[21] also betokens total detachment from earthly bonds, and at the same time it describes the desire to be spiritually fruitful in the Church in a spirit of sacrifice, even to the point of surrendering one's will to the perfect will of God and renouncing one's personal desires or expectations of reward.[22]

Moreover, in the Old Testament, harlotry, adultery, and fornication are common metaphors for idolatry and superstition, that is, spiritual unfaithfulness to the monotheistic God (e.g., Isa 1:21). Hence, these apocalyptic "virgins" are symbolic of all those who do not indulge in the cult of the beast and do not follow the impieties of Jezebel and Babylon (2:20; 14:8; 17:5–6). They uncompromisingly constitute the Church as the chaste and faithful Bride betrothed to the Lamb (19:7–8). Just as Moses required the Israelites to exercise sexual self-restraint as a purifying and consecratory sacrifice that prepared them for Sinai's theophany (Exod 19:15), and priests abstained from marital relations during seasons of temple sacrifice (Luke 1:23–24), and just as warriors practiced military celibacy (1 Sam 21:5), so also our spiritual continence signifies

20. The verb *molýnō* (μολύνω, *coinquinare*), "to besmear with mud, stain, pollute" (3:4), cannot be interpreted as a disparagement of the sacrament of holy matrimony, although in the Old Testament sexual union, including that of wedlock, was indeed regarded as ritually defiling (Lev 15:18), likely as a consequence of the postlapsarian curse (Gen 3:16); thus, interestingly, we owe to the two celibate apostles, John and Paul, the highest appreciation of Christian marriage (Rev 21–22; Eph 5:23–33).

21. Cf. RD, 1091; this singular occurrence of the Greek noun *parthénos* (παρθένος, *virgo*), "virgin," especially in its masculine grammatical gender, is equally applicable to men and women, figuratively showing those who are faithful to Christ as their heavenly Bridegroom (2 Cor 11:2); it was later adopted in ecclesiastical language as a title for St. John the Evangelist himself.

22. Cf. AvS, 454.

our desire to be holy as God is holy (1 Pet 1:16), to worthily offer priestly worship, and to be soldiers for Christ in this world.

A second characteristic of these singers of the new song is that they obediently "follow the Lamb wherever he goes" (v. 4), foreshadowed by Old Testament events such as the Hebrews following Moses into the howling wilderness, and figures such as Ruth (Ruth 1:16) and Ittai the Gittite (2 Sam 15:21). In their unreserved devotion, the sheep follow the divine Lamb-Shepherd as a sure guide to every good and truth, all the way to the Cross. This earthly loyalty of theirs springs from the religious conviction that ultimately there are only two ways (Ps 1) and no middle ground.[23] In the here and now, whether in prosperity or adversity, an authentic disciple imitates Christ's example, receives him as his or her counselor, and obeys his commandments, not shunning even the path of suffering.[24] To always be able to follow Jesus entails scrutinizing the Sacred Scripture and conforming one's life to it,[25] and as a fitting reward, Christians are promised to enjoy espousal proximity to the Lamb in heaven (21:2).

Separation or unworldliness is the third mark of those who "have been redeemed from humankind as first fruits for God and the Lamb" (v. 4). Becoming the first fruits of the human family complements their new song. Although mentioned only here in Revelation, the idea of first fruits is rooted in the Old Testament where it designated the first ripe crop of the year to be solemnly offered to Yahweh (Lev 23:10). It embodied an earnest of a more plentiful harvest in succeeding seasons. Applied to the followers of the Lamb, they are the elite, so to speak, representing ripened humanity before the throne of God, who sanctifies the whole batch (Rom 11:16). Hand-picked out of the vastness of human history, they are his peculiar possession and servants of his glory.[26] Not because of generational blood (John 1:13), nor through their own works (Titus 3:5), but rather bought back in Jesus' Death and Resurrection,[27] they are the primordial gift of the Holy Spirit to his Church, from the birthday of Pentecost up to full maturation in the canonized saints of the Catholic Church.

23. By secular comparison, there existed the *sacramentum militare*, that is, the oath taken by Roman legionaries, pledging their allegiance to the emperor, and swearing that they would never desert their military service even in the face of death (cf. Vegetius, *Epitoma rei militaris*, 2.5).

24. The double historic present tense in the Greek verbs *akolouthoûntes* (ἀκολουθοῦντες, *sequuntur*), "they follow," and *hypágei* (ὑπάγει, *abierit*), "he goes," in this v. 4, provides narrative vividness and relates them to the present life of each Christian.

25. Cf. RD, 1094.

26. Cf. RD, 1095; elsewhere, the saints are redeemed *by*, not *for*, the Lamb, as expressed by the dative case (*Deo et Agno*, "for God and for the Lamb") in this verse (cf. 5:9).

27. Associated with the concept of first fruits is the image of Christ the "first born of all creation" and "first born from the dead" in Col 1:15, 18.

Interwoven with this is the complete absence of mendacity or any other cause for blame in them (v. 5), as they worship the one true God as his guileless children. By employing the adjective "immaculate" (*sine macula*),[28] John adds another tinge of sacrifice, already expressed by the first fruits, since it is the Septuagint designation of unblemished sacrifices (Lev 22:21). This word also alludes to the immaculateness of the paschal lamb (Exod 12:5), as well as to the person of Mary most holy. Thus, the Lord Jesus makes those one hundred forty-four thousand a sweet sacrificial offering pleasing to God, unblighted by the consequences of sin (Jude 24), and wholly conformed to himself as the Crucified One.

Before proceeding deeper into this chapter, however, let us briefly reflect on the spiritual message of these opening verses 1–5. What immediately piques our interest is the prospect of learning that new song, so mysteriously held in reserve for souls already ransomed from the earth (v. 3). Revelation motivates us to enter deeper into an experiential knowledge of salvation enkindled by the electing grace of God. To sing the new song means experiencing the Spirit of truth, speaking the language of praise, enjoying the moments of sacramental absolution from personal sin, receiving the Lord's Body and Blood in Holy Communion, and cherishing that interior certitude that Christ protects us from the many perils of spiritual captivity, illness, and eternal death. It is a supernatural doxology that is born out of all those incomparable joys in him and that the carnal-minded human nature neither knows nor can receive.

Unending newness awaits the soul that remains receptive to ever-surprising benefits showered on it from on high, enabling it to radiate toward others some of the immaculateness of that novel life. One could also prayerfully share this experience with one's guardian angel, since those good spirits have never been made familiar with the rescuing force of the Blood of the Lamb, and they surely "long to catch a glimpse of these things" (1 Pet 1:12; Eph 3:10; 1 Tim 3:16). Similarly, we can lend our voice to the mute and inanimate creation, praising God in its stead, as so beautifully taught in the canticle of Shadrach, Meshach, and Abednego (Dan 3:52–90). Chanting this heavenly anthem also entails a sincere and persevering effort to live the virtue of Christian chastity in accordance with one's state of life in the Church, giving concrete expression to one's turning away from the world and following the Lamb. And may this Scripture passage sustain us in trials and comfort us in persecution, removing all distress and fixing our thoughts on the eternal reward.

28. The Greek adjective *ámōmos* (ἄμωμος), "without blemish," also connotes fragrance and aroma (see āmomum, a plant native to China and India, valued for its aromatic properties).

14:6–12, Judgment as Good News

Worldwide evangelization (14:6–7)

[6]Then I saw another angel flying in midheaven, with an eternal gospel to proclaim to those who live on the earth, to every nation and tribe and language and people. [7]He said in a loud voice, "Fear God and give him glory, for the hour of his judgment has come; and worship him who made heaven and earth, the sea and the springs of water."

Now that the main actors in the apocalyptic drama of human history have been made known, apart from the great harlot (17:1), this vision paints a picture of the proclamation of God's Good Tidings to the whole world, against the concurring backdrop of the beasts' persecution and the worship on Zion. Verses 6–20 present a unique type of septet, namely, the appearance of two angelic trios revolving around the central figure of the Son of Man (v. 14), hinting at the perfection of the announcement in vv. 6–12 and of the proleptic execution of his final judgment in vv. 13–20.[1] They also predict that three chief attempts will be undertaken in view of a spiritual reform of humanity, symbolized by a trivium of angels coming into sight one after another: a worldwide evangelization, an alert regarding the world-city's fall, as well as a forewarning of eternal torment.

John's attention is now all engrossed by "another angel flying in midheaven, with an eternal Gospel to proclaim to those who live on the earth, to every nation and tribe and language and people" (v. 6). Though there is no explicit reference to previous angels, the last mentioned having been Michael and his angels (12:7), this one is in the lead of two trios of angels taking shape in vv. 6, 8–9 and vv. 15, 17–18, with the Son of Man in the center like a textual

1. Eberhard Nestle and Kurt Aland, *Novum Testamentum Graece et Latine* (Stuttgart: German Bible Society, 2013) captions 14:6–20:15 as *De Iudicio Dei*, 659.

hub.[2] His flight across the sky's zenith shows the universal import of his message that leaves no room for a periphery (8:13; 19:17). From this loftiest of positions, he can swiftly impart the Good News over all parts of the earth.[3] His Gospel, recalling the little scroll and the *mysterium Dei* (10:2, 7), is everlasting[4] because, like its divine Author, it remains unaltered, yesterday, today, and forever. That makes it so unlike the many novel doctrines of the beast and the false prophet that will be uprooted (Matt 15:13). Its essence was established from all eternity according to the counsel of the Almighty, and it shall abide unchanged until the end of time, inexpugnable even amid the opposition of the world and the onslaught of hell. It will never be antiquated nor made void by another Gospel, for there will be no other. This is the immutable doctrine of salvation resulting in the Kingdom of Christ and the joys of heaven. Hence, the preeminent embassy of this angel has substantially the same purpose as the foregoing vision, namely, to cheer the despondent heart and to sustain the faith of the Church in the hardships of her pilgrimage.

Of note is that the audience, namely, every nation, tribe, language, and people (7:9), is the same as the one claimed by the pseudo-authority of the sea-beast (13:7), setting up an eschatological conflict.[5] Now, since the actual dissemination of God's Good News has not been entrusted primarily to the angels but to us humans, the above messenger could be interpreted as the Church herself, clergy and laity alike, engaged in the task of evangelization across the ages (Matt 28:19). These are the diligent sentinels of Zion who cannot be silenced and who remind the Lord to "take no rest until he establishes Jerusalem and makes it renowned throughout the earth" (Isa 62:6–7).

The angel's message is inculcated with a loud voice:[6] "Fear God and give him glory, for the hour of his judgment has come; and worship him who made heaven and earth, the sea, and the springs of water" (v. 7). Further underlining

2. Only the New Vulgate distinguishes between the first of each tercet by designating them as *alter*, an adjective meaning "other, second" (vv. 6, 15), while introducing the subsequent two as *alius*, an adjective meaning "another, different" (vv. 8–9, 17–18), lending symmetry and cohesion to this septenary formation.

3. The repetition of the preposition *epí* (ἐπί, *super*), "onto, upon, against, at," in this verse, translates the unconquerable descent or approach of the Gospel toward humanity.

4. Every single word of the Greek phrase *euaggélion aiṓnion euaggelísai* (εὐαγγέλιον αἰώνιον εὐαγγελίσαι, *evangelium aeternum, ut evangelizaret*), is mentioned only here in Revelation, giving them extraordinary weight within the overall narrative.

5. Cf. AvS, 456.

6. Another typical solecism is the nominative participle *légōn* (λέγων, *dicens*), "saying," that should read *légonta* (λέγοντα), to agree with the accusative case of the noun *ággelon* (ἄγγελον) at v. 6.

its earnestness is the threefold imperative "Fear!" (*timete*), "Give!" (*date*), and "Adore!" (*adorate*), expressive of one and the same idea, that is, of true Christian worship. Emphatic, too, is the fourfold description of creation as "heaven, earth, sea, and springs of water," matching the quadruple characterization of the human family as "every nation, tribe, language, and people" in v. 6, both phrases denoting the universality of the angel's assertion. And incentivized by the ever-imminent judgment, the brethren of Christ live God-fearing lives.[7] Could the zenithal angel of v. 6 be a figure of an eschatological Elijah Redivivus?[8] In any event, here we have the very first mention of the word "judgment" (κρίσις, *iudícium*) in Revelation, and its hour is announced with certainty; indeed, it is at hand, and in due season will be fully carried out against all those who persist in impenitence and unbelief.

That this angelic exhortation is aimed principally at non-Christians can be inferred from its resemblance to the speech addressed by Barnabas and Paul to the pagan audience in Lystra (Acts 14:15); it is very much in opposition to the second beast deceiving people to make an image of the first beast instead of glorifying God (13:14). Such a solemn admonition to forsake the world's idolatry and superstition, and to stand in awe before the Blessed Trinity, is exactly the core teaching of the Gospel. It is also permeated with the "springs of water," i.e., with the streams of his grace, empowering the human heart to not only inwardly revere the Lord, but also outwardly give him glory.

How can the angel's Gospel illuminate our spirituality as sons and daughters of the Church today? On the one hand, the soul is stirred to await one's own judgment with alertness and sobriety every day, every hour, of our lives.[9] Anticipating the moment that will decide one's eternity means to continuously surrender, body and soul, to God's infinite justice in every area of Catholic faith and morals. Jesus himself reminds us that his divine word is already now our judge and sanctifier (John 12:48; 15:3), which should make the daily Bible meditation a desire and a must-do. Part of this lifelong preparation to meet the divine Judge is to contemplate him as the Maker of heaven and earth, of all things visible and invisible, as we profess in the Nicene Creed (v. 7; cf. Rom

7. In the Apocalypse, the verb *phobéomai* (φοβέομαι, *timēre*), "to fear," never depicts the reaction to satanic forces.

8. Especially since according to later Jewish literature, Elijah was considered an angel in human form, while some Church Fathers thought him to be a priest, awaiting his return into this world just before the end-time arrival of the Messiah. Nevertheless, for most Christians, the Malachian prophecy (4:5–6) has already been fulfilled by his appearance alongside Moses on Mount Tabor (Matt 17:3), and in the person of John the Baptist (Matt 11:14).

9. Cf. AvS, 457–58.

1:19–20). In this way, the Christian trope *Memento mori* ("Remember that you have to die") that urges us to be conscious of our earthly limitations and mortality, will turn into a window opened toward afterlife's immortality, and the Gospel of Judgment becomes Good News.

On alert for the world-city's fall (14:8)

[8] *Then another angel, a second, followed, saying, "Fallen, fallen is Babylon the great! She has made all nations drink of the wine of the wrath of her fornication."*

Not missing a beat, the second[10] angel of this first angelic triptych makes his appearance (vv. 6, 9), citing a fateful oracle of Jeremiah (Jer 51:7–8),[11] as he proclaims: "Fallen, fallen is Babylon the great!" (v. 8). This is the unforeseen introduction of the mother of all metropolises of world-power in Revelation, convicted and doomed by the proclamation of the eternal Gospel. This "Gate of the gods"[12] was a large urban reality situated astride the Euphrates River in the plains of Shinar of ancient Mesopotamia, founded by Nimrod (Gen 10:10). God himself halted the construction of the tower of Babel by scattering humanity across the earth and confusing its language. Henceforth the city's Semitic name was "Confusion," as stipulated in Genesis 11:9.[13] Residence of the Babylonian dynasties (Dan 4:30), it was celebrated as the world's most powerful city in Old Testament times, especially from 605 till 539 BC, one of the most influential empires of antiquity, a center of commerce, art, and learning, and yes, the figurehead of the pagan world.

She appears in descriptions of the invasion of the Holy Land, the destruction of Jerusalem, and the subsequent national trauma of the Babylonian exile (Matt 1:11; Acts 7:43). Without fail depicted by the prophets as the ungodly power on earth par excellence, it became symbolic of oppressive force, of

10. Made explicit in the Greek text by the ordinal number *deýteros* (δεύτερος, "second"), not received into the NeoVulgate, however.

11. Arguably the most vehement among the "prophecies against the nations" (Jer 46–51), following the battle of Carchemish (605 BC), after which Nebuchadnezzar established Babylonian supremacy in the Middle East; Jeremiah considers Babylon as God's instrument for punishing other nations, yet she is not to escape vengeance herself; cf. Bernard Orchard et al., *A Catholic Commentary on Holy Scripture* (New York: Thomas Nelson & Sons, 1951), 587–90.

12. According to a possible native Babylonian etymology.

13. Deriving from the Hebrew verb *balál* (בָּלַל), meaning "to confound, to babble, to speak foolishly"; the Septuagint renders it as *Sýgchysis* (Σύγχυσις), i.e., "Confusion, Mixing."

idolatry and immorality (Isa 21:9), against which righteous Jewish believers must fight. Then, in the early centuries of Christianity, due to its proverbial worldliness and wickedness, Babylon came to be a dysphemism for the Roman Empire as the most corrupt seat of idolatry, hopelessly inimical to the Church (1 Pet 5:13). Typifying the materialistic world or any historical rerun of apostate imperialism, and identical to "Sodom and Egypt" (11:8), Rome was magnificent, strong, insolent, and oppressive, just as Babylon was before it, actively seeking to exploit and oppress the peoples of the world. One might say that what Babylon was to ancient Israel, Rome has been to the Church, the Israel of God (Gal 6:16). In it, Rupert recognizes the "reign of sin, the princedom of this world, the brigandage of the devil."[14]

That allegorical Babylon, the beast's earthly satrap, has now fallen, and she will rise no more, as is asserted with absolute certainty by the prophetic perfect of the Latin verb *cecidit* ("she has fallen"); and to transmit the sheer magnitude, the annihilatory outcome, and, at the same time, the mirth of that event, the angel restates this verb in the guise of an exclamation mark. Although she pretends to be "great," her worldly might will turn into powerlessness, and the vanity of her self-assertion only precipitates her total overthrow. Nothing remains of the veneer of her earthly invincibility; instead, she is doomed to implode and be shattered with startling briskness. This whole scene could be interpreted as a flashback toward the destruction of cities in the Old Testament, such as Sodom and Gomorrah (Gen 19:24–25) or Jericho (Josh 6:20–21). Yet more importantly, it anticipates 16:19–19:4, where the profane features of this world-city, her actual chastisement, and the ensuing dirge, are fleshed out.

Her destiny is *sui generis*, distinct from the beasts, and she is judged separately, her perennial sin being that she cajoles all nations into the drinking of the wine of the wrath of her fornication (v. 8). Astounding, and at the same time typical of this biblical genre, is that dissonance in combining the otherwise unrelated notions of fornication and wrath. The meaning here seems to be that humanity drinks of that inflammatory cup of impurity, bringing on itself God's indignation. Likewise, the Greek noun *thymós* (θυμός, *ira*) carries the idea of inebriation, exciting the passions that can precipitate a person into depravity. Besides, it occasionally renders the Hebrew word for venom (Job 20:16), making this a sort of Circean cup[15] that intoxicates souls to allure them into spiritual fornication, that is, idolatry. Hence, the wrath-wine signifies the

14. RD, 1098.

15. Circe is the quintessential enchantress amid the classical Greek pantheon, said to transform her victims into wild animals by offering them a magically poisonous potion.

way in which the demonic world-city operates through moral vice for the ruin of entire nations. All of which is deeply at odds with the chaste demeanor of the followers of the Lamb (v. 4) who refuse to adulterate true Christian worship and love.

Turning again to our spiritual life, Babylon's sudden fall and utter demolition suggests that personal vices are torn down when confronted with Christ-like moral choices. Sin and imperfections are suddenly smashed, making room for the workings of God's grace in our souls, as implied in the word to Jeremiah: "See, today I appoint you over nations and over kingdoms, to pluck up and to pull down, to destroy and to overthrow, to build and to plant" (Jer 1:10). Babylon means confusion, and so her downfall may be a metaphor for the overcoming of spiritual disorientation brought on by the random trials and disorders of this present life.[16] Interior insobriety, errors, uncontrolled passions, and the various agitations of mind and heart, can now be surmounted by the light and wisdom of our Lord. That clarity comes to us by drinking the cup of blessing that we bless, a participation in the blood of Christ (1 Cor 10:16).[17] This Eucharistic chalice contains the wine transubstantiated into the God-Man's Blood, no longer a vehicle of wrath and fornication, but rather of peace and purity, the ultimate remedy for the sin of all peoples. Hence, each one of us is called to foster a fervent devotion to the Most Precious Blood in the Blessed Sacrament of the Altar.[18] Incidentally, at the time of John's writing, Mediterranean cultures gave much prominence to wine, worshipping Dionysus-Bacchus, the frenzy-inducing and murderous deity of grape-harvesting and winemaking in Greco-Roman mythology. Both the seduction by harlot Babylon and by Bacchus are now unmasked and exorcized as diabolical idolatry: "You cannot drink the cup of the Lord and the cup of demons" (1 Cor 10:21).

Forewarning of never-ending torment (14:9–11)

[9] Then another angel, a third, followed them, crying with a loud voice, "Those who worship the beast and its image, and receive a mark on their foreheads or on their hands, [10] they will also drink the wine of God's wrath, poured unmixed into the cup of his anger, and they will be tormented with fire and sulfur in the presence of the holy angels and in the

16. Cf. RD, 1099; AvS, 460.

17. On a pertinent etymological note, the word "blessing" stems from the Proto-Germanic **blodison*, that is, "to mark and hallow with blood," in allusion to the blood sprinkled on pagan altars.

18. Cf. *CCC*, §§1374–77.

presence of the Lamb. [11]*And the smoke of their torment goes up forever and ever. There is no rest day or night for those who worship the beast and its image and for anyone who receives the mark of its name."*

Rounding out the first angelic trio (vv. 6, 8), a third angel now broadcasts the doom of all idolatrous worshippers (v. 9). By citing the beast, its image and mark, he takes the hearer back to the previous chapter, witnessing to the fact that Babylon is just another dimension of the machinations of God's enemies. That everyone will be answerable for his or her free choices and actions is foregrounded by the grammatical singular of all Greek verbs in vv. 9–10, shifting to the plural only in v. 11. Unsurprisingly, when keeping v. 8 in mind, such a person will also drink the wine of God's wrath, poured unmixed into the cup of his anger (v. 10), which is proleptic toward the scenes at 16:19; 17:4; 18:6. Hence, the beast-worshipper's retribution shall fit the crime: as he drank of the entrancing wine of Babylon's fornication, so he will be made to consume the foaming wine of God's ire. To do so means to experience the severity of divine justice, often expressed by the biblical figure of a cup of fury, which, once taken, will inebriate the nations, making them reel and totter toward their self-ruin (Jer 25:15). What exacerbates the situation is that this wine is apportioned undiluted,[19] that is, it will be poured out in full alcoholic strength without any admixture of water, signifying unmitigated chastisement. Thus, no hope is mingled into it, grace is no longer part of the blend, nor is mercy in the mix. Instead, evildoers will feel the untempered impact not only of the Lord's outburst of wrath,[20] but of his fury or passion for just vengeance, too.[21] Incidentally, both words, wrath and fury, appear together already, albeit in an inverted order, in a similar context in the first messianic psalm (Ps 2:5). At this point, Dante's spine-chilling inscription over the gates of hell impresses itself again on the mind: "Abandon all hope!"[22]

Borrowing imagery from Sodom and Gomorrah's destruction (Gen 19:24), John goes on to describe the fate of the wicked, who will be "tormented with fire and sulfur in the presence of the holy angels and in the presence of the Lamb" (v. 10). In this image, inextinguishable flames are combined with odoriferous

19. Literally, and somewhat paradoxically, "mixed unmixed" (*kekerasménou akrátou*, κεκερασμένου ἀκράτου, *mixtum est mero*), a phrase drawing on Ps 75:9; it is also reminiscent of the spiced wine offered to Jesus on the Cross (Matt 27:34; Mark 15:23).

20. The Greek noun *thymós* (θυμός, "wrath,") derives from the verb *thýō* (θύω), "to get heated up, to boil."

21. The Greek noun *orgḗ* (ὀργή, "fury") stems from the verb *orgáō* (ὀργάω), "to swell."

22. Dante Alighieri, *Divine Comedy, Inferno*, Canto 3:9.

fumes, hazardous to human breathing. This hellish scene foreshadows the eternal punishment reserved for the devil and his agents, human and angelic, as illustrated in more detail in chs. 19–21. What is more, this severe torture (20:10) is said to unfold in the very sight of all the good angels and even in the presence of the divine Lamb himself. Only on this occasion do we learn of such spectators of doom, implying that after passing judgment on the acolytes of the beast, the angels and the Lamb remain present to witness their eternal torment at the hands of the demons. That acquiescing presence in power and glory will inevitably maximize the excruciation of the inhabitants of Gehenna. While on earth, the evildoers despised the Lamb and persecuted his followers, and now they suffer their reprobation with all its dire consequences before his eyes. And although no explicit mention is made here of the glorified saints, their presence can be assumed, too, especially considering v. 4, and given their perfect oneness with the just sentiments of God in the blessed world above. Does this not also intimate that the beatific vision of heaven somehow involves a peripheral vision of those condemned to hell?[23] Again, from the latter's vantage point, to know of those heavenly onlookers, coupled with the inability to ever leave their place of separation from God (Luke 16:23–26), cannot but escalate their agony to an extreme. Be that as it may, the apocalyptic concept of vengeance and torture should be taken as a metaphor for distance from God, not as implying that he physically tortures anyone.

Rising from the ashes of such affliction and desperation of the condemned is a sulfurous smoke that evokes, among others, the obliteration of Sodom and Gomorrah (Gen 19:28), of Gibeah (Judg 20:38, 40), and of Babylon itself (19:3). It can be related to the infernal abyss and its emissaries (9:2–3, 17–18) but is antithetical to the incense of prayers and glory in the Lord's presence (8:4; 15:8). Nevertheless, in a paradoxical way even this repugnant haze seems to serve a liturgical purpose, glorifying God forever and ever (v. 11). By squaring the plural of the noun "age" in the phrase "for ages of ages" (*in saecula saeculorum*), the apostolic seer indicates an unbroken cycle of epochs stretching into infinity. It bespeaks the humanly unfathomable notion of eternal punishment for those who freely chose to be lost. Acerbating their condition and its perpetuity is that for them there is no rest day or night (v. 11; Matt 12:43), in opposition to the reward of eternal rest in heaven. Unlike the unceasing praise offered to God by the living creatures (4:8), the condemned are perennially

23. Thomas Aquinas quotes Isa 64:24 to make the argument that the blessed in heaven will see the suffering of the damned to increase their bliss and thankfulness, and that they will be unable to feel pity for them (*Summa Theologiae*, Supplement, 94, a. 1–3).

deprived of inner rest and outer refreshment. Instead of eventually becoming altogether extinguished in their existence, their pain will have no hiatus, no sleep will be granted to them in their gloomy detention, nor the slightest cessation from their consciousness of sin, remorse, and doom. On the contrary, they are unremittingly terrorized by the company of demons and fellow accursed humans in hell (Matt 25:41). Just as they had worshipped the beast on earth, they doggedly keep on prostrating themselves before it after their death in unending hopelessness.

On a spiritual plane, vv. 9–11 should be pondered as an unembellished forewarning of eternal punishment, a reminder that each one will be held personally accountable for the way we made use of our human freedom. For Christians, there can be no hiding behind anonymous masses, no proverbial "going with the flow" when it comes to moral choices. Whatever trickery the devil may come up with to seduce the soul into worshipping him, one's decision is still voluntary, and one is always free to say No to his dissimulation. Once yielding to the temptation, however, personal sin has broad repercussions: besides the damage inflicted on body and soul, it offends God and his good angels, and injures the Mystical Body of Christ, too. By the greater fear of potentially incurring everlasting torment, we are persuaded into overcoming any fright one might have of the beast.[24] Sin is deceptively presented to us as gain and pleasure, then embraced as a delight, but it soon becomes a pitiless slave-driver, strongarming us into bad habits, vice, and ultimately death. Before long, one falls into a vicious cycle of self-loathing, renewed craving, and unrest, deforming us into waterless clouds, fruitless trees, wild waves, and stars wandering into deepest darkness (Jude 12–13). While this dark potency of sin does stamp its disfiguring contours upon human nature, punishing us already here and now, it also heartens us to labor at our ongoing conversion, as is suggested also in the upcoming verse.

Third call: Patience (14:12)

[12]Here is a call for the endurance of the saints, those who keep the commandments of God and hold fast to the faith of Jesus.

If the above prospect of divine chastening is an admonishment for weak-minded Christians, it is at the same time consoling to the faithful ones, "those who keep the commandments of God and hold fast to the faith of Jesus" (v.

24. Cf. AvS, 462.

12). This is already the third out of four of such sapiential appeals to what is noblest in man, with one more to follow at 17:9. Not least due to its contextual anonymity, this quartet of Wisdom calls keenly draws the audience's attention. One textual clue, however, is the demonstrative adverb *hôde* (ὧδε, hic), "here," prefacing each of these four calls; this word recurs only two other times in the Apocalypse (4:1; 11:12), and both are affiliated with the heavenly sphere, making it plausible that God the Father, the Lamb, or an angel is speaking; alternatively, St. John himself could be imagined as the one pronouncing this phrase.

At any rate, here is a summons to the sons and daughters of the Church to respond to tribulation and persecution with saintly patience: "But the one who endures to the end will be saved" (Matt 24:13). This long-suffering readiness to wait for the Lord is shown by those who keep God's commandments, clinging to the virtue of Jesus' faith despite ongoing temptation, and who refuse to pay homage to the god of this world. All the children of the apocalyptic Woman (12:17), those one hundred forty-four thousand (7:4), are encouraged to practice constancy in the certitude of the eventual ruination of the anti-Christian Babylon. To avoid the fellowship of the beast, they are prepared to suffer any distress, and take comfort at the thought that the final collapse of the wicked is necessary for the ultimate triumph of truth and holiness.[25]

25. The first-century AD Jewish pseudepigraphical *Apocalypse of Baruch* carries a comparable encouragement: "For if you endure and persevere in [God's] fear, and do not forget his law, the times shall change over you for good, and you shall see the consolation of Zion" (44:7).

14:13–20, Judgment as harvest and vintage

Second makarism: Holy death (14:13)

[13]And I heard a voice from heaven saying, "Write this: Blessed are the dead who from now on die in the Lord." "Yes," says the Spirit, "they will rest from their labors, for their deeds follow them."

What is about to transpire in these remaining verses of ch. 14 is an anticipatory snapshot of the final judgment on the world. Setting the tone for it is a solemn declaration regarding the sacredness of a Christian death. John hears another heavenly voice bidding him to "write this: Blessed are the dead who from now on die in the Lord" (v. 13). And herewith the second of a heptad of beatitudes in Revelation is revealed (cf. 1:3; 16:15; 19:9; 20:6; 22:7, 14). Although there is no certainty of its identity (cf. v. 12), this voice probably belongs to that angelic chargé d'affaires of John's visionary experience,[1] often indistinguishable from Jesus' own speech. These otherworldly words, worthy of all attention, are recorded for the consolation and encouragement of God's people, perhaps dispirited by the adversity they are bound to meet. It goes without saying that the reign of the antichrist has already claimed many martyrial victims, and untold numbers of Christians will likely be put to death still, before the Lord returns. Of course, since death denotes the disjunction of body and soul as the bitter fruit of sin, it cannot be desirable in itself; on the contrary, it is universally dreaded. However, the Son of God has removed its sting (1 Cor 15:55), and thus, to die no longer means the loss of union with him, and "the second death has no power over them" (20:6). Now there is blessedness in a tasting a holy death (Mark 9:1), even if it seems a defeat in the eyes of the world: "Take courage; I have overcome the world!" (John 16:33). It now marks the blissful moment of finally joining the visible communion of saints, to enjoy the nuptial banquet of the Lamb, and to partake of the Tree of Life (19:9; 22:14). These

1. Cf. RD, 1101.

happy victors are to be congratulated, since they miss nothing, even if their lives ended in martyrdom (Eccl 4:2). Not all the dead, however, but only those who die "in the Lord" (*in Domino*), that is, those truly configured to Christ. Obviously, the eschatological coordinate "from now on" (*ap'árti*, ἀπ' ἄρτι, *āmodo*)[2] pertains to the Death and Resurrection of Christ, without excluding those righteous men and women of the Old Testament who have gone before him in faith (Heb 11:13).[3]

A celestial dialogue ensues as the Spirit lends his own weight to the above makarism: "Yes, they will rest from their labors, for their deeds follow them" (v. 13). One should also remember, however, the paradoxical oneness and distinction between Jesus' voice and that of the Holy Spirit in the seven letters (chs. 2–3). In any case, the divine Spirit now specifies the relation between God's love and justice, uniting heaven and earth, yoking together life and labor.[4] Enjoying the outcome and purpose of their pious dying in the Lord,[5] the just will finally be able to rest, as foreshadowed by Elohim's own sabbatical ceasing after finishing his creative work (Gen 2:2). Similarly, Israel was granted all-round tranquility after settling in the Promised Land (Josh 21:44). Only Jesus can give perfect repose from earth's trouble and toil,[6] and he alone can empower them to join their fellow servants, the souls under the heavenly altar, until their number will be complete (6:9–11). Their relaxation stands in contrast to the fate of the wicked as described above (v. 11). Far from being overlooked (cf. 2:2–3, 19, 23), the good deeds of the saints accompany them to their judgment as witnesses, reaping an eternal reward.[7] What will be forgotten, however, are any material possessions; they do not survive (Job 1:21), as the dour saying goes, "Shrouds have no pockets."

Before turning to the subsequent scene, let us internalize what we have exegeted regarding v. 13. That we are all doomed to "die of death" (*morte moriéris*, Gen 2:17) is a truism, yet our Christian faith teaches us to look forward to our

2. This rendition by the New Vulgate emerges as the "more difficult reading" (*lectio difficilior*) of several variants that place "from now on" differently: the Ethiopic version, for instance, connects it with the word "write!," resulting in "write now!"; and the Vulgate affixes it to the next clause, "Hereafter already says the Spirit" (*Amodo jam dicit Spiritus*).

3. Commemorated by the Roman Martyrology on December 24.

4. Cf. AvS, 468.

5. Expressed by the Greek conjunction of finality and result *hína* (ἵνα, *ut*).

6. The Greek noun *kópos* (κόπος) literally means the striking of one's breast in grief (cf. Liddell and Scott, *Greek-English Lexicon*, 978), while the New Vulgate's translation *lábor* implies weariness and sorrow.

7. Such a concept of divine recompense is reflected already in early Jewish writings (e.g., 2 Esdras 7:35).

departure from this world, since it will not signal separation but, if found worthy, definitive union with Jesus, whom we have loved all our life. Like weary travelers we can finally come home, like harried exiles we are allowed to return to the fatherland. Instead of pushing the topic away altogether, as something that brings on feelings of anxiety, fear, or gloom, we now can look beyond our earthly death, and look forward to our ultimate destiny, and that of our loved ones, with supernatural faith. Nevertheless, Revelation does not share in misguided and pessimistic beliefs that death is preferable to the miserable existence on earth; on the contrary, life is considered a boon, crowned by a holy death. One should pray to be granted the spiritual favor of dying in the company of Jesus, Mary, and Joseph.[8] That way we have hope to partake one day of the Yes of Christ's and the Holy Spirit's promises to the glory of God (2 Cor 1:20). With eyes fixed on the realities above, we are sustained here on earth, even in moments when courage faints or trust wavers. In fact, we can enjoy that spiritual rest already now, sustained by our belief in the meritoriousness of our good actions done in the state of grace.[9] By the same token, we must detach ourselves from any conceitedness of personal achievement, since it is the Lord who accomplishes the good in us: "In crowning their [saints] merits you crown your own gifts."[10]

Crop ripened (14:14–16)

[14] Then I looked, and there was a white cloud, and seated on the cloud was one like the Son of Man, with a golden crown on his head, and a sharp sickle in his hand! [15] Another angel came out of the temple, calling with a loud voice to the one who sat on the cloud, "Use your sickle and reap, for the hour to reap has come, because the harvest of the earth is fully ripe." [16] So the one who sat on the cloud swung his sickle over the earth, and the earth was reaped.

Having set the tone by reassuring the hearer about the blessings of dying in the Lord, and with all his visionary senses marshalled into a comprehensive prophetic experience ("I heard," v. 13; "I saw, and behold," v. 14), John now receives

8. Cf. AvS, 465.

9. Catholic theology has expounded on the condignity or congruency of eternal merit and reward, cf. *CCC*, §§2006–11; Thomas Aquinas, *Summa Theologiae* I-II, q. 114.

10. Roman Missal, *Preface I of the Saints*; cf. St. Augustine, *Enarrationes in Psalmos*, 103.6; *De gratia et libero arbitrio*, 6.15; see also AvS, 469.

two visions, one of a harvest (vv. 14–16), the other of a vintage (vv. 17–20). Both taken together foretell the Lord's final judicial dispensations portrayed with more detail in chs. 15–16 and again in chs. 19–20. Such reiterated and complementary perspectives, so iconic in this apocalyptic genre, bring about one cumulative picture of those crucial events. Nevertheless, one distinction must be underlined: when compared to 20:12–15, which concerns the resurrection and judgment of those who were dead by the time of Christ's parousia, this twin image of harvest and vintage appears to portray the judgment of those who will be alive at that point in time.

Thus, he sees "a white cloud, and seated on the cloud one like the Son of Man" (v. 14). Unparalleled is the fourfold mention of this radiant cloud in vv. 14–16, giving eschatological prominence to some of the most salient realities in the life of ancient Israel, of Christ himself, and of his faithful people.[11] Not unlike the Woman positioned on the moon with a twelvefold crown (12:1), this likeness of a Son of Man is seen sitting down as the eternal Judge in accomplishment of his filial mission. This similarity also intimates that his virginal Body was assumed from his Immaculate Mother, that his human flesh shrouds his divinity, and that he is sovereign Lord over the Church.[12] Reinforcing this image are the "golden crown on his head, and a sharp sickle in his hand" (v. 14). He who bore the scornful crown of thorns will one day be seen with many diadems (19:12), and he whose hand carried the mocking reed (Matt 27:29), is now wielding the reaper's scythe. That this Judge comes with regal, sacerdotal, and human dignity is shown by his crown;[13] that this will be the hour of victory is conveyed by the sevenfold reiteration of this farming implement (vv. 14–19); and that he will act with great precision and swiftness is told by the adjective "sharp."[14] This sharpness and rapidity recalls Jesus' sword that would not allow for mediocrity. At long last he reveals himself as the "Lord of the harvest" of the whole world (Matt 9:38), true to his own prophecy: "His winnowing fork is in his hand, and he will clear his threshing floor and will gather his wheat into the granary; but the chaff he will burn with unquenchable fire" (Matt 3:12).

At this juncture the seer on Patmos notices yet another angel, the first of the second angelic triplet (vv. 17–18), exiting the temple, "calling with a loud voice to the one who sat on the cloud, 'Use your sickle and reap, for the hour to

11. To wit, the Exodus (Exod 13:21), the Temple (1 Kgs 8:11), the Transfiguration (Matt 17:5), the Ascension (Acts 1:9), the parousia and Final Judgment (Matt 24:30), the transcendence of the God-Man (Dan 7:13), as well as his promise of eternal life (Rev 1:7; 11:12).

12. Cf. RD, 1100; AvS, 471–72.

13. Cf. RD, 1101.

14. Cf. AvS, 473.

reap has come, because the harvest of the earth is fully ripe'" (v. 15). This is the first mention of God's heavenly sanctuary since 11:19, and the angelic mise-en-scène stirs up memories of that at 8:3–5. If the Lord's work of redemption began with the annunciation by the Holy Spirit's angel, then it will find its completion in a like manner.[15] Curiously enough, Rupert understands this angel to be a figure of John the Baptist, "preacher and precursor" (*praeco et praecursor*).[16] His reverberating voice, on par with that of the first, third, and sixth angels (vv. 7, 9.18) appears to certify his message as an incontestable verity. However, that he addresses himself so vehemently to the Son of Man is uncommon and puzzling: just as crown and sickle are contradictory images representing king and peasant (v. 14), so also the seemingly subordinate and colorless character of the God-Man appears to clash with his majesty expressed in other passages (1:5–8, 13–19; 19:10–13). Unfamiliar, too, is the fact that he as God is not only summoned to his task by one of his creatures, but that his action will be followed up by another angel's more decisive operation (vv. 17–19), making Jesus almost equal to an angel himself (10:1–3), perhaps as "first among equals" (*primus inter pares*). Although such an angelological concept appears to be inconsistent with John's otherwise lofty Christology, he may have maintained it for its dramatic effect. It conveys the idea of an almost shy pursuit of final justice by God the Father through his Son. Nevertheless, that the apocalyptic Messiah should receive divine instructions through one of his companions is not stranger than that he should necessitate an angel to expose his Revelation to the eyes of his servants (1:1).[17]

Be that as it may, this fourth angel now clamorously informs Jesus of the hour set by his heavenly Father (Mark 13:32); and as Redeemer, Jesus is subordinate to the Father, performing the work that has been given him to do (John 5:19). By surrounding himself with these six angels, he manifestly arrives as the Judge of heaven and earth. From Matthew 13:39–42 we understand that the harvest is the end of the age (*consummatio saeculi*), and that the angels are the reapers who gather in his elect from the four winds, bind up the tares in bundles, and burn them. Likewise, the Latin verb *aruit* (v. 15),[18] that is, "com-

15. Cf. AvS, 475.

16. Cf. RD, 1102.

17. Cf. AvS, 474.

18. The Greek verb *xēraínō* (ξηραίνω) also means "to pine away, to parch, be ripe, fully desiccate, shrivel," hinting at wheat stalks whose moisture has been lost, making the fields look white for harvest (John 4:35); magnifying that notion of dryness is the fact that the noun *therismós* (θερισμός), "harvest," derives from the verb *thérō* (θέρω), "to heat," and is related to the noun *théros* (θέρος), "late summer."

pletely dried up," can only point to the final judgment of the world (e.g., Isa 17:5). Christ through his holy Church had sown the good seed (Luke 8:11), and as the fully grown grain of the fields is gathered in, so are the righteous received into the Kingdom. In Cana, the Lord obliged at his Mother's request, and now he promptly obeys the angel: "So the one who sat on the cloud swung his sickle over the earth, and the earth was reaped" (v. 16). It is the reaping of the Church's first fruits (v. 4), the glorious crop of God's people across the centuries, including the final salvation of all of Israel (Rom 11:26). On a symbolic level, the reapers could also be said to be the ministers of the Gospel, and the sickle is the way its teaching cuts to the heart.

Which brings us to reflect again on the spiritual dimension of this image. For the eternal Judge to appear seated on a white cloud may suggest that he rewards his followers with the enjoyment of eternal life, after their sins have evaporated in the warmth of his endless mercy.[19] There is also a touch of Marian presence, she who was foreshadowed by a little cloud rising out of the sea announcing a reviving rain that would end the drought in Elijah's day (1 Kgs 18:44), and she who was overshadowed by the Holy Spirit in the hour of the Incarnation (Luke 1:35): with her we can always take refuge as sinners, finding help and guidance, especially in view of passing the final judgment.

Moreover, contemplating Christ's golden crown can energize us to strive with all our heart, soul, strength, and mind (Luke 10:27) to obtain that imperishable wreath of glory promised to each one of us (2:10). Moreover, considering the angel entreating him, we as witnesses to his Gospel should never tire to beseech him for the salvation of souls. While God's patience toward sinners will always be extraordinary and miraculous, it will not be everlasting: on the one hand one should take care not to become rife with evildoing, and on the other hand that ripeness in sin of worldly people is the measure of afflictions that the saints will be asked to bear in atonement until the second coming of the Lord Jesus. Lastly, the biblical figure of harvest indicates the fruitfulness of the good seed sown by the Savior and his apostles in the fertile soil of our hearts (Mark 4:8).[20] That those fruits shall be gathered into the barns of eternity ought to sustain us especially in times of trial and persecution: "Rejoice and be glad, for your reward is great in heaven" (Matt 5:12).

19. Cf. AvS, 472.
20. Cf. RD, 1103.

Grapes matured (14:17–20)

[17]Then another angel came out of the temple in heaven, and he too had a sharp sickle. [18]Then another angel came out from the altar, the angel who has authority over fire, and he called with a loud voice to him who had the sharp sickle, "Use your sharp sickle and gather the clusters of the vine of the earth, for its grapes are ripe." [19]So the angel swung his sickle over the earth and gathered the vintage of the earth, and he threw it into the great wine press of the wrath of God. [20]And the wine press was trodden outside the city, and blood flowed from the wine press, as high as a horse's bridle, for a distance of about two hundred miles.

A fifth angel, the chapter's second-last, exits the heavenly temple like the previous one (v. 15), but wielding a sharp sickle (v. 17). If God's dwelling place is typically the locus of worship and contemplation, here it becomes the origin for administering the vintage of the earth. Concluding this veritable chain reaction of angels is a sixth one, coming from the altar and having authority over fire (v. 18). His provenience from the altar suggests a flashback not only to the souls crying out for vengeance from beneath the altar (6:9–11), but also to the fiery scene in 8:3–5, as well as to the sixth trumpet angel in 9:13; yet it looks forward to 16:7, too. What all these images have in common is that they allude to God's eternal judgments. Located in the front of the temple, the altar was the place where burnt offerings were made (Luke 1:11), signifying the all-important meeting place between God and the true worshiper. At this juncture, it marks the starting point of the righteous judgment of the Lord, inflicting vengeance on those who refuse to obey the Gospel and who afflict the saints (2 Thess 1:5–8). Furthermore, and in line with common Jewish speculation,[21] the Book of Revelation suggests that cosmic elements are committed to the jurisdiction of particular angels, in this case, fire.[22] It may be allusive to the priestly office of keeping the sacred fire on the altar, but it also implies the operation of God's Spirit in baptism (Matt 3:11), as well as his eschatological judgment, awaiting new heavens and a new earth (2 Pet 3:7).

21. E.g., *Sefer Raziel*, 39:2; *Targum* on 1 Kgs 19:11; *Pesachim*, 118; *Gittin*, 68a; *Yalkut Simeoni*, par. 2. 58:4, 167:4.

22. Cf. the "angel of the waters" (16:5), and the "four angels standing at the four corners of the earth, holding back the four winds of the earth" (7:1); also worth mentioning is the extra-biblical association with the Persian semi-divine archangel Asha Vahishta, who, according to Zoroastrian mythology, presides over fire and holds out the path toward goodness, truth, and justice.

Mirroring the scene of the fourth angel calling out to the Son of Man (vv. 15–16), here the sixth angel entreats his fellow angel, the fifth to be precise, in the name of God to execute the vintage (v. 18). That the harvest is reaped by Christ (v. 16), but the vintage is gathered in by a mere angel (Matt 13:39),[23] seems to indicate that the latter refers to the fair and square judgment of the wicked part of humanity.[24] This dual logic also corresponds to the announcements of the former angels, who first preach the everlasting Gospel, and afterwards denounce those who serve the beast (vv. 6–11).[25] Their evil is now coming to its "acme" as intimated by the Greek verb *akmázō* (ἀκμάζω), meaning "to reach maturity," and they are finally cut down with inexorable justice, as suggested by the triple reiteration of the adjective "sharp" (*acutus*) in vv. 17–18. Despite its careful cultivation (Isa 5:1–10), this earthly grapevine turned out to be the "vinestock of Sodom, the vineyards of Gomorrah" (Deut 32:32–33), producing nothing but wild grapes, bitter and poisonous, with all the unrighteous cohering in one mass like a bunch of unpalatable grapes. Not excluded from this scene is the final reckoning that will befall all those who became unworthy members of the Lord's vineyard, that is, his Church (John 15:1–6). As a dutiful servant of God, the angel carries out the above command at once, throwing the grape-clusters "into the great winepress of the wrath of God" (v. 19), and simultaneously suspending, as it were, Jesus' work of redemption.[26] Mindful of Babylon's idolatrous wine (v. 8), and portending the superlative "winepress of the fury of the wrath of God the Almighty" (19:15), the symbolism merges the prophecies of Isaiah 63:1–6 and Joel 3:13. Divine wrath[27] in this apocalyptic

23. Rupert, incidentally, surmises that this angel embodies Moses calling for the judgment of Israel, cf. RD, 1104.

24. See also the midday prayer on Mondays of the First Week in the *Liturgia Horarum*, calling God the Lord and Custodian of harvest and vineyard ("Deus, qui messis ac víneae Dóminus es et Custos").

25. Intriguingly, for Adrienne, harvest symbolizes mortal sin, while vintage stands for the judgment of venial sins, cf. AvS, 479.

26. Cf. AvS, 477.

27. There is a grammatical mismatch in the Greek text between the feminine noun *lēnós* (ληνός), "winepress," and the masculine adjective *mégas* (μέγας), "great, large," making the latter appositional to the masculine noun *thymós* (θυμός), "anger, sorrow" in this v. 19; in which event, despite the clash between the accusative and genitive cases (see the perfect match between *lacum* and *magnum* in the Neo-Vulgate), it gives more emphasis to the terrible nature of divine wrath, than that of the winepress, and in that sense should be taken as a *constructio ad sensum*. There is also the possibility that the Greek word for winepress, deeply ingrained in the pagan Bacchanalia, was of either grammatical gender at the time of writing, making it more inclusive.

genre is synonymous with God's judiciary power and authority, eventually exercised against those who sided with the antichrist in this world.

More elaborate and dramatic than the harvest is the description of the vintage: "And the winepress was trodden outside the city, and the blood that flowed from it rose as high as the bridles of the horses for a distance of 1,600 stades" (v. 20). Just as the Gentile nations had trampled over the holy city (11:2), so now a great winepress awaits them, to be trodden into their violent destruction. These crushed grapes fittingly image the unbelievers' missed opportunity of redemption as well as their punishment (Lam 1:15). They had crucified the Lord outside his city, effectively excommunicating him (Heb 13:12), and now they suffer their own fate of extermination apart from the pure and the just, outside the Church and outside the Heavenly Jerusalem (22:15). They have fallen away along with Babylon, the offal of the world.[28] Symbolically, therefore, the anti-Christian forces are humiliated and defeated in proximity to the sacred capital where the Messiah set up his Kingdom.

By way of metalepsis, the grape juice turns into an inundation of sinful blood across a vast area of land (Ezek 32:6),[29] an antithesis to the blood of Christ and his martyrs (7:14). Featured between the four earthly horsemen (6:1–8) and the equestrian armies of heaven (19:14), the blood of evil people rises to the unimaginable height of those horses' bridles.[30] As an additional, unique, and ghastly hyperbole, the flood's length of forty stades squared[31] sets forth the largeness and universality of the destruction of sinners, a veritable lake of blood, corresponding to Babylon's red wine of seduction.[32] Yet, it also hints at the impossibility of an escape: this judgment-carnage is not only

28. Cf. RD, 1105; regarding the tradition that pagan nations were to be judged and obliterated outside Jerusalem, see Zech 14:2–3, 12–13; Ezek 38–39; Joel 3:2, 12, 14.

29. Imagining the freshly crushed grape must overflowing or leaking from what Mark 12:1 more technically designates as the *hypolḗnion* (ὑπολήνιον), that is, the vat dug in the ground beneath a winepress to receive the fruit-juice.

30. Rupert interprets them as malignant spirits, unbridled until the last judgment, and the blood of the wicked, their partners in crime, now seen gruesomely intermingled with them, cf. RD, 1105.

31. An ancient Greco-Roman measure of length, the "stade" (*stádion*, στάδιον, *stadium*) consisted of 600 English feet, equal to one-eighth of a mile; thus, approximately two hundred miles are implied here; unlike 144,000 (14:1), 1,600 cannot be evenly divided by three, which makes it a symbol of an earthly reality, or derivative of "four," to the exclusion of the divine "three."

32. A Preterist interpretation would see in this vision the siege, capture, and destruction of Jerusalem in the year AD 70 during the First Jewish-Roman War led by the future Emperor Titus.

fearful, but also global and complete.[33] And those who fall under its implacable weight are the ones who during their lives on earth refused the defense of Zion, the true city and sanctuary of God (14:1). Thus, ch. 14 marks the end of another cycle of visions begun in ch. 12, depictive of an arc beginning with the Birth of Christ and spanning all the way toward the final judgment.

What is this copious imagery trying to tell us about our Christian discipleship? Beginning perhaps with the sharpness of the sickle: it seems to remind us of keeping the word of God alive and efficacious in our hearts and on our lips (Heb 4:12–13). Related to this is the aspect of ripening to maturity (v. 18), hinting at our spiritual growth that ought to overflow into a habitual readiness for conversion of personal *mores*. As we are pressed in conscience, our love for the Lord and the conviction of his truth redounds to more perfect sorrow for our sins, apprehensive of God's wrath. Besides, the process of being trodden down in a winepress could connote the period of cleansing after death in purgatory,[34] the thought of which spurs us on to be conscientious in seeking to avoid even venial sin and imperfection.[35] Furthermore, when meditating on the combined figure of grain and grape (vv. 16, 19), apart from its exegetical allusion to the just and unjust, we are strongly reminded again of the Holy Eucharist: "Wine to gladden the human heart, . . . and bread to strengthen the human heart" (Ps 104:15). By falling into the earth like a grain, dying, and thereby bearing much fruit (John 12:24), but also by abiding in the vine like branches (John 15:5), our souls will be able to avoid the terrible harvest and wrathful winepress of eschatological reckoning. Moreover, the horrifying torrent of blood should be a steady pull in our hearts not to reject Christ's offer of salvation, and to preserve in us a healthy dose of fear of God. Why not also take the cue of those horse bridles to determinedly work on controlling our inner passions and temper (Ps 32:9; Jas 3:3)? Above all, however, we are resolved to face any trials and embrace all tribulation with Christian hope, as this biblical passage comforts and reassures our spirit that God will bring about final justice.

33. Instead, early commentators understood the 1,600 stades to be the circumference of solely the Holy Land.

34. Cf. *CCC*, §§1030–32.

35. Cf. AvS, 481.

15:1–8, Pantocrator globally acknowledged

A great and marvelous sign (15:1, 5–8)

[1]Then I saw another portent in heaven, great and amazing: seven angels with seven plagues, which are the last, for with them the wrath of God is ended.

[5]After this I looked, and the temple of the tent of witness in heaven was opened, [6]and out of the temple came the seven angels with the seven plagues, robed in pure bright linen, with golden sashes across their chests. [7]Then one of the four living creatures gave the seven angels seven golden bowls full of the wrath of God, who lives forever and ever; [8]and the temple was filled with smoke from the glory of God and from his power, and no one could enter the temple until the seven plagues of the seven angels were ended.

If chs. 12–14 are taken as an interlude of visions recapitulating the entire history of salvation, then the septet of plague-bowls in ch. 16 fleshes out the seventh trumpet, which in turn is considered equal to the third woe (cf. 11:14–15). That trumpet had rounded off a septenary originating in the last of the seven seals (cf. 8:1–2), thus narratively interlocking the three septenaries of seals, trumpets, and bowls. Of the latter, ch. 15 is a heavenly prelude, announcing the very last cataclysmic plagues that will conclude the inter-advent age, and as such it is also the shortest of all chapters in Revelation. In all this, one should keep in mind John's view that the eschatological period, that is, the end time, begins with the earthly life of our Lord Jesus (1 John 2:18). Although these three septets can be seen as largely overlapping in their portrayal of divine trials and chastisements, perhaps with a touch of narrative progression or intensification, the plague-bowls appear to be preliminary to the "last" events of history (v. 1), contrasting with the "first" happenings of the Egyptian plagues (Exod 7–12). From now on the plot becomes increasingly futurist and referential to the very end of the eschaton, imbued with a temporal linearity that will chronicle the eventual ruin of the world-city (chs. 17–18), the final battle between the forces of good and evil (ch. 19), the universal judgment leading to the condemnation of all wickedness (ch. 20), as well as the descent of the heavenly city, complete with a postlude (chs. 21–22).

John's vision of the Son of Man and his reaper-angels now segues into three scenes ("I saw," *vidi*, vv. 1–2, 5) that culminate in an audial experience at 16:1 ("I heard," *audivi*). He sees "another portent in heaven, great and marvelous (*signum magnum et mirabile*)" (v. 1), that is, a sight so awe-inspiring (v. 3) that it stirs the beholder's deepest emotions, twinned with a dramatic sense of wonder. It appears to be a culminating moment compared to the plain "sign" (*signum*) of the dragon (12:3) and the "great sign" (*signum magnum*) of the cosmic Woman (12:1). Anticipating vv. 5–8, in v. 1 we are told about the appearance of seven angels with seven plagues, which are the last, for with them the wrath of God is ended (v. 1; cf. Ps 78:49). Again, the number seven denotes the universal nature of the plagues.[1] Also, the anarthrous introduction of this angelic septet, that is, lacking the definite article, proves that it cannot be identified with any previous trumpet or harvest angels. That they are carrying plagues or wounds (*plagas*) takes us back to Egypt, where they showed forth God's righteous power, exposed the idolatrous pretensions of Pharaoh's magicians, and inflicted widespread devastation on the eve of Israel's Exodus. Here, however, they seem to be typologically broadened to apply God's apocalyptic wrath to unbelievers around the globe. When added to the three blows of 9:18, these mirror the ten disasters of Egypt (Exod 7–12). That they run up to the final consummation of the ages is underscored by the double expression "last" (*novíssimas*; 21:9) and "completed" (*consummata*; v. 8), foreboding chs. 18–20. Thus, they coincide with Jesus' being "the Last," the cosmic "Goal" and "Omega" of all (20:13).

Before reflecting on the upcoming narrative entr'acte of the chanting conquerors in vv. 2–4, let us first complete the picture of these seven bowl angels by turning to their fuller portrayal at vv. 5–6: "After this I looked, and the temple of the tent of witness in heaven was opened, and out of the temple came the seven angels with the seven plagues, robed in pure bright linen, with golden sashes across their chests." This vision is of special importance, since the alliterative *templum tabernaculi testimonii* ("temple of the tent of witness"), in continuity with the scene of 11:19, appears to telescope the entire history of the people

1. Adumbrated also by the prophet Amos's phrase "For *three* transgressions . . . and for *four*, I will not revoke the punishment" (*passim* in Amos 1–2), making numbers and divine chastisement converge, albeit on a more local scale.

of God into one image: from the tent in the desert (Exod 25:9), to the temple in Jerusalem, all the way to the two witnesses of the Church (11:3).[2] Considering that the wilderness-tabernacle or *shekhinah* housed the ark of the covenant (Heb 9:1–5), the symbolism here includes divine truth, mercy, worship, as well as Christ's Incarnation and presence in the Holy Eucharist.

Similar to the open door set before the bishop of the Philadelphian church (3:8), the opening of heaven in v. 5 signals increased liberty to preach the Gospel and hasten the downfall of the antichrist. As if leaving behind the Old Testament ceremonies, this septet of angelic actors in the eschatological drama, representative of the Holy Spirit (1:4),[3] emerges from the cultic place of the temple, implying that they are here to execute a command that comes from God himself.[4] In absolute contrast to those plagues, they present themselves in the splendor of Christ the Risen High Priest, their linen garb symbolizing the righteous deeds of the saints (19:8).[5] Across their chests they wear golden sashes like girdles to signify the righteousness of the imminent judgments.[6] Also implied in their dazzling raiment is their enthusiastic readiness and majesty, befitting the ministers of divine justice who do everything in a pure and holy manner, their angelic hearts filled with love toward the saints.

The moment these seven exit the celestial sanctuary, one of the four living creatures consigns to them "seven golden bowls full of the wrath of God, who lives forever and ever" (v. 7). One can only speculate about him being the first among the four, the one resembling a lion (4:7), whose fortitude and thunderous voice would aptly represent those servants of the Gospel eventually defeating all untruth on earth. Associated earlier with one of the first septenaries in Revelation (6:1–8), these living beings are now implicated in the unfolding of the last one, too. What can be affirmed with conviction is that they stand for God's life in creation.[7] Like the shallow bowls of incense in 5:8, these vessels are semi-liturgical implements just as the seals and the trumpets, intimately

2. Cf. RD, 1111.

3. Cf. AvS, 498.

4. Cf. RD, 1112.

5. Some manuscripts carry the variant reading of *líthon* (λίθον, *lapis*), "stone," instead of *línon* (λίνον, *lino*), "linen," possibly in allusion to the priestly breastplate (Exod 28:15–30), or the regalia of a king (Ezek 28:13).

6. That they are not to be confused with the Son of Man is evidenced by the differentiated phrases in the Nova Vulgata and in the Greek: *ad mamillas* (*pros toîs mastoîs*, πρὸς τοῖς μαστοῖς, "toward his breast") in 1:13, and *circa pectora* (*perì tà stḗthē*, περὶ τὰ στήθη, "around his chest") in this v. 6.

7. In the Greek text, both, the noun *zṓon* (ζῴων), and the verb *zôntos* (ζῶντος) in this verse stem from *záō* (ζάω), "to live, to be alive."

related to priestly service in the temple, and regularly used for offerings or else to carry fat and ashes of sacrifices outside the sanctuary precinct (1 Chron 28:17).[8] No longer mere warning signs like the seals, nor calls to repentance like the trumpets, these deep saucers are now replete with plagues for those who have refused to return, who rejected the tabernacle of witness that the Lord had pitched among us in his flesh.[9]

At this juncture, "the temple was filled with smoke from the glory of God and from his power" (v. 8), reminiscent of theophanic events like at Mount Sinai, at the *shekhinah*, or in the Jerusalem temple. With the liturgy of divine justice getting underway, the focus is on God's awesomeness and omnipotence, but also on the incomprehensibility of his judgments involving inescapable calamity. Just as the people were not allowed to approach the holy mountain in the wilderness (Exod 19:12), so also now, "no one could enter the temple until the seven plagues of the seven angels were ended" (v. 8). Does John realize that the time for intercession has passed? that no one can procrastinate the hour of judgment? that nobody can turn away the wrath of the Almighty? that no one can distract him from his purpose? Yes, it is true, nobody can stay his righteous hand until justice is done (Dan 4:35). In former days, it was impossible to enter the shrine during its ritual dedication, and it is impossible now because of the purification and consummation of the cosmos as the dwelling of the Pantocrator. Also, a narrative *inclusio* is brought about using the verb *teléō* (τελέω, *consummare*, "to finish, carry out") in vv. 1, 8, confirming the promise of the completion of God's mystery in 10:7, with further details to follow in ch. 16.

On a spiritual note, there is the awareness that the seven plagues can apply to the individual soul, in the here and now: "If you continue hostile to me, and will not obey me, I will continue to plague you sevenfold for your sins" (Lev 26:21).[10] If the trumpets were tokens of warning for those who waver, to continuously find the path of repentance, then the plagues will be providential goads prodding us during the times when the soul obstinately refuses to return. When we vacillate or willfully harden our heart, then they will strike in the form of innermost remorse to bring the heart to reform itself. Moreover, when we read of the opening of the temple displaying the tent of witness, we should remember to gladly exercise true religion and give religious witness, especially in times when society allows for the freedom to do so.

8. Not to be overlooked is the lexical connotation of a goblet filled with poison and given to convicts as one of the methods of capital punishment in ancient times, and thus symbolic of divine wrath, too.

9. Cf. RD, 1106–7.

10. Cf. AvS, 485.

Also, in contemplating the robes of pure bright linen, we are reminded that in baptism we have become priestly, royal, and prophetic, called to surround ourselves with the righteousness of Jesus himself. Having put off the sackcloth of mourning in the absolution of personal sins, we can now joyfully live in his purity and spotlessness.[11] Related to the heavenly attire is the golden girdle, a metaphor for the preciousness of the Christian faith to be deeply appreciated. It encompasses the whole person in perfect charity,[12] keeps us ready through hope (Luke 12:35), and sustains us in truth (Eph 6:14). We remain girded, too, in service to others and asceticism toward ourselves (Mark 1:6). When thinking of divine wrath, we should take note that the Lord pursues his just judgments at times despite human opposition, since any kind of evil will be incompatible with his holiness: "Nothing unclean will enter" heaven (21:27).[13] Lastly, the smoke of God's glory could be taken as a reverse symbol of obfuscation in unbelief,[14] as well as our longing to see the Father's face.[15]

Canticle of the conquerors (15:2–4)

[2]*And I saw what appeared to be a sea of glass mixed with fire, and those who had conquered the beast and its image and the number of its name, standing beside the sea of glass with harps of God in their hands.*
[3]*And they sing the song of Moses, the servant of God, and the song of the Lamb: "Great and amazing are your deeds, Lord God the Almighty! Just and true are your ways, King of the nations!* [4]*Lord, who will not fear and glorify your name? For you alone are holy. All nations will come and worship before you, for your judgments have been revealed."*

In vv. 2–4, John inserts another ebullient canticle just like he did in 7:9–12. He first notices "what appeared to be a sea of glass mixed with fire" (v. 2). It is hardly coincidental that the Apocalypse teems with allusions to the sea, given the island setting of Patmos where it was received and written down (1:9). From

11. Notice that the Greek adjective *katharós* (καθαρός), v. 6, literally designates an object without admixture of stain or other undesirable elements; spiritually, it suggests a state of innocence, purified by God from any contaminating influences of sin.

12. Cf. RD, 1112.

13. Adrienne uncovers a relationship between the seven bowls, the seven capital sins, the seven heads of the dragon, and the seven gifts of the Holy Spirit, describing how the human heart alone is the place where all these divine and satanic vectors meet, cf. AvS, 500–501.

14. Cf. RD, 1113.

15. Cf. AvS, 502.

its shores, the apostolic visionary would have routinely witnessed the sun rise or set, sending red-glowing rays across the calm expanse of the Aegean Sea on windless days. In any event, among the biblical connotations of the above "sea of glass mixed with fire" would be Genesis's cosmology involving a celestial firmament (Gen 1:7), Israel's passage through the Red Sea (Exod 14), the ratification of the covenant at Sinai (Exod 24:10), the incandescent reflection in the bronze lavers of Solomon's Temple (1 Kgs 7:38), the evil monster arising out of its pelagic abode (13:1), yet also the great prostitute seated on many waters (17:1). Metaphorically, the sea means the profundity of supernatural designs (Rom 11:33), and in that quality it becomes the graveyard of all diabolical forces forever. Not unlike the crystalline sea illuminated by flashes of lightning and torches at 4:5–6, the present one has a meta-conceptual admixture of glass and fire as a symbol of divine sanctity and judgment. Uniting three naturally incompatible elements, i.e., water-glass-fire, John suggests new aesthetic dimensions in blazing translucency, not exclusive of the saints' afflictions and the sinners' punishment. Most importantly, this glassy ocean of fire signifies the cleansing Blood of Christ, the sevenfold gifts of the Holy Spirit, the Church proclaiming the Gospel, and, last but not least, the sacrament of baptism (1 Cor 10:2). Those who have been washed in its waters become priests, prophets, and kings, transparent, simple, and pure.

Subsequently John's attention is drawn toward "those who conquer the beast and its image and the number of its name" (v. 2). These victors are the faithful members of the seven churches addressed by the Spirit (2:7), followers of the Lamb and of God's holy people. They prevail by escaping from the beast's sphere of influence, intimated by its image, number, and name, separating themselves from any of its allegiances, fighting their way clear of all agnosticism, and marching forth triumphant.[16] No longer an exodus from Pharaoh's bondage, but a conflictual recovery of inner freedom from the antichrist, they now stand "on the sea of glass with harps of God in their hands" (v. 2), redolent of Jesus' nighttime walk over the water (John 6:19–21). While their static position implies rest, the uncommon use of the Greek preposition *epí* (ἐπί, "upon") with the accusative case (*tèn thálassan*, τὴν θάλασσαν, "the sea") gives an inkling of motion toward that glassy surface,[17] meaning that they have come

16. In the Greek, the curious phrase *nikȏntas ek toû thēríou* (νικῶντας ἐκ τοῦ θηρίου), literally means "they battled their way *out of* the beast"; it has been smoothed out in the Neo-Vulgate's rendition *vicerunt bestiam*, "they overcame the beast."

17. Similarly unusual is the way the New Vulgate links the preposition *supra* ("above, upon"), which normally calls for the accusative case, with the ablative case *mare* ("sea"), to be rendered in a locative sense.

to the sea, and are now standing *on* it. Hence, allusion is made to the Israelites standing on the shore at the Red Sea, after having passed through it safe and sound, and after Yahweh had ravaged the Egyptian charioteers in it. Put differently, their arrival, and ours by implication, implies a prolonged journey of faith toward this eschatological fulfillment. While Peter began to sink into the waves (Matt 14:30), the saints now share in the power of the Risen Lord and the glorious stability of the Woman (12:1), taking a firm stance on top of the demons' abode and amidst the world's instability.[18] Symbolized is also the Gospel, solidly founded on prophets and apostles and faithfully practiced by Christians, who give it steadfast continuance and thereby gain victory over the beast. In their virginal hands are the harps of God that excel the tambourines of Miriam (Exod 15:20–21), denoting that their lives have become true music before God in spiritual joy and gratitude (Ps 150).

As was the case with the previous scourges, the seven bowls are launched amidst heavenly worship, with voices joining the melody of harps, and involving "the song of Moses, the servant of God, and the song of the Lamb" (v. 3). We are to imagine the ancient Israelites rising from the past into the realm of eternity, reenacting Moses's paean that reflected on and celebrated their deliverance from Egypt (Exod 15:1–21).[19] This servant hymn equals the ode of the Lamb in this verse, underlining its typological fulfillment; together they complement 5:9–10 and 14:1, 3, since new mercies call for new praises. By appearing here conjoined,[20] they recall the twenty-four elders who represent both dispensations, i.e., of the Old and New Testaments (4:4). Isaiah seems to have foretold such a song of the redeemed at Isaiah 12:1–6. At this juncture, however, it is the Lamb himself who appears to honor his Father "in the great assembly" (*in ecclesia magna*, Ps 22:25), that is, the redeemed in heaven (7:4–17). If Israel was mystically baptized by its passage through the Red Sea, and thereafter led by a pillar of cloud toward the Promised Land, then also the faithful will be born of water and Spirit (John 3:5), and met by the Lord coming with the clouds (1:7).[21] Before discussing the actual tenor of the song, it should be noted that it is unique among all those occurring in this book in that it presents a synonymous parallelism in quasi-metrical pattern of classical Hebrew poetry. Also, as could be expected, in its entirety it is a magnificent montage of

18. Further stressed by the timeless present tense of the Greek *nikōntas* (νικῶντας, "they are standing") in this v. 2.

19. See also his testamentary song at Deut 31:30–32:44.

20. That these are not two separate songs, but one, is expressed by the epexegetical conjunction *kaí* (καί, *et*), meaning "even so, that is, namely."

21. Cf. AvS, 491.

Old Testament citations.[22] It is composed in two hymnic strophes, the first one being a doxology that honors prerogatives of the Almighty followed by a divine title (v. 3), while the second one offers a parallel glorification of his holiness and justice (v. 4).

In a spirit of adoration, they chant: "Great and marvelous are your deeds, Lord God the Pantocrator!" (v. 3). Clearly, among those deeds is also the sign of v. 1, performed by the All-Ruler in his unrestricted power. This exercise of absolute dominion recalls the God Sabaoth of the Old Testament (Mal 1:11), now solemnly applied to his work of redemption (*opera*). "Just and true are your ways, King of the nations[23]!" (v. 3), a righteousness that finds its truest manifestation in the Cross of Christ. His rule holds all the potentates of this world in submission, responding to the agonizing cry of the slain witnesses: "How long!?" (6:10). In Jesus, God is true to his creation, true to humanity, and true to the fulfillment of all his promises, too (2 Cor 1:20).

All this is worthy of praise: "Lord, who will not fear and extol[24] your name? For you alone are holy" (v. 4). Answering this rhetorical question is an unanticipated Greek word choice for "holy," namely, *hósios* (ὅσιος, *sanctus*), instead of the conventional *hágios* (ἅγιος), since the former commonly bespeaks pious human action and not divine holiness. Perhaps it is intended as a hint at the dwelling of the God-Man among us in faultlessness, and mindful that as Judge he will reward those who hallowed his name by good works in their generation. Echoing the *Shema Yisrael* (Deut 6:4), which is the monotheistic Jewish religion in a nutshell, and is the most important part of Judaism's daily prayer, the adjective "alone" (*mónos*, μόνος, *solus*) exalts the absolute uniqueness of the Lord's reign. It found its way into the Greater Doxology of the *Gloria in excelsis Deo*: "For you alone are the Holy One, you alone are the Lord!"

Mirroring v. 3, the victors add one more acclamation: "All nations will come and worship before you, for your judgments have been revealed" (v. 4). At last, Simeon's blessing has found its scriptural match: "Behold, this Child is appointed to cause the rise and fall of many in Israel, and to be a sign that will be spoken against, so that the thoughts of many hearts will be revealed" (Luke 2:34–35). Since Christ is the knower of all thoughts, he is the most flawless Judge of human sin. In the end, all nations will acknowledge God's glory,

22. Cf. Exod 34:10; Deut 32:4; Pss 58:11; 85:10; 86:9–10; 92:6; 97:2; 98:1–2; 111:2–4; 139:14; 145:17; Jer 10:7.

23. The reading "nations" (cf. Sinaiticus, A; Neo-Vulgate *gentes*) is preferable to the variant "ages" (cf. P^{47}, Sinaiticus*).

24. Instead of the New Vulgate's *glorificabit* ("glorify"), Latin codices W, S, V, read *magnificabit* ("magnify").

willingly or forcibly. However, this should be understood as a hyperbolic statement in light of 16:9 and considering the Eucharistic concept of "for you and for many" (*pro vobis and pro multis*). Thus, John, the beloved disciple, is chosen from among the apostles to convey to the Church God's justice and truth.[25]

How can these apocalyptic conquerors inspire our Christian lives in the world today? Meditating firstly on the tranquil and translucent sea, we might discern in it a symbol of God's holiness and omniscient love, shot through with the fire of his eternal justice. Hence, as servants of Christ, we are called to become similarly transparent to others, by repenting of, confessing, and atoning for our sins. As a figure for deep-rooted faith, too, this oceanic expanse is meant to let the Lord's own glory shine through our very being, reflecting his light toward the brethren.[26] In this way, any bewilderment or obfuscation in the face of God's mystery and designs, which could otherwise alienate the soul, dissipates. Instead, we are empowered to foreshadow the illumination of the Heavenly Jerusalem.

Secondly, and flowing from the above, there remains the lifelong obligation to mortify and conquer the beast of godless egocentrism lodging in one's soul. Let us be resolved to keep our spiritual heels on the neck of that brutish animal within our hearts, who tries to dominate and ruin us through rude selfishness, worldly seductions, and all sorts of unchecked impulses of human passion. Sustained by God's grace, we refuse to be dragged away captive, "like sheep destined for Sheol" (Ps 49:14). In fact, every year, that is, during the Eastertide, we are invited to make that rejection official again: "Do you renounce Satan? I do. And all his works? I do. And all his empty show? I do."[27] And although proneness to self-degradation is the original woundedness affecting all children of Adam, we are now prepared to heed the summons of victory and of inner freedom through the blood of the Warrior-Lamb. And precisely by faithfully embracing his meekness and innocent self-sacrifice, we triumph.

Thirdly, those harps of God could be taken as a metaphor for our souls, tuned by joy and a deep sense of thankfulness for Jesus' endless mercies toward them.[28] Then, a life of sincere piety and selfless service turns into welcome music in the ears of God, reechoing from the interior strings smitten with sorrow and suffering: "Be filled with the Spirit, as you chant psalms and hymns and spiritual songs among yourselves, singing and making melody to the Lord in your hearts" (Eph 5:18–19).

25. Cf. AvS, 493–95.
26. Cf. AvS, 487–90.
27. Roman Missal, *The Renewal of Baptismal Promises* during the Easter Vigil.
28. Cf. AvS, 491.

16:1–21, Final effusion of divine wrath

First bowl: Plague on the earth (16:1–2)

[1]Then I heard a loud voice from the temple telling the seven angels, "Go and pour out on the earth the seven bowls of the wrath of God." [2]So the first angel went and poured his bowl on the earth, and a foul and painful sore came on those who had the mark of the beast and who worshiped its image.

If the previous chapter was a mere résumé of God's final judgment, then the present one tenders a narration in full of those events. Like the septenary of seals and trumpets, the outpouring of the seven bowls will bring a succession of cataclysms, modeled in part on the plagues of Egypt (Exod 7–12), unfolding either in rapid chain reaction or even simultaneously. Still in consonance with the apocalyptic genre, this final septet suggests unalleviated severity of castigation, striking not just a fourth (ch. 6) or a third portion (ch. 8), but the totality of creation, epitomized by the elements of earth, water, fire, and air.

While his eyes are still fixed on the wide-open temple in heaven, observing that phalanx of seven angels exiting, John now hears from that same direction a full-throated command issued probably by the living creature of 15:7, "Go and pour out on the earth the seven bowls of the wrath of God!" (v. 1). Reverberating in this imperative are all the gravity and urgency of God's indignation,[1] impeccably timed and measured by his justice.[2] This imminent effusion (*effúndere*) recalls the sacrificial blood sprinkled toward the curtain at the entrance of the Israelites' tent of meeting in the wilderness, and liberally poured out onto the base of its holocaustic altar, cleansing it from any defilement of sin (Lev 4:6–7).

1. Cf. RD, 1113.
2. Cf. AvS, 503.

With lightning promptness so typical of the angelic spirits, "the first [angel] went and poured his bowl into the earth, and a foul and painful sore came on those who had the mark of the beast and who worshiped its image" (v. 2). Having kept themselves in alertness, stationed at the gate of heaven's sanctuary, they now depart[3] to pour forth the destructive contents of their goblets. One envisages them as approaching the edge of the celestial arena, from where they now look down upon the earth, implying a fair distance (Luke 16:26). "Earth" here must be taken as synecdochical for the dry land only, contradistinguished from the sea, the rivers, the air, and the sun.[4] The earlier embargo against damaging the earth has been quashed (7:3), and at this time the pernicious liquid is literally emptied right into it.[5] As a consequence, festering boils (Luke 16:21) heave into view on those who repudiate the one true God, universalizing, as it were, the chastisement of the sixth Egyptian plague. According to Exodus 9:8–12, it also struck Pharaoh's two professional idolaters, the magicians Jannes and Jambres, so that they could not stand before Moses; thus, this first apocalyptic plague could be said to vex all the spiritual descendants of ancient sorcery and idolatry. At any rate, the earth, identified with the irreligious sectors of humanity, symbolizes any and all promoters of evil world-power and its oppression of the faithful, now afflicted with bodily pain of utmost virulence.[6] Those who contemptuously submitted to the prideful mark of the beast will now have to bear the scar of an avenging God, in whose retributive exercise of justice the penalty seems to fit the crime.[7]

For each of these plagues, let us ponder their relevance for our spiritual life. To start with, the outpouring of divine anger by way of wicked sores may signify the ongoing proclamation of the Gospel intended to invite to personal conversion. As we know that suffering is the unescapable result of sin, there is also the aspect of penance: in the grand scheme of Christian life and death, we can

3. In the New Vulgate, the verb *íre* ("to go") in v. 1 is intensified in its compound version *abíre* ("to go away") at v. 2, illustrating that departing movement directed toward the earth.

4. Cf. AvS, 504.

5. The repetition of the Greek preposition *eís* (εἰς), "in, into," governing the accusative case, sets the first three bowls (vv. 2–4) apart from the last four, which are preceded by the preposition *epí* (ἐπί), "on, upon, toward" (vv. 8, 10, 12, 17). The Neo-Vulgate, on the other hand, translates all the prepositions with *in* ("in, into"), except for the fifth and sixth, which are rendered as *super* ("on, onto").

6. "Foul and painful" is a phraseological superlative expressing utmost intensity; the two Greek adjectives *kakós* (κακός) and *ponērós* (πονηρός) emphasize the downright evil nature of the punishment (1 Cor 5:8).

7. Cf. RD, 1114.

accept and embrace bodily or spiritual pain in union with the crucified Lord,[8] not only to avoid the torments of hell, but also to reduce the punishment for sins in the afterlife, namely, in purgatory. Or else, by way of atonement, we can offer them up for sinners to the glory of God. In this way, suffering can become even a source of joy, as St. Paul avows: "I fill up in my flesh what is lacking in regard to Christ's afflictions for the sake of his body, which is the Church" (Col 1:24).[9] It must be maintained, of course, that one cannot always assert a direct correlation between sin and suffering.

Furthermore, the image of an ulcer could be indicative of the noisome distraction that the sinner feels, disturbing one's inward self-complacency, to the point of rendering the person hateful and contemptible to oneself. That inner perturbation can be due to the various forms of beast-worship plaguing humanity. Once, however, the soul becomes aware of its wounded conscience, or a heart filled with evil intentions that defile the person (Matt 15:18–20), one should recognize in it the prompting of Christ to trustingly ask for his mercy and grace: "Come to me, all you who are weary and burdened, and I will give you rest" (Matt 11:28).

Second bowl: Plague in the sea (16:3)

3 *The second angel poured his bowl into the sea, and it became like the blood of a corpse, and every living thing in the sea died.*

As if synchronously to the first, "the second [angel] poured his bowl into the sea, and it became like the blood of a corpse, and every living thing in the sea died" (v. 3). Jointly with the upcoming bowl, this second one represents a global escalation of the archetypal first Egyptian plague (Exod 7:14–24), but also of the partial scourge brought on by the second trumpet (8:8–9). As will be clarified in 17:15, the "sea" is just another metaphor for those members of the human family who inanely deny God the adoration that is his due.[10] It, therefore, is synonymous in John's Apocalypse with "the great city where the Lord was crucified" (11:8), "Sodom," "Egypt," "Babylon," and "earth." Out of it rises the beast that signals malignant world-power, and by its dark restlessness it epitomizes the tumultuous impulses and blind passions of the masses,

8. Cf. St. John Paul II's 1984 Apostolic Letter *Salvifici doloris*, on the Christian meaning of human suffering.

9. Such a spiritual partnership in redemptive suffering is made explicit in *CCC*, §618.

10. Cf. RD, 1118.

hostile to the virtues of God's people. Lack of godliness and selfishness produce corpse-like corruption in the end. Whenever material and spiritual resources are swelling and tossed about like waves in opposition to their Creator, they become loathsome and deadly.

Furthermore, divine judgment reveals the cosmos's share in all suffering caused by man's sin, resulting in death. Its metaphysical unsightliness is presented under the image of discolored, coagulated, and putrid blood, oozing from a dead body.[11] Could the expiration of everything that has the breath of life (Gen 1:30)[12] not also be an innuendo to those many naval battles fought among nations with their untold fatalities, spilling their blood into the watery depths? In that case, the symbolism as *pars pro toto* would include the judgment on all instances of self-destruction, suicidal, fratricidal, and genocidal, rendering civilized life difficult or impossible. Moreover, and in foreshadowing of chs. 17–18, one could interpret the lethal putrefaction of bloody oceans as a sign of eschatological disintegration of evil economical world systems, and the ill-gotten gain that so often goes with them. Spiritless prosperity derived from maritime commerce, among the many other patterns of profane self-enrichment, is doomed to meet its demise when the Almighty rises in judgment on the boundary of human history.

Turning to the spiritual message borne out by this second plague, one could regard the angel aggravating the waters of the oceans as a figure for God's attempt to stir up our individual moral conscience, and shake it out of a state of complacency, helping it to finally arise from the sleep of wickedness. Indeed, the redundant way the Greek text expresses the death of all "soul-life" (*psychè zōēs*, ψυχὴ ζωῆς) might be an allusion to the reality of mortal sin, from which only contrition, repentance, and divine forgiveness can free us.

This wrath-vial appears to chastise the sins of those who rebuff God's designs: instead of cooperating especially in the generating of life, they engage in a culture of death, abortive of his many gifts.[13] Not least of all, the changing of water into corpse-like blood sounds like a diabolical perversion of the transformation of water into wine in Cana (John 2:9), and even more crucially, of the transubstantiation of wine into the Eucharistic Blood of our Lord. Let us

11. Cf. Philo of Alexandria, *De vita Mosis*, 1.100.

12. Arguably including both animal and human, as is hinted at in the Greek text by the solecistic neuter plural relative pronoun *tá* (τά), "who, which," which can also be read as a definite article ("the") or a demonstrative pronoun ("those"), expanding as it does, albeit discordantly, the feminine singular noun *psychḗ* (ψυχή) with its appositional *zōḗs* (ζωῆς); this syntactic awkwardness is smoothed over by the New Vulgate's flush *anima vivens . . . quae*.

13. Cf. AvS, 505.

take, then, every opportunity to participate in that Sacrament of love, celebrating his Death and Resurrection, knowing full well that the alternative eventually means to metaphorically consume the putrescent blood on his *Dies Irae* ("Day of Wrath").

Third bowl: Plague in the rivers and fountains (16:4–7)

[4]The third angel poured his bowl into the rivers and the springs of water, and they became blood. [5]And I heard the angel of the waters say, "You are just, O Holy One, who are and were, for you have judged these things; [6]because they shed the blood of saints and prophets, you have given them blood to drink. It is what they deserve!" [7]And I heard the altar respond, "Yes, O Lord God, the Almighty, your judgments are true and just!"

Then, in rapid succession, reminiscent of the targets of the third trumpet (8:10–11), and resembling the second bowl in its universal effect (v. 3), "the third [angel] poured his bowl into the rivers and the springs of water, and there was blood" (v. 4).[14] Thus, it is not only the great sea that turns into blood, but also its worldwide tributaries flowing seawards, and even their respective fluvial sources, become blood-red too. Feeding into the oceans, they contribute to their corruption, allegorizing individual persons and their sinful earthliness that make up the popular sentiment and culture of entire peoples, smitten by the same degeneracy. Humans cannot pretend to worship idols without in the process degrading all of society and even the Church. Once the streams of life grow fetid, the refreshing gifts of God are polluted, and the pelagic expanses of public opinion become unhealthful. Like the previous bowl, these reddened waters become metaphorical for worldly prosperity, now stricken with economic trials and material destitution.

But it is the good spirit himself, as an interpreter of a higher order, who offers a deeper meaning to this dreadful transformation of water into blood: "I heard the angel of the waters say, 'You are just, who are and were, O Holy One, for you have judged these things; because they shed the blood of saints and

14. There is yet another syntactic roughness in the Greek phrase *kaì egéneto haîma* (καὶ ἐγένετο αἷμα), carried over into the Neo-Vulgate *et factus est sanguis*, whose grammatical singular in both cases disconnects itself from the preceding plural of "the rivers and the springs of water," and which can only be translated as "and there was blood," with its inherent universalization.

prophets, you have given them blood to drink. It is what they deserve!'" (vv. 5–6). God evidently entrusts the element of water to the stewardship of this angel under his supreme authority (Job 26:10–12).[15] It conceptually accords with the four living beings as representatives of earthly creatures (4:6). For the fifth and last time in Revelation, the ungrammatical and unchronological phrase "who are and who were" (v. 5) aims at expressing the Pantocrator's timelessness and eternity.[16] Unlike the first three recurrences, the one at 11:17 and the present one, while addressing him directly, lack the future segment "who is to come," since God has now come to execute end-time judgment in messianic righteousness and holiness.[17] Although still shrouded in uncertainty, this impending wrath seems also to answer the cry for vengeance by the souls stationed beneath the altar at 6:9–11, and at the same time it is antiphonal to the canticle in 15:3–4.

World-powers and idol-worshippers have shed the life-blood of the Lord's servants and witnesses,[18] yet in a stinging reversal of fortune, they are now made to consume the blood of death themselves, as if reviving the ancient Egyptian plague (Ps 78:44). Not without sarcasm, the *angelus aquarum* subjoins his own persuasion: "It is what they deserve!" (v. 6). Such chastisement manifests the grim equivalence between sin and sin's wages, giving a definitive signification to the Old Testament's law of retaliation (*lex talionis*), but also offering an interpretive key for this chapter's entire septet of bowls. One might add that this dire prophecy received its initial fulfilment in the violent deaths of so many of those earliest Christian persecutors.[19]

In the guise of a responsorial, a personified altar emphatically assents: "Yes, O Lord God, Pantocrator, your judgments are true and just!" (v. 7).[20] Hence, this eternal Judge is not only "fair" (*iustus*) and "hallowed" (*sanctus*, v. 5), but also in agreement with reality, that is, "all-powerful" (*omnipotens*) and "true"

15. Cf. 7:1 (winds); 14:18 (fire); 9:11 (abyss); see also 1 Enoch 66:1–2.

16. Identical with 1:4, 8; 11:17; the order is inverted to a more logical "who was and who is" in 4:8; also, aside from the first one (1:4), the remaining four (1:8; 4:8; 11:17; 16:5) feature the above divine title in their immediate context.

17. Cf. AvS, 508.

18. Cf. RD, 1117; AvS, 510.

19. See also the early Christian author Lactantius's work *De morte persecutorum*, in which he describes the deaths of those Roman emperors who persecuted the Church, both before his time (Nero, Domitian, Decius, Valerian, Aurelian), as well as his contemporaries (Diocletian, Maximian, Galerius, Maximinus, Maxentius), leading up to the AD 313 Edict of Milan.

20. There is yet another strange use of the Greek genitive case, *toû thysiastēríou* (τοῦ θυσιαστηρίου), literally, "I heard of the altar," or "I heard from the altar."

(*verus*).[21] This solemn "Yes" is the last mention of this personified heavenly altar in the Apocalypse, a final link to the voice of those martyred souls at its base awaiting their vindication (6:9). In the ultimate analysis, to be sure, this altar symbolizes Christ himself, anointed by the Spirit of justice, sanctification, and truth, echoing the worshipful sentiments of his Mystical Body regarding his heavenly Father.[22]

But how do we make this third bowl valuable for our interior lives as Christians? There is the simple recognition that the God-Man Jesus desires to guide each one of us to the springs of the water of life (21:6), to slake our spiritual thirst, and to make rivers of that water gush up from our hearts and flow into eternal life (John 4:14). Another thought revolves around the immutability of God Almighty, impressed on our hearts by the truly sublime but also mysterious phrase used by the water-angel: "You are just, O Holy One, who are and were!" (v. 5). In other words, surrounded as we are by the never-ending midstream changes of direction affecting all worldly affairs, our minds can turn to the One who remains unchanged, whose throne is from everlasting to everlasting. That timeless stability continues in his divine Son and his sacrifice (Heb 13:8), recalling the Carthusian motto, "The Cross is steady while the world turns." In wrapping up, here is one more spiritual insight, centered on the trifecta of "justice-holiness-truth" in God: they are the solid reason why we should always praise the Lord, both Church militant and Church triumphant, for fulfilling his promises. He is worthy of all glory and love for saving his chosen people, but also for punishing his enemies. This is God's work *in fieri*, that is, already accomplished but not yet done.

Fourth bowl: Plague on the sun (16:8–9)

[8] The fourth angel poured his bowl on the sun, and it was allowed to scorch people with fire; [9] they were scorched by the fierce heat, but they cursed the name of God, who had authority over these plagues, and they did not repent and give him glory.

Marking the septenary midpoint and escalating the apocalyptic libations from merely terrestrial to cosmic dimensions, "the fourth [angel] poured his bowl

21. Tellingly, the Greek adjective *alēthinós* (ἀληθινός) stems from the root *a-lantháno͞* (α-λανθάνω), having the lexical meaning of "not concealed, of undeniable fact, fully tested, worthy of credit."

22. Cf. RD, 1119; AvS, 511.

on the sun, and it was allowed to scorch the humans with fire" (v. 8). Thrillingly, these first four bowls advance in the same order as the first four trumpets, harming the earth (8:7; 16:2), the sea (8:8; 16:3), the rivers and springs (8:10; 16:4), and the sun (8:12; 16:8). Yet, while the trumpets strike only a third part of the physical world with natural disasters, mirroring the partial damage inflicted by the ten plagues of Egypt, the present cups of God's wrath perturb the totality of those creational targets.[23] Nor should it go unnoticed, at least as a scriptural coincidence, that "the greater light" (*lumināre maius*), known as the sun, was created on the fourth day (Gen 1:16) and is now upset precisely by the agency of this fourth bowl. Commentators have put forward a broad assortment of elucidations in its regard, interpreting the sun in a literal sense, as an allegory of Christ (1:16) or of his Gospel, or else of idolatrous world-powers in their illusory anti-Christian heaven. Just the same, under God's absolute control ("he was allowed," *datum est illi*), this celestial body no longer grows dark, as during the ninth Egyptian plague (Exod 10:21–23), or at the sixth seal (6:12), or at the fourth trumpet (8:12), or at the fifth trumpet (9:2), or even at the fifth bowl (16:10), but rather, its bright scorching power becomes excessive. Originally meant as a chief source of light and warmth, whose gentle rays bless the earth and call forth the flowers, it is now perverted into an instrument of divine punishment. In other words, for those who dared to alter God's law in sin, the natural order is changed to their detriment and judgment, unleashing shockwaves of consuming fire.

Contrary to the salvific promise of immunity made to the followers of the Lamb at 7:16, the human acolytes of the beast (v. 2) suffer the torment of fierce heat, likely resulting in the perishing of a vast number of people. Yet, despite being chastened with such severity, and mirroring the outcome of the sixth trumpet (9:20–21), "they cursed the name of God, who had authority over these plagues, and they did not repent and give him glory" (v. 9). Instead of being enlightened by the rays of Jesus' word, and recognizing the hand of God, who had mercifully struck every other creature before them, to bring them to their senses and spare them, they will, like clay in an oven, be even more hardened by this scorching hotness. In imitation of their devilish master, they blame God for their suffering, a response recurring under the fifth and seventh bowls incidentally (16:11, 21), instead of willingly submitting to his perfect will (11:13). Inklings of the Lord's parousia, blasphemy and unrepentance

23. As indicated already under the first bowl, for the outstanding four bowls, the Greek text prefers the preposition *epí* (ἐπί), "on, upon," instead of *eís* (εἰς), "in, into," delicately relaying the idea of motion toward the sun to effectively reach and touch its surface.

are morally identical in that they deepen a person's allegiance to the dragon. Surely, such failure to honor the one true God is a primary trait of the heathen spirit, too, perpetuating the reaction of the Egyptian Pharaoh who hardened his heart (Exod 9:12).

The wrath-bowl of the scorching sun illustrates how things that are naturally or supernaturally beneficial to body and soul may become sources of sorrow. True, the Lord rose as the Sun of Justice whose radiance is meant to brighten every human heart, but the wisdom and knowledge he diffuses turn into searing soreness to the consciences of those who choose to follow paths of malignity. The light and warmth of his grace, if not received single-mindedly, will end up cauterizing and dehydrating the soul. Cautioning, for instance, against an undiscerning reception of the word of God, St. Peter writes: "Some parts of his [Paul's] letters are hard to understand, which ignorant and unstable people distort, as they do the rest of the Scriptures, to their own destruction" (2 Pet 3:16). It is not too far-fetched to see here also an allusion to the heat of human passions that, if left unchecked, deteriorate into vices that in turn ravish the person physically and morally. To exemplify the tragic aftereffect of a life lived in such sinfulness, Jesus employs the related figure of agonizing flames that emblematize all torment in Hades (Luke 16:23–24).

Besides, as Christians, we ought to be aware of the lethal consequences of all forms of idolatry, of which ancient and neopagan heliolatry, i.e., sun-worship, is just one example.[24] To intentionally cold-shoulder or even quench the Spirit of God and his offer of redemption amounts to signing one's own death-warrant (1 Thess 5:19). What is more, suffering due to divine punishment, if not accepted as a remedial force in humility and obedience, will result neither in blessed purification nor repentance of the soul; quite the opposite, it will unfortunately vex it, harden it, and enrage it, making it miserable and even desperate.

Blasphemy, fury, and envy are also frequent companions of those who resent the progress of Christ's Gospel and his Church on earth, irrationally accusing God of injustice and unfaithfulness. In doing so, the person *ipso facto* reveals himself as rebellious and impenitent.[25] Hence, instead of giving in to temptations of wickedness and irreligion, may we again and again embrace the gift of *metanoía*, interiorly melting into the heart of our heavenly Father. To recall the beseeching of *Second Clement* to the Corinthians:

24. See also the inauspicious revival of pre-Christian forms of paganism in the ever more de-christianized Western world today.

25. Cf. RD, 1121; AvS, 515.

> While we have an opportunity of being healed, let us yield ourselves to God that heals us, and give to him a recompense. Of what sort? Repentance out of a sincere heart; for he knows all things beforehand, and is acquainted with what is in our hearts. Let us therefore give him praise, not with the mouth only, but also with the heart, that he may accept us as sons.[26]

And with that, let us now give our attention to the looming fifth plague-angel.

Fifth bowl: Plague on the beast (16:10–11)

10 The fifth angel poured his bowl on the throne of the beast, and its king-
dom was plunged into darkness; people gnawed their tongues in agony,
11 and cursed the God of heaven because of their pains and sores, and they
did not repent of their deeds.

Continuing to aim at worshipers of the antichrist, and meting out cumulative punishment for them, the fifth plague-bowl comes into play, poured "on the throne of the beast, and its kingdom was plunged into darkness; people gnawed their tongues in agony" (v. 10). To put it in another way, all preceding judgments had some bearing on this one, and were preliminary to it, yet now a nerve-center is reached, the very seat of evil, which the dragon had bequeathed to the sea-beast (13:2), established in diabolical mimicry of God's own throne (4:2). This beastly kingdom is symbolic of the heartbeat of anti-Christian dominion and its human idolatry on earth.[27] Preparatory to their final overthrow under the seventh goblet of wrath (vv. 17–21), all demonic forces and their worldly cohorts are reduced to a condition of spiritual obscurity and blindness. Such an eclipse of their whole realm will make it even more oppressive, comfortless, and confusing, not least due to the beast's inability now to rule with any measure of lucidity. Its Old Testament counterpart is the ninth Egyptian plague, Pharaoh being the antetype of the antichrist (Exod 10:21–23).[28]

This current manifestation of wrath leaves the reign of the ancient serpent in a state of permanent disorganization, disquiet, and disease, as oftentimes

26. Clement of Rome, *Second Epistle*, 9.7–10 (trans. John Keith, ANF 9:253). The "Second Epistle" of St. Clement of Rome is an early Christian homily composed by an anonymous author around AD 95–140, which at one point was regarded as canonical by the Eastern Orthodox Church and the Coptic Orthodox Church.

27. Cf. AvS, 516.

28. Ironically, Egyptian Pharaohs were considered incarnations and protégés of the most radiant deity in their pantheon, namely, the sun god Ra, to the point of being referred to as "Sons of Ra."

presaged in ancient prophecy (e.g., Jer 13:16). Wickedness is now smitten to its core, and Satan's will-o'-the-wisp is unmasked as shadow; without the Sun of Justice, there can be no reliable light in this world and in our hearts: "Take heed, therefore, that the light which is in you is not darkness" (Luke 11:35). An unending "gnashing of teeth" as a shuddersome accessory of hell, repeatedly warned about by the Lord Jesus (Matt 8:12), is here preceded by a desperate biting of tongues in extreme pain.[29] Blasphemy and impenitence spawn writhing anguish and acts of self-destruction.[30] Part of this ungodly sorrow is their fury and envy at the dismantling of their kingdom, succumbing to powerlessness and remorse, incapable of procuring revenge, and by now unable to turn back.

At this juncture, there is no softening of hearts, no opening of minds, no blaming themselves, no humbling themselves before their Maker, but only a frenzied slithering into their spiritual suicide: they "cursed the God of heaven because of their pains and sores, and they did not repent of their deeds" (v. 11; cf. 2:22). "Like small children called to clean up the mess they have made, they are quick to blame each other, and slow to take responsibility for the task of restoration."[31] Paradoxically, however, this refusal to engage in acts of conversion is at the same time an acknowledgment of God's sovereignty.[32] All evil passions are doomed to end in exasperation and defeat. Tragically, while in 11:13 the rest gave glory to the God of heaven, here they detest him. Hence, this fifth plague-angel provides us with a timeless snapshot, so to speak, of all those who stiff-neckedly and often unaware of impending doom, continue down their primrose path, deeper into the state of sin.

Before delving into the sixth scene of God's wrathful dealing with humanity, a few items of interest for our spiritual life should be addressed. To begin with, the symbol of the beast's throne, unlike the divine throne of mystical dominion, is constituted exclusively of illusory riches, depraved opulence, and empty promises (Matt 4:8). Knowing about this diabolical deceit regarding ungodly materialism, as baptized Christians we seek to cultivate a lifestyle of

29. The Greek verb *masáomai* (μασάομαι), "to gnaw," cited only here in Scripture, is sharpened by the Nova Vulgata translation *commanducáre*, meaning "to thoroughly masticate, to chew to pieces"; also of note is the fourfold reiteration of the preposition *ék* (ἐκ), "out of," in these vv. 10–11, emphasizing, as it were, the root cause of their agony ("out of their pain, sores, works").

30. Cf. RD, 1122.

31. Leo Zanchettin, *Revelation: A Devotional Commentary* (Ijamsville, MD: The Word Among Us, 2007), 122.

32. Cf. AvS, 518.

simplicity and even frugality. Countless saintly monastics of all ages have made themselves mendicants, heeding, like Anthony the Great, the Gospel stirrings: "If you want to be perfect, go, sell what you have and give to the poor, and you will have treasures in heaven" (Matt 19:21).

Additionally, and in opposing contrast to the maximum solar blaze above (v. 8), here the image of total lightlessness is transmitted, bespeaking all forms of spiritual darkness, so obviously prevalent among the devil's vassals. Brought on by the willful separation of the interior person from his or her Maker, it carries confusion and fear in its wake. Among the many other attendants are the inward fretting of mind, the galling of conscience, the incremental clouding of the intellect, as well as the utter indifference to or horrified anticipation of one's judgment.

Moreover, one notices a seemingly irreconcilable dichotomy between the two extremes of total redemption and absolute destruction: on the one hand, all nations are said to ultimately find to the true religion (15:4), whereas in other places it appears to be certain that all godless nations will be condemned in the end, as intimated in the fourth, fifth, and seventh bowls (vv. 9, 11). In reality, however, it is part of the two possible ways mapped in Wisdom literature, typified by Psalm 1, the magnificent gateway into the Psalter, as well as the opposing female figures of Lady Wisdom and Dame Folly (Prov 7–9). In that vein, the early Christian treatise of the Didache begins with these words: "There are two ways, one to life and one to death, but the difference between the two ways is great."[33] And the Catechism of the Catholic Church expands: "The way of Christ leads to life; a contrary way leads to destruction. The Gospel parable of the two ways remains ever present in the catechesis of the Church; it shows the importance of moral decisions for our salvation."[34] Hence, this stark ethical dualism, coupled with Christ's warnings about the few who will find the narrow road (Matt 7:14) and the many unable to enter the narrow door (Luke 13:23–24), is meant to jolt us out of our spiritual apathy and spur us to an unwearied reforming of our lives, in union with him and his Blessed Mother Mary.

33. *The Didache: A Commentary*, by Kurt Niederwimmer, trans. Linda M. Maloney, ed. Harold W. Attridge (Minneapolis: Fortress, 1998), 1.1.

34. Cf. *CCC*, §1696.

Sixth bowl: Plague on the Euphrates (16:12–14)

[12]The sixth angel poured his bowl on the great river Euphrates, and its water was dried up in order to prepare the way for the kings from the sunrise. [13]And I saw three foul spirits like frogs coming from the mouth of the dragon, from the mouth of the beast, and from the mouth of the false prophet. [14]These are demonic spirits, performing signs, who go abroad to the kings of the whole world, to assemble them for battle on the great day of God the Almighty.

While the first five wrath-bowls were descriptive of the eschaton, the two remaining ones are more descriptive of the last judgment. Such an interpretation continues a similar rationale concerning the first six trumpets as compared to the seventh and last one. With that in mind, we watch how the sixth plague-angel empties "his bowl on the great river Euphrates, and its water was dried up, in order to prepare the way for the kings from the sunrise" (v. 12). If this most storied and majestic Euphrates River, mentioned already at the sixth trumpet at 9:14, served as a mere geographic dividing line in prophetic literature, it now signifies an idealized eschatological frontier highlighting the strife between the Kingdom of Christ and an unspiritual world. Just as it had formed a natural barrier between Israel and the hostile northern and eastern kingdoms in bygone biblical eras, its topographic partition had always been viewed as a quasi-insurmountable check on war. Nevertheless, its sudden and sensational drying up, as if by the glowing breath of the angel,[35] seems to foretell the stripping and burning of the great harlot at 17:16. Could it be an allusion to the Persian rulers Cyrus (539 BC) and Darius (515 BC) who cunningly diverted this waterway, permitting their armies to traverse it, enter Babylon unexpectedly and defeat it? Eventually, of course, that conquest led to the release of Israel's exiles from captivity.[36]

But who are the kings from the sunrise? Allusion may be made to the first-century AD legend of a Parthian incursion from the vulnerable eastern border of the Roman empire under *Nero redivivus*,[37] understood as a shadow

35. Unlike the preposition *eís* (εἰς), "in, into" (*in flumina et in fontes aquarum*) in v. 4, here *epí* (ἐπί), "on, upon" (*super flumen*) is used, suggesting that this blowing wind issues from the angel's mouth.

36. Cf. 2 Esdras 13:39–47; 2 Bar 77:22; Herodotus, *The Histories*, 1.190–91; Xenophon, *Cyropaedia*, 7.5.

37. Cf. 13:3; 17:9–11; Tacitus, *Histories*, 1.2.3; Suetonius, *Life of Nero*, 40, 50, 57; Cassius Dio, *Roman History*, 46.19.3; Sibylline Oracles, 4.119–24; 5.137–41, 361–96.

of the antichrist.[38] Viewed from a positive angle, and considering especially the reference to the prophetic "paving the way" (*ut praepararetur via*) and the "oriental sun" (*ab ortu solis*), this verse hints at the messianic coming of Christ, both in his birth and in his parousia. He is the head, at the same time crowned with thorns and glorious, of a priestly Kingdom.[39] He commands the victorious armies of heaven (19:14), on a mission to convert the "occident" of Satan's kingdom, culminating in the grand finale of the salvation of Israel itself (Rom 11:25–27). When, however, speculating negatively, the way to wage war is made easy for "the kings of the east," namely, all mundane power (vv. 14, 16). Long-restrained forces of evil will exploit opportunities to rise up and advance in revolt against Jesus and against all sanctity of life. They are instruments of the dragon and of the beast (v. 13), and their evil agency wreaks great temptation. Hence, this bowl signals divine judgment on the "west" of this world. And just as the beast at 11:7 is proleptic toward ch. 13, so here the kings foreshadow 17:12–14, adding to the extraordinary interwovenness of these apocalyptic visions.

John's reemergent *Et vidi* at this juncture vibrates with intense revulsion: "I saw three foul spirits like frogs coming from the mouth of the dragon, from the mouth of the beast, and from the mouth of the false prophet" (v. 13). This visionary perception of his is the only activity in this otherwise verbless and, therefore, quite motionless scene. Digressing somewhat from the previous plot of invading kings, John's attention is now drawn toward the mouths of the anti-trinity of "dragon-beast-pseudoprophet." With chameleon-like dissembling, the former land-beast (13:11) magically restyles itself as a false prophet, out to bewitch entire populations into Satan worship. Counterfeiting the inner-trinitarian communion and processions of Father, Son, and Holy Spirit, this mystery of iniquity also arrogates to itself humanity's joint adoration. Giving away their true nature, each one of this evil triumvirate vomits the likeness of a frog (*velut ranas*), symbol of impure demon-spirits. Of seemingly inferior status on the hierarchical ladder of hell, and evocative of the second Egyptian plague (Exod 8:1–14), these devils adumbrate the uncleanness of Babylon, the mother of all harlotry and idolatry (17:4–5).

Starkly contrasting with the dove-like form of the Holy Spirit, their amphibian silhouette embodies all the pestilential sliminess, formlessness, and ugliness of the ancient serpent. Their senseless and irksome croaking can only be taken as a symbol of idolatrous incantation, as well as of confusingly soulless

38. Cf. Encyclopædia Britannica, "Antichrist."

39. Cf. AvS, 519.

speech.[40] Like Pharaoh's magicians capable of performing pseudo-miraculous signs, they now "go abroad to the kings of the whole world, to assemble them for battle on the great day of God the Pantocrator" (v. 14). Copycatting Christ who sent his apostles to all the nations (Matt 28:18–20), the antichrist dispatches his minions into the *oikuménē* (οἰκουμένη, *universi orbis*) in an attempt to affect all political authority of the impious world-systems, arguably one with the oriental kings of v. 12. As a matter of historical fact, no class of people has been more deluded and taken captive to pagan superstition than earthly royals. Mustering them for battle means that the two hostile kingdoms, that of the Lamb and that of the dragon, are gradually jostling into overt antagonism, driving theological and moral issues toward a decisive test: "If the Lord is God, follow him; but if Baal is God, follow him" (1 Kgs 18:21). Far removed from false neutrality, this war against God by the forces of evil is being waged all through history, from the fall of Adam right until the last judgment day. In the usual interpenetration of visionary vignettes, this final mobilization for battle will be highlighted one more time at 19:19 and 20:8, coinciding with the great day of universal judgment.[41] Thus, just as the sixth trumpet digressed into an account of the two miracle-working witnesses of God (ch. 11), so also here, the penultimate bowl excurses into a depiction of the three pseudo-testifiers for Satan's cause.

Third makarism: Being on guard (16:15–16)

15 "See, I am coming like a thief! Blessed is the one who stays awake and is clothed, not going about naked and exposed to shame." 16 And they assembled them at the place that in Hebrew is called Harmagedon.

At this point, and with delightful abruptness, Jesus interjects himself: "Behold, I am coming like a thief!" (v. 15). And that it is the Lord, indeed, is easily discerned by his familiar voice recorded in the Gospels (Luke 12:39).[42] Before the visionary segment of this sixth bowl is completed in v. 16, he wants the reader to urgently fix his or her eyes on him and behold him (*Ecce!*), as he so frequently does throughout this book (e.g., 1:18). A parenthetical word of exhortation, it rephrases some of his message to the churches of Sardis (3:1–6) and Laodicea (3:17–18), intended to further acquaint his beloved people in these challenging

40. There may be an implicit polemic against the frog-headed god Nu and goddess Heqet (or Hathor) of ancient Egyptian mythology; see also those fiery locusts proceeding from the mouth of the beast in *The Shepherd of Hermas*, Vision 4, ch. 1.

41. Cf. RD, 1125; AvS, 524.

42. Cf. AvS, 525.

times with his near and sudden return. In using the well-known simile of a thief, the emphasis is not on violence, but rather on stealth. He who had asked his disciples to shout his message from rooftops (Matt 10:27), will return furtively. And yet, paradoxically, he does not come to steal or destroy, but to enrich and save. This apocalyptic insight should suffice to refute any endeavor at computing the times and seasons of his parousia, for Christ will arrive unannounced.

Adjoining Revelation's third beatitude,[43] "Blessed is the one who stays awake and is clothed, not going about naked and exposed to shame" (v. 16), the Lord praises the one who is vigilant, that is, attentive to his various ways of blessing and testing his brethren. Still, watchfulness is not enough: the garments of righteousness must be kept, too. While sloth and pleasure might tempt the watcher to lay aside his garments and to indulge in sleepiness or immorality, the baptized have clothed themselves permanently with Christ (Gal 3:27). They are awake to duty and danger, never found drowsy at their post, lest they lose the graces, and others see their spiritual nakedness, i.e., the deformity of sin and punishment (17:16).[44] Daily perseverance in the ways of truth, consistent preparedness for one's personal death, and for the coming of the Son of Man, protects them from the slumber of a worldly mindset. His faithful await him enthusiastically, clad in wedding robes, to walk with him toward the marriage chamber, and participate in the supper of the Lamb: "Keep awake therefore, for you know neither the day nor the hour!" (Matt 25:13).

After this interposed wisdom appeal, the train of thought is resumed from v. 14: "And he assembled them at the place that in Hebrew is called Harmagedon" (v. 16). Although in that former verse, the trio of demon-spirits was said to marshal those in earthly power ("they proceed," *procedunt*), it is now their singular figure-head, Satan himself, who with God's permission galvanizes them into one fighting force ("he congregates," *congregavit*). Now, given the obscure etymology of the biblical *hapax legomenon* Harmagedon[45]—which, unlike the

43. Cf. 1:3; 14:13; 19:9; 20:6; 22:7, 14.

44. The Greek noun *aschēmosýnē* (ἀσχημοσύνη, *turpitudo*) derives from the privative *a* (ἀ), "not," and *schēma* (σχῆμα), "fashion, shape," literally meaning "a formless, shapeless, deformed, improperly fashioned object"; figuratively, it refers to conduct that lacks in what is fitting, i.e. "unseemliness, impropriety, immodesty, indecency, shame, nakedness, lewdness" (cf. Rom 1:27).

45. The Greek *Harmagedōn* (Ἁρμαγεδών) is an indeclinable name not found in the Septuagint; it is derivative of a Hebrew compound stem that can mean "mountain," "city," "destruction," or "slaughter" of "Megiddo." Today, Tel Megiddo, identified with the above biblical place, is an archaeological World Heritage Site close to the village of Lajjun, south of Haifa in Israel.

translation of Abaddon into Apollyon at 9:11, the sacred author does not further explain for his Hellenistic audience in Asia Minor—one is directed toward a spiritual interpretation of it based on its history. Hence, the most plausible Old Testament antetype would be the Galilean Megiddo, a city of the tribe of Manasseh within the limits of Issachar (Josh 17:11). Originally one of the royal Canaanite cities, it was not conquered by the Israelites until later, and then rebuilt and fortified by King Solomon (1 Kgs 9:15). Adjacent to the vast Plain of Esdraelon-Jezreel near Mount Carmel in the proximity of Mounts Tabor and Hermon, it dominated the strategic coastal pass. Its geography as a high tableland surrounded by hills predestined it as a great battlefield of the Holy Land in antiquity.[46] It became memorable for a double slaughter: that of the Canaanite armies led by Sisera, destroyed by the Israelites under Judges Deborah and Barak (Judg 5:19), and that of King Josiah and his Israelites, allies of Babylon, at the hands of Egyptian invaders under Pharaoh Neco (2 Kgs 23:29–30). Since those military disasters, "the plain of Megiddo" became a byword for misadventure (Zech 12:11) and eventually a symbol of the final rout of the forces of evil.[47]

Ergo, John, himself a Galilean native, conflates these scriptural passages into a novel image, namely, the apocalyptic place of the final conflict fought between the hosts of good and evil just prior to the Day of Judgment (20:9). In a textual *inclusio* with the figurative Euphrates at the beginning of this sixth wrath-bowl (v. 12), Harmagedon, therefore, functions as the figuratively fabled battleground of that decisive meta-historical struggle, occurring in the world and also in the heart of every human being. In a way it is complemented by Joel's "valley of Jehoshaphat" (Joel 3:2), which in Hebrew means "God judges." Allegorically, it signifies the holy mountain of the Gospel, humanity's ultimate touchstone.

Investigating further into the spiritual message of this sixth plague, let us briefly look back at the Euphrates (v. 12). Standing as it does as a symbolic boundary between good and evil, the unrestrained passage through its drained riverbed implies not just the times of secularization and persecution in different historical eras and various parts of the world, that saw a Christian culture invaded, defiled, and occasionally demolished; but it reminds each one of us,

46. From the days of Assyrian King Nebuchadnezzar to the Jews, Persians, Egyptians, Gentiles, Saracens, Christian crusaders, Druses, Turks, and Arabs, soldiers down the centuries, all have crossed the valley of Jezreel, facing the hill of Megiddo.

47. Comparable perhaps to other household names that memorialize world-historical battles such as Marathon (490 BC), Carthage (149–46 BC), Tours (AD 732), Tenochtitlan (AD 1521), Vienna (AD 1529), Lepanto (AD 1571), Trafalgar (AD 1805), Waterloo (AD 1815), Gettysburg (AD 1863), Stalingrad (AD 1942–43), or Iwo Jima (AD 1945).

members of the holy people of God, not to let the sacred soil of our faith be encroached on by false principles, or by tolerating corrupt manners of life. With the Lord's help one will be able to prevent any unscrupulous neglect of conscience, that inner sanctuary of purity, dignity, and freedom. On the other hand, the image of the waterless river reassures the soul that no matter the circumstances, God can make a path where heretofore an obstacle existed.[48]

Moreover, when reflecting again on those amphibian-like fallen angels (vv. 13–14), their triplicity intimates some of the radical foes of divine presence in our hearts, as brought to the fore by John in his first Epistle: "For all that is in the world, the lust of the flesh, the lust of the eyes, and the pride of life, is not of the Father" (1 John 2:16). St. James in his letter denounces yet another tercet of inimical attitudes rising within the Christian soul, namely, jealousy, strife, and lies (Jas 3:14).[49] In their relative ugliness and formlessness, frogs also signal opposition to the dogmatic teachings of the Church, obviating the forming of the child of God in the image of Christ.[50] By their proverbial noisiness and uncleanness they also embody a spirit of empty verbosity and complaining against God, disturbing the necessary silence and serenity of the soul.[51]

By trying to exalt themselves in the nothingness of their demonic signs (v. 14), they instill in us an aversion toward all manner of self-glorification as a major obstacle on our earthly pilgrimage as servants of God. But they also remind us of the reality of diabolical activity in this world, and the need for our constant readiness to discern and resist it. Included in their portfolio of deceit is to tempt men and women into becoming "kings of the whole world," that is, hearts that delight in possessing the pleasures of this world yet become impoverished before God (Luke 12:21). May this biblical text vitalize us to keep up our spiritual combat by daily climbing Harmagedon, that is, the embattled mountain of decision, never tiring of choosing the Lamb over the dragon, and thereby bit by bit conquer all evil of mind and body: "Behold, the Kingdom of God is inside of you!" (Luke 17:21).[52]

48. Cf. AvS, 518.

49. Rupert comments on the frogs as metaphors for religious sects, black magic, and atheistic philosophies, cf. RD, 1123.

50. Cf. AvS, 521.

51. Cf. RD, 1125; AvS, 522.

52. Cf. AvS, 529.

Seventh bowl: Plague on the air (16:17–21)

[17]The seventh angel poured his bowl into the air, and a loud voice came out of the temple, from the throne, saying, "It is done!" [18]And there came flashes of lightning, rumblings, peals of thunder, and a violent earthquake, such as had not occurred since people were upon the earth, so violent was that earthquake. [19]The great city was split into three parts, and the cities of the nations fell. God remembered great Babylon and gave her the wine-cup of the fury of his wrath. [20]And every island fled away, and no mountains were to be found; [21]and huge hailstones, each weighing about a hundred pounds, dropped from heaven on people, until they cursed God for the plague of the hail, so fearful was that plague.

Curiously, there is no appreciable intermission ahead of this seventh *phiala*,[53] unlike the ones observed before the seventh seal and trumpet, except perhaps for Christ's reassuring makarism at v. 15. Notwithstanding that structural rift, one can expect this last wrath-goblet to be climactic. Thus, without delay, "the seventh [angel] poured his bowl on the air, and a loud voice came out of the temple, from the throne, saying, 'It is done!'" (v. 17). Another part of creation is now smitten, that is, the atmosphere, thereby completing the visitation of the fourfold division of the universe, in addition to earth, water, and fire. Vaguely recollective of the sixth plague of Egypt, when Moses tossed handfuls of kiln-soot in the air in Pharaoh's sight (Exod 9:8), but also of the fifth trumpet that saw the air darkened by hellish smoke (9:2), this atmospheric element can be read as a symbol of the vastness of cosmic space and the entire spiritual realm.[54] St. Paul portrays it as the residence of the devil encompassing the whole world, ruling over the children of unbelief (Eph 2:2).

Then, as if acknowledging the completion of the seven angels' mission at v. 1, the Lamb's own powerful voice appears to resonate from the throne, conveying authority and majesty, rejoicingly proclaiming that all is finished (v. 17; cf. 10:7). On the Cross he had bowed his head and given up his Spirit with a similar solemn cry (John 19:30), and his apocalyptic singular *Factum est!* on this occasion will only be outclassed by his finalizing plural *Facta sunt!* in the new heaven (21:6).[55] Even though the seventh seal and the seventh trumpet had already signaled a gradual approach of the end, this one is truly final.

53. The Neo-Vulgate's rendition of the Greek *phiálē* (φιάλη) throughout Revelation, meaning a broad shallow bowl or a flat saucer (5:8).

54. Cf. RD, 1127.

55. Cf. AvS, 530.

Then, as if unleashed by a furious tempest, "there came flashes of lightning, rumblings, peals of thunder, and a violent earthquake, such as had not occurred since people were upon the earth, so violent was that earthquake" (v. 18). Set in motion at this point is a flurry of events enumerated in vv. 18–21, more widespread in its scope and more effective in its ferocity than the previous six bowls. They seem to provide a closure correlative to those of the septets of seals (8:5) and trumpets (11:19), albeit on a maximal scale.[56] This previously unknown whirlwind of cosmic cacophony evokes the image of the theophany at Mount Sinai (Exod 19:16–19), demonstrative of God's power and wisdom as the Giver of Israel's Law; now his final visitation is announced, during which he will punish its violators. Especially in emphasizing the earthquake's enormity, the seer on Patmos confirms that the build-up from 8:5 and 11:19 has reached its highest potential, flowing into a global cataclysm in which God finally settles accounts with his creation.[57] Just as a natural earthquake rends asunder the surface of the earth leaving nothing concealed, so also here, metaphorically, everything is laid bare before the eternal Judge (Heb 4:13). With unsurpassable severity, the overthrow of the anti-Christian kingdom is about to be completed, of which earlier judgments were mere precursors.

Due to the unprecedented scale of that apocalyptic earthquake, "the great city was split into three parts, and the cities of the nations fell" (v. 19). Babylon, the unspiritual metropolis of the world, a figure for sinful humanity,[58] has already lost a tenth part (11:13), and now the remaining nine parts are torn apart, too. Her pitiless dismemberment can be ascribed to Christ's sword of division on earth (Matt 10:34) and will be looked at in detail during the upcoming visions of chs. 17–18. While the three frog-shaped demons undertook to bring all ungodly power in this world together for a final assault (vv. 14, 16), that entity is now losing all cohesion since its only bond is hatred of God and man. Could the city's tripartition be a reflection of the trinitarian wrath directed at her?[59] In any event, the triple fractionalization implies that she as the capital is reduced to a state of total ruination, and with it all subordinate, dependent, or allied powers of unconverted nations.

Indeed, "God remembered great Babylon and gave her the wine-cup of

56. Signaled by a fifth element ("hail," v. 21) added to the customary four ("thunder, rumblings, lightning, earthquake," 8:5, and "lightning, rumblings, earthquake, hail," 11:19), and by underscoring the extreme violence of the earthquake (v. 18) and the extraordinary magnitude of those hailstones (v. 21).

57. Cf. AvS, 531.

58. Cf. RD, 1128.

59. Cf. AvS, 533.

the fury of his wrath" (v. 19). He seems to have overlooked sin in the past (Rom 3:25), leaving it unchecked and suspending judgment, not least due to his patience in awaiting the fruits of conversion (2:21). But at this time, he recalls it for the purpose of punishment since neither mundane magnificence nor repute can cover up the world's malefactions against the moral order. Well-deserved is the drinking of divine indignation boiling over in anger,[60] resulting in the destruction of the antichrist and his damnation, in fulfillment of 14:10.[61]

Unable to resist the brunt of judgment day, and as a direct effect of the devastating earthquake, "every island fled away, and no mountains were to be found" (v. 20), a vanishing that goes far beyond the mere displacement sketched at 6:14. Reversing some of God's work of creation, earth's landscape returns to a state of protological formlessness and void (Gen 1:2, 9), an unambiguous sign of the eschatological end.[62] Driving this universal convulsion to a breaking point, "huge hailstones, each weighing about a hundred pounds, dropped from heaven on people, until they cursed God for the plague of the hail, so fearful was that plague" (v. 21). Hail is yet another biblical symbol of divine might and wrath,[63] contrasting with the gentle rain of manna coming down from heaven (Exod 16:4). In this end-phase of judgment, however, its monstrous size (*sicut talentum*)[64] conveys the idea of the crushing fierceness of God's ire, vastly exceeding the phenomena of the seventh Egyptian plague (Exod 9:23), as well as of the first (8:7) and seventh trumpets (11:19). If the Almighty's hailstone-shower trounced the five Amorite kings in Joshua's day (Josh 10:11), then he will also overthrow every hostile federation that might array itself against the King of Justice.

Tragically, however, and contrary to the outcome of 11:13, the vehemence of this peak-bowl makes humans stubbornly persist in their impenitence, as is implied by their blasphemies. This is now the third recurrence of the grievous act of blaspheming in this chapter (vv. 9, 11), underscoring man's refusal to acknowledge anything that is good and worthy of respect or veneration;

60. Notice the epexegetical genitive in the Greek *toû thymoû tēs orgēs* (τοῦ θυμοῦ τῆς ὀργῆς, *indignationis irae*), a superlative expressing the exceeding fierceness of castigation.

61. Cf. RD, 1128.

62. Cf. *Assumption of Moses*, 4.4.

63. Conversely, 1 Enoch declares that "the spirit of the hail is a good angel," 60:17.

64. A "talent" was an ancient unit for measuring weight or value in Greece, Rome, and the Middle East; in the Old Testament, it measured precious metals like gold and silver; in the New Testament, it was the largest coin for monetary exchange, equaling 6,000 drachmas or denarii; at the same time, it standardized the heaviest measurement, equivalent to 75–100 pounds or 34–45 kilograms.

it is humanity's futile attempt to overturn religious values and to vilify sacred things.[65] Unrepentance was sadly already the reaction to the fourth and fifth goblets. In the people's incorrigibility, they would rather be destroyed than be reformed by the Lord's love and grace. In closing, one realizes a pattern of progression and intensification: while the seven seals are natural tragedies, the trumpet-septet escalates them into regional disasters for repentance, and the bowl-septenary constitutes a global cataclysm ahead of the final judgment. Even on a mere textual level, within the last septet of wrath-bowls, this narrative crescendo is reflected in the swelling of verses from one (v. 2) to five (vv. 17–21).

Let us again try to glean some grain of spiritual insight from our exegetical reading. By touching the air of the sky (v. 17), this final plague-angel reminds us of Paul's stupendous promise about meeting the Lord in the air at his second coming (1 Thess 4:16–18). Also refreshed in our minds is Jesus' own cry from the throne of his Cross, "It is finished!" (John 19:30), a cry that should never cease to shake up the conscience, like an earthquake preceding and accompanying a spiritual resurrection. In that awareness, the Christian soul will not lose its interior strength and focus, it will not undergo splintering like Babylon, the great city and matrix of all sinfulness, prior to its ruin. Furthermore, even though the Almighty in his forgiveness does not remember our sins (Heb 8:12), let us never presume his mercy. Sacramental absolution will keep us whole and united with the Lord.[66]

Rupert in his commentary on this passage offers the thought-provoking suggestion of the islands as metaphors for local churches, and the mountains as figures for the saints, who, the more they are pressured and persecuted, the more they preach the Gospel, represented by the hailstones from heaven.[67] And again, the flight of islands and mountains could be an allusion to the transformative power of divine grace in the soul, as it expeditiously works at rooting out all traces of idolatry. Additionally, it also nudges us to not overly rely on concepts, calculations, and securities in this world, for there is nothing that will not be removed eventually: "We brought nothing into the world, so we cannot carry anything out of it" (1 Tim 6:7). Only the Cross of Christ remains stable

65. Etymologically, the Greek verb *blasphēméō* (βλασφημέω) is a composite of either (a.) *blax*, "slow, stolid, dull," and *phḗmē*, "reputation, fame," signifying one's sluggishness in recognizing what is godly, or (b.) *blapto*, "to hurt, injure," and *phḗmē*, suggesting any evil-speaking or slandering of God, vitiating his all-holy name.

66. Cf. AvS, 534.

67. Cf. RD, 1129.

and dependable, our "only hope" (*spes unica*).[68] Like a sailor's lodestar, it will aid the human heart to overcome any wrong sense of self-reliance, and not to experience a state of abandonment, disorientation, or loneliness. In this way, one can embrace even the most stinging trials of life by recognizing in them the perfect will of God.[69] But let us now listen to one of the bowl-angels who is approaching and about to speak up.

68. A pious motto borrowed from the sixth stanza of an ancient Roman hymn to the True Cross of Christ, *Vexilla Regis*.

69. Cf. AvS, 536–37.

17:1–18, Anti-Marian mystery

Irreligious inebriation (17:1–6)

[1]Then one of the seven angels who had the seven bowls came and said to me, "Come, I will show you the judgment of the great whore who is seated on many waters, [2]with whom the kings of the earth have committed fornication, and with the wine of whose fornication the inhabitants of the earth have become drunk." [3]So he carried me away in the spirit into a wilderness, and I saw a woman sitting on a scarlet beast that was full of blasphemous names, and it had seven heads and ten horns. [4]The woman was clothed in purple and scarlet, and adorned with gold and jewels and pearls, holding in her hand a golden cup full of abominations and the impurities of her fornication; [5]and on her forehead was written a name, a mystery: "Babylon the great, mother of whores and of earth's abominations." [6]And I saw that the woman was drunk with the blood of the saints and the blood of the witnesses to Jesus. When I saw her, I was greatly amazed.

As we cross the threshold into the closing section of the Apocalypse at this point, a narrative pattern should be pointed out. There is the aspect of history or chronology being expressed in structural linearity in the way the forces of evil are vanquished, the dead are judged (chs. 17:1–20:15), creation is made new, and saved humanity is united with the New Jerusalem (21:1–22:5), with the added finishing touch of an epilogue (22:6–21). But there is also a hermeneutic key to be kept in mind when reflecting on these concluding chapters of Revelation, and that is the sapiential dualism between two female figures, i.e., Lady Wisdom and Dame Folly, mentioned above already. As delineated in the Book of Proverbs, the son, representative of the individual soul, along his life's journey encounters both women, who invite him, and the reader with him, into an intimate relationship. The young man must decide between the personification of true wisdom of the Lord (Prov 8:1–9:6) and worldly foolishness

(Prov 9:13–18). Both women's houses, incidentally, sit on the heights overlooking the city (Prov 9:3, 14), suggesting ancient temples: thus, the choice is between the true God and false deities. Such an ongoing ethical challenge can serve as an interpretive backdrop as we now learn about another pair of female figures, namely, the great whore of Babylon and the bridal Virgin-Mother of the New Jerusalem. The former's judgment, which was already displayed in summary at the sixth and seventh plague-goblets (16:12–21), now comes into a more detailed view in chs. 17–19. Beginning here at 17:1 is a depiction of the punishment of Babylon in the prophetic past, a metaphor for ungodly societies, led astray into idolatry, immorality, and sundry crimes.

Up to this point, the seven bowl-angels have departed for their missions (16:2), but now John observes one of them approach and address him: "Come, I will show you the judgment of the great whore who is seated on many waters" (v. 1). This personal invitation is reminiscent of that of the four living creatures to draw closer and witness the opening of the first four seals (6:1, 3.5, 7). His presence not only reconnects with the notion of God's final judgment (15:1), but it is also a logical continuation of the last plague that already had the great city of Babylon in its crosshairs (16:17–19). In all likelihood, this is that selfsame seventh angel. A verbatim reference to his angelic septet is again made at 21:9, initiating the contrastive vision of the heavenly city, that is, the Bride of the Lamb. Hence, God entrusts the execution of the judgments prior to the advent of his reign and their communication to his good spirits. In the ultimate analysis, this act of revelatory "showing" (*ostendere*) is part of God the Father's resolution to "make public" (*palam facere*) his Son's mystery (1:1).

Despite the prominent placement of this word in the angel's behest, and its rhetorical anticipation at 14:8 and 16:19, the actual "damnation" of Babylon happens only in ch. 18,[1] in definitive response to the witnesses' plea at 6:10. Although the concept of harlotry as religious infidelity or idolatry is a frequent one in the Old Testament (e.g., Isa 1:21), none of those antetypes were called a "great harlot" like in this verse. She is the apocalyptic personification of unfaithfulness par excellence, a prime symbol of the alluring nature of Satan's schemes, to attract followers and snatch them away from Christ. One might say that she epitomizes the diametrical opposite of the great Virgin-Mother of God, a quintessential anti-Mary. Adopting what is normally the posture of God

1. This is the very first occurrence of the noun *kríma* (κρίμα) in Revelation, rendered as *damnatio* by the New Vulgate; the Greek conveys the idea of "judgment, account, reckoning, decree, decision"; cf. 18:20; 20:4.

or Christ or the saints,[2] this figurative prostitute is sitting down in her presumption of exercising well-established influence, control, and uncontested sovereignty; at the same time, her recumbence denotes self-delusional ease, rest, and queen-like grandeur.

Her pompous throne is made up of many waters, the habitat of the sea-beast (13:1), into whose corruption she settles, in open defiance of the upcoming image of her barren environment.[3] There is perhaps a concrete reference here to the famous irrigation systems of ancient Babylon, situated on the Euphrates, if not also to Rome as the city on the Tiber. Of course, it also evokes the prototypical deluge, illustrating Yahweh's resolve to cause the earth to revert to a primordial state of watery chaos, and to remake it in the image of the microcosm of Noah's ark (Gen 6–9). And if that ark is symbolic of the saving vessel of the Church in the flood of world history, then the great harlot represents its antithesis: instead of renewal, she instigates rebellion and destruction.

In the same tradition as the Thyatirian Jezebel (2:20–23), "the kings of the earth have committed fornication [with her], and with the wine of whose fornication the inhabitants of the earth have become drunk" (v. 2). Contemplated through the allegorical prism of the undefiled virgins at 14:4, the powerful of the world choose to partake of idol worship, and cast the spell of irreligious inebriation and spiritual adultery even on their subjects, namely, the faithless portion of humanity. Such was the case, for instance, with the numerous pagan nations in John's time that had submitted as tributaries to Rome in its godless suzerainty, imbibing its infatuation with the imperial cult and ensuing enmity toward the one true God and his people. By extension, such intoxication is intrinsically contrary to a sober and pure relationship with Christ, the heavenly Bridegroom not only of humanity, but of every single soul.[4] His Mystical Body, the Church, must carefully avoid such extramarital poisoning, and persistently prepare for the marriage feast of the Lamb (19:7–8).

As he experienced before (1:10; 4:2), the sacred author is again ecstatically taken into the visionary action: "So he carried me away in the spirit into a wilderness, and I saw a woman sitting on a scarlet beast that was full of blasphemous names, and it had seven heads and ten horns" (v. 3). Such pneumatic

2. The angels are never seen sitting down in the Apocalypse, which seems only logical, given their spiritual nature and their mission as messengers.

3. Cf. Dante Alighieri, *Divine Comedy, Inferno*, Canto 19:107.

4. Also mindful of the Old Testament theonym "Baal" (בעל, Βάαλ), that Canaanite-Phoenician deity, part of the Mesopotamian and Semitic pantheon, whose name means at the same time "Lord, master, owner" and "husband," further illustrating the scriptural association between idolatry and adultery (e.g., 1 Kgs 18:18).

teleportation, as it were, was lived through already by the pre-Noahic patriarch Enoch (Gen 5:24), the prophets Elijah (1 Kgs 18:12), Ezekiel (Ezek 8:3), and Habakkuk (Dan 14:36), the deacon Philip (Acts 8:39–40), as well as the apostle Paul (2 Cor 12:1–4), to mention but a few. Jesus himself was transported by the tempter from the desert both to the temple's pinnacle and to a very high mountain (Matt 4:5, 8), and as Risen Lord he frequently appeared to his disciples, seemingly autonomous as regards time or space (e.g., Luke 24:15). Thus, inserting himself into that long-standing biblical tradition, John is now transferred into a desert with all its positive and negative connotations. Certainly a classical site of contemplation, fit for spiritual combat, this austere setting becomes his apparent vantage point for his visions up to 21:10.

Even though in its desolation, the wilderness was regarded as a prime haunt of demons and renegades (Lev 16:10), it was also chosen as the woman's refuge (12:6). That she is now joined by another female figure, the great prostitute, constitutes a challenge for the reader: are the two somewhat indistinguishable like the parabolic wheat and tares (Matt 13:24–30)? Upon further discernment, however, one realizes that the desert is a place of mere pilgrimage for the former woman, but a home for the latter. Here, the former shall be delivered from the ancient serpent, whereas the latter is doomed to destruction by it. Seen together, water and wilderness (v. 1; cf. 12:15) in their borderless vastness signal the inherent magnitude and universality of human sin, and, consequently, the reality of Christian hardship and persecution across the centuries.

Speaking of the beast, it now functions as the whore's mount[5] in addition to the many waters (v. 3), antithetical to the eagle-winged or non-sedentary Mother (12:14). Its scarlet color, seven heads, ten horns, and blasphemies betray its affiliation with both the dragon (12:3) and the sea-beast (13:1). In its bloody livery the beast symbolizes any empty show of mundane independence, oppressive authority, and cruelty not only of the Roman empire, but of all agnostic world-power ever since. To draw support from it is the reason why the woman allies herself with it, not unlike the land-beast or false prophet that is inspired by the first beast (13:12), even though she also has control over it and gives it guidance. One might say that Satan, in addition to his violent stratagems, tries to seduce her by the allurements of the world. While Jesus resisted him in the desert, she is overcome by this temptation, again in representation of the apostate world. If the living creatures are full of eyes all around and inside (4:6), tokens of true intelligence and ready obedience, this beast

5. See also the mythological depictions of Dea Roma riding on a beast, Bacchante on a lion, or Astarte on a panther.

is now teeming with blasphemous names, no longer limited to its head (13:1), attempting to rival and usurp divinity (2 Thess 2:4).[6] This seems to mark a final development of its hostility against God under the harlot's superintendence, putting forth pretensions of lawlessness and self-sufficiency. By its seven heads of plenary dominion on earth and its ten horns of temporary plenitude of ungodly might, it signals a concentration of sinfulness and embodies humanity's self-divinizing philosophy opposed to God.[7]

After having accounted for some of the sea-beast's exterior, John now reverts to the central female character: "The woman was clothed in purple and scarlet, and adorned with gold and jewels and pearls, holding in her hand a golden cup full of abominations and the impurities of her fornication" (v. 4). Arrayed in utmost pomp (18:12, 16), she is even more reddish than the beast, adding scarlet[8] to the purple.[9] While employing these two adjectives, the visionary does not finish the line of thought and define the type of dress in which she is clad, but only highlights its colors, discontinuing this first part of the verse. Among Mediterranean cultures, incidentally, the much-prized purple often symbolized times of peace, while scarlet stood for epochs of war. Tellingly, in the Apocalypse, the faithful are arrayed in white (3:5), in sackcloth (11:3), or in bright and pure linen (19:8), but never in self-congratulatory purple and crimson. These dazzling insignia unmask the woman's ambitions to rule like a queen (18:7), yet her earthly power is sadly perverted by vanity and homicidal cruelty (v. 6), a veritable anti-Mary (Ps 45:9). Her meretricious trappings are intended to make people compromise the truth of God through flattery and fear.[10] Further aggravating her ostentation is the fact that she is literally covered in finest gold, jewels, and pearls,[11] clashing with her deserted milieu.

6. Cf. AvS, 546.

7. Another solecism should be noted in this verse, where the masculine of the participle *échōn* (ἔχων, *habentem*) is disconnected from both the preceding feminine noun *gynaîka* (γυναῖκα, *mulierem*) and the neuter noun *thēríon* (θηρίον, *bestiam*); this discrepancy could be construed as a cue to reconnect it with the masculine *drákōn* (δράκων, *draco*) at 12:3, as the real mastermind behind those subsequent iterations of evil in the world; several manuscripts, in an effort to rectify this tension, read the correct neuter participle *échon* (ἔχον) in its relation to the beast.

8. Designating a bright red color (*coccinus*) at times with an orange tinge produced by the cochineal dye, lighter than the deep red crimson or carmine.

9. Specifying a spectrum of colors with hues between red and blue (*purpura*), customary in ancient times for royal attire.

10. Cf. RD, 1132.

11. In the Greek original, the participle *kechrysōménē* (κεχρυσωμένη), "gilded," naturally labels the noun *chrysíō* (χρυσίῳ), "gold," but it also stands zeugmatically to the collective

She also exposes herself as a travesty of the bejeweled Bride of the Lamb, that is, the New Jerusalem (21:2, 9–23). Decked out as she is in excessive adornments, she makes it clear that she is not related to a legitimate husband, but that she indulges in the hypocrisy and deceit of brothels.[12] These sparkling diamonds and shimmering pearls of hers become an antipode of God's Kingdom. The glittering cup she is holding evokes the drugs and potions that prostitutes would offer their clients to inflame lustful desire, such as in ancient Babylon. Figuratively speaking, this intoxication means the alluring arts by which the harlot incites human hearts to immorality and idolatry. It amounts to seduction into sin as the ultimate drunkenness and degradation, changing their divine likeness into some brutish form. Using Old Testament cultic language, John interprets the goblet's contents as abominable corruption, referring to the filthiness of idolatrous and sexual depravation (Lev 18:22–30). Thus, this high-society courtesan, empowered by her beastly mount, and made prosperous by the donations of her unchaste clients, suggests an intrigue between impious state power and world economy. And until she is made to consume the cup of divine wrath, she will not only invite spiritual drunkenness, but also, in a perverse twist of fortunes, use her own cup to scoop up and then ingest the blood of saints and martyrs (v. 6).

In a steady upward movement, the apostle's eye has passed from the scarlet beast to the harlot's dazzling attire, and from the gesture of her hand it is now completely lifted up as he depicts this feature of her face: "On her forehead was written a name, a mystery: 'Babylon the great, mother of whores and of earth's abominations'" (v. 5). This name is noteworthily dissimilar from the inscription etched upon the high priest's miter (Exod 28:36), but also from the title affixed above Christ's head on the Cross (John 19:19). As a badge of identity, it upholds the contraposition between those who are sealed by God and those who have fallen victim to the devil. A possible innuendo to the ancient Hellenic-Roman practice of notorious prostitutes, who had their names emblazoned on a circlet around their foreheads or even upon the fronts of their houses,[13] the name brazenly advertises the impudence of this spiritual harlot: she openly declares the shame and guilt of her idolatrous worship, she pleads for it, and ensnares souls to join in it with her.[14]

expression *lítho timíō* (λίθῳ τιμίῳ), "precious stone," and the plural noun *margarítais* (μαργαρίταις), "pearls."

12. Cf. AvS, 547.

13. Cf. Seneca the Elder, *Controversiae*, 1.2; Juvenal, *Satire*, 4.114–35.

14. Cf. RD, 1133–34.

The appositive "mystery" (v. 5) means that her name is not to be understood literally, but rather as a symbol (11:8). It is something hidden and enigmatic, impossible to be unveiled by mere reason, yet now about to be revealed (v. 7), and to become manifest in due time also through "the man of lawlessness" (*homo iniquitatis*) as the embodiment of all evil (2 Thess 2:3). Hers is the mystery of iniquity, a murky secret of confusion (Gen 11:9), of deceptive haughtiness, of spiritual tyranny and of idol worship. She is the leaven of original sin, its proliferation through the ages, the carcinogen of false religion, the glorification of wickedness, the travesty of divine mysteries, and the precise antipode to God and his pilgrim people.[15] Introduced in Revelation at 14:8, and in literary proximity to Daniel 4:30,[16] the woman's mysterious name is "Babylon the great" (*Babylon magna*), conjuring up painful memories of Israel's exile (Matt 1:11; Acts 7:43). What Babylon had been in the days of the Old Testament prophets, namely, "the hammer of the whole earth" and "a horror among the nations" (Jer 50:23), Rome would have been at the time of John's writing (1 Pet 5:13).[17]

She is synonymous, too, with the worldly Jerusalem that crucified Jesus, also known as Sodom and Egypt (11:8). All of these place-names are bywords for idolatry of the unfaithful, as well as persecution of the righteous. Here she becomes the metaphorical capital of the entire anti-Christian empire, the city of sinful humanity, intensifying the fate of the wilderness.[18] Despite her global expanse and influence, she is not the maternal "Jerusalem above" that Christians await (Gal 4:26). Instead, she is the progenitor of irreligious and impure offspring, the ringleader of her ungodly satraps on earth. Nourisher and patroness of countless children, she promotes mental and carnal vice of every kind.[19] Thus, "Babylon the great" is the apocalyptic code name for the matrix of anybody opposing the *Mater Ecclesiae*. In antithesis to the glorious Mother of 12:1–2, she exists to counter the Church of Christ as the anti-Mary, the figurehead of faithless souls. World-history, therefore, becomes the epic theater for the unequal battle between the great harlot and the beast on the one side, and the Bride and the Lamb on the other, until the former alliance is conquered by the Lord of lords and King of kings (v. 14).

It must have taken the apostle a little while to observe her behavior before

15. Cf. RD, 1135; AvS, 549.

16. Spoken immediately before King Nebuchadnezzar's downfall, cf. Dan 4:31–33.

17. Cf. John Tickle, *The Book of Revelation: A Catholic Interpretation of the Apocalypse* (Liguori, MO: Liguori Publications, 1983), 109.

18. Cf. Dante Alighieri, *Divine Comedy, Inferno*, Canto 19:109–17.

19. Called "universality of wickedness" (*universitas impiorum*) by Rupert, cf. RD, 1134.

he was able to provide the following detail: "And I saw that the woman was drunk with the blood of the saints and the blood of the witnesses to Jesus" (v. 6). Not only is she responsible for the worldwide delirium of godlessness, but she herself is in a state of acute insobriety.[20] This her loathsomeness puts on display her utter lack of self-awareness, of a female sense of dignity and self-control. By now the reader has gathered a comprehensive picture regarding the harlot's intimate association with the sea-beast, her luxurious attire, her profession as a prostitute, and her licentious activities. This embodiment of secular power adversarial to God is culpable of the double crime of inciting apostasy and large-scale murder. Both were traits of pagan Rome yet perpetuate themselves throughout the ages and cultures; both are of utmost gravity, making the reign of the antichrist infamous and detestable. Her clothing reflects the lifeblood of her victims, denoting another point of contrast with the woman clad with the sun (12:1): the former is a drunken persecutor, while the latter maintains her sobriety to flee from persecution (12:14). To see someone intoxicated is a shameful sight; but to notice that the person is drunk with human blood, is unspeakably monstrous and jarring.

Hence, this mystical Babylon is closer in nature to the red dragon (12:3), the murderer from the beginning, than to humans. Her animalistic and devilish blood-slurping will find its match in the cannibalistic flesh-eating of the kings at the time of her own demise (v. 16). She gorges herself on the precious blood of saints and witnesses of our Lord, those who believe in his Gospel of life, among them the early protomartyrs Stephen (Acts 7:60), John's own brother James (Acts 12:2), and Pergamum's Antipas (2:13). They themselves had been redeemed by Christ's blood and offered their own in atonement for their persecutors and hangmen. Yet, the more the great harlot consumes this sacred stream of blood, enraged in drunken stupor and obstinacy against the Author of all good, the more she rejects God's work of salvation.[21] John subjoins: "When I saw her, I was greatly amazed" (v. 6). With a touch of Semitic phrasing ("to wonder . . . with wonder"), and unlike those earthly-minded persons who marvel at or are impressed by the blasphemous brilliancy of the beast (13:3), he is struck by the vile alliance between the whore and the wild beast, wondering how Satan can disguise himself as an angel of light (2 Cor 11:14). There may also be wonderment about the fallen angels being governed by this anti-Marian

20. The active participle of the Greek verb *methýō* (μεθύω) underscores the process of drinking freely, whereas the Neo-Vulgate's adjective *ēbria* suggests the end-result of being fully intoxicated.

21. Cf. AvS, 550.

entity, since at the dawn of time they refused to serve the mystery of the forthcoming Incarnation of the God-Man, born in Bethlehem of a humble woman.

These initial six verses of the chapter are so replete again with imagery that it seems necessary to pause for a moment, take a deep breath, and digest the spiritual undercurrent of what has been shown to us. As always, it is a matter of translating symbols into the Christian life today, as Jesus encourages us to do (Luke 12:56). Such a spiritual-theological roundup might start with the insight that the harlot is only "great" in her own subjective estimation and vainglory. Objectively, she represents the worst that has ever existed.[22] And so, in the sanctuary of our hearts we must remain unassuming and avoid doing things out of haughtiness or selfish ambition (Rom 12:16; Phil 2:3).

Also worth pondering is the clash between John's virginal purity and the whore's impurities, whose sight he must endure (Hab 1:13). In response to that painful showdown, we continue to commit ourselves to Christian chastity, praying to obtain this precious gift both for ourselves and for others, combining the beatitudes of a pure heart (Matt 5:8) with that of hungering and thirsting for righteousness (Matt 5:6).[23] There ought to be a sense of hope and satisfaction, too, knowing that the Almighty will bring about that justice one day.[24] Is it not also reassuring that it takes just one angel to reveal the vanquishing of the totality of evil? So much for the harlot's "greatness"![25] Moreover, while she is sitting down in torpidity, we must prefer the status of being pilgrims, tirelessly walking through the wilderness for the "forty years" of our earthly lifetime (Josh 5:6). Then also, why not interpret the "many waters" (v. 1) as a sign of the fluidity of our human nature with its weakness and passions? As an antidote, a personal devotion to the Virgin Mary will both strengthen our interior life, protecting us from the anti-Marian scheming, and lead us deeper into the loving heart of the Church.[26]

Furthermore, Babylon's intoxication (v. 6) cautions the faithful to not get caught up in the anesthetizing effect of earthly addictions, making one lose the virtue of vigilant discernment.[27] Since the apostle is carried away into the desert (v. 3), we should imitate him by cultivating a type of interiority that is able to reconcile worldly activity with heavenly contemplation.[28] Only then will

22. Cf. RD, 1131.
23. Cf. AvS, 540.
24. Cf. RD, 1130.
25. Cf. AvS, 539.
26. Cf. St. Thérèse of Lisieux, *Story of a Soul*, ch. 9.
27. Cf. AvS, 541.
28. Cf. AvS, 543–45.

the soul be able to trust God more than temporal realities (Ps 146:3), as implied by the woman supported by the beast. The attraction of her and the beast's femininity[29] might also symbolize Satan's attempt to control the human heart with sentiments of false surrender, commitment, and devotion. Then there is the aspect of blatant hypocrisy in the way she decks herself out with finery and gems all the while being morally rotten on the inside, teaching us to keep the interior and the exterior dimensions of our earthly existence in harmony.[30]

What is more, the empty enticement of the diabolically scintillating goblet and mystery (vv. 4–5) must not distract us from the mystery of our Christian Catholic faith (*mysterium fidei*), that is, the participation in the Body and Blood of Christ. If the apocalyptic prostitute suggests the blinding unanimity of the world's socioeconomic guilds of powers, then the followers of the Lord Jesus are well-advised to practice evangelical simplicity or even poverty for the Kingdom (Matt 19:21), which has entailed in the past, and can still do so in the future, becoming marginalized from the contemporary mainstream, or even excluded from cultural and economic conveniences: "*Timeo Dánaos et dona ferentes.*"[31] Lastly, St. John's amazement (v. 6) is in solidarity with all sinners who again and again fall for the siren songs of the devil.[32] Similar to the apostle, we should be astonished at the perverted logic of instrumentalizing good, such as womanhood, water, wine, or even human blood, for the purpose of evil.[33] But let us now advance into the second part of this chapter.

Cryptic fascination (17:7–8)

[7]But the angel said to me, "Why are you so amazed? I will tell you the mystery of the woman, and of the beast with seven heads and ten horns that carries her. [8]The beast that you saw was, and is not, and is about to ascend from the bottomless pit and go to destruction. And the inhabitants of the earth, whose names have not been written in the book of life from the foundation of the world, will be amazed when they see the beast, because it was and is not and is to come.

---

29. See the feminine gender of the Latin word for "beast," *bestia*.

30. Cf. RD, 1132.

31. Paraphrased as "Beware of Greeks bearing gifts," a phrase from Virgil's *Aeneid*, spoken by the Trojan priest Laocoön: it refers to the Trojan Horse used by the Hellenes during the Trojan War, warning against trusting the adversary, even when they appear to be making an enticing offer.

32. Cf. RD, 1136.

33. Cf. AvS, 550.

Drawing heavily again on the imagery of the prophet Daniel (chs. 7–8), and at the same time expanding on Revelation 13, vv. 7–18 have a pronounced futuristic touch, with no fewer than seventeen verbs set in the future tense according to the New Vulgate. Resuming the scene of v. 3, the seer continues: "But the angel said to me, 'Why are you so amazed? I will tell you the mystery of the woman, and of the beast with seven heads and ten horns that carries her'" (v. 7). Doubtlessly struck by his startled reaction, the angel seems to read it as an amazement of stupefaction or incomprehension, mixed with dismay and even distress at the woman's bloodthirstiness.[34] Was John perhaps also perplexed by the fact that he has not yet seen the harlot's actual condemnation as promised him by the angel at the outset of this vision (v. 1), or confused about her identity, since her attire will turn out to be very similar to that of the Lamb's Bride (21:11–21)? Acknowledging, therefore, his bafflement, the angel's rhetorical question "Why?" cannot be a reproof, but rather an introduction to his own upcoming interpretation of the vision.

Interestingly, the images perceived are clearly not sufficient per se, but call for an inspired voice to illuminate their secret meaning, appropriately offered by a supernatural messenger (Dan 4:17). This, incidentally, will be the only vision expounded on by an angel throughout Revelation, and its tenor can henceforth serve as a hermeneutic key to unlock the significance of much of the remaining symbolism, wisely shepherding the reader through the book's intricate labyrinth.[35] That mystical elucidation ensues in vv. 8–18: woman and beast will be decrypted in an inverted order, that is, beginning with the story of the beast (vv. 8–14), followed by that of the woman (vv. 15–17), and reaching a finale in her renewed identification as Babylon (vv. 1, 5, 18). This palistrophic pattern[36] might be an intimation that the great city, the woman, and the beast are ultimately one and the same reality. It should not go unnoticed that the beast's act of carrying the woman is now characterized by the Greek verb *bastázō* (βαστάζω, v. 7b), frequently connoting the bearing of a burden (e.g., Matt 20:12). Thus, it could be an inkling of the lurking hatred that will explode in a shockingly brutal way between the two at v. 16. That same verb also has the overtone of a child carried in its mother's womb (Luke 11:27), further consolidating the quasi-identicalness of beast and woman, if not even parodying the virginal pregnancy of 12:2.

34. Cf. AvS, 551.

35. Rupert terms the exemplary nature of the angel's interpretation as a "paradigm of universal truth" (*forma universæ veritatis*), cf. RD, 1137.

36. Other designations for this common literary device are thematic chiasmus, *inclusio*, concentric circle, or symmetric ring structure.

Here is the beginning of the angel's elaboration: "The beast that you saw was, and is not, and is about to ascend from the abyss and go to destruction. And the inhabitants of the earth, whose names have not been written in the book of life from the foundation of the world, will be amazed when they see the beast, because it was and is not and is to come" (v. 8). As an introductory overview, vv. 8–14 are organized in two waves, the first of which explains the beast's seven heads (vv. 8–10), and the second, while puzzlingly identifying it with an eighth head, shedding light on its ten horns (vv. 11–14). It is useful to underline that the main point of vv. 8–18 is the subdividing of the devil's activities, camouflaged as the beast, along world-history into three periods, namely, past, present, and future.

His *past* existence, that is, before and until the Incarnation of the Son of God, is articulated three times as "it has been" (*fuit*) or "it was" (*erat*) in vv. 8, 11. That describes the time when Satan ruled supreme in the world, mainly through tyrannical and idolatrous forms of government, but also over individual consciences by tempting them into sin. But then, and as suggested already by the mortal wound back in 13:3, as well as by the "five [that] have fallen" at v. 10, the devil's power is vanquished through the Death and Resurrection of the Lord, putting limits on his influence on earth (20:1–3).[37] Now, in the eschatological *present*, therefore, "it is not" (*non est*), repeated twice at vv. 8, 11. Simultaneously, however, and paradoxically so, it is still among us, as stated in v. 10, "one is living" (*unus est*), also symbolized by the healing of the sea-beast's fatal blow (13:3). Those ongoing tribulations in the concurrent nonexistence and existence of diabolical action are likewise indicated in 12:14, 17. Hence, a *future* undoing of all evil is being prepared, and it will take place on the last day, when it is cast into eternal perdition (20:7–10). That forthcoming epoch is communicated by the six phrases "and is about to ascend from the abyss and go to destruction" (v. 8), "is to come" (*aderit*; v. 8), "the other has not yet come" (v. 10), "it goes to destruction" (v. 11), "have not yet received" (v. 12a), and "are to receive for one hour" (v. 12b).

While these verses seem to accentuate the future, they describe the entire duration of the created visible world and its human history. All those who are corrupt and ungodly, and whose names are not enrolled in heaven (13:8), will rejoice at the sight[38] of the beast's revivification and its anti-Christianity, sym-

37. "For the days of his saving Passion and glorious Resurrection are approaching, by which the pride of the ancient foe is vanquished, and the mystery of our redemption is celebrated" (Roman Missal, *Preface of the Passion of the Lord* II).

38. Some manuscripts read the nominative *blépontes* (βλέποντες, "they are seeing") to harmonize with the preceding subject of the principal clause, i.e., the nominative *katoikoûntes* (κατοικοῦντες, reflected in the Neo-Vulgate *inhabitantes* [...] *videntes*), instead of the difficult

bolized by its sixth, seventh, and eighth heads (vv. 10–11). In typical Johannine fashion, humanity will always remain divided into just two groups, namely, those who follow the Lamb (14:1–5), and those who succumb to a cryptic fascination regarding the dragon, the self-proclaimed god of this world.

At the burning bush, Elohim revealed himself to Moses by the Hebrew phrase *Ehyē ašer ehyē* ("I Am Who I Am," 'Εγώ εἰμι ὁ ὤν, *Ego sum qui sum*; Exod 3:14), later framed as "Yahweh," stemming from the tri-consonantal root h-y-h (היה), meaning "to be" or "to come to pass," and traditionally spelled in four sacred letters or the tetragrammaton as YHWH (יהוה). This most holy name can be considered the archetype of the Apocalypse's periphrastic title of the Father, "who is, who was, and who is to come" (1:4), and of the Son: "I am the first and the last, and the living one" (1:17b–18a). When the beast is portrayed here as one who "was, and is not, and is about to ascend from the abyss," or as one "who was, and is not, and is to come," or again in v. 11 as one who "was and is not . . . and goes to destruction," then this intentional alteration could be called the anti-tetragrammaton, a travesty of the divine title and nature. All this diabolical monster can do is to ridicule God's historical ways of redemption.[39]

What is more, in its promise to be the one who "is to come," there is an antithetic parody of Christ's own parousia (3:11). That comparison is implied by the Greek word here employed, namely, *páreimi* (πάρειμι, *adesse*), functioning as the verbal stem of the cognate noun *parousía* (παρουσία, *adventus*), ordinarily used in the New Testament of the second coming of the Lord (e.g., Matt 24:27). Ominously, and unlike the angel that ascended from the sunrise (7:2), the beast shall come up out of hell, or, as the text says, the "abyss," i.e., the netherworld or bottomless pit. It should be remembered that throughout Revelation, this term is used to depict the abode of the devil while being operative in the world as an antichristic power. Its release on the boundary of history, corresponding to Satan's career as detailed in 20:1–10, will be most devastating, but is also a mere march to the grave, as it will end in its annihilation within the lake of fire that burns with brimstone (19:20). While God lives forever, his enemy will suffer total ruin, a wreckage that is preprogrammed, as it were.

What about the spiritual relevance of these first few words of angelic explanation to John on Patmos? His inquiring "Why are you so amazed?" (*Quare miraris?* v. 7) should make us ponder the needfulness of maintaining the highest

absolute genitive *blepóntōn* (βλεπόντων), that solecistically connects with the genitive pronoun *hṓn* (ὧν) of the subordinate clause.

39. Cf. RD, 1138.

level of admiration and awe for God's revelation and our acceptance of it with sincere faith, a faith that seeks also to understand. As baptized Christians, we experience the divine transcendence as something that makes us tremble (*mysterium tremendum*), and yet at the same time we feel irresistibly drawn to its truthful beauty and glory (*mysterium fascinosum*).[40] That overwhelming attraction then translates into prayerful reverence and adoration, but also into never-fading joy at the awareness of having been chosen to be a child of the Most High destined to live in him eternally.[41]

Related to that point is the encouragement to attentively listen to and discern the otherworldly voices of God, of his angels and saints, who communicate with our individual conscience, offering light, guidance, and understanding of the awesome *mysterium Christi* (Eph 3:4). Additionally, the unrelenting mockery of God's name on the part of the beast and its satraps in the anti-Christian world can inspire us to nurture the virtue of reverence for the Lord, habituating ourselves to always know the difference between the Creator and the creature. His faithful servants distinguish themselves in their use of speech in sacred matters, too, as directed by the Second Commandment of the Decalogue.[42]

And finally, no spirituality would be complete without a sound preparation for the hour of one's death. Just as Christ's return at the end of time will be preceded by the beast's rising from the infernal pit to wreak havoc (v. 8), so we can be certain that the demons will fight hard to snatch away our soul when our days on earth draw to a close. The Christian writer Sulpicius Severus chronicled this regarding the moment of St. Martin of Tours' death: "He saw the devil standing near: 'Why do you stand there, you bloodthirsty brute?' he cried. 'Murderer, you will not have me for your prey. Abraham is welcoming me into his embrace.' With these words, he gave up his spirit to heaven."[43]

40. The theologian Rudolf Otto (d. 1937) highlights the concept of the "numinous" (cf. Latin *numen*, meaning "divine presence and will"), or that which is "wholly other," having to do with divine power that undergirds all religious experience, and elicits silence and moral perfection; cf. *The Idea of the Holy*, trans John W. Harvey, 2nd ed. (Oxford: Oxford University Press, 1923).

41. Cf. AvS, 555.

42. Cf. *CCC*, §2142.

43. *Epistle* 3.14–17, 21 (SC 133:340–44); trans. from *Liturgy of the Hours*, vol. IV (New York: Catholic Book Publishing, 1975), 1553.

Fourth call: Sense of wisdom (17:9a)

[9a] This calls for a mind that has wisdom.

Unlike the previous three sapiential interjections that are articulated by the apostolic seer himself (13:10, 18; 14:12), the exhortation "This calls for a mind that has wisdom" (v. 9a) is most likely part of the angel's interpretive discourse. Even though its interpolation at this point appears to break the train of thought, much like Jesus' adjuration at 16:15, it also heightens the reader's focus on the explanation about to ensue. That this is the fourth and final such wisdom call in the Apocalypse is tied to the use of the Greek adverb for "here, thus" (ὧδε, *hic*) featured at the head of each one of them. There are only two more recurrences of this word in Revelation, and those are supernatural invitations to "come up here!," that is, into heaven (4:1; 11:12), enhancing the contextual meaning of this present pronouncement by the plague-angel.

When viewed together, not only do these four appeals occur in direct conjunction with visions of demonic darkness versus divine light, but they are also organized in an alternating rhyme scheme with two matching couplets (A-B-A'-B'): the first and the third remind one of the patience and faith of the saints (13:10; 14:12), whereas the second and fourth solicit wisdom and understanding (13:18; 17:9). This second couplet contains the additional commonality of investigating the sense of mysterious numbers, namely, "six hundred sixty-six" (13:18), and "one, five, seven, eight, ten" (17:9–12). There is a noticeable syntactic difference between 13:18 and 17:9, however, in that in the latter the human faculty of understanding is positioned ahead of wisdom and rendered by the Neo-Vulgate as *sensus* instead of *intellectum*. And when looking at the phrase in the original (*hôde ho noûs ho échōn sophían*, ὧδε ὁ νοῦς ὁ ἔχων σοφίαν), it translates as "this is the mind having wisdom." Hence, while 13:18 underlines the virtue of wisdom refined by human reason, this current call conversely emphasizes the mind's intellectual acumen enriched by wisdom.

Thus, the angel urges John, and consequently his audience, to make full use of one's God-given mental capacity, and to exert oneself in reflective thinking. Such religious intelligence, or "sense of the faithful" (*sensus fidelium*), is evinced in the ability to discover the deeper meaning of God's word and counsel (Rom 11:33). Intriguingly, the Greek noun *sophía* (σοφία) derives from the adjective *saphēs*, expressing the notion of being transparent: hence, a mind of wisdom is a mind ennobled by clarity and insight. That quality is equally conveyed by the Hebrew counterpart for wisdom, i.e., *chokmâh* (חָכְמָה), pointing to the broadest sense of cognitive power and knowledge, acquired by reason and experience, by learning and science. Therefore, this is not an occasion for simplistic or amateur interpretation, but it takes an earnest application of the mind illuminated by true sagacity from above, to spiritually discern the incongruity between the destinies of Lamb and dragon, and not be scandalized by the stumbling blocks of history.[44] Taking into account that watermark adverb "here," we feel impelled to acquire and embrace that wise comprehension in the present moment, in the "here and now," especially by paying sincere attention to Sacred Scripture. A requisite for upright living, such wise thinking will lift us up to grasp what must take place, to rescue us from our enemies, and ultimately to find salvation in Christ, "in whom are hidden all the treasures of wisdom and knowledge" (Col 2:3).

Hour-long collusion (17:9b–14)

9b The seven heads are seven mountains on which the woman is seated;
also, they are seven kings, 10 of whom five have fallen, one is living, and
the other has not yet come; and when he comes, he must remain only
a little while. 11 As for the beast that was and is not, it is an eighth but it
belongs to the seven, and it goes to destruction. 12 And the ten horns that
you saw are ten kings who have not yet received a kingdom, but they
are to receive authority as kings for one hour, together with the beast.
13 These are united in yielding their power and authority to the beast;
14 they will make war on the Lamb, and the Lamb will conquer them,
for he is Lord of lords and King of kings, and those with him are called
and chosen and faithful."

Having been given the above sapiential impetus, the reader is now ready for the angel to lift the veil of the secret: "The seven heads are seven mountains on which the woman is seated; also, they are seven kings" (v. 9b). With a puzzling ability to adapt herself to changing whereabouts, the woman is said to not only be seated on many waters (v. 1) and on the scarlet beast (v. 3), but now also on seven mountains that in turn are identical with as many kings. By reiterating the auxiliary verb "are," the angelic illustrator decrypts the symbolism unambiguously. Mountains in the language of the Old Testament, had already been taken as images of hindrance against God's cause on earth (e.g., Ps 68:16). Curiously, infamous Babylon, even though geographically situated on a vast plain, becomes "a destroying mountain," too (Jer 51:25). Yet the most obvious

44. Cf. AvS, 555.

application, especially for the first-century Christians, would have been to the seven-hilled city of Rome (*Roma septicollis*) upon which reclined its eponymous goddess.[45] Later on, Byzantine Constantinople was also known as the City on the Seven Hills.

In any case, seven mountains signal the fullness of world-power in a state of rebellion against the Lord's designs in history, turning themselves into bastions of idolatry and tyranny. As such, they are antipodean to sacred mountains like Sinai, Jerusalem's Zion, Tabor, Golgotha, and the "great high mountain" of the holy city (21:10). The latter could be said to be foreshadowed in the mysterious stone that grows into a mountain of planetary dimension according to Daniel's interpretation of King Nebuchadnezzar's dream (Dan 2:34–35), embodying the Messiah's universal Kingdom about to supplant all earthly dominions (Cant 2:8). This is why the seven heads of the beast are also seven kings, intimated already by the crowned heads of the locusts at 9:7, suggesting a complete succession of secular governments present in every generation. They shall be subdued, however, by the King of the universe, "The Word of God," in his coronation with many diadems (19:12–13).

Concerning those seven royals, the good angel continues, "Five have fallen, one is living, and the other has not yet come; and when he comes, he must remain only a little while" (v. 10). This is simply a rephrasing of the formulaic notion found in vv. 8, 11, namely, the triadic division of human history[46] into past, present, and future, leading to Satan's defeat and the establishment of God's reign. The verb "fallen," incidentally, is a Septuagint coefficient for the tragic demolition of regal power (e.g., Isa 21:9), also in accord with the archetypal vision of Daniel 7. Therefore, when John wrote this prophecy, "five"[47] worldly empires had already suffered their cyclical breakdown, as the case may have been. Included among them were the well-known yet God-opposing superpowers of antiquity, namely, Egypt, Medo-Persia, Assyria, Babylon, and Greece. As stated above, the "living one," the sixth, would have been Rome, but

45. See the effigy of Dea Roma on a Vespasian sesterce (AD 70); of note here, too, is the ancient Roman fall festival of "Seven-Hills" (*Septimontium*).

46. Akin, for instance, to the Gospel of Matthew's opening genealogy, organized in a trichotomous way (Matt 1:17).

47. A congenial number for us humans, as it can be naturally counted on one hand; as such it is a common feature in the New Testament, mainly as part of Jesus' parables, like the "loaves" (Matt 14:17), "foolish and prudent virgins" (Matt 25:2), "talents" (Matt 25:15), "months" (Luke 1:24), "sparrows" (Luke 12:6), "family members" (Luke 12:52), "yoke of oxen" (Luke 14:19), "brothers" (Luke 16:28), "pounds" (Luke 19:18), "cities" (Luke 19:19), "husbands" (John 4:18), "porticoes" (John 5:2), "days" (Acts 20:6), and "words" (1 Cor 14:19).

signifies any despotic regime in our own day, contemporaneous to our lifespan. Its singularity might hint at the relative imminence of the eschatological seventh power as the final onslaught of the antichrist.

Hence, we are today, as Christians have been for two millennia for that matter, in the middle of this epic plot, characterized on other occasions as "ten days" (2:10), "a time, and times, and half a time" (12:14), "forty-two months" (11:2), "twelve hundred and sixty days" (11:3), and "a thousand years" (20:2). Before long, the Apocalypse will retell the same paradigm pivoting around the idea of a chiliastic reign at 20:1–10, and how at the end of it Satan will be let out just for a little while. This short period represents the eschatological remainder of the time of the world's existence, likely identical also to the "one hour" at v. 12, and to the "three and a half days" at 11:9.

Referring to his words in v. 8, the angel carries on: "As for the beast that was and is not, it is an eighth, but it belongs to the seven, and it goes to destruction" (v. 11). In intertextual closeness to "Noah the eighth" (2 Pet 2:5), the eminent figurehead of his family, the body of the monster remains the chief manifestation and support for the its collection of heads.[48] No eighth kingdom shall emerge, but it symbolizes Satan as the unchanged and meta-historical sum-total of "seven" iterations of worldly power. In him all devilish might is concentrated and consummated, outstripping everything in wickedness, just prior to its convulsive ebbing away when Christ returns. That this antichristic messiah, this apocalyptic *Nero redivivus*, is spoken of in this verse as a personal entity can be proven by the grammatical switch from the neuter *thēríon* (θηρίον), "beast," to the masculine pronoun *autós* (αὐτός), "he." His final doom is reasserted, the savage sputtering and flickering of dying power, as he is headed toward his eternal ruin, as narrated once more at 20:7–10. He does not merely fall like his seven minions, but his is a total loss and complete severance from all hope and from all that is good.[49] His treacherous eighth existence may be mocking the Lord's Resurrection after the sabbatical day, but this monster will go down in shameful destruction, while the Church passes on toward her supernal glory.

Further elaborating on the future appearance of the beast, and the seventh king yet to come, the angel announces: "And the ten horns that you saw are ten kings who have not yet received a kingdom, but they are to receive authority as

48. One could contend that the absence of the article before *ógdoos* (ὄγδοος), "eighth," demonstrates that the beast is not one more element in succession of the previous seven, but rather that it is their synthesis.

49. Considering that the Greek noun *apṓleia* (ἀπώλεια, *interitum*), occurring only here and in v. 8 in Revelation, stems from the verb *apóllymi* (ἀπόλλυμι), conveying the idea of being cut off entirely, to perish utterly, or be lost violently and permanently.

kings for one hour, together with the beast" (v. 12). Methodically, he reminds John of the individual facets of his earlier vision (vv. 1–6), interpreting them one by one. No fewer than five times he repeats the indicator "that you saw," including here. In the present case, he calls his attention to the ten horns described in vv. 3, 7, and through them back to the sea-beast at 13:1, and even to the dragon himself (12:3), as the frontman, as it were, of hostility against the Lamb. It is conceivable that the number "ten"[50] also brought back to the seer's mind the specter of the devil imprisoning some of the Smyrnaean Christians, causing ten days of tribulation (2:10).

Be that as it may, ten is an apocalyptic cipher for temporal or spatial completeness and sufficiency that bears within it earthly finiteness as opposed to divine infinity. In Revelation, it is consistently coupled with "seven" in speaking about dragon and beast. Together with the "horn" as a biblical figure for untamed power, this decemvirate of forthcoming regality enjoys widespread but not unlimited worldly influence. Unlike the first six superpowers, these ten yet uncrowned kings are identical to the seventh king of v. 10 in the scriptural tradition of Daniel's approaching "fourth kingdom" (Dan 2:40). While it is true that they are much more numerous, they are also imbued with much less might. There is vagueness about the character of this tenfold collectivity due to the indefinite relative pronoun *hoítines* (οἵτινες) in the original, meaning "whosoever has not yet received a kingdom." This relative inscrutableness of the text is an intentional cue for the reader not to take it in a literal sense; the same holds true for the expression "analogous to kings" (*tamquam reges*). Nevertheless, for the Christians of the apostolic age, this might have conjured up the legendary scene of a revived Nero surrounding himself with Parthian cohorts to accompany his march on Rome, in a desperate attempt to regain governance.

What is made abundantly clear again, this time by reiterating the verb "to receive" (v. 12a), is that these upcoming manifestations of ungodly rule will not be autonomous in any way, but will ultimately act under God's providential control and sovereignty. Although it is not disclosed from what source this power is received, God or Satan, it is simply implied that it will in fact be imparted on them as on ignoble vassals. Which lays bare yet another infernal paradox, namely, that these kings or kingdoms are at the same time royals

50. In logical correlation to the above "five," "ten" is also an important part of Jesus' parabolic teachings regarding the "virgins" (Matt 25:1), the "talents" (Matt 25:28), the "silver coins" (Luke 15:8), the "lepers" (Luke 17:12), the "servants" (Luke 19:13), the "pounds" (Luke 19:16), and the "cities" (Luke 19:17).

and underlings, contemporary serfs with the beast, and simultaneous with the eighth king, who in turn embodies the antichrist. Previously called "a little while" (v. 10), this hour-long alliance between these mundane rulers and the wild beast is yet another parody of God's own workings:[51] it apes not just Jesus' own promise of "a little while" (John 16:16), but also derides his salvific hour of mutual glorification with his heavenly Father (John 17:1). Satan parrots the Divine since in his corruption he is incapable of imaginativeness or originality, let alone of creating anything out of nothing (*creatio ex nihilo*). No longer forty-two months of struggle, this short duration of diabolical onslaught, which yet again encapsulates the whole period of the world's existence,[52] also predicts the arrival of the Lord's permanent Kingdom, a byproduct of which will be eternal damnation.

More is said now about the collusion between that royal decennary and the monster, namely, that they are "united in yielding their power and authority to the beast" (v. 13). Perfect unison is what characterizes the forces of evil in this world, forming "one single council" (*unum consilium*; cf. v. 17)[53] to render wholehearted support and intellectual submission to the beast. And they purposely abuse their position of leadership to corrupt their peoples.[54] That this hour-long collusion is in fact an ongoing one is exposed by the narrative present tense of the New Vulgate's predicate *tradunt* ("they yield"). This verb also makes known the thoroughness of iniquitous surrender, as those feckless kings become the upholders and dependent allies of the authority of Satan, who aspires to nothing more than to be the despot of all despots.

What will happen next is then foreshown: "They will make war on the Lamb, and the Lamb will conquer them, for he is Lord of lords and King of kings, and those with him are called and chosen and faithful" (v. 14). Warfare has been in the air since 9:7 and 12:7, remaining an unabating travel companion for all generations, a dreary shadow that will not dissipate until the final battle is fought (20:8). As indicated by the main verbs' future tense (*pugnabunt*, "they will make war"; *vincet*, "he will conquer"), at issue will be a climactic

51. Cf. Sophie Laws, *In the Light of the Lamb: Imagery, Parody and Theology in the Apocalypse of John*, GNS 31 (Wilmington, DE: M. Glazier, 1988).

52. In accord with the logic of "one day like a thousand years" (2 Pet 3:8), as well as "sufficient time" (Luke 20:9).

53. The Greek noun *gnṓmē* (γνώμη), "purpose, intent, consent, opinion," stems from the verb *ginṓskō* (γινώσκω), meaning "to learn" and "to know," and thus stresses intellectual judgment based on experiential knowledge.

54. See the Latin adage "Corruptio optimi pessima" ("the corruption of the best is the worst of all").

moment of that perduring conflict that sees secularity pitched against spirituality. Whenever and wherever policies are decided on in favor of ungodliness or oppression, they are at war with the Lamb (Luke 11:23). This decisive conflict marks the first time in the Apocalypse that the divine Lion-Lamb involves himself in earthly action, and he does so as the one true King of all kings, as fully unveiled at 19:16.[55]

That sublime quality is his by virtue of being the Firstborn of all creation and of the Church (Col 1:15, 18), and it winds up being the reason for his smashing victory at the figurative Harmagedon. To be triumphant is nothing new for him, however, since he has vanquished countless enemies in the past, beginning with the Egyptian Pharaoh during Israel's Exodus. What is more, he has accomplished these feats oftentimes through the weaker party involved.[56] Those who follow the Lamb wherever he goes (14:4), joining him in his victory, receive a trifecta of honorific cognomens. First, they are "called" (*vocati*)[57] into sainthood through divine purpose. Second, they are the few who are "chosen" (*electi*)[58] in grace for glory and have reciprocated with loyalty, unlike the admirers of the beast. That is why they have also earned the third epithet of "faithful" (*fideles*),[59] that is, worthy partakers in Jesus' own title and word. These are the persons of integrity and uprightness who steadfastly adhere to the Lord and his Gospel even amidst protracted trials. Heretofore unseen in heaven, now they appear with him, his dependable soldiers and servants. Reference is also made to the inherent progression of Christian life: in baptism one is *called* to serve God; then, by devoting one's life to him becomes his *chosen* one; and by remaining *faithful* to him one shares in his victory.

After having inclined our ear and applied our mind to the angel's decoding of the symbolism of the beast's heads and horns in these vv. 9b–14, may his message now become spiritual and lift up our heart. To start with, there is the realization that mundane authority, implied by the above conga line of kings, is

55. Scriptural precedents to this majestic title are found in Deut 10:17; Ps 136:2–3; 2 Macc 13:4; 1 Tim 6:15.

56. E.g., David and Goliath (1 Sam 17:50), Judith and Holofernes (Judith 13:15), Queen Esther and Haman (Esther 7:10).

57. The adjective *klētós* (κλητός), "called," surprisingly a *hapax legomenon* in Revelation, derives from the verb *kaléō* (καλέω), "to call," which in turn is at the root of the noun *ekklēsía* (ἐκκλησία), meaning "Church," or literally, "a people called forth," i.e., out of the world toward God.

58. The adjective *eklektós* (ἐκλεκτός), "chosen," is yet another *hapax legomenon* in this book, implying a personal preference, an intentional pick of a favorite.

59. The adjective *pistós* (πιστός), "faithful," is derivative of the verb *peíthō* (πείθω), which in its passive voice signifies someone who is persuaded of something trustworthy.

most susceptible to working hand in glove with demonic corruption and collusion. Or, as the English historian Lord Acton once quipped: "Power tends to corrupt, and absolute power corrupts absolutely; great men are almost always bad men."[60] Jesus' stern proviso regarding the rich in this world also comes to mind: "It is easier for a camel to pass through the eye of a needle than for a rich man to enter the kingdom of God" (Matt 19:24). And if heads and horns are viewed as a grotesque parody of the seven gifts of the Holy Spirit and the Ten Commandments, then let us be resolved never to compromise with evil, lest one suffer eventual downfall through it like the five kings. Rather, iniquity in the human heart must be wrestled down and into oblivion, even though the very percentile of five out of seven (vv. 9–10) would indicate that it cannot be overcome completely. Naturally, the image does not only refer to heads of state, but possibly to the heads of bodies as well, meaning, the human spirit given to a mentality of anarchy or revolt against the Spirit of God.

Also worth meditating upon is the satanic contradiction of simultaneously "being" and "not being" in its rejection of salvation (v. 11), a volatility that can only result in perdition. What the Christian can learn from that power-hungry decuplet of kings, awaiting their hour of wicked fame, is not to act in premeditated or presumptive pride.[61] Along with it, may our spiritual association with a local ecclesial community such as a diocese, a parish, or a religious order, prevent us from falling for the unethical unanimity of the guilds of the anti-Christic or anti-Marian beast (v. 13).[62] In addition to that, the gallant defeat of the devil showcases how the relative dualism of the Apocalypse will end, and how each one of us, disciples of the Lord, must take sides with determination.[63] By embracing his holy Gospel and receiving God's grace, the soul will be fitted even for the toughest combat and will surely share in its unfaltering successes and eventual victory.[64]

60. From his letter to Mandell Creighton, Archbishop of the Church of England (April 5, 1887), par. 7, in *Historical Essays and Studies*, ed. John Neville Figgis and Reginald Vere Laurence (London: Macmillan, 1907).

61. Cf. AvS, 563.

62. Cf. RD, 1141.

63. Cf. AvS, 564–65.

64. Cf. RD, 1142.

Evil's cannibalization (17:15–18)

[15]And he said to me, "The waters that you saw, where the whore is seated, are peoples and multitudes and nations and languages. [16]And the ten horns that you saw, they and the beast will hate the whore; they will make her desolate and naked; they will devour her flesh and burn her up with fire. [17]For God has put it into their hearts to carry out his purpose by agreeing to give their kingdom to the beast, until the words of God will be fulfilled. [18]The woman you saw is the great city that rules over the kings of the earth."

As the angel continues to unriddle the mystery, John hears him say: "The waters that you saw, where the whore is seated, are peoples and multitudes and nations and languages" (v. 15). Taken back to the beginning of his vision (v. 1), he is offered another hermeneutic key that not only unlocks a further facet of imagery but consolidates the concept that all these images ought to be interpreted not literally, but symbolically: that is now an established datum, in order to accurately understand this apocalyptic genre, so unique in the New Testament. Here, the unambiguous equivalency between figure and reality is again conveyed by the verb "are" (*sunt*; cf. 1:20). Although no longer classified as "many" (v. 1), but still in the grammatical plural (*aquae*), these waters represent the teeming and faceless mass of humanity under the unfortunate jurisdiction of the global harlot. She continuously bewitches, enslaves, and tosses them about with her extensive power. Also suggested by this aquatic metaphor are the easily-manipulated passions of fickle multitudes seduced by the enemy. As such it stands in contraposition to the fountains of living water, epitomizing the faithful flock of the Church tended by the divine Shepherd (7:17).

Then, pointing back to v. 3, the angel explains: "The ten horns that you saw, they and the beast will hate the whore; they will make her desolate and naked; they will devour her flesh and burn her up with fire" (v. 16). This now is the third depiction of Babylon's fall, from yet a different angle (14:8; 16:19). Her doom will be due to internecine strife fueled by outright hatred (2:6; 18:2). As she loses her aura as a spiritual "fornicator,"[65] the secular world and its satrap powers will arise in open hostility, not only lording it over nations (Luke 22:25),

65. In the New Vulgate there is a noticeable change from *meretrix*, "prostitute" (vv. 1, 15; cf. 19:2), to the even crasser *fornicaria*, "fornicator," in this verse (see *fornicationum*, "fornications," already in v. 5), the single occurrence of this noun in the New Testament, giving more prominence to the harlot's acts of immorality and unfaithfulness.

but now also turning on her in raw detestation. It could be called an eschatological aggravation of Amnon's revulsion toward his half-sister Tamar (2 Sam 13:15). Hence, in addition to Satan's warfare against the Lamb (v. 14), his house is ruined by internal division (Mark 3:26). Instead of hating sin, the forces of evil lash out at each other in suicidal execration.[66]

This mutual abhorrence will manifest itself now in four ruinous actions: After rabidly dismounting or rather dethroning the harlot, the wild beast will isolate and abandon her in desolation. Next, she will be stripped naked (Ezek 16:37), that is, shamefully dispossessed of her immoral attractiveness and plundered of her tainted wealth. Following is one of the most gruesome images in Revelation, namely, the downright cannibalization of the devil's kingdom, devouring carnality in its entirety, as implied by the rare plural of the Greek noun *sárkas* (σάρκας, *carnes*), "all flesh." This unspeakable savagery anticipates the scene of 19:18, 21, and also has antecedents in prophetic writings of old (e.g., Jer 10:25). It will be perpetuated in the all-out hatred present within the ranks of the loyalists of the devil: *homo homini lupus*.[67] Fourth and last, there is the great whore's redundant annihilation by incineration (18:8), carrying subtle overtones of Noah's primordial burnt offering (Gen 8:20), of the ritual cremation of the Exodus lamb (Exod 12:10), but also of a prostitute's legal punishment according to Levitical law (Lev 21:9). This apocalyptic inferno is a foretaste of the beast's and the devil's own conflagration in the lake of fire (20:10).

That the Lord has sovereign control over evil's maneuvering and eventual self-defeat is nowhere more forcefully expressed: "For God has put it into their hearts to carry out his purpose by agreeing to give their kingdom to the beast, until the words of God will be fulfilled" (v. 17). By divine permission and causation, therefore, Satan's malice accomplishes the holy will of the Most High. Put differently, the mystery of iniquity becomes an instrument of divine vengeance by merely carrying out God's design and "what is pleasing to him" (*quod illi placitum est*). That divine pleasure and purpose is ironically conveyed by the same Greek noun *gnómē* (γνώμη) as in evil's "one single council" (*unum consilium*), repeated in this same verse. And the latter's reiteration from v. 13 shows that the devil in his blindness indulges in the fantasy that he is fulfilling his own plans, independent of the much greater counsel of God.

66. Mindful of the denotation of the Greek verb *miséō* (μισέω), signifying a moral choice that elevates one thing or person over another to the point of loving one and detesting the other (Matt 6:24).

67. As the Latin proverb goes, meaning "a human is like a wolf to another human," cf. Plautus, *Asinaria*, line 495.

Hence, evil is left to its own reprobate mind as it drives toward self-destruction. It must be said, however, that divine providence, giving all this into the hearts of the ungodly, and thereby permitting it to happen, neither encroaches on their free will, nor again acquits them of the sinfulness of their choices. It is not some irrational determinism, but the relative dualism of apocalyptic hue that affirms the dichotomy between good and evil, and also affirms that the Pantocrator will indeed reign supreme in the end.[68] Thus, a permanent strife will not exist, but only until the words of God be brought to consummation at some unspecified future juncture (v. 17). In that sense, the adverbial particle *áchri* (ἄχρι, *donec*), meaning "until, as far as, up to," should be rendered in its fullest lexical force here, i.e., as the uninfringeable boundary-marker of the eschaton. He sets this temporal limit for the exercise of diabolical authority to usher in his eternal Kingdom, where his children enjoy unchallenged freedom and peace in his presence.

In a recapitulating fashion, the heavenly messenger confirms: "The woman you saw is the great city that rules over the kings of the earth" (v. 18). With these words his exegesis of the mystery of the great whore so intimately associated with the beast closes. Even though the city of Rome, then capital of the known world, would have been the foremost embodiment of all hostility against the Lord in John's time, there is more spiritual depth to the image (11:8), especially when understood as the fulfillment of Daniel 7 with its snapshot of the entire economy of salvation. Also, this female figure of Babylon instantiates the oppositeness to the other woman at 12:1, contrasting a prostitute with a Virgin, a widow with a Bride, a mother of whores with a Mother of faithful progeny, and a faithless world with the Church.

While both traverse the wilderness of history, one is dressed up in the attire of earthly seduction, the other is robed in heavenly glory; one offers the hypnotic wine of idolatry, the other exemplifies sober maternal love for her divine Son and all humanity; one mounts a wild beast, the other is transported by the aquiline wings of the Holy Spirit; one enlists the powerful of this earth, the other embraces lowly pilgrims; one incites to war against the Lamb, the other suggests obedience to the Prince of peace; and finally, one is cannibalistically obliterated, the other divinely protected and delivered. Now, to be sure, this provisional tally of dissimilarities between Blessed Mary and the blasphemous anti-Mary, between the New Jerusalem and Babylon, will not

68. As opposed to a type of manichaeistic or absolute dualism that professes a perpetual and insoluble conflict between good and evil, between spirit and matter, between light and darkness in history.

be complete until "the Spirit and the Bride say, 'Come!'" toward the very end of this book (22:17). After having communicated judgment and mystery (17:1, 7), the angelic interpreter recedes from John's view, only to be replaced by yet another angel in at 18:1.

Before becoming engrossed in the demise of that doomed city in the upcoming chapter, let us again take a moment to reflect on the spiritual import of these vv. 15–18. Starting off with those "many waters" (v. 15), symbolizing the nameless multitudes of all generations of human beings who allowed themselves to be led astray by the devil's tactics of irreligiosity: They can motivate us to nurture a strong sense of identity as children of God and followers of Christ, and not to be overwhelmed or intimidated by the masses: "Do not be afraid, little flock, for your Father is pleased to give you the kingdom" (Luke 12:32). Also, the image of extreme mutual odium and depredation, eager to assist in tormenting the other to the point of cannibalizing and incinerating one another alive (v. 16), illustrates what sinfulness is capable of in its ultimate stages of shame, rage, despair, and viciousness.[69] And yet, the Lord permits his eternal counsel (v. 17) to be perverted into its opposite because he knows that those who commit this error and perpetrate evil things, and persist in unrepentance, will destroy themselves in the end.[70]

Hence, instead of worrying about what wicked people might do, the Christian carefully preserves the baptismal garb of grace, and will patiently await spiritual consolation after periods of desolation. A heartfelt devotion to the Blessed Virgin Mary will be instrumental, too, in steering clear of a legion of anti-Marian pressures in contemporary cultures: through an act of filial consecration we can profess to her our *Totus Tuus*.[71] There is also the insight that the human heart subjugated by sin and concupiscence fools itself regarding its self-importance and illusory power, not realizing that it is subservient to Luciferian authority materialized in "the great city" (v. 18).[72] Conversely, those who follow the Lamb gladly bend their knee before him, and their tongue confesses his Lordship, glorifying God the Father. To worship the name that is above every name in humble obedience of faith is true self-fulfillment engendering endless joy and life (Phil 2:9–11).

69. Biblical hamartiology calls the most grievous moral transgressions sins that cry to heaven for vengeance (*peccata clamantia*), cf. Gen 4:10; 18:20–21; Exod 22:21–23; Deut 24:14–15; Jas 5:4; Jude 1:7.

70. Cf. AvS, 572–73.

71. St. John Paul II's spiritual motto, based on the Mariology of St. Louis de Montfort.

72. Cf. AvS, 574.

18:1–8, Anti-Marian demise

Haunted city (18:1–3)

[1]After this I saw another angel coming down from heaven, having great authority; and the earth was made bright with his splendor. [2] He called out with a mighty voice, "Fallen, fallen is Babylon the great! It has become a dwelling place of demons, and a haunt of every foul spirit, and a haunt of every foul and hateful beast. [3]For all the nations have drunk of the wine of the wrath of her fornication, and the kings of the earth have committed fornication with her, and the merchants of the earth have grown rich from the power of her luxury."

Now that the mysterious complicity of harlot and beast has been unraveled, John is about to witness the doom in store for them, that is, the actual judgment that had been promised at 17:1, making that chapter a mere prelude to this present one. From 17:16, one can deduce that those worldly kings are the principal garroters procuring Babylon's ruination. Endorsing some of the most scathing prophecies of the Old Testament directed against cities like Babylon, Tyre, Edom, and Nineveh, the vengeful phrasing is intended to expose God's demands of justice and sanctity. As we peruse this chapter, a tripartite structure emerges: first, the portrayal of the great city's fall (vv. 1–8); second, a fourfold dirge weighing in on its devastation (vv. 9–19); and third, an exhortation to rejoice followed by an obituary (vv. 20–24).

There are only a handful of times that the sacred author introduces a vision with the formula "After this" (*Post haec*), and when he does, the emphasis seems to be on both the chronological sequence or segmenting of scenes, and on their great intrinsic relevance within the overall narrative. And so, following the previous angel's disquisition, he "saw another angel coming down from heaven, having great authority; and the earth was made bright with his splendor" (v. 1). As is conventional in the Apocalypse, the communication of supernatural realities is entrusted to such a heavenly ambassador who humbly descends from on high, from God's presence, in opposition to the ancient serpent that fell from those heights due to its pride (12:9).[1] In his awesome power and glory, he mirrors the empyrean splendor as if he were Christ himself (10:1) or possibly the Holy Spirit.[2] Bestowed on him is an exceptional amount of authority to declare the overcoming of evil under the figure of Babylon, as determined in the counsels of God the Almighty. He likely belongs to a higher rank of angelic choirs, potent enough to execute even the exterminating part of his mission.

Adding to the magnificence of the picture is the burst of light[3] emanating from him, capable of illuminating the whole world. By employing the rare verb *phōtízō* (φωτίζω, *illuminare*), "to give light," John not only anticipates the effulgence of the New Jerusalem (21:23; 22:5), but he also hints at the Lord's prowess in exposing every mundane darkness of ignorance and sin. That radiance recalls the numerous theophanic moments in salvation history, including Sinai (Exod 24:16), the fields of Bethlehem (Luke 2:9), and Tabor (Matt 17:2). All the nations are enlightened by his holy Gospel, shining an uncontainable ray of light on the garish glamor of Babylon, making evident that what has been prized and applauded by unspiritual persons, is worthless in the eyes of God. This simile of light at its core is affiliated with the glory of the parousiac Jesus: "Arise, shine; for your light has come, and the glory of the Lord has risen upon you" (Isa 60:1).

From within that blast of gleaming light "he called out with a mighty voice, 'Fallen, fallen is Babylon the great! It has become a dwelling place of demons, and a haunt of every foul spirit, and a haunt of every foul and hateful beast'"[4] (v. 2). Similar to other angels, he proclaims his message with intense loudness (*forti voce*), reminiscent also of the souls under the altar (6:10), of those saved (7:10), and of the pregnant woman (12:2). This vocal vehemence of his is at the same time indicative of triumphant joy, of the inherent importance of the message, but also of warning to the whole world, spoken in a way that all may hear. It also aims at arousing the world-city from her lethargic slumber, even though she will show herself insensible and nonresponsive in the face of the destruction about to befall her, as was the case with ancient Babylon. While the

1. Cf. RD, 1148.

2. Cf. AvS, 575.

3. The original *dóxa* (δόξα), "glory," in this verse is rendered as *claritas* ("splendor, luminosity") by the Neo-Vulgate.

4. This translation follows the New Vulgate's text, omitting the Greek variant reading of "and a haunt of every foul bird," which is probably a copyist's misreading due to the visual similarity of *ornéou* (ὀρνέου) and *thēríou* (θηρίου); it may also be a proleptic harmonization with the birds featured at 19:17, 21.

doomful end of Sodom and Gomorrah remains the undisputed biblical archetype (Gen 19:24–25), the wording of the angel's announcement is modeled especially on Isaiah 21:9 and Jeremiah 51:8. And even if the historical capital city of the Babylonian empire in Mesopotamia was never entirely razed to the ground, the Old Testament prophecies bespeaking her utter ruin, will at last find their fulfillment in apocalyptic times.

More spectacular than the fall of the star *Absinthius* (8:10), the collapse of the ungodly city will have reached its lowest conceivable point, as expressed by the woeful call: "Fallen, fallen!" Intriguingly, Rupert holds forth the idea that this reiteration signals the judgment of humans and demons alike.[5] But at any rate, this rousing shout, coupled with the prophetic past tense,[6] denotes the certainty of destruction as if it had already taken place, in accord with God's predetermined design: "How the mighty have fallen!" (2 Sam 1:19). In that sense, Revelation has prepared for this crucial moment by alluding to it on previous occasions already (e.g., 14:8). Although the actual leveling of the urban perimeter is neither acted out nor depicted here, it satisfies the prophetic purpose, as Simeon spoke of the falling and rising of many for the unveiling of their inner thoughts (Luke 2:34–35).

What is in fact illustrated, and in no uncertain terms, is the ghastly aftereffect of her collapse, lyrically amplified, as it were, by a triple stanza ("dwelling place-haunt-haunt"). *First,* and not unlike the throne of Satan at Pergamum (2:13), Babylon has now turned into a natural habitat for the fallen angels or demons, especially those of lesser rank, as implied by the neuter diminutive form of the masculine noun *daímōn* (δαίμων), that is, *daemonium*, meaning a miserable little devil (9:20; 16:14).[7] That word, incidentally, was also a common name for heathen deities. It implies their complete powerlessness compared to their moral counterpart, Christ, and his work of salvation. Moreover, this scene is an allusion to mythologies that assigned satyrs and demons to otherwise uninhabited places, like abandoned towns, decrepit ruins, deserts, and oceans. And Christ himself speaks of such places in his teaching on unclean spirits (Matt 12:43).

Second, the rebellious city appears to have metamorphosed into a place

5. Cf. RD, 1151.

6. To be exact, the Greek *épesen* (ἔπεσεν) is conjugated in the aorist tense, undergirding the factuality of the event, whereas the perfect tense of the Latin *cecidit* emphasizes the city's fall as an anticipated *fait accompli.*

7. This is also the Neo-Vulgate's rendition of the Hebrew masculine noun *sa'iyr* (שָׂעִיר) at Lev 17:7, meaning "hairy, shaggy"; by derivation, it designates a goat-like demon (cf. the Greco-Roman gods Pan and Faun).

of damnation, traditionally known as hell. This is strongly suggested by the repeated word for "prison" (*phylakḗ*, φυλακή, *custodia*; v. 2), which Jesus used to describe purgatory as a holding place or antechamber of heaven until the last penny is paid (Matt 5:25). Here, however, it characterizes that situation of permanent separation from God; at the end of the thousand years of the eschaton, Satan will be released just once more, before being confined there definitively, i.e., eternally (20:7). Another possible rendition would be that of a cage: Babylon the great whore having been disowned of her mundane façade, then brutalized and burned, now seems to reveal a charred skeletal rib cage teeming with unclean creatures and sundry filth. One can also imagine demonic monsters frozen into immobility, lining the gloomy thoroughfares of the fallen city, eerily staring down at passersby, and watching for a deliverance that will never be granted to them: truly a haunted city. An additional connotation would be that of prison-guards stationed on their watch-posts, ensuring that none of the jailbirds, demonic or human, will break free. No longer is it a mere ten days' penitentiary inflicted by the devil to test the people of God (2:10), but now damned souls will be watched unceasingly in their unescapable captivity of hell. What makes their torment even more excruciating is that those jail-watchers are foul spirits of all infernal stripes.

And *third*, the haunting presence of "every foul spirit" and "every foul and hateful beast" is recorded (v. 2), there to perpetuate the hatred that has already simmered among all the entities of evil, i.e., whore, beast, and earthly kings (17:16). How much they detest one another was already on full display when the legion of unclean spirits in the Gerasene country begged the God-Man to send them into a herd of swine which they deemed more tolerable than their own company of demonic brutes in hell (Mark 5:12). It is possible, too, that these three semi-strophic units, "dwelling place-haunt-haunt," portraying the dystopian Babylon, are hinting at the threefold offense, caused by angelic and human sin, against the Triune God, against themselves, and their neighbors.[8]

As the fallout continues, and subjoining the cause for her condemnation, the angel declares: "For all the nations have drunk of the wine of the wrath of her fornication, and the kings of the earth have committed fornication with her, and the merchants of the earth have grown rich from the power of her luxury" (v. 3). While at 14:8, the personified Babylon offered her impure potion to the world population (*potionare*), at this juncture it is affirmed that people also willingly accepted and imbibed it (*bibere*): "The world wants to be deceived,

8. Cf. RD, 1150.

so let it be deceived!"[9] One can only imagine the anguish that the virginal and beloved apostle, who reclined on the Lord's chest at the Last Supper (John 13:25), must have endured when seeing such immoral and idolatrous delirium brought over humanity. And just as in the previous verse, he has recourse again to a ternary refrain, "nations-kings-merchants," testifying that in addition to narcotizing all the nations, leading them into estrangement from God, she also seduces kings and corrupts commercialists.

When reporting on those royals, the visionary simply recapitulates what he previously communicated (17:2, 4.13), but now we learn about that third group comprised of tradespeople. Although the original noun *émporos* (ἔμπορος) generally designates a person traveling by land or by sea, the Neo-Vulgate prefers its connotation of "merchants" (*mercatores*), who, as we will discover in v. 23, are parabolic of the powerful business tycoons of this world, managing global finance centers and commercial networks. In ruthless avarice, they bankroll themselves into affluence, unable to resist the prostitute's overpowering luxuriousness (*virtus deliciarum*, v. 3). They pursue her overweening possessions with wantonness, sensuality, and stubbornness.[10] In their hedonism, these merchants do not realize the shocking contradiction between her trappings and the actual destitution of the world-city and its bogus influence. If the Roman empire of John's lifetime fits this description, the apocalyptic message transcends and universalizes it, referring not so much to earthly greed and consumerism, but rather to spiritual idolatry, irreligious compromise, and all guises of anthropocentrism, that tend to drown out authentic Christian worship and commitment.

Looking back over these opening verses of the chapter (vv. 1–3), let us further internalize them and make them more meaningful for our Christian life. Before anything else, there is the apparition of that tremendous angel (v. 1) that makes us reflect: if a single servant of God is so dazzlingly radiant, then how majestic must the Lord himself be, who has thousands upon ten thousands of them attending to him?! Yet that otherworldly splendor is mirrored on earth by the truth of his Gospel and of his Church. May each one of Christ's followers willingly receive such supernatural illumination, especially through the gifts of baptism and the Holy Eucharist, "so that, with the eyes of your heart enlightened, you may know what is the hope to which he has called you, what are the riches of his glorious inheritance among the saints" (Eph 1:18).

9. "Mundus vult decipi, ergo decipiatur," cf. Augustine, *De civitate Dei*, 4.27.

10. The noun *strē̂nos* (στρῆνος), cited only here in the New Testament, means "insolent luxury, excessive delicacy," and is akin to the adjective *stereós* (στερεός), conveying the idea of "straining, strenuousness, strength, arrogant hardness, immoveable firmness."

Next, the bodeful cry "Fallen, fallen!" (v. 2) should reecho in our innermost being and impress deeper on our mind the awareness that one can collapse under the sheer weight of one's own sins. Truth be told, insatiable licentiousness, unconscionable profligacy, impurity, and idol worship will spawn desolation and self-destruction, until and unless the heart feels remorse and seeks divine forgiveness and healing.

Furthermore, when listing three different types of diabolical beings, that is, "demons," "every unclean spirit," and "every foul and hateful beast" (v. 2), the apostle seems to signal that every type of satanic testing will be unleashed against every human being along the span of one's lifetime, tempting us into all sorts of sin, bodily and mental, venial and mortal, pulling out all the stops to make us fall. Unfortunately, or even inevitably, we do lapse into imperfection and moral fault, but those occasions ought to turn into moments of grace and an invitation to immediately get up and return to our merciful God (2:5).[11]

Also, Babylon's consumeristic inebriation, recounted in v. 3, should be a caveat for us to circumnavigate all mindless superfluity, to curb inordinate desires for material goods, and to exercise restraint in the use of them. Jesus himself warns us against the blinding effect of excessive materialism, especially in the parable of the foolish rich man who failed to store up treasures in heaven (Luke 12:16–21). In Paul's mind, the love of money is the worst, and, unless shunned, it can endanger our fidelity to Christ (1 Tim 6:9–10). He also cautions against the fleetingness of earthly riches that tend to make the heart haughty, instead of putting its trust in God's providence (1 Tim 6:17–19).

What is more, true spiritual wealth consists in finding and treasuring the Kingdom, to the point of ridding oneself of all other earthly ballast (Matt 13:45–46).[12] In fact, and happily so, many men and women will heed the interior call to pursue perfection through evangelical simplicity (Matt 19:21), perhaps even under vow in monastic or other religious settings, in imitation of the One who chose to become poor for our sake, to enrich us, his brethren, in many surprising ways (2 Cor 8:9). And although material affluence should never be the sole purpose of our labor on earth, we may find ourselves in situations of abundance, which will be an opportunity to be generous, but also to stay vigilant, calling to mind Paul's good counsel one more time: "I know how to live humbly, and I know how to abound. . . . I can do all things through Christ who

11. Cf. AvS, 576.

12. Unlike King David, who lived in his cedar palace while God's ark stayed in a poor tent (2 Sam 7:2).

gives me strength" (Phil 4:12–13). But let us now continue to exegete the text, listening with St. John to another heavenly voice addressing him.

Evacuation order (18:4–5)

[4]Then I heard another voice from heaven saying, "Come out of her, my people, so that you do not take part in her sins, and so that you do not share in her plagues; [5]for her sins are heaped high as heaven, and God has remembered her iniquities.

Given that the addressee of the command in v. 4 is "my people," this voice can only be trinitarian, meaning that God the Father, in unison with the Son and the Holy Spirit, is issuing an appeal that bears the semblance of a formal covenant renewal. When Elohim was about to bring the Hebrews out from under the Egyptian yoke, he promised to adopt them as his people (Exod 6:7). That sacrosanct pledge had undergirded the long and involved history of salvation, commencing with his theophany at Mount Sinai. But it will come to completion only when God's pilgrim people is perfectly severed from the symbolic Babylon of this world, as if in an apocalyptic Exodus, at the end of time. Encouraging the exiled Israelites to flee the historical Babylon, God spoke to them in similar terms through his prophets (Isa 48:20). He was calling on his people to realize that the years of their captivity had expired, and that they must not linger, but should seek liberty by going back to Jerusalem.

Likewise, that heavenly voice (v. 4) reminds us of Noah and his family taken out of a hopeless society ahead of the deluge and preserved for a divine covenant (Gen 6:18). Later on, Yahweh spoke to Abraham to abandon his native city, namely, Ur of the Chaldeans, and depart for Canaan, to become the ancestral patriarch of the chosen people (Gen 12:1). Similarly, his nephew Lot was ordered to leave Sodom and Gomorrah, lest he and his family perish along with those cursed cities (Gen 19:15). And again, the Hebrews were ordered to avoid the tents of Korah, Dathan, and Abiram in the midst of the assembly, before the earth split open and swallowed them, and they went down alive into Sheol (Num 16:21). Recalled is also the angel's apparition to Joseph in Bethlehem, commanding him to take the divine infant and his Mother and take flight to Egypt (Matt 2:13). Moreover, Jesus in his Olivet Discourse advises his disciples to evade Jerusalem's destruction (Matt 24:16). But the most obvious precedent is the woman's apocalyptic flight into the desert to escape the serpent's tyranny (12:6).

What is intimated here is that those faithful who are found in the idolatrous world-city are in acute danger from the impending ruin, and their only way to secure purity and liberty is to come out of her at once. Fair warning is given to all who hope in the Lord's mercy, that the strict separation of sinners and saints will be necessary (3:10), since God's judgment will make no discrimination among those who are still found there. On the contrary, they will be regarded as partakers of her vice and corruption and must expect to suffer the same calamitous consequences that will come upon her. Here is, therefore, the Lord's paternal warning out of infinite love, to take radical steps to steer clear of the peril of falling under Babylon's spell and contamination. Because those who willfully share in her wickedness, must also receive her punishment, like Lot's wife, who lingered near the ill-omened cities; she was soon overtaken by their fate, simply because her heart was not detached from their misdeeds (Luke 17:32). Thus, the reader is cautioned not to entertain close fellowship with idolaters.

Just as in v. 3, a deeper rationale ("for," *quia, quoniam*) for the above command is subjoined: "For her sins are heaped high as heaven, and God has remembered her iniquities" (v. 5). Unique here is the metaphor of sins literally becoming glued to the sky's cloud-ceiling. In other words, when guilt is ripe for judgment, it can be said to press unto heaven's door, touching the very face of God (*pervenērunt*). Thus, Babylon's sticky pile of crimes is towering to its highest limit, crying out for vengeance, and inevitably attracting God's attention. Similar expressions can be found regarding the innocent blood of Abel spilled by his brother Cain (Gen 4:10), the condemnation of Sodom and Gomorrah (Gen 19:13), the deplorable situation at Nineveh (Jonah 1:2), and the cry of defrauded harvesters against their oppressors (Jas 5:4). There is a hint, too, at the methods of justice systems where criminals are prosecuted when their evildoing is brought to light before the court of judgment. Perhaps it even alludes to the usage of this Greek verb *kolláō*, "to glue," in ancient medical literature concerning the bandaging of wounds, suggesting that the world's festering traumas, lacerations, and lesions are crying out for treatment, but that the *kairós* or opportune time for healing is now running out.

Sometimes the oppressed may have had the impression that the Lord has forgotten the voice of the enemy (Ps 74:10), yet such divine forbearance amounts to opportunities for salvation (2 Pet 3:9). Even if he formerly seemed not to notice human sin, now he will act as if they had come to his recollection recently and more forcefully. Put differently, just as the pardoning of our transgressions is symbolized by God's non-remembrance of them (Heb 8:12), so also the punishment of sinners is expressed by his recalling of them (16:19). But what exactly is being remembered for retribution, if not the overflowing number of acts of unrighteousness? Belonging to the realm of jurisprudence, the Greek noun *adíkēma* (ἀδίκημα) in this v. 5 conveys the notion of legal wrongdoing with which one is charged, and for which one awaits the judge's verdict. To sin, therefore, means to violate God's righteousness and justice. When the New Vulgate renders this word as *iniquitas*,[13] it intimates a different nuance of meaning, namely, the fact that it is unfair or inequitable for humans to offend their Creator and Redeemer. So, now the time has come when God will punish the great harlot for her idolatry and persecution, and all the other abominable things committed by her.

For the sake of further internalization of vv. 4–5, let us first and foremost appreciate Jesus' exact knowledge and gracious care as to our wellbeing, and how he provides opportunities for us, his beloved people, to reach places of safety so as not to perish with the world. There is no doubt that it is his will that his faithful be *in* this world, but not *of* this world, and kept from evil (John 15:19). In many ways, we are set apart from attitudes of worldliness in that we strive to spiritually immunize ourselves from erroneous and corrupt aspects of present-day culture (Rom 12:2).[14] That is how we live the *Exite de illa!* ("Come out of her"), God's veritable evacuation notice, amid our own generation. As baptized members of Christ's Body, we seek to flee, as much as that is feasible, any fellowship with the unfruitful works of darkness (1 Cor 5:9–11). This duty of separation may sometimes take the form of a severance and literal exodus from a milieu that is judged too disreputable or even perilous for one's spiritual welfare. Sustained by a personal prayer life, the heart will discern the voice of God's Spirit urging us to gradually retreat from sin as a matter of Christian priority, and to dissociate ourselves from all forms of evil (1 Tim 5:22).[15] St. Paul instructs the Philippian church to "be blameless and innocent, children of God without blemish in the midst of a crooked and perverse generation, in which you shine like stars in the world" (Phil 2:15).

What cannot be sidestepped altogether, of course, is some measure of ill-treatment that everyone must endure, since that is needed for our

13. This Latin noun derives from the adjective *inīquus* or *in-aequus*, signifying something that is "unfair," "unjust," or "unequal."

14. Tellingly, the Hebrew word for "holy," i.e, *qadôsh* (קָדוֹשׁ), has the original meaning of being "set apart for a special purpose," just as Israel was separated from the other nations as the son and servant of Yahweh; and a similar significance is found in the Latin word for "temple," that is, *fānum*, as opposed to *profānus*, the latter indicating time and space outside or before (*pro-*) the temple (*fānum*).

15. Cf. AvS, 577.

purification and prepares us for Christ's glorious return, as the apostolic seer himself attests: "I, John, your brother, who shares with you in Jesus the persecution and the Kingdom and the patient endurance" (1:9). Another possible takeaway from the apocalyptic text is the resolve to cultivate a clear conscience, not allowing personal sins to pile up to the sky, which would leave little space for God's grace and light.[16] Also, in imitation of his divine remembrance, the soul ought to practice some form of contemplative recollection, accompanied by a wholesome introspection that flows into an examination of conscience. This must be considered a privileged way to boost one's inner cooperation with the promptings of the Holy Spirit, holding on to "faith and a good conscience, which some have rejected and thereby shipwrecked their faith" (1 Tim 1:18–19).

Double payback (18:6–8)

6Render to her as she herself has rendered, and repay her double for her deeds; mix a double draught for her in the cup she mixed. 7As she glorified herself and lived luxuriously, so give her a like measure of torment and grief. Since in her heart she says, 'I rule as a queen; I am no widow, and I will never see grief,' 8therefore her plagues will come in a single day, pestilence and mourning and famine, and she will be burned with fire; for mighty is the Lord God who judges her."

Summoning now the agents of vengeance, the divine voice insists on a double payback for Babylon's sins (v. 6), but who are these executioners of just retribution if not the saints themselves, given that the Lord is still speaking directly to his people (v. 4)? "Do you not know that the saints will judge the world? . . . Do you not know that we will judge angels?" (1 Cor 6:2–3). Undoubtedly included here are the seven plague-angels (15:1) and the ten kings (17:16), too, who thus become unsuspecting vehicles of divine justice. This command reassures all those who have been wronged and persecuted by Babylon the great whore, since the day has dawned for exact retaliation. She is being paid back in kind for what she inflicted on the followers of the Lamb throughout history; they now requite her hatred, deceit, and violence. Scripture proves that it is God's prerogative to take vengeance (Heb 10:30) and that he is not to be mocked (Gal 6:7).

16. Cf. AvS, 578.

Drawing on the biblical concept of "an eye for an eye" (Exod 21:23–25) or retaliation,[17] divine justice is delineated as punishing the offender, namely, all ungodly power-structures on earth, for their idol worship and Christian persecution. In certain cases, the Torah demanded acts of double restitution (e.g., Exod 22:4), which is recalled three times in this v. 6 (*duplicate, duplicia, duplum*), suggesting vindication to the fullest and fitting the crime. Out of her own cup of impurity, Babylon is now made to drink abundantly of the wine of God's wrath, duplex in volume and intensity of what she had dealt out to others. Babylon is double-stained in wickedness, and thus, brought upon her is the twofold amount of calamity in divine revenge (Ps 137:8–9).

Yet is not this vengefulness altogether against Gospel principles that instill the virtue of Christian meekness and forgiveness, even of one's enemies (Matt 5:44)? In response to this soul-stirring question it is important to note that the mode of the saints' payback is not made explicit, and indeed, that one nowhere sees them taking private or public vengeance into their own hands (6:10). Which may be a hint at a more spiritual signification of this certainly thought-provoking passage: the idea seems to be that the impious part of the human family will receive the adequate punishment for its iniquities not in this world but in the world hereafter. Hence, the puzzling duplication of the law of retaliation is not exclusive of God's mercy, but rather points to the second or eternal death as meted out after the final judgment and with the implied consent of the good angels and saints. With that unanimous consignment of evil to hell, divine justice will be definitively served.

Carrying on the above line of thought, the divine voice issues this directive: "As she glorified herself and lived luxuriously, so give her a like measure of torment and grief. Since in her heart she says, 'I rule as a queen; I am no widow, and I will never see grief'" (v. 7). Instead of giving honor and praise to God (15:4), the great harlot seeks to bestow glory on herself in all things,[18] exposing a profound misconception regarding her own identity. She errs substantially and diabolically in attributing value and weight only to herself, and thereby perverting the relationship between Creator and creature.[19] In her boasting,

17. A word stemming from the Latin *re-*, "back," and *talis*, "such like" (*retaliāre*), literally, "pay back, return in kind, repay, requite, exacting a payment in kind"; it inspired the phrase *lex talionis*, i.e., the law of commensurate retribution or reciprocal justice.

18. That is the connotation of this correlative pronoun *hósa* (ὅσα) in the neuter plural at the beginning of v. 7, rendered by the New Vulgate as *quantum* in the neuter singular, stressing how much, how great, and in how many ways something happens.

19. In the Scripture, the verb *doxázō* (δοξάζω), "to glorify, extol, venerate," itself lexically akin to *dokéō* (δοκέω), meaning "to form an opinion, have a personal esteem of value, acknowl-

pomp, and lustful self-indulgence she ran riot, fallaciously thinking she could deify herself. And now, in double proportion to her dissoluteness ("as-so," *quantum-tantum*) she will be made to suffer. God's justice will precipitate her into vexation and grief, which are thinly veiled innuendos, for sure, to the pains of hell. What a nauseous antithesis between her arrogant self-image and the dreadful reality in which she will find herself at any moment now, further fleshing out the symbolic double payback of the foregoing verse.

Only the all-knowing God can design and hand down a sentence of such consummate correspondence between guilt and punishment. For the third time (cf. vv. 3, 5), a deeper rationale[20] not only for the prostitute's deranged self-glorification, but also for her castigation is offered, an insight into the thought-world of her wicked heart (v. 7). As a matter of fact, she deludes herself with a triple miscalculation, the first of which has to do with her pretense of impregnable regal power as the "daughter Chaldea" (Isa 47:5–11). John had seen her securely enthroned on many waters (17:1), on the scarlet beast (17:3), as well as on seven mountains (17:9); and now, like a miserable caricature of God's own throne in heaven (4:2), of that of the elders (11:16), and of the Son of Man's white cloud (14:14), she obstinately dreams of queenly fame. But this empty claim of hers is made even worse by the second false reasoning of never experiencing the emotional void of widowhood (Bar 4:12, 16). Which ties also into her third inner misjudgment, this time concerning her future, of never being affected by sorrow. Her unconcernedness and outright denial, however, stand in crass opposition to the impending calamity that will soon bereave her of all her children.

And as for her dead husband, she had considered her imaginary world-power to be her spouse and supporter. But since pride goes before the fall, and since she refused to be betrothed to Jesus, the true and undying Bridegroom of humanity, she will indeed be widowed in everlasting damnation. Her idolatrous fornication with earthly kings left her childless like Jezebel (2:23), powerless like the dragon ambushing the childbearing woman (12:4), and in utter desperation like a desolate Jerusalem: "How lonely sits the city that once was full of people! How like a widow she has become, she that was great among the nations! She that was a princess among the provinces has become a vassal" (Lam 1:1).

edge true character," renders the Old Testament word for "glory," that is, *kāḇôḏ* (כָּבוֹד), which etymologically expresses something that is literally heavy, or figuratively weighty.

20. Intimated by the subordinate conjunction *hóti* (ὅτι), "since, because," denoting cause or reason, reflected in the Nova Vulgata's *quia*, "because."

At this juncture of John's vision, the otherworldly voice passionately exclaims: "Therefore, her plagues will come in a single day, death and mourning and famine, and she will be burned with fire; for mighty is the Lord God who judges her" (v. 8). All of Babylon's demonic narcissism and immoderation, as well as the blight she brought on countless others down the centuries, will result in fatal consequences. In sharp contradiction to her perfidy and presumption, her final afflictions will befall her when she deems herself at ease and secure, and they shall be poured out on her very speedily, if not all at once. It will be that fearsome *Yōm Adonai*, the "Day of the Lord," as prophesied of old (Joel 2:1). That single "day" will be as short as an "hour" (14:7), that is, it will happen instantaneously, like a sudden implosion. Unlike the seven plagues of ch. 16, these wounds of hers (v. 4; 22:18) are intimately linked to the death-blow of the sea-beast (13:3), and the plagues suffered under the sixth trumpet (cf. 9:18, 20).

And her ordeal will be fourfold, as if thrashing her from the four corners of the world (7:1), not unrelated to the four horsemen (6:2–8) and the horns of the golden altar (9:13). Death is mentioned first, since it is metonymical for eternal damnation to mourning, starving, and burning.[21] Death is also in retribution for her contempt concerning the prospect of widowhood. Cited second is her perpetual wailing, which she pretended she would never experience; it will be the punishment for her overextravagant reveling. It is the diametrical opposite of heaven's consolation, too (21:4). Third, and in punition for her decadent feasting, she will be condemned to famine in perpetuity. And fourth is fire as the worst torment (17:16), proleptically hinting at the annihilation of evil in the second death, following the decisive battle at Harmagedon, when beast and devil, death and Hades, will be arrested and cast alive into the lake ablaze with fire and brimstone.[22] Yahweh-Elohim cursed the soil upon which Adam stood (Gen 3:17), he flooded the earth beneath Noah's ark (Gen 7:6), he rained sulfurous fire on Sodom and Gomorrah (Gen 19:24), and he will overthrow an unfaithful world again by fire when that heartrending day arrives. And lest anybody should doubt, Babylon's Judge is omnipotent, and will not hesitate to bring all these calamities upon her: Jesus is the Alpha and Omega, the one who is to come for the infallible execution of that judgment (1:8).

Humanly speaking, it may be tempting to resort to some form of vindication, or even downright revenge, when it comes to injustice and injury suffered

21. Cf. AvS, 582.

22. Elsewhere in the New Testament, the verb *katakaíō* (κατακαίω) suggests the eternal fire of hell (e.g., Matt 3:12).

innocently in our lives at the hands of the forces of darkness. However, when pondered in the context of the New Testament, that does not appear to be a viable option. And so, how are we to understand this double payback encouraged by the Lord in these verses? Well, knowing that he himself will one day set all things right, all we need to do here and now is to wait for him, to conform our will to his perfect will, which means to humbly aspire to Christian holiness, to truly detest our personal sins, and then to patiently endure whatever suffering God may send our way in his eternal wisdom.

Moreover, with the help of his grace, we strive to counter those sinful and dangerous tendencies that ultimately cause moral corruption, namely, self-glorification, a lifestyle of excessive luxury, presumptive confidence in one's own prestige or earthly securities, but also the obsessive and futile avoidance of all pain, be that in the form of grieving, suffering, or even dying. Instead, the soul was created to acknowledge the supreme and intrinsic worth of its Maker, and to worship him in word and deed. Such sincere and loving *opus Dei* will outstrip inner pride as the foremost cardinal vice, and it will dampen its manifold offshoots such as moral complacency, incorrigibility, and arrogant denial of reality.[23]

Almost countless are the examples from the lives of the saints, who were more partial to temporal suffering and weeping with Christ, than living out the fleeting joys of their age. St. Katherine Drexel, the wealthy American heiress, comes to mind, as she donated her entire inheritance to charities to become a religious, and selflessly served the missions of her time. It is also worth listening again to how Paul embraced personal adversity: "Who will separate us from the love of Christ? Will hardship, or distress, or persecution, or famine, or nakedness, or peril, or sword? . . . No, in all these things we are more than conquerors through him who loved us" (Rom 8:35, 37). Hence, when we shoulder Jesus' easy yoke (Matt 11:30), that is, accepting the difficulties and sorrows of life out of love, they are transfigured into a privileged way of holiness, that of the glorious Cross, which opens onto the horizons of a greater good.[24]

23. Cf. AvS, 581.

24. Homily by St. John Paul II, on the occasion of the canonization of St. Pius of Pietrelcina (Vatican, June 16, 2002), §1.

18:9–19, Funereal quadrilogy

First threnody: Royals (18:9–10)

[9]And the kings of the earth, who committed fornication and lived in luxury with her, will weep and wail over her when they see the smoke of her burning; [10]they will stand far off, in fear of her torment, and say, "Alas, alas, the great city, Babylon, the mighty city! For in one hour your judgment has come."

At this beginning of the chapter's second part (vv. 9–19), there is a transition from the celestial voice of vv. 4–8 to a direct utterance by John himself, which in turn will lead us up to the third part of the chapter (vv. 20–24), pronounced arguably by yet another agent. Hence, circumstantial to the overthrow of the great world-city are two opposite responses, namely, the lamenting of the wicked (vv. 9–19) and the euphoria of the godly (vv. 20–24), patterned on Ezekiel's elaborate lamentation over Tyre (Ezek 26–27), as well as Jeremiah's extensive oracle against historical Babylon (Jer 50–51). The reader is about to witness a stirring elegy, consecutively declaimed by four groups representing the totality of socioeconomic power structures on earth: by kings (vv. 9–10), financiers (vv. 11–14), merchants (vv. 15–17a), as well as seafarers (vv. 17b–19). In this way, another apocalyptic tetrad, this time of mourners, embodies all global dealings with the great harlot by land and by sea.[1]

1. Most commentators identify three sections in this dirge, headed up by (a.) "kings" (v. 9), (b.) "merchants," twice designated by one and the same noun in Greek, namely, *émporoi* (ἔμποροι, vv. 11, 15), and (c.) "seafarers" (v. 17b), all of whom reiterate the cry "alas, alas" (vv. 10, 16, 19). However, considering the Neo-Vulgate as the standard text, one can distinguish four crowds of mourners, that is, in addition to kings and seafarers, there are "bankers" or "financiers," translating *émporoi* as *negotiatores* (v. 11), and "traders or merchants," this time rendering the selfsame *émporoi* as *mercatores* (v. 15); and such a quadruple grouping is supported by the fourfold expression "weep and wail" (v. 9) or "weep and mourn" (vv. 11, 15, 19), attributed to those four bands of people.

Unquestionably, the Book of Lamentations with its bevy of five poetic laments on occasion of the destruction of Jerusalem in 586 BC, a veritable gold standard of biblical funeral song, served as a paradigm. It inserts itself into the ancient Near East genre of City-Lament, oftentimes voiced by the lost city's tutelary deity, presenting suffering as overwhelming while God remains silent on the sideline and his redemption out of reach. Additionally, there is an affinity to the structure of the Song of Songs, which dramatizes the dialogue between bride, bridegroom, and the chorus. Aside from these Semitic inspirations, however, the obituary poetry of ch. 18 also bears a remarkable resemblance to classical Greek tragedy. Among its parallels are ethical antitheses, illustrations of catastrophes complete with the protagonist or antagonist reacting to them, dialogue as action, a plot driven toward a cathartic denouement, reversal of fortune with an intrinsic irony, and the emphasis on pathos, to mention but a few.[2] Yet without further ado, let us now scrutinize the first of these four apocalyptic laments.

John himself now appears to comment on his vision: "And the kings of the earth, who committed fornication and lived in luxury with her, will weep and wail over her when they see the smoke of her burning" (v. 9). Presented as the chief mourners, the kings of this world, *pars pro toto* for the nations they rule, but also epitomizing all earthly authority, wail because they had derived substantial support from Babylon's power now in shambles. They understand that with their anti-Christian ally destroyed, the source of their influence is taken away, too. She had flattered them into immorality and idolatry, inciting them to be tyrannical over their subjects. Saddened by the swift reverse of fortune they bewail her, without being able to afford her any defense. It is conceivable that the ten kings who cannibalized her (17:16) are excepted here. The only royals who are somehow moved to commiseration are those who persisted in their stubbornness of heart and are still living in unholy fellowship with her. Their inconsolable sobbing is the first in a tetralogy of dirges, setting the tone for the three classes of mourners yet to step up and take center stage (vv. 11, 15, 19).

What is eye-catching is that the verbs expressing grief in this first lament are set in the future tense (*flebunt et plangent*), the ones in the second in the present tense (v. 11, *flent et lugent*), the ones in the third again in the future (v. 15, *stabunt . . . flentes ac lugentes*), whereas the ones in the fourth and last dirge in

2. Cf. Jo-Ann A. Brant, *Dialogue and Drama: Elements of Greek Tragedy in the Fourth Gospel* (Peabody, MA: Hendrickson, 2004); Harold W. Attridge, *History, Theology, and Narrative Rhetoric in the Fourth Gospel*, Pere Marquette Lecture in Theology 2019 (Milwaukee, WI: Marquette University Press, 2019), 31–40.

the past tense (v. 19, *clamabant, flentes et lugentes*). Once again, this apparent syntactic oddity only underscores the a-chronological or meta-historical tone of Revelation, where the future judgment is portrayed as a *fait accompli* in the prophetic past or eschatological present. By articulating this grief in those four couplets of verbs, the seer may also hint at inward desolation accompanied by outward gestures of sorrow (Job 1:20; 2:8), in opposition to the world's celebratory gloating earlier over the dead bodies of the two witnesses (11:10). Tragically, the anguish described here is the net result of sheer terror tempered with frustrated selfishness, as earthly potentates regret the vanishing of their voluptuous lifestyle and of their quick-growing commercial profits.

There is no trace of sympathy, altruism, repentance, or fear of God, but only the realization that the trappings of mundane impurity and riches will avail them nothing. That the kings have indeed been seduced into such practical idolatry by the great harlot has been conveyed several times already (e.g., 17:2). Although the ancient Roman empire again almost perfectly fits the description, with its voracious appetite for materialism and lustful indulgences, sustained by corrupt trade guilds and patronal deities opiating people's consciences, Babylon the great transcends such historical strictures. This imagery is meant to apply to all forms of irreligiosity in this world until the final judgment. In aberration from the worshipful incense arising in God's presence and the magnificent smoke filling his temple in heaven (8:4), the infernal fumes looming over the prostitute's incineration are but harbingers of the end of her impious autarchy. True to the apocalyptic style, the gory details of execution are withheld from the visionary's eyes; and so, shrouded in a bloodcurdling blanket of smog, she meets her demise in crushing solitude.[3]

With a touch of grim humor, the apostle continues to flesh out the picture of this first in a quartet of elegy: "They will stand far off, in fear of her torment, and say, 'Alas, alas, the great city, Babylon, the mighty city! For in one hour your judgment has come'" (v. 10). Their stance from afar (vv. 15, 17) brings back the painful memories of Peter and the pious women keeping their distance from our Lord in his hour of suffering and dying (Matt 26:58; 27:55). Unwittingly, the kings here are acting on God's command for his people to come out of the reprobate city (v. 4). More than happy to have partaken of her sins in despicable self-interest, worldly power is unwilling, however, to share in her fatal ordeal, contenting itself with idle whimpering.

No attempt whatsoever is made to rescue her; they are too dispirited, and the fire will be too hot for them anyway. Instead, like a death knell in the

3. Cf. AvS, 584.

distance, they simply shout their "woes" in disbelief, reechoing in vv. 16, 19, reflective of the double payback of v. 6, and capping the triple "woes" of previous occasions, too (8:13). That repetition corresponds to the extremity of pain, as well as their being thunderstruck by the rash ruin of such a formerly splendid world-city.[4] Even though a "day" had been set aside for her judgment (v. 8), it all took just "one hour" (vv. 17, 19), underscoring the Almighty's eternal justice in terms of punctuality and inexorability.[5] Such a fixed time of judgment was promised by the angel in 17:1, and God surely does not renege on his promises.

When contemplating this first dirge from a spiritual vantage point, one realizes that no matter how powerful or influential one might be, a life lived in sins of immorality and material abundance, especially while remaining tone-deaf to the indigence of others in the guise of the parabolic rich man (Luke 16:25), will result in profound dejection of the soul. Thoughtless self-interest is a sure path to self-destruction, unless remedied or at least tempered by Christian altruism flowing from a heartfelt union with the Lord. And as we behold the catastrophic burning of the unfaithful city, we ought to remind ourselves that the eternal fire of hell can be avoided by cultivating an Emmaus heart (Luke 24:32), permanently set on fire by our openness to the word of God and its Christocentric message of salvation. But we must also learn to bravely endure the many blazing trials that our heavenly Father sends us his children: "Beloved, do not be surprised at the fiery ordeal that is taking place among you to test you, as though something strange were happening to you. But rejoice insofar as you are sharing Christ's sufferings, so that you may also be glad and shout for joy when his glory is revealed" (1 Pet 4:12–13).

Not to be overlooked is the enormous smokescreen created by Babylon's cremation, nudging the members of the Church to maintain a level of transparency and clean conscience. That purity of the heart is powerfully aided by a regular celebration of the sacrament of penance and reconciliation, allowing the light of grace to push away any fogginess of sin or imperfection. Spiritually stimulating, too, is the fact that the kings' wailing is anticipated by John's own profuse weeping at creation's inability to decipher the scroll's designs (5:4). Likewise, the soul should find moments to mourn its own unworthiness before its Creator, and to make oneself vulnerable to the torturous vicissitudes of human history, whose darkness is so in need of the light of redemption. In this

4. Rupert recognizes in the sixfold reiteration of woes the "six ages of the world," never reaching the sabbath, but left with only labor and restlessness, cf. RD, 1154.

5. Cf. AvS, 585.

way we mystically anticipate Christ's parousia, a return that will elicit universal wailing (1:7).

Furthermore, the way the regal onlookers distance themselves from the ravaging of Babylon (v. 10) can teach us to persevere close to Jesus' Cross, like the pious women on Golgotha (John 19:25), but also to eagerly approach him like the Gerasene man who had an unclean spirit by the name of legion (Mark 5:6), begging for healing. This will strengthen us for the hour of our own bodily death when his presence will drive away the tears of despair. As a closing thought, the inanity of giving credence to the fallen city's hypocritical "grandeur" and "might" (v. 10), should enlighten us to not place our trust in worldly things, as the God-Man reassured Paul: "'My grace is sufficient for you, for power is made perfect in weakness.' So, I will boast all the more gladly of my weaknesses, so that the power of Christ may dwell in me" (2 Cor 12:9).

Second threnody: Bankers (18:11–14)

[11]And the merchants of the earth weep and mourn for her, since no one
buys their cargo anymore, [12]cargo of gold, silver, jewels and pearls, fine
linen, purple, silk and scarlet, all kinds of scented wood, all articles of
ivory, all articles of costly wood, bronze, iron, and marble, [13]cinnamon,
spice, incense, myrrh, frankincense, wine, olive oil, choice flour and
wheat, cattle and sheep, horses and chariots, slaves, and human lives.
[14]"The fruit for which your soul longed has gone from you, and all your
dainties and your splendor are lost to you, never to be found again!"

Joining the kings of the earth in their grief is a second group of people exerting great clout on the global stage: "And the bankers of the earth weep and mourn for her, since no one buys their cargo anymore" (v. 11). What the Neo-Vulgate phrase *negotiatores terrae* (cf. *magnates*, v. 23) appears to convey is that class of chief financial executives and business tycoons who control the world's commercial nerve centers, industriously going about their business, wheeling and dealing unrelentingly.[6] Ironically, they weep not so much for the collapsed Babylon, but for their lost transnational markets and dissipated profits with their untold cargos and supplies. Their sorrow is even more purely selfish than that of the kings (v. 9), as they think only of their missed opportunities to sell countless

6. Tellingly, the original Latin noun *negōtium* is a compound noun that couples *nec* ("not") with *ōtium* ("leisure"), signifying the negation of inactivity, or a state of restlessness.

freighters laden up to a maximum.[7] With a heightened narrative vividness of the historical present tense (*flent et lugent*), those top financiers on earth are frustrated that buying and selling under the aegis of the beast is now broken up (13:17), and with that, also their illusion to unite the whole world into a single marketplace of greed and consumerism.[8]

What follows in vv. 12–13 constitutes one of the most extensive biblical lists of merchandise, second only to the one in Ezekiel 27, granting a thrilling glimpse into the mercantile activities of ancient markets. Highlighted are no fewer than twenty-nine commodities, the majority being products of luxury, and an impressive nine of which are absolute New Testament *hapax legomenoi*, that is, occurring only once. Taking a cue from the placement of commas in the text of the Nova Vulgata, one can subdivide the merchandise into seven categories, epitomizing the totality of tradable earthly commodities: *first*, jewelry ("gold, silver, gems, pearls"; v. 12a), *second*, haute couture ("fine linen,[9] purple, silk, scarlet"; v. 12b), *third*, palatial décor ("all kinds of scented wood, all articles of ivory, all articles of costly wood, bronze, iron, marble"; v. 12c), *fourth*, upmarket goods ("cinnamon, spice, incense, myrrh, frankincense"; v. 13a), *fifth*, food ("wine, olive oil, choice flour, wheat"; v. 13b), *sixth*, livestock and transportation ("cattle, sheep, horses, wagons"; v. 13c), and *seventh*, commercialized human life ("slaves, human souls"; v. 13d).

These are understood to be managed by the international banking magnates of all historical eras on earth. One cannot help but notice that most of these items are elsewhere mentioned in Scripture as either to be placed at the service of God's greater glory, or, as something to be avoided like unnecessary ballast on our spiritual journey. Put differently, these wares can be used as tokens of true worship, or as means for egocentric idolatry, creating a certain tension and challenge for our moral choices. While the great harlot is preening herself in the crème de la crème of that mundane splendor (17:4), she acts like an anti-Marian travesty of the aesthetic that shines through the Old Testament

7. The Greek noun *gómos* (γόμος), "cargo," derives from the verb *gémō* (γέμω), "to fill up or load to capacity."

8. Any transfer of ownership from seller to buyer is lexically indicated by the verb *agorázō* (ἀγοράζω, *emere*), which stems from the noun *agorá*, signaling "a place of assembly, marketplace, typically in the town-center"; that noun in turn is derivative of *ageíro*, meaning "to bring together, to assemble in one public forum."

9. Notice how the Neo-Vulgate renders the Greek adjective *býssinos* (βύσσινος), "made of fine linen," with the noun *byssus* ("sea-silk") to smooth out the awkwardness of having an adjective within a list of nouns; the same goes for the ensuing adjectives *sirikós* (σιρικός) and *kókkinos* (κόκκινος), likewise translated by the nouns *sēricum* and *coccus* (v. 12).

shekhinah and priesthood, Solomon's temple, the tokens of mystical love (Cant 4:14), Jesus' own earthly life and Kingdom teachings, the efficacy of Christian prayer, the elements used in the holy sacraments of the Church, particularly baptism, confirmation, and the Blessed Sacrament, and most importantly, God's throne with his angels and saints in the New Jerusalem.

Adding insult to injury, and with intensified drama, those worldwide fiscal barons and business moguls then address themselves to this dying, smoldering world-city, just like the other three grieving parties do: "The fruit for which your soul longed has gone from you, and all your dainties and your splendor are lost to you, never to be found again!" (v. 14). All that ever mattered to Babylon the great prostitute, that is, whatever was superficially pleasant to the senses, will evaporate eventually. Her degenerate nature and materialistic soul relished the ostentation of her luxuriousness, the sumptuousness of her global markets, as well as domestic delights and fineries. Two triads of contrasting concepts communicate the final dissolution of it all: *First*, the doomed trifecta of pleasures, namely, the "autumnal fruitfulness" (*fructus*), the "fatty richness" (*pinguis*[10]), and the "shiny magnificence" (*clarus*), the last two being attractively set in Greek alliteration (*lipará-lamprá*). And *second*, a terzetto conveying the idea of disintegration, i.e., "gone" (*discedere*), "ruined" (*perire*),[11] and "no longer found" (*non invenire*). It is a tautological way of signaling the breaking up of all commercial traffic that had the formerly splendid city as its pivot, the perishing of all articles of pleasure and prestige, which she had procured by her diabolical intrigues.

What light can the bankers' elegy cast on our inner life as baptized children of God and of his Church? To begin with, if the great harlot behaves like a bad shepherd, fleecing the flock to feed only herself, then we are called to discover the boundless riches of Christ (Eph 3:8). Instead of habitually lusting after earthly possessions, the soul ought to be a *homo negotiator* (Matt 13:45), searching day in and day out for the fine pearls of the Kingdom, to be able to enrich the brethren (Acts 3:6). Next, there is a stern warning that the idol worship of consumerism inevitably ends up reducing others to inhuman servitude and subjugating the human heart (v. 13d). Such a sin, the underbelly of ruthless mercantilism, makes the soul unable to soar to the heights of contemplation.[12]

10. This Latin adjective also connotes insipidness of taste, obtuseness of mind, and a comfortable easiness.

11. This is the singular occurrence of the Greek verb *apóllymi* (ἀπόλλυμι) in Revelation, a compound of *apó*, "away from," intensifying *óllymi*, "to destroy, cut off entirely," depicting utter perdition and death, viewed as miserable and certain.

12. Cf. AvS, 587.

Conversely, Jesus purchased us for his Father by his precious Blood (5:9); we are now his personal possession, his very own slaves in the service of his glory.

Furthermore, and in the same logic as the river in the wilderness (12:16), global marketplaces flush with material goods create the illusion of a pseudo-paradise, enticing the soul not to wait for heaven, but to engage in unscrupulous pleasure-seeking, carnal luxury, and gain in the "here and now." For the planet, such ruthless avarice does not have such paradisiac consequences; on the contrary, it is being looted in the long run. And what must be stated with great clarity and urgency, too, is that it is not first and foremost international politics or trading agreements that bring humanity together, but the Mystical Body of Christ, the sole truly global unifier on earth.

In addition, faithful Christians seek to lay their life's foundation in the holiness and merits of his grace, symbolized by the gold, silver, gems, and fine linen (1 Cor 3:10–15). Thus, those freighters carrying highly priced goods are an image for the saints themselves, spreading the fragrance of the Gospel into the four corners of the world; in the process, they become a source of light for all generations.[13] A discerning heart will surround itself with as little temporal goods as possible, but search for ways to employ abundant means for God's glory and in charity toward the neighbor.[14] For those who pray to receive a docile heart like King Solomon (1 Kgs 3:9), and who leave everything behind to follow Christ, can hope to inherit eternal life (Matt 19:29). Hence, we strive first for the Kingdom of God and his righteousness, and all these things will be given to us as well (Matt 6:33).

Third threnody: Traders (18:15–17a)

[15] The merchants of these wares, who gained wealth from her, will stand far off, in fear of her torment, weeping and mourning aloud, [16] "Alas, alas, the great city, clothed in fine linen, in purple and scarlet, adorned with gold, with jewels, and with pearls! [17a] For in one hour all this wealth has been laid waste!"

Coming as they do on the heels of the bankers (*negotiatores*, v. 11), and under their supreme economic management, are the actual *mercatores* or marketeers (v. 15), i.e., those who commercialize products by making them available to the

13. Notice how in the Apocalypse the adjective "splendid" (*lamprós*, λαμπρός, v. 14) is normally applied to the Lord and to his angels and saints (15:6; 19:8; 22:1, 16).

14. Cf. AvS, 588.

masses: "The traders of these wares, who gained wealth from her, will stand far off, in fear of her torment, weeping and mourning" (v. 15). They constitute the third group of mourners in this tetralogy of apocalyptic dirges. That these middle-persons between producers and consumers are often well-traveled[15] makes them also instruments of considerable cosmopolitical and cultural influence. With a slight emphasis on the eschatological dimension suggested by the future tense "will stand" (*stabunt*), they position themselves at a safe distance from the burning blaze of Babylon, like the kings and upcoming sailors (vv. 10, 17), frightened at her torture, loudly squealing and moaning. They know that an end has come to all her corrupt affluence and renown, and now they experience a blend of terror and heartbreak, sorely unequipped to render relief. They sense the real possibility that they might be next in line for punishment, suffering a similar fate together with their bosses and customers, all partners in crime.

Resuming the doleful refrain "Alas, alas, the great city," parallel to kings and sailors (vv. 10, 19), they add, true to form, a portraiture of the great whore's attire: "Clothed in fine linen, in purple and scarlet, adorned with gold, with jewels, and with pearls" (v. 16), thereby reiterating what was hinted at already at 17:4 and 18:12.[16] When these attributes are put as collective singulars, universalizing her appearance, she becomes a parody for the sacred vestments of Aaron and his sons (Exod 28), but also another manifestation of unfaithful Israel (Ezek 16:13) and not least an antithetical foretaste of the heavenly Jerusalem (21:11–21). Bewailing the abrupt decay of this her fortune, they adjoin: "For in one hour all this wealth has been laid waste!" (17a). While they are synchronized with the kings and shippers in saying "For in one hour" (vv. 10, 19), they differ in the focus on *what* so rapidly happens: the royals stress Babylon's judgment, whereas these merchants lament the ruination of her trading affluence. In that, they echo the financiers' perspective (v. 14), and at the same time prepare for the forthcoming funeral song of the sailors (v. 17b).

And again, from a spiritual angle, the traders' fear (v. 15) reveals the deep-seated remorse of their conscience, convicting them for their callous business practices, but also for their sinful greed and attachment to ephemeral things

15. As implied by the Greek noun *émporos* (ἔμπορος), deriving from *en*, "in," and *póros*, "a way of passage, transport," literally designating someone on a journey; by connotation, it means a merchant, using a particular area or venue to ply his trade.

16. Flavius Josephus offers a captivating backdrop to the harlot's colorful clothes and adornments when he describes the temple curtain as being of Babylonian origin, embroidered with a quadruple color scheme, blue-white-scarlet-purple, interpreting it as a mystical image of the universe (cf. *The Jewish War*, 5.4); by extension, the apocalyptic prostitute could be viewed as an epitome of secularity, antagonistic to God's cosmic designs.

on earth. On the other hand, faithful Christians will maintain a healthy dose of detachment, freeing them from fright in the face of possible material deprivation, and keeping them mindful of Jesus' behest: "Store up for yourselves treasures in heaven, where neither moth nor rust consumes and where thieves do not break in and steal" (Matt 6:20).[17]

Fourth threnody: Mariners (18:17b–19)

[17b]And all shipmasters and seafarers, sailors and all whose trade is on the sea, stood far off [18]and cried out as they saw the smoke of her burning, "What city was like the great city?" [19]And they threw dust on their heads, as they wept and mourned, crying out, "Alas, alas, the great city, where all who had ships at sea grew rich by her wealth! For in one hour she has been laid waste."

Rounding out the tetralogy of laments (vv. 9–17a) is the entirety of nautical personnel, more germane to seagoing Rome than to landlocked Babylon. By dividing this group into four, namely, shipmasters,[18] seafarers, sailors, and whoever labors across the oceans, unlike the uniform entities of the preceding three dirges (kings, bankers, traders), John seems to give more relevance to this maritime sector of world commerce. With all these naval characters, who gain their living by the sea, the loop of international economics is completed. Positioning themselves at distant coastlines, albeit not "in fear of her torment" like royals and merchants (vv. 10, 15), the shippers naturally take a keen interest in the wastage of a city with which they were accustomed to do trade, and that in turn enriched them by the import and export of manifold merchandise. In a climactic intensification compared with the previous three, they cry out as they watch the conflagration take its course.

Mirroring the first elegy, they are shocked at the sight of the billowing smoke, and repeatedly comment on the former grandeur of the city, bringing about a literary *inclusio* with regard to vv. 9–10. Their rhetorical challenge "What city was like the great city?" (v. 18) not only establishes an intimate bond with the sea-beast, of whom its worshipers boast, "Who is like the beast, and

17. Cf. AvS, 589.

18. The original Greek masculine noun *kybernētēs* (κυβερνήτης) covers a wide range of lexical meanings, including "ship captain, steersman, helmsman, pilot, navigator, driver, director, manager, administrator"; it is rendered as *gubernator*, i.e., "governor, leader, guide," by the New Vulgate.

who can fight against it?" (13:4), but it also mocks the praise of Yahweh directly after Israel's Exodus, "Who is like you, O Lord, among the gods? Who is like you, majestic in holiness, awesome in splendor, doing wonders?" (Exod 15:11). How is it not also a sarcastic allusion to Babylon's former self-deification as she is now consumed by fire: What city has suffered as she has?! Rather than sincerely commiserating with her agony,[19] there is merely a self-centered lingering of the memory over delights now vanished (v. 19): is this really the proud city that claimed queenship, that disdained widowhood, and that thought to herself that she would never see unhappiness (18:7)? Her outward show and inward idolatry and impenitence have now turned into irretrievable ruin.

Redolent of grief-stricken Job, scraping himself with a potsherd and sitting among the ashes (Job 2:8, 12), all the shippers "threw dust on their heads, as they cried out, weeping and mourning" (v. 19). This gesture of intense sorrow and humiliation, together with their continued outcry, compounds the stereotypical "weeping and mourning" (vv. 9, 11, 15), making theirs the culmination point of the entire elegiac quadruplet (vv. 9–19). Borrowed from the sailors' lamentation over Tyre (Ezek 27:30), it also recalls Jesus' own warning against the unrepentant cities, located around the northern shore of the Sea of Galilee (Luke 10:13–14). Ironically, the seafarers' dust of grief is the exact opposite of the luxury items that were channeled in and out of the unfaithful world-city (Isa 47:1).

And for a third and last time (vv. 10, 16), the stomach-turning "Alas, alas!" rings out toward "the great city, where all who had ships at sea grew rich by her wealth!" (v. 19). And since it would be nonsensical to acclaim her power, the adjective "mighty" (*fortis*) of v. 10 has now reverted to the generic, yet no less sarcastic, "great" (*magna*). Despite the wreckage of a third of all ships at the blow of the second trumpet (8:9), mariners of all stripes still found a productive and lucrative market in Babylon, bringing abundant bargains of precious treasures from all ports of the world. By employing the abstract Greek noun *timiótēs* (τιμιότης), "abundance," John stresses a brand of affluence that has obsessive value in the eyes of the beholder. Thus, it is not private property or generally the possession of goods that is ethically problematic, but their arrogant use, exclusively trusting in the security they offer, which amounts to idolatry. It is translated by the Neo-Vulgate as *opes*,[20] meaning plenty and

19. Such coldness of heart is connoted by the Greek verb *blépō* (βλέπω, v. 18), descriptive of the mere act of seeing, without further thought of or reflection on the object perceived.

20. Etymologically related to Opis, the divine matron of queenly status, representing earthly prosperity and fertility according to ancient Roman mythology; in iconography, she is

munificence, akin to *opus*, "work," which in turn implies the sacredness of human work to procure these riches.

Closing the shippers' dirge is the stunned affirmation "for in one hour she has been laid waste" (v. 19), the third and last recurrence of this refrain (vv. 10, 17). Hence, Babylon's doomsday, predicted at v. 8, seemed to the disturbed onlookers but "one hour." And this concludes the quadrilogy of parallel elegies, dramatically proclaimed by kings, bankers, traders, and mariners, as if in attendance of a requiem for the wicked world-city, on the heels of her cremation and preceding her interment.

This fourth and final dirge contains cues for our interior life, as well. To begin with, the trade by sea can remind us of the Church as a ship, the bark of Peter, prefigured by the saving ark of Noah. Her "trade" is to reach out to the four corners of the earth in a missionizing effort: "Go therefore and make disciples of all nations, baptizing them in the name of the Father and of the Son and of the Holy Spirit!" (Matt 28:19). And if the God-Man seems asleep on the cushion in the stern, i.e., the rear, of the boat (Mark 4:38), he prods each one of us, his brethren, to take charge of, or at least participate in, those salvific endeavors. In fact, the Christian life is a voyage across the ocean of temporality heading toward the harbor of heaven.

Moreover, the text appears to illustrate the various aspects of sin especially when it becomes a habit: the indulging of the kings, the masterminding by the top financiers, the self-enriching of the mercantile folks, and the stabilization of supply lines by the seafarers.[21] Spiritual remedy should be sought in evangelical simplicity, in a humble pursuit of personal holiness, a charitable attitude toward the needy, and the avoidance of occasions of sin. And what is so unsettling about that whole set of laments in vv. 9–19 is its air of barefaced insincerity and hypocrisy, with no sign of authentic repentance or conversion. Which can inspire the Christian today and of all time to be unfeigned in the way we worship God, work for his Kingdom, and return to the embrace of our merciful Father. Also, there is the urgency of seizing every opportunity to take advantage of the kairotic "hour" with its means of salvation.[22] True disciples of Jesus will not procrastinate in accepting the Cross as the royal path to fulfillment: "Father, the hour has come: glorify your Son, that your Son may glorify you!" (John 17:1).

depicted as sitting down, holding a scepter, a spray of corn, and a cornucopia; the sum of these attributes is clearly suggestive of Babylon, the great apocalyptic harlot, too.

21. Cf. AvS, 590.

22. Cf. AvS, 591–92.

And in closing, the dust of the mourners brings Ash Wednesday to mind, the starting point of the Lenten journey of *metanoía* toward Easter. A metaphor for humility and fasting, the dust reminds us that every baptized person will be brought low at some point in life, down to the ground, even near the ashes of death, as a test of one's faith, hope, and love. It also intimates that sanctity cannot be achieved without self-mastery, but that self-control will not come without some measure of asceticism and indeed, material renunciation. If our divine Master had to suffer greatly, since "without the shedding of blood there is no forgiveness of sins" (Heb 9:22), then we, the members of his Body whose Head is crowned with thorns, are also called to share in his affliction: "Earth to earth, ashes to ashes, dust to dust; in sure and certain hope of the resurrection to eternal life through our Lord Jesus Christ."[23] Or, as Paul puts it: "The saying is sure: If we have died with him, we will also live with him; [12] if we endure, we will also reign with him" (2 Tim 2:11–12).

23. From "The Order for the Burial of the Dead," *Book of Common Prayer* (1928) of the Church of England.

18:20–24, Supernal eulogy

Just jubilation (18:20)

[20]Rejoice over her, O heaven, you saints and apostles and prophets! For God has given judgment for you against her.

Wholly antipodal to the earthly laments of the chapter's second part (vv. 9–19) is the heavenly euphoria of the forthcoming third and final part (vv. 20–24), both being reactions to Babylon's fall as depicted in the chapter's first part (vv. 1–8). This jubilant response arising in this v. 20, heralded already in 11:17–18, 15:3–4, and 16:5–7, simultaneously answers the cry for retributive justice by those slain Gospel witnesses at 6:10, and it will brim over into yet another quadrilogy, this time of Hallelujahs, in 19:1–8. While it illustrates the radical separation between the realm of darkness and the Kingdom of light, it also constitutes a certain disruption of the train of thought between verses 19 and 21. Nevertheless, instead of considering it an awkward interpolation later made by the hand of an editor, we should rather view it as an enlivening literary apostrophe like the one at 16:15.

Without identifying the one who is speaking, here is the galvanizing exhortation: "Rejoice over her, O heaven, and you saints and apostles and prophets, for God has given judgment for you against her!" (v. 20). Now, even though the Neo-Vulgate's punctuation seems to put these words still into the mouth of the villainous shippers wrapping up their direct speech (vv. 18–19), it seems more logical not to associate this celestial invitation with them, but to attribute it either to an angel, to some unspecified supernatural voice, or to John himself. A compelling connection can be made between the one calling upon the saints to come out of Babylon, to avenge themselves of her (vv. 4–8), and this appeal to be happy at her undoing. It is impossible to overstate the contrast between the foregoing wailing and the injunction here to rejoice, in bold imitation of Jeremiah 51:47–49. As a matter of fact, there is more joy in heaven at the harlot's downfall than at that of the two beasts (19:20) and even of the devil himself (20:10).

The seer employs the Greek verb *euphraínō* (εὐφραίνω, *exsultare*), "to rejoice," aware of its eloquent connotation, namely, the combining of the prefixed *eú*, "good," with *phrḗn*, meaning "midriff, heart, intellect," conveying the idea of visceral gladness governed by one's personal conviction, or a cheery state of mind based on a deep inner sense of triumph, expressed in hearty jubilation. Solemnly and vividly addressed with the vocative "O heaven!" are all the saints dwelling in the presence of God and of his angels. Now that the great enemy of the Church and corrupter of the world is removed, there is occasion to delight in the victory. This is supplemental to the reality expressed earlier, where all the human worshipers of the beast are said to be tortured in the presence of the holy angels and in the presence of the Lamb (14:10). After this *genus* of sanctity, a first of two *species*, as it were, is enumerated, namely, the "apostles," not the college of the Twelve chosen directly by Christ (21:14),[1] but a unique designation for Christians of all generations (2:2). It could be argued that the apostolic successors, the bishops of the Church, are envisioned in a special way. In a broader sense, however, these are all those who promote the values of the Gospel down the centuries by way of evangelization. Making the cross-section of Church triumphant and militant complete are the "prophets," beginning with those whose inspired oracles are preserved in the canon of the Old Testament. Additionally, there are all those baptized men and women, clerical and lay, who have witnessed to the truth regarding faith and morals in revealing God's will to their brethren throughout the ages (Eph 3:5).

Thus, in yet another fourfold summary, heaven, saints, apostles, and prophets, are summoned to revel in the final destruction of evil. Heaven and earth rightly ratify Babylon's elimination, now that God has avenged his elect. To "judge a judgment" (*iudicavit iudicium*) is a Hebraic way of emphasizing that the Lord reveals himself as the definitive executor of justice. With strong overtones of the ancient law of "an eye for an eye," but also conclusive to the biblical Courtroom Motif,[2] there is a threefold perspective on this exercise of God's justice: *first*, it is "your judgment" (*iudicium vestrum*), i.e., *our* judgment, in that it reflects the discernment of Christians concerning evil in this world; *second*, it is the divine judgment of the great harlot's annihilation (17:1); and

1. Of whom St. John would have been the last survivor by the time he wrote Revelation on Patmos, traditionally toward the end of the first century.

2. Also known as the *Rîb*-Motif, according to which Jesus and his followers are the defendants, ungodly humanity is the plaintiff, Satan the prosecuting adversary or accuser, the Holy Spirit the defense attorney, and God the Father the judge; the final sentence is an acquittal of humanity in the Resurrection of Christ from the dead.

third, we see God taking our cause out of her wicked hands (*ex autḗs*, ἐξ αὐτῆς, *de illa*) into his own, to fully satisfy his justice. Put differently, he vindicates us, his beloved children, by exacting vengeance "out of her," condemning her for her condemnation of us. And all of these three aspects taken together will "avenge the blood" of the slain souls at 6:10.

There are several ways in which this verse can enlighten our Christian spirituality. To begin with, there is the inner joy at seeing good separated from evil, light from darkness, truth from falsehood, the god-fearing from the godless.[3] Since Babylon is a metaphor for the presence of evil in the heart of every human being wounded by the consequences of original sin, it ought to be a lifelong endeavor to discern between the two, making it "our judgment," convinced that following the path of righteousness generates a profound sense of bliss already here on earth. Yet also, the soul must patiently wait for the Lord to vindicate it, not seeking immediate or delayed vengeance in conflictual situations. Moreover, we should heed the warning regarding the ultimate takedown of wickedness, oftentimes observable even in the lives of people that surround us, but also wisely judge the general volatility of earthly affairs and set our affections on things above (Luke 13:2–3).

By the same token, each one should foster a wholehearted devotion to the angels and saints, who delight in God's glory, and at the same time feel sorrow for us, their friends, in our trials down here in this valley of tears. And perhaps most importantly, we are reminded that each one of us is "heaven, saint, apostle, prophet," by living out our triple office (*munus triplex*) conferred to us in baptism, which incorporates us into Christ, the Priest, the Prophet, and the King. In the universal call to holiness,[4] each member of his Church is called to give witness to the truth in word and deed as prophets, using our talents to advance his Kingdom.[5] As St. John Paul put it on occasion of the joint beatification of the first married couple, Luigi and Maria Beltrame-Quattrocchi:

> Drawing on the word of God and the witness of the saints, the blessed couple lived an ordinary life in an extraordinary way. Among the joys and anxieties of a normal family, they knew how to live an extraordinarily rich spiritual life. At the center of their life was the daily Eucharist as well as devotion to the Virgin Mary, to whom they prayed every evening with the Rosary, and consultation with wise spiritual directors.[6]

3. Cf. AvS, 593.

4. Cf. Second Vatican Council, *Lumen gentium*, §§39–42.

5. *CCC*, §898.

6. John Paul II, Homily for the Beatification of Luigi Beltrame Quattrocchi and Maria Corsini, October 21, 2001, Vatican City, §2; English trans.: "Bl Luigi Beltrame Quattrocchi

Hurled into irrelevance (18:21–24)

[21]Then a mighty angel took up a stone like a great millstone and threw it into the sea, saying, "With such violence Babylon the great city will be thrown down, and will be found no more; [22]and the sound of harpists and minstrels and of flutists and trumpeters will be heard in you no more; and an artisan of any trade will be found in you no more; and the sound of the millstone will be heard in you no more; [23]and the light of a lamp will shine in you no more; and the voice of bridegroom and bride will be heard in you no more; for your merchants were the magnates of the earth, and all nations were deceived by your sorcery. [24]And in you was found the blood of prophets and of saints, and of all who have been slaughtered on earth."

And suddenly, John's attention is pulled away from the smoke of the burning city (vv. 9, 18) toward the unfolding of a different scene: "Then a mighty angel took up a stone like a great millstone and threw it into the sea, saying, 'With such violence Babylon the great city will be thrown down, and will be found no more'" (v. 21). With graphic detail, therefore, the visionary observes this powerful spirit stoop down to the ground and physically lift up (*sustulit*) an object similar to a colossal millstone from the earth. He is the last of three apparitions of a "mighty angel" in Revelation, the first one inquiring about the opening of the large scroll (5:2), the second one holding the little scroll (10:1), and this present one arguably heralding the fulfillment of their mysterious contents. In his preternatural muscularity he now raises the millstone up high, maybe even over his head, as sometimes depicted in iconography, only to hurl it into the sea.[7]

Like one of the Old Testament prophets, he performs this symbolic action to reassure the spectator with utmost energy that this is the doom awaiting those who cause God's children to stumble (Matt 18:6), but possibly also to hint at the abruptness and swiftness of his return. In her rage, the world-city ground so many of God's holy ones to powder, and now, sarcastically, her fate is sealed by a millstone, an implement of pulverization. To be dashed into the ocean, an image speaking a thousand words, mainly signals irretrievable riddance. As she sinks down far past recovery into the deep sea, a hopeless victim of her own

(1880–1951) and Bl Maria Corsini (1884–1965)," *L'Osservatore Romano*, English Edition 1713 (October 10, 2001): 11.

7. Because of his power and decisive symbolic action, Rupert sees in him a representative of Christ himself as an eschatological "Angel of the Lord" (*Malak Yahweh*), cf. RD, 1156.

weight, she is met with abysmal chill and darkness. Just as the beast surfaced from the sea (13:1), and as she arrogantly lounged on the many waters (17:1, 15), so she is now tossed back into that same element of frigidness and gloom.[8] This imagery also evokes the contrast between Pharaoh's chariots plunging into the Red Sea like rock and lead (Exod 15:5, 10), and the God-Man walking on the waters of Lake Tiberias by night (John 6:19), the latter signifying the victory over sin and death through his Resurrection.

And promptly following is a clarification of the angel's gesture, namely, that Babylon will be violently destroyed without leaving a trace for posterity (v. 21). With that begins a rhythmic song of doom up to v. 24. That this will happen with God's permission and with absolute certainty at the end of history is expressed by the future passive voice: "She surely shall be thrown down at that point" (*blēthḗsetai*, βληθήσεται, *mittetur*). Not by gentle or natural decline, but by an irresistible impetus will she be declassed and annihilated, swiftly and irreparably, not unlike the herd of swine perishing in the Gadarene territory (Matt 8:32). Now that she is flung down out of sight, she will never again harm the children of God (Ezek 26:21). And somberly pealing no fewer than six times in vv. 21–23, again like a death knell for the deceased, are the words "no more!" In the wake of the bankers' rebuking the world-city to her face back in v. 14, these vv. 22–23 are the last time that she is addressed directly with seven second person pronouns ("you, your"), interwoven with five verbs inflected in the future tense.

Besides Babylon herself (v. 21), there are five items that will be found "no more" in her, and they are symmetrically arranged to feature the noun *vox* (*phōné*, φωνή), "sound, voice," in the first, third, and fifth stanza (vv. 22a.c.; 23b), as an innuendo to Jeremiah 25:10. Banished *first* are musical tunes as a prime expression of human life and culture: "And the sound of harpists and minstrels and of flutists and trumpeters will be heard in you no more" (v. 22a). An oriental ensemble comprised of four types of musicians is envisaged, therefore, and their tragic disappearance will forever sever all ties to the arts of the muses[9] and to the mirth of heavenly worship. Only the principal instruments are mentioned here, representing all forms of festivity and joy on earth. And a

8. Cf. AvS, 594.

9. The Greek adjective *mousikós* (μουσικός) springs from the noun *moûsa* (μοῦσα), which at the time the Apocalypse was written, would have referred to the nine deities in Greek mythology called Muses, considered the source of all human knowledge, namely, astronomy, history, poetry, tragedy, comedy, lyrics, music, hymns, and dance. Theogonically speaking, they were daughters of Zeus, the king of the gods, and of Mnemosýne, the goddess of memory, but their mission was to facilitate obliviousness in people concerning their earthly suffering.

second skill will vanish: "An artisan of any trade will be found in you no more" (v. 22b). Artificers and craftsmen were supposed to imitate God the supreme Architect and Builder of all things (Heb 11:10). Yet their creativity[10] utterly deteriorated, and the sculptures, paintings, and statuary that were supposed to adorn life, turned into vehicles of idolatry and immorality.

Thirdly, "The sound of the mill[11] will be heard in you no more" (v. 22c), indicating the permanent disruption of supplies for the necessities of life, such as preparing flour to bake bread. This image may not so much hint at the tedious creaking and grating of the rotating runner-stone against the massive bed-stone, as at the voice of singing that ordinarily accompanied grinding (Eccl 12:3–4). Hence, the mill was a sign of cheerfulness and comfortable living, and its ceasing is a terrifying metaphor of decline.[12] *Fourth* in line of the five things that will vanish as a direct consequence of the harlot's fall is the means of illumination: "And the light of a lamp will shine in you no more" (v. 23a), creating an alliteration in the Latin text (*lux lucernae non lucebit*). For the first-century audience of Revelation, it would have been a matter of oil-fed portable lamps usually placed on a stand in the house. But these cheerful sources of luminescence in homes and during festivals are now extinguished, bringing about a frightening absence of light,[13] yet another image of total desolation, in polar opposition to the radiance of the heavenly city (22:5).

But it all culminates in the *fifth* and final reality to completely evaporate: "The voice of bridegroom and bride will be heard in you no more" (v. 23b). This is also the third and last time, following music and mills, that a specific sound will disappear forever. Hence, nuptial companionship and communication are silenced, that is, marriages will be absent, and with that the propagation of the human family: the evil world-city will be depopulated and desolate. Neither rich nor poor will be able to live there anymore, and everything that signaled festivity (music), prosperity (mill), and familial joy (matrimony), will

10. Given that the Greek noun *téchnē* (τέχνη), "art, craft, trade, skill," stems from the verb *tíktō* (τίκτω), meaning "to beget, yield, bring forth, produce, give birth."

11. Whereas in v. 21a, the Latin adjective *molāris* (*mýlinos*, μύλινος) meant a "millstone" proper, here it is the noun *mola* (*mýlē*, μύλη), signifying the entire "mill."

12. In antiquity, mills came to be seen as a chief hallmark of a culture's prosperity and expertise, invaluable for economic advancement. Biblical authors acknowledged how critical milling and grain were to a nation's survival, and thus proscribed anyone from unlawfully monopolizing them (Deut 24:6). A millstone even came to symbolize civilization itself (Exod 11:5), and for the Hebrews, it would have carried an unforgettable overtone of the Exodus and their sojourning in the wilderness that saw them grinding the manna as sustenance on their way to the Promised Land (Num 11:7–8).

13. Cf. AvS, 604.

have disappeared. All that is, of course, in startling antithesis to the presence of Bridegroom and Bride in the New Jerusalem, a city enlivened by a never-ending wedding banquet, and inhabited by the demographic plenitude of the nations.

Three reasons for Babylon's destruction follow: *First*, there is the self-sufficient and impudent arrogance of the global socioeconomic systems:[14] "For your marketeers were the magnates of the earth" (v. 23c). They thought of themselves as the ultimate great ones in this world and the lords of the universe,[15] while they allowed themselves to be led into numberless sins by their avarice. Fallowing is the *second* cause of the great whore's fall, and another enormous scandal: "All nations were deceived by your sorcery" (v. 23d). This witchcraft is simply synonymous with satanic deception.[16] Hence, by her artful policies and attractiveness, she drew into the meshes of her secularism all the surrounding nations (13:14). And the *third* reason for her ruination is that "in her was found the blood of prophets and of saints, and of all who have been slaughtered on earth" (v. 24). Reverting to the grammatical third person of v. 21, Babylon becomes again the now distant object, not the close subject, of conversation; the seer passes from reporting the good spirit's denunciation of her to his personal characterization of her guiltiness.

There is also a marked polarity between the double "will be found no more" in v. 21–22, and the phrase "was found" here (v. 24). Now, her true scarlet is showing (17:3–6), since her seductive hands are defiled with the blood of prophets and saints (v. 20; 11:18), of all those, therefore, whose holy lives were a disapproval and protest of her depravations, and so infuriating to her. The apex of her iniquities is couched in the simple Semitic concept of bloodshed that cries out for vengeance. Cain sadly inaugurated the reign of Babylon by shedding his younger brother's lifeblood (Gen 4:10), and from that moment an arc has stretched all the way to the Lamb himself (5:6), as well as to all his intrepid followers, killed on account of their faith-filled witness to his name till the end of time. Only in Christ's own saving Blood is the desecration expiated, yet those violent acts will continue to cry out until they are appeased by the punishment of the killers. The apocalyptic harlot's bloodthirsty persecution of the saints is the one single deed that summarizes her transgression of God's law, and here it

14. Here, the New Vulgate's *mercatores*, "merchants," is to be taken in the generic sense of world-economic managing agents (vv. 11, 15).

15. The noun *megistán* (μεγιστάν, *magnātus*), meaning "chief, a great one, lord, nobleman" (6:15; Mark 6:21), derives from the adjective *mégistos* (μέγιστος), which in turn is the superlative form of *mégas* (μέγας), signifying "the very greatest, the ultimate, the most magnificent one."

16. Cf. AvS, 605.

concludes the entire judgment pronounced against her since 17:1. And now, she will be hurled into never-ending irrelevance.

But how do the angel's action and words (vv. 21–24) translate into our spiritual life? For one thing, the grinding motion of the millstone (v. 22) can be taken as an allegory for the gravity of personal sin, tending to crush and fragment the soul's inner disposition of virtue and strength.[17] It also reminds us of Jesus' realism regarding scandals: "Occasions for stumbling (*scandala*) are bound to come, but woe to the one through whom they come! It would be better for him to have a millstone hung around his neck and to be thrown into the sea, than to cause one of these little ones to stumble" (Luke 17:1–2). What is more, the image of that millstone plunged into the sea conjures up associations with hell, and how only Christ himself was able to return from visiting those depths on Holy Saturday,[18] and how each one of us is eternally grateful for that redeeming visitation.

Also, when hearing about Babylon being "found no more," we are reminded of Rachel's grieving for her children (Matt 2:18), and the serious or even permanent consequences of our moral decisions. At the same time, the contemplation of the annihilation of that great prostitute should motivate us to look forward to those dwellings that Jesus has gone to prepare for us (John 14:3).[19] But there should also be the realization of how excruciating it must have been for John, the Lord's beloved disciple, to face the reality of hell, the necessary outcome of demonic and human hatred and unbelief, and how he endured that visionary agony for our sake, to help us fear eternal death, to do everything in our power to avoid it, and to intensify our prayers for the conversion of sinners.[20] Additionally, there is a lesson about the spiritual benefits of sacred music (v. 22a) that is capable of lifting up the human heart to the heights of religious sentiment, but also of how the perversion of that great gift can result in dangerous expressions of satanism.[21] Likewise, the followers of Jesus cherish the

17. Cf. RD, 1156.

18. Hans Urs von Balthasar in his book *Mysterium Paschale: The Mystery of Easter* (1970) offers a reflection on that momentous day, opining that Jesus suffered not only physical death on the Cross, but also spiritual death in hell as the farthest reach of his vicarious suffering; nevertheless, given the difficulty of harmonizing his position with traditional Christology, theologians have typically argued that the Lord did not enter the actual precincts of hell but stopped short at a place called the limbo of the fathers, where the Old Testament righteous men and women resided at a safe distance from the burning flames awaiting their admittance into heaven.

19. Cf. AvS, 595.

20. Cf. AvS, 598–602; see also the vision of hell shown to the children of Fatima on July 13, 1917.

21. Cf. RD, 1157.

fruits of artistic effort and genius (v. 22b), as well as the pure joys of sacred art, as prime interpreters of theology and Christian humanism.

Moreover, bridegroom and bride (v. 23) are synonymous with the beginnings of family life, which contemporary culture tries to undermine especially by the promotion of contraception and the heinous crime of abortion. Speaking of which, the *pharmakeía* (φαρμακεία, *veneficium*, "sorcery, magic")[22] of v. 23d, that is, the preparation of magic potions in pagan antiquity, is a timeless appeal to use the science and skills of medicine for the advancement of healing and health.[23] Lastly, the savage slaughter and the spilling of innocent blood in this world, especially that of Christian martyrs (v. 24), makes us devotedly turn to the most precious Blood of our Savior: "In him we have redemption through his blood, the forgiveness of our trespasses, according to the riches of his grace" (Eph 1:7).

22. See also the remarks on *pharmakós* at 9:21.
23. Cf. AvS, 605.

PART 4

19:1–8, *Ecclesia sponsalis*

First Hallelujah: Vindication (19:1–2)

[1]After this I heard what seemed to be the loud voice of a great multitude in heaven, saying, "Hallelujah! Salvation and glory and power to our God, [2]for his judgments are true and just; he has judged the great whore who corrupted the earth with her fornication, and he has avenged on her the blood of his servants."

In unmistakable polarity to the condemnation of Babylon as the seat of the anti-Christian and anti-Marian kingdom, and ensuing funereal threnodies in the preceding chapter, the seer on Patmos is about to witness an outburst of celestial joy in continuation of 12:12 and 18:20. The great harlot's doom signals the commencement of triumph (19:1–8), and her defeat sparks the manifestation of victory, expressed by the end-time appearance of Jesus as Warrior-King, leading his Church via a final battle into the eternal wedding chamber of heaven. Just as on previous occasions (7:9–12; 14:1–5), the forthcoming exultant anthems serve as narrative relief, but also as an overture to the final movement or *coda* of the apocalyptic symphony. At the same time, this quadruple Hallelujah will be the concluding strophe of Revelation's hymnology.[1]

Up to this moment in time, John has been listening to the mighty angel's declaration (18:21–24) but is now enraptured by another voice: "After this I heard what seemed to be the loud voice of a great multitude in heaven, saying, 'Hallelujah!'" (v. 1a). This is the sixth and last recurrence of the introductory "After this" (*Post haec*) in this book, denoting the beginning of another heavenly vision, and it is possible that the seventh *post haec* will be Christ's parousia itself. Since the apostle does not identify the exact nature of the utterance, one can only imagine the immense chorus of all the saints, rejoicing again in

1. Robert E. Coleman distinguishes a total of fourteen spiritual canticles, cf. *Songs of Heaven* (Old Tappan, NJ: Fleming H. Revell, 1980).

the accomplishment of divine justice in response to the promptings of 18:20. It is the Church's bridal thanksgiving for the toppling of the great whore at the consummation of history, a cosmic anthem of consolation and exultation, a worshipful song of pilgrims who at last have arrived at their heavenly homeland, leaving behind the lamentations of the world below.[2] Joining in the triumphant harmony are the good spirits and even all of creation, recognizing God's supreme goodness.[3]

Nothing could ever be more evincive of those sentiments than the resounding quartet of Hallelujahs (vv. 3–4, 6), featured at this closing juncture of the New Testament like a final exclamation mark. This fourfold praise is not just a perfect response to the foregoing quadrilogy of laments (18:9–19), but can also be read as a reference to the Lord's victory over the vicissitudes of this earth whose apocalyptic emblem is precisely the number four. Analyzed in its Hebrew etymology, "Hallelujah" (הַלְלוּ־יָהּ, ἀλληλουϊά, *Alleluia*) is a communal exhortation to gratefully adore God the Most High, indeclinably composed of the plural imperative verb *hallelu* (הַלְלוּ), "you all praise!," and a theophoric suffix, i.e., the noun *Yah* (יָהּ), an abridged form of the tetragram Yahweh, "God." True to his custom (9:11), John paraphrases it at v. 5, "Praise our God!" Implied in this four-letter theonym YHWH (יהוה) is the broadest notion of "being" or "existence in past, present, and future," suggesting the Lord's never-failing help and protection (1:4). Phonetically, the prominence of the aspirated consonant "h" in Yahweh evokes the breath of life insufflated into Adam's nostrils (Gen 2:7), but also the pneumatic breath of forgiveness by the Risen Christ (John 20:22).

This apocalyptic Hallelujah exhibits the union between the Old and New Testaments, between the Jewish and the Christian peoples, the former being the latter's "elder brothers."[4] To this day, synagogal worship, especially during Passover (or *Pesach*), Pentecost (or *Shavuot*), and Tabernacles (or *Sukkot*), involves the chanting of the Hallel, that is, Psalms 113–118, all of whom contain the Hallelujah. There may even be a hint at the Jews' final re-inclusion in the Church (Rom 11:26). Yet in its present context, this heavenly doxology also signals the definitive punishment of the ungodly (v. 2). And to preserve the beauty of this superlative expression of thanksgiving, joy, and triumph, the early Christians left this Hebrew word simply untranslated like an untouchable spiritual treasure.

2. Cf. RD, 1158.

3. Cf. AvS, 608–10.

4. From St. John Paul II's discourse during his visit to the Synagogue in Rome on April 13, 1986.

All these countless voices converge into one pivotal acclamation: "Salvation and glory and power to our God" (v. 1b). In its biblical uniqueness, its sequential order follows its own logic, giving absolute importance to the fact that God has redeemed his children, who consequently glorify him and his boundless might. Inversely, that it does not reflect the progression from divine power, to bringing about salvation, and thereby deserving all honor, again proves that chronological categories do not necessarily apply to this apocalyptic genre, where the dimensions of space and time are sublimated into transcendence. But since this chant reacts to the disintegration of diabolical Babylon, its opposing force, that of God's salvation, is highlighted. In a trinitarian way it exalts the loving work of his hands ("salvation"), the fruit of his grace ("glory"), but also the perfection of his nature ("power"). And although the attributes are equally common to each person of the Triune God, one might credit especially the Son-Redeemer with "salvation," assign "glory" to the Father-Creator, and allocate "power" to the Holy Spirit-Sanctifier.

Three rationales for extoling God are now adjoined, the *first* being that "his judgments are true and just" (v. 2a). Put differently, his punishment of idolatrous and immoral Babylon vouches for his trustworthiness and righteousness. Ergo, those calamities that come upon the evil world-power here referred to are well-deserved. The Lord's "judgments" can also signify his precepts or his providential designs in history, worthy of glorification (15:3; 16:7). A *second* motive for divine praise is that "he has judged the great prostitute who corrupted the earth with her fornication" (v. 2b). At this point, therefore, irrevocable judgment has been passed on her who was never married,[5] but instead engaged in whoredom of every type. And that this judgment is presented as already accomplished is implied by the perfect tense of the Latin verb *iudicāvit*, "she has been judged." Here we find the singular mention of the verb *phtheírō* (φθείρω), "to corrupt," in Revelation, stressing the extreme degree of moral depravity in her relationships. What is remarkable is the consistency with which John characterizes the whore's four chief sins, i.e., deception, idolatry, immorality, and Christian persecution.

And the *third* ground for jubilation is that "he has avenged on her the blood of his servants" (v. 2c; cf. 18:20). Impatient was the cry at 6:10, but it has finally been answered,[6] as if by applying this ancient biblical principle: "Whoever

5. Tellingly, John nowhere employs the term that contrasts with *porneía* (πορνεία), "fornication," namely, *moicheía* (μοιχεία), meaning "adultery, marital unfaithfulness," underscoring that Babylon was always promiscuous, and never truly espoused to anybody.

6. The Greek compound verb *ekdikéō* (ἐκδικέω, *vindicare*), "to vindicate, exacted retribution, judge thoroughly," recurs only in these two verses in Revelation.

sheds the blood of a human, by a human shall that person's blood be shed; for in his own image God made humankind" (Gen 9:6).[7] There appears to be a rather mysterious bond in this book between the Blood of the Lamb and that of his servants, one redemptive, the other martyrial. Since both are shed at the hands of the great city, it will be avenged "out of her hands":[8] "Why should the nations say, 'Where is their God?' Let the avenging of the outpoured blood of your servants be known among the nations before our eyes" (Ps 79:10). Equally enthralling is the similarity between Christ, portrayed by Isaiah as the Suffering Servant of God (Isa 42:1), and all his servants on earth. They were so cruelly put to death for their faith, but Jesus shows himself to be their true Savior, redressing their loss, and repaying their persecutors.

Second Hallelujah: Condemnation (19:3)

[3]Once more they said, "Hallelujah! The smoke goes up from her forever and ever."

This continued chanting constitutes the last allusion to parabolic Babylon in Revelation. By prefacing it with an emphatic "a second time" (*deúteron*, δεύτερον), John seems to suggest that the four Hallelujahs in vv. 1, 3–4, 6 should be viewed as a deliberate quadrivium, similar to the several other sequences of ternaries, quaternaries, and septenaries in this book. Those heavenly throngs commenced their solemn worship with "Praise the Lord!" (v. 1), and now they close it out in the same way, just as some Psalms begin and end with such an antistrophic Hallelujah (e.g., Ps 149). So momentous is the final defeat of the Church's enemy, that it calls for an amplification and repetition of the praise of God, arising from hearts inflamed with gratitude and joy (18:20).

Amazingly, the observation regarding the ascending smoke is not prosaic but lyrical, it is part of the canticle, stirring up memories of the wiping out of Sodom and Gomorrah (Gen 19:28), as well as the prophet Isaiah's oracle against Edom (Isa 34:9–10). That demonic exhalation as a result of the city's incineration, antithetical to the rising incense at 8:4, serves as an unending testimonial of God's punishment of sin (14:11); it indicates that evil world-systems will be permanently neutralized, that they are past recovery and will never rear

7. "And the hearts of the holy were filled with joy; because the number of the righteous had been offered, and the prayer of the righteous had been heard, and the blood of the saints been required before the Lord of Spirits," 1 Enoch 47:4.

8. In that way, the Greek phrase *ék cheirós autḗs* (ἐκ χειρὸς αὐτῆς), translated in the plural by the Neo-Vulgate *de manibus eius*, complements *éx autḗs* (ἐξ αὐτῆς, *de illa*) at 18:20.

their ugly heads again.[9] As such, the smoke embodies the reality of eternal hell, too (9:2).[10] Yet, that the latter also unfolds under the supreme control of God Almighty is testified to by the Greek idiom "into the ages of the ages" (*eis toùs aiṓnas tṓn aiṓnōn*, εἰς τοὺς αἰῶνας τῶν αἰώνων, *in saecula saeculorum*) which is invariably descriptive of the Lord's own eternity (1:6, 18). Thus, the revolting miasma of Babylon's demise shall never be quenched, and the city never restored again, even though earthly kingdoms might label themselves as "eternal."[11] This is the epitome of the antichrist's ultimate condemnation.

Third Hallelujah: Laudation (19:4–5)

4And the twenty-four elders and the four living creatures fell down and worshiped God who is seated on the throne, saying, "Amen. Hallelujah!"
5And from the throne came a voice saying, "Praise our God, all you his servants, and all who fear him, small and great."

Like inverted ripples encircling the blessed Trinity, the celestial praise now approaches its very throne (v. 4). Following a lengthy intermezzo of divine judgments on earth, the elders and living beings make a joint reappearance on the apocalyptic stage. They were last seen together listening to the new song reechoing from Mount Zion (14:3), and now they actively take part in the chorales of praise over the great harlot's ruin, which also marks their final mention in Revelation. These are not only lieutenants, as it were, of God's creation, but also representatives of the beginning and end of the economy of salvation, and, therefore, of the Jewish people and of the Church.[12] As such, they are adverted to one more time as rejoicing in the final triumph of God's elect, and in the razing to the ground of their last foe. With tremendous reverence they now adore God the Most High for what he has done in delivering his pilgrim people from all its persecutors and causing it to conquer the whole world. They express desire for the Lord to eschatologically fulfil what he has begun earlier in his grace: and how their jubilant vivacity contrasts with the hate-fueled bloodthirstiness of the dragon, the beasts, and the great whore!

9. That unendingness is also intimated by the narrative present tense of the verb *anabaínei* (ἀναβαίνει, *ascendit*).

10. Cf. AvS, 614.

11. E.g., the "everlasting empire" of ancient Chinese dynasties; the city of Rome as *Urbs Aeterna*; the former Japanese capital of Kyoto as "eternal city"; or, infamously, the so-called "thousand-year Reich" of Nazi Germany.

12. Cf. AvS, 616.

Ratifying the worship of the communion of all the saints (cf. vv. 1–3), they subjoin their "Amen," "So let it be": may God be forever praised, who manifests his infinite perfections on earth. Based on the triconsonantal Hebrew *a-m-n* (אמנ), this indeclinable noun Amḗn (אָמֵן, Ἀμήν) signifies firmness, trustworthiness, and dependability. It features as a title for the monotheistic God at Isaiah 65:16 (*Deus Amen*), as well as for Christ himself in 3:14 and 2 Corinthians 1:20. Here, it shows solemn approbation of what he has accomplished as Creator and Redeemer. From these scriptural passages it passed over into synagogal and Christian liturgies. What is unique on this occasion is its conflation with "Hallelujah,"[13] as in the manner of antiphonal chanting, where vv. 1–2 signal the invitation, v. 3 responds, and vv. 4–8a reflect three more rejoinders in harmony. Naturally, this third reiteration of divine laudation allows us to gauge well the intensity of the joy in heaven over the unfathomable gift of salvation (Luke 15:7, 10).

Antiphonary to the "Rejoice!" (*Exulta*) in the imperative mood at 18:20, as well as to the implied hortative mood of the three intervening Hallelujahs (vv. 1, 3–4), is the cohortative "Praise!" (*laudem dicite*) in what John hears next: "And from the throne came a voice saying, 'Praise our God, all you his servants, and all who fear him, small and great!'" (v. 5). Now, if God the Father is the one seated on the throne, worshiped by living beings and elders (v. 4), then it is conceivable that the voice issuing from the very midst of it belongs to his Son, the Lamb (5:6). However, Christ nowhere in Scripture speaks of him as "our God," but rather the opposite: after the Resurrection he carefully distinguished between "my Father and your Father, my God and your God" (John 20:17). By the same token, however, is it conceivable that this voice resounding from the center of God's throne could be anything less than divine? To reconcile these two poles of the ellipsis remains theologically hairy, and probably explains why some manuscripts carry the variant reading of a more generic *ouranoû* (οὐρανοῦ), "heaven," instead of *thrónou* (θρόνου), "throne," to allow for a non-divine origin of that voice, and perhaps also to it harmonize with that of v. 1. Hence, it is more supposable that it is a response proceeding from those nearest the throne, calling on all to unite in praising the Lord God Almighty.

Or again, could this be the voice of the mighty angel at 18:21, who in turn may be indistinguishable from the one who will interact with the visionary momentarily (19:9–10)? Quite surprisingly, the Greek word for "praise," that

13. With a single precedent in the Old Testament, namely, the Hebrew version of Ps 106:48; this psalm, incidentally, praises the covenant God for delivering his captive people from historical oppression.

is, the verb *ainéō* (αἰνέω, *laudem dicere*), occurs only once in Revelation,[14] and within the phrase "praise our God," it could be taken as a translation of "Hallelujah," except that it refers specifically to "our" God, which the latter does not, at least not explicitly. Tellingly, in the Septuagint, too, the two words appear next to each other in several psalms.[15] There is concordance between the angels and the saints in this triumphant song, and all of heaven shows great interest in the destinies of the Church, inviting all of God's servants to unite in thanksgiving (v. 2).

It is noteworthy that the title of "servant" (*doûlos*, δοῦλος, *servus*) is used exclusively in the Apocalypse to describe the beloved children of God, except on two occasions, where it signifies the slaves of Satan (13:16; 19:18). Whereas the previous chanting celebrated the Lord's faithfulness and justice as manifested in the punishment of all persecuting power (vv. 1–3), this one praises him for the glorious state of his Church which is about to blossom. Sons and daughters of God in the Son, they are no longer enslaved to sin, but willingly and cheerfully serve the Lord. In their hearts is found no trace of servile fear, but solely filial reverence,[16] flowing from faith and love, sustained by God's gracious goodness. Without a trace of mundane discrimination among them, the formerly poor and the rich, the young and the old, the lowly and the exalted (11:18), all shall accomplish in unison their doxological, royal, and sacerdotal function, namely, to worship him for ages unending.

Fourth Hallelujah: Espousal (19:6–8)

[6]Then I heard what seemed to be the voice of a great multitude, like the sound of many waters and like the sound of mighty thunderpeals, crying out, "Hallelujah! For the Lord our God the Almighty reigns. [7]Let us rejoice and exult and give him the glory, for the marriage of the Lamb has come, and his bride has made herself ready; [8]to her it has been granted to be clothed with fine linen, bright and pure," for the fine linen is the righteous deeds of the saints.

What happens in v. 6, is in sweeping response to the bidding of the antecedent verse. This vast crowd (*turba magna*) is indistinguishable from the ones

14. Related to the noun *aînos* (αἶνος), a frequent term in classical Greek poetry for "story," "proverb," or "laudatory discourse."

15. Cf. Pss 112:1; 116:1; 134:1; 150:1.

16. Incidentally, this is the sixth and last recurrence of the Greek verb *phobéō* (φοβέω), "to fear," in this book.

at v. 1 and 7:9, symbolizing the totality of the redeemed from among Jews and Gentiles, now gathered in the Church of Christ.[17] From the threefold repetition of the particle of comparison "like" (*quasi, sicut*) in this verse one might infer that the overall sound is louder, yet also more indiscernible, due to the larger throng that by now has swollen to its maximum capacity. In an obvious crescendo from those previous mentions, however, their voices are now more like immense cataracts or oceanic billows, that is, of the same volume as that of the Son of Man himself (1:15), and as that of the hundred forty-four thousand followers of the Lamb on Mount Zion (14:2). And from 17:1, 15 we understand that those waters symbolize all the nations on earth. Forever reliving the theophany on Mount Sinai (Exod 19:16), this divine praise also resembles the most earsplitting of thunderclaps, superlative in comparison to all the preceding ones.[18] Having been called a Boanerges, i.e., a "son of thunder" by Jesus himself (Mark 3:17), John must have been touched by this phenomenon in a special way. Lifted up before the throne of God, therefore, is a worshipful symphony of nature's voices, human, oceanic, and atmospheric, truly representative of heaven and earth.

This combination of images well conveys the magnitude and majesty of the forthcoming extolment of God's designs. Nevertheless, by employing a solecistic masculine plural participle *legóntōn* (λεγόντων, *dicentium*), syntactically disconnected from the anterior feminine, neuter, or singular nouns of this v. 6, the sacred author seems to surpass the symbolism of the multitude, and hint at the individual persons engrossed in the heavenly worship. Bearing close resemblance to the seventh trumpet (11:15–19), the ensuing divine epithalamium[19] is the last song of praise in the Apocalypse (vv. 6–8). It is the closing chorus opening with a fourth and final Hallelujah, pointing forward to the marriage of the Lamb, and thus, to the completion of the Lord's covenant with his children in glory. After all enemies have been overthrown, his faithful people can now enjoy imperishable bliss. That full triumph is transmitted both by the perfect active verb *regnavit* in the Neo-Vulgate ("he has reigned"), as well as the ingressive aorist tense of *ebasíleusen* (ἐβασίλευσεν), "has taken the Kingdom, has begun to reign," in the Greek original. Even though the God-Man has

17. Cf. AvS, 618.

18. In fact, this is the last of eight recurrences, quite evenly interspersed with the entire narrative plot of Revelation (4:5; 6:1; 8:5; 10:3; 11:19; 14:2; 16:18).

19. A classical wedding poem, composed specifically for the bride as she approaches the nuptial chamber (i.e., *thálamos*); tradition holds that the Canticle of Canticles may have been such a lyrical celebration of King Solomon's marriage to Pharaoh's daughter (1 Kgs 3:1).

always ruled due to his glorious Resurrection and Ascension,[20] at this juncture he enters the plenary phase of his reign, and hence is deserving of consummate adoration, as highlighted by the causative conjunction "because" (*hóti*, ὅτι, *quoniam*, *quia*; cf. vv. 2, 7). Having moved on from the defeat of the failed Babylonian queen, all eyes are now focused on the awesome presence of the Pantocrator,[21] who in his sovereign power has made the whole world a footstool for his feet (Eph 1:22). He himself, as the Maker and Upholder of the universe, is the culminating and permanent reason for authentic worship.

And at this midpoint of the anthem, the multitude's acclamation reaches an apogee: "Let us rejoice and exult and give him the glory, for the marriage of the Lamb has come, and his bride has made herself ready" (v. 7). With overflowing enthusiasm, the praise becomes pluri-dimensional, so to speak, as implied by the triple hortatory "let us rejoice!," "let us exult!," and "let us give him the glory!" (*gaudeamus-exsultemus-demus*). Foretasted in its ubiquitous use within the Psalter, the verb *agalliáō* (ἀγαλλιάω), "to exult, rejoice," especially expresses messianic joy, one's delight in the faith, and its makaristic recompense in the afterlife (Matt 5:12). Unlike their former adversaries (11:10), the saints never reveled in evildoing, but now their gladness explodes at the prospect of the union between the Lamb and his Bride. After its absence from the previous chapter, this divine Lamb abruptly reappears here, and will then not be reintroduced till 21:9. By means of the threefold prophetic perfect "has come," "has prepared," and "has been granted" in vv. 7–8 (*venerunt-praeparavit-datum*), this scene also anticipates the marriage between the Messiah and his people in chs. 21–22. Noteworthy, too, is the synthetic parallelism between vv. 1–2 and vv. 6–7, displaying the same sequence of a "Hallelujah" followed by a dual conjunction *hóti* (ὅτι, *quia*, *quoniam*), correlating God's judgment (v. 2), his pantocratorial sovereignty (v. 6), and the Lamb's wedding plans (v. 7).

Speaking of which, marriage as a universal institution is praised by all cultures and exalted in their respective forms of art and literature. Painting with a broad brush, the customary storyline involves mastering various challenges before bridegroom and bride, often imagined as prince and princess, can enjoy a happy marriage as husband and wife ever after. And so, too, it happens in John's Apocalypse: after overcoming the nefarious influence of the great harlot,

20. Cf. AvS, 620.

21. It is noteworthy that this divine title is unique to Revelation in the New Testament, excepting 2 Cor 6:18 (which in turn quotes 2 Sam 7:8, where it means "Lord of hosts," Yahweh Sabaoth, *Dominus exercituum*).

the earthly Bride is ready for her heavenly Bridegroom.[22] Of course, matrimony remains also the chief Old Testament metaphor to capture the covenant relationship between Yahweh and his people Israel, and hence, acts of idolatry and apostasy are viewed as adultery and harlotry (Ezek 16:17). And in the New Testament, the union of Christ with his Church is portrayed under the same simile (Eph 5:23, 32). Hence, and as a matter of metaphysical and theological fact, the earthly sacrament of marriage ultimately symbolizes the fruitful union to which God will raise his spousal Church as he inaugurates his eternal Kingdom.

It is also worthwhile to scrutinize the etymology of the biblical terminology involved in v. 7. There is the Greek masculine noun *gámos* (γάμος), meaning "betrothal, marriage, wedding-festival," probably derived from the Proto-Indo-European root **ǵem-*, meaning "to bind, unite," which underscores the unitive aspect of the mystically monogamous and everlasting relationship between Jesus and his faithful.[23] Translated in the Neo-Vulgate by the noun *nuptiae* ("nuptials"), another layer of meaning is added: it derives from the verb *nūptus*, signifying the act of veiling oneself for the bridegroom; it is based on the adjective *nubilis* ("marriageable"), which itself originates in the word *nubes*, meaning "cloud."[24] That in turn would have the connotation of Mary's overshadowing by the Holy Spirit in the Incarnation (Luke 1:35). Moreover, the English rendition "wedding," from the Proto-Germanic **wadja*,[25] has to do with the notion of "promise, pledge,[26] entrustment, betrothal." Thus, the trust and faith that bind the people of God to its Savior are brought to the fore, as well. English Bible translations have traditionally employed the term "marriage," springing from the Latin *maritāre*, "to wed"; the latter is a derivative of *marītus*, "husband, suitor," from *mās*, meaning "man, male." Implied, one might say, is the maleness and femaleness of the protoparents Adam and Eve, redeemed in the bridal relationship between Christ and Mary, or between him and each Christian soul.

Since this divine betrothal appertains to the end-phase of human history, it presupposes that the momentous "all Israel will be saved" (Rom 11:26) has taken place already, and that this chosen people will have finally been added

22. Cf. RD, 1159.

23. Notionally akin to the word "conjugal," stemming from the Latin *con*, "with, together," and *iugum*, "a yoke": the idea is that husband and wife are yoked together like two oxen as they plow the field of family life.

24. Cf. Alfred Ernout and Alfred Meillet, *Dictionnaire Étymologique de la Langue Latine: Histoire des Mots*, 4th ed. (Paris: Klincksieck, 2001), "nubo," 449.

25. Related to the Latin *vās*, "bail, security, surety."

26. Perhaps in allusion to the custom of offering a dowry at the time of marriage.

to the Mystical Body of Christ. In this way, on eschaton's boundary, they will be the very last heirs of his salvific "life from the dead" (Rom 11:15), before the resurrection of all flesh takes place. By the same token, it will give final proof that the Lion-Lamb is the Redeemer of world-history, the one who was able to open all seven seals of the scroll (5:5). The "Israel of God" (Gal 6:16) was never fully divorced, just temporarily separated from her Husband, and will now be reunited with him as a constitutive part of the New Jerusalem.

After all, the celebration of his espousals on earth is nothing other than the distribution of the eternal reward of grace to his believers, who then enter with him into his heavenly glory. That will also mark the fulfillment of all promises given earlier to the conquerors within the seven churches, namely, to eat from the paradisiac tree of life (2:7), to never die again (2:11), to attain to the hidden manna together with a white stone that has a new name (2:17), to secure the iron rod and morning star (2:27–28), to be clothed in white robes with one's name etched in the book of life (3:5), to be a temple pillar with Jesus' new name (3:12), and to be enthroned with Christ (3:21). And what would be the wedding day if not the day of his second advent or parousia, ushering in the most intimate aspect of his *Basileía* (v. 6), namely, the consummation of his union with the One, Holy, Catholic, and Apostolic Church? And for that moment, his "wife" (*gynḗ*, γυνή, *uxor*)[27] has intently prepared herself, as befits a spouse who joyfully awaits the arrival of her bridegroom.

Nevertheless, as a complement to her own preparations, God is doing his part in view of the wedding festival: "To her it has been granted to be clothed with fine linen, bright and pure: for the fine linen are the righteous deeds of the saints" (v. 8). All her good qualities of virtue and sanctity have their source in God (Jas 1:17). John ordinarily conveys that supernatural initiative and control of historical events through the divine passive "it has been granted" (*edóthē*, ἐδόθη, *datum est*). Hand in hand with her own generous contributions, the nuptial garment is given to her by the Lord as she enters paradise (Isa 61:10), just as he clothed Adam and his wife Eve before they were driven out of Eden (Gen 3:21). Ergo, she receives her nuptial dress, but now it is up to her to cover herself wholly with it, as expressed by the Greek subjunctive verb *peribálētai* (περιβάληται, *cooperiat*), to the point of resembling the Immaculate Conception herself, without stain, wrinkle, or blemish (Eph 5:27). And by the way, numerous are the scriptural connotations of that compound verb *peribállo* in Revelation, connected as it is with the cosmic woman (12:1) and the antithetical harlot (17:4; 18:16), with the faithful members of the Church (3:5, 18; 11:3), with

27. Cf. 21:2, where the proper noun for "bride" appears, namely, *nýmphē* (νύμφη, *sponsa*).

the heavenly realm (4:4; 7:9, 13; 10:1), as well as with Christ himself (cf. 19:13).[28] Contrary to the ostentations of the great prostitute, the Bride arrays herself in simple yet dignified linen[29] almost like a Matron, demonstrative of her purity in the Holy Spirit (Matt 22:11). Besides, bright and pure bridal dresses are universally taken as an emblem of virginal innocence, rendering the apocalyptic spouse almost angelic (15:6).

"For the fine linen is the righteous deeds of the saints" (v. 8b): this phrase is one of the several intra-textual interpretations in Revelation,[30] which, according to the New Vulgate's punctuation, forms the closing sentence of this hymn (vv. 6–8). Thus, the radiant espousal garb made of linen "are" (*sunt*)[31] the "saints' justifications" (*iustificationes sanctorum*). Considering this Latin rendition of the original *dikaíōma tôn hagíōn* (δικαίωμα τῶν ἁγίων), one can hardly avoid the impression that again a certain synergy between the human and the divine are intended here. On the one hand these are the meritorious works and virtues of the saintly children of God, done in the state of sanctifying grace and in fidelity to his ordinances; they are robed entirely, as it were, in the holy will of Christ, and thereby advancing the beauty and perfection of his Church. These deeds will even follow them straight into the communion of all the saints (14:13). And on the other hand, they are the divine acts of justification and sanctification of the individual baptized soul. God is the one who judges its righteousness by washing it in the blood of the Lamb; he is the one who bestows imperishability on the human body (1 Cor 15:53),[32] and apart from him we can do nothing (John 15:5). Thus, all the preparations have been made for an indissoluble union between the elect and their Redeemer, redounding to consolation and happiness; it also means a change in marital status and the reception of a "new name" that accompanies it (2:17; 3:12): the spousal Church of Christ (*Ecclesia sponsalis Christi*).

28. See the several citations of the above verb already in the Gospels' Passion and Resurrection narratives (Mark 14:51; 16:5; Luke 23:11; John 19:2).

29. Byssus (*byssinum*) was an exceptionally fine and valuable fiber or cloth of ancient times, also known as "sea-silk" of a beige-golden hue, sourced from the extensive silky threads secreted by the large Mediterranean pen-shell. Linen was also the textile used for the high priest's vestment in the Old Testament (Lev 16:4).

30. Cf. 1:20; 5:8; 13:18; 17:15.

31. Whereas the Greek singular verb *estín* (ἐστίν), "is," unconventionally reconnects with the singular "linen" earlier in the clause.

32. See also the incorrupt bodies of several Saints and Blessed in the Catholic Church (e.g., Rita of Cascia, Francis Xavier, Virginia Centurione, John Vianney, Catherine Labouré, Pier Giorgio Frassati).

Looking back over this symphonious adoration in heaven, Apocalypse's last, with its quadrivial echoing and reechoing of Hallelujahs (vv. 1–8), we are further inspired to learn its language and to acquire its spiritual tune already here on earth. Because in praising God for what we already possess, we pray for what is yet to be done for us. Just as the Lord Jesus, after having instituted the holy Eucharist, sang the Hallel on his way into his Passion and Death,[33] so should we love the Hallelujah and affectionately chant it especially in the difficult moments of our life. We Christians should also often thank God for the unfathomable gift of salvation, for having been called to magnify his glory, and to humbly extol his power (v. 1). And if our calling and its inherent fragility and vulnerability means to shed tears and blood in testimony of his name, then we can rest assured that in the end he will vindicate and reward us (v. 2): "You have kept count of my tossings, put my tears in your bottle; are they not in your record? Then my enemies will retreat in the day when I call; this I know, that God is for me" (Ps 56:8–9).

Additionally, by repeating their praises "once more" (*iterum*, v. 3), the saints in light teach us to discover the spiritual benefit of reiterating certain prayers, like the *Ave Maria* of the Holy Rosary, or the Prayer of the Heart: "Lord Jesus Christ, Son of God, have mercy on me." Moreover, Babylon's smoke going up forever ought to encourage the soul to regularly contemplate the Last Things, i.e., death, judgment, heaven, and hell. It will increase its detestation of all sin, its fear of eternal damnation, its love of God, and its desire for heaven: "In all you do, remember the end of your life, and then you will never sin" (Sir 7:36). And how much each one should cherish the short but powerful prayer "Amen" (v. 4), expressing our joyful trust in the Lord, especially when we receive Holy Communion: "The Body of Christ: Amen!" What is more, in addition to supernatural love, as Jesus' brethren we treasure servanthood buoyed by the fear of God, indicative of true piety and adoration (v. 5). No longer enslaved to vice, we willingly serve him as his sons and daughters in virtue.

When reflecting on v. 6, showing how the Pantocrator reigns supreme, the soul should take heart in its battle to overcome sin and to improve on its imperfections. By persevering in this spiritual combat, rejecting the harlotry of idolatry and immorality, we live out that bridal relationship with him (v. 7) and prepare ourselves for his eternal wedding banquet. That way, the Yes of the Church in her present stage of courtship or engagement is made up of the nuptial Yes

33. Cf. Mark 14:26; this Hallel consists of Pss 113–118, sung by the Hebrews in connection with the Passover meal and other festivals, reflecting on God's redemption of his people, particularly from their bondage in Egypt.

of all her children, awaiting the mystical meal of the beatific vision.[34] Bathed by him in water and word (Eph 5:26), our whole life becomes an ongoing enjoyment of that intimate oneness with Jesus, singing an ongoing wedding song.[35] And lastly, the fine linen (v. 8), ensign of our regal and priestly dignity, liturgically expressed by baptismal gown and priestly alb, is a constant reminder of what Christ bestowed on us and of the need for our cooperation with his grace.[36] On the feast day of St. Aloysius Gonzaga (June 21), this espousal reality is communicated during the prayer over the offerings at Holy Mass: "Grant us, O Lord, that . . . we may take our place at the heavenly banquet, clothed always in our wedding garment, so that, by participation in this mystery, we may possess the riches of your grace. Through Christ our Lord, Amen."

34. Cf. AvS, 623.

35. Cf. RD, 1060.

36. Not least by gaining partial and plenary indulgences to recapture that baptismal uprightness.

19:9–10, The Lamb's nuptial supper

Fourth makarism: Wedding invitation (19:9)

[9]And the angel said to me, "Write this: Blessed are those who are invited to the marriage supper of the Lamb." And he said to me, "These are true words of God."

The contrastive recurrence of the word "supper" (*deîpnon*, δεῖπνον, *cena*) helps the reader to subdivide the remaining verses of this chapter (vv. 9–21): In v. 9, an invitation is extended to humanity to partake of the nuptial banquet of the Lamb, whereas in v. 17, all birds are summoned from midheaven to the gruesome scene of the great supper of God, becoming the ultimate carnivores of the eschaton. Hence, the demarcations of the two textual segments of vv. 9–16 and vv. 17–21 crystallize. It is presumptively the angel from 18:21 who is now addressing the seer on Patmos; he had already commented on the bridal theme in v. 23 and was the last angelic voice to communicate with him. And he commands John: "Write this!" (v. 9), the penultimate of thirteen such instructions issued to him in Revelation (21:5).[1] It asks him to keep a record of the truth, importance, and certainty of the upcoming message, so it may be preserved for and remembered by future generations. Indeed, it amounts to another apocalyptic beatitude, the fourth and central one of the seven, and arguably the most superb among them,[2] inspired by the Lord's parables at Matthew 22:1–14 and 25:1–13. Jesus began his public ministry by accepting a wedding invitation in Cana ("is invited," *vocatus est*, John 2:2), and now he invites his brothers and sisters ("are invited," *vocati sunt*) to join him for his own wedding in conclusion of human history. And how could anyone resist the meekness of the Lamb?!

Now, according to Talmudic traditions of John's time,[3] two formal stages

1. Cf. 1:11, 19; 2:1, 8, 12, 18; 3:1, 7, 14; 10:4; 14:13; 21:5.

2. Cf. 1:3; 14:13; 16:15; 20:6; 22:7; 22:14.

3. Cf. "Marriage," in *The New Standard Jewish Encyclopedia*, 7th ed. (New York: Facts on File, 1992), 632.

were involved in bringing about a marriage. *First*, the betrothal, then and now called *kiddushin*, which means "sanctification." By this nuptial ceremony a young couple was legally joined to each other in marriage, contractually confirmed by the marriage writ or *ketubah*,[4] without living together yet. For the man, the average age would have been around eighteen, whereas the marriageable woman would have been fourteen. It marked the beginning of yearlong preparations for the wedding proper, during which the bridegroom would ready the home and bridal chamber. It also meant time for the groom's father to pay a dowry to the bride's family, to acquire her for his son. Once the future family's place was completed, the groom would return to fetch his bride without her being privy to the exact time of his coming. His arrival was announced with a trumpet call or a shout. This first part of the wedding is reflected in vv. 7–8.

After which, the *second* phase commenced, that of the full-fledged marriage and wedding party, also known as *nisuin*, meaning "elevation." A day before, bride and groom would fast; then she would engage in ritual cleansing, bathing, veiling, and adorning herself. Then, surrounded by her friends she would be led in a bridal procession, while the groom, too, went out to meet her, taking her to his house to live together. At this point the marriage was consummated, and the wedding festival took its course, normally for not fewer than seven days of joyful celebration. This second stage is symbolized by this present v. 9. And so, all are invited now "into" (*eís*, εἰς) the Lamb's nuptial banquet, made possible by the expense or dowry[5] of his precious Blood offered to the heavenly Father.

As typified by the Lord's Supper on Holy Thursday, this espousal supper takes place in the evening, that is, at the completion of the economy of salvation, ushering in the dawn of eternity. Eating and drinking become metaphors for the beatific vision of the Blessed Trinity. Also, this wedding invitation is signed and sealed, so to speak, by a reiterated "and he said to me" (*et dicit mihi*), that is, with a solemn declaration of infallibility as in 21:5 and 22:6. The idea is, that in periods of trial and despondency, the Church as the Bride of the Lamb, should receive it as an undoubted truth, that Christ will eventually prevail, and that all persecution and sorrow here below will one day be replaced by triumph and jubilation in heaven.

4. Dissolved by the *libellus repudii* (Matt 5:31).

5. The Greek noun for "dinner" (*deîpnon*, δεῖπνον) derives from *dapánē* (δαπάνη), meaning "expense, cost, consumption."

"No" to angelolatria (19:10)

[10] Then I fell down at his feet to worship him, but he said to me, "You must not do that! I am a fellow servant with you and your comrades who hold the testimony of Jesus. Worship God! For the testimony of Jesus is the spirit of prophecy."

John then humbly admits to his reaction to what he saw, and how the angel corrects him by saying: "Look, you must not do that!"[6] This is the first of two such responses (22:8–9), perhaps to show the reader that even saintly persons may repeatedly commit the same error. That he prostrates himself at the angel's feet gives proof that the latter appeared not only in quasi-divine splendor, but also in an anthropomorphic way. This impulsive gesture of adoration is dissimilar to the seer's sorrowful wonder with which he gazed at the doomed prostitute (17:6). It does accord, however, with the ancient custom in the Orient to do homage to persons in authority, and to express reverential obeisance (3:9). Above and beyond that, it may be inferred that John thought it was the Lord himself, overawed by his majestic appearance (1:17). Yet, his angelic interpreter (*angelus interpres*) brusquely refuses it and immediately rebukes him. In the Greek, he seems to force the apostle to make eye contact with him, only to forcefully stop him in his tracks with a rather colloquial "Look at me! Don't!" (*hóra, mḗ*; ὅρα, μή). This abrupt incompletion of speech is a rare aposiopesis in the New Testament.[7]

This incident can be viewed as evidence for the authenticity of Revelation, too, not allowing for any unorthodoxy, in this case, angel-worship, against which Paul had warned already (Col 2:18). Humble yet determined, the angel renounces divine honors for himself, and immediately advises John regarding the unsuitability of his prostration. When it comes to their common worship of God, angels and humans do not outrank one another but are on equal footing, they are fellow-servants (*sýndoulos*, σύνδουλος, *conservus*, 22:9). That is why

6. There are two grammatical options for the translation of the Nova Vulgata's *nē fēceris*: (a.) as a future perfect active indicative of *faciō*, rendered as "you will not have done this!," paraphrased in the above translation; and (b.) complementing the negative conjunction *nē* with the perfect active subjunctive *fēceris*, literally "you may not have done this!," which, however, is less logical in this context.

7. A literary device (Greek *aposiṓpēsis*, ἀποσιώπησις, literally "falling silent"), that is, where a phrase is interrupted and left unfinished due to the speaker's passionate anger, excitement, fear, or modesty, rendering him unwilling or unable to carry on with his speech; the ending must be supplied by guesswork and imagination.

the title "angel of the church" was so appropriate within the seven letters (2:1), since all are bonded together in witness, and engaged in divine service of the same God and Redeemer. And with a second imperative, the supernatural messenger then directs the apostle to the only true object of religious *proskynesis* or prostration (twice in v. 10), the Triune God alone: "Worship God!" Nothing could be more antipodal to the divine law than adoring a mere creature; amazingly, though, it was necessary to mentor even the beloved disciple on that subject.

With another explanatory "because, since, for" (*gár*, γάρ, *enim*), similar to the one at v. 8, the angel subjoins: "'For the testimony of Jesus is the spirit of prophecy'" (v. 10). His explanation amounts to a double epexegetical genitive, expressive of his intention to satisfy the heavenly Father's desire to have all worship him in Spirit and Truth (John 4:24). *First*, there is "the testimony of Jesus" that highlights the God-Man as both subject and object, author and goal, of Christian witness, even to the point of shedding one's blood for him: "He [Christ] is the mouth without a lie in whom the Father speaks truly."[8] And the *second* epexegetical genitive, "the Spirit of prophecy," denotes the Holy Spirit as subject and object of prophesying in the Church and in the world. Indeed, he "has spoken through the prophets."[9] This is meant to confirm Jesus' mission before humanity's mind and conscience, as previously attested by way of the Old and New Testament prophets, of whom John becomes a coequal. And as those prophets were inspired to proclaim God's word, so each believer is called to give witness to the Word of God made flesh.

Before moving on to Christ the Warrior (vv. 11–16), however, let us briefly reflect on the allegory of Christ the Bridegroom. It is no overreach to say that our Christian life is comparable to the two stages of a traditional Jewish wedding as the backdrop to the apocalyptic wedding feast of the Lamb. It all begins with our sacramental espousal to him in the *kiddushin* or sanctification of baptism. This has been made possible by the mystical dowry that Jesus and his heavenly Father paid in his own redemptive Blood. While he is currently preparing an eternal bridal chamber for us (John 14:2–3), we strive to live in Christian asceticism, virtue, and holiness, sustained by the other sacraments of the Church. Like a bride, the soul cleanses and adorns itself with his grace,

8. Ignatius of Antioch, *Letter to the Romans*, in *Ignatius of Antioch & Polycarp of Smyrna: A New Translation and Theological Commentary*, Revised and Expanded Edition, ed. Kenneth J. Howell, ECF 1 (Zanesville, OH: CHResources, 2009), 8 (p. 118).

9. Nicene-Constantinopolitan Creed.

as if waiting in the vestibule of this world to be admitted into the banquet hall of heaven (19:7–9). Not knowing the exact hour, we faithfully watch for the Lord's return (16:15). He arrives thief-like both in the hour of our death, and at the end of history in his parousia. Similar to the *nisuin* or elevation, he will then take us with him as in a bridal procession, commencing the second stage of his spiritual espousal with us (21:2–8). The blessedness of vigilance is then rewarded by the beatitude of partaking of the nuptial supper in consummate union with the Blessed Trinity (21:9–22:5). After the final judgment, each one of the saved shall spend the "seven days" of the eternal wedding banquet enjoying the Bread of Angels (*panis angelorum*), foreshadowed by the Holy Eucharist in our churches around the globe.[10] And whenever we approach Holy Communion, we will hear the celebrant reiterate the apocalyptic invitation: "Blessed are those called to the supper of the Lamb!"

This entire nuptial-matrimonial metaphor is summed up by the Lord's touching exhortation to the Laodicean Christians: "Behold! I am standing at the door, knocking; if you hear my voice and open the door, I will come in to you and eat with you, and you with me" (3:20). There should also be the abiding awareness that in promoting the Christian religion in this world, the human heart is profoundly communing with the good angels whom we ought to regard as brothers; to have them walk at our side day and night and to be protected and guided by them is truly the honor of our lifetime and an unmerited gift of divine providence. The mere thought of it should lift us up and deepen the desire of union with them, since they bring us nearer to God. Together, we are engaged in the selfsame work of evangelization through the word of God and his prophecy,[11] and, indeed, one day we will be "like angels" (*isággeloi*, ἰσάγγελοι, *aequales angelis*; Luke 20:36).

Notwithstanding such spiritual intimacy, however, the soul must resist any urges to idolize them: angel-worship or angelolatry do not conform to the revelation of their divine Master, the incarnate Son of God. Taking a cue from the visionary experience of the beloved disciple, who had to be reminded by the good spirit, one must be vigilant in this regard. By embracing Jesus' divinity in adoration (*latria*), we are no longer in need of seeking divine mediation in any other creature, but content ourselves with venerating angels and saints (*dulia*), primarily St. Joseph and John the Baptist (*protodulia*), and having a maximal

10. Cf. AvS, 626.
11. Cf. AvS, 627–29.

devotion to their heavenly Queen, the Blessed Virgin Mary (*hyperdulia*).[12] By maintaining such an undivided focus on the one true Lord, we will surely lead those who do not yet have faith to him: "After the secrets of the unbeliever's heart are disclosed, that person will bow down before God and worship him, declaring, 'God is really among you'" (1 Cor 14:25).

12. Cf. Thomas Aquinas, *Summa Theologiae*, II-II, q. 103, a. 4; III, q. 25, a. 5.

19:11–16, Supreme Commander

His first name: Staunch Warrior (19:11)

[11]Then I saw heaven opened, and there was a white horse! Its rider is called Faithful and True, and in righteousness he judges and makes war.

The text of 19:11–22:5 seems to propound a definitive, because Christocentric, rereading of Ezekiel 38–48, describing an analogous arc of events: starting with the rout of every last enemy (Ezek 38–39 and Rev 19:11–20:15), and flowing into the glorious restoration of God's Temple (Ezek 40–48 and Rev 21:1–22:5). And so, in the remaining text of this chapter (vv. 11–21), the theme of warlike vanquishment of all hostility against God is again envisioned from a different angle. Running like a common thread through the Apocalypse, holy war surfaces under the ever-varying and antithetical imagery of the Son of Man against the Nicolaitans (2:16), of locusts against ungodly humanity (9:7, 9), of the beast against the two witnesses (11:7), of Michael against the dragon (12:7), of the serpent against the woman's offspring (12:17), of the sea-beast against the saints (13:4, 7), of the satanic trinity against God at Harmagedon (16:14, 16), of the ten kings against the Lamb (17:14), and finally of the devil against the encampment of the saints (20:8). Also, the foregoing motif of divine nuptials (vv. 7–9) is now enriched by the metaphor of the Messianic Warrior (vv. 11–16), developing the theological vision of Psalm 45, where the royal marriage (vv. 6–16) takes place only after the righteous king's return from glorious victory (vv. 2–5).

Moreover, there appears to be a remarkable scriptural complementarity between Revelation's Warrior-King and Isaiah's Suffering Servant[1] when it comes to the topic of establishing justice among the nations. Could this apparent contrast between King and Servant also account for the startling tension between the meek humility of the God-Man's first coming into this world, and his stern majesty when he returns at the end of time? In terms of textual

1. Cf. the four Servant Songs at Isa 42:1–4; 49:1–6; 50:4–11; 52:13–53:12.

arrangement of vv. 11–16, his three known names, i.e., "Faithful and True" (v. 11), "Word of God" (v. 13), and "King of kings and Lord of lords" (v. 16), make up somewhat symmetrical frames around two sets of three physical attributes: the first triad focuses on his eyes ("fire," v. 12a), his head ("diadems," v. 12b), and his clothing ("blood-stained robe," v. 13), whereas the second trio puts the spotlight on his mouth ("sword," v. 15a), his hand ("iron rod," v. 15b), and his feet ("treading the winepress," v. 15c). With this preliminary overview, let us now explore verse by verse.

Initially, John was shown just an open door in heaven (4:1), then the heavenly temple was disclosed to his gaze (11:19; 15:5), but at this point he "saw the heaven opened, and behold, a white horse; and the one mounted on it is called Faithful and True, and in justice he judges and wages war" (v. 11). While the exiled Ezekiel saw a horseless celestial chariot (Ezek 1), the apostle's eyes are riveted on this white horse, much more imposing than the one coming out to conquer after the opening of the first seal (6:2). There, it denoted the swift progress and purity of the Gospel, but this royal mount here symbolizes war. The time for peace, intimated by the donkey and its colt (Matt 21:2), is spent; now the God-Man is riding in the power of his virginal body[2] to triumph over all diabolical cavalries.[3] He does so in the authority of his victory over sin and death by his Resurrection, symbolized by the white color in this vision.

This impressive portrait of the exalted Christ "like a soldier, like a warrior" (Isa 42:13) commences with the mention of his first known name, "Faithful and True," which combines the characteristics of trustworthiness in all his promises, and truthfulness in executing just judgment, and thereby satisfying the desires of his sons and daughters. In him all hope is anchored, and all ideals are realized. Fulfilling the messianic representation of Psalm 2:4–9, and against the mystery of lawlessness preceding his parousia (2 Thess 2:1–12), Jesus valiantly wages a holy war, whose gory details, however, in keeping with the apocalyptic genre, are nowhere relayed. It is consoling that this *Christus Triumphator* ("Christ Triumphant") progressively wins his battles in divine justice, "for he is coming to judge the earth; he will judge the world with righteousness, and the peoples with his truth" (Ps 96:13).

2. Cf. RD, 1164.

3. That overpowering presence is implied also by the fivefold mention of horses in this chapter (vv. 14, 18–19, 21).

His middle name: Irrefutable Revealer (19:12–13)

[12]His eyes are like a flame of fire, and on his head are many diadems; and he has a name inscribed that no one knows but himself. [13]He is clothed in a robe dipped in blood, and his name is called The Word of God.

At this moment, John is able to make out some of the majestic Horseman's facial features (v. 12): Jesus' fiery eyes of infinite holiness and knowledge have not changed since he manifested himself to the seer early on as the glorious Son of Man (1:14). They are still piercingly transformative, but they also discern between the flame of divine illumination and the flickering light of hell. In this martial context they also signify the fierceness of his anger against the enemies of his people, against all who provoke it by their wickedness. His flaming eyes hint at the suddenness, inevitability, as well as thoroughness of their eventual incineration. He is also crowned with an infinite number of diadems, and no longer just a single crown (14:14), because he now arrives as King-Priest mirroring the many victories of his brethren on earth; he comes to judge, already certain of his total victory. They may also be taken as a token of his countless conquests in the material and the spiritual realms, and the fact that his dominion encompasses heaven and earth.[4] He is the Son of that Woman crowned with a cosmic wreath of twelve stars, and neither the dragon with his seven garlands (12:3), nor the sea-beast wearing ten of them (13:1) are a match for him.[5] Those are diabolical usurpers of power, whereas Christ is true royalty as Creator of the universe and Redeemer of humankind, and toward him the elders cast their crowns (4:10).

Visible probably on the frontlet of this compound diadem or on his forehead is a mysterious—because humanly unknowable—name (v. 12). It praises his work as Mediator between God and man, which for now remains inscrutable and ineffable. His divine Sonship and Incarnation are incomprehensible and unpronounceable, as was his Father's name, i.e., Yahweh, in the Old Testament.[6] And who can ever understand the profundity of salvation, or who can exhaust the fulness of his love and power, the depth of his omniscient wisdom?[7] Evidently, only God himself has that comprehensive knowledge of his own

4. Cf. RD, 1165.

5. As a historical reference, Ptolemy Macron, the general of King Antiochus IV Epiphanes (d. 164 BC), crowned himself with two crowns, that of Egypt and that of Asia (1 Macc 11:13; Flavius Josephus, *Antiquities*, 7.7.3).

6. Cf. AvS, 635.

7. Cf. RD, 1165.

infinite nature. This humanly insurmountable unknowability of the Divine also has the effect of stretching the meaning of his other three titles in this passage into infinity. It is possible, however, that in the future state of beatific vision the veil of its meaning will be lifted before each one of the saints, because "The Lord is there!" (Ezek 48:35).

John's eyes now fix themselves on Christ's garment: "He is clothed in a robe sprinkled[8] with blood, and his name is called The Word of God" (v. 13). His warfare with Satan involved the shedding of his own precious Blood, which now redounds to his decoration. Fulfilling the Mosaic gesture of sprinkling the blood of the covenant (Exod 24:8), the God-Man purchased his power as Mediator and Savior by undergoing his Paschal Mystery (5:9).[9] Yet also, after the manner of an ancient Roman general clad in a purple toga, this divine Victor wears the blood of his enemies like a badge of honor, confirming the archetypal passages at Isaiah 63:1–6 and Wisdom 18:14–16. He also seems to provide evidence that he has now avenged the blood of the saints, infamously spilled by the great harlot (17:6).

His middle name, as it were, is *Verbum Dei*, "The Word of God," and this revelation may have inspired John's mention of it at the very beginning of his Gospel (John 1:1). The Son of God is the consubstantial *Lógos* (λόγος), since through him the Father has created the universe, and through him it will also be made new. But the Father also entirely revealed himself through this one Word to the human family, and henceforth Jesus is the irrefutable Interpreter and Communicator of the Blessed Trinity (John 1:18). Just as in the beginning was the Word, so it shall be at the very end.

His loyal troops (19:14)

[14]And the armies of heaven, wearing fine linen, white and pure, were following him on white horses.

What is seen next explains why a single open door in heaven (4:1) would never have been sufficient (v. 14). According to ordinary usage in Scripture, these

8. There are several variant readings for this verb in the Greek manuscripts: some give *rerantisménon* (ῥεραντισμένον), meaning "sprinkled," reflected in the Neo-Vulgate's rendition *aspersa* (see Isa 63:3); others read *perirerамménon* (περιρεραμμένον), signifying "sprinkled around"; and there is also *bebamménon* (βεβαμμένον), that is, "dipped," possibly in allusion to Gen 49:11 or Lev 9:9; its verbal stem *báptō* (βάπτω), "to dip," could be taken as an innuendo to the sacrament of baptism.

9. Cf. RD, 1166.

heavenly hosts would betoken the angels (Jude 14) under the rule of "the Lord of hosts" or *Kýrios sabaóth* (Κύριος σαβαώθ).[10] However, in this apocalyptic context, it seems more appropriate to interpret these troops as the redeemed, the faithful companions of the Lamb (14:4), since it would be incongruous for the angels to be mounted on horses. Also, the Greek noun here employed for "army" (*stráteuma*, στράτευμα, *exercitus*) does not occur in the Old Testament as a designation for angelic hosts; but it is used several times for earthly troops in the Bible (Matt 22:7). And although white vesture certainly is a biblical hallmark of the angels (Mark 16:5), in Revelation it is reserved for Christ and his faithful followers. Affiliated with the linen of the Bride who has made herself ready (vv. 7–8), these armies also symbolize the nuptial procession following the Lamb as her Bridegroom through the heavens to celebrate their union.

Thus, the steadily advancing[11] retinue of the Lord is confirmed in a state of transfigured joy, as signaled by their radiant garments. It is the pure white of the conquerors (3:5) and of bridal love (19:8), far removed already from the idolatrous impurities of the great prostitute. Their armor of purity paradoxically contrasts with the blood-dyed one of their celestial Commander (v. 13), since his saving blood has washed theirs clean (7:14). Possibly, too, these chosen ones have no need to take part in the actual end-time battle that will trigger the slaughter of Satan's cavalries (9:16).[12] They may be simply attendant to the unconditional surrender of enemy troops, followed by their summary execution at the hands of their divine General and Judge (v. 21).

His last name: Absolute Sovereign (19:15–16)

15From his mouth comes a sharp sword with which to strike down the nations, and he will rule them with a rod of iron; he will tread the wine press of the fury of the wrath of God the Almighty. 16On his robe and on his thigh he has a name inscribed, "King of kings and Lord of lords."

Ahead of the unveiling of the Lord's last name (v. 16), there are three more attributes of his, that is, mystical observations regarding his mouth, hand, and

10. A transliteration of the Hebrew plural noun *Sabaoth* (צְבָאוֹת), denoting, among others, "hosts of angels, armies, expedition, warfare, services, the heavenly bodies, the entire creation" (Isa 6:3).

11. Expressed by the imperfect tense of the main verb of this verse, in both the Greek original (*ekoloúthei*, ἠκολούθει) and the Neo-Vulgate (*sequebantur*).

12. Cf. David Andrew Thomas, *Revelation 19 in Historical and Mythological Context*, SBLit 118 (New York: Peter Lang, 2008).

feet (v. 15). As if coming full circle, Christ is again seen with a sword, implying his mission as an eschatological Servant of the Lord or *Ebed Yahweh.*[13] It is reminiscent, too, of his sharp sickle at the time of harvest (14:14), as well as the readiness for battle of "the most handsome of men" (Ps 45:2–3). Since the heavenly Father has entrusted all judgment to his Son (John 5:22), he no longer appears with a "double-edged" sword as in the inaugural vision (1:16), epitomizing the efficacy of the Gospel, but now he punitively deploys only a sharpened javelin[14] to smite his enemies in this world. Since Jesus never used a sword in his earthly life, it must be understood as parabolic for his omnipotent word (v. 13) by which alone he created heaven and earth, and now that word suffices to defeat and judge all his enemies.[15]

John's eyes then pass down to his hand wielding an iron rod (v. 15), evocative of the messianic figure of the Good Shepherd (Ps 2:9). Whereas the Hebrew tradition of this text stresses the smashing quality of a metallic scepter, already conveyed in Balaam's oracle about the future Messiah (Num 24:17), the Greek rendition emphasizes the feeding, guiding, and protecting staff of a shepherd. The Neo-Vulgate prefers the notion of authoritative ruling.[16] Thus, Christ is portrayed as commanding and controlling the nations single-handedly, as is also intimated by the emphatic personal pronoun "he" (*autós*, αὐτός, *ipse*) by which he sets himself apart from the innumerable usurpers of power who have misruled on earth. Since the scepter's first occurrences in 2:27 and 12:5, people had the *kairós* or opportune time to repent, but now the time has arrived to enforce divine governance on all. This also reflects the tenor of what Psalm 110:2 states concerning the Priest-Messiah.[17] Hence, those who have fought his dominion of righteousness and meekness, now discover the staff of the Good Shepherd to have turned into an iron rod.

Next, John observes the Lord's feet vigorously treading grapes in a winevat (v. 15; cf. 14:19), a truly climactic metaphor of his divine "fury of wrath"

13. Cf. Isa 49:2, part of the second Servant Song.

14. Which is the other lexical meaning of the Greek noun *rhomphaía* (ῥομφαία).

15. Cf. George T. Montague, *The Apocalypse: Understanding the Book of Revelation and the End of the World* (Ann Arbor, MI: Charis Servant, 1992), 197.

16. The Hebrew text of Ps 2:9 has the verb *ra'a'* (רָעַע), signifying the act of breaking or smashing; both the Septuagint version of Ps 2:9, and its quotation in the Greek of Rev 19:15, employ the verb *poimaínō* (ποιμαίνω), denotative of the humble staff of a shepherd or *poimḗn* (ποιμήν); the Neo-Vulgate, instead, carries *regere*, "to rule," in both Ps 2:9 and Rev 19:15.

17. See the Hebrew verb *radah* (רָדָה) in that verse, meaning "to have dominion," rendered in the Septuagint with *katakyrieúō* (κατακυριεύω), "to exercise power, have lordship over"; the same concept is expressed in the New Vulgate by the verb *dominare*, "to rule, dominate."

(16:19) that neutralizes the convulsions of demonic rage. Afterwards, no one will be able to oppose the All-Ruler, who now has destroyed the most prideful of adversaries with as much ease as one crushes grape-clusters underfoot, releasing their blood like fresh purple must.

Lastly, John's attention is drawn to the God-Man's equestrian attire: "On his robe and on his thigh he has a name inscribed, King of kings and Lord of lords" (v. 16). Like the ensign of a medieval knight, his surname, so to speak, is displayed on the part of the vesture which is upon his thigh:[18] he is the absolute Sovereign (cf. 17:14; Eph 1:20–21). Syntactically, it is conveyed by a redoubled Semitic superlative, i.e., "King of kings" and "Lord of lords," akin to the Latin phrase *saecula saeculorum*, to denote its unsurpassable greatness and perpetuity. Echoing several biblical precedents (e.g., Deut 10:17), it suggests that he exists before all earthly rule, as implied by his earlier title, "Ruler of the kings of the earth" (1:5). He holds superiority over the satanic "king" Abaddon-Apollyon (9:11)[19] and "queen" Babylon (17:18; 18:7). But Christ also outranks all good earthly potentates as their supreme King and Lord (21:24), to the everlasting confusion of his enemies and the bliss of his chosen ones.[20] As Lord of lords he is also the sole and gracious husband of his covenanted people.

In closing our exegetical remarks on this passage (vv. 11–16), let us look back at some of the plenteous imagery to see how it can illuminate our Christian spirituality. That magnificent Rider, symbolizing Jesus as truthful and just Judge of all (v. 11), should stir our conscience to continuously refine our discernment between good and evil, and to surrender our will more fully to him.[21] It will remain a challenge to reconcile the feebleness of a lamb with the valor of a warrior needed in spiritual combat, to live the humility of a beast of burden and its colt together with the bravery of a war stallion, and to love the divine Bridegroom in a state of spiritual readiness (v. 14).

Moving on to his flaming eyes (v. 12), we are reminded that the soul should often seek eye contact with him, allowing his gaze to purify and transform its deepest recesses. By doing so, one will paradoxically come to comprehend more and more of the incomprehensibility of God's nature. Of great help in this

18. Notice how the femur was a part of ritual oath-taking in patriarchal times, cf. Gen 24:9; what is more, Rupert opines that it symbolizes the human aspect of Jesus' Mystical Body; cf. RD, 1170.

19. A number of ancient Hellenistic thigh inscriptions were found to have been dedicated to the god Apollo; cf. James R. Edwards, "The Rider on the White Horse, the Thigh Inscription, and Apollo: Revelation 19:16," *Journal of Biblical Literature* 137, no. 2 (Summer 2018): 519–36.

20. Cf. AvS, 641.

21. Cf. AvS, 634.

process will be not only the worthy reception of the Eucharist that douses the spirit with Christ's precious Blood, but the devoted study of his biblical word as well, allowing us to discover some of the depth of his Sacred Heart (v. 13).

Additionally, once our inner imperfections and ailments are recognized, we should give prayerful permission for the divine surgeon to apply the scalpel of his word for the cure (v. 15).[22] And as long as there is time on earth, we choose to bow under the gentle crook of the Shepherd, so there is nothing to fear when he returns wielding his iron scepter. Furthermore, the image of the winepress reminds us that we can implore the grace of patient perseverance for the hour of pressure or persecution.[23] Not least of all, as genuine servants of our King and Lord, let us never tire of bending our knee before him in everything we think, say, and do. Considered especially together with the title Pantocrator (v. 15), his wondrous names give credence to Jesus' cosmic Lordship: "Great is the Lord, and greatly to be praised; his greatness is unsearchable. On the glorious splendor of your majesty, and on your wondrous works, I will meditate" (Ps 145:3, 5).

22. Cf. Heb 4:12; see also RD, 1167; AvS, 637.
23. Cf. RD, 1168.

19:17–21, The birds' raptorial meal

Avian anthropophagy (19:17–18)

[17]*Then I saw an angel standing in the sun, and with a loud voice he called to all the birds that fly in midheaven, "Come, gather for the great supper of God, [18]to eat the flesh of kings, the flesh of captains, the flesh of the mighty, the flesh of horses and their riders, flesh of all, both free and slave, both small and great."*

As we now turn to the fourth and final segment of this so variegated chapter (vv. 17–21), a few lines of thought should be kept in mind. First, the awareness that these verses constitute another thumbnail of the entire eschaton, that is, the time of war between Lamb and dragon. They cover the same ground as those septenaries of seals, trumpets, and bowls earlier in the book. But there is one crucial distinction, namely, that in all those previous visions the ordinary or day-to-day Christian spiritual combat is brought to light, whereas this closing passage of ch. 19 concentrates on the final overthrow of those powers of evil. And the exact same topic will be addressed yet again in the upcoming ch. 20, which, however, will go one step further by showcasing Satan's eternal chastening, as well as that of his fawning cohorts. Another clue is that the macabre imagery of the foes' end-carnage is patterned on Old Testament typology found mainly in Ezekiel 39:4, 17–20, presenting a sacrificial feasting on Gog of Magog, but also in Psalms 2:10–12 and 74:14. Likewise symptomatic are two facets of messianic triumph, namely, its utter certainty, but also its truly apocalyptic scale and gruesomeness. And lastly, it will be critical to appreciate the ironic antithesis between the Lamb's supper and the forthcoming vultures' banquet.

One last time in Revelation, the apostolic visionary hears a message shouted out with a loud voice, that it might be heard far and near: "Then I saw one angel standing in the sun, and with a loud voice he called to all the birds that fly in midheaven, 'Come, gather for the great supper of God'" (v. 17). By now, many different angels have appeared to John, and each one came with a new message, making it likely that this one is distinct from the one ascending from the rising sun (7:2). He is bathed in the fullest sunlight, the symbol of divine presence, in association with Jesus the Sun of Justice (1:16),[1] and his Mother Mary, too (12:1). As such he commands the attention of the whole world, and that central spot also allows him to summon all the birds at the sky's zenith (8:13; 14:6). It is difficult to imagine a more sublime scene than this, and there is a possibility that he is the angelic steward of the sun as the main luminary, similar to those other elemental angels in authority over the winds (7:1), over fire (14:18), and over the waters (16:5). Consistent with his fondness for Greek diminutive words,[2] the sacred author here mentions the last one in this book, literally speaking of "birdlings,"[3] perhaps to underline their subordinate role in God's plan. In which case they are inferior to the fourth living being of aquiline features (4:7), or also to the great eagle transporting the woman into the wilderness (12:14).

That their flight takes them conspicuously across midheaven suggests that they are birds of prey, more ferocious than the other ornithological references in the New Testament.[4] Their symbolic hue in this context can be either negative, as a demonic humiliation,[5] or positive, signifying the countless Christian witnesses throughout the ages (14:6), or even the good angels, given the involvement of a sacrificial meal as divine punishment (8:13; 14:10). In anticipation of certain victory, these raptors are invited to gather beforehand, since the enemies' carrion will soon be ready to be torn into pieces by them. All the ungodly can do is overhear this frightening and humiliating invitation concerning their definitive extermination. It is the same "assembling" that is spoken about in 16:14, 16, yet now they are called to partake of God the Father's "great supper" (*cena magna*) which he prepares to ensure that the contrastive *cena*

1. Cf. RD, 1171.

2. See "little Lamb," "little scroll," "little flock," "little demon," and "little beast," "little lamp."

3. The noun *órneon* (ὄρνεον; cf. 18:2; 19:21) is the diminutive form of *órnis* (ὄρνις), which remains unreflected in the Neo-Vulgate's regular noun *avis*; it is the most common designation for "bird of prey" in classical Greek, and its secondary lexical meaning includes "domestic fowls," "bird of omen, from the flight or cries of which the augur divines," "good fortune," and even "astral constellation."

4. Namely, the generic "winged or flying animal, fowl" (*peteinón*, πετεινόν, *volātilis*), most common in the New Testament outside of Revelation.

5. Like the foul birds haunting Babylon (18:2), the birds that come to devour the seed of the word of God (Matt 13:4), human nature's superior value compared to them (Luke 12:24; Jas 3:7), their uncleanness (Acts 10:12–13), or their idolatrous abuse (Rom 1:23).

nuptiarum of his Son (v. 9) can be celebrated in perpetuity without any interference from the mystery of iniquity. It is a figurative way of announcing their final slaughter and the triumph of God's justice, also described as a sacrifice, that will shine forth with the clarity of the sun.

Having moved down from the highest heaven (v. 11) through the illuminated mid-sky (v. 17), John has now returned to the earth in his visionary journey. Those ominous feathered predators are getting ready "to eat the flesh of kings, the flesh of captains, the flesh of the mighty, the flesh of horses and their riders, flesh of all, both free and slave, both small and great" (v. 18; cf. Matt 13:4). Evil people appertaining to all classes of human society will be affected by the carnivorous onslaught, i.e., the demographic essence of the anti-Christian empire of this world. There is also a military nuance to the enumeration of those about to fall prey to divine wrath, especially by including chiliarchs or army tribunes (*tribunus*) with their rank and file, under royal high command, anticipating the next verse (v. 19).

Unique to the Apocalypse is the plural use of the Greek noun for "flesh" (*sárkas*, σάρκας, *carnes*), repeated here five times, dramatizing not only the gross carnality of those marked by the beast, but also the inescapable relentlessness of their damnation.[6] Simultaneously, it is an overdue retribution for their inhumanity in not burying the dead, but instead gloating over them and celebrating their murder (11:8–10). They had eaten food sacrificed to idols (2:14, 20) and cannibalized the great prostitute (17:16), but now, ironically, they themselves are torn to shreds and consumed in an orgy of avian anthropophagy. This spine-chilling scene stands not only in opposition to the Lamb's wedding banquet (v. 9), but it also caricatures the sacramental consuming of the Body and Blood of Christ in the Holy Eucharist, mysteriously adverted to by our Lord himself: "Wherever the corpse is, there the vultures will gather" (Matt 24:28).

Armies against a single army (19:19)

[19] *Then I saw the beast and the kings of the earth with their armies gathered to make war against the rider on the horse and against his army.*

Even though there had been many spiritual armies following their divine General (v. 14), they have now closed ranks into a holy unity, one single formidable fighting force, when attacked by the armies of Satan, themselves hopelessly

6. Cf. AvS, 642.

and debilitatingly divided into many units. Under the corrupt leadership of the sea-beast and the "ten kings" (17:12), these sinister hordes are bonded together only in their common hostility to good, demonically united in opposition to the progress of Christ's Gospel and the growth of his Kingdom. They are depicted as engaging in man-to-man combat, intimated by the reiterated preposition *metá* (μετά, *cum*) in this verse, which visualizes their direct and strategic engagement "with" and "against" Jesus and his loyal troops. Completely unarmed though they are, only clad in fine linen, these saints fear nothing, since the Captain of their salvation is their preeminent head (Col 1:18). Symbolically, these inimical armies clash at Harmagedon, mirroring King David's prayerful chant: "Why do the nations conspire, and the peoples plot in vain? The kings of the earth set themselves, and the rulers take counsel together, against the Lord and his Anointed, saying, 'Let us burst their bonds asunder, and cast their cords from us'" (Ps 2:1–3).

This ultimately cosmic conflict is not primarily among nations or societal classes, but rather between holiness and sin, justice and injustice, truth and falsehood, Christ and Belial. It is a paradigmatic war, a strife par excellence, as indicated by the definite article preceding "war" in the Koiné text (*tòn pólemon*, τὸν πόλεμον), against the "King of kings and Lord of lords" and his soldiers, *the* war perpetually waged between the powers of light and darkness, and it will not be won until the last judgment (20:9). Amazingly, anti-Christianity is so obtuse and deprived of sight that it deludes itself into thinking that it has a chance in fighting against God. Instead, it will be chastised and eventually defeated in the process, as the Risen Lord admonished Saul: "It hurts you to kick against the goads" (Acts 26:14). Herein lies the extreme Babylonian folly and confusion. Intriguingly, and in typical Johannine fashion, only the staging of the battle is shown, but not the actual warfare or its gore,[7] suggesting that it is over immediately due to the crushing stratagems of Christ's wisdom and grace, which now leads the reader into the next verse.

A beastly broil (19:20–21)

[20]And the beast was captured, and with it the false prophet who had performed in its presence the signs by which he deceived those who had received the mark of the beast and those who worshiped its image. These

7. Cf. R. Bauckham, "The Book of Revelation as a Christian War Scroll," *Neotestamentica* 22 (1988): 17–40.

two were thrown alive into the lake of fire that burns with sulfur. [21]*And the rest were killed by the sword of the rider on the horse, the sword that came from his mouth; and all the birds were gorged with their flesh.*

At long last, here is the end of the road for the two beasts (v. 20). Victory is immediate and total (17:14), making it unnecessary to waste even a single word on the tactical warfare itself, for what struggle can there be between the Pantocrator and a fallen creature? What an admirable and eloquent *argumentum ex silentio*. Both sea-beast and land-beast, the latter again closely identified as "the false prophet" or *pseudopropheta* (16:13; 20:10), are overpowered by Christ, signaled by the first of two verbs conjugated in the passive voice in this verse, i.e., *epiásthē* (ἐπιάσθη, *apprehensa*), "seized." Ironically, this word appears six times in John's Gospel describing his enemies' efforts to arrest Jesus (e.g., John 7:30). That the second or land-beast is nowhere explicitly identified with that false prophet until this point in the Apocalypse may suggest that it persists in its works of deception until the bitter end.

It continues, too, the theme of dual agents in this epic battle, namely, Balaam and Jezebel (2:14, 20), the two witnesses (11:3), the Woman and her male Child (12:1, 5), the two monsters (13:1, 11), Gog and Magog (20:8), as well as Death and Hades (20:14). Masterminded by the dragon, the two wild beasts were the true counsellors of all anti-Christian aspiration, of any unsanctified cultural, ideological, or political world-power, embodied by those diabolically marked idolaters. But this is their last mention as a relevant force, just as they had murdered those who would not worship them (13:15), and the feminine gender of the Nova Vulgata's name for them, namely, *bestia*, contains one last allusion to Babylon the great harlot's demise as well. As the eschatological plot is now propelled toward its grand closure, the definite article preceding the "signs" references their earlier depiction,[8] and how the false prophet had conspired with the sea-beast in hoodwinking the nations of the earth into boycotting the spread of the true religion; yet now they meet their doomful end.

That it is Jesus as the Rider on the horse and his army (v. 19) who cast these two beasts into the fiery lake is symbolized by a second verb conjugated in the divine passive, that is, "thrown" (*eblḗthēsan*, ἐβλήθησαν, *missi sunt*). This verb is a linguistic staple in the Gospels for consigning wicked people to hell (e.g., Matt 7:19). And here we also find the first mention of this "lake of fire" in Revelation: the Greek *límnē* (λίμνη) appears to be related to *limḗn* (λιμήν), signifying a harbor or haven, and thus hinting at the final destiny of those wild beasts.

8. Cf. 13:13–14; 16:14; see also Matt 24:24.

It is a concept important enough for the eschaton to be repeated another five times leading up to 21:8, based on the combined Old Testament imagery of the burning cities, Sodom and Gomorrah near the Dead Sea (Gen 19:24–25), as well as the terrestrial swallowing up of Korah and his company (Num 16:31–35).

Those two beastly generals captured during their apocalyptic assault are not merely detained in the bottomless pit (9:12; 20:3) but now meet their horrid because interminable punishment in "the gehenna of fire" (Matt 18:9). While the brimstone connotes intense and stenchful heat, it is not material fire, but the wrath of God poured out like lava, making for a torment more excruciating than their death on the battlefield. Since the demons, unlike their human minions, do not possess a physical body, which could be "killed" (v. 21), they can only be plunged into the underworld's flames of darkness alive. And the sheer horror of it is conveyed by the emphatic placement of "living, alive" (*zôntes*, ζῶντες, *vivi*) at the beginning of this clause in v. 20c (Ps 55:15). Hence, their chastisement is not only undying, but to be suffered fully conscious and unanesthetized, much more dreadful than bodily death. In other words, since the devil knowingly lodged his rebellious "I will not serve!" (*Non serviam*) before his Creator, then malignantly tried to brush aside the divine Redeemer, so also with all that knowledge his two surrogates now descend into hell.[9] They undergo a living death, a sentient annihilation, in a place "where their worm never dies, and the fire is never quenched" (Mark 9:48). All told, this vision expresses the utter awfulness, inevitability, and severity of their punishment, or in short, just a beastly broil.

As the hellish beast had made war, conquered, and killed God's innocent witnesses (11:7), so now its godless servants "were killed by the sword of the rider on the horse, the sword that came from his mouth" (v. 21). Thus, twofold is the endgame, in that the demonic leaders are made prisoners of war, whereas their earthly vassals are captured to be executed, making a clear distinction between deceivers and deceived. If the satanic duo of beast and pseudoprophet is anonymously discarded in hell, as it were, then it is the divine Commander on his white war stallion who slays his human enemies personally, all those who on earth chose to oppose him intellectually and spiritually. He does so not with laborious effort, but rather with "the breath of his mouth" (2 Thess 2:8), literally consumed "within" his sword (*en tē rhomphaía*, ἐν τῇ ῥομφαίᾳ, *in gladio*), that is, the word of prophecy as a mystical weapon of invincible might (1:16). Any and every resisting army will be cut down without delay, and not taken prisoners for protracted torture.

9. Cf. RD, 1175–76.

What follows, "and all the birds were gorged with their flesh" (v. 21), is modeled on the sacrificial festival on Israel's mountaintops, celebrating the defeat of the prince Gog of Magog, where wild animals and raptorial birds are bidden to glut themselves with carrion (Ezek 39:17–21).[10] With vulture-like eagerness and orgiastic ritualism, the carcasses of God's adversaries are cleaned up and consumed in their entirety. In the ancient world, this was the worst indignity imaginable for the dead, to lie unburied, a prey to wild birds.[11] And even Christ's witnesses had to undergo a similar humiliation and misfortune (11:8–10). As the birds flying in midheaven readily accept the invitation extended to them (v. 17), here their crude satisfaction in good cheer is portrayed. While the flesh of these fallen inimical fighters is eaten up on the battlefield, their living souls await their final judgment (20:12–13), prior to being hurled into the lake of fire (20:15).

Hence, bodily and spiritual death will come to those who arrogantly turn down Jesus' gentle offer to receive eternal life. One cannot help but notice the extreme irony in this metaphor of a grisly supper, where death and destruction provide pleasure and satisfaction. And as so often in the Apocalypse, the image can have a positive connotation, too, since the word "to feed, be filled" (*chortázō*, χορτάζω, *saturare*) recurs in the fourth beatitude (Matt 5:6) and at the miraculous multiplication of bread (John 6:26). And at the same time, it can be read in a negative key, perchance alluding to demons gorging themselves with the bodies of the damned. Be that as it may, the whole unspiritual world, even in its highest intellectual and material development, is but a rotting carcass around which the eagles gather. The pride and beauty of the human family is ephemeral, and if devoid of true worship and virtue, proves to be worthless: "As for mortals, their days are like grass; they flourish like a flower of the field; for the wind passes over it, and it is gone, and its place knows it no more" (Ps 103:15–16).

It goes without saying that this ghastly repast of vultures and their carrion represents a dramatic antithesis to the wedding banquet of the Lamb and his faithful (v. 9), the latter being the result of unconditional triumph over evil, achieved by the justice and omnipotence of the Lord. This entire scene also fulfills the foreshadowing at the conclusion of the first and foremost messianic psalm: "Now therefore, O kings, be wise; be warned, O rulers of the earth.

10. See also 1 Kgs 21:24; Ps 79:2; Jer 7:33; 15:3; 19:7; 34:20; Ezek 32:4.

11. One of the seven surviving fragments of the famous Stele of the Vultures, a Mesopotamian victory-monument (2350 BC), depicts enemy combatants lying bare on the battlefield and in the process of being devoured by vultures that carry severed heads in their beaks, while the corpses of the royal troops are carefully buried.

Serve the Lord with fear and with trembling; embrace discipline, or he will be angry, and you will perish in the way; for his wrath is quickly kindled. Blessed are those who trust in him" (Ps 2:10–12).

While the symbolism of these closing verses of the chapter (vv. 17–21) seems even more outlandish and unrelatable than usual, it was still shown to John and given to us for our spiritual edification. So, let us briefly revisit them to see how they might shed light on our Christian pilgrimage on earth. Still marveling at the sunlit zenith of v. 17, we could interpret the angel's summoning of the birds as God's call to holiness through victory over sin in our everyday lives. It then becomes a metaphor for our interior life in the sense that the soul allows itself to be drawn higher and higher above mundane affairs into the midheaven of grace and perfection. From that exalted vantage point, each one is urged to evangelize and prophesy about the nearness of the Kingdom and the defeat of anti-Christianity.[12] Contemplated from that angle, "both small and great" of humankind (v. 18) are meant to be "consumed" by the Gospel and eventually incorporated into the Mystical Body of Christ: "Get up, Peter; kill and eat" (Acts 10:13); irrespective of ethnic, cultural, socioeconomic differences, all are called to become members of the One, Holy, Catholic, and Apostolic Church.[13] And that oneness is particularly precious because it takes shape against the bewildering backdrop of the disunity and fragmentation of the armies of darkness (v. 19). Those benighted hordes are banding together, driven by evil intentions, hating the Lord and one another; and tragically, that total animus and reciprocal detestation is the only unifying factor among them.[14]

Moreover, when meditating on the capture of the sea-beast and false prophet and their eventual ejection (v. 20), one ought to always remember the truly glad tidings that "*now* is the judgment of this world; *now* the ruler of this world will be driven out" (John 12:31): the individual baptized soul believes that no matter how hard the spiritual combat might be, it always finds itself on the winning side of history, and that all inner untruth or pseudo-prophecy must be vanquished by the wisdom of God.[15]

Additionally, how can the soul not be shaken at the horrid thought of being burnt to death and being alive at the same time? That should invigorate us to strive to be always fully alive, body and soul.[16] Since "there is a sin that leads

12. Cf. RD, 1172.
13. Cf. RD, 1173.
14. Cf. AvS, 644.
15. Cf. RD, 1174.
16. Cf. AvS, 646–47.

to death" (1 John 5:16), in the event of committing such a mortal sin, we do well to seek out an occasion to confess that sin and be restored to the fullness of life. That way, the divine sword of the Prince of peace (v. 21) will be experienced as salvific and not punitive.

Still further, Jesus' mere appearance and overpowering presence as he fights on behalf of his people (Exod 14:14), makes a direct encounter with the devil innocuous, and exposes to full view the latter's nothingness (John 18:6). The God-Man's word is spoken performatively to great moral effect, capable of bringing about all kind of good and of subduing every guise of wickedness: "So shall my word be that goes out from my mouth; it shall not return to me empty, but it shall accomplish that which I purpose, and succeed in the thing for which I sent it" (Isa 55:11). Indeed, there is no exaggeration in stating that his word is the most efficacious reality in all respects, to the point that it conducts the spiritual battle in our souls on our behalf, without the need for us to bear arms ourselves (v. 14): a pure heart in union with him is sufficient.[17] And one day, the saints will be sated with the vision of that divine Word, without gloating over the damnation of many others.[18]

Second to last, there is no denying the fact that our good Lord does come across in this apocalyptic passage as a fierce, taciturn, and implacable subjugator, and not at all Lamb-like. Traces of evangelical tenderness and mercy seem to be absent, except perhaps in sparing his elect. This could be considered part of the divine pedagogy concerning us his children, not to permit us to slip into the naivete of thinking that willful antagonism against him would simply remain inconsequential.

And lastly, there is a subtle message in that beastly leaders and ungodly followers alike suffer severe punishment. There is no excuse in blindly carrying out unethical orders, but each one must follow his or her well-formed Christian conscience, which at times may necessitate a conscientious objection, as exemplified by Blessed Franz Jägerstätter, who was sentenced to death and executed for his refusal to fight for Nazi Germany; his last recorded words before his martyrdom were, "I am completely bound in inner union with the Lord."[19]

17. "What then, is there no need for you to fight? Yes, it is necessary to fight, but not to be distressed and toil. For it is not in fact war, but a solemn dance and feast-day, such is the nature of the arms, such the power of the Commander." John Chrysostom, *Homiliae in epistulam ad Romanos* 24 (commenting on Rom 13:12).

18. Cf. RD, 1177.

19. "Solitary, but not alone," *Denver Catholic*, magazine of the Archdiocese of Denver, Colorado, March 28, 2016, https://denvercatholic.org/franz-jagerstatter-solitary-but-not-alone/.

20:1–6, Millenary toward eternity

Chiliastic lockup (20:1–3)

[1]Then I saw an angel coming down from heaven, holding in his hand the key to the bottomless pit and a great chain. [2]He seized the dragon, that ancient serpent, who is the Devil and Satan, and bound him for a thousand years, [3]and threw him into the pit, and locked and sealed it over him, so that he would deceive the nations no more, until the thousand years were ended. After that he must be let out for a little while.

In narrative discontinuity with regard to the previous one, this chapter consists of three clearly discernible parts, beginning with the mysterious reign of a thousand years that culminates in a fifth apocalyptic beatitude or makarism (vv. 1–6), followed by a globalized end-battle (vv. 7–10), and closing with the "resurrection of the body"[1] that triggers the last judgment (vv. 11–15). It adds a finishing touch, as it were, to ch. 12, which constituted a sweeping delineation of crucial events within the entire economy of salvation, excepting only the work of creation itself (Gen 1–2). In an a-chronological fashion, it portrayed (a.) the primeval fall of Lucifer and his angels (12:4, 7–9), (b.) the incarnation of the Son of God (12:2, 5), (c.) his work of redemption on earth (12:10–12), (d.) the arduous life of his Church throughout the eschaton (12:6, 13–18), (e.) and her eventual glorification in heaven as depicted at the beginning (12:1).

Having recourse to a different set of images, which supplement that of ch. 12, this present chapter reflects a more logical timeline of events in its survey of that same history of salvation. Starting out with (a.) the implied victory of the Savior over Satan, albeit omitting the latter's previous fall from heaven (vv. 1–3), (b.) then summarizing the entire, or "millennial," existence of the Church militant and triumphant between the two advents of Christ (vv. 4–6), (c.) it flows into a new outbreak of diabolical activity triggering an end-conflict and the

1. As stated in the Apostolic Creed.

devil's expulsion (vv. 7–10), (d.) and closes with the last judgment that brings about the eviction of Death, Hades, and condemned humans (vv. 11–15). Thus, ch. 20 fills in the marginally more comprehensive storyline of ch. 12 by giving more weight to the happenings before the Lord's parousia. At that juncture, the way is paved for the revelation of the Bridal City in heaven (21:1–22:5), which in turn is a definitive unfolding of the great sign of the celestial Woman at 12:1.

For the third and last time, St. John observes a good spirit with anthropomorphic features descending from God toward the earth: "Then I saw an angel coming down from heaven, holding in his hand the key to the abyss and a great chain" (v. 1; cf. 10:1; 18:1). With the stereotypical phrase "Then I saw," the visionary weaves together a tapestry of four vignettes in this chapter alone (vv. 4, 11–12). Commissioned by the Most High and a minister of his providence, the angel symbolizes Christ's incarnation and its goal of destroying sin and death.[2] In one hand he secures a single key, the "key of David" (3:7), emblematic of his power over death and Hades (1:18). It is evocative, too, of the two metaphorical keys of binding and loosing in the Kingdom, entrusted to Peter in Caesarea Philippi (Matt 16:19). Ergo, this angel is the eschatological gatekeeper of hell,[3] that bottomless pit or "abyss," from which the devil and his hordes conduct their operations of hostility against God and his people for the time being (9:1–2). It is about to become Satan's everlasting prison, unveiled also as the lake of fire and sulfur (20:10).[4] In his other hand he clenches a complementary chain, an image occurring only here in Revelation; it is called "great" because of the extraordinary might of him whose power is to be curtailed. It is obviously not a material manacle, by which spirits could never be tied (Mark 5:3–4) but functions as a symbol of God's power over the devil.

And so, "he seized the dragon, that ancient serpent, who is the Devil and Satan, and bound him for a thousand years" (v. 2). Just as the dragon had been expelled from heaven by Michael, his peer according to the shared angelic nature (12:7), so he is now apprehended again by a mere angel. With superior might invested in him from heaven, he forcefully lays hold of the evil one, as implied by the verb "to arrest" (*ekrátēsen*, ἐκράτησεν, *apprehendit*; cf. 19:20). Pretending to be the prince of this world (Luke 4:6–7), in the eyes of God Satan remains the most powerless and grotesque of all his creatures. Robed, as it were, in a fourfold camouflage, appositionally put and descriptive of all

2. Cf. RD, 1177.

3. Cf. RD, 1178, AvS, 648.

4. In John Gill's *Exposition of the Bible* (1748), one finds this fascinating annotation: "The Ethiopic version reads, 'the key of the sun', where some have thought hell to be."

manners of wickedness by which he tries to perpetuate his sway on earth (12:9), Jesus' archenemy is first and foremost fierce and hideous as a dragon. Then, he is cunning and venomous like the ancient snake that beguiled our protoparents (Gen 3:1).[5] As *diábolos*, he is the "slanderous accuser" of the Lord and his saintly people, but also the archetypal *Śāṭān* (Hebrew שָׂטָן) or "obstructor" of all righteousness.[6] Even though he tries to hide behind all these aliases like an indicted criminal, they forever betray his *modus operandi* of ruling this fallen world. However, by virtue of Jesus' Incarnation and Paschal Mystery, his influence is shackled (*ligavit*) and will always remain under divine control.[7] Though he is unable to do anything without God's permission, his chain nevertheless seems elongated, as he is still relatively free to roam earth and air causing mischief (Eph 2:2). But that this restraint is prophesied to last for exactly one thousand years means that it is coextensive to the length of the Church's existence on earth evolving between the two historical comings of Christ, commonly defined as the eschaton.

Promptly the heavenly messenger "threw him into the pit, and locked and sealed it over him, so that he would deceive the nations no more, until the thousand years were ended. After that he must be let out for a little while" (v. 3). Satan's fall is incrementally ruinous, since after having been shamefully evicted from heaven and thrown to the earth (12:4), he is now also expelled from the earth and violently flung into the netherworld.[8] That "deep" (*abyssum*) in turn is only a temporary confinement (9:1; 20:7), which he absolutely dreads (Luke 8:31) and abuses to make destructive sorties around the world, before he will be cast into the lake of fire, his fateful destination (v. 10). Not to be interpreted as a spatial or geographic reality, the abyss symbolizes hell, that is, "the state of definitive self-exclusion from communion with God and the blessed," the existence and eternity of which the Church unequivocally affirms.[9]

And while heaven's gates are simultaneously shut to those not ready (Matt 25:10) and unlocked forever (21:25), the devil is locked up to leave the earth undisturbed for the eschatological millennium, which could be viewed

5. As one of the ambivalent metaphors in the Bible, the snake is also employed as a symbol of Christ at John 3:14.

6. Since the Greek *diábolos* has a next to identical lexical meaning to the Hebrew *satan*, i.e., "accuser, adversary," there is an undeniable affinity with the double name in 9:11, except that on that occasion the Hebrew *Abaddon* is mentioned ahead of the Greek *Apollyon*.

7. See also the binding of Azâzêl, the demon toward whom on Yom Kippur a scapegoat was driven, carrying the transgressions of the Jewish people (1 Enoch 10:4; 54:5).

8. Cf. RD, 1180.

9. Cf. *CCC*, §1033–34.

as contrasting with God's shutting Noah in the ark to save him (Gen 7:16). To make his relegation even more airtight, the mouth of the pit above Satan's head is also sealed (Dan 6:17). So now he is arrested and fettered, locked and sealed up, as opposed to Revelation's prophecy that remains unsealed and free (22:10), in the power of the one whose Resurrection could not be stopped by a sealed tomb (Matt 27:66). And hence, every precaution is taken to keep the one who thought he had defeated the Lord on Calvary imprisoned, yet more in the sense of restraint than complete suspension or let alone cessation of his influence over human history along the millennium, which seems puzzling. Indeed, in that paradoxical state, the ancient serpent comports itself like a modern escape artist, demonically adept at eluding the chains of detention. He knows that no change has happened to humanity's fallen nature, always prone to sin and corruptible by passion, and so he continues to harass and deceive the nations, as he did much more ferociously before the coming of the Redeemer in the fullness of time. That Satan will be released for a short period of time once the thousand years are completed, is proleptic toward v. 7 and will be reflected on at that juncture.

Millennial *basileia* (20:4–5)

4 Then I saw thrones, and those seated on them were given authority to judge. I also saw the souls of those who had been beheaded for their testimony to Jesus and for the word of God. They had not worshipped the beast or its image and had not received its mark on their foreheads or their hands. They came to life and reigned with Christ a thousand years. 5 The rest of the dead did not come to life until the thousand years were ended. This is the first resurrection.

Another visionary vignette crystallizes in the revelator's sight, initially focused on thrones (v. 4), recalling those of the twenty-four elders (11:16), but also anticipating the divine throne in v. 11. They are in opposition to Satan's throne (2:13; cf. 13:2; 16:10). The seats envisioned here, however, are not located in heaven but on earth, and the faces of their occupants, like that of God himself, remain anonymous for now. Referencing Daniel's vision (Dan 7:22), they not only receive favorable judgment,[10] but also exercise it in this world by virtue of their baptismal anointing as priests, prophets, and kings. Of course, so long as

10. Connoted, as is customary in Revelation, by the divine passive voice, i.e., *edóthē* (ἐδόθη, *datum est*).

they are pilgrims on earth, their kingship will remain intimately associated with the Lord's crown of thorns (John 19:2). Allegorically speaking, they occupy their tribunal chairs as assessors of the divine Judge in the power of the Holy Spirit, and their jurisdiction is over those who conspire and wage war against the Lamb. Intimated in this image are also the sees or cathedras of the shepherds of the flock, namely, popes and bishops across the ages, making up the hierarchy or "sacred reign" in his Church. Yet, since metaphors in the Apocalypse tend to be multidimensional, this one is probably no exception, and thus, those thrones also carry in them the seed of a future unfolding of the Kingdom in heaven (1 Cor 6:2–3).

Allusion is then made to a second assembly, and that is, of the communion of all the saints in heaven, under the synecdochical image of the martyrs' disembodied souls (v. 4). These are all those who down the centuries have served God by witnessing to his Son, Jesus, often amid great suffering. In fact, when John mentions their beheading by a grisly battle-axe, as denoted by the Greek verb *pelekízō* (πελεκίζω), he must have recalled his elder brother's martyrdom, that is, of James the Great, the first among the apostles to shed his blood for Christ. And like a refrain, for the sixth and last time in the Apocalypse,[11] the seer asserts their moral loyalty to the Lamb by rejecting the worship and mark of the beast or its image (v. 4).

Then all of a sudden, the scene comes to life: by employing an ingressive aorist tense of the Greek verb ("they came to life," *ézēsan*, ἔζησαν, *vixerunt*), the visionary recounts how these persons all began to live in the wake of the Lord's own Easter. And they are vivified either by the grace of baptism, bestowing divine life and faith on the soul, or by having been found worthy of eternal life after their earthly death, joining the ranks of the saints in heaven already now. Once alive, they also rule with Jesus, hinting at the spiritual influence that both Church triumphant and militant enjoy in this world. Their ascendancy will be chiliadal, that is, lasting "a thousand years," as is impressed on the reader by its sixfold reiteration in vv. 2–7. Since there is no other instance of a literal use of numbers in Revelation, the "thousand" ought to be viewed as one more numerical symbol conveying the state of terrestrial completeness but also finiteness.[12] And this millennium would signify the extended interval between the first and second comings of Christ, or, put differently, the period from his humble Incarnation to his glorious parousia, also thought of as Church history. It marks,

11. Cf. 13:16; 14:9, 11; 16:2; 19:20.

12. It is also possible that the Blessed Trinity is alluded to in the triple multiplication of ten times ten times ten (cf. Deut 7:9; Pss 90:4; 105:8).

therefore, the duration of the entire eschaton coinciding with the co-regency between the God-Man and both, the saints in heaven and faithful Christians on earth (Dan 7:27).[13] In that sense, the millennial Reign or *Basileía* is homogeneous with the symbolic timespans of the "ten days" (2:10), the "little while" (6:11), the "forty-two months" (11:2), the "one thousand two hundred sixty days" (12:6), the "short time" (12:12), as well as the "time, and times, and half a time" (12:14).

Upholding the strict ethical dualism, so characteristic of the apocalyptic genre, John subjoins: "The rest of the dead did not come to life until the thousand years were ended. This is the first resurrection" (v. 5). His reasoning is based on the Pauline concept of the general resurrection on the boundary of history (1 Cor 15:12). On that decisive day, marking the conclusion of the Christian millennium, God's plan or "mystery" will be completed (10:7). But until that morning dawns, those who have died or will die apart from a saving relationship with God through faith in his incarnate Son, are judged unworthy of the divine presence in heaven even before the final judgment. They will be part of the last judgment only to be condemned to eternal death. Thus, the "until" of the completion of the chiliastic reign does not imply that afterwards they will be saved for eternity.[14]

What is more, all those humans who refused the sacrament of baptism and the effort to live in the state of grace in union with Christ, are not included in the spiritual Kingdom of a thousand years.[15] Unless one dies to sin and awakens to a life of righteousness in his Church, one remains spiritually dead (Eph 2:1–7). Following this parenthetical remark regarding those who do not avail themselves of the Lord's redemptive offer, the sacred author now condenses what he had described in the previous verse into a unique definition. He declares that whoever in the sacrament of baptism imitates the Lord, once dead yet alive forever (1:18), experiences a "first resurrection," i.e., that of the soul, paving the way for a second resurrection, namely, that of the glorified body, at the end of time (John 5:28–29). That way, every Christian spiritually shares in Jesus' incarnational privileges of being the "Firstborn from the dead" (Col 1:18) and being "the First and the Last" (1:17). And that second resurrection will be more closely viewed at vv. 12–13.

13. Cf. RD, 1182; for an abstract of chiliastic interpretations, see Williamson, *Revelation*, 329–31; Smalley, *Commentary on the Greek Text of the Apocalypse*, 502–4.

14. Following the same logic as Matt 1:25, where the "until" of Jesus' Nativity does not indicate that Joseph and Mary engaged in marital relations afterwards, resulting in having more children, known as his "brothers" (cf. Matt 12:46).

15. Cf. RD, 1183.

Fifth makarism: Death-immunity (20:6)

6Blessed and holy are those who share in the first resurrection. Over these the second death has no power, but they will be priests of God and of Christ, and they will reign with him a thousand years.

With prayerful gravitas and vibrant joy, John now proclaims this fifth apocalyptic beatitude, which stands out in that it entwines bliss and sanctity: *Beatus et sanctus!* It is enormously consequential in the way it highlights the gifts and blessings lavished on our souls. As a literary hysteron-proteron, the verse commences with the climactic effect, as Christian holiness practiced on earth eventually flows into happiness in heaven. To be holy, in the sense of the first resurrection by baptism, implies a vivid relationship with the Triune God that spurs us on to turn away from sin, to nurture virtue of the heart, to consecrate one's action to his glory, and therefore be wholesome: "O Christian, recognize your dignity!"[16] Regenerated by the grace of the Holy Spirit, the soul experiences a certain immunity from the "second death," standing in opposition to the "first resurrection" (v. 5). It epitomizes eternal damnation as a spiritual and corporal separation from God in hell (v. 14), presupposing a first death which remains unmentioned.

That initial dying is temporal and refers to both the spiritual death in mortal sin, but also to the separation of body and soul in physical death, as alluded to already in the second makarism (14:13). Likewise, John's first resurrection, the spiritual millennium, implies a second resurrection which again he does not put forward. That second rising corresponds to the universal resurrection of all flesh as depicted in vv. 12–13. Ergo, the faithful who partook of the "first resurrection" rise twice, first spiritually and then physically, yet die only once when at the end of their earthly life they pass through the gateway of physical death. And the reverse holds true for unbelievers who die three times, first spiritually and physically on earth and then eternally, but will experience the resurrection only once, namely, in the resurrection of the body on the last day for their condemnation.

Already now, the sons and daughters of the Church, and all those who serve God with a sincere mind, are blessed by being priests not just "for God" (*tô̂ Theô̂*, τῷ θεῷ; 1:6; 5:10), but now also "of God [*toû Theoû*, τοῦ θεοῦ] and of Christ" in the Holy Spirit (1 Pet 2:9). This is, incidentally, the final of seven recurrences of the messianic title "Christ" (*Christós*, Χριστός, *Christus*) in this

16. Leo the Great, *Sermo I de Nativitate.*

book,[17] emphasizing his mission as the Anointed of the Father and divine High Priest. By adducing God and Christ together on this occasion, the apostle renders testimony to their coequal divinity or consubstantiality. During their existence in this world, yet without becoming conformed to it, these baptized priests worship the Lord by offering themselves as a living sacrifice, holy and acceptable (Rom 12:1). And if it was the sacred duty of the Aaronite priests to serve at the tent of witness in the wilderness and in the Holy of Holies in the Jerusalem temple on behalf of the people, then those who spiritually already dwell in the celestial regions enjoy God's glorious presence in intimate fellowship. A literary *inclusio* is brought about with the end of v. 4 by reaffirming their chiliastic reign, except that the perfect tense "they have reigned" (*regnaverunt*) is now complemented by the future tense "they shall reign" (*regnabunt*).

As we prepare to learn what will happen after the eschatological millennium in the upcoming verses, let us first take a short break and ruminate on the spiritual lessons that the apostle's visions in vv. 1–6 transmit. Thinking of the image of the key and chain (v. 1), we are invited to obediently persevere within the hierarchical authority of binding and loosing of Holy Mother Church, as outlined in the Catechism and in canon law, a power that can ensure the salvation of our souls.[18] By doing so, we are all but guaranteed not to become enchained in sin, vice, or addiction, but to enjoy interior freedom. Tied to this is the recognition that it takes heavenly might to subdue diabolical clout, yet also the reassurance that a mere angel can accomplish it. Indeed, when reflecting on the five verbs of angelic action against the devil in vv. 2–3 ("to seize, bind, throw, lock, seal"), one realizes how relatively powerless he is, caught in an unbreakable prison of doom. That in turn ought to inspire us to call on the holy angels in our spiritual battles. And that combat, to be sure, will continue so long as we live here below, albeit with reduced ferocity due to Satan's current defeat and confinement.

But if one takes the apocalyptic millennium also as a measure of one's personal lifespan (2 Pet 3:8), then the path to holiness is open and so are the opportunities to prove one's fidelity to the Lord in faith, hope, and love.[19] Also, the chiliadal metaphor, coupled with the first resurrection, could also be interpreted as the completion of one's personal vocation and mission on earth,[20] maturing into the full measure of the God-Man's stature (Eph 4:13), preserving

17. While his personal name "Jesus" occurs fourteen times or precisely twice as frequently.

18. Cf. Code of Canon Law, c. 1752.

19. Cf. RD, 1188; AvS, 651–52.

20. Cf. AvS, 658–60.

one's first love for him (2:4), doing the first works (2:5), and accomplishing even greater ones than those (2:19; John 14:12).

Moreover, how blessed we are to have embarked on the royal and priestly path (vv. 4, 6), sustained by the perfect and regal law of freedom (Jas 1:25; 2:8), and already reigning from the mystical thrones of grace. In this way, faithful Christians will avoid having a name of being alive but being practically dead (3:1); instead they will shun the first death of mortal sin and so escape the second death (v. 6). That avoidance of moral trespassing is itself a way of dying to oneself, in voluntary acts of mortification and asceticism, so that at the hour of one's physical death one has already died to this world. Not to be neglected either is the lively contact with the saints worshiping before God's throne on high, to implore their help and protection. And lastly, let us treasure the beatitude of having already risen with the Risen Lord as the most outstanding of divine favors, a grace that will give us patience and courage to persevere even in moments of hardship.

20:7–10, Siege broken

Sand against sand (20:7–8)

[7]When the thousand years are ended, Satan will be released from his prison [8]and will come out to deceive the nations at the four corners of the earth, Gog and Magog, in order to gather them for battle; they are as numerous as the sands of the sea.

If the millennial detainment had truncated Satan's interference on earth (v. 2), these forthcoming vv. 7–10 chronicle his irrevocable ruin, and in that sense the Apocalypse reaches its narrative anticlimax. During a brief post-chiliastic bout, he will be permitted to renew his rebellion and bluffing, and even engage in a final symbolic battle, but his fate is already sealed, and he is flung irredeemably into the lake that burns with sulfur. From then onward he will remain permanently incapacitated. As overtly predicted at the end of v. 3, yet still quite shockingly, "when the thousand years are fulfilled, Satan will be released from his prison" (v. 7). But then again, five circumstances evince divine control over the events on the boundary of human history.

First, there is the rhythmic restating of the consummation of the millennium (*consummare mille anni*, vv. 3, 5.7) as the timeframe purposely prearranged by God the Almighty. *Second*, a mysterious "necessity" is inculcated at the end of v. 3 (*deî*, δεῖ, *oportet*) that predicates the devil's future release as part of the methodic achievement of God's will and design. *Third*, there is also the indication of "a little while" (*modico tempore*) in that verse. This limited duration of the end-time (John 16:16) should not be confused with the similar-sounding phrase at 6:11, signifying the same amount of time as the millennium itself (*tempus modicum*).[1] That important distinction between the eschaton and its coda, so to speak, can be inferred from the transposed word order:

1. See the related phrase with the same connotation, yet divergent vocabulary, at 12:12b, *olígon kairón* (ὀλίγον καιρόν, *modicum tempus*).

while v. 3 emphasizes "brief" (*modicum*), 6:11 gives more prominence to "time" (*tempus*). As such, the short interval of Satan's release at the very conclusion of the eschaton could be identified with the equally figurative "half a time" (*dimidium temporis*) at 12:14. That hurried period will be the window for the final onslaught of the antichrist, global turmoil, but also perhaps for the conversion of the people of Israel to take place (Rom 11:26), directly preceding Christ's parousia.[2] *Fourth*, God's dominance is also shown in the divine passive "released" (*solvetur*, v. 7): although no hint is dropped as to the "why" or "how" of the devil's temporary discharge, the reader does know that it cannot be done by himself, but by the One who bound him, or by divine permission, so God can manifest both his judgment wrath and his saving power. And *fifth*, there is the eloquent future tense of this same verb, making everyone understand that those trials will happen according to the Lord's timetable, set for hour, day, month, and year (9:15).

What the reader had always suspected is finally spelled out, namely, that the abyss functions as the demons' prison where, to their utter humiliation, they are kept before being incinerated in the fiery lake. Once those restraints are eased one last time, Satan "will come out to deceive the nations at the four corners of the earth, Gog and Magog, in order to gather them for battle; their number is like the sand of the sea" (v. 8). Having been frustrated in his attacks on the Woman and her Child, he made his beastly minions create rival kingdoms and promote perfidious ideologies, to persecute and possibly annihilate her offspring in the Church. Never one to lie low, he now temporarily returns to the scene to instigate a pre-parousiac outbreak of wickedness as predicted by Jesus in his Eschatological Discourse (Mark 13), and by Paul, too (2 Thess 2:1–12). Although his assault will be planetary, that is, not sparing even the remotest regions on earth, as symbolized by the four corners of the world, as if it were one expansive square plain (7:1), his evil endeavor will soon be quelled. And that all those nations had already been exterminated at 19:21 puts the trans-historical pattern of the apocalyptic genre again on full display.

Those ends of the earth are neatly equated with "Gog and Magog," a paronomasia mentioned only here in the Bible. In Jewish tradition it came to symbolize an exceptionally savage and warmongering people, expected to either turn their dreaded forces against the Jews resettled in their own land, or to invade Israel itself. Once there, in the last days, they would wage an unprovoked battle against Jerusalem as their ultimate adversary, only to be eventually overthrown by the Messiah. John, as is his custom, universalizes the Ezekelian

2. Cf. RD, 1181.

prophecy by changing the phrase "Gog of the land of Magog" (Ezek 38:2)[3] to "Gog and Magog," and by adapting their origin "from the farthest north" (Ezek 38:6) to a globalized "four corners of the earth" (v. 8). Under his pen they now denote the ungodly inhabitants of this world, allies of Satan in the persecution of the saints at the end of the millennium.[4] Hence, like "Babylon," "Sodom," "Egypt," "Jerusalem," and "Harmagedon" earlier in Revelation, "Gog and Magog," too, become a symbolic toponym for the last-standing enemies of the Mystical Body of Christ, the ugly tail-end of the dragon, as it were. To rally them (*congregare*) for the final combat is the whole intent of the serpent's seduction, prepared by the war-posturings at 16:16 and 19:19.

That truly apocalyptic conflict, repeatedly foretold,[5] will be the war of all wars, so to speak. To visualize the sheer vastness of inimical forces, the apostle employs a number for the tenth and last time in his book, but its arithmetic value remains tantalizingly vague, like the grains of sand on the seashore.[6] And that location happens to be the place where the dragon took up his stance, intending to make war on the rest of the Woman's children (12:17–18). While this image recalls the parable of the demolition of a house built on sand (Matt 7:26–27), it also evokes Yahweh's covenant with Abraham: "I will surely bless you, and I will multiply your descendants like the stars in the sky and the sand on the seashore; your descendants will possess the gates of their enemies" (Gen 22:17). In other words, the final warfare will pitch "sand" against "sand," as it were, and result in the defeat of the "sand" of Satan's offspring at the hands of the "sand" of Abraham's children.[7]

Fire from above (20:9)

[9] They marched up over the breadth of the earth and surrounded the camp of the saints and the beloved city. And fire came down from heaven and consumed them.

To ascend toward the battlefield would have been common parlance for military expeditions in antiquity, but in this apocalyptic context it connotes the

3. Flavius Josephus proposes this ethnic identification: "Magog founded those that from him were named Magogites; but who are by the Greeks called Scythians" (*Antiquities*, 1.6.1).

4. Cf. RD, 1184; AvS, 663.

5. Cf. 9:7, 9; 11:7; 12:7, 17; 13:7; 16:14, 16; 19:19.

6. A common comparison in Scripture, incidentally, to signify a vast multitude (e.g., Josh 11:4).

7. Cf. RD, 1184.

resurgence of evil (e.g., 13:1). After the drying up of the Euphrates's riverbed to facilitate the strategic movement of all worldly kings and their confluence at Harmagedon's staging area (16:12–16), we now witness a final escalation of bellicose multitudes swarming like locusts and chariots (9:3, 9) across the full latitude of the earth. That breadth of the earth symbolizes the theater of God's victory over the final unleashing of Satan, the last cosmic upheaval of this passing world, causing the Bride of Christ to descend from heaven in the form of the New Jerusalem.[8] Hence, analogous to the previous image of the four corners (v. 8), the enemy forces invade all parts of this world where the Church sojourns. In a strangling move they press on to encompass and besiege her, but they find her well prepared, as if lodging in multiple military barracks (*castra*) in defense of their city. That protective stance of the Church militant between the ungodly attackers on the one side and the sacred city on the other is intimated by the Greek *parembolḗ* (παρεμβολή), literally meaning "to put in between." John appears to draw inspiration from the desert encampment of the Israelites, which, like a bulwark, surrounded the tabernacle of the covenant from east, south, west, and north (Num 2).

What we are given to understand is the apocalyptic exodus of God's people from this world. Another symbolic layer is added by equating this camp to the much-loved messianic city of Jerusalem (*civitas dilecta*), navel and center of the whole world. Despite being trodden under foot by the Gentiles (11:2), she will remain the mystical capital of the millennial Kingdom, the heavenly Jerusalem already present in history. She is the City of God surmounted by "Mount Zion, which he loves" (Ps 78:68), forever holding firm against the machinations of Babylon, the city of Satan. Like the repatriated exiles who never laid down their swords (Neh 4:17–18), she is bravely waging her spiritual warfare especially during this closing strife. And precisely because of that, she is already the beloved Bride of the Lamb.

Thus, the apostolic revelator is being shown four portrayals of one and the same end-time war, namely, (a.) 16:12–16, (b.) 17:14, (c.) 19:11–21, and (d.) 20:7–10, matched, incidentally, by four mentions of the fall of Babylon, i.e., (a.) 14:8, (b.) 16:19, (c.) 17:16, (d.) 18:21. Yet, what is perhaps most uplifting about this endmost version of opposition against the Church is the Lord's prompt response in eliminating the evil one. And so, without going into any detail whatsoever concerning a military confrontation, fire descends from on high to consume all enemies. They had come up for battle and are now trounced by the blaze that comes down on them, reminiscent of the two witnesses'

8. Cf. *CCC*, §677.

preliminary victory (11:5). Old Testament antetypes include again the conflagrant overthrow of the cities of the plains (Gen 19:24–25), the fiery destruction of the two hundred fifty Hebrew rebels (Num 16:35), Elijah's incineration of King Ahaziah's delegations (2 Kgs 1:9–12), and Gog and Magog's punishment by divine fire (Ezek 39:6). And that this climactic battle before Christ's return, in which God remains unconquerable, would be accompanied by such flames of his wrath, fulfills Hebrew and apostolic prophecy.[9]

Into fire below (20:10)

[10]And the devil who had deceived them was thrown into the lake of fire and sulfur, where the beast and the false prophet [were], and they will be tormented day and night forever and ever.

Through the lens of 12:3–4, 7–9 we caught a glimpse of the *diabolus*' existence, insurgence, and fall at the dawn of creation, and from Gen 3:1–5, 13 we were able to glean that he must be the chief seducer of humankind, yet at this juncture his eternal fate is revealed. And this will remain his last-ever mention in the Bible. No longer just restrained as before, this archenemy of God and his people is now cast into fiery and never-ending excruciation: "On that day the Lord with his cruel and great and strong sword will punish Leviathan the fleeing serpent, Leviathan the twisting serpent, and he will kill the dragon that is in the sea" (Isa 27:1). Satan shall never be permitted to enter the paradise regained, in direct punishment for having wrested the primeval one away from our first parents, Adam and Eve. Instead, he is condemned to reunite with his two top surrogates, the sea-beast and the land-beast or pseudo-prophet, a wretched anti-trinity, and an inerasable monument to his rebellion against the one true God.

And there he is, writhing in agony among his former vassals, aflame with hatred toward God and one another, suffering just punishment for attempting to lead men and women astray. A more painful torture cannot be imagined than to be incinerated alive in burning brimstone. To better appreciate the infernal symbolism, one has to recall that this type of fire burns slower, is next to inextinguishable, but also highly flammable and prone to ignite its surroundings; moreover, it produces blue flames hotter than red ones, it resembles the liquefied surface of a body of water ablaze, and produces copious amounts

9. Cf. Isa 66:15–16, 24; 2 Thess 1:8; Heb 10:27; 2 Pet 3:7, 10, 12.

of extremely malodorous smoke deadly when breathed in.[10] While "night" will no longer be part of the New Jerusalem due to the all-enveloping light of God (22:5), those in the state of damnation will have to endure the unbroken monotony of the old creation where God had called the light Day, and the darkness Night (Gen 1:5). Satan had accused the children of God "day and night" (12:10), and now he himself is tormented without intermission, restlessly and despairingly awaiting the break of yet another day of being burned and suffocated while living and breathing.

And how irrecoverable his exclusion is from the Lord's presence is ironically conveyed by the liturgical formula "forever and ever" (*saecula saeculorum*), in antithesis to those who are redeemed and "reign forever and ever" (22:5). And all of Scripture affords no starker expression for haunting endlessness and therefore hopelessness. This everlasting or meta-chronological horror of hell is intimated, too, by the omission of a verb that would imply the passage of time; thus, the clause simply reads, "where the beast and the false prophet" (*ubi et bestia et pseudopropheta*), completely removed from temporality.[11] This will be their full retribution, which, however, will not materialize before the time of the Last Judgment. With the neutralization of the great opponents of the Lamb, the way is now paved for the final consummation. This verse marks the completion of the entire series of visions begun at 12:3 regarding demonic activity in this world, the resolution of the antagonism between the Pantocrator and his followers on the one hand, and the dragon and his worshipers on the other. Herewith, the Apocalypse enters its extended conclusion.

Looking back over these past four verses, vv. 7–10, illustrative of events on the fringe of history, we should keep ourselves in a state of preparedness, always ready to witness the end of the spiritual millennium and the temporary unleashing of Satan (v. 7). Naturally, no one knows day or hour (Mark 13:32), but all are taken into the eager yearning and inward groaning with creation itself, awaiting full liberation (Rom 8:19–23). What *is* known, however, is that those end-trials can befall us at any moment, and one is well advised to prayerfully interpret the signs of the present time (Luke 12:56). And once those days are here, the Church will be intimately associated with Jesus' own Death and Resurrection, suffering her final Passover amid a cosmic upheaval of this passing world. May the Christian heart be watchful and ever ready for those prophecies to come true (Matt 24:42).

10. Cf. AvS, 667.

11. To smoothen the slight awkwardness of the text, most English translations add the auxiliary verb "were," which we have added in square brackets.

What can be of great encouragement, too, is that the devil's unmanacling is only of relative impact, since the Lamb-Lion has broken open the seals and conquered already (5:5), setting us free from our sins by his Blood (1:5). By the same token, the spiritual person will not belittle those latter hardships and religious deception either (v. 8), since they will shake the faith of many believers, and even drive them into apostasy.[12] Any internal tantalization to be god-like or to create an earthly paradise must be quashed, in order that we can withstand the evil resolve and determination of those who rally for war against Jesus' Kingdom.[13] At the end of the day, the demons are like unwitting sports coaches that constantly empower saintly souls to prove their stamina in faith and *mores*, going "from strength to strength" (Ps 84:7).

Furthermore, if the "camp" and the "beloved city" are taken as metaphors for the human heart (v. 9), then the ascent and siege of those inimical forces could be interpreted as thoughts of pride and insubordination that must be firmly resisted and brought low. Consequently, one will be able to break up the spiritual beleaguerment and achieve inner freedom.[14] And lastly, no interior life will be whole without earnest meditation on the truly frightening prospect of unending torment in hell (v. 10), always contrasting it to the eternal joys in heaven: "What no eye has seen, nor ear heard, nor the human heart conceived, what God has prepared for those who love him" (1 Cor 2:9).

12. Cf. *CCC*, §675.
13. Cf. RD, 1184.
14. Cf. RD, 1185; AvS, 664.

20:11–15, *Basileian* tribunal

Faith that worked (20:11–13)

[11]*Then I saw a great white throne and the one who sat on it; the earth*
and the heaven fled from his presence, and no place was found for them.
[12]*And I saw the dead, great and small, standing before the throne, and*
books were opened. Also another book was opened, the book of life. And
the dead were judged according to their works, as recorded in the books.
[13]*And the sea gave up the dead that were in it, Death and Hades gave up*
the dead that were in them, and all were judged according to what they
had done.

At last, it's judgment day in John's Apocalypse! To be precise, vv. 11–15 highlight the resurrection and Last Judgment of all those who will have been deceased by the time the final day of history dawns, whereas the final judgment of all the living was depicted under the twin images of harvest and vintage at 14:14–20. So, those two visionary vignettes supplement each other, accomplishing the entire mystery of divine justice, and clearing the way for the climactic unveiling of the Holy City, the New Jerusalem of heaven (21:2). Without further ado, let us delve into the sacred text. Here comes the book's fourth-last mystical scene ushered in by "Then I saw" (*et vidi*, cf. 20:12; 21:1, 2): "Then I saw a great white throne and the one who sat on it; the earth and the heaven fled from his countenance, and no place was found for them" (v. 11). What is described here dovetails chronologically with Christ's parousia. And when John nods toward "the One seated" on the throne, he gives an inkling of the presence of the Blessed Trinity, one God in three persons: while the third person, the Holy Spirit, typically remains unnamed or alluded to in his seven gifts in Revelation (1:4), the throne is shared by God the Father and his Son, the Lamb, and together, in that trinitarian logic, they are Lawgiver, Judge, Shepherd, and King.

With the Lamb's mediatorial role carried out, he submits the reign to his Father, so "that God may be all in all" (1 Cor 15:24–28). It marks the solemn moment when postlapsarian humanity for the first time comes into unmediated contact with the first divine Person, namely, the heavenly Father himself. At the same time, he entrusts judgment to his Son, because as *perfectus Deus, perfectus Homo*,[1] both omniscient and omnipotent, he is uniquely equipped to pass just sentence on every human conscience (John 5:22, 27). That glorious justice and pure sacrality of God's judging is brought across by the "great white throne" (v. 11), foreshadowed in the ivory seat at King Solomon's Jerusalem palace (2 Chron 9:17). After sinning, Adam and Eve tried to abscond in the Garden (Gen 3:10), and ungodly persons of all walks of life attempted to hide from God's wrathful face at the sixth seal (6:15–17), but here it is all of creation that appears to take flight from before his countenance (16:20). That face, shining like the blazing sun (1:16), is so awe-inspiring that it causes earth and heaven to shrink and then vanish into nothingness. They are not simply relocated but fade away to make room for the renewal of creation (21:1, 5). Given the uniqueness and relative vagueness of wording, it lends itself to two interpretations. On the one hand there is the idea of mere transformation in continuity with what was before. Such a change, that is, without annihilation of the cosmos's substance, might be scripturally supported by Lucifer's metamorphosis into Satan (12:8), as well as Babylon's mutation into hell (18:21). Besides, there is the transformative devastation of the primeval deluge, where a new world-order emerged out of a watery chaos.

On the other hand, one could speculate about a total dissolution or discontinuity of the old world, since "no place was found for them," v. 11 (2 Pet 3:10). That, however, would necessitate a second *creatio ex nihilo*, to bring about a new heaven and earth. In support of that opinion, i.e., of some guise of cosmic nonexistence without leaving a trace, one might adduce the reasoning that demonic and human sin has contaminated creation to the point of being unsalvageable, and thus deserves to be annihilated and replaced with another universe. But then again, how can one theologically reconcile such a concept of perfect annihilation with the intrinsic worth of the very good things made by God (Gen 1:31)? One way or another, there will be a transition into a new and definitive era, and that is the purport of this entire cosmic metaphor. Hence, instead of airing on the literalistic side of a physical obliteration of all creation like a *reductio ad nihilum*, the apostle seems to transmit a message of moral and spiritual regeneration of an obsolete world-order. And at this very moment, in terms of the visionary scene, there exists absolutely nothing between humanity and its Creator, setting the stage for the general judgment, which in turn will

1. Cf. the Athanasian Creed.

open the way for many to enter the beatific vision of the Lord's glorious countenance (22:4).

John then observes how the metaphorical void left by creation's disappearance is filled with another portentous spectacle: "And I saw the dead, great and small, standing before the throne, and books were opened. And another book was opened, which is the book of life. And the dead were judged according to their works, as recorded in the books" (v. 12). These dead are those persons who died before the Lord's parousia, and they have now risen, joining those who are living at that time. Worldly distinctions as to age, rank, or any other imaginable human condition, are nothingness before God, and all, saints and sinners alike, are summoned.[2] On that great and terrible Day of the Lord (Mal 4:5; Jude 6) they stand in his presence reverentially, facing his judgment seat, ready to render account for their lives and receive just sentence (11:18).

Books, not known up till now, are solemnly unclosed (Dan 7:10). They epitomize both God's unfailing memory, but also human accountability. Like a modern flight recorder or black box that captures the performance of an aircraft between takeoff and landing, all the moral decisions of a person's conscience made during a lifetime, good and bad, will be laid bare for all to see.[3] And everybody will be able to recollect, review, and thoroughly know the moral nature of all his or her past actions. Although formerly secret, they will then be exhibited for a final reckoning according to divine omniscience, and they constitute the basis for the individual sentence to be passed. Simultaneously, the Book of Life (21:27) is disclosed, God's eternal decree containing the names of the redeemed, those who responded to his foreknowing, preordaining, electing, and redeeming love (Rom 8:29–30).[4] It is the mystical register of the New Jerusalem identifying its heavenly citizens (Ps 87:6). By the same token, this "other book" (v. 12) represents the wisdom of God for his people as revealed in the God-Man Christ Jesus,[5] in the Sacred Scriptures, as well as in the law of nature and of grace. As such, it could be equated with the scroll sealed sevenfold (5:1), but also with the opened little scroll held by the mighty angel's hand (10:2).

Ultimately, the "books" of human consciences and works are now assessed by mirroring them in the light of the "book" of God's omniscience and law, to reveal the truth of history. In line with the well-known Thomistic dictum

2. Cf. AvS, 673.
3. Cf. RD, 1187; AvS, 673.
4. Cf. RD, 1187.
5. Cf. AvS, 673.

that "truth is the agreement of thing and intellect,"[6] from an apocalyptic viewpoint one might adjoin that truth is also the agreement of divine will and human conscience, which is the quintessence of each person's last judgment. By his earthly life and death, Christ earned the right to judge every single person according to their works in this world,[7] and he had emphasized their crucial importance already in the letters to the seven churches.[8] While it is true that one is justified by faith in him (Gal 2:16), it must be a faith that works; the former is known to God alone, but the latter gives evidence of it to all (Jas 2:14–26). "Works" (*érga*, ἔργα, *opera*) here and in v. 13 should be assumed as an umbrella designation for the practice of morally upright thoughts, words, and deeds. If done in union with the Lord Jesus and in conscious collaboration with his grace, they attain to degrees of personal holiness whose merit will be rewarded in the afterlife. Especially meritorious is the serene acceptance of trial, temptation, and suffering, which render the soul more cruciform. That way, God's Life-Book and the individual believer's work-book will harmonize toward a favorable judgment (22:12).

Given the monumental relevance of the general resurrection of the dead, the seer on Patmos appends some more specifics about where they come from: "And the Sea gave up the dead that were in it, and Death and Hades gave up the dead that were in them, and all were judged according to their works" (v. 13). Shortly before the sea melts into thin air altogether (21:1), it is pictured here personified as *Thálassa* (Θάλασσα, *mare*, "Sea"), the primordial goddess of the world's great bodies of water according to ancient Greek mythology, often depicted as a matronly woman half-submerged in the sea. Water was the element that enveloped the entire face of the earth at creation (Gen 1:2), and since even today about two thirds of its surface remain water-covered, it seems reasonable that this is the first place of origin referenced, that is, of the dead being resurrected. These are all those who over time perished at sea and were entombed in the depths of the oceans. At this juncture, and at God's command, she promptly "gives" (*dedit*) them back to him so he can judge and resettle them into their eternal destinations.

Second to be alluded to are those who died on land and were buried in cemeteries or random graves. They were held in the cold and rigid clutches of *Thánatos* (Θάνατος, *mors*, "Death"), the rarely appearing male personification of death in Hellenistic mythology. He was thought to have no father but was

6. In the Latin original: "Veritas est adaequatio rei et intellectus," *De veritate*, q. 1, a. 2.

7. Cf. *CCC*, §679.

8. Cf. 2:2, 5, 19; 26; 3:1, 8, 15.

the son of Nyx the goddess of night;[9] he receives the deceased through the services of Charon the ferryman who leads them across Styx, the river-boundary between Gaia ("earth") and Hades ("underworld"). Considered as compassionless and undiscriminating, he was universally loathed by gods, goddesses, and mortals alike, often portrayed as carrying a torch upside down symbolizing another human life extinguished and forever stolen. In John's vision, like Thálassa, so also Thánatos has no choice but to give up the dead and return them now to their Creator and eternal Judge.

Thus, swallowing the dead eventually would have been *Hadēs* (Ἅδης),[10] the ancient Greek god and king of the underworld. And here he is, the third embodiment in v. 13 of places that on the last day will have to surrender the dead to the Lord. It was imagined as the infernal regions in the very depth of the earth (*infernus*), the abode of departed and disembodied spirits. Its lowest and gloomiest sector would have been *tartarus* where severe punishment was doled out, the exact opposite of *elysium*, the mythic heaven brimming with comfort and unfailing sunshine. Hades was known among the ancients to strictly forbid those souls to leave his dreary and misty domain and would become enraged when anyone tried to escape. In the present apocalyptic scene, Thánatos and Hades are like two insatiable ghouls, co-conspirators who have swallowed all past generations in hell, yet are now constrained to disgorge their human prey to the One who has the keys of Death and of Hades (1:18).[11] This is the last mention of the dead in Revelation, and without exception, all are raised into a reunion of body and soul, and each one will be judged with an emphasis on individual accountability (*singuli*), emphatically restating the "according to what they had done" (*secundum opera ipsorum*) of v. 12.

9. Tellingly, mythological imagination saw him also shadowed by eight dreadful siblings, representatives of old age (*Geras*), doom (*Moros*), strife (*Eris*), sleep (*Hypnos*), blame (*Momus*), deception (*Apate*), pain (*Oizys*), and vengeance (*Nemesis*).

10. This Greek name (cf. 1:18; 6:8) stems from the negative prefix *a*-, "not," and *idein*, "to see," literally "the unseen place," as closer reflected in its variant spelling of Ἅιδης, pointing to the invisible realm in which all the dead reside; it is the Septuagint's translation of the Hebrew *sheol* (e.g., Gen 37:35).

11. Rupert posits that "Death" returns the souls of the saints, while "Hades" delivers the souls of the condemned; cf. RD, 1188.

Beneath the underworld (20:14)

[14]Then Death and Hades were thrown into the lake of fire. This is the second death, the lake of fire.

With inexorable divine muscle, Thánatos and his metonymical accomplice Hades (6:8), the grim repository for death's casualties, are flung down into the fiery lake, torturously reunited with the two beasts (19:20) and with the dragon-devil (20:10). What was not known heretofore is that this "lake" (*límnē*, λίμνη, *stagnum*) is lower than the underworld itself. Inferior to that nether region, it marks figuratively the farthest removal from God's throne, intimating that death as the last enemy (1 Cor 15:26) will be rendered powerless: "Death will be no more" (21:4). This eternal exclusion, that is, the fatal drowning and burning, of death and Hades is a precondition to the everlasting bliss of the glorified. Their evil reign will then have found a horrific termination with the whole realm of mortality being set ablaze at last, making way to a new order of things to be inaugurated very soon (21:1).[12] Following is the first of two explicit identifications of the second death with the lake of fire (21:8), which at the same time confirms Jesus' prophecy to the angel of the Smyrnean church (2:11; cf. 20:6).

Into the inferno (20:15)

[15]And anyone whose name was not found written in the book of life was thrown into the lake of fire.

With the destruction of Death itself, the stage is set for the delineation of the final act of judgment, the one that is most relevant for humanity, namely, of what happens to a person not found worthy of eternal bliss (v. 15). In typical apocalyptic fashion, this whole situation will be developed in more detail at 21:8, although without abandoning the stark simplicity of description. Just as vv. 12–13 formed a synthetic parallelism on the penultimate theme of judgment according to works, so also these vv. 14–15, only this time on the ultimate topic of destruction in the fiery lake. If the "first death" is understood as the spiritual death resulting from deadly sin (1 John 5:17) and the end of a person's physical life on earth, then

12. This final elimination of God's adversaries is commented on in other biblical passages as well (cf. Isa 24:21–22; 66:24; Hos 13:14; Matt 3:10, 12; 12:28–29; 7:19; 13:40–42; 18:8–9; 25:41–46; 1 Cor 15:24; Col 2:15).

the "second death" is the person's definitive separation from God, or total death in damnation.[13] It is a death of which the first or earthly death, now destroyed, was but a faint foreboding. When dying, body and soul are disjoined on earth, but will be reunited only to suffer death eternally in the inferno.[14] That state of continual agony affecting the unglorified body and soul defies human conceptualization; its loveless and hopeless horror is ultimately unimaginable.

What is so daunting is that existence is not turned into nonexistence but rather perpetuated in unspeakable lethal pain, the never-finished destruction of soul and body in hell, accompanied by an irrepressible sense of God's wrath and displeasure. In fact, they are being tormented under the eyes of the good angels and of the Lamb (14:10). Demonic spirits and demonized humans are eternally commingled in suffering as they drown in fire forever: "Trembling grips the ungodly: 'Who of us can dwell with a consuming fire? Who of us can dwell with everlasting flames?'" (Isa 33:14).[15] This apocalyptic portrayal of eternal condemnation seems to leave little room for speculation on a final reconciliation and restoration of creation, also known as apocatastasis or universalism, erroneously opining that all creatures endowed with morality, i.e., humans, angels, and demons, will eventually be saved and live in God's kingdom, to the exclusion of the notion of hell.[16]

Since a new creation will be announced at 21:1, making this v. 15 a relative narrative closure, a remark concerning the overarching structure of the Apocalypse is in order: in the gradual introduction and eventual elimination of anti-Christian entities, a fivefold chiasmus emerges (A-B-C-D-E | E'-D'-C'-B'-A'), that sees humanity introduced *first* as the servants of Christ (A: 1:1) with its unfaithful members permanently banished last (A': 20:15); set forth in the *second* place are Death and Hades (B: 6:8), which are destroyed second-last (B': 20:14); *third* to come on the scene is the dragon (C: 12:3), ousted third-last (C': 20:10); *fourth* to feature are the two beasts (D: 13:1, 11), and they are obliterated fourth-last (D': 19:20); and the *fifth* and final palistrophic element made known is Babylon (E: 14:8), which ends up being cast down first (E': 18:21). Thus, a very systematic narrative preparation has been made for the triumph of the angels and saints, the doxological state to which all things tend, and which will occupy the entire closing vision at 21:1–22:5.

13. Cf. AvS, 686.

14. In reference to the first part of Dante's *Divine Comedy*, although the Dantesque spectrum of punishment, the fruit of poetic imagination, is conspicuously absent from Revelation.

15. Cf. *CCC*, §682.

16. This heresy was condemned as anathema by the Fifth Council of Constantinople in 553.

But before resuming the exegesis of the upcoming vision of the New Jerusalem, like spiritual hummingbirds let us try to collect some of the nectar from these fascinating petals of the word of God. To begin with, the judgment seat of Christ representing his Father and the Holy Spirit (v. 11) should make us aware that each one of us will one day be summoned to appear before it. The Christian soul should frequently imagine itself already standing in his presence in holy fear, that is, before the God-Man who knows our conscience divinely well, he who "searches the heart and tries the reins" (Jer 17:10). This is the reason why before receiving absolution in the sacrament of penance and reconciliation one implores the light of the divine Spirit to assist in the examination of that conscience, striving to conform our lives, thoughts, words, and deeds, more thoroughly to the Lord's will.[17] And the same holds true for the commendable practice of a daily particular examen, equally useful in preparing for the reception of the Holy Eucharist, as St. Paul reminds us: "Examine yourselves, and only then eat of the bread and drink of the cup. For all who eat and drink without discerning the Body, eat and drink judgment against themselves" (1 Cor 11:28–29). If we approach those moments in our lives with reverence, then one has nothing to dread of the time when one is called to appear before God who through his Son will judge the secret thoughts of all (Rom 2:16).

May also the opening of the books (v. 12) be an inspiration to remain docile to the offers of God's grace in the here and now, conducting ourselves in ways that will make us unafraid of the general judgment when all hidden things will be brought to light.[18] All spiritual discernment should be not so much about good intentions, but about what can be done concretely for God, the Church, and for our neighbor, especially the sick, the dying, and the poor, knowing that each will be judged according to their works: "Whatever you did for one of the least of these brethren of mine, you did for Me" (Matt 25:40).

Furthermore, when meditating on the lake of fire as an image of hell (vv. 14–15), one is more profoundly motivated to make good use of our free will, that truly royal faculty bestowed on the human nature, that sacred potential which the Lord will respect it in all its consequences: "It is a fearful thing to fall into the hands of the living God" (Heb 10:31). Instead of the husks of the swine, we choose the joyous celebrations of the Father's house (Luke 15:16, 24). And that intentional and wholehearted embracing of divine wisdom impels us to do everything in our power to save the souls of others as well (2 Cor 5:11, 14),

17. Cf. AvS, 687.
18. Cf. *CCC*, §678.

convinced that they can be saved right up to the last moment of their life on earth. Authentic Christian charity and the consciousness that hell is real (v. 15), will compel the heart to steer clear of the works of the evil one, in order that one can experience the resurrection of life, and by no means the resurrection of condemnation (John 5:29). And in the end, what matters most is to make every spiritual effort not to be blotted out from the book of life, that is, the roll of those who have followed the Lamb wherever he goes.

PART 5

21:1–8, Theandric family

Immanuelian tabernacle (21:1–4)

[1]Then I saw a new heaven and a new earth; for the first heaven and the first earth had passed away, and the sea was no more. [2]And I saw the holy city, the new Jerusalem, coming down out of heaven from God, prepared as a bride adorned for her husband. [3]And I heard a loud voice from the throne saying, "See, the home of God is among mortals. He will dwell with them; they will be his peoples, and God himself will be with them; [4]he will wipe every tear from their eyes. Death will be no more; mourning and crying and pain will be no more, for the first things have passed away."

Crossing the narrative threshold into 21:1–22:5 is like stepping inside the Holy of Holies of the Book of Revelation, or like finally discovering the Holy Grail. Here the human mind and soul is presented with an overwhelmingly beautiful portrait of God's eternal Kingdom, a metaphorical mosaic composed of a new Heaven and a new Earth, a holy City, a Bride, and a refound Paradise. Their magnificence transcends even that of the first creation. Fully described in vv. 1–8, it is more elaborately contemplated in the passage that follows, and brought to a stirring conclusion in 22:6–21. If John has Ezekiel's futuristic temple in mind like a prophetic blueprint (Ezek 40–48), then he also contrasts Jerusalem the heavenly Bride with her earthly antitheses, namely, Babylon the great prostitute. And speaking of the image of the Bride, she is now fully adorned, ready to enjoy the wedding banquet and consummate the marriage (19:7–9). Moreover, this climactic vision should be viewed as the long-awaited fulfillment of all promises held out in the letters to the seven churches (chs. 2–3). Indeed, what is about to emerge is the most extensive and most splendid vision of heaven found in all the Scriptures, the Bible's punchline, so to speak, at the very end of its canon.

If the last Judgment had taken place in the total absence of earth and heaven (20:11), then this void is now replenished before the visionary's eyes: "Then I saw a new heaven and a new earth; for the first heaven and the first earth had passed away, and the sea is no more" (v. 1). New names (3:12) and the new song (14:3) will be heard in a renewed cosmos and a new city. Since the first creation and the tragic fall into sin, hope of liberation and renewal was cherished by humanity and foretold by prophets. A previously dualistic world is now recreated under the exclusion of evil and in perfect restoration of paradisiac peace between the Maker and his creatures. Paul's anthropological renewal (2 Cor 5:17) is now dilated into cosmic dimensions, and all corruption has been purified as through fire. In her catechetical teachings on life everlasting, the Catholic Church conveys the notion of a mysterious transformation and comprehensive reestablishment of all things in Christ.[1] Such a definitive realization of God's plan will confirm that common destiny conjoining humanity with the material and spiritual worlds.

Although neither time nor manner of this palingenesis is revealed, one is reassured that the universe will not only be restored to its original state of immaculate beauty and harmony but surpass it in glory.[2] And once the God-Man presents to his Father a universal Kingdom founded on this earth, the Father will reciprocate by gifting to his Son a glorified heaven, transfigured by his unmediated presence. Recreated heaven and earth will have melted into each other, since the Holy Spirit pours out his benefactions on all things without exception, and the Blessed Trinity will be all in all (1 Cor 15:28).[3] Christian tradition has also pondered the wondrous scenario of a heaven now fully populated with all the saints who will have occupied the thrones left vacant by the fall of the angels at the dawn of time.

As far as the sea in concerned (v. 1), as a symbol of chaos, or demonic scheming, and of the nations' restlessness, it will disappear, and in fact this is its final mention in the Bible. Its vanishing from the new creation will be complemented by the evanescence of nine additional realities emblematic of the old universe, namely, death, mourning, crying, pain, temple, sun, moon, lamp, and curse.[4] Formerly the abode of the sea-beast (13:1) as well as the throne of the great harlot (17:1), the sea's symbolic obliteration ahead of those other items

1. Cf. *CCC*, §§1042–50.

2. Rupert envisions a new species of universe, transformed into perfection ("speciem novam in melius commutatam"), RD, 1189.

3. Cf. AvS, 691–96.

4. Cf. 21:4, 22–23, 25; 22:3, 5.

of obsolescence signals God's comprehensive victory that no longer allows for demonic obscurity or terror. His infinite plenitude also makes earthly commerce across the oceans superfluous (18:17–19). All will be enveloped by an unruffled state of unity and prosperity, surpassing the covenant with Noah, since any threats of more flooding are altogether removed (Gen 9:15). And if the great bodies of water used to separate continents and peoples from one another, their future disappearance suggests the tranquil oneness of all humankind in the loving embrace of God.

What the apostle observes next is the unification of the renewed heaven and earth: "And I saw the holy city, the new Jerusalem, coming down out of heaven from God, prepared as a bride adorned for her husband" (v. 2). Another early promise, this one to the Philadelphian church (3:12), is about to be fulfilled, that is, for the conquerors to have the name of the city of Jesus' God written on them. At last, it is entirely sanctified[5] and deserving of the exalted title "New Jerusalem,"[6] since now it embodies the harmonious society of the Lord's servants of which the ancient Zion was a mere figure. As will be depicted in more detail beginning at v. 9, it now reflects that immaculate betrothal of humanity with its divine King in a restored cosmos, living up to its sublime reputation and fame (Isa 65:19). And how profoundly it stands in opposition to the hopelessly depraved and insubordinate worldly city, epitomized by Babylon, but also Sodom, Egypt, and Harmagedon. A certain irony lies in the fact that the latter is narratively encompassed and outshone by the former, since Jerusalem is announced as early as 3:12 and bespoken in chs. 21–22, whereas the evil city is introduced only in 11:8 and vanquished in ch. 18.

In terms of salvation history, the heavenly Jerusalem as the home of the communion of all saints marks the destination of a nomadic people that was chosen in Abraham and guided by Moses, as it journeyed through Exodus and the wilderness toward the Promised Land. Or, to widen the lens even further, there is no longer merely a garden (Gen 2:15), but the arrival of God's very own city, statelier and more glorious than anything that came before, and at the same time the result of laborious sacrifice, the true paradise of God (2:7). It was present to his divine mind as its Architect and Builder long before its manifestation on earth (Heb 11:10). Yet now, at the parousiac descent of Christ

5. Cf. AvS, 697.

6. It is notable that John in his Gospel exclusively employs the Greek form of this name, *Hierosólyma* (Ἱεροσόλυμα), which is rare in the Septuagint and often used with a political connotation; conversely, in his Apocalypse, he solely cites the original and more sacred Hebrew version *Ierusalēm* (Ἰερουσαλήμ), also by far the most common rendition in the Septuagint, perhaps to emphasize continuity with its Old Testament history as the messianic city.

his Son, the city comes along with him floating down from God like an immeasurable gift. Babylon was cast down from the earth into the abyss,[7] but the New Jerusalem floats gently downward from heaven toward a renovated world with irresistible majesty.

By choosing the present tense participle "descending" (v. 2), John suggests something of a current interim status between history and eternity, the characteristic "already but not yet" polarity of the eschaton in which we still live. It also denotes the progressive completion of Christ's descent of *katábasis* of his Incarnation, as he continuously draws humanity into his own hypostatic union, that is, the supernatural marriage between God and humankind. And to compare this holy city to a bride bears out the visionary's literary originality, as there is no precedent for it in the Old Testament. Given that she is identified with the saints at 19:8, the crucial conclusion must be drawn that the heavenly city should not be thought of as a physical or topographical place where the redeemed will gather and dwell, but that they themselves constitute that city, being its figurative pillars (3:12) and its living stones (1 Pet 2:5–6). And Christ will dwell in nuptial union with them in God's glory forever.

Adding to the uniqueness of John's imagery is the seemingly incongruent pairing of the word "bride" (*sponsa*) with "husband" (*vir*), instead of the more logical "husband-wife" (*vir-uxor*) or "bridegroom-bride" (*sponsus-sponsa*), which again plays into the trans-temporality of this genre. Christocentrism now necessarily involves androcentrism, that is, the simultaneous salvific focus on humankind.[8]

Her state of preparedness (*prae-parare*, 19:7) for the wedding has now advanced toward being completely ready (*parare*, v. 2). That she has consistently and actively cooperated in her nuptial arrangements and adornment is connoted by a couple of Greek perfect tense and middle voice verbs of reflexive nature (*hetoimasménēn*, ἡτοιμασμένην,[9] and *kekosmēménēn*, κεκοσμημένην). Especially the first of the pair, *hetoimázō* (ἑτοιμάζω), "to prepare," commonly refers in the New Testament to the coming of the Kingdom (e.g., Matt 3:3), while the etymology of the second one, *kosméō* (κοσμέω), "to adorn," underscores the New Jerusalem's blending into the rearranged *kósmos* (κόσμος).

7. Poetically called *pandemonium*, i.e., the "all-demon-place," the capital of hell, by John Milton (cf. the end of Book I of his 1667 "Paradise Lost").

8. Cf. Edmondo F. Lupieri, *A Commentary on the Apocalypse of John* (Grand Rapids, MI: Eerdmans, 2006), viii.

9. Here it is worth recalling the even more emphatic active voice of *hetoímasen* (ἡτοίμασεν) at 19:7.

Drawing on a wealth of scriptural precedents,[10] this connubial image tops and telescopes all other images regarding the covenant between God and his people, so central to this book and to the entire Bible.

At this moment, to the three images of a renewed universe, a new city, and a bride, a fourth is added: "And I heard a loud voice from the throne saying, 'Behold, the tabernacle of God with humanity! He will tabernacle with them; they will be his peoples, and God himself will be God with them'" (v. 3). Even though this resounding voice is not further identified, it can be attributed to the Holy Spirit in unison with the Lamb and reechoed by one of the living creatures, due to the message of joy and consolation proclaimed in these vv. 3–4. Their solemn proclamation will be completed by that of the Father himself at vv. 5–8. All generations are now urged to lift up their eyes and behold this heavenly tabernacle, obviously reminiscent of the tent of meeting that signaled Yahweh's faithful *shekhinah* or dwelling with his people on their way to the Promised Land. Tent and city are symbolic, like the two poles in the ellipsis, of humankind's journey from humble nomadic conditions toward highly evolved urbanization. This tent mainly connotes the incarnate Christ in whom "the whole fullness of divinity dwells bodily" (Col 2:9), and by extension his Mystical Body, the now glorified Church. In the tabernacle of his flesh, he offered up the one sacrifice, atoning for the sin of the world, and thereby bringing us nearer to God. From then onward, the Lord dwells "in" us (*in*, John 1:14), "over" us (*super*, Rev 7:15), and "with" us (*cum*, Rev 21:3), too.[11]

Thus, the nature of the new creation implies utter intimacy with God, an unending festival of tabernacles, and consummate bliss for the redeemed. They will hail from all peoples (*populi*, v. 3) and no longer just from a single people, Israel, highlighting the universal extent of salvation.[12] Indeed, God himself (*ipse Deus*) shall live with his people as the fulfiller of all covenant promises and as their Immanuel (Isa 7:14). After his Ascension, Christ is still present to his brethren in his "other Comforter" (John 14:16) and in the Eucharist, but on that day he will be visibly with them in person to rule together over all the earth. And while Babylon attempted to promote and glorify herself, the New Jerusalem receives her glory solely from God. Hence, this divine-human communion is the most blessed consummation of human history.

10. Cf. Isa 1:21; 49:18; 61:10; 62:5; Jer 2:32; 7:34; 25:10; Hos 2:19–23; Matt 9:15; 22:2; John 3:29; Eph 5:32; 1 Pet 3:4.

11. See also the intensified verb *kataskēnóō* (κατασκηνόω, *habitare*), used to depict birds nesting in the branches of the tree symbolizing the Kingdom (Matt 13:32).

12. Cf. 7:9; 10:11; 21:24.

Continuing the theme of what God the Father will do in the future for his beloved children,[13] the voice states, "'He will wipe every tear from their eyes, and death will be no more; mourning and crying and pain will be no more, for the first things have passed away'" (v. 4). God will not only be accessible to all, but with the tenderness of a parent will console each one individually (7:17).[14] Although tears did flow plentifully before, not even one shall be found on the face of any of them ever again, making God truly the eternal Comforter.[15] Elaborating on 20:14, death will not occur anymore, and consequently no graves will have to be dug nor funerary processions be held, in a mind-blowing reversal of the primordial curse imposed on our protoparents (Gen 3:19). Death and its sting now have been definitively swallowed up in victory (1 Cor 15:54–55).

And with that all humanly conceivable negativity has become immaterial, as is made clear through the triple negation "and no" (*neque*). Once that root cause of anguish has been removed, there can be no more grief, as Jesus pledged in the second beatitude of his Sermon on the Mount (Matt 5:4). Innumerable and implacable are the current sources of sorrow here below, brought on by our sins, by the loss of loved ones, by disappointment, affliction, oppression, persecution, violence, calamity, and the fear of dying. But all that will have vanished. Also absent will be any reason to cry, the wailing in sickness, dismay, despair, emotional distress, mental pain, psychological perturbation, remorse, or the outcry over immorality and evil in this world. And finally, human toil and its attendant weariness have evaporated since all earthly work has forever ceased. Whatever is not undisturbed restfulness, serenity, and happiness, and whatever is not glorious, incorruptible, and spiritual, will have permanently passed away.

From *Fiat* to *Facta* (21:5–8)

[5]And the one who was seated on the throne said, "See, I am making all things new." Also he said, "Write this, for these words are trustworthy and true." [6]Then he said to me, "It is done! I am the Alpha and the Omega, the beginning and the end. To the thirsty I will give water as a gift from the spring of the water of life. [7]The one who conquers will inherit these things, and I will be his God and he will be my son. [8]

13. Highlighted by the six verbs in the future tense in these vv. 3–4.
14. Cf. RD, 1191.
15. Cf. AvS, 704.

But as for the cowardly, the faithless, the polluted, the murderers, the fornicators, the sorcerers, the idolaters, and all liars, their place will be in the lake that burns with fire and sulfur, which is the second death."

Taking over from the Son and the Holy Spirit (vv. 3–4), here comes the sole proclamation of the heavenly Father in John's Apocalypse, breaking his otherwise hermetic silence: "And the one who was seated on the throne said, 'Behold, I am making all things new.' Also he said, 'Write: these words are trustworthy and true'" (v. 5). If the second and third divine Persons wanted the apostle to fix his eyes on the Immanuelian tabernacle (v. 3), the first Person of the Trinity urges him to now focus on the absolute renewal or recreation that is about to occur: "Behold!" (*ecce*). Intertextually associated, like vv. 1–2, with the first creation (Gen 1:1), it therefore links the scriptural teachings on the first things or protology to those of the last things or eschatology. That God is continuously engaging in creative work is implied by the present tense of the verb *poiô* (ποιῶ, *facio*), "I create," complemented by the "all things have come to be!" (*gégonan*, γέγοναν, *facta sunt*) in the next verse.[16] As out of the primeval chaos and darkness arose cosmic order and beauty, which God pronounced to be very good (Gen 1:31), so out of a world currently replete with disorder and sin, will emerge the new creation in which glory and holiness reign supreme.

This new order is being prepared today by a new teaching (Mark 1:27), new tongues (Mark 16:17), a new covenant (2 Cor 3:6), a new commandment (John 13:34), a new sacrament (1 Cor 11:25), and yes, a new humanity (Eph 2:15). And to accentuate the colossal impact of his utterance, God the Father commands his servant John to take note of it in writing without delay (v. 5); and it will remain the last and culminating instruction of this kind, preceded by twelve similar directives to make a record of his visionary experience.[17] Since this message is intended for a divinely appointed time, knowledge of and reflection on it are critical to keep up the spirit of Jesus' followers amid their unrelenting trials. Especially during the antichristic end-time, they will be able to read it again to find light, hope, and comfort, convinced that all will be fulfilled with certainty: indeed, these words are reliable (*fidelia*) *because* they are true (*vera*).[18]

After a brief pause to allow the apostolic seer to fully assimilate that momentous communication on God's recreation, he is now enlightened on its ultimate life-and-death implications: "Then he said to me, 'All is accomplished!

16. Cf. AvS, 707.

17. Cf. 1:11, 19; 2:1, 8, 12, 18; 3:1, 7, 14; 10:4; 14:13; 19:9.

18. Cf. 3:7, 14; 6:10; 19:9, 11; 22:6.

I am the Alpha and the Omega, the beginning and the end. To the thirsty I will give as a gift from the spring of the water of life'" (v. 6). While the perfect tense of the Latin phrase *Facta sunt!* ("They are done!") suggests that the process of renewing is now irreversibly completed, it also echoes several earlier biblical milestones: first, the divinely efficacious command *Fiat!*[19] ("Let there be!") at the morn of creation (Gen 1:3), followed by the humble yet courageous *Fiat!* ("Let it be done!") of the Virgin of Nazareth consenting to the Incarnation (Luke 1:38); then there was the theophanic *Factum est!* ("It is done!") that confirmed the finalization of the Lord's wrath poured out over the world-city (16:17), which can be contemplated in conjunction with the *Consummatum est!* ("It is finished!") of the dying Savior on the Cross (John 19:30). Unlike the *Factum est* in the grammatical singular at 16:17, however, the present resounding *Facta sunt!* is expressive of plurality, pointing to the consummation of God's plan of creation, redemption, and sanctification, engendering a new and glorious universe.[20]

Elohim revealed himself to Moses at the burning bush in the name "I Am Who I Am" (Exod 3:14), and likewise Jesus according to the Fourth Gospel identifies his Sonship of the Father with "I am" sayings: both phrases are meant to make known their divine nature that knows no beginning and no end. Yet, to all his creatures, the Lord is truly the Alpha and the Omega,[21] in that everything and everyone springs from him as the *causa prima*, and that to him they will return as their absolute end. Pivotal to the Good Tidings of Christianity is the conviction that the end will be more perfect and glorious than the beginning, and that Eden will be surpassed by the new Jerusalem, which can be accomplished only by God's infinite goodness. For the sake of emphasis, the alphabetical symbolism is then unfolded by two equivalent terms that are pregnant with scriptural meaning, i.e., *archḗ* (ἀρχή, *principium*) or "beginning, rule" and *télos* (τέλος, *finis*) or "goal, finality" (22:13). Both expressions are unique to the Apocalypse and are not found in the Old Testament, adding to the weight and beauty of their message. By elliptically withholding their grammatical object, however, the reader is free to use his or her imagination and fill in literally anything and everything between the two nodal points of creation and cosmic

19. Parsed as the third-person singular present passive subjunctive of the Latin verb *faciō*, "may it become."

20. Cf. RD, 1192.

21. Cf. 1:8; 22:13 (see also "First and Last" at 1:17; 2:8; 22:13); in the Greek original, for some obscure reason, only the first letter of the alphabet is spelled out (ἄλφα, *alpha*) in this verse, while the final one is not (ὦ, *ō*); the Neo-Vulgate, on the other hand, strikes a better balance by spelling out both letters as *Alpha et Omega*.

recreation. This awe-inspiring divine title illuminates the Lord's transcendence, perfection, and eternity.

And at this point, he seems to assume the role of a Good Shepherd, promising to tend his flock near life-giving water sources (v. 6; cf. 7:17). All that is needed is to live out the beatitude of thirsting for salvation (Matt 5:6), as exemplified by the Samaritan woman (John 4:15). It rounds out the apocalyptic imagery of life that includes a tree (2:7; 22:2, 14, 19), a crown (2:10), and a book (3:5). Astoundingly, all of it will be given for free (*gratis*), that is, an unmerited gift from God: in his grace we are created, justified, and glorified.[22] Already here on earth, the spiritual water of divine refreshment and enjoyment outshines the temporal order, as poignantly asserted by Paul: "I count all things as loss compared to the surpassing excellence of knowing Christ Jesus my Lord, for whom I have lost all things. I consider them rubbish, that I may gain Christ" (Phil 3:8).

Like a good parent or a skilled pedagogue, the heavenly Father adds this encouragement: "The one who conquers will inherit it, and I will be his God and he will be my son" (v. 7). This is the final echo of the promises made to the conquerors of the seven churches.[23] By overcoming all forces of evil, that is, sin, Satan, and the world, the individual believer will join the victorious Lamb, and will receive the allotted portion of the water of life.[24] In the Greek, what is inherited is a share in the totality of the recreated universe, just as Jesus himself exercises lordship as supreme heir over the whole creation.[25] Also recalled is the third beatitude in which Christ assures the meek that they will possess the earth (Matt 5:5). Thus, whoever fights the good fight and perseveres to the end will partake of the joys of heaven.

And in that capacity, each of us has become a true "son of God." This is the solitary place in John's writings where the singular noun "son" (*hyiós*, υἱός, *filius*) is employed to allude to that most intimate relationship with God, for which he elsewhere prefers the image of priests (e.g., 1:6). Essentially repeating the covenant formula of v. 3 (Lev 26:12), this one is unique in that it focuses on

22. Cf. RD, 1193.

23. Cf. 2:7, 11, 17, 26; 3:5, 12, 21.

24. According to the Neo-Vulgate, the feminine singular demonstrative pronoun *haec* in this v. 7 refers to *aqua* ("water") at the end of the previous verse; now, since it points to it as a direct object, it ought to be in the accusative case (*hanc*); however, it is inflected in the nominative, and this solecism could be viewed as further underscoring the magnitude of that gift of life.

25. As intimated by the correlation between the accusative neuter plural demonstrative pronoun *taûta* (ταῦτα), "these things," and the matching adjective *pánta* (πάντα), "all things" (*omnia*), in v. 5 (cf. Heb 1:2).

the individual "son." In this regard, a distinction is observable in the New Testament among four expressions concerning divine adoption of the baptized: *first*, "children of God" (*tékna*, τέκνα, *filii*), which is the most generic designation of redeemed women and men (John 1:12); *second*, "sons and daughters of the Father" (*hyioùs kaì thygatéras*, υἱοὺς καὶ θυγατέρας, *filios et filias*), emphasizing the equality of both genders in relation to their heavenly Father (2 Cor 6:18); *third*, the "sons of God" (*hyioí*, υἱοί, *filii*), highlighting their sonship in the Son of Man and Son of God (Rom 8:14), since in him all are one and there is "no longer male and female" (Gal 3:28); and *fourth*, there is the most radical and unique formulation "son of God" (*hyiós*, υἱός, *filius*) in this verse, stressing the individual believer's filiation by adoption in Jesus, the only-begotten Son of the Father (Heb 1:5).

In that sense, and metaphysically irrespective of gender, every man and woman saved in Christ becomes a "son of God." Hence, she or he are mystically assimilated, as it were, into the intra-trinitarian relations of Father, Son, and Holy Spirit. And that communion or incorporation could be called a theandric family, where the divine and the human are not merely conjoined but indissolubly interlaced, a match literally made in heaven. In God, the redeemed as his spiritual offspring will be rewarded and glorified just like the divine Son. Hence, Revelation teaches how the most cordial and congenial relationships in this world, namely, between spouses as well as between parents and their children, will one day be transfigured into divine betrothal and sonship. Incidentally, the word "he will be my son" proves the speaker in these vv. 5–8 to be God the Father, even though it is unfeasible to entirely divide the persons of the Blessed Trinity in these chapters so filled with unitive dynamics.

In his paternal love, and coupled with his universal will of salvation for all his children, God the Father issues a strict warning to those who refuse to conquer: "But as for the cowardly, the faithless, the polluted, the murderers, the fornicators, the sorcerers, the idolaters, and all liars, their place will be in the lake that burns with fire and sulfur, which is the second death" (v. 8). That the tenor is in fact threatening is made clear by the definite article *toîs* (τοῖς) at the beginning of this verse, followed by the adversative coordinating conjunction *dé* (δέ, *autem*, "but"), which in real life would translate to pointing or wagging the finger directly at the malefactor. In an antithetical way, eight representative groups of people are cited who will be barred from entering the holy city. It functions as a photographic negative of an ideal Church community, too.

Contrasting with the numerous virtue lists in Scripture, this is Revelation's third last vice catalogue (21:27; 22:15), and it has an anti-Decalogue, anti-Wisdom, and anti-Beatitudes ring to it.[26] Strange though it might seem to the reader, it starts off with the least glaring incrimination, that is, with those who act "cowardly" and who out of selfish fear end up apostatizing instead of boldly professing the Lamb. Equally inconspicuous is the fault of being "faithless," a trait of those who actively reject the proposition of Christ's Gospel. Arguably of greater profile are the "polluted" ones[27] or those whose detestable conduct makes them loathsome to God.[28] Next are the "murderers," that is, those who follow in the footsteps of Cain (Gen 4:8) and intentionally take someone's earthly life; they shall suffer exclusion from eternal life. Likewise, not admissible are those who persist in sexual immorality or "fornicators."[29] One is also put on guard against the sin of "sorcerers,"[30] a notion that includes witchcraft, poisoning, necromancy, magic, drug-fueled enchantment, drug-induced abortion, and every guise of occultism, all of which are quintessentially anti-Christian. Those who repudiate God's worship by prostrating themselves before cultic and irreligious objects are by definition "idol-worshippers" and will have no access to the Lord's presence in heaven. And lastly, those who maliciously pervert veracity into mendacity and hypocrisy, being intentionally misleading in their statements and their promises, i.e., "all liars," cannot commune with the God who granted "grace and truth through Jesus Christ" (John 1:17).

Concluding his solemn utterance, the Lord reminds the visionary and through him the readers of all times, that the lake of sulfurous fire awaits those evildoers. Additionally, not twice but three times, the "second death" had already been adverted to (2:11; 20:6, 14), and at this juncture, the heavenly Father subjoins his own confirmation of that terrifying possibility: "God has spoken once; I have heard this twice: that power belongs to God" (Ps 62:11).

It goes without saying that things of greatest import and certainty for the future of humanity have been unveiled in this first segment of the chapter (vv. 1–8), and so let us take that again as an occasion to distill them into a few spiritual keynotes for our present life as faithful followers of the Lamb. To make a start, the soul should prayerfully cherish the hope and anticipation of a renewal of all things (v. 1), especially when weighed down by the burden of personal sin

26. Cf. AvS, 716.

27. This Latin verb *exsecratis* derives from *ex-secrari*, signaling the exact opposite of "sacred," i.e., something devoted to destruction, cursed, or abominable.

28. The Greek verb *bdelýssomai* (βδελύσσομαι) denotes the effects of foulness and stench.

29. Etymologically rooted in the Latin noun *fornix*, meaning "arch, vaulted chamber, covered way," which came to designate a brothel, and hence, the lexical idea of prostitute-chasing or whore-mongering.

30. Cf. 9:21; 18:23; 22:15.

or imperfection. If we only ask him in the here and now, the Lord will never tire of revivifying and recreating us by his grace.[31] In that sense, the new heaven and new earth could be understood as a metaphor for the regeneration of mind and body in the holy sacraments, offering ourselves as a gift to the Father.[32] That continual transformation then becomes part of the preparations made by the chaste Bride for her Spouse, meaning the Church's union with the Trinity.[33] Inner integrity and the practice of Christian charity beautify the heart and ready it for the eternal betrothal.[34]

Moreover, what can inspire us to be more engaged in a local ecclesial community is the thought that each is called to dwell in the transfigured civilization of the New Jerusalem (v. 2) There should be a profound conviction within every baptized person that the world as we know it will never evolve into an ideal state, a golden age, a utopia, or an earthly paradise. True and lasting happiness will have to descend from the throne of God and be received in faith and love. When it comes to the tent of Immanuel (v. 3), one is reminded of God's presence in our innermost being, an indwelling that does not replace but rather coexists with our nature. The human heart should entertain the immanent divine guest with sentiments of adoration. And there is no better way to bring that about than to approach the Eucharistic tabernacle, to participate in the Holy Sacrifice of the Mass, to frequently receive Holy Communion, and in the process make visible the communion of all the saints.[35]

That tent is also a necessary reminder that so long as we are in this mortal body, we are pilgrims awaiting the unending festival of Tabernacles in heaven. And by resisting temptation, turning away from sin, and walking in his presence, the soul is already experiencing supernal consolation (v. 4). What is more, God's promise of making all things new (v. 5) can reassure us that, even after falling into the same temptation a thousand times, or being defeated by the same sin ten thousand times like a spiritual recidivist, the hope of ethical victory must be kept alive. That is the essence of spiritual conversion, that we become new creatures in the Lord. Furthermore, it is imperative to confidently cooperate with his grace to finish the work begun (v. 6), and wish it for others, too, "that the one who began a good work among you will bring it to completion by the day of Jesus Christ" (Phil 1:6).

31. Cf. RD, 1189.
32. Cf. AvS, 692–95.
33. Cf. RD, 1190.
34. Cf. AvS, 699.
35. Cf. AvS, 701–2.

As "the Beginning and the End" (v. 6), all love originates in him and must flow back to him, and thus, the heart is restless until it can repose in him.[36] And at that juncture all pure yearnings will find satisfaction in his life-giving water. Yet, as the soul thirsts for God, it is also united with the thirst of Christ on the Cross for the salvation of others (John 19:28).[37] Besides, among the most heartwarming of biblical revelations is the realization that each one is a "son of God" (v. 7), despite one's inner proneness to indulge in the sinful adventures of the prodigal son (Luke 15:13). To prevent that from happening, however, spiritual warfare is necessary in order to preserve the faith (v. 8),[38] to conquer worldliness, to be spared the second death, and to eventually inherit the Kingdom of heaven.[39]

36. Cf. Augustine, *Confessions*, 1.1.5.

37. Cf. AvS, 711.

38. Expressed so well in the classical Latin adage, "Si vis pacem, para bellum," or translated, "If you want peace, prepare for war."

39. Cf. AvS, 713.

21:9–27, *Ecclesia consummata*

Theo-gamic city (21:9–14)

[9]*Then one of the seven angels who had the seven bowls full of the seven*
last plagues came and said to me, "Come, I will show you the bride, the
wife of the Lamb." [10]*And in the Spirit he carried me away to a great,*
high mountain and showed me the holy city Jerusalem coming down
out of heaven from God. [11]*It has the glory of God and a radiance like a*
very rare jewel, like jasper, clear as crystal. [12]*It has a great, high wall*
with twelve gates, and at the gates twelve angels, and on the gates are
inscribed the names of the twelve tribes of the Israelites; [13]*on the east*
three gates, on the north three gates, on the south three gates, and on the
west three gates. [14]*And the wall of the city has twelve foundations, and*
on them are the twelve names of the twelve apostles of the Lamb.

Resuming both the announcement of the Lamb's wedding banquet (19:7–9), and the initial vision of the bridal New Jerusalem (21:2), but also corresponding to the new universe (21:1) while differing from the harlot-city Babylon (chs. 17–18), the exiled mystic now proceeds to narrate with more detail what he was shown regarding that nuptial city (vv. 9–27). It is safe to say that his descriptions resemble an assemblage of the most sublime imagery of the Old Testament, drawing especially on the adorned vestments of the high priest (Exod 28), on King Solomon's temple construction (1 Kgs 5–9), as well as on Ezekiel's temple prophecy (Ezek 40–48). Nevertheless, John's depiction also diverges considerably from the Ezekelian blueprint in that his heavenly city is much larger and more glorious, and that there will be no temple anymore. But what cannot possibly be overlooked is that the ruination of the historical Jerusalem in AD 70 intensified the expectations not only of a rebuilt earthly capital, but of a renovated transcendent city, too; and at the time of writing toward the end of the first century AD, that eschatological hope formed a crucial backdrop for the vision of an apocalyptic Jerusalem descending from heaven. At this point it also becomes a symbol of the Church triumphant, in her totality conformed to Christ and blissful in him.[1]

Still transfixed by the sublimity of what he saw and heard in the matter of the new creation (vv. 1–8), the apostle is now personally approached again: "Then one of the seven angels who had the seven bowls full of the seven last plagues came and spoke with me saying, 'Come, I will show you the bride, the wife of the Lamb'" (v. 9). As a direct flashback to the angelic apparitions at 15:1; 16:1; 17:1, the triple repetition of "seven" (*septem*) in this verse is the book's very last reminder of how God's wrath was accomplished in the destruction of Babylon. And since they were so instrumental in inflicting punishment on that great whore, ridding the earth of all evil, it seems fitting that one of them should now also be commissioned by the Lord to show forth[2] the pure Bride of the Lamb, set into a new heaven and a new earth.

He invites the seer to accompany him to a more suited vantage point so that he might have a clearer view of her. And if there was a mere allusion ("like, as," *sicut*) to Bride and Husband in v. 2, that symbolic connubiality is now on full display. What is so marvelous about her is that she remains a Bride (*sponsa*) while simultaneously being the Lamb's Wife (*gynḗ*, γυνή, *uxor*), virginally betrothed to him for a perpetual wedding feast. This is the mystical matrimony between the last, second, or new Adam (1 Cor 15:45) with the last, second, or new Eve,[3] heavenly progenitors, so to speak, of a regenerated human family. At last, the identity of the cosmic woman at 12:1 (*gynḗ*, γυνή, *mulier*) is wholly revealed, too. She is an image of the redeemed Church, glorifying the Son, just as he glorifies his Father.[4]

Hence, since the upcoming sight equates her completely with the New Jerusalem, the latter could metaphorically be called a theo-gamic city in the sense that an authentic spiritual marriage (*gámos*, γάμος; 19:7, 9) is celebrated and consummated between the divine Lamb and the human City-Bride, between God and humanity: "And in the Spirit he carried me away to a great, high mountain and showed me the holy city Jerusalem coming down out of heaven from God" (v. 10). Whereas in 17:3, the seer was "taken away" (*abstulit*)

1. Cf. Bruce J. Malina, *The New Jerusalem in the Revelation of John: The City as Symbol of Life with God* (Collegeville, MN: Liturgical Press, 2000).

2. It must be noted that the Greek verb *deíknymi* (δείκνυμι, "to exhibit, demonstrate, make known"), rendered by the New Vulgate as *palam facere* ("to make public") and *ostendere* ("to make clear, point out, display, exhibit, reveal"), is strategically placed at five additional narrative crossroads throughout the Apocalypse, cf. 1:1; 4:1; 17:1; 22:1, 6.

3. Cf. *Missal of Masses of the Blessed Virgin Mary*, no. 20: "Mary, the New Eve."

4. Cf. AvS, 720.

into the desert to be shown Babylon, here he is "taken up" (*sustulit*) to a massive mountain to take a good look at the holy city. This is the fourth and final occasion for him to be *in spiritu*,[5] meaning that the Holy Spirit transported his mind and soul, but not his body, to a place where he could communicate these apocalyptic scenes to him. Announced to the Philadelphian church at 3:12, the city was shown to him already in the form of royal Mount Zion at 14:1, then at a distance in 21:2, but now he is granted an unobstructed close-up view of her. In a characteristic, yet still flabbergasting layering of symbols, the greatness and exceptional elevation of the mountain emblematizes the New Jerusalem herself, beheld in all her glory. Her magnitude, now no longer hidden, is due not least to its untold number of enraptured inhabitants (v. 16), but mainly because she is the celestial *shekhinah* of the great King.[6]

Ultimately, this mountain signifies the holy Church, founded on, and at last also exalted to the heights of Christ's divinity.[7] And in her descent, heaven and earth are unified like never before into a quasi-urban civilization with a rural touch. That she originates in God (*a Deo*) suggests that we are his "workmanship" (Eph 2:10). He had descended for the first time in history to disunite and disperse the human family due to its haughtiness surrounding the construction of the tower of Babel (Gen 11:5); he then had his Son descend in his Incarnation to reverse that misfortune, and John here witnesses his eschatological and final *katábasis* to achieve universal reunion.

Launching now into a more detailed delineation of first the exterior (vv. 11–21) and then the interior (vv. 22–27) of the city, John states: "It has the glory of God; and a radiance like a very rare jewel, like jasper, clear as crystal" (v. 11). As an initial and most ravishing impression, he points to its divine luminosity (*dóxa*, δόξα, *claritas*) by comparing it to three gems, perhaps yet another innuendo to the Blessed Trinity. That "light-source" (*phōstḗr*, φωστήρ, *lumen*) had designated sun and moon when they were first created (Gen 1:16), and they ended up embellishing the apocalyptic Woman (12:1). In antiquity, this word was commonly used, other than for stars, for a house's windows, making the New Jerusalem an illuminator for the entire cosmos, but also underscoring its unmatched transparency. Its gem-like radiance cannot be divorced, however, from its durability, symbolizing heaven's gleaming perpetuity. Adding to the splendor is the red hue of jasper that was descriptive already of God's presence in 4:3, and redolent of Aaron's high priestly breastpiece (Exod 28:18).

5. Cf. 1:10; 4:2; 17:3; see also Matt 4:5, 8; Ezek 3:14.

6. Cf. Isa 2:2–3; 25:6–7; Ezek 40:1–2; Mic 4:1–2; Heb 12:22.

7. Cf. RD, 1195.

Shimmering with the bluish hue of crystal-clear ice,[8] the city's brilliance also seems to deliver an entire spectrum of temperatures between heat and cold (Isa 54:11–12).

Hence, its dazzling brightness illustrates the majesty and glory of God. Next, John's gaze is riveted by the urban circumference: "It has a great, high wall with twelve gates, and above the gates twelve angels, and on the gates are inscribed the names of the twelve tribes of the children of Israel" (v. 12). As mentioned above, mountain and city are two metaphors for one and the same reality, and thus, her wall has the same dimensions, namely, "great and high" (*magnum et altum*, v. 10), to exhibit its impregnable strength and safety under divine protection.[9] It also functions as a bulwark against all evils and enemies, the unpassable gulf between heaven and hell (Luke 16:26), a separation line from anything unholy,[10] and therefore, a safe place to store one's treasures (Matt 6:20).[11] At the same time, however, the city is wide open as embodied by its twelve gates, reminiscent of the wreath of twelve stars in 12:1.

Both emblematic notions, the perpetually unlocked gates and the salvific number twelve, will maintain a high profile in the forthcoming depiction.[12] Saints will be generously admitted in the New Jerusalem through the door which is Christ (John 10:9).[13] Just as the angels were the stewards of the Church's earthly apostolate, so now they are stationed above each gate as the guardians of the heavenly city's holiness, sentinels watching that nothing improper should enter, as they did at the evacuated Eden (Gen 3:24). They will be like brethren to the redeemed citizens (Luke 20:36) and will still wait on the heirs of salvation. Recalling the sealed out of every tribe of the people of Israel (7:4–8), and in fulfillment of promises made to them several millennia ago, the just of the Old Testament will be residents of the holy city, represented by the first half of those twenty-four elders encircling God's throne (4:4). Indeed,

8. The Greek adjective *krýstallos* (κρύσταλλος), "pellucid or resplendent like crystal," also connotes "ice," derivative of the noun *krýos* (κρύος), "icy cold, frost."

9. Cf. AvS, 727.

10. Fulfilling the concept of Old Testament cities of refuge in an unexpected way (cf. Deut 4:41–43; Josh 20:7–8; Isa 14:32).

11. Cf. RD, 1196.

12. There will be eleven recurrences of "gates" up to 22:14, and ten mentions of "twelve," leading up to 22:2.

13. Gates epitomized the socio-cultural center of Semitic urban life (e.g., Luke 7:12): it was there that important business transactions were made, court was convened, and criminals punished; there, prophets frequently delivered their messages, and personified Wisdom positions herself at the head of the streets to make her speech, to mention but a few aspects of the biblical relevance of city gates.

their sacred names will be inscribed ubiquitously above the gates, in contrast to the blasphemous names on the dragon's head (13:1) and on the scarlet beast carrying the great Babylon (17:3). No one can enter who does not belong to that chosen people, the spiritual Israel, i.e., the Church.

Another exterior feature of the New Jerusalem is that it has "on the east three gates, on the north three gates, on the south three gates, and on the west three gates" (v. 13). While the narrative continues to be interfused with arithmetic symbolism, now it is paired with a geographic one, too, expressive primarily of the handsome and harmonious proportions of the urban layout. Moreover, there is a messianic allusion in adducing the East (*oriens*) first and finishing with the West (*occasum*), its diametrical opposite, because the "dawn from on high" has broken upon us (Luke 1:78).

What is more, Israel's tribal arrangement within their wilderness encampment is referred to (Num 2), which, alongside the camp of the saints (20:9) indicates that eternal joys will be the fruit of lifelong battles (Cant 6:4, 10).[14] And that the gates lie open to all quarters without any refusal of admission toward any people signifies God's will for universal salvation (Luke 13:29). Previous diversities of nationality or culture, of age or race, have become irrelevant, since all the redeemed of the human family are brought into one happy fellowship. And there is ample opportunity of access to the Father's heart as suggested by the fourfold reiteration of trinitarian gates on each side of the holy city.[15]

Furthermore, its wall "has twelve foundations, and on them are the twelve names of the twelve apostles of the Lamb" (v. 14). Mirroring the triple "twelve" of v. 12 and prefigured in the twelve memorial stones carried across the Jordan (Josh 4:3), these symmetrical foundations symbolize the beauty, stability, and imperishability of the heavenly Jerusalem. This is also the sole citation of the apostolic college in Revelation (2:2; 18:20), including John the visionary himself, and only here they are characterized as the "apostles of the Lamb" (*apostoli Agni*).[16] And rightly so, because they were chosen to be part of the Church's foundation, they followed him wherever he went, and opened the gates of heaven for us by transmitting his faith and sacraments. Their twelveness[17] denotes the variety and excellence of the Gospel doctrines, the numerous

14. Cf. RD, 1196.

15. Cf. AvS, 734.

16. Cf.; see also *CCC*, §865.

17. To preserve its ecclesial symbolism, the apostles Paul, Barnabas, and Matthias are not incorporated in the tally, and no further emphasis is placed on Peter's primacy, just as Dan and Ephraim are omitted from the list of Israel's tribes at 7:5–8. Likewise, the argument that the

graces of the Holy Spirit, but also the personal excellences of the Lord Jesus, who alone is cornerstone and capstone of the renewed universe. And for all eternity, their work and witness will receive special recognition. Just as worldly leaders inscribe their names on buildings in their honor and for their memorialization, so also these spiritual architects have their sacred names etched into the foundations of the New Jerusalem in everlasting remembrance (Mark 14:9). Thus, the Old and New Testaments, as well as the entire history of the Church, are figuratively represented in her bridal appearance.

Theo-aesthetic city (21:15–21)

[15]The angel who talked to me had a measuring rod of gold to measure
the city and its gates and walls. [16]The city lies foursquare, its length the
same as its width; and he measured the city with his rod, fifteen hundred
miles; its length and width and height are equal. [17]He also measured its
wall, one hundred forty-four cubits by human measurement, which the
angel was using. [18]The wall is built of jasper, while the city is pure gold,
clear as glass. [19]The foundations of the wall of the city are adorned with
every jewel; the first was jasper, the second sapphire, the third agate, the
fourth emerald, [20]the fifth onyx, the sixth carnelian, the seventh chryso-
lite, the eighth beryl, the ninth topaz, the tenth chrysoprase, the eleventh
jacinth, the twelfth amethyst. [21]And the twelve gates are twelve pearls,
each of the gates is a single pearl, and the street of the city is pure gold,
transparent as glass.

After having poured out his plague-bowl (15:1) and then carried John to an exalted vantage point to be his angelic guide or *angelus interpres* (v. 9), this celestial messenger is now presenting himself as an architect holding "a golden measuring rod, to measure the city and its gates and its wall" (v. 15). Borrowing from Ezekiel's temple vision[18] and recalling the measuring of the earthly Jerusalem (11:1), this present symbolic action excels over those precedents since the reed is golden and the agent is angelic. What is denoted is the glorious state of the Church, no longer subject to desecration (11:2), but rather entirely protected by and consecrated to her divine Spouse. At long last, all things have

apostle John could not be the writer of Revelation due to his mention here in the third person is feeble, since Jesus, too, speaks of himself in the third person as the Son of Man (John 1:51; 17:3).

18. There are over thirty recurrences of "measuring" between Ezek 40:3 and 47:3; cf. Zech 2:1–2.

attained to the exact standard of his holy requirements, the perfection of faith in the incarnate Lord.[19] She was prepared with exactness and care even before the foundation of the world (Eph 1:4), and for all eternity she will be preserved (Amos 7:7–9) under his almighty guardianship, enjoying consummate peace.

Following is an overall geometric assessment made by the seer and the angel: "The city lies foursquare, its length the same as its width; and he measured the city with the reed, twelve thousand stades; its length and width and height are equal" (v. 16). Her perfect quadrangularity, recognized by the visionary even before the angel applies the measuring rod, conforms to the four directions of the universe mentioned earlier (v. 13), the four corners of the earth whence the inhabitants are arriving. This flawless square shape evokes Noah's ark (Gen 6:14), the holocaustic altar in the desert sanctuary (Exod 27:1), the high priest's breastplate (Exod 28:16), Solomon's historical temple (1 Kgs 7:42), Ezekiel's unrealized temple (41:21), as well as the Maccabean fortification of Mount Zion (1 Macc 10:11). Additionally, the vocabulary of "length" and "breath" recalls Abraham's exploration of the Promised land (Gen 13:17), the ark of the covenant and its mercy seat belonging to the wilderness tent (Exod 25:10, 17). Metaphorically speaking, creation's "four" and God's "three" are finally merged in perfect concord.

If taken literally, the gigantic perimeter of the holy city would be more that of a large country; but taken figuratively and hyperbolically, its twelvefold multiple of one thousand[20] signals eternity as the sacred completeness of God's people in an otherworldly millennium (Ezek 48:35). Adjoining the "height"[21] to the proportions, this bridal city turns out to be an enormous quadrilateral cube, redolent of the Holy of Holies in Solomon's temple (1 Kgs 6:20). Universally perceived, alongside the circle and the triangle, as an image of impeccable beauty, the cubical form in this apocalyptic simile inspires admiration for the symmetry and immovableness of the Lord's work of recreation, where nothing will be left distorted or uneven. Everything will revert into conformity with his wise plan, allowing the occupancy of all human generations, a truly beauteous or theo-aesthetic[22] outline of this celestial metropolis.

19. Cf. AvS, 744.

20. Most Bibles translate the "12,000 stades" (*stádion*, στάδιον, *stadium*) as 1,400–1,500 miles.

21. Indicative elsewhere in the New Testament of Christ's love (Eph 3:18) and of heaven (Luke 1:78; 24:49; Eph 4:8).

22. A notion made prominent by the Swiss theologian Hans Urs von Balthasar, especially in the first part of his 15-volume trilogy, *The Glory of the Lord*, celebrating the beauty of God and his salvation.

Finalizing its appraisal, the angel "also measured its wall, one hundred forty-four cubits by human measurement, which the angel was using" (v. 17). He not only bypasses the measuring of the gates (v. 15), but also transitions to a much smaller measuring unit.[23] With its approximately two hundred and sixteen feet, a mere fraction of a mile, the wall's height or thickness, even though still extraordinarily tall for a physical wall on earth, it stands disproportionately low when compared to the immensity of the holy city's circumference. Hence, its low profile is sufficient to intimate the state of security of heaven's inhabitants since Satan has been eliminated and any demonic surprise attack is forever inconceivable (21:27). By the same token, the wall's comparable smallness also guarantees that the celestial light can shine into the cosmos without obstruction.

Echoing the one hundred and forty-four thousand sealed of Israel (7:4) and the same number of redeemed on Mount Zion (14:1, 3), the present one hundred and forty-four, the mathematical square of twelve, epitomizes the people of God in its eternal consummation.[24] And just as the imperfect number of the beast was coopted by evil humans (13:18), so also the accomplished measure of angel and man become one and equal in the New Jerusalem (v. 17; cf. Luke 20:36). Thus, all of God's creatures graced with intelligence will be profoundly intertwined at the level of holiness and glory.[25] That conceptual sameness could also suggest that John saw the angelic measurer in human appearance.

After its measuring, John observes: "The structure of her wall is of jasper, while the city itself is pure gold, clear as glass" (cf. 18). Reflecting God's own radiance, the wall's masonry is jasper-like, but the city on a whole is made of gold as a sign of otherworldly wealth, infinitely surpassing that of King Solomon (1 Kgs 10:14). Its purity symbolizes the holiness and love of the glorified Church (3:18). In yet another meta-conceptual twist, this heavenly gold is translucent, too, like glass. In other words, excellent yet incompatible qualities of earthly objects are now found unified in the New Jerusalem, as if embedded in the eternal oneness of God with his beloved people. Perhaps one might say that the gold mirrors the Bride's beauty, whereas the glass conveys her humility in the thoughts of angels and saints shining with unfading wisdom.[26] Since every dimness of pride and all obscuration of self-interest have been overcome, the entire city is now encompassed and suffused with noble light not unlike a supernatural crystal palace.

23. From the 600 feet of a Roman stade all the way down to the 18 inches of a cubit.

24. Cf. AvS, 748.

25. Cf. RD, 1200; AvS, 752.

26. Cf. RD, 1202.

John then highlights one last, but no less stunning, aspect of her wall, supplemental to v. 14: "The foundations of the wall of the city are adorned with every jewel; the first was jasper, the second sapphire, the third chalcedony, the fourth emerald, [20] the fifth sardonyx, the sixth sardius, the seventh chrysolite, the eighth beryl, the ninth topaz, the tenth chrysoprase, the eleventh jacinth, the twelfth amethyst" (vv. 19–20). Resting on her apostolic infrastructure, the Church's grace and charisms, manifested in the individuality of her saints, resemble all sorts of precious stones.[27] In her nuptial adornment (v. 2) she infinitely outshines Babylon's promiscuous embellishments (17:4).

With the adroitness of a professional jeweler, the apostle describes the remarkable mix of shades and tints of those gems: the opaque red of the jasper arguably associated with Peter as "first among equals" (*primus inter pares*) and perhaps also with his martyrdom, followed by the sapphire's sky-blue with specks of gold (Exod 24:10; Cant 5:14); then there is the misty red of the chalcedony, the transparent green of the emerald, the black-white streaked and clouded red of the sardonyx, the blood-red of the sardius, the olivine green tinged with gold luster of the chrysolite, the sea-green of the beryl, the pellucid greenish-yellow of the topaz, the semi-translucent apple-green of the chrysoprase, the flashing orange-red of the jacinth, and also the vinous-purple of the amethyst. Standing again in direct opposition to the monotony and anonymity of hell, the holy city is encircled by a belt of rainbow shimmer, glorifying God by those variegated colors that glow and sparkle like an eternal dayspring.

Thus, the Church in her supernatural beauty is the Lord's crown jewel, as well as the veritable "*kosmos*"[28] of his renewed cosmos. And fleshing out what was said about the twelve gates in vv. 12–13, John affirms that they are "twelve pearls, each of the gates is a single pearl, and the square of the city is pure gold, transparent as glass" (v. 21). Pearls (*margaritae*) are the earliest gems known to humanity, highly priced worldwide and throughout the ages. Considered by the ancients as divine gifts, their natural gorgeousness was the expression of finest quality that no gem-cutter could ameliorate. Hence, pearls were admired as a symbol of unchangeable truth, and in their relative and simple uniformity they also suggest unity, both of which are illustrative of heaven.[29] Also, its citizens walk along a golden broadway of wisdom and love (Cant 3:2) and gather

27. Cf. AvS, 756.

28. Given that the verb *kosméō* (κοσμέω, *ornare*), "to adorn," is at the root of the noun *kósmos* (κόσμος), and exclusively employed to depict the Lamb's Bride in vv. 2, 19.

29. Cf. AvS, 758.

in a hyaline center square of utmost transparency.[30] What is denoted here is the overall delightfulness and preciousness of the glorified Christ, the pearl of great price (Matt 13:45), and our way to unending life (John 14:6). In sum, this apocalyptic parable transmits the magnificence of the future abode of angels and saints enjoying the beauty of God's embrace.

Theo-centric city (21:22–27)

[22]I saw no temple in the city, for its temple is the Lord God the Almighty
and the Lamb. [23]And the city has no need of sun or moon to shine on it,
for the glory of God is its light, and its lamp is the Lamb. [24]The nations
will walk by its light, and the kings of the earth will bring their glory into
it. [25]Its gates will never be shut by day, and there will be no night there.
[26]People will bring into it the glory and the honor of the nations. [27]But
nothing unclean will enter it, nor anyone who practices abomination
or falsehood, but only those who are written in the Lamb's book of life.

After having put into words his visionary impressions regarding the exterior of the New Jerusalem (vv. 11–21), John now dedicates an equal amount of text to her interior (cf. 21:22–22:5): "And a temple I did not see in her, for the Lord God, the Pantocrator, is her temple, and the Lamb" (v. 22). While Ezekiel had foretold the eschatological building of a glorious temple, which, however, remained unbuilt, such a temple will be discarded altogether from the apocalyptic city. Or, to be more precise, the biblical temple, and the heavenly one, too,[31] will have metamorphosed into God's presence in the heavenly city: neither mountain nor earthly Jerusalem, but Spirit and Truth (John 4:21, 23). Just as the historical Second Temple, destroyed by the Roman armies in 70 AD, was never rebuilt, so also there will be no more physical temple in heaven. There, all ground is holy and the dividing curtain between God and his children will have been permanently removed, indeed, it will have become superfluous. No outward shrine made with human hands, no altar of holocausts, no high priestly rituals, no peace offerings, no sprinkling of blood, and no incense will be needed any longer, because the communion with God and the Lamb will be unmediated, all-encompassing, and all-permeating. Yet, notwithstanding

30. By "street" (*plateîa*, πλατεῖα, *platea*; cf. v. 18; 11:8; 22:2) is meant the broadest place in an urban setting, like an ancient Hellenistic *ágora*, a Roman *forum* or *cardo maximus*, the main north-south-oriented thoroughfare; in Prov 8:2 it becomes symbolic for Wisdom herself.

31. Cf. 3:12; 7:15; 11:19; 14:15, 17; 15:5, 8; 16:1, 17.

the absence of the temple, the cubical configuration of the holy city will be a perennial reminder of the earthly Holy of Holies. Here is also the last mention of the Pantocrator, denoting the Lord God's unbounded approachability and fruition.[32] Indeed, "the Lord will be there" (Ezek 48:35), and he will be "all in all" (1 Cor 15:28).

Within that same logic, "the city has no need of sun or moon to shine on it, for the glory of God is its light, and its lamp is the Lamb" (v. 23). Like in the preceding verse and at v. 25, the explanatory Greek conjunction *gár* (γάρ, *enim* or *nam*), "because," serves as another hermeneutic key to correctly decode the symbolism. That the two great luminaries shall also disappear proves that the cosmic Woman of 12:1 had mainly symbolized the pilgrim people in the wilderness of this world, and that now her radiant embellishments have transmuted into the fullness of glory and light. No subsidiary or artificial light sources with their feeble glimmer can subsist any longer side by side with Light itself (1 John 1:5). Hence, the vulnerable beam of the Church's candlestick in this world will eventually have immingled itself with the great light which is the Lamb, "the reflection of God's glory and the exact imprint of God's very being" (Heb 1:3).[33] Since the plenitude of light is a universal metaphor for holiness, knowledge, and comfort, all fear and confusion due to darkness will no longer exist in the heavenly Jerusalem.[34] All the redeemed will enjoy total independence, as it were, from created things, wholly enveloped by the *shekhinah* or glorious presence of God and their Bridegroom, the Lamb.

While on earth we walk by faith and not by sight (2 Cor 5:7), but in heaven, according to the seer on Patmos, it will be quite different, because "the nations will walk by her light, and the kings of the earth will bring their glory into her" (v. 24). Basing his portrayal on Isaiah's prophecy regarding the splendors of a postexilic Jerusalem (Isa 66:20), he mystically sees people of all nations and of all generations, delivered at last from pain and persecution, flock within her walls. And all the righteous rulers of the earth, that is, those who did not fall for Satan's ruses, seduced by the great harlot, and warring against the Lamb, now join in to glorify the King of kings. Put in the prophetic present (*afferunt*),[35]

32. Cf. AvS, 760.

33. Notice how the sacred author distinguishes between the diminutive Greek noun *lychnía* (λυχνία, *candelabrum*), "candlestick, lampstand," used for the earthly churches and the witnesses (1:12–13, 20; 11:4), and the regular noun *lýchnos* (λύχνος, *lucerna*), "lamp," when pointing to the light of heaven (22:5).

34. Cf. AvS, 763–66.

35. Incidentally, the amazing oscillation of Greek tenses especially in this vision of the holy city, undulating between aorist, imperfect, present, and future, emphasizes the trans-

they already engage in universal worship, imitating those twenty-four elders who prostrate and cast their crowns before the throne in adoration (4:10–11),[36] unlike the diabolical self-enrichment by those loyal to Babylon. This picture conveys the Lord's supreme glory and unquestioned authority, and the theo-centric appeal and outlook of the heavenly cosmopolis, home of the blessed forever.

As a sign of the openness of God's heart, "her gates will never be shut by day, and night will be no more there" (v. 25; cf. 22:5). She welcomes and admits saints from all parts and all backgrounds,[37] granting them perfect security, liberty, and peace, since all evil threats are eliminated (Neh 13:19), no thieves are to be feared, and all unfaithful are excluded.[38] Her dwellers are not prisoners, but are allowed free ingress and egress, to leisurely explore the recreated universe, to visit every world, and survey every spiritual galaxy. They now reside *in* God and revel in unhindered communion with one another, angels and humans. Since solar and lunar revolutions will have ceased, there is consequently no more succession of days and nights, symbolizing the permanence and stability of all that is sacred, metaphorically dominated by the Sun of Justice.[39] With the darkness of sin, error, and sorrow banished, the everlasting daylight will prevent drowsiness, bewilderment, or inactivity, and allow the blessed to be fully awake: "That they may have life, and have it in all its fullness" (John 10:10).

Expanding on the idea of v. 24, the visionary adjoins, "They will bring into her the glory and the riches of the peoples" (v. 26). Their wealth[40] epitomizes their cultures purified and made excellent in Christ, contributing to the Church's glory. Without him they could do nothing, and now they return to him as the font of all their achievements.[41] Hence, for all eternity, whatsoever

temporality of the message, referring mainly to the present time and to the eschatological fulfillment.

36. "We celebrate the festival of your city, the heavenly Jerusalem, our mother, where the great array of our brothers and sisters already gives you eternal praise. Towards her, we eagerly hasten as pilgrims advancing by faith, rejoicing in the glory bestowed upon those exalted members of the Church" (Roman Missal, *Preface* on the Solemnity of All Saints).

37. Foreshadowed, among others, by the pagan Ruth becoming a daughter of Israel (Ruth 1:4).

38. Cf. RD, 1204.

39. Cf. AvS, 768.

40. Only on this occasion in Revelation, the Greek noun *timē* (τιμή) is rendered as *divitia*, "riches, value," by the Neo-Vulgate, whereas in the four remaining recurrences it prefers *honor*, "esteem, dignity, honor" (4:11; 5:12–13; 7:12).

41. Cf. AvS, 770.

was noble and desirable in this world shall be put at the disposal of the saints for their gratification.

At this juncture, John encourages the reader to strive hard to attain to these blessings, since "nothing unclean will enter her, nor anyone who practices abomination or falsehood, but only those who are written in the Lamb's book of life" (v. 27; cf. 22:15). As he is speaking from an eschatological perspective outside of history, anything inglorious is excluded. To convey this single idea, the apostle employs three terms as a literary hendiatris, namely, "profane,"[42] "abominable," and "mendacious." This is a forceful reminder that the only way to qualify for celestial citizenship is to be accredited in the Book of Life, which is the synopsis of the Lamb's work of redemption.[43]

Having mulled over the extraordinarily rich images contained in vv. 9–27 more from an exegetical standpoint, let us again seek to make them spiritually conducive to a life of holiness in the present. Stepping inside the seer's mind for a moment, we can reflect on how much he, the beloved disciple of the Lord, longed to enter the holy city as he watched her descending from God (vv. 9–10). But his time had not yet come, and he had to wait until his earthly death to have access. Similarly, we should foster a constant yearning for heaven, for perfect oneness with God and with all his angels and saints. That desire will be sustained by the Church's liturgy as heaven's foretaste,[44] and by continued climbing to the altitude of self-surrender, by frequently visiting the mountaintop of separation from the world and of prayerful reading of God's word. Also needed to obtain a clearer view of heaven is to already die to oneself in acts of self-mastery and Christian mortification, carried higher by the gifts of the Holy Spirit.

Further, inspired by the city's magnificent wall made passable by numerous gateways (v. 12), the human heart should be enclosed and guard itself from worldliness and evil like a garden locked and a fountain sealed (Cant 4:12), but at the same time remain unblocked and porous when it comes to receiving God's grace and loving one's neighbor in apostolic outreach. Hence, the wall suggests contemplation, while the gates intimate the active life of a Christian, interpenetrated by the Lord's own holiness and light. Also, with the help of one's guardian angel, a judicious distinction between the sacred (*fanum*) and

42. The Nova Vulgata translates the adjective *koinós* (κοινός), "common," with the more aggressive *coinquinatus*, which derives from the verb *inquinare*, meaning "to pollute, defile, corrupt, contaminate, befoul"; its lexical spectrum also includes the notions of "unclean, infected, tainted, stained, dyed"; it carries the Old Testament undertone of ritual impurity or Gentile uncleanness (1 Macc 1:47, 62).

43. Cf. AvS, 773.

44. Cf. *CCC*, §1090.

the mundane (*profanum*[45]) will preserve the gifts of grace in the inner sanctum of one's conscience.[46]

Moreover, Abbot Rupert interprets each side of the city's quadrangular blueprint (v. 13) as the openness to the Transcendent in each of the four seasons of our human life, viz., during infancy, adolescence, adulthood, and seniority alike.[47] Besides, the solidity of her apostolic foundations (v. 14) should motivate our mind again and again to found its thinking on them, to base its discerning and deciding on the teachings of Holy Mother Church, summarized by the Catechism and the biblical canon like a trusted measuring reed (v. 15). In this way, the interior life will be equally "squared" or surrounded by God's grace, capable of adapting itself to his supernatural standards (vv. 16–17).[48]

Additionally, the translucent gold that the New Jerusalem is made of (v. 18), encourages us to choose spiritual transparency and uprightness in all we do, not allowing faith to be befouled by worldliness (v. 27). And speaking of the multicolored sheen she exudes (vv. 19–20), it seems to hint at the Christian's willingness to reflect God's own glory in ever new and creative ways.[49] And perhaps there is a spiritual message hidden in the relative uniformity of natural pearls (v. 21), too, moving us to be individually strong in Christ Jesus, without, however, succumbing to unhealthy individualism, so conflicting with the ecclesial notion of communal life.

And what is more, the insight that there will be no temple in heaven (v. 22) reminds us that even when visiting a physical church, the inner eye should be fixed on Jesus' real presence in the tabernacle, and to then keep on walking in that illuminating presence (v. 24). Last not least, the unlocked state of heaven's gates (v. 25), a symbol for the openness of the Father's heart, reassures the sinner in us that so long as we live on earth there is the opportunity of salvation. To him we dedicate all we have and do in this world (v. 26), for our spiritual merit, for his glorification, as well as for the sanctification of souls, or, as St. Ignatius of Loyola would say: "For the greater glory of God."[50]

45. In line with the Old Testament concept of *qadôsh* (קָדוֹשׁ, *hágios*, ἅγιος, *sanctus*), "holy," which originally meant "distinct," that is, intentionally set apart from a sinful world (Lev 19:2; Isa 6:3).

46. Cf. AvS, 726–32.

47. Cf. RD, 1197.

48. Cf. RD, 1198; AvS, 744–45.

49. Cf. AvS, 725.

50. The complete version reads "Ad maiorem Dei gloriam inque hominum salutem," or "For the greater glory of God and the salvation of humanity," to this day the motto of the Society of Jesus (Jesuits).

22:1–5, Eden regained

Vitalized by river and tree (22:1–2)

[1]*Then the angel showed me the river of the water of life, bright as crystal, flowing from the throne of God and of the Lamb* [2]*through the middle of the street of the city. On either side of the river is the tree of life with its twelve kinds of fruit, producing its fruit each month; and the leaves of the tree are for the healing of the nations.*

This closing vision of the Apocalypse and the last page of the entire Bible, is still saturated with innuendos to Old Testament imagery and prophecy, adding one more facet to the marvelous collage that presented a new cosmos as bride and city,[1] and this final touch is a recovery of paradise, as promised to the church in Ephesus (2:7). Hence, the first and the last things, or protology and eschatology, come around to form a full circle in a comprehensive victory of grace and life over sin and death. Like the finale of a grand concerto, in which the melodic themes sounding throughout are bundled into a single symphonic salvo, here we are at the farthest and culminating point of Revelation into which mortal eyes are allowed to pierce. First, the apostle was shown the new universe and holy city (21:1–2, 9–23), then its citizens (21:24–27), and now its King, forever adored by his co-reigning servants (22:1–5).

John notices the angel from 21:9, 15–17 approaching him again: "Then he showed me the river of water of life, bright as crystal, flowing from the throne of God and of the Lamb" (v. 1). As a truism, humanity throughout the centuries has chosen to settle down and build its cities in the vicinity of the earth's coastlines, fountains, rivers, and streams, knowing well that its survival, prosperity, and happiness depended on the priceless blessing of their waters. So, too, at the original site of the historical Jerusalem there was a natural spring, called Gihon,

1. Cf. *CCC*, §1044.

channeled via a tunnel into the pool of Siloam as the city's principal freshwater reservoir;[2] from time immemorial it was used by pilgrims for ritual purification before visiting the Temple precinct (John 9:7).

Now, the image of the celestial river is intertextually layered, beginning with the river flowing out of Eden to water the paradisal garden only to break up into four branches (Gen 2:6, 10).[3] Then there is the water gushing out of the rock struck by Moses' staff, enabling the Israelites to slake their thirst; it then flowed through the desert like a river (Num 20:11). Another Old Testament prefiguration is the water rising from below the temple threshold and flowing toward the east, healing and sweetening everything along its course (Ezek 47:1). Likewise, the psalmist sings of a delightful river that gladdens God's city and sustains his people (Ps 46:4). Additionally, the prophet Isaiah predicts that we shall joyfully drink water from the wells of salvation (Isa 12:3); and a similar scenario is foretold by prophets Joel (3:18) and Zechariah (14:8). Then finally there is Jesus himself speaking of the Holy Spirit as a spring of living water gushing up from the human heart to eternal life (John 7:37–39).

Returning to the Apocalypse, however, this river is the divine antithesis to the serpent's death-dealing stream in the desert (12:15–16),[4] and its fluvial size bests the promise of "springs" in 7:17 and 21:6. Its brilliance blends in with that of the throne itself (4:6) and the Lamb's Bride (19:8). On a theological plane it could be argued that the mention of "God-Lamb-River" in one single verse is John's way of describing the Blessed Trinity, the river being a figure of the Holy Spirit spreading God's life, love, and joy. Originating in the heart of God and issuing from the pierced side of the crucified Savior, it now unstoppably flows from the foot of his throne toward his children, divinizing them as it gushes along.

While geographic rivers tend toward the sea, there is no mention of an estuary in this vision, suggesting that this celestial stream flows into the ocean of eternity. At the same time, saved humanity is ushered nearer than ever to God's throne, navigating the currents of its vivifying waters. And again, this radiant river cascades without the muddiness of natural watercourses, contrastive also with any stagnant body of water, and thus it becomes an emblem of a pure and wholesome life. How can one not think of the sacramental water that

2. As constructed by King Hezekiah approximately 680 BC (2 Kgs 20:20).

3. The circumstance that the river flows "out of Eden" into the paradise appears to foreshadow the differentiation between the inner sanctuary and the nave of the historical temple in Jerusalem.

4. Possibly in allusion to that episode, a Greek variant of this v. 1 reads "from the mouth" instead of "from the throne" of God.

connects the soul with the Lord in baptism, and how it now turns into abundance of life and happiness?[5]

Carrying on with the Edenic portrait of the holy city, John observes that "in the middle of her street, on either side of the river, is the tree of life producing twelve fruits, yielding its fruit each month; and the leaves of the tree are for the healing of the nations" (v. 2). Although the topographic layout here is kept rather poetic, especially with the unique biblical phrase "on both sides" (*ex utraque parte*), the basic idea is unequivocal, namely, that all three simultaneously, "main boulevard," "river," and "tree," are mystically central to and dominant in the New Jerusalem, as they all embody the presence of the Triune God. Rounding out, therefore, the picture of the refound paradise is this life-giving tree that was seen and touched by our protoparents (Gen 2:9). At this stage of human perfection, however, there is no more prohibition against taking and eating from it, and the redeemed relish plentiful knowledge due to their beatific vision.

Moreover, Ezekiel's description of countless trees, part of the messianic transformation of an arid landscape (Ezek 47:7, 12), is now adapted back to the single paradisiac tree of life. By using the Latin noun *lignum*, literally meaning "wood," the text hints at the Cross of Christ,[6] too, source of supernatural life. "For you placed the salvation of the human race on the wood of the Cross, so that where death arose, life might again spring forth, and the evil one who conquered on a tree, might likewise on a tree be conquered."[7] Intimated is also the staff of the Good Shepherd (Ps 23:4), now comforting the blessed souls beside the still waters of unending rest.

What is more, twelve[8] fruit harvests signal a never-ending supply from which the heavenly citizens can freely partake at all seasons. Unlike the barren and cursed fig tree (Matt 21:19), this life-tree is laden with delectable fruits, yielding plenty in perpetuity, the promised reward to the victors (2:7). By being all-fertile, it complements the all-pervading life-water. This tree, laden with delight, also symbolizes the ever fresh, recreating, and fructifying Spirit, as suggested by the present participle of the Greek verb *poiéō* (ποιέω), "to do, make, create" (Gen 1:1). This is the moment when those who had hungered

5. Cf. AvS, 775.

6. Cf. Acts 5:30; Gal 3:13; 1 Pet 2:24; see also its foreshadowing in the ark of Noah (Gen 6:14), the preparations for Isaac's holocaust (Gen 22:6), Moses' staff of deliverance (Exod 7:19), and the ark of the covenant (Exod 25:10).

7. Roman Missal, *Preface* on the feast of the Exaltation of the Holy Cross (September 14).

8. This is the last of nine recurrences of this numeric symbol in the holy city (cf. gates, angels, tribes, foundations, names, apostles, stades, and pearls).

and thirsted for justice will be satisfied (Matt 5:6), eating and drinking God's wisdom as the food convenient for them (Prov 3:18; 30:8).

Continuing to reminisce about the garden Eden, John comments on the tree's salutary leafage, perhaps also recalling the loincloths that Adam and Eve made for themselves by sewing fig leaves together after awakening to the dire consequences of their sin (Gen 3:7). Those heavenly leaves are of medicinal benefit and fragrance,[9] not to cure any malady or infirmity, nor to sustain some healing process (21:4), but to impart immortality. Or, to put it differently, the foliage emblematizes the fatherly presence of God with his children.

Thus, to dwell in heaven means to possess everything for which humanity yearned, namely, undying comfort, health, and happiness. Furthermore, there is the intriguing connotation of "service, care, attention" to the Greek term *therapeía* (θεραπεία): just as the righteous of all the nations serve the Lord (v. 3), so God himself will be at their service for all eternity, bringing his bilateral covenant to fulfillment. Indeed, the God-Man "will fasten his belt and have them sit down to eat, and he will come and serve them" (Luke 12:37). Lastly, this scriptural highpoint also coincides with the last citation of the "nations" (*gentes*) in Revelation, signifying that humanity has arrived at the end of its historical adventure, it has finally come home and is at rest.

To serve is to reign (22:3–5)

[3]Nothing accursed will be found there anymore. But the throne of God and of the Lamb will be in it, and his servants will worship him; [4]they will see his face, and his name will be on their foreheads. [5]And there will be no more night; they need no light of lamp or sun, for the Lord God will be their light, and they will reign forever and ever.

Pressing on with his elucidations to the apostle, the angelic guide negates yet another evil in the heavenly city,[10] this time the reality of curse itself, and, consequently, anything that is accursed (v. 3a).[11] This reverses not only the primordial curses inflicted on Adam still in paradise, and on his homicidal son Cain

9. One Latin variant reading of the Neo-Vulgate's *sanitatem*, "healing, health, wellbeing," is *medicinam*, "medicine, cure."

10. Cf. 21:1, 4.8, 22–23, 25, 27; 22:5, 15.

11. Cf. AvS, 780.

after their expulsion (Gen 3:17; 4:11),[12] but all subsequent ones, pronounced against any transgressors of God's law, as well (Deut 27:15).

Yet John here uses a word that bears further expounding: the neuter noun *katáthema* (κατάθεμα) is an absolute *hapax legomenon*, i.e., mentioned only once, in Greek literature, a contraction of the double compound noun *katanáthema* (καταναάθεμα), which in turn stems from the intensifying prefix *katá* (κατά), the infix *aná* (ἀνά), "up," and the verb *títhēmi* (τίθημι), "to place," literally meaning "to pledge or place up a votive offering." In antiquity, such an offering, after being consecrated to a deity, was suspended upon the walls or columns of its temple, or laid up in some other conspicuous place (2 Macc 2:13). More common in the Bible is the shorter term *anáthema* (ἀνάθεμα), which is the Septuagint translation of the Hebrew *harām* (חֵרֶם), denoting an object devoted to God without hope of being redeemed, and, in the case of animals or pagan towns, to be doomed to destruction and slaughter (Deut 7:26). Also, the related New Testament verb *anathematízein* (ἀναθεματίζειν) signifies both "to curse" and "to take an oath"; hence, the meaning of this unique *katáthema* would be an exacerbated "oath-curse, denunciation, malediction,"[13] that is, a divinely accursed thing or person deemed abominable. In this present context, given its elimination from the New Jerusalem, the apostle seems to say that any form of separation and excommunication from Christ and from his beloved people will no longer exist. With that, explicit wishes that misfortune would befall another person are eradicated, too.

And one last time, the presence of the divine throne is stressed (v. 3b), reiterating what was already visualized in v. 1: God's rule forever replaces the futile dominance of Satan and his evil schemes over a groaning creation (Rom 8:22). Turning then from the city and her King to the inhabitants, and unlike the poetic vision of Dante's *Paradiso*, where on his journey through heaven he encounters a variety of saints, and where St. John questions him about love,[14] the Apocalypse does not specify any individuals or their names but identifies the redeemed simply as "his servants" (v. 3c). At last, they can serve their Lord without hindrance, enthused by his unmediated presence. Earthly toil and labor are over and done with, but divine service remains (7:15), paradoxically increasing their regal honor. To serve is to rule, to glorify, and to be glorified.

12. Notice, on the contrary, how Yahweh's curse over the serpent (Gen 3:14) has not been and will never be undone.

13. That is the connotation adopted by the Neo-Vulgate, translating it as *maledictum*, a derivative of the verb *maledīcere*, "to speak ill of, curse, taunt, insult."

14. Cf. *Canto* 26.

And at that moment, the wearied dichotomy between action and contemplation is resolved into the everlasting priestly service or *latreía* of the undistracted beholding of God's beauty. Not to be disallowed, however, from the worshipful joys of heaven is the service to one's neighbor in mutual affection, edification, and enrichment.

What is communicated next can only be called a culmination point of biblical spirituality, and perhaps the most profound theological statement of the Apocalypse: "They will see his face, and his name will be on their foreheads" (v. 4). In heaven, therefore, to serve God means to contemplate his countenance, truly the greatest pleasure imaginable. No longer will it be necessary to hide from his face in the woods, filled with shame and fear, like humanity's protoparents in Eden (Gen 3:8). Over are the days, too, when the soul was compelled to seek his face without ever truly finding it (Ps 13:1). Like Moses on Sinai[15] and the chosen apostles on Tabor, and not least like the angels themselves, the saints will be fully contented as they look into the heavenly Father's eyes and converse with the God-Man Jesus: "As for me, I shall behold your face in righteousness; when I awake I shall be satisfied, beholding your likeness" (Ps 17:15).

In fulfillment of the promise to the Philadelphian church (3:12), the divine name imprinted conspicuously on their foreheads demonstrates that they are now completely reconfigured to the image and likeness of their Maker (Gen 1:27). Metaphysically speaking, they have been divinized: "We will be like him, for we will see him as he is" (1 John 3:2). Hence, three dimensions characterize their heavenly existence: to serve, to see, and to resemble the Lord God. And in those qualities they have reached their human perfection as his beloved children and his adoring priests.[16]

Restating what was unveiled already in 21:23, 25, to express its absolute certainty, the angel avows: "And there will be no more night; and they need no light of lamp or light of sun, for the Lord God will be their light, and they will reign forever and ever" (v. 5). Even in this closing verse of the portrait of the New Jerusalem, the eschatological strain between the "already and not yet" still manifests itself in the different tenses of the Greek verb *phōtízō* (φωτίζω): whereas in 21:23 it appears as an aorist (ephṓtisen, ἐφώτισεν) and the Latin perfect tense (*illuminavit*), suggestive of heaven as a *fait accompli*, here, it is inflected in the future tense (*phōtísei*, φωτίσει, *illuminabit*) as something that

15. Cf. Exod 33:11, whose "face to face" (*facie ad faciem*) is complemented by the "mouth to mouth" (*ore enim ad os*) at Num 12:8.

16. Cf. RD, 1207.

is not yet fully realized. Gone are the days of shadows: God's face will shine on us (Num 6:25–27), and Christ as the bright morning star (2:28; 22:16) will floodlight the day of eternity (2 Pet 3:18). His elect will reign as kings together with Christ their King, fully exposing the eschatological significance of his title "King of kings." And this marks the conclusion of the last and most majestic vision in Sacred Scripture (21:1–22:5), the theological pinnacle not just of St. John's Apocalypse, but of the entire Bible.

While it remains certainly true that no eye has seen, nor ear heard (1 Cor 2:9) what heaven really looks like, the above passage (vv. 1–5), in addition of course to ch. 21, does offer the most extensive scriptural glimpse of its glory, inviting us to further reflection and joyous anticipation. In typical Johannine manner, all divine blessings showered on us are summed up as "life" (v. 1), and the only true life is to live in the here and now as the Lord's servants. A river of sacramental graces gushes forth from his heart, the never-dwindling fountain of all vitality and happiness, and is poured into our hearts. From whence it wells up again like a spring and flows back to him in willing cooperation and glorification. Its steadily enlarging stream accomplishes our election, adoption, vocation, sanctification, and eventually everlasting life. Thus, like circulating water, there is a marvelous eddying movement of grace's issuance (*exitus*) from God's throne, and its return (*reditus*) from our souls back to him that will last for ages unending.

Along with that, the image of the healing tree (v. 2) suggests the centrality of the open side of the Savior on the Cross, source of the Church's fruitfulness.[17] By faithfully eating and drinking from it, each Christian shares in that divine fecundity, making us profitable in our apostolate in this world. At the same time, water and arboreal fruit allegorize the heavenly fulfillment of the earthly gift of the Holy Eucharist. Besides, our fallen nature stands in need of physical and spiritual redress, which we experience here on earth, albeit imperfectly, by touching the medicinal leafage of the *lignum Crucis*: and we are assured that one day, those leaves will make the body immortal and the soul immaculate. And that state of perfect welfare of our human nature should be anticipated with great joy. By the same token, if during our earthly pilgrimage we cling like foliage to that mystical tree, we ourselves are transformed into agents of healing for many:[18] "They are like trees planted by streams of water, which yield their fruit in its season, and their leaves do not wither. In all that they do, they prosper" (Ps 1:3).

17. Cf. AvS, 776–77.
18. Cf. AvS, 779.

Also, in reflecting on the absence of imprecation in the New Jerusalem (v. 3), we are encouraged to seek refuge with the Blessed Virgin Mary as her spiritual offspring, because there we are kept from the serpent's execration and enmity (Gen 3:14–15); indeed, to be sheltered under her safeguarding mantle as the Mother of Mercy is a foretaste of heaven. Also, may our prayer life be a humble anticipation of the beatific vision described in v. 4, that is, the plenary satisfaction of every aspiration uniting the whole human family.[19] In that deepening desire to explore the inexhaustible wealth of his countenance, the hour of our death will become our birthday or *dies natalis* into heaven, fusing continuity with newness of life.[20] A sense of belonging and undivided commitment to God, symbolized by the name borne on our foreheads, the avoidance of sin as an attempt at defacing him, and the effort to live out Christian purity, will eventually give us access to God's paradise. There, his servants reign in full knowledge and felicity, celebrating the unending feast of Tabernacles: "The glory of God is man fully alive, and the life of man is the vision of God."[21]

19. Cf. *CCC*, §1045.
20. Cf. AvS, 782.
21. Irenaeus, *Adversus haereses*, 4.20.7 (SC 100.2:648; author's translation).

22:6–21, *Maráná-thá*!

Sixth makarism: Keeping the prophecy (22:6–7)

[6]And he said to me, "These words are trustworthy and true, for the Lord, the God of the spirits of the prophets, has sent his angel to show his servants what must soon take place." [7]"See, I am coming soon! Blessed is the one who keeps the words of the prophecy of this book."

Revelation's closing portion (vv. 6–21) is commonly termed its epilogue, devised as an *inclusio* with regard to its prologue (1:1–3), albeit five times its length, and consisting of an aphoristic series of exhortations, testimony, warnings, as well as another two apocalyptic beatitudes or makarisms. With exceptional unction, several themes of the book are confirmed one last time, making the bulk of its narrative something of a paraphrase of previous material. Two traits are dominant, namely, the vital relevance of its divinely authenticated message, but also the nearness of the end. Both are intended to induce the reader to an obedient receptivity and encourage Christian perseverance. That said, let us go *in medias res.*

After having revealed the Bride of the Lamb as a holy City (21:9–10) and as a refound Paradise (22:1–2), the angel-interpreter now asserts their validity: "And he said to me, 'These words are most trustworthy and true, for the Lord, the God of the spirits of the prophets, has sent his angel to show his servants what must soon take place'" (v. 6). In words designed to round off the Apocalypse, he reminds John of its utter reliability (*fidelissima*),[1] that everything will be fulfilled as stated due to its infallible truthfulness. This, of course, repeats and ratifies a tenet that has been declared or implied several times before.[2] In

1. Strikingly, the New Vulgate translates the Greek adjective *pistós* (πιστός, "trustworthy, stable") in its positive degree with this superlative form of the adjective *fidelis*, "faithful."

2. Cf. 1:5; 3:7, 14; 6:10; 15:3; 16:7; 19:2, 9.11; 21:5.

other words, there has been no dissembling of the senses in these visions, but what was disclosed in them is of supreme authority, worthy of firm faith and interpretation. Implied, too, is the continuity and harmony between this revelation and what the Holy Spirit inspired in the Old Testament prophets, awaiting its certain fulfillment (19:10). All this is transmitted through God's angel to "his servants," that is, the loyal followers of the Lamb in the Church throughout the ages. Not restated from 1:1 at this time is the visionary instrumentality of John the apostle, the seer on the Dodecanese island.

What is reiterated verbatim from that opening verse 1:1 is the phrase "what must soon take place" and couched in between these two is the similar 4:1, lacking, however, the expression "in haste, with quickness" (*en táchei*, ἐν τάχει),[3] so charged with apocalyptic urgency. Thus, the angel presses vigilance and preparedness, and with that his voice becomes indistinct from that of Christ himself: "And behold, I am coming swiftly. Blessed the one who guards the words of the prophecy of this book" (v. 7). That velocity (*velociter*) of his parousia is typical of the genre and, thus, emphasized in Revelation no fewer than eight times to foster spiritual alertness and counteract foolish somnolence.[4] Moreover, this verse contains the sixth of seven apocalyptic makarisms[5] in close resemblance to the first one (1:3). With a favorite Johannine verb, "to keep" (*tēréō*, τηρέω, *servare*), the Lord exhorts each one to hold fast to these precious prophecies, and that to do so would amount to a wonderful benediction. Blessed is the one who preserves them in his or her memory, who ponders, understands, believes, observes, and puts them into practice: particularly in days of darkness and trial, they will be of light and comfort. This beatitude can be considered the embodiment of the spirit of the entire Apocalypse, namely, the revelation and watchful anticipation of the coming One.

3. This Greek noun is rendered by the Latin adverb *cito*, meaning "speedily, before long," perhaps in adaptation to the adverb *tachý* (ταχύ, "quickly, soon") in the upcoming v. 7.

4. Cf. 1:1; 2:16; 3:11; 11:14; 22:6, 12, 20.

5. Cf. 1:3; 14:13; 16:15; 19:9; 20:6; 22:14.

Swift return (22:8–13)

[8]I, John, am the one who heard and saw these things. And when I heard and saw them, I fell down to worship at the feet of the angel who showed them to me; [9]but he said to me, "You must not do that! I am a fellow servant with you and your comrades the prophets, and with those who keep the words of this book. Worship God!" [10]And he said to me, "Do not seal up the words of the prophecy of this book, for the time is near. [11]Let the evildoer still do evil, and the filthy still be filthy, and the righteous still do right, and the holy still be holy." [12]"See, I am coming soon; my reward is with me, to repay according to everyone's work. [13]I am the Alpha and the Omega, the first and the last, the beginning and the end."

What follows is the fourth and closing self-identification of Revelation's sacred author (1:1, 4.9): "And I, John, am the one who heard and saw these things. And after I had heard and seen them, I fell down to worship at the feet of the angel who showed them to me" (v. 8). By appealing repeatedly to his physical senses of hearing and seeing, he energetically confirms the veracity of his mystical experience, as he does also in his Gospel and First Epistle.[6] What should also be underlined is the very last recurrence of the crucial verb *deiknýō*[7] (δεικνύω, *ostendere*), denoting that salvific showing or disclosing of divine mysteries in the Apocalypse. Somewhat surprisingly, there is no trace of nostalgia or reluctance on his part to return to the dire reality of his earthly affairs, that is, to reenter his exiled life on Patmos and later at Ephesus.

Supposing that the angelic guide was Christ himself (1:17), especially since the latter had just proclaimed another beatitude, John prostrates himself again at his feet to express his wonder, homage, and gratitude (v. 8). This is now the second time he is carried away in rapt emotion and attempts to adore a mere creature (19:10), which is astounding for someone who had been the first to recognize the Risen Christ by the Sea of Tiberias, exclaiming, "It is the Lord!" (John 21:7). Yet one must be careful not to judge him rashly, given the splendor of the angelic appearance, all but blending into divinity just like the *Malak Yahweh* of Old Testament times (Gen 18:2; Josh 5:14). And there is one notable difference: whereas on that earlier occasion (19:10) the angel professed himself to be a fellow-servant of the seer's brethren holding the testimony of Jesus in

6. Cf. John 1:14; 19:35; 20:8; 21:24; 1 John 1:1–3; 4:14.

7. This exceptional spelling does not differ in meaning from the more common *deíknymi* (δείκνυμι), found at 1:1; 4:1; 17:1; 21:9–10; 22:1, 6.

the Church, here he appears to rank himself and John among the great Old Testament prophets, whom he calls "brothers" (*fratres*).[8] And that articulation of continuity between the prophetic and apostolic ministries in both Testaments is something unparalleled in the Scriptures (Deut 18:18). But be that as it may, the good spirit here again vehemently redirects the seer's attention, now that his mission of writing the book is accomplished and his soul enlightened by the visions received. He is to return to what is essential, namely, to worship and adore God alone![9]

Unlike at 10:4, where he is ordered not to take note or publish,[10] the visions are now complete, and John is commanded to communicate them to the world: "Do not seal up the words of the prophecy of this book, for the time is near" (v. 10). By committing this Revelation to writing and arranging for its wider circulation, he makes it available for the constant use of the Church henceforth. Although their ultimate unfolding will extend to the end of the ages and even into eternity, the events predicted were about to begin to be fulfilled at the apostle's own time, and therefore their advance knowledge would aid in consoling Christians during their hardships. It would reassure them that the dogma of their religion would go on to eventually triumph, and thus, they would be able to endure adversity patiently. Part of the immediate crisis would have been the explosion of violent persecutions under emperors Nero and Domitian in the second half of the first century AD. That the Son of God's second advent is near, too, was already announced in the prologue (1:3), reflecting the Baptizer's and Jesus' own initial proclamation of the Kingdom (Matt 3:2; Mark 1:15). Ergo, by hearing repeated what was communicated already at v. 7, the listener senses the urgency to prayerfully watch for his coming.

Nevertheless, the Lord evidently is not unrealistic about the chances of widespread or radical change of lives: "Let the evildoer still do evil, and the filthy still be filthy, and the righteous still do right, and the holy still be sanctified'" (v. 11). This dual antithetical parallelism, i.e., "evil-filthy" vs "righteous-holy,"[11] again stresses the palpable ethical dualism undergirding the entire Apocalypse, which will reecho twice more in this its afterword (vv. 15, 18–19). While obviously not inferring that the time to reform is too short, we are forewarned that we must reckon with the obduracy of wicked hearts and

8. Cf. AvS, 799.

9. Cf. AvS, 801.

10. Cf. Isa 8:16; 30:8; Dan 8:26; 12:4, 9–13; Rev 5:1.

11. Visualized especially in the polarity between the Greek verb *adikéō* (ἀδικέω), "to act unjustly," and its cognate adjective *díkaios* (δίκαιος), "just."

their persistence in evil, but also with the perseverance of the saints in doing good. One should never be surprised that ongoing and upcoming crises will accentuate and accelerate moral character, corroborating positive or negative habits. Surely, the message of Christ will displease those of morally unfit and polluted souls,[12] yet it must not be concealed, because no matter the conduct of humans, the divine plan will be accomplished. Also intimated is that no more opportunities will be granted to save one's soul than what is contained in the word of God and proposed by the Church (Luke 16:29–31).

Now is the time to heed the warnings and to exercise one's free will to further God's glory,[13] now is the acceptable time and the day of salvation (2 Cor 6:2). In fact, the fourfold verbal imperative expressing commands in this verse has an ironic ring to it to stir us up to timely repentance, like the Lord's agonized remark to Peter, James and John in the garden, "Sleep on now, and take your rest!" (Matt 26:45). Unquestionably, there is also the realization that one can still obtain God's mercy until one's last breath on earth, yet it will be impossible to make moral adjustments beyond the grave: following the Last Judgment, the punishment for sin will be quickened sin, and the reward for holiness will be immense bliss.

Lest anyone give in to indifference or tepidity, Christ declares again: "See, I am coming soon, and my reward is with me, to repay according to everyone's work" (v. 12). This is the penultimate occasion where the speediness of his return is brought to the fore (v. 20). And when he comes, he will certainly not be empty-handed; to the contrary, he will be true to his promise first made to Abraham, our father in faith, and bring his eternal recompense (Gen 15:1). In opposition to the great harlot's wages of sin (18:6), each person shall be rewarded in accordance with what he or she has done on earth (20:13). Jesus' knowledge and memory of those works are flawless (2:2),[14] and the good shall receive the crown of life in heaven, while the wicked collect the curse of death in hell, and nothing and nobody can hinder the full execution of his intention.

In that sense, Christ is the origin and consummation of his creatures: "I am the Alpha and the Omega, the first and the very last, the beginning and the end" (v. 13). God had affirmed himself to be the "Alpha and Omega" at the opening of

12. The Greek adjective *rhyparós* (ῥυπαρός, *sordidus*), "shabby, impure, dirty," recurs solely in Zech 3:3 and Jas 2:2, and its correlative verb *rhypaínō* (ῥυπαίνω, *sordéscere*), a biblical *hapax legomenon*, here refers to moral defilement or the stain of personal sin; see also the related nouns *rhyparía* (ῥυπαρία), "impurity," at Jas 1:21, as well as *rhýpos* (ῥύπος), "squalor," at 1 Pet 3:21.

13. Cf. RD, 1210; AvS, 804.

14. Cf. AvS, 806.

Revelation (1:8), followed by Jesus' speaking of himself as the "First and Last" (1:17; 2:8);[15] then, like a crescendo, at 21:6, it is again God who calls himself the "Alpha and Omega, Beginning and End," and in this present verse, at the book's close and appropriately framing it, Christ cumulatively applies the three clauses to himself. In its triplicity, the title carries a trinitarian overtone, since Father, Son, and Holy Spirit together conceived of the plan of creation, salvation, and sanctification, and they will determine its consummation. Besides, this climactic appellation, indeed the longest Christological title in Scripture, pays tribute to the divinity, infinity, and perfection of our Lord.

Seventh makarism: Pure garments (22:14)

[14]Blessed are those who wash their robes,[16] so that they will have the right to the tree of life and may enter the city by the gates.

As he affixes one more apocalyptic makarism to the litany of the previous six, the Lord offers a threefold retrospect to those who washed their robes in the blood of the Lamb (7:14), to the healing of nations by the leaves of New Jerusalem's tree (v. 2), as well as to the generous gateways or porches leading into that same heavenly city (21:12). To be clothed in that nuptially pure linen (19:8) as a logical opposite to the shabbiness of evil (v. 11) means true blessedness.[17] There seems to be another image-vector, as it were, progressing from the time when Yahweh Elohim expelled Adam and Eve from the garden of Eden and clothed them with garments of skin (Gen 3:21), through Jesus' parable in which a guest is questioned about not wearing a wedding attire (Matt 22:11–12), through the best robe put on the prodigal son by his exultant father (Luke 15:22), even to Paul's metaphor of clothing ourselves with the Lord and a new self (Rom 13:14; Eph 4:24). All these are figurative of the baptismal bath that enables the person to enter the heavenly wedding banquet.

But having arrived at the close of this septenary of beatitudes in Revelation, we are now in a position to give a short synopsis: the *first* and the *sixth* are

15. Cf. Isa 41:4; 43:10; 44:6; 48:12; John 1:1.

16. In lieu of the Greek phrase *hoí plýnontes tás stolás autôn* (οἱ πλύνοντες τὰς στολὰς αὐτῶν), "those who wash their robes," a variant reads *hoí poioûntes tás entolás autoû* (οἱ ποιοῦντες τὰς ἐντολὰς αὐτοῦ), meaning "those doing his commandments": these two phrases resemble each other so closely that a scribe in a moment of haste or carelessness might very easily have mistaken the one for the other.

17. Foreshadowed in Naaman immersing himself seven times in the Jordan, according to prophet Elisha's word, cf. 2 Kgs 5:14.

related in their emphasis on receiving and guarding the prophecy (1:3; 22:7); also linked are the *third* and this present *seventh* one in their reference to the symbolic clothing of grace (16:15; 22:14); quite unique, however, are the *second*, which extols a holy death (14:13), the *fourth*, with its exquisite invitation to the Lamb's marriage celebrations (19:9), and finally the *fifth*, magnifying the sanctity of baptism as a first resurrection (20:6). And even though entirely different in wording and tenor, this septet of makarisms is also complementary to the octet of the Matthean beatitudes (Matt 5:1–12).

Amazingly, that state of supernatural bliss means a share in the power of the Messiah himself (12:10) and access to the tree of life through the city's pearly gates, making the consummation even better than the beginning. Eden was fair, but the heavenly garden-city shall be fairer, because her inhabitants are assured in the Holy Spirit, the giver of life, of living forever (Gen 3:22) in the presence of the Son, its gardener (John 20:15), and of the Father, its husbandman (John 15:1; Matt 15:13).

Pneumatic betrothal (22:15–21)

15 Outside are the dogs and sorcerers and fornicators and murderers
and idolaters, and everyone who loves and practices falsehood. 16 "It is
I, Jesus, who sent my angel to you with this testimony for the churches.
I am the root and the descendant of David, the bright morning star."
17 The Spirit and the bride say, "Come." And let everyone who hears say,
"Come." And let everyone who is thirsty come. Let anyone who wishes
take the water of life as a gift. 18 I warn everyone who hears the words of
the prophecy of this book: if anyone adds to them, God will add to that
person the plagues described in this book; 19 if anyone takes away from
the words of the book of this prophecy, God will take away that person's
share in the tree of life and in the holy city, which are described in this
book. 20 The one who testifies to these things says, "Surely I am coming
soon." Amen. Come, Lord Jesus! 21 The grace of the Lord Jesus be with
all the saints. Amen.

Coming right on the heels of that final beatitude, and in antithesis to it, is this additional exclusionary catalog at v. 15. This is now the second-last such listing (vv. 18–19), comprised of six categories of people, of which five are shared, albeit in altered sequence, with the total of eight cited in 21:8, namely, murderers, fornicators, sorcerers, idolaters, and liars. This most disconcerting concept of distinguishing between the inside and the outside (*éxō*, ἔξω, *foris*) of the Kingdom of heaven first surfaces after the Exodus, when Yahweh instructs Moses and Aaron to exclude foreigners from the Passover festivities (Exod 12:43). And many are the New Testament instances or parables that are allusive to such noninclusion;[18] but here it simply shows how the Lord respects the ultimate consequence of human free will, that is, of what happens to those who deliberately chose not to be counted among his beloved people.

What remains without scriptural equal, however, is the disqualification of dogs. For better understanding one must remember that the dog served as an archaic metaphor among oriental nations and nomads for what is most degraded or disliked and was proverbially used against one's enemies (Ps 22:16, 20). In Hebrew tradition, it was pronounced an unclean animal (Lev 11:27), considered dirty, foolish, and voracious, and as such it came to designate the biblical Gentiles. Specifically, in Deut 23:18, it denounces the moral profligacies of heathen worship involving female and male prostitutes. All five citations of dogs in the New Testament are found in extremely negative circumstances (e.g., Matt 7:6), and in due course, they became an epithet marking out heretics, apostates, and persecutors of the Church (Phil 3:2). In this present context, they seem to epitomize all those who choose a life of vileness despite having been justified in baptism. And one other item stands out in this penultimate exclusion formula (v. 15), and it has to do with those who engage in mendacity (14:5; 21:27); only on this occasion the aggravating condition of being intentional, inventive, and even pleased (*philéō*, φιλέω, *amare*) about practicing such hypocrisy is pointed out. In any event, and in contradistinction to those who are promised never to be excluded from heaven (3:12), the above list implies that the names of those malefactors are not written in the life-book, and that they are thrown into the fire-lake (20:15).

Yet, going from darkness back to light, here is the first-person reassurance by Christ himself to the seer: "I, Jesus, sent my angel to testify to these things to you about the churches. I am the root and the descendant of David, the bright morning star" (v. 16). It should not astound us that we find here at the very end of the New Testament canon the Lord's most emphatic self-identification, "It is I, Jesus!" (*Egò Iēsoûs*, 'Εγὼ 'Ιησοῦς, *Ego Iesus*). What is affirmed here enhances the tenor of 1:1–2 in that now aside from the Father, it is also the Son who sends his angel to communicate with the churches (chs. 2–3), and to initiate the writing of the Book of the Apocalypse. For Jesus to speak of "my angel" recalls the angelic protection following the Hebrews' Exodus (Exod 23:20), as well as the

18. E.g., Matt 5:13; 13:48; 21:39; Mark 4:11; John 12:31; 15:6.

parousiac expectation of the messenger of the covenant (Mal 3:1). And that this angel entrusts his testimony to a collective recipient "you all" (*vobis*) probably denotes an ecclesial plural rather than a plurality of visionary authors (John 21:24).

Furthermore, here we find the last of five "I am" sayings in Revelation,[19] this time to identify the Lord not just as the root of King David (5:5), but paradoxically also as his descendant, signifying that he inherits the messianic throne by being at the same time Lord and Son of David, that is, Lord in his divinity, and Son in his humanity. Also, he had promised to bestow "the morning star" on the Thyatiran faithful, but it turns out that by virtue of his glorious Resurrection, he himself has become "the splendid morning star" (2:28), able to put an end to the night of ignorance, sorrow, and sin.[20] Now he is the harbinger of the rising sun, of a never-diminishing day of pure light and joy. Thus, the Lord ratifies the divine authority of this revelation, ready to be communicated to the universal Church.

At this moment, overwhelmed by her love for Christ, the Church, in intimate union with the Holy Spirit here on earth, expresses her bridal desire to become one with her divine Spouse, imploring him to come back and take her to the wedding banquet: "The Spirit and the bride say, 'Come!'" (v. 17a). Put differently, the third divine Person in union with the pilgrim people of God in this world requests the second divine Person to return into human history, to gather them all into the first divine Person, effectively merging the redeemed with the Blessed Trinity in heaven. This exclamation reverberates with the full force of creation's and humanity's longing for Christ, the desire for him to celebrate his eternal nuptials with us (19:7). It is in direct response to Jesus' own assertion of the imminence of his parousia (vv. 7, 12). This impatient anticipation of his second advent is also the Church's eschatological *Fiat* ("Let it be done!") toward her pneumatic betrothal.[21]

And now every reader, every hearer, every believer is urged by God through John to join in the cosmic cry of yearning, the enormous intensity of which is conveyed by five verbal imperatives in this verse ("come!," "say!," "come!," "come!," "take!"). Made present to the worshipper notably during liturgical celebrations, this eschatological expectation must be repeated from the bottom of the heart, hoping that we may draw near to him, who never ceases to draw near to us: "Let everyone one who hears say, Come!" (v. 17b; cf. v. 20). Restless

19. Cf. 1:8, 17; 2:23; 21:6.
20. Cf. RD, 1212.
21. Cf. AvS, 822.

is the soul for God, the heart longs for his love, and the human will desires nothing more than to be mastered and possessed by the Father's embrace. And with irresistible warmth and benevolence, Jesus subjoins his own invitation, reiterating what he had already declared during the feast of booths in the temple (John 7:37) and at his death on the Cross (John 19:28): "Let the one who thirsts, come; let anyone who wishes take the water of life as a gift" (v. 17c). No monetary means on earth could ever cover the cost of drawing water from the springs of salvation (Isa 12:3; 55:1); it remains a gift from our Redeemer. All we can do in response is to desire it: "My soul thirsts for God, the living God. When shall I come and appear in God's presence?" (Ps 42:2).

And then John in the name of Christ subjoins a closing adjuration for his listeners of all generations, discharging his grave duty and sealing the Apocalypse's authenticity (vv. 18–19). Constructed as a synthetic parallelism that hinges on the contrastive use of "to add" (*apponere*) and "to take away" (*auferre*). What is betokened is that this sacred book contains a measure of divine revelation whose inspiration and inerrancy warrants no further modification.[22] Ergo, any slightest addition or subtraction would amount to heretical falsification.[23] This anticlimactic peroration reflects the religious eagerness to safeguard the apostolic tradition as a body of authoritative doctrine that must not be tampered with. Testified against are not the copyists or translators who might inadvertently insert or omit something in the transmitted text, but rather anyone who purposely rejects even a single word of it,[24] for it means rejection of the book altogether. Jesus announces repayment in kind, namely, plagues for the one who dilutes the force of its warnings, and exclusion from heaven for the one who attempts to diminish the fullness of its promises. And by restating the word "prophecy" in vv. 18–19, the seer contrasts this admonition with the blessedness of reading and hearing it at 1:3.

Christ's final word in Revelation confirms his witness of 1:2 and adds eschatological hope: "The one who testifies to these things says, 'Surely, I am coming soon.'" (v. 20a). This resounding "Yes!" (*naí*, ναί, *etiam*) of the Son evokes that of the Holy Spirit (14:13), as well as the one affirming the Father's truthfulness (16:7). And that it is urgent for us to watch for his return in glory is shown by the Lord's own threefold insistence on it in this final chapter (vv. 7, 12). And at this point, with firm faith each one of us assents to this Revelation, cheerfully

22. In due course, the ecumenical Council of Trent officially approved of its canonicity (*De canonicis Scripturis*, April 8, 1546).

23. Cf. RD, 1213; AvS, 825.

24. As intimated by the repetition of the noun "word" (*lógos*, λόγος, *verbum*) in vv. 18–19.

saying "Amen. Come, Lord Jesus!" (v. 20b). If translated into Aramaic, the Lord's mother-tongue, it would be *Marána-thá* (מרנא-תא, μαράνα θά; 1 Cor 16:22), an acclamation that would soon become a watchword of the early Church: "Our Lord, come!"[25] If, however, one divides its syllables differently, that is, *Máran-átha*, it becomes a statement of faith regarding his Incarnation: "Our Lord has come!" Overall, the prayerful and faith-filled yearning for Christ's coming could be called the quintessence of the Apocalypse.[26]

Similar to the greeting he extended to the seven churches in Asia (1:4), John here subjoins his closing salutation, ultimately addressed to all the children of the Church scattered throughout the world: "The grace of the Lord Jesus [be] with all" (v. 21).[27] Paul before him had opened and closed most of his epistles with that gracious wish (e.g., 1 Cor 16:23). As if trying to clasp all humanity in his arms, this parting benediction of the aging apostle on our upturned heads is also the way the New Testament canon is finalized and promulgated, and with it the whole deposit of divine revelation. Thus, the rolling thunders of Mount Sinai have crystallized in the gentle dew of God's compassionate blessings. May the Lord make haste to come in his Kingdom, so that we can be with him forever.

Although the language of this epilogue (vv. 6–21) is mostly non-metaphorical, and thus contains a straightforward message to further interior life, it may be worthwhile to make some of it still more clear. To begin with, there is the trustworthiness of what has been unveiled in this Book of the Apocalypse (v. 6), evincing our human capacity of receiving and assimilating the objective truth.[28] If duly considered, these prophetic words are a powerful encouragement to mind and soul, making a persuasive case to purify and corroborate the practice of the faith, no matter the difficulties or dangers it may face. Also, that God sends his angel to his servants (v. 6) should inspire each member of the Church to discern with self-awareness and humility one's specific place in his Kingdom, acknowledging that in the end all are called to serve the Lord and our neighbor, his brothers and sisters.

Not only that, but his avowal to return quickly (v. 7) should be received as referring primarily to the present moment, meaning that he makes himself

25. It also appears in the Didache, ch. 2, in a passage on the Holy Eucharist; see also *CCC*, §451.

26. Cf. AvS, 830.

27. Variant readings add "with the saints" or "with all the saints," while the Vulgate carries this version: "Gratia Domini nostri Jesu Christi cum omnibus vobis. Amen" ("The grace of our Lord Jesus Christ [be] with all of you. Amen").

28. Cf. AvS, 795.

present right here and now in the faithful one's heart.[29] And what consummate happiness it is to commit his words to memory, to cherish and ponder them, and to conform one's inward and outward life to them. Particularly in days of darkness and trial, they will be of light and comfort, making the believer truly blessed or *makários*. Moreover, there is John's recurring attempt to worship the angel (vv. 8–9), proving beyond doubt that the proneness to misunderstanding and sin is found even in the greatest saints. Likewise, it demonstrates that there is a profound propensity to idolatry lodged in our fallen human nature, requiring constant vigilance and discernment to remain focused on the genuine *opus Dei*.

Besides, when the apostolic visionary is asked not to conceal these words (v. 10), it signals to all followers of the Lamb to not be spiritually inert or parsimonious, but rather share them freely and generously with the people of our time, too. This can be accomplished by fostering habits of justice and holiness (v. 11) by which in turn we perseveringly weave and wash the spiritual robe that will eventually admit us to the marriage feast in heaven (v. 14). What should also animate us to be singlehearted in our commitment to the baptismal vow is the healthy fear of being chased away at the end of the day by the Lord like a dog (v. 15). It goes without saying that malicious intentionality and scheming falsehood have no place in the life of a member of Christ's Mystical Body.

Just as the God-Man is at the same time root and scion of David, that is, eternally preceding him and also outliving him (v. 16), so his presence should surround and transfix our every thought, word, and action. What is more, in that inner union with him, with his Spirit, and with his Church, the desire for his prevenient or anticipating grace steadily increases: Lord, come into my life today! (v. 17). And how grateful the soul is for the preservation and faithful transmission of the word of God through the ages (vv. 18–19). In his providence, the Sacred Scriptures, and the Book of the Apocalypse of St John in particular, have been handed down to us and have remained the inerrant north star, nudging us not to leave them unstudied or unprayed over, but to discover and rediscover in them spiritual sustenance. Likewise, we do well to accept and believe them in their entirety, careful to neither attach anything to them nor subtract from them.

In that spirit of filial obedience, one can breathe the aspiration "Amen. Come, Lord Jesus!" (v. 20), the prayer of the heart, awaiting his return with loving impatience (6:10). And as far as we are concerned, his return cannot

29. Cf. AvS, 790.

come early enough. Yet "until he comes" (1 Cor 11:26), that hope will be nourished by the Holy Eucharist, keeping us awash in his grace, so we can wish it on others as well (v. 21).[30] Together then, as brothers and sisters in the Lord during this last hour (1 John 2:18), we fulfill Revelation's purpose, that is, the holiness lived today that gives glory to him forever: *Marána-thá*!

30. Cf. AvS, 832.

Conclusion

Having now arrived at the final mile-marker of our exegetical-spiritual journey through John's Apocalypse, let us subjoin some closing thoughts regarding the panhistorical spiritual drama that it depicts. As an overarching assessment, the apostle's visions are by no means Kafkaesque, but uplifting and permeated by mercy and consolation, offering authentic hope springing eternal. A case should be made that their magnificence, uncompromising Christocentricity, and all-encompassing import earn him the distinction of being the greatest among all biblical prophets. Nobody has lifted the veil on the secrets of history and eternity more eloquently and creatively than he did.[1]

His book has shown us conflict and confusion caused by humanity's blood-drenched yet vain rebellion against God's law, begging the vexed question of why the All-Ruler allows these heartbreaking scenes in the first place? And the answer resides in his truth, faithfulness, and righteousness with which he judges, and by which he grants courage and deliverance to his faithful ones. With its most developed theology of the Blessed Trinity and eschatology, Revelation gives also great prominence to human freedom and to Christian witness.[2] In the prologue to his commentary, Rupert affirms that by reading the Apocalypse, the soul experiences its exodus from spiritual darkness and enters the Promised Land of the knowledge of God, preparing it to see him face to face.[3]

1. Cf. Frederick James Murphy, *Fallen Is Babylon: The Revelation to John* (Harrisburg, PA: Trinity Press International, 1998), xiii–xiv.

2. Cf. R. Bauckham, *The Theology of the Book of Revelation*, NTT (New York: Cambridge University Press, 1993), 164.

3. Cf. RD, 826.

And how can we not recall Jerome's valuation that it "has as many mysteries as words; in saying this I have said less than the Book deserves; all praise of it is inadequate; manifold meanings lie hidden in its every word"?[4] In that sense, its world cannot be understood as being monolithic or self-contained, but is forever open to interpretation, able to be incorporated into any culture of any generation, and also, as was the purpose of this present commentary, to relate its symbolism to the spiritual realities of the Christian soul. Nevertheless, Revelation is overtly and unapologetically critical of human history, uncovering good and evil in their origins. In our effort to contemporize its message, it must remain compatible with the Christocentric norms laid down in the Gospels and in the Spirit's letters to the seven churches, to avoid falling into self-congratulatory naïveté, empty complacency, or vain celebration of violence.[5]

There must be that constant alertness, too, that John does not conjure up false hopes of miraculous divine intervention, but rather reinterprets our individual sufferings by promising strength in witness and perseverance amid our trials. That is the overall and enduring Paracletic purpose of the Apocalypse, that even as traumatized, wounded, and seemingly powerless victims in this world, we shall be victors in Jesus our Lord who has already won the war and defeated the enemy. Whenever the soul resists temptation and strives to be obedient and pure in Christ's radical discipleship, it shackles Satan and relegates him again to the abyss of the human heart.

If in the early Christian centuries the book struggled against Gnosticism, then today it can guard us against syncretism, large-scale apostasy, and neopaganism, encouraging continual discernment that involves putting oneself faithfully on God's side. No one can serve two masters, and by rallying with the Lamb, Revelation offers us a firm spiritual foothold amid the quicksand and riptides of our postmodern world.[6] And the stupendous anthology of facets of the Lord's countenance in Revelation will not fail to corroborate our faith: he is Son of God and Son of Man (ch. 1), Pantocrator (ch. 4), Lamb and Lion (ch. 5), Shepherd (ch. 7), male Child (ch. 12), King and Lord, Warrior and Judge (ch. 19), and Bridegroom (ch. 22), all in consummate harmony with the Jesus of the Gospels.[7] To live in a loving covenant with him ultimately means to discern the

4. Jerome, Letter to Paulinus, bishop of Nola, 53.8 (trans. W. H. Fremantle, G. Lewis, and W. G. Martley, NPNF 2/6:102).

5. Cf. Judith L. Kovacs and Christopher Rowland, *Revelation: The Apocalypse of Jesus Christ* (Malden, MA: Blackwell, 2004), 248–50.

6. Cf. H. M. Féret, *The Apocalypse of St. John* (Westminster, MD: Newman, 1958), 136.

7. Cf. Dan Lioy, *The Book of Revelation in Christological Focus* (New York: Peter Lang, 2003), 172.

falsehood of his satanic counterfeits in one's everyday life, and to firmly reject them.

By way of a concluding outlook, if the Apocalypse is conceived of as a portrayal of the spiritual way of purification and illumination toward union between an individual soul as bride and Christ as its Bridegroom, then it has no longer to satisfy unwise curiosity concerning concrete historical events but summons each one to diligent conversion. And while the spiraling repetitions of apocalyptic scenes hint at the need for this to take place many times, the continuous interchange of grammatical tenses spotlights it as a timeless truth, too.

That repetition of eschatological confrontations between good and evil is also at the core of Revelation's grand theology of history, meaning that human history despite our best efforts is bound to repeat itself, and that historical epochs come in rhymes, precisely because there will be no ceasefire in the spiritual warfare between the serpent and the Lamb until the end of the world. And if that is true on a cosmic scale, then it also goes for the spiritual combat that takes place incessantly on the battlefield of our hearts. In response, everything depends on how the believer transforms his or her life, aware that in the end Christ will be victorious. Overcoming every test in timely repentance, sincere reconciliation, and most of all in love, we decide between curse and blessing, making sure blessing wins out.[8]

This sacred book is a call to actively engage in bearing witness and in resolutely changing the world we live in, and thereby contribute to building up the Kingdom through the imitation of Jesus, a meek Lamb sacrificed for the salvation of the world. That testimony will engender much joy and certitude to sustain us within the tension of his solemn words of returning like a thief. Aside from that, willingness to suffer for Christ will be the sure path to ultimate triumph,[9] and if the apocalyptic millennium is not a period of time, but rather a way of speaking about the eschaton as a totality,[10] then we are all given the millennial *kairós* or measure of opportunity of our individual lifespan to attain to that cruciformity in him.

And part of that suffering is the recognition that the Bride of the Lamb in heaven is *one*, but the Church on earth is still painfully disunited. Living the message of the Apocalypse, therefore, implies a personal participation in the search for Christian unity, making this principal concern of the Second Vatican

8. Cf. J. Ramsey Michaels, *Revelation*, IVPNTC (Downers Grove, IL: IVP Academic, 1997), 260.

9. G. K. Beale, *Revelation: A Shorter Commentary* (Grand Rapids, MI: Eerdmans, 2015), 32–34.

10. Cf. Augustine, *De civitate Dei*, 18.53.

Council and of the Church ever since, our own.[11] Intimate contact with this sacred book should also gradually change our way of thinking, adopting its biblical viewpoint: "If you lead a life of faith, you will look on things through the eyes of Christ, and will be able to see the eternal dimensions. Then . . . you must fervently pray, Thy Kingdom come!"[12]

Furthermore, in all our hardships we should allow ourselves to be borne along by the hymnology of the heavenly liturgy and by the intercession of the *mārtyres* beneath the supernal altar (6:9).[13] That will be the way to learn the new song already, and to sing it to our contemporaries as an invitation to partake freely of the promises and privileges of the Gospel. In this way we also remain restless and yearning for fulfillment according to God's perfect will. Integrated cosmic worship is the goal, coalescing humankind into one communal act of adoration before the throne of the Lamb, and thereby definitively overcoming individualistic fragmentation and idolatry. Everything redounds to that hymnic focus, pervaded by mystical multidimensionality, and pointing to the doxological finality of our very human existence.[14]

But let us not neglect either to appreciate Revelation's multiculturalism, since it is steeped in ancient Near Eastern spirituality, composed by a Jewish author in the Hellenistic language and addressed originally to an Asian and Roman audience. How can this not inspire us to make our own personal cultural background contribute to the broader fabric of the Church today? Mutually enriching one another, we always expect his second advent and the dawn of the Kingdom, without, however, fearing judgment as a threat; instead, that final day will be a vindication, reward, and honor for all those who have kept the testimony of Jesus.

But after two millennia, the Lord has not yet come, and neither does his Church resemble entirely the image of the apocalyptic Bride adorned for her divine Husband. And precisely that constitutes the fundamental spiritual challenge and task at hand.[15] In fact, John's visions appear to depict a steady dete-

11. Cf. Second Vatican Council, Decree on Ecumenism *Unitatis redintegratio* (November 21, 1964); see also Roland James Faley, *Apocalypse Then and Now: A Companion to the Book of Revelation* (Mahwah, NJ: Paulist, 1999), 176–77.

12. Cardinal Nguyễn Văn Thuận, *The Road of Hope: A Gospel from Prison*, trans. John-Peter Pham, Kindle edition (North Palm Beach, FL: Wellspring, 2019), line numbers 628–29.

13. Cf. *CCC*, §2642; Joseph L. Mangina, *Revelation* (Grand Rapids, MI: Brazos, 2010), 254–55.

14. Cf. Leonard L. Thompson, *The Book of Revelation: Apocalypse and Empire* (New York: Oxford University Press, 1990), 69–73.

15. Wilfrid J. Harrington, *Revelation: The Book of the Risen Christ* (Hyde Park, NY: New City, 1999), 164.

rioration or devolution of the cosmos to the point of eventual dissolution of its natural order, which collides with the Western notion of improvement and evolution toward something higher and nobler. Simultaneously, one notices the gradational augmenting of the Lamb's supernatural influence, as if to encourage us to detach ourselves from worldly things, and not to grasp at an elusive and illusional worldly pseudo-paradise, but rather seek to magnify the Lord in our lives.[16]

Moreover, the attentive reader of the Apocalypse is enveloped by constant insights regarding the resurrection of the flesh on the boundary of world history, informing a pilgrimage that we share with both those who intentionally go forth to salvation, yet also with those tragically heading toward perdition. But since we have already risen in the God-Man Jesus, we are not insensately sucked into a gloomy or unspecified future but drawn into the sharply luminous contours of advance knowledge about heaven and hell.[17] Christ makes of us an eternal offering to his Father, so that one day we may obtain an inheritance with his elect.[18]

At the close of his commentary on Revelation, Andrew of Caesarea appends this pious aspiration:

> May it be that we who desire to see and enjoy these things might by an eager longing for obedience to the divine commandments receive them by long-suffering, meekness, humility, and purity of heart. From such a heart is engendered an unwavering and confident prayer that presents to God, who sees all that is hidden, a mind free from every earthly thought and uncorrupted by the deceits and seductions of the demons.[19]

And all that remains for me to do as I bring this book to its conclusion, is to wholeheartedly echo what Apringius of Beja sighs in the postscript of his exposition on John's Apocalypse: "I give thanks to God, now that this labor is ended."[20] So, once again, let us gather in the hope that we be saints, and cry out from the bottom of our hearts. Come Lord Jesus!

16. Cf. Bruce J. Malina and John J. Pilch, *Social-Science Commentary on the Book of Revelation* (Minneapolis, MN: Fortress, 2000), 237–39.

17. Cf. Michael Patrick Barber, *Coming Soon: Unlocking the Book of Revelation and Applying Its Lessons Today* (Steubenville, OH: Emmaus Road, 2005), 286.

18. Cf. *Eucharistic Prayer* III.

19. Andrew of Caesarea, *Commentary on the Apocalypse*, 114–207 in *Greek Commentaries on Revelation*, ed. Thomas C. Oden, trans. William C. Weinrich, ACT (Downers Grove, IL: IVP Academic, 2011).

20. Apringius of Beja, *Explanation of Revelation*, 23–62 in *Latin Commentaries on Revelation*, ed. and trans. William C. Weinrich, ACT (Downers Grove, IL: IVP Academic, 2011), 62.

Appendix: Detailed Outline of the Book of Revelation

Bibliography

Abbott, Edwin A. *Johannine Grammar.* London: Adam and Charles Black, 1906.

Acton, Lord (John Emerich Edward Dalberg). *Historical Essays and Studies.* Edited by John Neville Figgis and Reginald Vere Laurence. London: Macmillan, 1907.

Allen, Garrick V. *The Book of Revelation and Early Jewish Textual Culture.* Society for New Testament Studies Monograph Series 168. Cambridge, UK: Cambridge University Press, 2017.

Attridge, Harold W. *History, Theology, and Narrative Rhetoric in the Fourth Gospel.* The Pere Marquette Lecture in Theology 2019. Milwaukee, WI: Marquette University Press, 2019.

Augustine of Hippo. *The Confessions of St. Augustine: A Modern English Version.* Translated by Hal M. Helms. Orleans, MA: Paraclete, 1996.

Barber, Michael Patrick. *Coming Soon: Unlocking the Book of Revelation and Applying Its Lessons Today.* Steubenville, OH: Emmaus Road, 2005.

Barclay, William. *The Revelation of John.* Vol. 2 (Chapters 6 to 22). 2nd edition. Philadelphia: Westminster, 1960.

Bartusch, Mark W. *Understanding Dan: An Exegetical Study of a Biblical City, Tribe and Ancestor.* Journal for the Study of the Old Testament Supplement Series 379. Sheffield: Sheffield Academic, 2003.

Bauckham, R. "The Book of Revelation as a Christian War Scroll." *Neotestamentica* 22 (1988): 17–40.

———. *The Theology of the Book of Revelation.* New Testament Theology. New York: Cambridge University Press, 1993.

Beale, G. K. *Handbook on the New Testament Use of the Old Testament: Exegesis and Interpretation.* Grand Rapids, MI: Baker Academic, 2012.

———. *The Book of Revelation.* The New International Greek Testament Commentary. Grand Rapids, MI: Eerdmans, 2013 (reprint).

———. *Revelation: A Shorter Commentary.* Grand Rapids, MI: Eerdmans, 2015.

Beale, G. K. and D. A. Carson. *Commentary on the New Testament Use of the Old Testament.* Grand Rapids, MI: Baker Academic, 2007.

Bernardine of Siena. *St. Bernardine's Sermon on St. Joseph.* Translated by Eric May. Paterson, NJ: St. Anthony's Guild, 1947.

Boxall, Ian and Richard M. Tresley, eds. *The Book of Revelation and Its Interpreters: Short Studies and an Annotated Bibliography*. New York: Rowman & Littlefield, 2015.
Brant, Jo-Ann A. *Dialogue and Drama: Elements of Greek Tragedy in the Fourth Gospel*. Peabody, MA: Hendrickson, 2004.
Coleman, Robert E. *Songs of Heaven*. Old Tappan, NJ: Fleming H. Revell, 1980.
———. *Singing with the Angels*. Old Tappan, NJ: Fleming H. Revell, 1998.
Daniels, T. Scott. *Seven Deadly Spirits: The Message of Revelation's Letters for Today's Church*. Grand Rapids, MI: Baker Academic, 2009.
Dante Alighieri. *Divine Comedy*. Translated and annotated by Henry Wadsworth Longfellow (1867). Aeterna, 2021.
Davis, John James. *Moses and the Gods of Egypt*. Grand Rapids, MI: Baker, 1971.
D'Souza, John. *The Lamb of God in the Johannine Writings*. Allahabad: St. Paul Publications, 1968.
Doyle, Stephen C. *Apocalypse: A Catholic Perspective on the Book of Revelation*. Cincinnati, OH: St. Anthony Messenger, 2005.
Duff, Paul B. *Who Rides the Beast? Prophetic Rivalry and the Rhetoric of Crisis in the Churches of the Apocalypse*. Oxford: Oxford University Press, 2001.
Edwards, James R. "The Rider on the White Horse, the Thigh Inscription, and Apollo: Revelation 19:16." *Journal of Biblical Literature* 137, no. 2 (Summer 2018): 519–36.
Ernout, Alfred and Alfred Meillet. *Dictionnaire Étymologique de la Langue Latine: Histoire des Mots*. 4th edition. Paris: Klincksieck, 2001.
Faley, Roland James. *Apocalypse Then and Now: A Companion to the Book of Revelation*. Mahwah, NJ: Paulist, 1999.
Féret, H. M. *The Apocalypse of St. John*. Westminster, MD: Newman, 1958.
García Ureña, Lourdes. *Narrative and Drama in the Book of Revelation: A Literary Approach*. Translated by Donald Murphy. New York: Cambridge University Press, 2019.
Giblin, Charles Homer. *The Book of Revelation: The Open Book of Prophecy*. Good News Studies 34. Collegeville, MN: Liturgical Press, 1991.
Gorman, Michael J. *Abortion and the Early Church*. Downers Grove, IL: InterVarsity Press, 1982.
Harmless, William. *Mystics*. Oxford: Oxford University Press, 2007.
Harrington, Wilfrid J. *Revelation*. Sacra Pagina series 16. Collegeville, MN: Liturgical Press, 1993.
———. *Revelation: Proclaiming a Vision of Hope*. San Jose, CA: Resource Publications, 1994.
———. *Revelation: The Book of the Risen Christ*. Hyde Park, NY: New City, 1999.
Heine, Ronald E. *Origen: An Introduction to His Life and Thought*. Eugene, OR: Cascade, 2019.

Hemer, Colin J. *The Letters to the Seven Churches of Asia in Their Local Setting.* Grand Rapids, MI: Eerdmans, 2001.

Ignatius of Antioch. *Letter to the Romans.* In Kenneth J., Howell, ed., *Ignatius of Antioch & Polycarp of Smyrna: A New Translation and Theological Commentary.* Revised and Expanded Edition. Early Christian Fathers Series 1. Zanesville, OH: CHResources, 2009.

John Paul II, Pope. Address to the Participants of the Roman Symposium on Cardiology, May 30, 1989. English translation: "Address to Participants in a Cardiology Symposium Urging Them to Continue to Defend Life in All Its Phases." *L'Osservatore Romano,* English Edition 1096 (July 3, 1989): 5.

———. Homily for the Beatification of Luigi Beltrame Quattrocchi and Maria Corsini, October 21, 2001. English translation: "Bl Luigi Beltrame Quattrocchi (1880–1951) and Bl Maria Corsini (1884–1965)." *L'Osservatore Romano,* English Edition 1713 (October 10, 2001): 11.

Koester, Craig R. *Revelation and the End of All Things.* Grand Rapids, MI: Eerdmans, 2001.

Kovacs, Judith L. and Christopher Rowland. *Revelation: The Apocalypse of Jesus Christ,* Malden, MA: Blackwell, 2004.

Laws, Sophie. *In the Light of the Lamb: Imagery, Parody and Theology in the Apocalypse of John.* Good News Studies 31. Wilmington, DE: M. Glazier, 1988.

Liddell, Henry George and Robert Scott. *A Greek-English Lexicon.* 9th edition. Oxford: Clarendon, 1940.

Lioy, Dan. *The Book of Revelation in Christological Focus.* New York: Peter Lang, 2003.

Lupieri, Edmondo F. *A Commentary on the Apocalypse of John.* Grand Rapids, MI: Eerdmans, 2006.

MacArthur, John. *Revelation 1–11.* MacArthur New Testament Commentary Series 32. Chicago: Moody, 1999.

Malina, Bruce J. *The New Jerusalem in the Revelation of John: The City as Symbol of Life with God.* Collegeville, MN: Liturgical Press, 2000.

Malina, Bruce J. and John J. Pilch. *Social-Science Commentary on the Book of Revelation.* Minneapolis, MN: Fortress, 2000.

Mangina, Joseph L. *Revelation.* Grand Rapids, MI: Brazos, 2010.

Marckwardt, A. H., F. G. Cassidy, S. I. Hayakawa, and J. B. McMillan, eds. *Funk & Wagnalls Standard Dictionary of the English Language,* International Edition. Vol. 2. New York: Funk & Wagnalls, 1967.

Mathews, Mark D. *Riches, Poverty, and the Faithful: Perspectives on Wealth in the Second Temple Period and the Apocalypse of John.* New York: Cambridge University Press, 2013.

May, Eric Edward. *Ecce Agnus Dei: A Philological and Exegetical Approach to*

John 1:29,36. Studies in Sacred Theology, Second Series 5. Washington, DC: Catholic University of America Press, 2013.

McDonald, Lee Martin. *The Formation of the Christian Biblical Canon*. Nashville, TN: Abingdon, 1988.

Metzger, Bruce Manning. *Breaking the Code: Understanding the Book of Revelation*. Nashville, TN: Abingdon, 1993.

Metzger, Bruce Manning and Michael David Coogan, eds. *The Oxford Companion to the Bible*. London: Oxford University Press, 1993.

Meyer, Heinrich. *Critical and Exegetical Commentary on the New Testament*. Springfield, OH: Funk & Wagnalls, 1893.

Michaels, J. Ramsey. *Revelation*. IVP New Testament Commentary Series. Downers Grove, IL: IVP Academic, 1997.

Michaels, Lawrence R. *Revelation in Its Original Meaning*. San Diego, CA: Bovee Productions, 1999.

Moloney, Francis J. *The Gospel of John*. Sacra Pagina Series 4. Collegeville, MN: Liturgical Press, 1998.

Montague, George T. *The Apocalypse: Understanding the Book of Revelation and the End of the World*. Ann Arbor, MI: Charis Servant, 1992.

Muller, David G. *Testing the Apocalypse: The History of the Book of Revelation*. Bloomington, IN: WestBow (Nelson & Zondervan), 2016.

Murphy, Frederick James. *Fallen Is Babylon: The Revelation to John*. Harrisburg, PA: Trinity Press International, 1998.

Nestle, Eberhard and Kurt Aland. *Novum Testamentum Graece et Latine*. Stuttgart: German Bible Society, 2013.

Neyrey, Jerome H. *Hearing Revelation 1–3: Listening with Greek Rhetoric and Culture*. Catholic Biblical Quarterly Monograph Series 56. Washington, DC: Catholic Biblical Association of America, 2019.

Nicholas of Lyra. *Apocalypse Commentary*. Translated by Philip Krey. Teams Commentary Series. Kalamazoo, MI: Medieval Institute Publications, 1997.

Niederwimmer, Kurt. *The Didache: A Commentary*. Translated by Linda M. Maloney. Edited by Harold W. Attridge. Minneapolis: Fortress, 1998.

Nusca, A. Robert. *The Christ of the Apocalypse: Contemplating the Faces of Jesus in the Book of Revelation*. Steubenville, OH: Emmaus Road, 2018.

Oden, Thomas C., ed. *Greek Commentaries on Revelation: Oecumenius, Andrew of Caesarea*. Translated by William C. Weinrich. Ancient Christian Texts. Downers Grove, IL: IVP Academic, 2011.

Orchard, Bernard, Edmund F. Sutcliffe, Reginald C. Fuller, and Ralph C. Russell, eds. *A Catholic Commentary on Holy Scripture*. New York: Thomas Nelson & Sons, 1951.

Osborne, Grant R. *Revelation*. Baker Exegetical Commentary on the New Testament. Grand Rapids, MI: Baker Academic, 2002.

Otto, Rudolf. *The Idea of the Holy*. Translated by John W. Harvey. 2nd edition. Oxford: Oxford University Press, 1923.

Pao, David W. *Acts and the Isaianic New Exodus*. Grand Rapids, MI: Baker Academic, 2000.

Paulien, Jon. *Decoding Revelation's Trumpets*. Andrews University Seminary Doctoral Dissertation Series 21. Berrien Springs, MI: Andrews University Press, 1987.

Pius XII, Pope. Encyclical Letter *Doctor mellifluous*. May 24, 1953. In *The Last of the Fathers: Saint Bernard of Clairvaux and the Encyclical Letter* Doctor Mellifluus, 91–118. Translated by Thomas Merton. New York: Harcourt, Brace and Co., 1954.

Pontifical Council for Justice and Peace, *Compendium of the Social Doctrine of the Church*. 2nd edition. Rome: Libreria Editrice Vaticana, 2005.

Prévost, Jean-Pierre. *How to Read the Apocalypse*. Translated by John Bowden. New York: Crossroads, 1993.

Prigent, Pierre. *Apocalypse et Liturgie*. Cahiers Théologiques 52. Neuchâtel: Delachaux et Niestlé, 1964.

Ramsay, William Mitchell. *The Letters to the Seven Churches of Asia and Their Place in the Plan of the Apocalypse*. London: Hodder & Stoughton, 1906.

Reardon, Patrick Henry. *Revelation: A Liturgical Prophecy*. Yonkers, NY: St Vladimir's Seminary Press, 2018.

Resseguie, James L. *The Revelation of John: A Narrative Commentary*, Grand Rapids, MI: Baker Academic, 2009.

Rupert of Deutz. *In Apocalypsim Joannis Apostoli commentaria* [AD 1129]. PL 169. [RD]

Schüssler-Fiorenza, Elisabeth. "Composition and Structure in the Book of Revelation." *CBQ* 39 (1977): 344–66.

Second Vatican Council. Dogmatic Constitution *Lumen gentium*. November 21, 1964. In *The Sixteen Documents of Vatican II*, 107–90. Boston: Daughters of St. Paul, 1965.

———. Dogmatic Constitution *Sacrosanctum Concilium*. December 4, 1963. In *The Sixteen Documents of Vatican II*, 13–58. Boston: Daughters of St. Paul, 1965.

Smalley, Stephen S. *The Revelation to John: A Commentary on the Greek Text of the Apocalypse*. Downers Grove, IL: InterVarsity Press, 2005.

von Speyr, Adrienne. *Apokalypse: Betrachtungen über die Geheime Offenbarung*. 4th edition. Freiburg: Johannes Verlag Einsiedeln, 2019. [AvS]

Stanglin, Keith D. *The Letter and Spirit of Biblical Interpretation: From the Early Church to Modern Practice*. Grand Rapids, MI: Baker Academic, 2018.

Stock, Klemens. *Das letzte Wort hat Gott: Apokalypse als Frohbotschaft*. Vienna: Tyrolia, 1985.

Sutton, Matthew Lewis. *Heaven Opens: The Trinitarian Mysticism of Adrienne von Speyr*. Minneapolis, MN: Fortress, 2014.

Taushev, Averky, and Seraphim Rose. *The Apocalypse in the Teachings of Ancient Christianity*. 2nd ed. Platina, CA: St. Herman of Alaska Brotherhood, 1998.

Thomas Aquinas. *Summa Theologiae*. Translated by Fathers of the English Dominican Province. 2nd revised edition. London: Burns, Oates, & Washbourne, 1924.

Thomas à Kempis. *The Imitation of Christ*. Translated and with an Introduction by Leo Sherley-Price. New York: Dorset, 1986.

Thomas, David Andrew. *Revelation 19 in Historical and Mythological Context*. Studies in Biblical Literature 118. New York: Peter Lang, 2008.

Thompson, Leonard L. *The Book of Revelation: Apocalypse and Empire*. New York: Oxford University Press, 1990.

Thompson, Steven. *The Apocalypse and Semitic Syntax*. New York: Cambridge University Press, 1985.

Thuan, Cardinal Francis Xavier van. *The Road of Hope: A Gospel from Prison*. Translated by John-Peter Pham. Kindle edition. North Palm Beach, FL: Wellspring, 2019.

Tickle, John. *The Book of Revelation: A Catholic Interpretation of the Apocalypse*. Liguori, MO: Liguori Publications, 1983.

Vanni, Ugo. "Un esempio di dialogo liturgico in Ap 1,4–8." *Biblica* 57, no. 4 (1976): 453–67.

Voortman, Terence Craig and Jan A. du Rand. "The Language of the Theatre in the Apocalypse of John: A Brief Look at the Apocalypse as Drama." *Ekklesiastikos Pharos* 79, no. 1 (1997): 78–93.

Weinrich, William C., ed. and trans. *Latin Commentaries on Revelation: Victorinus of Petovium, Apringius of Beja, Caesarius of Arles, Bede the Venerable*. Ancient Christian Texts. Downers Grove, IL: IVP Academic, 2011.

———, ed. *Revelation*. Ancient Christian Commentary on Scripture. Downers Grove, IL: InterVarsity Press, 2005.

Wilder, Amos N. *Early Christian Rhetoric: The Language of the Gospel*. Cambridge, MA: Harvard University Press, 1971.

Williamson, Peter S. *Revelation*. Catholic Commentary on Sacred Scripture. Grand Rapids, MI: Baker Academic, 2015.

Yee, Gale A. *Jewish Feasts and the Gospel of John*. Zacchaeus Studies. Wilmington, DE: M. Glazier, 1989.

Zanchettin, Leo. *Revelation: A Devotional Commentary*. Ijamsville, MD: The Word Among Us, 2007.

Index of Names and Subjects

Index of Scripture References

NOTE: *page numbers in bold indicate where a passage is the focus of an entire section.*

Genesis

Proverbs

Mark

Luke

Acts of the Apostles

Romans

Other Books in This Series

The Transcendent Mystery of God's Word: A Critical Synthesis of Antioch and Alexandria, ed. John Martens and Paul V. Niskanen (2024)

The Word of Truth, Sealed by the Spirit: Perspectives on the Inspiration and Truth of Sacred Scripture, ed. Matthew C. Genung and Kevin Zilverberg (2022)

Augustine's Confessions *and Contemporary Concerns*, ed. David Vincent Meconi, SJ (2022)

In the School of the Word: Biblical Interpretation from the New to the Old Testament, Carlos Granados and Luis Sánchez-Navarro (2021)

Piercing the Clouds: Lectio Divina *and Preparation for Ministry*, ed. Kevin Zilverberg and Scott Carl (2021)

The Revelation of Your Words: The New Evangelization and the Role of the Seminary Professor of Sacred Scripture, ed. Kevin Zilverberg and Scott Carl (2021)

On Earth as It Is in Heaven: Cultivating a Contemporary Theology of Creation, ed. David Vincent Meconi, SJ (2016: repr., 2021)

Verbum Domini *and the Complementarity of Exegesis and Theology*, ed. Scott Carl (2015: repr., 2021)